# ROME'S PATRON

# Rome's Patron

## THE LIVES AND AFTERLIVES
## OF MAECENAS

### EMILY GOWERS

PRINCETON UNIVERSITY PRESS
PRINCETON & OXFORD

Requests for permission to reproduce material from this work should be sent to permissions@press.princeton.edu

Published by Princeton University Press
41 William Street, Princeton, New Jersey 08540
99 Banbury Road, Oxford OX2 6JX

press.princeton.edu

All Rights Reserved
ISBN: 978-0-691-19314-4
ISBN: (e-book): 978-0-691-25598-9

British Library Cataloging-in-Publication Data is available

Editorial: Ben Tate and Josh Drake
Production Editorial: Jenny Wolkowicki
Jacket design: Katie Osborne
Production: Danielle Amatucci
Publicity: William Pagdatoon

Jacket image: Florilegius / Alamy Stock Photo

This book has been composed in Arno Pro

Printed on acid-free paper. ∞

Printed in the United States of America

10  9  8  7  6  5  4  3  2  1

For Ann Arnold, Stephanie Jamison, Juliet Mitchell
and
Caroline Montagu, and in memory of Judith Ogden Thomson

# CONTENTS

GENEVA, 2011. Among the upmarket stores that skirt the lake and reflect the mountains in their glass fronts stands the Montblanc pen shop. Something in one of the windows catches my eye. Cushioned on silk lies the latest in the Patrons of Art series: the limited edition "Gaius Maecenas" pen. An objet de luxe for the businessman with everything, it's oddly restrained, at least compared with the other pens in the series: Elizabeth I, Catherine the Great, Frederick the Great, Peter the Great, Lorenzo de' Medici. In fact, it murmurs "classical" in every detail. I learn that the standard issue features cap and fittings of sterling silver, a lacquered and fluted barrel to simulate a marble column, together with an 18-carat gold, rhodium-plated nib and laurel wreath trimmings, while the luxury edition is upgraded to solid gold cap (Maecenas's name wrapped around a ring), gold nib and fittings, and genuine marble barrel. In both versions, a portrait is engraved on the base of the cone, like a seal ready for stamping. Around the cap is inscribed the opening dedication to Horace's *Odes*—"MAECENAS ATAVIS EDITE REGIBVS" (Maecenas, issued from kingly ancestors)—followed by four more lines and ending with the reassuring word "NOBILIS" (noble).[1]

Unaffordable for most window shoppers, this small object is one of many attempts across different centuries and media to capture the identity of a historical figure about whom very little is known. If his name is recognized at all, it evokes the wealthy enabler and protector of the leading poets of Augustus's time—Virgil, Horace and Propertius among them. Indeed, "Maecenas" remains the type-name for "patron" in most European languages other than English. In antiquity, however, this was a man known equally for his unusual career and inconsistent behaviour, someone who cut an exotic, transgressive figure in the streets of Rome, unsettling political and ethical norms alike. The Montblanc pen takes inspiration from the two phenomena that he bound together: the Augustan regime, long associated with a classicizing aesthetic, and

---

1. *Carm.* 1.1.1–5. An error crept in in the early stages of production—CVRRICOLO for CVRRICVLO—which the manufacturers offered to correct free of charge. Released in 2011 to mark the twentieth anniversary of the Patrons of Art series, the edition is now sold out.

FIGURE F.1 Patrons of Art Gaius Maecenas pen.
©Montblanc/Bonhams

Augustan poetry, in the shape of Horace's masterwork and its dedication. Together, they do duty for Maecenas, the invisible conduit between them.

Montblanc's accompanying brochure, meanwhile, promotes the following legend:

> As the first recorded patron in the history of the arts and culture, Gaius Maecenas became a symbolic figure and representative for cultural responsibility and selfless commitment—today, his name lives on in many Germanic and Roman [*sic*] languages as the root of the synonym for "patron of the arts", while his philosophy endures around the world in the hearts and minds of all those people who feel a moral commitment to the provision of selfless patronage to artists and the creative community.

Maecenas is hardly a household name now, nor do we know very much about his "philosophy". But perhaps the most surprising element here is the focus on "selfless patronage". Everything we know about patronage, at all periods of history, suggests that the benefits of a relationship with a protégé flow both ways. Anyone who supports a promising individual or artistic project can reasonably expect their good judgment and generosity to be commemorated in creative form, resulting in a satisfactory circulation of cultural capital and prestige. Indeed, the Montblanc Foundation sees itself as an active patron in this very mode: "initiating and supporting worldwide projects since 1992 in terms of patronage of art, contemporary arts, young theatre and classical music". It is a nice thought—and one presumably in the designers' minds—that the pen might itself have been used to award generous grants and sign large cheques.

On reflection, though, where posterity is concerned, how could Maecenas be considered anything other than "selfless"? Hailed at the start of so many Latin poetry books, he risks being taken for granted as a source of "commitment" and "support". He is much written to, by poets and Emperor Augustus alike, but all we have from his own pen are a few decontextualized fragments: such a singular individual has paradoxically little to say about himself. It may not be so strange, then, that Montblanc's eulogy denies Maecenas any agency in the creation of culture.

In another respect, Maecenas gets the benefit of the doubt, in that he is portrayed not as a stern dictator of themes but as a liberal and enlightened patron. Yet while the twentieth-century "minister of propaganda" label is long out of fashion, he continues to be regarded as the active and purposeful mediator who steered poets towards serving Emperor Augustus's "cultural programme".[2] This accounts conveniently both for the coincidence of a regime with a golden literary moment and for Maecenas's disappearance from the surviving texts, as his poets move on to higher genres and unmediated encounters with Augustus.[3] Even so, we cannot know what conscious influence he had on those poets' work, or whether, as Montblanc maintains, art and culture were his "main passion". All that can be said is that the poets use Maecenas to urge or allow them to go in whatever direction they want.

This book, the fourth monograph on Maecenas in a decade, needs some extra justification. In the interval since Jean-Marie André's dazzling psychobiography (André 1967), most attempts to recover Maecenas's subjectivity have been reluctantly but wisely abandoned. On the other hand, the twin goals of historical reconstruction and coherent explanation are alive and well. Three recent studies (Le Doze 2014; Chillet 2016; Mountford 2019) have reinstated Maecenas as an active influence, a linchpin of political and cultural change.[4] Philippe Le Doze's *Mécène: Ombres et flamboyances* has the best subtitle. Surprisingly, none of the three shows much interest in Maecenas as a forerunner of queerness and gender fluidity.

My approach here to Maecenas's role in the evolution and legacy of Augustan poetry and culture is far more sceptical. I presuppose very little about his motives, stress the inconsistencies of his textual appearances, and focus

2. Le Doze 2014.

3. Gordon Williams 1990.

4. Chillet (2016) meticulously reconstructs what can be known of Maecenas as a political operator, reinterpreting his Etruscan posturing as the symbolic façade of a political "fixer", well placed to amalgamate centre and periphery in late first-century BCE Italy.

instead on his symbolic versatility.[5] I ask why he is such a faceless outline in Augustan poetry but such a Protean shapeshifter (patron, friend, aesthete, snob and slippery courtier) after his death, and how he came to be both a mascot for aristocratic nonchalance and a cautionary focus for elite anxieties about masculinity, pleasure, retirement, and ethnic and social identity. Instead of trying to update the life story, reassess the realities of Roman patronage or make more accurate deductions about Maecenas's relationships with his poets and the emperor, I treat him as a movable rhetorical figure, deployed to suit different agendas and contexts.

What has emerged in the process is something of an anti-biography, one that highlights gaps and contradictions in the evidence and gives full credit to the murkier aspects of textual representation. Persistent features of the personality—sleeplessness, nervous hypochondria, trailing robes—are questioned and often dismantled. More positively, I promote "Maecenas"—that is, the perception of the man by other people—as a motivating force, a reflector of alternative values and a focus for new directions in Roman poetry, whose notional seal of approval endorsed some very ambitious literary experiments. Far less "classical" than the Montblanc pen suggests, and far more of an outlandish foil to Augustus: Etruscan, womanish, unfixed, a boundary crosser split between public and private identities. In fact, one could imagine a very different Maecenas pen altogether: wreathed with snaking ivy, studded with gold and jewels, and decorated with curlicues and grotesques.[6]

In what follows, I start by looking at the many lives of Maecenas, not just the various compartments into which his life was divided in antiquity, but also the split biographies written by his observers, ancient and modern. After considering his reputation as statesman and courtier, I ask how the scenes and metaphors used by his poets mark his position in the long history of Greco-Roman patronage. Close readings of three central Augustan works—Virgil's *Georgics*, Horace's *Odes* and Propertius's *Elegies*—have an eye to Maecenas's absent presence in all of them. Next, I explore his posthumous fortunes in the imperial period and reconsider his relationship to the material objects and topographical sites associated with him. Finally, I offer a survey of his transformations in later Western culture, asking what remains of his cachet and influence for contemporary models of artistic patronage and fundraising. How do we—or should we—remember Maecenas?

---

5. Shannon Byrne has been a pioneer in this area.

6. Unwittingly, I have described the thyrsus of Bacchus, Maecenas's avatar, at *Elegiae in Maecenatem* (*Eleg. in Maec.*) 1.63–64: "et tibi thyrsus erat gemmis ornatus et auro: / serpentes hederae uix habuere locum".

# ACKNOWLEDGEMENTS

MAECENAS WAS NEVER in a hurry. He has set me a very leisurely pace, and this book has taken far too long to write. In any study of the pitfalls and hypocrisies of patron–author relationships, it is especially hard to make thanks ring true, so I will keep them brief. Even so, I owe them from the bottom of my heart to many individuals and institutions:

First to the Leverhulme Trust, most benign of benefactors, for its practical generosity and Olympian patience in awarding me a Major Research Fellowship (2014–16), with almost no strings attached. Long may its support and bounty for overworked scholars continue.

To colleagues at St John's College, Cambridge, who provided me with extended family and a warm atmosphere: Erica Bexley, Elena Giusti, Geoff Horrocks, Talitha Kearey, Ester Salgarella, Malcolm Schofield, Oliver Thomas, John Weisweiler and Tim Whitmarsh, not forgetting David McMullen and the late Joe McDermott for the best chats about Chinese literature, and Siobhan Chomse, who expertly proofread two chapters.

To Cambridge's Faculty of Classics, including David Butterfield, Ingo Gildenhard, Philip Hardie, Stephen Oakley, Carrie Vout and Chris Whitton. Two exceptionally generous colleagues, John Henderson and Richard Hunter, read everything I sent them and gave me vital suggestions for improvement.

To two groups of remarkable students in my graduate seminars "Maecenas and the Poets" at Stanford in 2011 (David Driscoll, Matthew Loar, Carolyn MacDonald, Jackie Montaigne and Dan-el Padilla Peralta) and at Princeton in 2014 (Stephen Blair, Emma Curran, Leon Grek, Aaron Kachuck, Amanda Klause, Noah Levin, Caroline Mann, Andrea Placidi and Clem Wood). They are the future of Classics.

To Christopher Smith, Tom True and the staff of the British School at Rome, who hosted two productive visits in 2016. To friends and colleagues at two Classics departments that welcomed me as a visiting scholar in 2019: UCLA (including Sander Goldberg, Bob Gurval, Francesca Martelli, Kathryn Morgan, Sarah Morris, Alex Purves and Amy Richlin) and UC Berkeley (including Leslie Kurke, Kathleen McCarthy, Nelly Oliensis and Dylan Sailor).

I also thank Jim Zetzel of Columbia, Alessandro Barchiesi of NYU, Janja Soldo of Edinburgh, and the Princeton Department of Classics.

To Emma Barker (who always asked the best questions), Peter and Jantien Black, Catharine Edwards, Usha Goswami, Rebecca Laemmle and Cédric Scheidegger Laemmle, Subha Mukherji, Alex Press and Mario Telò, who had my back through thick and thin. To the late Ian Jackson, Joshua Katz and Jim Lycett. And to three special lockdown friends: Julia Griffin (herself author of a brilliant sketch of Maecenas), Robert Jones and Juliet Mitchell.

To my parents, Keith and Valerie Thomas, and my brother, Edmund Thomas.

To Cambridge University Library, for picture permissions, and to Oxford University Press, for kind permission to adapt a section from "Girls Will Be Boys and Boys Will Be Girls, Or, What Is the Gender of Horace's *Epodes*?" (Gowers 2016b) in chapter 2 and to reprint much of "Under the Influence: Maecenas and Bacchus in *Georgics* 2" (Gowers 2016a) in chapter 3. And to Boatwhistle Books for kind permission to quote part of a poem by C. Perricone from *Footnotes* (2018).

To Ben Tate, Bob Bettendorf, Lisa Black, Josh Drake, Rob Tempio, Maia Vaswani (my wonderful copy-editor), Jenny Wolkowicki and the superb staff at Princeton University Press, without whom nothing. To Virginia Ling, for compiling the index. And to two anonymous referees, for their invaluable advice.

Finally, to my beloved dedicatees: Ann Arnold, Stephanie Jamison, Juliet Mitchell, Caroline Montagu and Judith Ogden Thomson (the last sadly no longer with us). Not patrons but matrons—wise women all.

I HAVE USED the Oxford Classical Texts of Latin and Greek authors where available. Translations are my own, unless otherwise specified. Abbreviations follow those used in the *Oxford Classical Dictionary*, 4th edition. The list of abbreviations is available online at https://oxfordre.com/classics/page/ocdabbreviations.

OLD = *Oxford Latin Dictionary* (1976), ed. Peter G. W. Glare. Oxford.

### Fragments of Maecenas

L = Lunderstedt, Paul (1911) "De C. Mecenatis fragmentis", *Commentationes philologae Ienenses* 9. Leipzig.

H = Hollis, Adrian S. (2007) *Fragments of Roman Poetry, c. 60 BC–AD 20*. Oxford.

C = Courtney, Edward (2003) *The Fragmentary Latin Poets*. Rev. 2nd ed. Oxford.

# ROME'S PATRON

# 1

# The Parallel Lives of Maecenas

Maecenas was the wisest counsellor, the truest friend, both of his prince and
his country, the best governor of Rome, the happiest and ablest negotiator, the
best judge of learning and virtue, the choicest in his friends, and thereby the
happiest in his conversation that has been known in story; and I think, to his
conduct in civil, and Agrippa's in military affairs, may be truly ascribed all the
fortunes and greatness of Augustus, so much celebrated in the world.

—WILLIAM TEMPLE, *THE GARDENS OF EPICURUS* (1685)

How Maecenas lived is too notorious to need narrating.

—SENECA, *EPISTLES* 114.4

And a third (is it myself?) whom I see even more dimly than the others . . .

—JOHN WILLIAMS, *AUGUSTUS* (1972)

LET US START with the life of Maecenas—or rather his several lives and the
multiple biographies that bind them together. He is like a coin with two faces.
On one side, a figurehead; on the other, a more complex knot of images.

What follows is a cautious summary of his career, a mixture of certainties
and "maybes" digested from the ancient sources.[1] Gaius Cilnius Maecenas was
born on April 13 sometime between 78 and 64 BCE, in or near Arretium (modern
Arezzo) in Etruria.[2] The name Maecenas derives from an Etruscan settlement,

1. Based on Kappelmacher (1928) and La Penna (1987, 1996); Gowers (2017a) is a thumbnail
summary. Chillet (2016: 476–84) transforms an eccentric outsider into a central political figure.
See Graverini (1997) for a comprehensive twentieth-century bibliography.

2. April 13: Hor. *Carm.* 4.11.14–16. Guesses at his birth year are extrapolated from his date of
death, helped by a rough sense that Virgil was his coeval and Horace his slight junior.

otherwise unknown.[3] The Cilnii (perhaps his mother's family) were wealthy but insular Aretines.[4] The Maecenates were a more upwardly mobile family (including a knight, C. Maecenas, mentioned by Cicero, and a *scriba*, L. Maecenas, present at the murder of Sertorius in 72 BCE).[5] Maecenas met and befriended the young Octavian and may have participated in the military campaigns of the forties and thirties BCE: Philippi, Perusia and even Actium. His contacts and fund raising in north-east Italy may have assisted Octavian's rise to power.[6] But he was probably busier acquiring the estates of proscribed individuals and boosting his wealth. There are papyrus records of his property holdings in Egypt.[7] He acquired an estate on the Esquiline Hill in Rome, said to have been confiscated from Favonius, a supporter of Cato.[8]

Along with Marcus Agrippa, Maecenas became unelected adviser to the future emperor and was known as a diplomat and swift suppressor of conspiracies.[9] As caretaker of the city of Rome in Octavian's absences (36–33 and 31–29 BCE), he was invested with exceptional ad hoc executive power, yet chose to remain in the ranks of the knights (*equites*), never holding a formal magistracy.[10] Tacitus speaks of his "downwardly mobile ambition" (praepostera ambitio).[11] Brokering Octavian's first marriage, with Scribonia, in 40 BCE, he was instrumental in peace negotiations between Octavian and Antony at Tarentum (40) and Brundisium (37).[12] Meanwhile, he fostered an outstanding group of poets, including Horace and Virgil. He married, divorced and perhaps remarried

3. Varro, *Ling.* 8.41

4. Chillet 2016: 34. Livy 10.3. *Cilnius* at Tac. *Ann.* 6.11.3 may indicate either a suppressed Etruscan-style matronymic *gentilicium* (family name) or that Tacitus was confused by Augustus's nickname for Maecenas, "emerald of the Cilnii" (Macrob. *Sat.* 2.4.12); Simpson 1996; Graverini 2006: 53–56.

5. Cic. *Clu.* 153; Sall. *Hist.* fr. 3.79 McGushin; Chillet 2016: 34.

6. Chillet 2016: 171–233.

7. Estates in Egypt: *PIR*[2] M 37 (p. 134); Rostovtzeff 1957: 2.671; Parassoglou 1978; Sijpesteijn 1985; Capponi 2002. Wallace-Hadrill (2008: 411) guesses that he was involved with the lucrative Arretine pottery trade.

8. Schol. *ad* Juv. 5.3.

9. The first of the fluctuating groups of friends who informally advised Roman emperors: Crook 1955: 21–30.

10. Equestrian status: Cresci 1995; Dakouras 2006. Octavian's deputy: Vell. Pat. 2.88.2 ("urbis custodiis praepositus"); Tac. *Ann.* 6.11; *Eleg. in Maec.* 1.14 ("Romanae tu uigil Vrbis eras"); Dio Cass. 49.16, 51.3, 55.7; Porph. *ad* Hor. *Carm.* 3.29.25 ("urbis praefectum"; a title that did not exist in Maecenas's time); Syme 1939: 292.

11. Tac. *Ann.* 16.17.

12. App. *B Civ.* 5.53.

Terentia, sister of L. Licinius Murena, who plotted against Augustus (23 BCE).[13] Maecenas is said to have warned Murena that the conspiracy had come to light, whereupon the emperor rejected him for his indiscretion.[14] Alternatively, it was because of Augustus's very public affair with Terentia (16 BCE) or because the two men grew apart and became bored with each other that the friendship cooled and became, in Tacitus's words, "more an image than a reality".[15] At any rate, from this point we hear no more about Maecenas. Either he fell out of favour or was simply allowed to withdraw from public life.[16] Nothing is known about his death, allegedly in 8 BCE, two months before that of Horace, who was buried next to him.[17] He left no children and bequeathed everything to Augustus.

So far, this is the story of an efficient multitasker who managed the transition from Republic to Empire while overseeing a "golden age" of Latin poetry—a man who rose from obscure origins to become a friend, mediator and kingmaker, then equally mysteriously disappeared from view. But glaringly absent from this account are the many notorious traces of Maecenas's private life (or rather, his confusion of public and private life): passions, pleasures, whims, habits, postures and weaknesses that together suggest a distinctive personal style, an idiosyncratic way of being in the world.[18] Seneca single-handedly serves up the most shocking picture of Maecenas, accusing him of cutting a scandalous figure in the streets of Rome and conducting official business while wearing trailing robes and flanked by two eunuchs "more man than he was".[19] Elsewhere, he is cited as an expert on wine, jewels and fish and credited with various innovations, from a new system of shorthand to

---

13. The couple are cited as colluding in the payment of a *donatio* (which enticed a divorcing wife to return to her husband; *Dig.* 24.1.65); Guarino 1992: 145n38; Martini 1995; Urbanik 2016: 479–80.

14. Suet. *Aug.* 66.3; Gardthausen 1964. Gordon Williams (1990: 260) objects that the smoking out of the conspiracy would have pleased Augustus. Pliny's list of Augustus's tribulations (*HN* 7.147–59) omits Maecenas, suggesting that the breach was unconnected with the conspiracy or Augustus's succession problems (White 1991: 130–32; Reckford 1959: 198–99; Syme 1939: 333–43).

15. Tac. *Ann.* 3.30, dismissed by White (1991: 133–34, citing Schomberg [1766: 62–63] on Maecenas's "happy retirement, consecrated to his pleasure which consisted in study"). White (1991: 135) reads Tac. *Ann.* 14.53.3—"otium . . . permisit"—as a euphemism for compulsory retirement.

16. Gordon Williams 1990: 261–62; White 1991.

17. Suet. *Vita Hor.*

18. Labate 2012: 413.

19. Sen. *Ep.* 114.6.

heated swimming pools and serving baby donkey meat.[20] Fragments remains of his experimental poetry and rule-breaking prose.[21] His park on the Esquiline is said to have included a viewing tower, the one from which Nero fiddled while Rome burned.[22]

Maecenas's emotional life, meanwhile, seems to have been complex and fretful.[23] Augustus, who seduced Terentia, called him *malagma moecharum*, "putty in married women's hands", "butterer-up of unfaithful wives" or "the married woman's mattress".[24] Seneca sneered that he was "even more womanish than his spouse", subject to "daily rejections" by his sulky wife.[25] Meanwhile, he was besotted with a celebrity pantomime actor, Bathyllus.[26] He may have been an Epicurean, a flawed one.[27] For Seneca, his name was as synonymous with pleasure-seeking or self-indulgence (*deliciae*) as Apicius's was with cookery.[28] But this devotion to pleasure was double-edged. If Maecenas is depicted alone in his gardens, enjoying the sensory pleasures of running water and birdsong, he is also imagined as tossing and turning with lovesickness on a feather bed, barely soothed by the sound of fountains and far-off music.[29] Along with dinner parties and ball games, we read about insomnia, hypochondria, three-year-long fevers and a morbid fear of death.[30]

Everything in the collage of biographical "facts" in the paragraphs above has been pasted together out of scattered literary testimony from the age of Augustus to the third century CE, from lyric poetry to historiography to encyclopaedias. Except for a few new inscriptions, the sources have not expanded; what varies is how they have been assessed.[31] For many observers, Maecenas's private habits have carried far more weight than his public achievements. Sir Ronald Syme's verdict is typically searing:

> The Roman [Agrippa] loathed the effeminate and sinister descendant of Etruscan kings who flaunted in public the luxury and the vices in which his

---

20. Plin. *HN* 14.67; 37, *praef.*; 23, *praef.*; 8.170; Dio 55.7.6.

21. Lunderstedt 1911; Avallone [1962/63]; Makowski 1991; Mattiacci 1995.

22. Suet. *Ner.* 38.

23. Dio 54.30.4; Sen. *Ep.* 114.6; *Prov.* 3.10.

24. Macrob. *Sat.* 2.4.12.

25. Plin. *HN* 14.67.

26. Bathyllus: schol. *ad Epod.* 14.9; schol. *ad Pers.* 5.123: "libertus Maecenatis"; Sen. *Controv.* 10 *praef.* 8, Tac. *Ann.* 1.54.2; Dio 54.17.5.

27. André 1967: 15–61; Graverini 1997: 243–46.

28. *Ep.* 120.1.

29. *Eleg. in Maec.* 1.33–36; Sen. *Prov.* 3.10.

30. Vell. Pat. 2.88; Sen. *Prov.* 3.10; Plin. *HN* 7.172; Hor. *Carm.* 2.17; Sen. *Ep.* 101.10–11.

31. *AE* 2011, 1703 and 1708; Chillet 2016: 8–9.

tortured inconstant soul found refuge—silks, gems, and the ambiguous charms of the actor Bathyllus; he despised the vile epicure who sought to introduce a novel delicacy to the banquets of Rome, the flesh of young donkeys. (Syme 1939: 341–42)

Here is Jasper Griffin in more indulgent vein:

He was a byword for effeminate fabrics . . . and was teased by Augustus for his interest in jewels; his house was palatial . . . and his gardens never lost their celebrity. (J. Griffin 1994: 13)

From Henri Richer in the eighteenth century to Francis Cairns in the twenty-first, biographers have highlighted Maecenas's associations with luxury, effeminacy and literary affectation.[32] An aura of neurosis and melancholy still clings to him. Hints of physiological and psychic discomfort add to the impression that there is an intense subjectivity to be recovered, if only the sources allowed.[33] Pathology is reported as fact: "As early as 29 or 28, Maecenas was a very sick man. Once at least he had a very close escape from death; a psychological terror of death may have joined with insomnia to torture him in later life."[34] As we will see, however, this tortured Maecenas is usually a function of the rhetorical purposes to which his personality was put: as the troubled recipient of soothing lyric poetry (in Horace) or as a deficient antitype in Stoic metaphysics (in Seneca the Younger).

In Maecenas's case, the split personality was central to his reputation, whether conceived as agile movement between public and private domains or as failure to separate them. He was technically speaking *priuatus*, in that he had no elected public role. Yet "public" and "private" are hard concepts to separate in the relationships of prominent late-Republican and early imperial figures. The association with the poets, for example: was that a public or a private matter? The erotic triangle between Maecenas, Terentia and Augustus: public or private? Maecenas's activities turn out to be typical of, even constitutive of, "the interleaving of the 'personal' (not necessarily the 'intimate') and the public", in a period where personal alliances served political aims and political alliances were represented in terms of the friendships (*amicitiae*) from which they arose.[35]

---

32. Richer 1746; Cairns 2006.

33. André 1967: 61.

34. Reckford 1959: 198.

35. Pelling 2009: 45; Hor. *Sat.* 1.5.29 ("auersos soliti componere amicos"), *Carm.* 2.1.3–4 ("grauisque . . . amicitias"). Kennedy (1992) deconstructs the terms "political" and "private" for the Second Triumvirate. Still, the dialectic distinction had legs: e.g., Cic. *Mur.* 76 ("odit populus Romanus priuatam luxuriam, publicam magnificentiam diligit").

As an abrupt transition in Plutarch's life of Lucullus suggests, the half-statesman-half-voluptuary was a familiar biographical type:

> And it is true that in the life of Lucullus, as in an old comedy, one reads in the first part of political measures and military commands, and in the latter part of drinking-bouts, and banquets, and what might pass for revelry, and torch-races, and all kinds of frivolity. (Plut. *Luc.* 39.1)

If his character can be captured at all, Maecenas turns out to be a composite of many historical characters, future as well as past. Not only do his biographical portraits break down into specifically Roman types or Greco-Roman cultural norms, they have subsequently been fleshed out with stereotypes retrojected from later periods: aesthete, millionaire, gourmet, decadent, culture minister, dandy, hippy.[36] Judging from the nationalities of recent biographers, Maecenas has translated especially comfortably to the lands of *bella figura* and *hommes de l'ombre*.[37] British writers, meanwhile, tend to "other" him as a continental European: *éminence grise, petit maître* . . .[38]

How has this contradictory bundle of attributes arisen? There are three ways in through the ancient textual legacy. First, there are the various biographical details found in imperial histories, rhetorical treatises and miscellanies: Velleius Paterculus, Seneca the Elder, Pliny the Elder, Suetonius, Plutarch, Tacitus and Cassius Dio, among others. Anachronistic though it is to start with them, they are the backbone of our testimony. It cannot be stressed enough that no contemporary accounts of Maecenas survive, from the Augustan period or earlier, except for what the poets tell us, and a few extracts from the alleged correspondence of Augustus. The fullest ancient lives belong to the post-Augustan period, and, even then, are usually no more than paragraph-length. Particularly precious is the short chiaroscuro sketch by Velleius Paterculus, writing under Tiberius in the twenties CE, that portrays Maecenas as an efficient statesman who confined devotion to luxury to his spare time:

> At that time C. Maecenas was put in charge of internal affairs, a knight but one born into a distinguished family. When vigilance was required, he was utterly insomniac, far-sighted and resourceful; but when it was time to relax after work, <u>he sprawled in pampered ease, almost out-womaning women</u> [otio ac mollitiis paene ultra feminam fluens]. (Vell. Pat. 2.88)

36. Graverini 2006: 51: "Forse in Mecenate c'era un po' del ricco Americano"; Bardon 1949: 164: "le premier en date des baroques latines"; Henderson 1996: 79: "the hippy patron".

37. Fougnies 1947; Avallone [1962/63]; André 1967; Paturzo 1999; Le Doze 2014; Chillet 2016.

38. Buchan 1937: 144, 187. See p. 408 below.

More straightforwardly negative is the celebrated "symphony of griev-ances" in Seneca's *Epistle* 114, written under Nero, which culminates in this climactic passage:[39]

> How Maecenas lived his life is too notorious now to need retelling, how he sauntered, how pampered he was, how he wanted to be stared at, how he did not care for his vices to be concealed. In short, was his speech not as loose as it was louche? Were his words not as distinctive as his dress sense, his entourage, his home, his wife? He would have been a brilliant man if he had followed a straighter path, if he had avoided being unintelligible, if his lan-guage had not been so dissolute. You will see the involved expression of a drunken man, wandering and licentious. . . . [Don't you know] that this was the man who always processed through the city wearing trailing robes (even when he stood in for Caesar in his absence, the signal was requested from a man in civilian dress); this man who on the tribunal, on the rostra, in every public context appeared to have covered his head with his cloak, with just his ears peeking out at the side, a bit like a rich man's run-away slaves in a mime; this the man who in the raging din of civil strife, with Rome in a state of emergency under martial law, appeared in public flanked by two eunuchs, more men than he was; this the man who had only one wife but married her a thousand times? (Sen. *Ep.* 114.4–6)

Maecenas is here famously condemned in the language of "letting it all hang out", relevant to every aspect of his personality from his trailing garments to his uncontrolled use of metaphors. His literary style was as *discinctus* ("un-belted") as his flowing robes.

To the rescue (or rather, party to the same debate, given the uncertain chro-nology) come two anonymous imperial texts. In the *Laus Pisonis*, which cites him as a model for all patrons, the word "Maecenas" is first used as a type-name. A pair of elegies, *Elegiae in Maecenatem*, are devoted to rehabilitating their sub-ject as an all-round civilized human being, one who richly deserved a life of ease after his executive career and military service (the latter implausibly over-played). Maecenas takes a supporting role in Suetonius's *Lives* of Augustus and Horace, which appear around the time that imperial memories of the Augustan Age, primarily nostalgic or envious, start to crystallize in Martial, Quintilian, Tacitus and Juvenal.[40] These authors remember Maecenas for his generosity, luxury and affected literary style, which they cast in frothy metaphors that only

39. André 1967: 19: "orchestration de tous les griefs". See p. 256–66 below on this passage.

40. The Horatian commentaries of Porphyrio (second century CE) and pseudo-Acro (fifth century CE) and Servius's commentaries on Virgil (fourth century CE) contain further testi-mony, often extrapolated from the relevant texts; Costa 2014.

reinforce his reputation for actual personal adornment.[41] Emperor Augustus speaks of the "myrrh-drenched ringlets" (myrobrechis cincinnos) of Maecenas's poetic flourishes, so plaiting together literary and personal style.[42] Seneca refers to his "drunken speech" (ebrius sermo) and "effeminate poetry" (carminis effeminati), and Tacitus to his rhetorical "curling tongs" (calamistros); for Quintilian, his words "frolic and flirt" (exultent atque lasciuiant).[43] After his death, Maecenas's voice is ventriloquized, first in an imaginary deathbed apologia (Elegiae in Maecenatem 2) and then in the long but incomplete speech to Augustus advocating monarchical rule fabricated for him by Cassius Dio (third century CE).[44] Both fictions suggest a strong need to compensate for the unnerving silence of the contemporary testimony.[45] Dio also leaves a sympathetic sketch in the form of an embedded obituary (55.7.1–6), which praises Maecenas for his forbearance and records his good influence on Augustus.

A second category of material, thin but hugely influential, is found in poems addressed to Maecenas by Virgil, Horace and Propertius. A central claim of this book will be that the poets give him a role far more significant than their brief name-dropping suggests. We will see how often the later biography is extrapolated from their meagre testimony, then reapplied by scholars and other readers to interpret the poems from which it is derived. Overwhelmingly, the poets portray Maecenas as a crucial supporter and role model, almost a muse—while revealing frustratingly little about the man himself. One scholar notes "his curious diffusion, almost his ubiquity. . . . [H]e is everywhere in the poems. . . . Yet he is . . . almost nowhere in them . . . so pervasive as to be almost transparent."[46] Barely a presence in Virgil, Maecenas becomes something abstract to push against in Propertius. He also appears on the margins of a famous *auto*biography, the many-faceted self-portrait in Horace's poetic corpus, where he remains a shadowy sketch, a mirror or yardstick for the poet himself.

It is generally Horace who gives us the best snapshots of Maecenas. The *Satires* and *Epistles* reveal his taste for ball games after lunch, his squeamish objection to jagged fingernails, his fondness for play (pranks, puzzles, comedy and mindless chitchat).[47] Meanwhile, the grander *Odes* supply the sleeplessness, the love of oriental perfumes and wine and the troublesome wealth (all unreliable

---

41. Mart. 1.107.4, 7.29.7, 8.56 (55), 10.73.4, 12.3.2; Tac. *Ann.* 1.54, 3.30, 14.53, 55; Juv. 1.66, 7.94, 12.39.

42. Suet. *Aug.* 86.2.

43. Sen. *Ep.* 19.1, 101.13; Tac. *Dial.* 26; Quint. 9.4.28.

44. Dio Cass. 52.14–40. The speech (and the companion piece ascribed to Agrippa) is no true record but reflects third-century CE debates; R. Meyer 1986.

45. For ancient *pseudepigrapha* (fakes) as creative attempts to fill gaps, see Peirano (2012).

46. W. Ralph Johnson 1993: 33.

47. Hor. *Sat.* 1.5.48–49; *Epist.* 1.1.104; *Epod.* 3, *Carm.* 3.8, *Sat.* 2.6.44–45.

attributes, we will see, inspired by concerns specific to lyric poetry). Overall, the continuity of Maecenas as dedicatee across Horace's work offers a unique chance to test the role of genre as a determining factor in his portraits. At the same time, the controlled frequency of these glimpses reinforces the impression of a credible, three-dimensional figure, one kept slightly out of view.[48]

A third way towards Maecenas is through his own voice. This is hard to hear authentically in a relatively thin corpus of decontextualized prose and poetic fragments, mere titles (*Prometheus, Symposium*, a paean to the emperor's sister Octavia's hair) and recherché Catullan verse-forms (galliambics, hendecasyllables, Priapeans).[49] Gleaned from moral tirades, imperial biographies and grammatical treatises, the fragments often come stripped of their original settings and dramatic personae. For all that, one recent editor is confident that "the preciosity and neuroticism of the author come through strongly".[50] Much has been made of an intriguing title, *De cultu suo*, "On His Own Style", which sounds like a personal manifesto or apology but may be only a scribal gloss on the letter (Sen. *Ep.* 114) in which it appears.[51] As with the ethical assessments, modern readers tend to parrot the verdicts and the metaphors of ancient critics. Eduard Fraenkel, for example, dismissed Maecenas as "a hopeless epigone" of the poetic school of the previous generation (Catullus and the other *neoteroi*), while Theodor Mommsen, picking up Tacitus's curling-tongs metaphor, named him "most disagreeable of all heart-withered, word-crimping court-poets".[52]

Even so, the fragments are remarkable, and not just for being eccentric. There is often something almost too neat about them. They seem to plug a gap, supply exactly what we might expect to be the other half of Maecenas's mutual exchanges with his friends. Take two letters allegedly written by Augustus to Maecenas. One makes Horace the desired object in a jealous love triangle, with the emperor intervening to try to seduce him away from his current friend:

> I used to be capable of writing letters to friends, but now that I am very busy and in poor health I want to steal our friend Horace from you. He will come from that parasite's table of yours to this royal one [ueniet ergo ab ista parasitica mensa ad hanc regiam] and help me with writing my letters. (Suet. *Vita Hor.*)

---

48. Cf. Most (1993: 91) on the "discrepancies and distortions, self-corrections, and self-contradictions" that make Hesiod such a paradoxically unified textual individual.

49. Lunderstedt 1911 (verse and prose); Courtney 2003 and Hollis 2007 (verse only).

50. Courtney 2003: 276.

51. See p. 230 below.

52. Fraenkel 1957: 17; Mommsen, 1856: 215: "den unleidlichsten aller herzvertrockneten und worteverkräuselnden Hofpoeten".

The other teases Maecenas with a parody of his precious style, playfully combining Etruscan adjectives with exotic stones:

> Farewell, my honey of Medullia, ivory of Etruria, silphium of Arezzo, diamond of the Adriatic, pearl of the Tiber, Cilnian emerald, jasper of Gubbio [or: of potters], beryl of Porsenna, carbuncle of Italy—may you get one!—in short, you butterer-up of married women. (Macrob. *Sat.* 2.4.12)

Together, the letters line up almost too perfectly with a counterpart fragment by Maecenas (on which more later), in which he seems to protest that Horace is worth more to him than all the jewels in the world:

> Flaccus, love of my life, I do not seek out shining emeralds or sparkling beryls or gleaming pearls or rings that Bithynian files have polished or jasper gems. (2C = 3L = 185H)

The literary fragments help to flesh out the interpersonal relationships.[53] Even so, the circularity is tricky to negotiate. Did the febrile literary output determine the physical delicacy, or was it the other way around? Did the taste for rhetorical novelty and rarity derive from the jewel collecting, or did the jewel poem and matching letter feed the myth of the jewel collector?[54] Did the notion of Maecenas as collector of literary talent shape his reputation as a collector of other kinds of art? The sources are so patchy and the various strands of authenticity and fiction, metaphor and materiality, so hard to disentangle as to make any rigorous historical biography virtually impossible to write. For all the hints of sensory or anguished engagement with the world, specific delights and intimate friendships, the reality is that no individual consciousness can ever be recovered.

Nor is there much scope to discover for Maecenas what Patricia Fumerton, writing about the Elizabethans, has called a "memorable self". Historical personalities have often been parcelled up in symbolic relics (gifts, scents, monuments, gems, seals, trinket-like poems, wills) that testify to uniqueness, fellow-feeling, taste and authority, and foster remembrance, longing and delight.[55] In Maecenas's case, no such material objects survive. But underpinning his story is a web of associations with surrogacy and sentimental exchange, attempts by himself and others to conjure up and prolong his presence. Plutarch tells us, for instance, that Maecenas used to present Augustus with a drinking

---

53. See below pp. 324–28 on this exchange.
54. Bernoulli (1882: 1.239) uses letter and poem as evidence of Maecenas's interest and pins his identity to certain gem portraits. See Petrain (2005) on the poem's "jewelled" style.
55. See Fumerton (1991: 17) on the miniature mementos Charles I took to his execution.

bowl every year on his birthday (*Mor.* 207c). Scents of balsam, cinnamon and saffron waft around his tomb in the *Elegiae*. He used Augustus's seal as proxy for imperial authority, while his own seal, with the figure of a frog on it, "struck fear into the hearts" of those who received his tax demands.[56] He begged Augustus to "remember" his beloved Horace. For Augustus, meanwhile, Maecenas's death left a gap that could not be filled, even by a generous bequest.[57] But there is almost no physical legacy to contemplate beyond the still-disputed outline of Maecenas's Esquiline estate, long buried beneath Rome's Termini Station.

For all the ancient emphasis on Maecenas's bodily performance, we also have little idea what he looked like. Few antique portraits survive, and of those none can be securely identified.[58] As one nineteenth-century antiquarian put it: "It was long a cause of wonder and regret, that no gem, medal, or statue of a man so illustrious had ever been discovered."[59] Hopes of finding an authentic likeness remain wishful thinking on the part of archaeologists and biographers alike. Predictably, jewelled rings have been a favourite hunting ground. A portrait-type of a high-browed beardless man in profile was first optimistically identified as "Maecenas" by Philip, Duke of Orléans (1672–1723), based on an amethyst ring signed "Dioscorides" (an Augustan engraver). Decisively dismissed by Adolf Furtwängler in 1900 as a Renaissance fake, it is now stored in the Cabinet des Médailles in Paris. Another, a sardonyx signed by "Solon", once in the Piombino-Ludovisi collection in Rome, was similarly discredited, and is now lost.[60] Other examples include carnelians in Paris and Boston, a sardonyx in Naples and a garnet in New York. The British Museum has a possible head of Maecenas in intaglio at the end of a tiepin, repurposed to suit some eighteenth-century dandy.[61]

Sculptural types are equally hard to identify. The wreathed man who hovers, wizened and conspiratorial, in the background of the parade on the south frieze of the Ara Pacis has suggested "*éminence grise*" to some observers.[62]

---

56. Plin. *HN* 37.4.10; Dio 51.3.5–6.

57. Suet. *Vita Hor.*; Dio 55.7.5; cf. Sen. *Ben.* 6.32.3 ("tota uita Agrippae et Maecenatis uacauit locus").

58. Bernoulli 1882: 1.237–45, "Maecenas"; André 1967: 10.

59. Charles Bryce, quoted in *Report of the Seventh Meeeting of the Advancement of Science.* London (1838: xliii–iv ); cf. *Athenaeum* 519 (1837): 754.

60. Ridley (2020) tells the full history, one of increasing scepticism among connoisseurs.

61. Bernoulli 1882: 1.238–41; Richter (1956: 104) is suspicious (the type is often confused with Cicero). Tie pin: Tait 1984: 127 (no. 850).

62. Moretti 1948: 231; cf. Andreae 2005–6; Coarelli 2014: 303; *contra* Ridley 2020. Rossini (2006) prefers the orthodox identification with Sextus Appuleius, consul in 29.

FIGURE 1.1 Gems of Solon and Dioscorides.
*Source:* E. Visconti (1818): vol. 1, pl. 12.4–5

Marble busts of an anonymous man and woman found in Arezzo and conveniently labelled "Maecenas" and "Terentia", are now installed in the Museo Gaio Cilnio Mecenate.[63] Outside, near the ruins of an ancient amphitheatre, stands a portrait bust with broad features and high forehead.[64] The original was excavated on the Via Flaminia in 1830 and identified as Maecenas on the basis of resemblance to the Dioscorides ring, before being consigned to the seventeenth century. Now it languishes in the storerooms of Palazzo dei Conservatori, but several copies were made by Danish sculptor Bertil Thorvaldsen: one presented to the Grand Duke of Tuscany and placed in Petrarch's House in Arezzo; another given to the King of Naples and deposited in the Borbonico Museum, now the Museo Archeologico. A third found its way into the art collection of Paul McCartney and George Harrison's alma mater, the Liverpool Institute, but has not been seen since the school's collection was auctioned in 1992.[65] Later, we will follow a fourth replica to rural Ireland and see it reanimated in a new context.

Ancient paintings of Maecenas, unsurprisingly, are even rarer. A fresco found on the Palatine, then lost, but preserved in an engraving in George Turnbull's *Treatise on Ancient Painting* (1740),

63. Andreae 2005: 134–40.

64. A nineteenth-century copy; Faralli (2019) gives the history of its installation. André (1967: 10) detects "a broad hairless forehead, deep-set eyes, pursed lips and a contemptuous set to the mouth".

65. On the bust's reception, see the report of Dr Charles Bryce (above, n. 59). Tiffen (1935, pl. 8) provides a photo of the bust in situ. School historian Jim Lycett has kindly shared his boyhood memories (which include crashing into the bust and rocking it on its plinth).

FIGURE 1.2 Possible figure of Maecenas, Ara Pacis, Rome.
*Source:* Wikimedia Commons; photo: Saliko

depicts a tight huddle of figures, which contemporaries interpreted as a laurel-wreathed Augustus holding out a diadem to a subject king (perhaps Phraates of Parthia), with Maecenas the balding robed figure in the centre, Agrippa at his ear and Horace wrapping an arm around his shoulder.[66] In later eras, Maecenas was painted in many guises. He is a wreathed patron dispensing gold coins to a recumbent female in Dutch Golden Age painter Gerard de Lairesse's *Gaius Maecenas Supporting the Arts* (1690s); a swarthy impresario in Giambattista Tiepolo's *Maecenas Presenting the Liberal Arts* (1743); a tonsured swami listening to Virgil reciting in Charles-François Jalabert's neo-classical *Horace, Virgil and Varius at the House of Maecenas* (1846); and a balding gangster-king in Fedor Andreevich Bronnikov's *Horace Reading His Satires to Maecenas* (1863). In Jean-Auguste-Dominique

66. Turnbull 1740: pl. 3. This discovery inspired Wicar's portrait of Maecenas (Missirini 1835: 11).

FIGURE 1.3 Gerard de Lairesse, *Gaius Maecenas Supporting the Arts* (1690s), National Museum, Warsaw.
*Source:* Wikimedia Commons; photo: Wilczyński Krzysztof

Ingres's *Virgil Reading the "Aeneid" before Augustus, Livia and Octavia* (1812), Agrippa and Maecenas are conspiratorial figures in the shadows.[67]

It is thanks to the vagueness of the ancient record that these various visualizations are possible. We will never know whether Maecenas was fat or thin, tall or short, fair or dark. The focus in antiquity was not on his face but on his style: rings and ringlets, swishing skirts, poultices, ointments, and oriental perfumes like myrrh and sandalwood. Nature was clearly less important for his memory than culture and the arts of care. To complicate matters, his sartorial choices are hard to separate from the bodily metaphors in which the

67. In Jean-Baptiste Wicar's similar painting, *Virgil Reading the "Aeneid" to Augustus* (1819–21, Villa Carlotta, Tremezzo), the collector and commissioner of many of the Villa's artworks, Giovanni Battista Sommariva, plays a mild, concerned Maecenas to Napoleon's Agrippa.

FIGURE 1.4 Giambattista Tiepolo, *Maecenas Presenting the Liberal Arts* (1743), Hermitage, Saint Petersburg.
*Source:* Wikimedia Commons

FIGURE 1.5 François Jalabert, *Horace, Virgil and Varius at the House of Maecenas* (1846), Musée des Beaux Arts, Nîmes.
*Source:* Wikimedia Commons

FIGURE 1.6 Fedor Andreevich Bronnikov, *Horace Reading His Satires to Maecenas* (1863), Odessa Art Museum.
*Source:* Wikiart; photo: mabrndt

FIGURE 1.7 Jean-Auguste-Dominique Ingres, *Virgil Reading the "Aeneid" before Augustus, Livia and Octavia* (1812), Musée des Augustins, Toulouse.
*Source:* Wikimedia Commons; photo: Daniel Martin

Romans couched literary taste and mannerisms.[68] When Horace praises Maecenas for not being a snob about his social origins—"You do not dangle me
from a hooked nose"—there is no way to tell whether that nose belongs, or
does not belong, to him, regardless of his liberal social attitude.[69] In any case,
as the poet Cesare Caporali wrote in his *terza rima* skit *Vita di Mecenate* (1604),
this hardly constitutes sensational information:

> Mecenate era un' uom, che aveva il naso
> Gli occhi e la bocca, come abbiamo noi,
> Fatti dalla Natura, e non dal caso.
> Si dilettava aver due gambe, e doi
> Piedi da camminare, e aver due mani,
> Da farsi da se stesso i suoi fatti.

(CAPORALI, *VITA DI MECENATE* [1762 = 2018]: 1–6)

Maecenas was a man who had a nose, eyes and mouth, like the rest of us,
created by nature, not by chance. He rejoiced in having two legs, and two
feet for walking, and two hands, to do his business all by himself.

If it signifies anything, Maecenas's nose in Horace is a traditional metaphor for
the patron or literary consumer's powers of discrimination. Fastidious features
and fastidious tastes have blended into one indissoluble personality.

For all that, Horace (short and portly, by his own account) leaves us with
strong physical impressions of an aquiline, smooth and towering presence. One
of Maecenas's poetic fragments begins with a Catullan expression of devotion:[70]

> ni te uisceribus meis, Horati,
> plus iam diligo, tu tuum sodalem,
> hinnulo uideas strigosiorem

(2L = 3C = 186H; H PRINTED HERE]

If I don't love you, Horace, more than my own guts [or offspring], may you
see your comrade scraggier than a little mule

"Quite the opposite of how we might imagine Maecenas' normal appearance"
is how one modern editor defines *strigosior* (stringier, scraggier). He adds that
he imagines Maecenas more similar to Horace's Epicurean self-portrait in

---

68. Bramble 1974.
69. Hor. *Sat.* 1.6.1–5. Bernardi Perini (1966–67), for one, is convinced.
70. *hinnulo* is Oudendorp's conjecture for MS *nimio*.

*Epistles* 1.4: "plump and sleek with a well-cured hide".[71] But since Maecenas is describing an unfulfilled condition (in this case, that he might ever *not love* Horace), we cannot infer anything about his actual physique. Such assumptions are a direct consequence of the poets' tendency to include detailed self-portraits in their works, which readers then modify to fit the patronal addressee, as part of a general phenomenon of back-reflection. If the physical Maecenas is conceived as being a bit taller, a bit sleeker, a bit more effeminate than Horace, this impression, as we will see, is conditioned by ethnic and gender stereotypes and the aura of wealth. Equally to blame is the poet's typical oscillation (on which more in the next chapter) between identifying with a patron and marking his difference, as someone more socially elevated or more discriminating.

In short, Maecenas functions as a chameleon, a dummy board to be inserted wherever it is needed to make a contrast. He is the mysterious tertium quid that alters the chemistry of any existing relationship.[72] His personality shifts according to whether it is seen in relation to Augustus or Agrippa, or to the poets themselves. Rather than trying to reconstruct him, we should ask how and why his literary portraits are so contradictory (sometimes camouflaged, sometimes flamboyant) and what kinds of mutation they allowed. Why did Maecenas's reputation fluctuate so drastically between his own era and the next? Why was he transformed in the space of two generations from a role model and intimate friend into a despicable, abject figure? How can he split into Petronius and Nero, and Trimalchio and Jay Gatsby, stand for exquisite taste one moment and flagrant vulgarity the next? The debate over ethics played its part: some notions of Roman civility accommodated enjoyment and luxury, others did not.[73] Opinions also shifted according to historical perspective, whether Maecenas was seen as a standard-bearer for a certain climactic moment in Roman civilization (the Augustan Age), as a relic of earlier, degenerate civilizations, or even as a forerunner of future decline.[74] His life, like his style, is often imagined as being out of step with his time: happening either too soon or too late.[75]

Where Maecenas's imagined poetic "circle" is concerned, it is often a sense of inclusion or exclusion that determines whether he is admired or resented. On the inside, in the minority, are the poets whose self-worth is reinforced by this great friend's acceptance. On the outside, the unprivileged majority—whether

---

71. Hor. *Epist.* 1.4.15 ("pinguem et nitidum bene curata cute"); Hollis 2007: 321–22. Horace as short: Hor. *Sat.* 2.3.308–9; as tubby: Suet. *Vita Hor.*

72. Cf. Henderson (1998b: 170) on "Menalcas-Maecenas" in Calpurnius Siculus: "The *tertium quid*, the presently absent motor of the poetic plots".

73. Edwards 1993: 173–206.

74. The title of Sklenář's 2017 *Plant of a Strange Vine* (on Seneca's Maecenas) alludes to the degenerate plant at Jeremiah 2:21.

75. On anachronism as a feature of dandyism, see Gelder (2007: 123).

in Maecenas's own time or in later eras—who devalue him and his nest of pampered cronies. For their part, the poets construct Maecenas as unreachable, exaggerating their own achievement in being close to him. Everyone else, contemporary or post-Augustan, sees him from the outside looking in: shielded in his study, curtained carriage, shady garden or impregnable palace.[76] Virgil and Horace speak from a position of tight-lipped mutual dependence. Horace says, "It was important for me that you singled me out, you who can tell real from fake." Virgil calls Maecenas "deservedly the greatest part of my fame".[77] Yet Maecenas is startlingly minimized in their poetry.

It is, frankly, in the poets' interests not to give away too much. Their Maecenas is a fetishized commodity, carefully guarded, sparingly revealed—conspicuous by his absence, or at least never more than a silent presence, like the non-speaking actor in a Greek tragedy.[78] Blanks in the record screen him from capture by rivals, biographers and literary critics alike, which only enhances the value of any rare sighting. The story of encounters with the patron is a story of noises off. In the distance: the tinkle of music and the hum of conversation and laughter. Something beautiful, important and valuable is going on in the next room.[79] Dinner with Maecenas is a sought-after ticket, but the evening's secrets can never be relayed.[80] The desired object is kept out of reach; the mystification is the message. "What's life like with Maecenas?" (Quomodo Maecenas tecum?) is a question that only an enfant terrible can ask. In the mouth of the anonymous social climber who pesters Horace in *Satires* 1.9, it is both compulsive and unanswerable.[81]

## The Perils of Softness

By contrast, post-Augustan biographies and commentaries offer an overload of small details, many of them scurrilous, to fill the void. One trait stands out: *mollitia*, variously translatable as "softness", "effeteness" or "effeminacy".[82] Spanning physique, sexual behaviour, and diplomatic and literary style, this functions as a virtual algorithm for generating Maecenas's biography,

---

76. Study: Hor. *Sat.* 1.3.63–65; carriage: Hor. *Sat.* 2.6.42; garden: *Eleg. in Maec.* 1.33–34; palace: Hor. *Sat.* 1.9.49, 54–58.

77. Hor. *Sat.* 1.6.62–63; Verg. *G.* 2.40.

78. See Labate (2005: 48–49) on Maecenas as tragic mute, alluding to Cicero's perception of his role in his own dialogues (*Att.* 13.19.3).

79. Cf. the title of Stefan Bakałowicz's 1890 painting (figure 1.8): *In Maecenas' Reception Room.*

80. Hor. *Sat.* 2.7.32–37.

81. Hor. *Sat.* 1.9.43; Dufallo 2015.

82. Edwards 1993: 63–97; C. Williams 2010: 137–76.

FIGURE 1.8 Stefan Bakałowicz, *In Maecenas' Reception Room* (1890), Pavlovsk Museum, Saint Petersburg.
*Source:* Wikimedia Commons

especially when defined against "harder" individuals like Augustus and Agrippa.[83] It is softness that automatically produces the eunuchs, the feather beds, the heated swimming pools, the debilitating enslavement to both a wife and a male mime actor, even Augustus's risqué nickname, *malagma moecharum* (amalgamating softness and Greekness). It is also what predicts Maecenas's erotic susceptibility and his passivity as an accommodating cuckold who lent his wife to Augustus.[84]

None of this is to say that his softness made Maecenas unique. In Roman Republican invective, *mollis* was ubiquitous as a slur against male opponents, when Latin *uirtus* derives from *uir*, "man" (thus normalizing the supremacy of *male* virtue), and when masculinity was conceived of as a fragile, acquired condition that needed to be maintained across all aspects of behaviour, from

83. Bourdieu (1984: 546–60) describes a 1970s parlour game where participants were asked to match contemporary politicians to people or objects. The items associated with Jean-Jacques Servan-Schreiber (narcissus, hairdresser, grasshopper, Porsche, Brigitte Bardot, sofa, straw boater) reinforced his identity as racy and lightweight—and distinct from solid rival Valéry Giscard D'Estaing (oak tree, Rolls Royce, Queen of England, top hat).

84. Dio 54.19.3; Plut. *Mor.* 207c.

gesture to dress to speech.[85] Seneca's blistering demonization of Maecenas's unmanliness in *Epistle* 114 has been seen productively in the context of Stoic beliefs about restraint, "holding together" (Latin *tenor*/Greek *tonos*), a quality that should manifest itself in every aspect of a Roman male's behaviour, from his sexual activity to his metaphors.[86] Each aspect of deviancy predicts the next one: flowing womanly robes implies corrupt sexual behaviour implies incoherent writing style.[87] Maecenas's prose and clothes alike are "diffuse, lacking in cohesiveness".[88] If, according to a well-known definition, ancient manhood was an achieved state that "remained fluid and incomplete until firmly anchored by the discipline of an acculturative process", then Maecenas was a staggering underachiever.[89] If Roman masculinity was "a house of cards", where if just one card was dislodged the whole precarious edifice toppled, then Seneca's biography makes all the cards go down at once.[90]

Even so, it is too simple to assume that *mollitia* was a wholly negative quality in Rome or that Seneca is exclusively responsible for Maecenas's effeminate reputation. Writing about Roman elegy, the self-abasing genre that signals its difference from epic and history, real men and conventional power dynamics, Duncan Kennedy invokes Maecenas as a living paradigm of softness, rightly pointing to the acceptability of effeteness as a marker of civility, humanity, refinement and social distinction in many places and eras.[91] Even in puritanical Rome, Maecenas might be considered an example of "*mollitia* successfully lived". Drawing on Pierre Bourdieu's observations of upper-class behaviour in twentieth-century France, Kennedy comments: "Accusations of *mollitia* need not have done [Maecenas] social harm even in a society in which masculinity was apparently so aligned with superiority as in the Roman, and he can be represented as having appropriated the discourse of *mollitia* to his own benefit."[92] It is not clear whether Kennedy thinks that Maecenas was con-sciously "camp" or "limp-wristed" or just constructed as such by others. Nor

---

85. C. Williams 2010: 137–76.

86. Graver 1998: 621–23.

87. Graver 1998: 620. Again, not exclusive to Maecenas: cf. Dion. Hal. *Comp.* 4.11 on Lydian rhetorician Hegesias of Magnesia's "precious, degenerate, effeminate [malthakon] way of ar-ranging words".

88. Graver 1998: 619.

89. Gleason 1995: 59, 81.

90. C. Williams 2010: 156.

91. Kennedy 1993: 31; Edwards 1993: 67–68. Under the Abbāsid rulers, lovesickness was positively encouraged as a civilizing process for young courtiers (Algazi and Drory 2000).

92. Kennedy 1993: 39; see Bourdieu (1984: 380) on "real men's" disdain for personal care or mollycoddling.

who those others were: perhaps not the socially inferior, in this case, but the more morally conventional. Softness, in short, was a contentious concept across all ancient moral discourse, not a purely negative one. It could even be a corollary of power. The fountain of Salmacis in Halicarnassus (modern Bodrum in Turkey), rumoured to unman those who swam in it, was heralded by its citizens as a civilizing and emollient source that marked their proud status as a Hellenized colony.[93]

One crucial factor is that the poets who enlisted Maecenas in their dedications had their own interests in celebrating this trait. To them, "soft" was nothing less than a defiant, self-ironizing badge of identity (much as "queer" is today), a label for literary or countercultural alternatives to conventionally masculine themes—world domination, size, power and authority—along with their literary equivalent, a mythical, essential version of martial epic.[94] Most Augustan poets performed the rhetorical gesture now known as *recusatio*, a formal refusal on grounds of weakness to produce the grand, glorifying or comprehensive poetry supposedly demanded by their patron.[95] Instead, they rebelled by siding with more delicate forms of expression, like elegy and lyric. Maecenas presided sternly over these refusals as the bearer of Augustus's demands for some military monolith, but often ended up exposed as an undercover collaborator. After all, what better role model for refusal to oblige than someone whose defining political act was his rejection of traditional career paths?[96] What more appropriate mascot for soft poetry than a man whose softness was his defining characteristic? Or should the phenomenon be looked at the other way around? Were Maecenas's attributes enhanced by the poets in their own image, so that "weak" decisions (the refusal to write epic, in particular) could be endorsed by someone whose sympathetic weakness was underpinned by significant power, soft but real?

## Paradoxical Personalities

In the next chapter, I consider Maecenas's role as patron against the long history of ancient poetic patronage. For now, my focus is on the other roles (social, political and diplomatic) that made him such a versatile figure in Roman

---

93. Ov. *Met.* 4.285–87; Strabo 14.2.16; Vitr. 2.8.12. See Lloyd-Jones 1999; Nugent 1990; Sourvinou-Inwood 2004; Gagné 2006.

94. Hinds 2000.

95. On literary *recusatio*, see pp. 74–76 below, Wehrli (1944: 69–76), Wimmel (1960), Race (1978) and D'Anna (1997). On emperors' parallel refusals of honours, see Wallace-Hadrill (1982: 37) and Freudenburg (2014).

96. Zetzel 1982.

ethical and cultural discourse, particularly in relation to Augustus and the Augustan regime. The portraits or fragments that we have are not just minibiographies of a singular personality: they are interventions in a broader debate about the merits of consistency versus many-sidedness and about the proper limits of pleasure in a life lived well.[97] And here we have the first of many paradoxes. This singular individual turns out to be a variant on a deeply entrenched cultural stereotype: the so-called "mixed" or "paradoxical" personality.

The paradoxical portrait is an ancient cliché with deep roots.[98] Traces can be seen in figures as diverse as Socrates, with his ugly exterior and beautiful interior, and Hannibal, who started heroically but burned out too soon.[99] Gods and demigods could be paradoxical, too, especially those enlisted in the *Elegiae* to vindicate Maecenas's "soft" behaviour—beefy Hercules, doing time as wool-spinning slave to Lydian Queen Omphale, and androgynous Bacchus, hot from war in India, carousing with his maenads and satyrs: "O Bacchus, after we conquered the dark-skinned Indians, you drank sweet wine from your helmet, and in your carefree hour your robes flowed loose—at that moment I believe you wore two robes, both brightly coloured."[100]

From the late Republic on, these historiographical vignettes feature able and efficient statesmen whose private leisure or passions threatened, if unchecked, to compromise their public performance. From Sulla to Catiline, Sallustius Crispus to Otho, brief lives form interludes at the middle or end of a historical narrative. Just as the suicide chamber to which paradoxical characters like Plato's Socrates or Tacitus's Petronius retreated offered definitive freedom of expression, a final summing-up, in the last moments of life, so these memorable cameos provide a space in which to contemplate an individual's freedom to tear up behavioural stereotypes.[101] Often, regret is expressed that the protagonist defaulted on his early promise: according to Sallust, Catiline might have done something great.[102] Seneca grudgingly concedes (*Ep.* 92.35) that Maecenas wrote a few manly hexameter lines with neat caesuras, "high-belted" ones; he had talent "both ambitious and masculine", which was "loosened", "unbelted", by good fortune. A consistent feature is the idea of sapped potential, sabotaged by luxury or weakness. Individuals' lives track the overarching narrative of

97. Aigner-Foresti 1996, La Penna 1981. Cicero was criticized (Sen. *Controv.* 2.4.4) for lack of *constantia*. On the debate about behavioural and artistic consistency, see Möller (2004).

98. La Penna 1976.

99. Pl. *Symp.* 215a4–222b7; Livy 21.3.6, 21.10.4.

100. *Eleg. in Maec.* 1.57–60.

101. Haynes 2010.

102. Sall. *Cat.* 5.5: "uastus animus immoderata, incredibilia, nimis alta semper cupiebat" (his expansive soul always desired the excessive, the implausible, the too ambitious).

world history: great cities undermined by moral failure. Only the gods find it effortless to keep their multiple identities in balance.

The paradoxical portrait, it has been argued, is a peculiarly Roman phenomenon.[103] Frustratingly, Maecenas never qualified for one of Plutarch's parallel Greek and Roman lives. Still, it is interesting to speculate about a hypothetical Greek counterpart. One important precedent must be Alcibiades, whose biography was distilled by Plutarch from a mass of earlier testimony into a masterpiece of paradox.[104] This androgynous figure carried a shield with a figure of Eros on it (*Alc.* 16.2), wore trailing purple robes in the agora (16.1), touted his promiscuous favours around the East, was well-preserved at forty but died a Dorian Gray, wearing rouge applied by a prostitute (39.2). He was an ephemeral Adonis (the herms were mutilated during the Adonia; Tissaphernes even created a garden named "Alcibiades", 24.5); a chameleon (23.4) who adapted his personality to each new lover, each new city-state, from Sparta to Persia; a flower that wasted its fruit (4.1). "They love him and hate him, and cannot do without him," says an Aristophanic character of the Athenian people, while Archestratus pronounced: "Greece can only take one Alcibiades."[105] For all the obvious differences, the two portraits share similar elements: erotics, luxury, Eastern tyranny, adaptability, ephemerality, fruit and gardens, decay, and pampered exceptionality. Other striking precedents for Maecenas include Agathon, both the elegant host of Plato's *Symposium* and the effeminate, parasol-carrying poet of Aristophanes's *Thesmophoriazusae*, as well as Agathon's Roman equivalent, the mincing orator Hortensius, whose precocious talent, according to Cicero, withered prematurely.[106]

On closer inspection, most of the qualities ascribed to Maecenas have parallels in other biographies. Accusations of effeminacy flood Roman Republican invective: not even Julius Caesar, Cicero, Pompey or Octavian escaped unscathed.[107] The "mixed personality" tout court had recently been exemplified by Lucullus, with his war medals on the one hand and his fishponds, dining rooms and Babylonian gardens on the other.[108] Less sustainable contradictions are found in Antony, an exceptional soldier brought low by luxury, drink

103. La Penna 1976.

104. Plut. *Alc*: J. Griffin 1977: 21; Alcibiades and Eros: Wohl 1999, 2002: 124–70. The character Alcibiades in Plato's *Symposium* (216a) claims a life split between politics and philosophy.

105. Ar. *Frogs* 1425; Plut. *Alc.* 16.8.

106. Agathon: Snyder 1974, Muecke 1982; Hortensius: Cic. *Brut.* 317.

107. C. Williams 2010: 61, 88, 191–92, 212, 237.

108. Lucullus's gardens: Broise and Jolivet 1998; Tac. *Ann.* 11.1, Frontin. *Aq.* 1.22. Luxurious living: Cic. *Sest.* 93, *Leg.* 3.30–31; Vell. Pat. 2.33.4; Plin. *HN* 8.211; Plut. *Luc.* 39; Swain 1992; Tröster 2008, ch. 3; Jolivet 1987.

and female domination.[109] Maecenas's reputation for political mildness and restraint can be traced back to Pericles of Athens.[110] Another affable, wealthy man, Cicero's alter ego Atticus, managed to be "everyone's friend", even when challenged by the special circumstances of civil war.[111]

In turn, Maecenas offered a model to his imperial successors and a template for historians to ponder and reapply. In Tacitus's view, the Tiberian statesman Sallustius Crispus specifically "emulated Maecenas", not just in limiting his ambition for office but also in combining political vigour and private relaxation in a modern, suspiciously controlled way, as this subtle "puzzle-portrait" suggests:

> Crispus was of equestrian descent and grandson of a sister of Caius Sallustius, that most prolific Roman historian, who adopted him and gave him his name. Though he soon gained access to offices, he emulated Maecenas, and without rising to a senator's rank overtook in power many who had won triumphs and consulships. He differed from old school manners in his elegance and refinement, and in his wealth and affluence he verged on luxury [diuersus a ueterum instituto per cultum et munditias copiaque et affluentia luxu propior]. But beneath all this was a vigorous mind, equal to important business, all the sharper for looking somnolent and apathetic. (Tac. Ann. 3.30)

Another bon viveur was Lucius Piso, who slept off his hangovers in the morning but served Augustus and Tiberius responsibly in the afternoon.[112] But the most exquisite variation on the theme is Tacitus's description of Petronius's deceptively casual suicide.[113] It is tempting to extract from Maecenas's literary fragments a nonchalant approach to life: "nec curo" (I don't care), "benest" (it's all good), "nec . . . quaero" (nor do I want).[114] Yet along with misplaced frivolity in serious contexts, he sometimes displays odd intensity in trivial ones ("If I didn't love you, Horace, more than my own guts").[115]

He also spawned less acceptable acolytes. While decadence and sensuality were traditionally attributed to Greece and places further east, later Greek sources suggest that the streets of imperial Rome were positively crawling with

---

109. J. Griffin 1977.

110. Swan 2004 ad Dio 55.7.1 compares Thuc. 2.65, 2.59.3.

111. Graverini 2006: 64–66; Nep., Att. 6.2. Cf. Dio 55.7.4 on Maecenas's likeability.

112. Sen. Ep. 83.9–10.

113. See pp. 284–88 below.

114. 6L = 8C = 191H; 1L = 4C = 187H; 3L = 2C = 185H. At Sen. Ben. 4.36.2, Maecenas is quoted as saying "I shall not be held accountable for 100,000 sesterces."

115. Quintilian (9.4.28) complains of 16L: "The word-order is playful in a grim context" (in re tristi ludit compositio).

Maecenases. The Jewish historian Philo spreads scare stories about an epidemic of purple-clothed "men-women" (androgunoi) virtually volunteering for castration (*On the Special Laws*, 3.40–41). In the speech written for her by Dio in the third century BCE, Boudicca denounces the Romans as "those men (if we can call them men) who bathe in warm water, eat artificial dainties, drink unmixed wine, anoint themselves with myrrh, sleep on soft couches with over-age boys for bedfellows and are slaves to a lyre-player [Nero], and a poor one at that" (62.6.4). With the Romans defined ironically here in terms of their traditional opposites, Maecenas and his type remained no less of an outrage. But the counterarguments we have already seen, that "loose" private behaviour was a sign of refinement or a rounded life, suggest that the debate was ongoing and that more flexible models of *Romanitas* had long been in circulation.

Critically, history's verdict on Maecenas hinges on how well he was judged to have maintained the divisions in his life between business and leisure, duty and relaxation, or how well he used his private time.[116] The effective leader who sank into leisure in his spare time would become crucial for shaping a new ideal of the imperial courtier and statesman.[117] During the Republic, strange beasts like Catiline, who slept by day and went to business at night, were suspected of tyrannical aspirations. Under the Empire, visible indolence, cast as *luxuria* or *otium*, had a reassuring political dimension. As well as promising a velvet-gloved style of operation, it indicated that its possessor was not in the running to become *princeps*.[118] Such an alibi enhanced Maecenas's reputation for harmlessness. At the same time, it ensured that he died in his bed.

This makes the algorithm that generates Maecenas's paradoxical biography more complex than simply "softness". Perhaps "hard-soft paradox", instead? Maecenas's public efficiency excused his private luxury, so long as the two did not flow into each other. Even within this framework, individual features attracted mixed interpretations. Take Maecenas's notorious sleeplessness. Velleius makes him a vigilant public servant, who works all hours. Seneca, on the other hand, gives quite a different impression of the nocturnal Maecenas—tossing and turning on his feather bed, sick with sexual rejection and debauchery: "[Maecenas,] debilitated by self-indulgence and worn out by too much good fortune [uoluptatibus marcidum et felicitate nimia laborantem], was troubled more by the reason for his suffering than by the suffering itself."[119]

---

116. La Penna 1981; Leppin 1992. Cic. *Brut.* 9 contrasts *inertia* and *desidia* with free time well spent ("oti moderati atque honesti").

117. Woodman 1983: 240–44.

118. See Woodman 1983: 244; J. Griffin 1977: 21–23 = 1994: 38–40.

119. Sen. *Prov.* 3.10.

The simple act of going to bed and not sleeping makes Maecenas either an ever-watchful statesman or a tortured neurotic.[120]

Where public service was concerned, Maecenas's tactful style tended to be rated positively, as a scaled-down version of (or inspiration for) imperial *clementia* (or, later, *indulgentia*). Cassius Dio tells us that he "not only made himself liked by Augustus . . . he also pleased everybody else" (55.7.4). The *Elegiae* praise his restrained use of his authority: "Although you had infinite power, thanks to your closeness to a great friend, no one ever felt you use that power."[121] Even Seneca concedes: "His most praiseworthy feature was mercy: he spared the sword, he abstained from blood."[122] Maecenas and Agrippa oversaw peace negotiations between Octavian and Antony (Plut. *Ant.* 59). In Horace's account of tagging along with Maecenas and other delegates in 37 BCE to seal a further peace treaty at Brundisium (*Sat.* 1.5), triumviral dissent is cosily domesticated into a squabble between friends, patched up by natural peacemakers.[123] Maecenas was also known for defusing the emperor's tantrums and putting him in a calmer mood, acting as a buffer between ruler and people.[124] The signature mildness is on display in an anecdote about Octavian's war crimes tribunals. Observing his friend handing down one death sentence after another, Maecenas pushed through the crowd and casually threw a tablet into his lap inscribed with the words "Time's up, executioner."[125] Still, "clemency" in a political context could easily slide into "softness" in a personal one: "non mitem sed mollem" (not mild, but soft), in Seneca's crisp formulation (*Ep.* 92.35).

## The Flow of Pleasure

Restrained at court, to the point of being invisible, Maecenas was positively flagrant in his pursuit of pleasure. Seneca regards him as synonymous with every kind of sybaritic delight:

120. André (1967: 76) reads sleeplessness as a physiological "symptom" of Maecenas's deployment of night police (*vigiles urbani*, established 6 CE); cf. Dio 52.24.6; *Eleg. in Maec.* 1.14; cf. Sall. *Cat.* 5 (Catiline's superhuman contempt for sleep).

121. *Eleg. in Maec.* 1.15–16.

122. Sen. *Ep.* 114.7.

123. Hor. *Sat.* 1.5.29 "auersos soliti componere amicos"; cf. App. *B Civ.* 5.64 on the peace-lords (Cocceius, Pollio and Maecenas) who promoted universal "friendship".

124. Longinus's description (*Peri hupsous* 32.5; cf. Pl. *Ti.* 70) of the lungs as a "soft [malakēn], bloodless, porous cushion [malagma] between the hot angry heart and the rest of the body" nicely suggests the buffer role played by the "married woman's mattress". See Graverini (1999) on Maecenas as diplomat and engineer of the *pax Augusta*.

125. Dio 55.7.2; Bauman 1982: 102–10.

It is consistency that lasts; falseness does not. Some men are like Vatinius or Cato, by turns; sometimes they don't think Curius is stern enough, or Fabricius poor enough, or Tubero frugal enough and content with simple things; at other times, they vie with Licinus in wealth, Apicius in dining and Maecenas in pleasure-seeking [Maecenatem deliciis]. The greatest proof of an evil mind is unsteadiness and continual wavering between the simulation of virtue and the love of vice. (*Ep.* 120.1.19–20)

In this tirade against behavioural inconsistency, Maecenas is ironically identified with a single quality: *deliciae*, "delights". The word signifies not just pleasurable amusements, such as love affairs, but also a favourite pet or toy boy, or in a literary context one's pet rhetorical tropes or figures (Seneca uses the word of Maecenas's literary "darlings" in *Ep.* 114).[126] It often has an intimate or naughty feel. Catullus is fond of it, despite the double stigma involved, and uses the word in both subjective and objective senses: "The negative associations of the word . . . include the implication of effeminacy that to the Roman mind goes with any form of nonpurposive or nonessential activity. . . . [T]o call someone your *deliciae* is to point in two opposite directions, to the object and to oneself, and it is also to mark one's behavior, quite self-consciously, as questionable."[127]

For all his disapproval, Seneca gives Maecenas a lasting place in the history of the senses, as someone so perversely hypersensitive that his pleasures were often indistinguishable from torture and pain. In the ancient world, yielding to pleasure was imagined as an intense physiological experience, a chemical process of osmosis between inside and outside.[128] Suspended in a state of heightened sensibility, Maecenas's body seems to melt into boneless pulp and feverish flux; his membranes become porous and dissolve; external pleasures seep into marrow and muscles.[129] Corporeal metaphors characterizing his manner as "loose", "soft" or "fibreless" are reflected in the symbolic markers of his physique, environment, writing and costume: flowing robes, tossing neck, unfettered gait and liquid, wandering style.[130]

---

126. Cic. *Orat.* 39 ("deliciis uel potius ineptiis"). See also Pomeroy 1992; Graver 1998: 616; Sen. *Ep.* 114.7.

127. W. Fitzgerald 1995: 36. Bayet (1956: 20) notes the etymological link with *delicere*, "seduce".

128. Seneca, *De vita beata* 5.4: "pleasure flows round [circumfundatur] on every side and seeps [influat] through every opening"; Edwards 1993: 173, 175.

129. Sen. *Ep.* 114.25: "luxurious habits descend into the marrow and sinews".

130. Sen. *Ep.* 114 turns Maecenas's idiosyncrasies into generalities: "The speech of a pampered man is soft and fluid" (21); "The soul's functions and actions grow limp and any impulse comes from a weak and fluid source" (23). Cf. Polemo on the androgynous orator (Gleason

The same language of high temperature, rapid ripening and excessive fluid-ity marks Maecenas's erotic entanglements. As Tacitus puts it, he "overflowed into passion for" or "went all soppy over" the mime actor Bathyllus (*Ann.* 1.54: "effuso in amorem Bathylli"), a passion that Augustus indulged by instituting a popular dramatic festival. In the Tacitean context, *amor* ("passion") might simply indicate exuberant fandom (as in the gangs of supporters who favoured Bathyllus or his rival Pylades), not personal obsession.[131] But similar terms are used by Horace in his *Epodes* of the lovesickness he and Maecenas experi-ence together; metaphors of burning and stewing (*arsisse, ureris, macerat*) sug-gest a steady boiling down of masculine muscle ("like a long soak in a hot tub").[132] Seneca, meanwhile, describes the operations of unlimited pleasure and consistent good fortune on Maecenas as premature "decay" ("wasting away in the pursuit of pleasure [*marcidum uoluptatibus*] and ground down by excessive good fortune") tantamount to castration: "if good fortune had not snipped his sinews, or, to be blunt, castrated him [*castrasset*]".[133]

With a curious symmetry, again, Maecenas's fractured literary corpus offers matching glimpses of loose or flaccid bodies, from the tossing head (*flexibile caput*) of the castrated followers of the Phrygian goddess Cybele (in his effete galliambics) to the floppy neck (*ceruice lassa*) of the "tyrants of the grove" (in a prose quotation) and the limp, quivering physique of a hunchback, captured in what Seneca calls "effeminate" verse (actually, Priapeans): "Make me weak in my hands, make me weak and lame in my feet. / Heap up a crooked hump on my back, shake my teeth till they rattle."[134] Pliny's account, allegedly derived from Maecenas and Agrippa, of the dropsy Augustus suffered while hiding in marshland during the civil wars ("aqua subter cutem fusa turgidi" [swollen with the water that seeped under his skin], *HN* 7.148), is curiously reminiscent of Seneca on Maecenas's porous body.

---

1995: 63): "His head is tilted to the side, his loins do not hold still, and his slack limbs never stay in one position." Cramer (2000) terms such popular connections between physical symptoms and sexuality "folk-endocrinology".

131. For the public performance of infatuation by the powerful, cf. Plut. *Alex.* 67: Alexander kissing his favourite eunuch Bagoas in the theatre; Vout (2007: 52–135) on Hadrian and Antinous.

132. McDermott 1982: 220. In Hor. *Epod.* 14, "debilitating lassitude" (mollis inertia) "has dripped" (diffuderit) oblivion into the poet's lovesick heart. Impotence in the *Epodes*: W. Fitzgerald 1988, Oliensis 1998: 64–101.

133. Sen. *Prov.* 3.10 (*marcidus* is from Proto-Indo-European *merk- "decay"); *Ep.* 19.9; cf. *Ep.* 114.23 *marcent*.

134. 4L = 5–6C = 188H; Sen. *Ep.* 114.5 = 11L; Sen. *Ep.* 101.11 = 1L = 4C = 187H ("debilem facito manu, debilem pede coxo, / tuber adstrue gibberum, lubricos quate dentes").

Vulnerability and lack of control—not just flow, but overflow—also identify Maecenas with what the Romans saw as a stereotypically feminine temperament. Velleius expresses the statesman's transition from political action to leisure in terms of gender transgression as much as physical fluidity ("He sprawled in pampered ease, almost out-womaning women"). Seneca makes the hint more explicit: any man, he says, who would rather be Maecenas, the spoiled courtier, than Regulus, the resilient soldier, must ultimately long to be Maecenas's wife Terentia (*Prov.* 3.10).[135] Such below-the-belt insinuations and hard-soft contrasts exploit ancient stereotypes of uncontrolled desire as constitutional in women and pathological in men. In Anne Carson's words: "Greek men ascribe to the female in general a tendency to 'let herself go' in emotion or appetite, a tendency encouraged by her wet nature and by the liquid or liquefying nature of emotions and appetites themselves."[136] Like Maecenas's thermal diving pool, ancient desire immerses its subject in a fusion of liquid and heat: "*Erōs* pours, drips, heats, softens, melts, loosens, cooks, boils, dissolves."[137]

## Etruscans and Lydians

Such concepts of "softness", "looseness" or "fluidity" in Maecenas's biographies turn out to be overdetermined, generated as much by ethnic stereotyping as by gender ambiguity or behavioural choice. The name "Maecenas" is Etruscan; his poets hail him as "descendant of Etruscan kings".[138] It is unclear whether Maecenas himself initiated this pretentious claim, but it is likely enough, given how many other Roman aristocrats were busy tracing descent from the legendary Trojans who emigrated with Aeneas.[139] Contemporary interest is signalled by fake Etruscan "antiques", such as the funerary urn of Volumnius or the Corsini Throne.[140] Even so, only a tiny minority of political players in Rome laid claim to "Etruscan" origins (a handful of families in the Republic and just a few more under the Empire).[141] Sometimes they suppressed their origins by adopting Roman names; sometimes they suppressed their political ambitions. Maecenas

135. Cf. Beulé 1868: 280: "comme une femme de l'orient se rendant au bazar".

136. Carson 1991: 156.

137. Carson 1991: 138. Cf. ibid. 155–56: "We encounter a deep and abiding mistrust of τὸ ὑγρόν [the wet] in virtue of its ability to transform and deform." Cf. Agathon at Pl. *Symp.* 195e–196a on the moist fluidity of *Eros*.

138. Hor. *Carm.* 1.1.1 ("Maecenas, atauis edite regibus"), 3.29.1 ("Tyrrhena regum progenies"); Prop. 3.9.1 ("eques Etrusco de sanguine regum"); *Eleg. in Maec.* 1.13 ("regis eras, Etrusce, genus").

139. Erskine 2001.

140. Wiseman 1987; Erskine 2001: 21–24; Chillet 2016: 66.

141. Farney 2007: 125–50.

chose neither option, except in that he exercised unofficial power without following the *cursus honorum*.

To identify oneself with regal Etruria was to risk associations with delicate, soft behaviour of a very un-Roman kind (what the Greeks called *truphē*, "luxury") and provoking old prejudices against the Etruscans as cruel, lascivious and weak.[142] From their productive hinterland, Etruscans acquired a reputation for physical lushness or pulpiness: a "sleek Etruscan" (pinguis Tyrrhenus) plays the flute for a rustic festival in Virgil's *Georgics*.[143] Writing in Maecenas's own time, Diodorus Siculus pushes environmental determinism in his account of Etruscan lassitude and overflow: "Not the least of the things that have contributed to their luxury is the fertility of the land; for since it bears every product of the soil and is altogether fertile, the Tyrrhenians lay up great stores of every kind of fruit."[144] Politically, Etruscans were stereotyped as stealthy or sluggish, like Maecenas's courtier successors Sejanus and Otho, or dominated by women, like Kings Tarquin and Servius Tullius (thanks to their tradition of matrilinear descent).[145]

If Maecenas had more to lose than gain by parading these origins, why did he parade them—if he really did—along with royal pretensions that were probably bogus? Claiming descent from gods was not unique, but kings were a scandal of early Rome (the expulsion of Etruscan Tarquin was its crisis) that must never be repeated.[146] Maecenas's immediate family may have been somewhat humbler. A Gaius Maecenas, shakily identified as our Maecenas's grandfather, is mentioned by Cicero in *Pro Cluentio* as a Roman knight who opposed Drusus in 91 BCE.[147] A later Maecenas, possibly his father, was present, according to Sallust, at the banquet where Sertorius was murdered in 72 BCE. As one of Sertorius's *scribae*, thus a member of an upwardly mobile bureaucratic class, he

142. Farney 2007: 133–40. See Macfarlane (1996) for Etruscan stereotypes in Latin literature; Bitarello 2009 lists laziness, effeminacy, cowardice, luxury, cruelty and religious difference. Theopompus (*ap*. Ath. 12.517d–518b) calls the Etruscans preening and sexually liberated; Y. Liebert 2006: 112–14.

143. Verg. *G*. 2.193; cf. Catull. 39.11 ("obesus Etruscus"). On Etruscan fertility, see Varro, *Rust*. 1.9.6 ("agro pingui").

144. Diod. Sic. 5.40.3–5.

145. Sordi (1995) emphasizes Etruscans' reputation as trusty servants to Rome (*fortitudo, pietas, fides*). On their obesity, see Y. Liebert (2006: 229–30) and Giugliano (2001: 206).

146. Dunkle 1967.

147. Cic. *Clu*. 153. See Kappelmacher (1928: 209) and Syme (1939: 129n4) on the connections between the various Maecenases. Chillet (2016: 100–123) suggests that the family were already Caesarians through friendship with L. Marcius Philippus, Octavian's stepfather, possibly as his bankers.

may even have been a recent freedman. As historian Louis MacKay once mockingly asked: "In what luster could the vanity of an elegant neurotic better hide the shabby paternal shadow of Perperna's scribe than in the legendary glories of Etruscan royalty?"[148]

Two seating plans from different generations of the family register the rapidity of the ascent. Describing Sertorius's murder, Sallust pictures the *scriba* Maecenas sandwiched on a dinner couch between two other Etruscans, Tarquitius and the host, Perperna.[149] While Maecenas sits "medius in imo" (in the middle of the bottom couch), Sertorius occupies the place of honour, "inferior in medio" (at the bottom of the middle couch). By contrast, at the fictional dinner of Nasidienus (Hor. *Sat.* 2.8), our Maecenas is the guest of honour, seated "imus in medio" (at the bottom of the middle couch), surrounded by *umbrae*, or hangers-on.[150] According to this narrative, Maecenas's wealth and connections mushroomed overnight. Like the freedman at Trimalchio's dinner who tricked a hobgoblin out of his treasure, he "grew from nothing".[151] Such a meteoric ascent was by no means exceptional. Poets from the margins, like Catullus, Propertius, Horace, Virgil and Ovid, "fitted comfortably into a Roman society dominated in their time by Maecenas of Arretium, the obscurely born Vipsanius Agrippa, and the *princeps* himself from a small town in Latium".[152]

Otherwise, the evidence that Maecenas exploited either his Etruscan or his regal connections is thin. A small legacy of his time in power may be the praetorian guard, developed from the police force he organized in Rome during Augustus's absence, which contained a large Etruscan component ever after.[153] But when poets hail him as "descendant of Etruscan kings", it is usually as prelude to a counterargument, that ancestry does not in fact matter. This is not to rule out the element of romance in the aura of kingliness. So long as Augustus was wary of that role himself, Maecenas could be safely cast as a fantasy king with whom to converse in the literary tradition of talking to rulers: "The relationship with Maecenas could serve the poets as a smoked glass, as it were, between them and the naked glare of the sun of Augustus."[154] The final sentence of the speech Dio invents for Maecenas to advise Augustus on his monarchy runs: "You will enjoy fully the reality of kingship without the odium which

---

148. MacKay 1942: 80. He suspects that the contrast "between the rough parvenu and the cultured scion of an ancient house" is exaggerated.

149. Sall. *Hist.* fr. 3.79 McGushin = Serv. *ad Aen.* 1.698.

150. Chillet (2016: 144) maintains that everyone at Perperna's banquet was of at least equestrian status.

151. Petron. *Sat.* 38.7: "de nihilo creuit".

152. Wiseman 1971: 52.

153. Sordi 1995: 154–55.

154. J. Griffin 1984: 195.

attaches to the name of 'king'" (Dio Cass. 52.40). Meanwhile, Maecenas and his poets enjoyed the pretence and glamour of limited, obsolete, fantasy kingship while deflecting attention from Augustus.

In Horace's case, Maecenas the descendant of kings is a character special to his lyric poetry. In his first book of *Satires*, where he cements their relationship, he gives a more modest account of the illustrious pedigree: "Notwithstanding your noble descent from all those Lydians who colonized Etruscan land, and despite the fact that your maternal and paternal ancestors once commanded great legions, you do not dangle nobodies like me, a freedman's son, from an aquiline nose."[155] This Maecenas, despite his descent from Republican generals, is no snob about his friend's origins (Horace, a freedman's son, had himself made landfall as a *scriba*, a bureaucrat, after fighting on the wrong side at Philippi). Now he claims that the gulf between him and the great man is purely one of birth; the two see eye to eye on the question of innate worth versus hollow ancestry. Around the same time, Livy portrayed Etruscan Queen Tanaquil (seventh to sixth century BCE), who pushed her husband Tarquin towards kingship in Rome despite his humble outsider status and encouraged her adopted son, Servius Tullius: "Think who you are, not from whom you were born."[156] Conversely, Livy's account (1.34.12) of Tarquin infiltrating King Ancus's court through hospitality, benefactions, liberality, efficiency and good advice, in both peace and war, public and private life, may well derive from Etruscan Maecenas's current "intimate friendship" (*familiaris amicitia*) with a ruler.

Despite their recent comeback, the longer trajectory of Maecenas's family and their Etruscan ancestors was one of decadence and decline. This is reflected in the narrative arc of his own life: from obscure beginnings to the peak of fame, followed by disappearance (whether caused by disgrace, sickness or lazy retirement). The "indefinitely prolonged civilized lassitude" that the orientalist imagination of later Western culture attributes to crumbling backwaters like Byzantium or Alexandria holds for Maecenas's Etruria, and for Maecenas himself.[157] His name suggests links with earlier doomed Etruscans: Mastarna, the ancient condottiere identified by Emperor Claudius with Servius Tullius, and Mezentius, tragic loser in the later books of the *Aeneid*.[158] Even Virgil's Tarchon (ancestor to Tarquin), an artificially contrived model for

---

155. Hor. *Sat.* 1.6.1–6.

156. Sordi 1995: 151; Livy 1.34, 1.41.

157. Vance 2004: 571.

158. The Lyon tablet (*CIL* 13.1668) names Servius Tullius as Vibenna's "most faithful friend and companion in all his adventures" (Vi/vennae sodalis fidelissimus omnisque eius casus comes), alleged to have changed his name from "Mastarna"; Cornell 1995: 135–41; *Etruskische Texte* Ager Tarquiniensis 1.1. I owe to John Henderson the attractive link with Mezentius (the discarded patron as tragic Etruscan failure), though a linguistic connection is hard to prove.

Roman–Etruscan collaboration, reinforces old stereotypes when he slams his own men as "always inert Etruscans" (semper inertes Tyrrheni), more inclined to brawling in the bedroom and holding drunken feasts than to serious fighting.[159] The Etruscans were the also-rans of history. Against a decayed aristocrat, Roman poets could measure their own ascent.

Uniquely in Satires 1.6, however, Horace makes Maecenas trail the residue of not one but two ruined civilizations, tracing his roots beyond the Etruscans to their supposed ancestors, the Lydians, said to have emigrated from what is now modern Turkey (Hdt. 1.94). Despite their associations with legendary kings like Croesus and Gyges, whose cities were still of interest to Roman antiquarians, Lydians were now more commonly found among the slave population of Rome.[160] As Cicero sneered (Flac. 65): "How many times do you find a comedy with a slave in it who is not called Lydus [or: is not of Lydian origin]?" Horace sneaks in a subversive message right under Maecenas's (aquiline) nose: far from being indigenous or irreproachably blue-blooded, even he, like so many of the Romans, descends from immigrants.[161] The "haunting question of whence", which plagued Etruscan history in antiquity, is deflected to probe the origins of its most recent representative.[162]

Any claim to Lydian descent would have made Maecenas unusual among late-Republican Etrusco-Romans.[163] There remains just one hint of his personal interest, a galliambic fragment featuring a Lydian river: "Here, every nymph encircles old Achelous."[164] But the Lydian connections can be pressed harder, and will be later, because they open up other, more exotic theatres for his textual performances as a kingly figure. Like Etruria, Lydia was seen as tyrannical, decadent and dominated by women: this double genetic inheritance helped to shape the personality and reinforce specific traits in the invective.[165] In particular, Maecenas's famous loose-beltedness could be understood either

159. Verg. Aen. 11.732–33; cf. 11.733 ("ignauia"), 736 ("segnes"), 749 ("pinguis"). Tarchon: Drew 1927; R. Tanner 1970–71. Cf. Nielson 1984: 33: Tarchon is "tactfully softening [Etruria's] involvement in [Rome's] history".

160. See Rojas (2010, 2013) on Roman antiquarian interest in ancient Lydia.

161. Gowers 2012: 220; Shackleton Bailey 1982: 17: "Maecenas too was a parvenu from the traditional Roman standpoint, a 'foreigner' like Cicero."

162. Scullard 1967: 18; Dion. Hal. 1.28.3.

163. Farney 2007: 146. M. Perperna, consul in 130, perhaps exploited his Etruscan ancestry while campaigning in Asia; Massa-Pairault 1999: 553.

164. 7C = 5L = 190H ("hic nympha cingit omnis Acheloum senem"). This sexualized paraphrase of Hom. Il. 24.616, on Sipylus in Lydia, confirms that the Lydian, not the Aetolian, Achelous is meant; Hollis 2007: 324; Courtney 2003: 280.

165. Farney 2007: 166–71.

as effeminate or as a visible display of Etrusco-Lydian ethnicity. It is just about possible to imagine him walking the streets in eccentric historical dress, like Lawrence of Arabia.[166] But whether the long skirts had any basis in fact, they persisted because they were good shorthand for the dubious associations of the pedigree, not just in the present but stretching back into the distant past.

To understand the full resonance of the outfit, we need to look still further back. Confusions in Maecenas's case between ethnic markers and effeminacy are typical of a long-lasting Mediterranean tradition of fascination with and hostility towards those who lived further east. From the sixth and early fifth centuries BCE, Greek writers depicted aristocrats inspired by luxurious living (*habrosune*, a word derived from ideas of softness and ripeness) in the courts of Lydia to wear trailing robes, jewellery, long hair and turbans (*mitrai*).[167] Long-haired lovers of Lydia came to be regarded as alien to democratic ideals, which originated in an eighth-century concept of civic *metriotēs*, "moderation". Against this, certain aristocrats (or would-be aristocrats) claimed a different authority through links to gods, heroes and the East, "and the great rulers of Lydia".[168] The groups who "sashayed" through the agorae of Greece became the mysterious figures who dance around Athenian vases, bearded but wearing long skirts, ear-rings and even parasols.[169] Once wrongly interpreted as transvestite men, or even women wearing men's clothes and false beards, they are now assumed to be members of exclusive male drinking groups whose dress represented a specific cluster of aesthetic and political values (loosely speaking, *to kalon*, "beauty" or "the good", and aristocracy, in league with Eastern luxury).[170]

Figures such as these can be regarded as Maecenas's cultural ancestors. Lydianizers live on in Horace's briefly mentioned mincing satirical character Malthinus, a cover for Maecenas according to Porphyrio.[171] More seriously, claims to Etruscan and Lydian regal or aristocratic ancestry may have been entwined with Maecenas's avoidance of a traditional political career and cultivation of exclusive sodalities and alternative value systems. There is, of course, a huge difference between playing the Lydian in sixth-century BCE Athens and doing so in first-century BCE Rome.[172] For the Romans, Lydia represented a far more distant origin, in time and space, for the "contagion" of

166. See Heurgon (1961: 219) on the Etruscan *tebenna*, supposed forerunner of the Roman toga and the knights' *trabea*: Dion. Hal. 2.60.2, 3.61.1.

167. Kurke 1992.

168. I. Morris 1996: 32.

169. Kurke 1992: 105; Boardman and Kurtz 1986; Frontisi-Ducroux and Lissarrague 1990.

170. Kurke 1992: 97–99.

171. Hor. *Sat.* 1.2.25 ("Malthinus tunicis demissis ambulat"); Kurke 1992: 105n59.

172. See Spawforth (2001: 380–84) on Lydian stereotypes in the Roman Empire.

*truphē* (delicate living) that had spread from East to West. The association made Maecenas an even more outrageous throwback to lands of debilitating heat, soft fruit and sexual incontinence.[173] Geo-determinism, as much as effeminacy, explains the vocabulary of overflow, stewing and effeteness (*effusus, fluens, marcidus, eneruare, macerare*), both in the friendly poetry and in the hostile invective. Faced with the stigma of decadence and luxury, Roman poets often put forward a "counter-Maecenas", a restrained proponent of moderation.[174] Dio's fabricated speech is guardedly Periclean in tone: his aristocratic Maecenas counsels against *malakia* ("softness") in those advantaged by wealth and nobility (Dio Cass. 52.26.4) and encourages public opulence without extravagance (52.30.1). Across the biographies, a few salient markers of culture, gender and ethnicity—Etruscan, Lydian, feminine, unorthodox—flower into a full-blown personality, one whose component parts are hard to disaggregate.

## Maecenas, Agrippa and Augustus

Maecenas's rise to power in Rome is always credited to his close personal friendship with Octavian, which continued unbroken when Octavian became Augustus. Without evidence for the motives of either party, any assessment of Maecenas's contribution to the survival and operation of Augustus's regime must remain speculative. He was around until he wasn't, and that is the limit of what we can reliably say. Scandalous as his transition was from personal intimate to unelected adviser, it is still worth considering how Maecenas's Etruscan-Lydian-Roman, "hard-soft" identity might have been useful, both to himself and to Augustus. Not only did his outsider status exempt him from stereotypes of competitive office-seeking, it also gave him flexibility, distinction, glamour and an alternative perspective on centralized power. His eccentricity may have been an asset, and not just in the superficial sense that he made the emperor look more modest, masculine and home-grown. Maecenas's aloofness and lack of obvious social fit may have inspired some of Augustus's own calculatedly free-wheeling behaviour: turning up to dinners late, disregarding senatorial precedent, refusing honours and bypassing the standard senatorial career.[175]

In some respects, the combination with Agrippa looked too good to be true. The trio "Augustus-Maecenas-Agrippa" is often compared to a "third triumvirate", a personalized sharing out of power among friends, cemented by

173. Compare Cyrus's apophthegm that "soft lands breed soft men; marvellous fruits and brave warriors do not grow from the same soil" (Hdt. 9.122.3); Sall. *Cat.* 11.5–6: "The lovely, pleasant land [Asia] and leisured surroundings had easily softened [molliuerant] the soldiers' fierce minds."

174. E.g. Prop. 3.9.31–32.

175. Suet. *Aug.* 74, 35.4, 52.

marriage alliances (in this case, Agrippa's marriage to Augustus's daughter Julia in 21 BCE, allegedly encouraged by Maecenas). At the core of imperial power, the presence of Etruscan Maecenas and Italian Agrippa bolstered the image of an idealized *tota Italia*. In Trajanic historian Florus's words: "Because the Roman people mixed with themselves Etruscans, Latins and Sabines and consider that there is one bloodline from all of these, they have made one body from these parts and one people composed from all of them."[176] At the imaginative level, Virgil's incorporation of obsolescent Etruscans and rugged Italians into the proto-polity of the *Aeneid* only reinforces this idea.[177]

Equally, Maecenas's decision to remain a knight (*eques*), another salient feature of the biographies, meant that imperial favour and political power could be seen as being distributed unusually widely and representatively. Suetonius describes him and Agrippa (consul in 37 BCE) as "leaders of their respective orders" (*Aug.* 66.5: "sui quisque ordinis principes"). Maecenas's "contentment" with his position strongly contrasts with a sharp influx of Etruscan families into the senate, along with artificial efforts to maintain a delicate equilibrium between knights and senators.[178] According to Cicero, to keep a knight's rank (and he names an earlier C. Maecenas among his examples) was to preserve a "tranquil and peaceful life removed from the storms of envy and other such judgments".[179] The equestrian order had ancient dignity (Horace addresses Maecenas as *equitum decus*, "glory, or ornament, of the knights"). Even so, Maecenas's status remained an anomaly.[180] Dio supplies Augustus with the necessary misgivings, alleging that he sent Agrippa back to Italy to cover for Maecenas during his regentship, ostensibly on some other mission, but really because he was afraid that the veterans would despise his friend "on the grounds that he was only a knight" (Dio Cass. 51.3.5).

Liability that he was in some respects, Maecenas functioned more as a symbolic supplement to Augustan power. Unconventional foil to both the emperor and Agrippa, he was for a time fully integrated into the imperial executive, so reinforcing the heft and spread of Augustan authority. He has been described as Augustus's "right-hand man" (*Eleg. in Maec.* 1.1.11–12:[181] "tu Caesaris almi [or: alti] / dextera," [You were the right hand of bountiful [or: high]

---

176. Flor. *Epit.* 2.6.1.

177. Le Doze 2014; Feeney 1999: 191–94.

178. Cresci 1995. Cf. Torelli 1969: 342–43; Nicolet 1966: 703–4, 718.

179. Cic. *Clu.* 153. See Cresci (1995: 174) on ambitious knights like Salvidienus Rufus and Cornelius Gallus who came to bad ends.

180. Hellegouarc'h (1963: 413–15) associates *decus* with decency (*uirtus, dignitas, salus, libertas, claritudo*). Mart. 10.73.3 calls Maecenas "eques Caesarianus".

181. *Eleg. in Maec.* = *Elegiae in Maecenatem*.

Caesar]). But the same title has been claimed for M. Agrippa by his latest bi-ographer.[182] Did Augustus have two right-hand men—or even one right and one left?[183] The two are often paired in the historical record, as joint proxies for use of the imperial seal and as witnesses of the emperor's most humiliating and intimate experiences, like the dropsy he endured from hiding in a marsh after the battle of Philippi.[184] When Seneca records Augustus's angry response to his daughter Julia's adultery, he has him refer to the pair as an item: "None of this would have happened to me had Agrippa or Maecenas been alive!" (*Ben.* 6.32.2). Both men made Augustus their primary heir; both were irre-placeable to him when they died.[185]

Despite the "diptych" formation, however, there remained a moral and cul-tural gulf between the virile Italian general and the effete Etruscan.[186] This translated into a rhetorical antithesis that would remain productive in the later reception of the Augustan Age: the urbane courtier versus the old-fashioned soldier ("a man closer to country ways than to pleasure-seeking").[187] Differ-ences in political style were sharply marked, too.[188] Agrippa, not Maecenas, was associated with public beneficence.[189] Dio's obituary emphasizes Agrippa's popular appeal and his bequests of gardens, baths and cash to the Roman people; the death of Maecenas, who kept his estate private and left everything to Augustus, is said to have been felt by the emperor more as a personal loss (if also a personal gain).[190] In the debate Dio stages between two imperial advisers, it is Maecenas who advocates a form of monarchy while Agrippa promotes Republican values. These speeches are an imaginative reflection of the reality that, for a time, the limits of Augustan power were up for negotiation:

> What we are dealing with . . . is not straightforward repression or straightfor-ward tolerance, but, as always, a developing and shifting relationship, without any precedents, where all the parties involved are feeling their way; habits and patterns of behaviour firm up as time goes on, of course, but it remains an essentially provisional and improvisatory atmosphere. (Feeney 1991: 9)

---

182. L. Powell 2015.

183. Pelling 2009: 43.

184. The source may be Augustus's memoirs: Pelling 2009; L. Powell 2015: 178–79.

185. Sen. *Ben.* 6.32.3; Dio 54.29.5; 55.7.1.

186. Agrippa's portrait-types: Bernoulli 1882: 1.252–63.

187. Plin. *HN* 35.26 ("uir rusticitati propior quam deliciis"). Hor. *Carm.* 1.6.1–2 (Agrippa): "fortis et hostium uictor". Agrippa's hometown is unknown. See Star (2012: 265n16) on the duo in Seneca's *Epistles*; Beugnot (1985: 287) on their early modern afterlife.

188. Della Corte 1992.

189. Dio 54.29.3–4 calls Agrippa a devout friend to the people (*dēmotikōtatos*).

190. Dio 54.29.1–8 (Agrippa), 55.7.1–6 (Maecenas).

In short, "Maecenas and Agrippa" came to represent in bipartite form the same oppositions or split existence that paradoxical characters like Maecenas encompassed in one person: war/peace, business/leisure, public/private, duty/pleasure, old/new. This is nicely illustrated by their joint role as dedicatees of Augustus's lost memoirs. While Sulla's memoirs had been dedicated uniquely to soldier-voluptuary Lucullus, it was as if Lucullus's personality had been split between two men: Maecenas the peaceful and civilized companion, Agrippa the military henchman.[191] Together, they incarnated the tensions and personalized the policy decisions in establishing the new regime, so that its different and often contradictory facets could be attributed to competing strands of advice (*consilium*). As Augustus's smooth-talking counsellor, Maecenas helped mitigate the outward signs of triumviral butchery, so Dio's anecdote about Augustus's reprisals suggests.[192] No surprise, then, that his seamless efficiency and feline swiftness aroused suspicions of "hushing up". When Velleius describes him quashing Lepidus's conspiracy in 31 BCE "without a ripple" (nulla . . . cum perturbatione), that is a euphemism for the summary execution of its ringleader.[193] Where posterity is concerned, Maecenas becomes a key symbol (or explanation) of the elusiveness of Augustan violence, a token sweetener for the onset of totalitarianism.

Nor did Maecenas simply promote clemency on the political plane. He also fostered a new model of Roman civility that embraced pleasure, indulgence and play and extended the ethics of private, Hellenizing sodality into public life. Take Augustus's inauguration of the Ludi Augustales in 19 BCE. Tacitus presents this as a one-off sop to Maecenas and his passion for Bathyllus, but in the wider scheme it allowed a *princeps ciuilis* ("citizen prince") to mingle at play with his people, in stark contrast with his austere, remote successor, Tiberius:[194]

> Augustus had granted [indulserat] these theatrical exhibitions to indulge [dum obtemperat] Maecenas, who had fallen violently in love with Bathyllus [effuso in amorem Bathylli]. Besides, he had no personal dislike for amusements of this type, and considered it an act of civility to mingle in the pleasures of the crowd [ciuile rebatur misceri uoluptatibus uulgi]. The temper of Tiberius had other tendencies, but as yet he lacked the courage to force into the ways of austerity [ad duriora uertere] a nation which had been for so many years pampered [populum per tot annos molliter habitum]. (Tac. *Ann.* 1.54; Loeb translation, adapted)

191. Plut. *Luc.* 1.3; *Comp. Dem. et Cic.* 3.1. Pelling (2009: 46) speculates that the joint dedication was designed to defuse jealousy.

192. See Sen. *Clem.* 1.9–11 on Augustus's imperfect *clementia*, with Berno (2013).

193. Vell. Pat. 2.88.3; cf. Livy *per.* 133; App. *B Civ.* 4.50.

194. On the *ciuilis princeps*, see Wallace-Hadrill (1982).

A caustic observer of the Augustan regime, Tacitus saw how the codes of indulgence (*indulserat, obtemperat*) and shared pleasure (*uoluptatibus*) appropriate for a personal favourite and a private friend could be openly paraded, and in due course rolled out wholesale into public policy. As Pylades, Bathyllus's rival, rejoined: "It is to your advantage, Caesar, that the people should devote their spare time to us" (Dio Cass. 54.17).

That Maecenas was instrumental in bringing out the emperor's softer side is reinforced by the teasing jewel letter from Augustus we saw earlier. Macrobius explicitly introduces it as a glimpse of the emperor in playful mood:

> Again, knowing his friend Maecenas's playful, effete, loose style [quia Maecenatem suum nouerat stilo esse remisso, molli et dissoluto], he would often adopt a similar style in the letters he wrote to him; in contrast to the moralizing tone [castigationem loquendi] he used in his writings elsewhere, he wrote an intimate letter to Maecenas spilling out this supplementary catalogue of joke-names [in epistula ad Maecenatem familiari plura in iocos effuse subtexuit]. (Macrob. *Sat.* 2.4.12)

Augustus can be seen embracing Maecenas's relaxed style, "going with the flow" (*effuse subtexuit*), as he flirts with Greek and Etruscan and invents paradoxical combinations of local and exotic terms. The letter showcases intimacy and exuberance as part of an emperor's life. For a brief interlude, Augustus is playing at being Maecenas.[195] In a broader context, the defence of Maecenas's softness in the *Elegiae* celebrates elite *mollitia*, not a cause for shame but a symptom of victorious jubilation, the winning side letting its hair down: "The Roman male, liberated from rigid masculine sex roles, delights in the freedom of playing a slave and a woman."[196] No permanent loss of face was risked by godlike Octavian and his coterie.[197]

Yet Augustus took no dynastic measures to consolidate the friendship. It was Agrippa who entered the imperial family through marriage to Julia, while Maecenas remained outside it. Indeed, Dio presents Maecenas as a pragmatic observer of Augustus's dilemma over the succession: "Either make him [Agrippa] your son-in-law [by divorcing Marcella and marrying Julia] or slay him" (Dio Cass. 54.6). He was associated far more with proxy relationships. Most obvious is that of Augustus's "darling" friend or naughty overage toy boy

---

195. Cf. Suet. *Aug.* 86.2 ("myrrh-drenched ringlets"): "imitando per iocum irridet".

196. C. Barton 1994: 92.

197. Compare the notorious secret "Banquet of the Twelve Gods" (Suet. *Aug.* 70) or the legendary woodland frolics and festive transvestism of the US political establishment at the Bohemian Club of San Francisco: Garber 1992: 65.

(*deliciae* or *exoletus*), as the frisky tone of the letters suggests (Maecenas was about five years older). Another is pimp (for his own wife), once the emperor took amicable sharing to a logical extreme:[198] "Some even suspected that [Augustus] had gone away on account of Terentia, the wife of Maecenas, and intended, since there was much talk about them in Rome, to live with her abroad free from all gossip" (Dio Cass. 54.19). A third role is that of imperial parasite, the name Augustus explicitly gives Maecenas in the letter where he asks him to entice Horace to leave "that parasite's table" (*ista parasitica mensa*) for the grander "king's table" (*regia mensa*).[199] When Marcus Aurelius draws up a list of Augustus's associates in a jeremiad on human mortality, Maecenas revealingly appears almost as an afterthought, not next to Agrippa but among the philosophers, physicians and priests, the hangers-on and care-givers:[200] "Wife, daughter, descendants, ancestors, sister, Agrippa, kinsmen, intimates, friends, Areius, Maecenas, physicians and sacrificing priests—the whole court is dead" (M. Aur. *Med.* 8.31). Otherwise, Maecenas is rarely described anywhere in the vicinity of Augustus's wife, Livia.[201] This may be because he is often cast as her less matronly substitute, an alternative wife or concubine, matchmaker and long-skirted caretaker of the city in his lord's absence, indulged with jewels, games and boyfriends. His poets, as we will see, associate Maecenas with familial surrogates, both male and female, but these tend to be voluntary ones: adoptive parent, guardian, midwife, lover and intimate friend.

There is another compromising factor for the ancient biographies to negotiate. Taken together with his supposed ethnic origins, Maecenas's career trajectory (from unelected power to withdrawal, rejection or disgrace) made him a forerunner in the narrative of Roman imperial decline. The relative earliness of emperors like Nero and Caligula already complicates the history of decadence.[202] But Maecenas must complicate it further—out of joint with his own time, whether as relic of the past or risk-taking pioneer. His image draws on historical oriental advisers (Alexander's eunuch Bagoas or Xerxes's Artabanus, for example) and later imperial courtiers. His travelling entourage of buffoons (Sarmentus, Balatro), parasites (Vibidius, Porcius), freedmen (Melissus, Sabinius Tiro), concubines (Licymnia) and actors (Bathyllus) resembled a miniature,

---

198. Suet. *Aug.* 69.1: friends acted as pimps to Augustus, stripping and inspecting matrons and young women "as if Toranius the slave-dealer were putting them up for sale"; 71.1: Livia as pimp.

199. Suet. *Vita Hor.*

200. Plutarch (*Mor.* 207c) calls Maecenas Augustus's συμβιότης (*sumbiotēs* household companion = *conuictor*).

201. An exception is *Eleg. in Maec.* 2.31.

202. Vance 2004: 563.

pre-imperial court on the Persian or Hellenistic model. His critics even went so far as to assimilate him to those whose company he kept: eunuchs, courtesans, actors, pimps, pantomimes, parasites and freedmen, all notorious for underhand influence. His smooth efficiency and invisible modus operandi laid him open to suspicion. If Maecenas and Agrippa were alive in his own day, Seneca predicted that "they would be among the dissimulators" (*Ben.* 6.32.4). Maecenas was thus a pioneer of imperial court mores, and not always in a positive way.

In relation to Roman civic space, Maecenas occupied a similarly liminal position. Along with fellow libertines Lucullus and the two Sallusts, he set a trend for later emperors and rich freedmen to move business to their estates in the half-urban, half-rural periphery of the city.[203] The park (*horti*) on the Esquiline Hill allowed him to withdraw from public life, originally part-time, then permanently, if Tacitus's Seneca is to be believed when he claims that Augustus allowed Maecenas to enjoy "retirement abroad within the city".[204] This may have been a consciously historicizing move; the Etruscan-born primeval king Servius Tullius had also shifted his seat of power to the Esquiline Hill.[205] But the detail that Augustus went to his friend's house to convalesce (Suet. *Aug.* 82.2) suggests that Maecenas avoided the conventional performance spaces of imperial power and haunted what sociologist Ervin Goffman would call its "back-regions".[206] Even so, this apparent opposition between centre and periphery has been soundly deconstructed: "The garden . . . flags an abstinence from politics of a particular sort; and yet because it is in fact in easy reach of the centre and a powerful advertisement of wealth, it is after all a bid for power. . . . Maecenas and Sallust set a model for others."[207] Maecenas's Esquiline estate was not just a place of retreat: it was also a panoramic lookout post.[208]

## Maecenas between Emperor and Poets

Maecenas's special position of middleman, halfway between subject and emperor, has another, symbolic consequence. It allows him to function as a sliding indicator of scale, magnified by those below and minimized by those

---

203. Wallace-Hadrill 1998: 6.

204. Tac. *Ann.* 14.53 ("in urbe ipsa uelut peregrinum otium").

205. Ampolo 1996; Chillet 2016: 47–52.

206. Goffman 1956. Cf. Suet. *Tib.* 15.1 ("in hortos Maecenatianos transmigrauit totumque se ad quietem contulit").

207. Wallace-Hadrill 1998: 5–6; Lucullus: Tröster 2008.

208. See chapter 9 below. Velleius uses *speculari*, "to spy", of Maecenas's stealthy operations at court: 2.88.3.

above. An anecdote in Plutarch, for example, approaches the scandal of Maecenas's wife Terentia's drift to Augustus from the bottom up:

> Many have allowed others to share in their erotic pleasures, prostituting not
> only their mistresses but their wives, like the Roman Galba [or Gabba], who
> used to ask Maecenas to dinner, and once he saw from his nods and winks
> what he had a mind to do with his wife, turned his head gently aside as if
> asleep. But when one of his slaves came up to the table and stole some wine,
> his eyes were wide open enough, and he said, "Villain, don't you know that
> I am asleep only for Maecenas?" This is not perhaps so strange, considering
> Galba [Gabba] was a <u>buffoon</u> [gelōtopoios]. (Plut. *Amat.* 760a)

What is striking about this fable is not just the cynical humour it ascribes to
one of Augustus's subjects but also the self-replicating trickle down of behaviour from high to low. Just as Augustus took advantage of Maecenas, so
Maecenas took advantage of his inferiors. As the emperor's courtier was
forced to bow to droit de seigneur, so the *scurra*-underling Galba (or Gabba)
defers to his superior, while remaining vigilant with his own slave.[209] "Turned
his head gently aside as if asleep" mimics the habitual connivance and faked
sluggishness of an imperial courtier in the face of royal prerogative (as do
"nods and winks").[210] As it turns out, this story is a common urban legend
with Republican origins.[211] Transferred to an imperial setting, the buffoon
comes to exemplify dissimulation under tyranny. Another *scurra*, Iortios, at-
tended Maecenas's banquet (or perhaps appeared in Maecenas's *Symposium*)
and praised a rectangular table as "perfectly round and spherical", flattery that
provoked loud laughter among the guests.[212]

Augustus, too, alludes to this "trickle-down effect" when he tries to entice
Horace away from the "parasite's table" to his own king's table, as though Maecenas were aping court dinners. Meanwhile Horace, lower in the pyramid,
pictures himself as a *scurra* (a freeloading entertainer like Galba/Gabba and
Iortios), one who in turn lords it over his own minor followers or parasites.[213]
In *Satires* 2.3, he puts into the mouth of Damasippus, a bankrupt property-
speculator-turned-Stoic, an Aesopic fable that fuses ideas of the miniature and
the replica. When a baby frog tries to express to its mother the size of the giant
calf (*ingens belua*) that has just fatally stepped on its siblings, the mother blows

---

209. Dio 55.7.5: the only event to unsettle Maecenas's sweet temper was Augustus's affair
with Terentia.

210. Lucilius fr. 251 W ("non omnibus dormio"); cf. Juv. 1.55–57.

211. Byrne 1999a: 35.

212. Plutarch, unassigned fr. 180 in Sandbach, *Moralia*, vol. 15.

213. Hor. *Sat.* 2.7.32–37; Turpin 1998.

herself up in emulation until she bursts, so caricaturing Horace's self-important but foolish imitation of Maecenas: "Or is whatever Maecenas does right for you as well, though you are so different and such a pathetic rival to him?" (Hor. *Sat.* 2.3.312–13). Not only is this a cartoon version of the poet's absurdly little attempts to follow his patron's example (in Damasippus's words: "You copy the high-rise guys, even though you're two feet high from top to toe").[214] It also logically reflects satirical victimhood back from replica to archetype. Dwarfing Horace's more limited aspirations is an unflattering reveal of Maecenas's megalomania. The brief inventory of his ambitious building schemes, extravagant lifestyle, and voracious appetite for boys and girls alike that follows effectively catapults the "Maecenas scandal" into the public domain.[215]

## Further Voices

In her compelling discussion of Seneca's 114th Epistle (which consolidates negative views of Maecenas two generations after his death), Margaret Graver concludes: "Seneca's real object is not Maecenas himself but an abstract principle which Maecenas serves to illustrate."[216] This is a crucial insight for his textual portraits in general. To paraphrase a well-known verdict on Augustus, we need to look less at Maecenas as a person and more at Maecenas as an "idea".[217] Not only did he serve as agent and maker of Augustan policy, he was equally a cautionary focus for the choice between political involvement and sybaritic withdrawal, as well as for anxieties about gender confusion and issues of ethnic and social identity.

Where Augustus and his moral programme are concerned, Maecenas has often been considered a frank embarrassment, an eccentric who eventually had to be bundled out of the way. Syme's intuition, for example, is that he was there on sufferance: "The way of his life, like the fantastical conceits of his verse, must have been highly distasteful to Augustus as to Agrippa. Augustus bore with the vices of his minister for the memory of his service and the sake of his counsel."[218] Miriam Griffin views him as similarly regrettable: "Maecenas was a political mistake. He cut a deplorable figure as the Princeps' representative."[219] But the figure he cut, as we will see, is central to our understanding of Maecenas.

---

214. Hor. *Sat.* 2.3.308–9 ("aedificas, hoc est, longos imitaris, ab imo / ad summum totus moduli bipedalis").

215. On ambitious private building, see Edwards (1993: 137–72) and Nichols (2010).

216. Graver 1998: 607.

217. Kennedy 1992: 35.

218. Syme 1939: 342

219. M. Griffin 1976: 211.

Indeed, his fascination is as a figure of style (*cultus*)—sartorial, sensual, literary and moral—an aesthete and a pleasure lover in a society that usually frowned on pleasure. He was not "deplorable" so much as pioneeringly queer (marginal, gender fluid, oriental, coming from a different orientation).[220] Like his beloved superstar, the pantomime actor Bathyllus, Maecenas bent and squirmed, deviating from the straight and narrow, "a man of great talent had he only kept to a straighter path [uia rectiore]", as Seneca puts it.[221] This signature queerness inflected every aspect, social and cultural, of his performance, so a recent definition of the "performative turn" suggests, using the very metaphors of detour and off-kilter sailing that his poets find so expressive:

> A turn that is alternately a technique of dance (pirouette), leads to an unconventional routing (detour), champions social change (revolution, social or otherwise), bends for new use (deflection), proudly questions the culturally normative (deviation), like a sail propels us forward yet is obliquely positioned to the wind (tack), and though unsteady is wide open (yaw), depending upon what is apt. (T. Davis 2008: 2)

From an anthropological perspective, Maecenas could be seen as the human equivalent of that unclassifiable beast the pangolin. Half-mammal, half-reptile, this scaly anteater is notoriously excluded by the Lele people of Tanzania from their normal diet as an inedible boundary-crosser but celebrated as "kingly" in a cult in which it is sacrificed and eaten to release its special powers. Mary Douglas, who brought the practice to Western fame in *Purity and Danger*, made much of this cult because she believed it offered a key to a phenomenon that was socially and culturally universal. By focusing on the pangolin in their rituals, the Lele choose, in her words, to "confront ambiguity in an extreme and concentrated form".[222] Just so, some people in antiquity who wanted to live up to Maecenas made him the focus of a cult of specialness. For Seneca, for one, he was too far out all his life (*Ep.* 19.9). Yet the author of the *Elegiae* specifically defends Maecenas's loose robes—in other words, tells us that after his death or even during his lifetime this paradoxical figure generated a debate about demeanour, sexuality, style, culture and the knee-jerk prejudices that allow image to write off all other aspects of a person.

Seneca's conflation of outer appearance and inner character recalls a notorious critique in Aristophanes's *Thesmophoriazousae*, when a cross-dressing

220. See also Ahmed 2006. Cf. *diuersus*, "deviating", used of Maecenas's Tiberian imitator, Sallustius Crispus (Tac. *Ann.* 3.30).

221. Sen. *Ep.* 114.4. See chapter 6 below on Maecenas's links with *controversiae*.

222. Douglas 1966: 201.

version of the tragedian Agathon appears, depilated and sporting a womanly hairnet along with his lyre. His defence of his outré appearance is that it is a badge of artistic integrity:

> It is bad taste [amouson] for a poet to be coarse and hairy. Look at Ibycus, at Anacreon of Teos, and at Alcaeus, who handled music so well; they wore headbands [emitrophoroun] and found pleasure in the lascivious dances of Ionia. And have you not heard what a dandy [kalos] Phrynichus was and how careful in his dress? For this reason his plays were also beautiful [kala], for the works of a poet are copied from himself. (Ar. *Thesm.* 159–67)

In other words, Agathon's dress is homage to the Lydianizing sodalities who are his aesthetic models.[223] Had Maecenas had the chance to counter Seneca, he might have claimed something similar. Like Anacreon, he loved a Bathyllus; like Agathon, he hosted a *Symposium*.[224] Posterity dresses him in the costume of his cultural forebears. The missing link here is Cicero's rival, the orator Hortensius, who used a similar defence when accused in court by L. Torquatus ("a coarse, unamusing man") of resembling a female dancer, Dionysia. Turning on his opponent, Hortensius uttered a reply "in a low, sultry voice" (uoce molli atque demissa): "I'd rather be Dionysia than be like you: a stranger to the muses, to Venus and to Dionysus [amousos, anaphroditos, aprosdionysos]!"[225]

In his first ode, Horace calls Maecenas his "bulwark" (praesidium), and in *Carm.* 2.17 his "pillar" (columen).[226] In each case, the word is paired with "glory" or "beautiful decoration" (decus).[227] This double tribute, conventional though it is, may be as good an assessment of his twofold significance as any. The biographies skew his reputation by stressing his luxury and superfluity: ornate tables, fish, rings, ringlets, hot water, trailing skirts. But if Maecenas was a prop of the Augustan regime, he equally functioned as its ornament—not so much in our sense of something frivolous and time-wasting but rather as its central, enhancing embellishment.[228] Strung between statecraft and pleasure, he single-handedly disrupted monolithic distinctions between the "Augustan" (straightforward, frugal, solid, inclusive, masculine, un-erotic, classical and

---

223. Snyder 1974; Muecke 1982: 50; Frontisi-Ducroux and Lissarrague 1990.

224. Horace's allusion to Anacreon's love for a Bathyllus in *Epodes* 14 is often seen as a dig at Maecenas's love for his Bathyllus; Tac. *Ann.* 1.54; Dio 54.17.5.

225. Hortensius *ap.* Gell. *NA* 1.5.2–3. See C. Williams (2010: 174): "Despite the black-and-white rhetoric of Roman masculinity . . . real life is often a gray zone."

226. A. Powell (2017: 187) calls him Virgil's "roof", in the Russian sense of high-level political protector.

227. Hor. *Carm.* 1.1.2 (praesidium), 2.17.4 (columen), 1.1.2, 2.17.4 (decus).

228. See Barham (2018: esp. 294) on ornament as conceptually central to Roman art.

grand) and the "non-Augustan" (extravagant, self-indulgent, fanciful, exclusive, feminized, erotic, baroque and miniature).[229] It is no coincidence that the adornments and scenes that accompany his textual portraits challenge more conventional equivalences associated with the Augustan regime: between value and size (jewels), power and size (seal rings), power and substance (perfumes), and power and centrality (peripheral gardens). These are points of tension to which we will return.

The fact that Maecenas was intimately involved with the Augustan establishment while standing aloof from what we normally think of as its ethical and aesthetic centre suggests that conventional notions of Augustan classicism can no longer give us the full picture (contrary to what the Montblanc pen suggests). So a ground-breaking discussion from the 1980s concludes:

> There is little sign of Atticism among Augustan and early imperial prose writers, or in the declamations recorded by the elder Seneca. It was the triumviral Sallust, not the Augustan Livy, who imitated Thucydides. Moreover, if Augustus' own style was a model of moral simplicity, what are we to make of Maecenas, notorious equally for the laxity of his morals, and the perfume-dripping ringlets of his style (Aug. 86 and Seneca, Ep. Mor. 114)? It was Maecenas, after all, who was Augustus' patron of the arts. (Wallace-Hadrill 1989b: 161)

Recent explorations of Augustan culture have built on these hints by exploring contemporary art and poetry through such lenses as the paradoxical, the marvellous, the Dionysiac and the irrational.[230] These elements turn out to be so intrinsic to the works in which they appear, even those where Augustus plays a central part, that it no longer makes sense to keep them distinct from any notional core or official programme. As we will see, Maecenas is often summoned as a privileged observer to marvel at the spectacles paraded before his eyes. As a living personification of the marvellous himself, he belongs by rights at the heart of Augustan culture, not at its margins. Hostile though he was, Seneca was right about one thing. This magnetic, liberated individual, who breached social norms with aplomb, enjoyed transcendent, immeasurable power, and said "no" or "yes" as he pleased was, as much as anyone, an icon of his age.[231]

229. On the former, see Zanker (1988: 239–64).

230. Paradoxical and marvellous: P. Hardie 2009a. Dionysiac: Wyler 2013; Mac Góráin 2013, 2014; Schiesaro 2009. Irrational: P. Hardie 2016.

231. *Ep.* 114.1, 8.

# 2

# Maecenas the Patron

It was one of those rare smiles with a quality of eternal reassurance in it,
that you may come across four or five times in life. It faced—or seemed to
face—the whole eternal world for an instant, and then concentrated on you
with an irresistible prejudice in your favor.

—F. SCOTT FITZGERALD, *THE GREAT GATSBY* (1925)

What do I know to do and what do I know to say of thanks; how can the ground
thank the clouds that pour down rain?

—FARRUKHĪ SĪSTĀNĪ (C. 980–1037), *DĪVĀN*

## Approaching the Patron

Sometime in the first century CE, an anonymous nineteen-year-old wrote a
poem pitching his verse-writing skills to a potential patron:

> All you need do is lend me your joyful presence: perhaps I will sing better
> songs; your very support will give me strength and hope will itself give me
> fertile inspiration. Just do me the favour of opening up your home: this is
> my sole request. It is not all-consuming hunger for gold or relentless desire
> for possession that has driven me on: it is the love of glory. I wish, best of
> men, to spend my life with you, and through all my years create poems that
> compete in excellence with your virtues. (*Laus Pisonis* 216–23)

The raw enthusiasm on show here is typical of the so-called "Encomium of
Piso" (probably the aristocrat of that name who conspired against Nero in 65
CE).[1] Piso is congratulated not just on his military and political exploits but
also on his creative use of his leisure time (which makes him a promising target

---

1. C. Calpurnius Piso. Di Brazzano (2004) puts the date at *c.* 38–40 CE.

for a poet in search of equally carefree conditions). As it happens, this poem is also our earliest source for the use of "Maecenas" as a generic noun. The enlightened champion who launched Virgil, Varius Rufus and Horace on their paths to eternal fame (*Laus Pisonis* 235, 238, 239) is named three times before, building to a climax, the young poet appeals to Piso to become *his* Maecenas:

> But if there is any room for my prayers, if my wishes have reached your heart, then <u>you will one day be sung in smooth verse entreaties of mine, enshrined in memory as my Maecenas</u> [memorabilis olim / tu mihi Maecenas tereti cantabere uersu]. (*Laus Pisonis* 246–48)

How did Maecenas achieve this status of "Über-patron" and what kind of patron did his poets imagine him to be? This chapter has little to add to scholarly debates about his real-life dealings. Other studies of Roman literary patronage are more systematic and put more trust in the texts as historical evidence.[2] Instead, my overarching assumption will be that poets construct their patrons on the page and that Maecenas's individuality is not recoverable from their works.[3] More positively, though, I believe that literary texts can themselves be read as meaningful performances of patronage, interventions in a discourse whose codes were determined as much on the page as in the audience chamber.[4] While they may not reveal what a relationship was really like, they tell us how it ought to be, and sometimes where it fails. They help to answer other questions, too. What is a patron for in a text (as opposed to in life)? How unique is Maecenas and how stereotypical? What part does genre play in his representations? And what do the scenes and metaphors poets use tell us about how they viewed his style of patronage?

At the opposite end of the spectrum from Piso's lavish encomium is Horace's account of his first meeting with Maecenas (constructed as having taken place around 40 BCE):

> I wouldn't say that luck was part of it, that I became your friend by chance. There was no stroke of fortune: it was excellent Virgil followed by Varius who once told you what I was. When I came before you, I blurted out a few words—bashful shyness prevented me from stammering more. I didn't claim to have a famous father, or ride around my estates on a Tarentine nag;

---

2. See, above all, White (1993).

3. Zetzel 1982: 98: Maecenas is "an element in poetry, and as such is subject to the same creative transformations as anything else in poetry is". (Feeney 1994: "a bracing corrective".)

4. Hunter 1996: 109. Cf. Barchiesi (1996: 13n16): patronage is "the thing itself, i.e. the social practice, plus the manifold discourses that construct and affect and contest and imagine the thing itself", as opposed to White (1993), "interested in the thing itself without the discourses".

I just told you what I was. You replied briefly—in your usual manner; I went away, and nine months later you called me back and invited me to join your group of friends. It means a lot to me that I met with your approval, when you know how to pick an upright man from a crooked one, not because he has a famous father but because he has an unstained heart and record. (Hor. *Sat.* 1.6.52–64)

By contrast, this is an object lesson in downplaying upward mobility. Horace tells it without frills, stressing his blameless morals, not his poetic talent. Fellow poets Virgil and Varius bear the burden of his literary ambition, just as the freedman father who brought a nervous schoolboy from Southern Italy to Rome bears the burden of his social and educational aspirations.[5] The stammering interview is embedded in a far more articulate simulated conversation (*sermo*) with Maecenas.[6] Nothing of interest is leaked; there is only tautology and denial. Horace's mini-vita states "what I was" through what he was not, a landed aristocrat with estates and a pedigree (like his satirical predecessor Lucilius).[7] Maecenas takes his time to add Horace to his group of friends. Their exchange is symmetrically brief, a mutually affirming "touchstone" of their future relationship.[8]

Between them, the *Laus Pisonis* and Horace's account represent two strands of ancient "narratives of patronage".[9] In one, the initiative comes from the aspiring protégé. In the other, a protégé, comfortably inside a relationship, remembers having patronage thrust upon him. Neither passage is more genuine a record than the other. Anonymous imperial suits for patronage are probably exercises in filling the gaps in Horace's version.[10] On the other hand, Horace's (dis)ingenuous account is in turn based squarely on a legendary literary scene, the overture to King Antigonus of Macedonia by an ancestor for the satirical voice, Cynic philosopher Bion of Borysthenes (third century BCE), who also told "the plain truth" about himself: his father was a fishmonger "who wiped his nose on his sleeve".[11] While Piso's poet offers uninhibited praise, Horace holds back, maximizing the value and effortlessness of what he has achieved.

5. Gowers 2012, *ad loc.*

6. Gowers 2003: 233.

7. Building on Virgil and Varius's preview of "what I was" (54–55). Cf. Bion *ap.* Diog. Laert. 4.47: "Such is my story. It is time for Persaeus and Philonides to stop recounting it. Judge me on my own account."

8. Labate 2005: 53: "pietra di paragone".

9. Hunter 2003: 38–39.

10. Peirano 2012: 117–72.

11. Diog. Laert. 4.47 = fr. 1 Kindstrand.

His account is a fantasy of instant mutual attraction. It is also a fantasy of power reversal, of being wanted without having to try. Later in his career, he will laugh at every poet's deluded hope that the emperor might spontaneously issue a summons offering his protection: "while we live in hope that, as soon as you know we are not composing poems, you will summon us of your own accord [ultro] and banish need and insist that we write [scribere cogas]."[12] But this is precisely what he claims to have managed himself.

Horace leaves us so many narratives of patronage, his own and other people's, that most of my illustrations here come from his works (the *Satires, Epodes* and *Epistles*; the *Odes* are discussed in a later chapter).[13] Key scenes will recur: the first interview; the "Journey to Brundisium" in the patron's entourage (*Sat.* 1.5); the successful rebuff of a rival poet, the "Pest" (*Sat.* 1.9); and the parables Horace tells Maecenas when he eventually wants to loosen his ties (*Epist.* 1.7). From the first line of *Satires* 1 (36/35 BCE), through the *Epodes* (30 BCE), *Odes* 1–3 (23 BCE) and *Epistles* 1 (21 BCE), Maecenas remains the long-term addressee.[14] Horace tracks their relationship from hesitant beginnings to familiar routines to attempts at separation, with strategic doses of antagonism and irritation thrown in, before he encounters a higher power on the page in his verse-letter to Augustus (*Ep.* 2.1). Until then, Maecenas plays involuntary witness to meditations on life, love, war, virtue, aging, social worth, literary criticism and patronage itself, and sounding board for anecdotes, entertainments, even gothic horror (*Sat.* 1.8, *Epod.* 5, 17). By contrast, we learn little about him from Virgil's *Georgics* (29 BCE), while Propertius addresses him only twice, less as a fleshed-out personality than as a yardstick for his own career choices.

If Horace's account of his life with Maecenas became *the* patron-poet bond in Western culture, that is quite an achievement. At the same time, it set an impossibly high standard for the duration and authenticity of such relationships. Horace is very good at persuading us that this exceptional meeting of minds dissolved the hierarchies and short-circuited the mechanics of mainstream patronage—that pervasive network of connections and obligations that oiled the wheels of Roman life at all levels, civic, local and personal. Yet his very exceptionalism is typical of the discourse of most patronage, especially literary patronage.[15] So is his language of "friendship" (*amicitia*). When Horace calls Maecenas *amicus* "friend" from the beginning to the end of their textual relationship,

12. Hor. *Epist.* 2.1.226–28.

13. See Granados de Arena and Lopez de Vega (1993) on Horace's partial portrait of Maecenas.

14. *Satires* 2.1 breaks the thread, addressed to Trebatius, not Maecenas.

15. Gordon Williams 1990: 270.

he suggests that together they transcended the mutual arrangement that Richard Saller has defined as a voluntary, socially unequal relationship of some duration, where one party wields influence to protect and assist the other, and goods and services are exchanged.[16] From the outside, though, this definition applies to Horace and Maecenas as much as to any other patron and client. Those inside patronage relationships tend to idealize them, replacing rank, dependence, obligation, dependence and payment with equality, autonomy, loyalty, abstract "bounty"—and friendship.

If there was a "tense dialectic between *amicitia* and clientship" in the Roman world, this was because the word *amicus*, "friend", did duty for both concepts.[17] The ideal is extolled by Aristotle, Cicero and Seneca: a partner in an altruistic, affective relationship where payment never passed hands. But *amicus* was also the standard term for a financial backer, or an acquaintance who performed a client's duties: sharing a journey, attending the morning audience, providing votes and even funds, according to principles of mutual obligation (*fides*, "loyalty"; *beneficium*, "benefit"; *munus*, "service").[18] It was not so much, then, that the second usage was a euphemism for "fake" (*amicitia*). The antithesis is a false one when *amicus* covers both affect and duty. Etiquette, rhetoric and position (interestedness or objectivity) complicate the picture.[19] All we can be sure of is that Horace is addressing someone he wanted to suggest was an *amicus*: "It is one thing . . . to argue that a relationship which calls itself *amicitia* is not really friendship, but quite another to claim that it is not really *amicitia*."[20] The performance of *amicitia* in his textual relationship with Maecenas explores every shade of that term.[21] Alongside *amicus* (of both parties) and *conuictor* ("living partner", "fellow diner", of the protégé) are many franker indicators of power difference: *rex* ("king", "boss", "host") versus *parasitus* ("parasite"), *scurra* ("freeloading entertainer") and *umbra* ("shadow"). Horace uses these terms pre-emptively of himself and Maecenas, with an eye to envious critics.

So far, I have used "patron" unreflectively. But this word, too, presents a challenge for translators—a reverse one. Our word clearly derives from Latin *patronus*, originally the term for an ex-master and subsequent sponsor of a

---

16. *Epod.* 1.2 ("amice"); *Epist.* 1.7.12 ("dulcis amice"). Saller 1982b: 1. To which Millett (1989) 16 adds the potential for exploitation.

17. C. Willliams 2012: 17.

18. Lucretius's "longed-for pleasure of sweet friendship" (1.140–41) may refer to either a patronal bond or authentic (or idealized) Epicurean closeness.

19. C. Williams 2012: 44–54. In short, *amicus* is a "false friend", as my student Cecilia Yearsley once aptly put it.

20. C. Williams 2012: 47.

21. C. Williams 2012: 70, 208.

slave, later applied analogously to broader support systems, legal, political and financial.[22] The term was rarely used by those inside Roman patronage relationships, even if they followed similar protocols and borrowed the language of *clientela* in moments of protest or self-loathing.[23] Our "patron", in the sense of a supporter of artistic endeavour, has no equivalent term in the ancient world, and yet the ancient world set the template for what such a supporter should be, starting with the Greek tyrants who maintained poets in return for fame and praise. Indeed, one radical (unthinkable?) possibility is that Maecenas's poets constructed a mere *amicus* as the ideal patron by casting him in the image of those earlier collectors of talent.

In that case, is the quest for what we think of as a patron in an ancient text an entirely circular one? And if not, can we better understand what we are looking for by considering not personal or historical attributes but the role such a person plays in that text?[24] Is being named as primary addressee of a collection, for example, a qualification? Clearly not, when it is still debated whether Catullus's Nepos, Propertius's pre-Maecenas addressee Tullus and Lucretius's student Memmius count as patrons.[25] A better clue is the hint of some benefaction or obligation between two parties each of whom has something the other desires. A patron is often enlisted as the pretext (genuine or not) for a text to come into being, whether this consists in a plea for attention, thanks for a gift or a response to a request. Ancient literary patronage modelled itself outwardly on broader social systems of gift exchange rooted in principles of voluntary, disinterested, excessive generosity. Patrons and protégés alike conspire in what Pierre Bourdieu calls "misrecognition agreements", strenuously substituting gifts, hospitality and services for their cash equivalent.[26] When texts enter this system as analogous tokens of gratitude or virtual recompense, they add a further level of sublimation. What matters, then, for a patronage relationship to continue is not the discharge of debt but "a perpetual disequilibrium of indebtedness" between parties, sustained and prolonged by the protégé's delivery of his work.[27] In other words, keying literary production

22. Miriam Griffin (1990: 402) speaks of a "healthy ambiguity". On Roman patronage, see Brunt (1965), Wallace-Hadrill (1989a) and Eilers (2002; a metaphor for relations between Roman supporters and Greek cities). Roman literary patronage: Gold 1982a, 1987, 2012; Zetzel 1982; White 1993. Patronage more widely: T. Johnson and Dandeker 1989.

23. Cicero famously called labels *patrocinium* and *cliens* "tantamount to death" (*Off.* 2.69).

24. Female patrons are rare but found, e.g., in Martial.

25. See pp. 198–200 below on Tullus.

26. An inhibition that applies in the practice as much as in the discourse of patronage; Bourdieu 1977: 171.

27. Bowditch 2010: 56.

to broader exchanges and individual benefactors creates both a context for gauging its incalculable value and an artificial stimulus for a two-way flow between poet and world.

Another clue to identifying a patron, as opposed to a friend, is inconsistency about distance and closeness (or difference and sameness) in the relationship.[28] A crucial aspect of the dynamics of patronal address is staking out differences and obstacles, then attempting to bridge them. Again, Horace is typical in alternating intimacy (spiritual, cultural and intellectual) with inequality (social, political and financial). His Maecenas has a grand house, wealth, ancestry, an entourage, even a noble nose: all the paraphernalia of "the great man". He is far ahead, in all senses, thanks to better grooming, higher status and faster transport. His poets bow to his ancestry and build up the privilege of admission to his company ("pure honey", Hor. *Sat.* 2.6.32). They praise his meritocratic judgment and use him as an aspirational goal, an *exemplum* to be imitated:

> at tua, Maecenas, uitae praecepta recepi,
>     cogor et te superare tuis.

> (PROP. 3.9.21–22)

But I have learned your advice for living, Maecenas, and I am forced to surpass you by your own example.

Just as often, familiarity and intimacy are stressed. Maecenas is cast as soulmate, drinking partner, hunting companion and prankster, and in his weaker moments as degenerate pleasure lover, vulnerable warrior and fragile patient. But even shared experience is marked by stratification and difference. In *Epodes* 14, Horace and Maecenas wilt side by side from lovesickness, but one loves a freedwoman, the other a noblewoman.[29] When Horace speaks as Priapus, custodian of a humble cabbage patch, he shadows Maecenas, owner of a great park and warden of the entire city (*Sat.* 1.8). As one of Horace's interlocutors puts it:

> an, quodcumque facit Maecenas, te quoque uerum est,
> tanto dissimilem et tanto certare minorem?

> (SAT. 2.3.312–13)

Is whatever Maecenas does right for you to do, too, when you are so different and at such a disadvantage when competing with him?

28. Sharlet 2011: 22–28.
29. Cf. the different categories of sex objects in *Sat.* 1.2.

A conclusion from medieval Islamic patronage fits Rome well: "Patronage relationships are about transcending boundaries of status while also clarifying who belongs in which category."[30] This helps explain what a patron is for in a literary text: to be a stimulus for literary production, a buffer between author and world, a bridge to what he wants to achieve (or reject), someone who for all his hovering mediation and support is never fully knowable or entirely reliable. Maecenas is where a poet wants to go—and later, what he wants to overtake.

## Patrons of the Past

Maecenas is also recognizable as a patron because of literary tradition. His portraits are shaped by images, scenes and crises from the long history of Greco-Roman literary patronage, which saw textual offerings of praise, wisdom, consolation and amusement injected (often by out-of-state individuals) into old systems of exchange. Patronage narratives overlap with travel, pilgrimage and conversion narratives.[31] They contribute to a stock of mythical conversations between the rich and powerful and their outspoken interlocutors (Croesus and Solon, Xanthus and Aesop, Antigonus and Bion).[32] When Horace and his peers frame Maecenas as a patron, they are not just considering contemporary Roman systems, they are also looking back to patrons of the past, fictional as well as historical, from different political and cultural contexts.

Literary patronage is as old as Greek literature itself, starting with the begging bards who sing for their supper at Homer's primeval feasts. But it is with lyric poetry (seventh to fifth centuries BCE) that it first becomes an institution (seen, that is, from the Hellenistic and Roman periods). Lyric poets are said to have travelled the Mediterranean offering their services to local autocrats (such as Polycrates, Peisistratus and the Sicilian tyrants) in an almost mercantile paradigm for the circulation of cultural capital and prestige.[33] Ideally, their songs promoted individuals, made communities cohere, and gave cities a history and divine provenance. A poet's trump card was his ability to give a patron something sublime and intangible: immortality. In return, as representatives of earthly power, patrons helped create their poets' posterity. The neatest statement of this "*kleos*-bargain" is lyric poet Ibycus's promise to Polycrates, tyrant

---

30. Sharlet 2011: 22.

31. E.g., Socrates's account of peripatetic interviews with wise men in the *Apology*, or the playboy Polemo's sudden conversion from drunken hedonism after attending a Stoic lecture (Hor. *Sat.* 2.3.253–57).

32. Whitmarsh 2013; Richlin 2016.

33. Hunter and Rutherford 2009.

of Samos:[34] "You too, Polycrates, will have undying fame in proportion to my song and my fame" (fr. S151.47–48).

Yet these mutually enmeshing transactions were neither as simple nor as static as they seem. When Pindar offered his patrons an overload of praise, designed to stimulate further cycles of gratuitous generosity (*charis*) and subsequent indebtedness (*chreos*), the smooth circulation of symbolic and other capital relied heavily on mystification.[35] Ideals of equality, autonomy and like-mindedness veiled social differences between *philoi* ("friends"), while abstract by-products like friendship, loyalty, benefit and fame were celebrated beyond (or as) wealth, and, given their cultural currency, were no less valuable and real.[36] This worked well enough in pre-capitalist societies, invested in competitive gift giving and united by distrust of money. Yet the more poets filled their works with images of wealth, the more their piles of "gold" and "silver" became hostages to fortune. Provoked by his mercenary rival, Simonides, Pindar himself came to admit the venal possibilities of language, expressing nostalgia for a time when "the Muse was not yet avaricious or a working-girl, nor yet were sweet, gentle-voiced songs sold with faces painted silver by sweet-talking Terpsichore" (*Isthm.* 2.6–8).

These tensions in lyric poetry crucially shaped the later discourse of literary patronage: insulated by ambiguity and battered by envy and suspicion about its workings. As tyrants turned into godlike world leaders, new models and antitypes evolved. Now, the *rex* (patron) of a feast might also be a real king. The itinerant bard of lyric became the kept court poet or sycophant (the Ptolemies' "bookish scribblers", or Choerilus with Alexander). The flatterer (*kolax*) was a staple accessory, while freak examples of candour (Aesop with Xanthus, Bion with Antigonus) fed larger debates about the relative merits of tact and free speech in unequal relationships.[37] The military framework that began with Alexander suited early Republican Rome, which generated stories of poets picked up or taken on campaign to commemorate a great lord's *res gestae*: Ennius (from Calabria) with Cato, Scipio Africanus and Fulvius Nobilior; Theophanes (from Lesbos) with Pompey.[38] These are tales of travel, war, migration and empire, with citizen rights traded for literary commemoration, Roman *amicitia* for Greek culture, in a far more capacious framework than

---

34. Martin 2009.

35. Bourdieu 1977: 177, cited in Kurke 1991: 81.

36. Bowditch (2001: 5) sees poetry as one form of capital among many, mystified and obfuscated, but with material exchange as the "reality" it disguises. Yet Lowrie (2002: 306) questions whether economic interests are "any more fundamental than . . . gratitude, voluntarism, and liberty".

37. Hunter 1985.

38. Horsfall (1988: 269) notes the continuity of the military model: "talk, reading, composition, even, in the general's tent on campaign . . . from Alexander to Messalla, via Julius Caesar".

traditional parochial, patriarchal models allowed.[39] Outsider Ennius, for example, integrated himself and Greek epinician poetics into a Roman aristocratic "economy of remembrance".[40]

Within this new framework, Ennius's "Good Companion" sketch (perhaps a self-portrait based on his own relationship with a noble patron) established a lasting ideal of the frank but discreet confidant who upheld, rather than disturbed, the aristocratic system that embraced him:[41]

> Having said this, he summons the man with whom he often cared to share his table and conversation and his thoughts on private matters when exhausted from spending most of the day managing the highest affairs of state, giving advice in the forum and the sacred Senate. To him he would speak with confidence of matters great and small and jests and would unburden himself of things worth saying and not, whenever he wanted, and would confide in him safely. Someone with whom he could share many pleasures . . . joys, privately and in public; someone whom no fickle or evil thought could persuade to do a bad deed; a learned, faithful, lovely man, pleasant, content with his lot, fortunate, clever, saying the right thing at the right time, obliging, taciturn . . . (Enn. *Ann.* 268–82 Sk.)

Meanwhile, unrulier stereotypes from New Comedy—the fawning parasite (*parasitus*) and swaggering mercenary (*miles gloriosus*) who compete for the attention of a vain and unpredictable king (*rex*)—suggested less containable scenarios: global adventuring and insane competition for every pampering niche.[42] Ennius himself was tainted by the double-edged concept of *praeconium*, promoting great men's deeds (a *praeco* being not just a military herald, spokesman on the field for a general or city, but also a loud-mouthed salesman).[43] Terence was stigmatized as an African ex-slave (from his cognomen *Afer*), a parasite at the table of senior playwright Caecilius and a dependant of Scipio Aemilianus and Laelius, whose coterie was known not just for its boyish antics but also for rumours of sexual exploitation and ghostwriting (Suet. *Vita Terenti*).

Stories like these fed anxieties about the permeability of patronage systems to opportunistic intruders irreconcilable with civic ideals. Patronage was not just an arena for practising *amicitia* (or Greek *philia*): it was also politics in

---

39. Transport words (*deducere* and *transferre*) are central to Ennius's biography; Suerbaum 2002: 121–22.

40. Gildenhard 2003: 104–5; Cic. *Brut.* 79.

41. Gell. *NA* 12.4. Ennius and his patrons: Goldberg 1989; Gildenhard 2003: 111.

42. Ter. *Eun.* 397–429; Skutsch 1968: 92–94; and see P. Hardie (2007b: 130–36) on what Horace takes from this scene.

43. Val. Max. 8.14.1. Cic. *Tusc.* 1.34 condemns the epigram written on a statue of Ennius: "He demands the reward of glory from those whose fathers he gave glory."

miniature, or politics displaced, a voluntary version of community that cut across kinship and other hierarchical systems. But what kind of politics? A relationship between a social superior and an inferior could be conceived as tyrannical (absolute power cutting across conventional aristocratic groupings), aristocratic (if both partners saw themselves as belonging to the same elite) or democratic/ meritocratic (if the lesser partner was elevated as a result of exceptional qualities or speaking his mind), an ambiguity that reflects broader interests and tensions.[44] One man's duty and fidelity was another man's dependency, one man's beneficent patron another's exploitative overlord (*rex, tyrannus*), one man's gifted protégé another's freeloader or parasite (*scurra, parasitus, umbra*).[45] In fourth-century Athens, patronage was associated with corruption and preferential treatment; in oligarchic Rome, it was enshrined practically and ideologically at all levels of society.[46] When Peter White calculates that positive representations of Roman patronage outnumber negative ones by a factor of four to one, that tells us only who was invested in what kind of representation.[47] As Cynthia Damon puts it: "The Romans perceived both the problems in and the limitations of a system based on patronage."[48]

For some observers, the disjunction between exclusive bonds and broader ideals of civic life was barely tenable. While his peers hosted pet poets, like Hellenistic dynasts, Cicero idealized patronage as a civic institution, defending Syrian-born Archias not as Lucullus's poet in residence but as an ornament to the entire state.[49] Yet *Pro Archia* (62 BCE) is equally a document of personal patronage, the implied quid pro quo for citizen rights being a tailor-made epic on Cicero's consulship.[50] Meanwhile, in *In Pisonem*, Cicero spares no mercy for another poet—the "little Greek . . . flatterer" (Philodemus) "trapped in friendship" and "asked, entreated, forced" to write about Piso's lusts, banquets and adulteries, so that "anyone who wishes can see the man's life reflected as in a

---

44. Netz 2020: 279: "[Cultural patronage] highlights a relation of subordination between two members of the elite. In a word, it is tyrannical"; but cf. 281: "patronage is constrained by the ideologies of egalitarianism".

45. See Damon (1997) on comedy and satire. On the *scurra*, see Corbett (1986) and Habinek (2005).

46. Brunt 1988: 382–442.

47. White 1993: 29.

48. Damon 1997: 276.

49. Damon 1997: 268–76; Gold 1987: 3.

50. Dugan 2001: 47. Archias, a noble in his home city Antioch (Cic. *Arch.* 4) and a teacher-cum-protégé, complicates the exchange of Greek culture for Roman hegemony; Whitmarsh 2013: 138–39. Cicero (*Arch.* 25) cites Sulla's use of proceeds from the proscriptions to pay off a bad provincial poet for unsolicited doggerel as a perfect storm of incompetence, pushiness, hostility and ill-gotten cash.

mirror".[51] Later, he imagines an ideal system where friends of high status answer each other's cultural and financial needs (*Off.* 2.62–63, 65–71).[52] Soon after Maecenas's death, Dionysius of Halicarnassus gave patronage a stable foundation myth going back to Romulus in which patrons were always patricians, clients always plebeians and bonds remained mutually supportive down the generations.[53] Both he and Cicero camouflaged an institution marked by volatility and competition, driven as much by transient protégés as by fickle patrons.[54]

Seen in this context, Horace's long-term relationship with Maecenas amounted to an anachronism that needed justifying. Having fully digested the history of literary patronage and internalized the strategies that protected its discourse, Horace knew that wealth, praise, and the motives of patrons and poets alike had long attracted suspicion.[55] Accordingly, he marks his relationship as exceptional, distinct from broader Greco-Roman contexts such as city-states locked into treaties or hordes of clients waiting for handouts in grand entrance halls. After all: "An ordinary client could not offer you immortal glory, nor would posterity have its eye on the nature of your relationship with him."[56] Piso's poet, likewise, credits his would-be patron with the ability to discern creative types among run-of-the-mill followers:

> Your whole house echoes with the varied arts of those who frequent it, every one motivated by the love of culture. You do not want a rough, untrained mass of clients, who only know how to push with all their sorry efforts to make you a path through the crowds. What you admire is talent in all its different aspects. (*Laus Pisonis* 133–37)

Both know better than to ask for money. When White finds evidence in the texts of "intimate, sustained" contact with patrons, with "visibility" (introductions, social cachet, and so on) as the poets' main reward, this may well be authentic (most of Maecenas's poets are likely to have been financially independent from

---

51. Cic. *Pis.* 70–71.

52. Stroup (2010) gives the name "society of patrons" to first-century BCE literati (Cicero, Catullus, Varro, Brutus) who exchanged works. Such a community of social equals with matching gifts does not fit the differential model.

53. Dion. Hal. *Ant. Rom.* 2.9.2–3. The inherent stratification of Roman society made patronage seem "natural"; Gold 1987: 65.

54. T. Johnson and Dandeker 1989: 240: "fluidity, ambiguity and flexibility"; see Gruendler (2005) on Abbasīd patrons.

55. J. Griffin 1984: esp. 190–92.

56. J. Griffin 1984: 217n43; cf. Gold 1987: 6. White (1993: 29) minimizes the difference between poets and other "friends". But Roman poets never describe hobnobbing with their Greek *conuictores*; Feeney 1994.

early in their careers).[57] At the same time, the rhetoric is entirely predictable.[58] Poets' success in concealing the "scandal" of monetary payment does not rule out the possibility that they were paid, in cash, gifts or land.[59] Horace hints throughout his poetry at the one-off gift of the Sabine Farm (on which more later) and a similar story is supplied for Virgil as a pretext for the *Georgics*. Conversely, the absence of "financial considerations" does not guarantee the presence of genuine friendship. Horace alone creates that impression.[60]

Still, Maecenas's poets depart from the effusive mainstream in several ways. First, they never compliment him on his own poetry. If this adds to the suspicion that it was embarrassingly bad, it also enhanced the value of their productions for him.[61] Secondly, any overt praise is managed obliquely: no monuments or inscriptions, just informal traces of friendship, generosity and laissez-faire. Nor is there a grand panorama of leisure activities, as in the *Laus Pisonis*. Instead, scattered snapshots illustrate an ideology of patronage as relaxed friendship, while the name itself, *Maecenas*, repeated at the start of many collections, becomes a badge of belonging and a pledge of lasting fame.

## Horace and Maecenas

Much has been written on how the arc of Horace's relationship with Maecenas evolves across his satires, iambics, odes and epistles, and what follows owes much to earlier discussions.[62] Some basic observations are worth repeating. First, the figure of Maecenas is always subservient to Horace's development, rather than the other way around. After all, it was his choice whether and when to enlist Maecenas on the page. The patron is portrayed not just as a supporter and friend, he is directly linked to the poet's self-construction and the evolution of his work, from crude to polished, personal to political: Maecenas "*became* the poetry".[63] Secondly, Horace performs a kind of rhetorical striptease, so that anything nakedly transactional comes into view only when it has become obsolescent or irrelevant and so useful for other purposes, such as asserting his

---

57. Zetzel 1982: 89–90: Horace qualified financially for equestrian status even before the civil wars.

58. White 1993: 34. Luc. *De mercede conductis* 20 mentions would-be protégés who paid to be in their patrons' contact lists.

59. J. Griffin (1984: 192) is certain that all three poets profited considerably; Virgil left 10 million sesterces in his will, some of it to Maecenas and Augustus (Donat. *Vita Verg.* 37).

60. Feeney 1994.

61. Bernhardy 1865: 258. Contrast Verg. *Ecl.* 1.3.86 ("Pollio et ipse facit noua carmina").

62. E.g., Reckford 1959; Freudenburg 1993, 2001; DuQuesnay 1984; Damon 1997: 105–45; Oliensis 1998; Bowditch 2001; C. Williams 2012.

63. Gold 1987: 141; cf. Zetzel 1982: Maecenas is "an element in a work of art" (95).

self-sufficiency; by contrast, he is explicit from the start about other people's manoeuvres. Thirdly, two-way vision helps him to see himself as others see him, as a movable token in a multi-tiered system where Maecenas is to Augustus as Horace is to Maecenas, and as a slave, parasite or bailiff is to Horace.[64] As patron and protégé in one person, Horace gives us patronage in the round, routine and transcendent, shot through with tensions, hopes and hypocrisies. His different poetry collections make it uniquely possible to assess the role of genre and literary history in Maecenas's portraits, to understand why he plays prickly interlocutor in the *Satires* and *Epistles*, combative drinking partner in the *Epodes*, and neurotic tyrant in the *Odes*.

If *Satires* 1, Horace's debut, fixed Maecenas's posthumous reputation as an informal, egalitarian figure, that is partly because this chimes with its generic ethos. Horace's serio-comic "conversations" (*sermones*) take their cues from Lucilius's cosy antics with great men and adapt them to a more cautious environment, telling the journey of a freedman's son from Southern Italian nobody to urban somebody. It is ironic that two books of "conversations"—sermons, anecdotes, travelogues, literary criticism—make Maecenas dumb witness to Horace's developing speech, overhearing generalized homilies that jab at his weak spots (wealth, sexual weakness and intolerance; *Sat.* 1.1–3). In other ways, he functions as a benchmark. Horace's history of satirical speech (a progressive tamping down of unrestrained expression) mirrors the history of his socialization, from the brute mumbling of the first interview to naive interruption:

> simplicior quis et est, qualem me saepe libenter
> obtulerim tibi, Maecenas, ut forte legentem
> aut tacitum impellat quouis sermone: "molestus,
> communi sensu plane caret" inquimus.
>
> (SAT. 1.3.63–66)

Take someone a bit gauche, like myself, who has often butted in on you unasked, Maecenas, when you were perhaps reading, or interrupted you with some conversation or other when you wanted to be quiet. "What a pain, he clearly lacks all social sense," is our reaction.

... and from that to knowing when to stay quiet:

> haec ego mecum
> compressis agito labris; ubi quid datur oti,
> illudo chartis.
>
> (SAT. 1.4.137–39)

---

64. Gold 1987: 119.

I talk to myself like this with lips sealed; whatever leisure time I have, I fritter it away on paper.

"Quietly reading" is exactly where Horace wants Maecenas. Indeed, it has been suggested that the relationship Horace creates with him is, above all, an allegory of reading.[65] It will never be clear whether Maecenas really incarnated casual, sexually adventurous, entertainment-loving sprezzatura or whether that is just how Horace constructs him as his satirical ideal.[66] But one man's way of being in the world is modelled on the other's (*Sat.* 1.6.60: "ut tuus est mos" ~ *Sat.* 1.9.1: "sicut meus est mos"), so that the urbane patron becomes the ever-receding end point of a bumpkin's polishing process. Ever alert to the chutzpah of his meteoric rise, Horace downplays ambition and dependence at every opportunity while exaggerating the outrage he provokes.[67] He travels separately, dines separately, flaunting his independence.

Meanwhile, his rivals' manoeuvring is made all too explicit. The pushy Pest who accosts him in the street asking for an introduction to Maecenas is best seen as an excruciating caricature of Horace's former self, who lays bare the mechanics of patronage while trampling on its delicate aesthetic sympathies.[68] For instance, the Pest does not hesitate to use the crude *tradere*, "introduce" (so conspicuously missing from Horace's first interview) while parading his accomplishments:[69]

> "haberes
> magnum adiutorem, posset qui ferre secundas,
> hunc hominem uelles si <u>tradere</u>." "dispeream, ni
> summosses omnis."

(SAT. 1.9.45–48)

"You'll have a great ally, prepared to be number two, if you agree <u>to introduce</u> yours truly." "Blow me if you don't jump straight to the front of the queue."

"Life with Maecenas isn't what you think," says Horace, again anticipating the critical tradition by protecting the coveted residence from mud-slinging. Just so, he deals with insulting names for his own condition—parasite, puppet, garden gnome, pet poet, court jester—by assuming all those roles

---

65. Lowrie 2002: 309, citing De Man 1979: writing has power to shape the world imaginatively.

66. The smooth, elusive Aristius Fuscus (*Sat.* 1.9.60–74) is Horace's ideal satirist; Gowers 2003: 86.

67. Rhetoric typical of the *nouus homo*; Wiseman 1971: 73.

68. Henderson 1993.

69. Cf. the blander correlative *assumere* (*Sat.* 1.6.51, of Maecenas).

pre-emptively.[70] Cartoon characters distort "Horace and Maecenas," grotesquely pairing boorishness and hyper-civility, exhibitionism and decadence: stinking Gargonius and scented Rufillus; a shameless flasher and mincing Maltinus; the obscene god Priapus and the ornamental gardener Maecenas; the free-loader (*scurra*) Pantolabus and the playboy (*nepos*) Nomentanus; the band of strippers, street people and drug dealers who weep crocodile tears at the funeral of their sugar daddy (*benignus*) Tigellius.[71]

Five or six years on, *Satires* 2 charts the increasing strain of a patronage relationship. As establishment figure and owner of an idyllic farm, Horace continues to attract envy, fighting his way to Maecenas's house through crowds of lobbyists and gossipmongers in the streets where he once peace-fully wandered (*Sat.* 2.6). The "child of Fortune" has become a middleman in Maecenas's image, suspended between client and patron. Surrogate speakers partly unstopper the secrets, or the cost, of Horace's success. He "belatedly" silences a ruined antique dealer turned Stoic, Damasippus, who accuses him of aping Maecenas in grandiose building, philandering and living beyond his means (*Sat.* 2.3). He allows a free-speaking slave, Davus, to nail him as others see him, as the servile parasite who jumps at every last-minute invitation (*Sat.* 2.7).[72] He displays his credentials as Maecenas's Good Companion, re-gurgitating dull trivia about sport, the weather and the time of day rather than state secrets (*Sat.* 2.6). Even so, he has already allowed the scandal of his pa-tron's decadent habits (extravagant building, love affairs) to be "unintention-ally" exposed (*Sat.* 2.3.307–26). Images of patrons and clients become more twisted. Indigent Ulysses is desperate to learn the art of legacy hunting (*Sat.* 2.5). Nasidienus hosts a disastrous soirée where the guests, including Maecenas, stifle their guffaws while rejecting the food (*Sat.* 2.8), suggesting an uneasy model for the reception of Horatian satire: schadenfreude with a sour aftertaste.

Meanwhile, Horace was experimenting with overt aggression towards his patron. The *Epodes*, evil twin of *Satires* 2 (also published in 30 BCE), revives the iambics of Archilochus and Hipponax, refracting contemporary upheaval via the spats of archaic drinking factions. The reticent speaker of the *Satires* ex-plodes into malicious, self-destructive abuse, destined to backfire when he is all too similar to the upstarts, witches, malodorous pariahs, limp males and unap-pealing old women he derides.[73] Not even the patron, cast as aristocratic

70. Turpin 1998; Damon 1997: 105–45.

71. Gowers 2003: 85. *Sat.* 1.2.27, 4.92, 2.25, 1.8, 1.8.11, 1.2.3–4. The scholiasts identify Maltinus with Maecenas.

72. On Horace's pre-emptive self-identification as parasite, see Gordon Williams (1982: 3–27), Turpin (1998), Oliensis (1998: 157–65) and Damon (1997: 105–45).

73. Henderson 1987: 111.

boon-companion, escapes the poet's mood swings between passionate loyalty and vicious attack. Horace professes himself a devoted follower when Maecenas leaves for Actium (*Epodes* 1), but soon tears into him (*Epodes* 3) for "poisoning" him with indigestible garlic, his exhalation serving as both a physiology of iambic anger and a perversion of gift exchange.[74] The abuse is interrupted by a parenthetical "you joker, Maecenas" (*Epodes* 3.20; "iocose Maecenas"), which arguably neutralizes the blast of verbal venom. Cursed later in the book for his unwelcome pressure (*Epodes* 14.5: "occidis rogando", "You're killing me with your demands"), Maecenas is called *candide* (literally "white"; "well-meaning" or "supportive")—another protective casing for Horace's words? Is this horseplay among friends or barely diluted vitriol?[75] Denis Feeney writes: "We are still told nothing whatever about Maecenas' reaction to what he had read (*although it must have been favourable*)."[76] But perhaps Maecenas hated the *Epodes*; perhaps he was meant to.

Following the *Odes*, Horace's anxieties about the outward appearance of patronage relationships—a lordly dictator's dealings with a favoured toady or entertainer—undergo a sea change. In *Epistles* 1, older, wearier and more confident, he begins to shift the mask of exceptionalist deference to Maecenas, resisting his entreaties for more lyric by returning to hexameter verse. Now, "letters" replace face-to-face "conversation" (*sermo*) with geographical, temporal and emotional distance. Horace defaults to an unkempt philosopher with something to teach a superficial dandy. Against a background of physical maladies (catarrh, summer fever, dropsy, gout), quarantine and spa cures, he offers talking therapy to a patron in need of mental equilibrium.[77] As patron in his own right, he hosts a dinner party, writes a recommendation letter to Tiberius for a young hopeful and offers tips to those further down the queue—"outrageous" mock advice to social climbers on attending to a patron's every whim (*Epist.* 1.9.3, 1.17, 1.18.78), lessons in point-by-point compliance that threaten the integrity and innocence of his earlier success.[78] In *Epistles* 1.7, Horace takes the ultimate risk of publicly unpicking his relationship with Maecenas by exposing the overload of debt that underpins it. He ends by seeing the desire for control from the other side, reluctantly releasing his fledgling

74. Gowers 1993: 306–7.

75. Oliensis (1998: 89) reads simmering aggression here. Earlier uses of *occidere* tend to be comic: McDermott 1982.

76. Feeney 2009: 26, emphasis added.

77. *Epist.* 1.1.108, 1.7.9, 1.2.34, 52. Epistolary greetings *Salue*, "I hope you're well," and *Vale*, "Be well," are reanimated at *Epist.* 1.7.3 ("si me uiuere uis sanum recteque ualentem"); cf. *Epist.* 1.2.49, 3.12, 6.66, 8.13, 10.1, 13.19, 18.50.

78. Oliensis 1998: 155.

book into the world like a newly freed slave or pick-up artist, vulnerable to touching and exploitation by others.

As a performance of long-term *amiticia*, Horace's works hold every shade of the word up to the light. In *Satires* 1, friendship is the meaning of life, society's affective glue, pitched somewhere between frankness and civility: *Satires* 1.3.135–36, "sic dulcis amicis / occurram" (That's how to get on with friends); *Satires* 1.5.44, "nil ego contulerim iucundo sanus amico" (I'd be mad not to put a cheery friend at the top of my list); *Satires* 1.6.70, "si et uiuo carus amicis" (If I'm popular with my friends).[79] On the Journey to Brundisium, politics and patronage are figured as *amicitia* on split levels. Maecenas's finest diplomatic achievement is domesticated into "patching up squabbles between friends" (*Sat.* 1.5.29; auersos . . . componere amicos), while lunchbreaks are filled with ball games, siestas and joyful reunions.[80] Attention switches from "important business" (28; magnis . . . rebus) to entertainments and sideshows; shared laughter consolidates this mafia in mufti.[81] In the *Epistles*, where Horace spills the beans on how to grease up to a patron, he appears at last to clarify the underlying hierarchy, using phrases like "rich friend" (*Epist.* 1.18.24; diues amicus), "powerful friend" (44; potens amicus), "friend to be revered" (73; uenerandus amicus). From one viewpoint, "We are seeing a relationship of 'patronage' being described as one of 'friendship.'"[82] Alternatively, we are seeing a relationship of "friendship" finally revealed as one of patronage. The shattering of the illusion allows Horace to highlight the affective bond with Maecenas and negotiate a longer leash (*Epist.* 1.7).

Along with the mechanics of patronage, Horace exposes "financial considerations" only retrospectively. At the end of his career, a sob story emerges about the harsh realities of his early life: first, dispossession and poverty (*paupertas*) made him write (*Epist.* 2.2.50–52); now, the duties of an establishment figure (recommendations, sick visiting, etc.) have removed the peace in which to do it (67–76).[83] His earlier poetry collections hold wealth at arm's length while making it unclear what, if anything, he has already received. *Satires* 1.1, a mock sermon to Maecenas on the futility of wanting more than one needs, ends with the motto "Enough is enough" (iam satis est), an elastic disclaimer that can

79. Cf. *Sat.* 1.3.54 ("haec res et iungit iunctos et seruat amicos").

80. Kennedy 1992. Even off duty, he never sleeps. Sporting companions: *Sat.* 2.6.48–49 ("ludos spectauerat, una / luserat in campo"). Fancy footwork as the mark of a practised *scurra*: cf. Lucil. 211–12W: "scius ludet et eludet". Cf. *Sat.* 2.8.79 (Nasidienus's dinner as sport): "nullos his mallem ludos spectasse".

81. 70: "iucunde cenam producimus illam"; 98: "dedit risusque iocosque".

82. C. Williams 2012: 47.

83. Horace only ever calls himself the "client" of a god ("cliens Bacchi"); *Epist.* 2.2.78.

be read as moral or stylistic, abstract or highly personal. In *Epodes* 1, when Horace declares, "Your generosity has enriched me enough and more than enough" (31–32; satis superque me benignitas tua / ditauit), it is unclear whether "generosity" (benignitas) equates to tangible wealth or spiritual benefit, or both.[84] What is important is the priority of any gifts and the resulting burden of gratitude: any debt now lies with Horace to fulfil.[85] Writing explicitly about his beloved country estate in *Satires* 2.6, Horace deflects his gratitude to Mercury instead.[86] Even when he washes his hands of Maecenas's gifts in *Epistles* 1.7 (34; "cuncta resigno" [I renounce everything]), we still do not know what they were.

The scholiasts are quick to blow Horace's cover.[87] Scholiast Porphyrio takes "generosity" to refer directly to the Sabine Farm.[88] A mirage shimmering through Horace's poems, the farm is hinted at only in its surroundings and by-products (Sabine wine, jar, woods, valley, climate, hills) or as an unspecified location.[89] It has been understood as a proverbial expression, a scholiast's invention, a real gift with an actual site, a "symbol of benefaction", or, by a further sublimating remove, a metaphorical stand-in for the poetic domain, flourishing self-sufficiently thanks to the patron's hands-off generosity.[90] It is "at once the clearest reminder of Horace's dependence and the site and figure of his independence".[91] As a one-off gift, a face-saving substitute for hard cash, not only did a farm delicately satisfy the "misrecognition agreement": it could even be stored up to Horace's credit as an emblem of modest means. "Why would I exchange a Sabine valley for more bothersome riches?" (*Carm.* 3.1.47– 48; Cur ualle permutem Sabina . . . diuitias operosiores?). This dynamic site could generate surplus from an initial outlay and offer a return on the patron's bounty, whether a respectful tithe, unwelcome glut or disappointing harvest.

84. Echoed in Canidia's overload of punishment: *Epod.* 17.19 ("satis superque poenarum").

85. Oliensis (1998: 84) notes the perfect tense of *ditauit*. DuQuesnay 2002: 30: "Maecenas' generosity was perhaps already legendary." Cf. Reckford 1959: 201: "Horace voluntarily incurred a tremendous material and social obligation to Maecenas even though, having *satis superque*, he asked for nothing more. . . . The crucial question then arises, what was the *quid pro quo?*"

86. Oliensis 1998: 48.

87. As Horace had already done, in the voice of a would-be farmer (*Epod.* 2).

88. Porph. *ad Epod.* 1.31: "donatum sibi in Sabinis fundum a Maecenate Horatius saepe testatus est".

89. Sabine: *Sat.* 2.7.118; *Carm.* 1.9.7–8, 1.20.1, 1.22.9, 2.18.14, 3.4.21–22; *Epist.* 1.7.77. Unidentified: *Sat.* 2.6.1; *Epist.* 1.16.1.

90. See Bradshaw 1989 (gloriously sceptical); Frischer et al. 2006 (an actual site); Leach 1993; Bowditch 2001: 5 ("a symbol of benefaction"); Dang 2010; Roman 2014: 113: "The reality of the farm is less important than the literary work it is made to perform."

91. Oliensis 1998: 165.

## The Circle of Maecenas?

Without Horace's understated PR, would Maecenas ever have stood out as the preeminent patron? In his favour was a rare alignment of politics, aesthetics, zeitgeist and a singular career. Mario Labate compiles an impressive list of the factors that converged to make him an ideal backer: exceptional social and political prestige, financial generosity, the appearance of friendship between patron and protégé, and a complex of personal qualities—culture, literary education and refined taste.[92] Everything here, however, hinges on the word "ideal". As Labate observes elsewhere: "The positive moral and intellectual substance of Maecenas and his friends is more tautologically affirmed than concretely illustrated."[93] Horace validates the relationship in circular fashion: "It means a lot to me that I met with your approval, you who know how to sift a straight man from a crooked one."[94] Or, as the crooked legacy expert Tiresias puts it to the equally crooked opportunist Ulysses: "It is my worth that makes me your friend" (*Sat.* 2.5.33; tibi me uirtus tua fecit amicum). Such tautologies have provoked suspicion: Maecenas had inexpressible charisma, he was Augustus's puppet, his "friendships" were propped up by untold wealth . . .

What, if anything, then, made him objectively special? For a start, his legendary "circle" of poets. Greco-Roman literary history clusters around such formations, the most celebrated in Rome being that of Scipio Aemilianus and Laelius (which included Terence, Lucilius, Panaetius and Polybius, among others). However, the "Scipionic Circle" has long been suspected of being a myth invented by Cicero in his dialogues: "The idea of a 'circle' is a seductive one."[95] Not only because it allows a batch of roughly contemporaneous authors to be considered productively in the same sightline: it also maps well onto the coteries and salons of later eras. Other powerful figures with literary associates include Julius Caesar (Varro Atacinus, Furius Bibaculus, Cinna, Calvus, Gallus and Asinius Pollio—mostly elegists from Cisalpine Gaul—and Catullus as a more detached sparring partner) and Pompey (Lucceius, L. Scribonius Libo, M. Terentius Varro and Theophanes of Mytilene—mostly prose writers).[96] Philodemus's poetic invitation to Piso (*Anth. Pal.* 11.44) became a canonical

---

92. Labate 2012: 406.

93. Labate 2005: 59.

94. *Sat.* 1.6.62–63; cf. 1.6.51 ("praesertim cautum dignos adsumere").

95. Zetzel 1972: 173; arguing that Cicero created the circle in the image of his own friendship groups.

96. Gold 1987: 91. On the influence of Alexander's *philoi* on Pompey's companions, see Anderson (1963) and Gruen (1974: 62n5).

example of a response to a patron's bounty.[97] Even in Augustan Rome, Maecenas had rivals: Messalla Corvinus, soldier and consul in 31 BCE, and (the same) Asinius Pollio, politician and orator, for whom Virgil had written the *Eclogues* and who instituted the first public library in Rome and public recitations.[98]

The notion of a "circle" has particularly attracted scepticism when linked to organized literary strategy.[99] Maecenas was a different doyen from Scipio, Julius Caesar, Pollio and Messalla. As an unelected politician, he did not need his protégés' votes.[100] Nor did the military model of poets as camp followers picked up on campaign apply in his case. In fact, when Horace vows to follow Maecenas to Actium in *Epodes* 1, he constructs a shared world alien to soldiering, where "duty" to the patron pivots on a paradox: military loyalty is construed as rebellion when one's marching orders are to share a life of ease (7; "iussi persequemur otium"), more suitable for "soft men" (10; mollis uiros). By contrast, Tibullus's patron Messalla is a virile warrior, the opposite of the elegiac lover, while Propertius's Tullus is a soldier turned decadent; neither shares the poet's sympathies. If Republican patrons used leisure activities (*otium*) to build up friendships (*amicitiae*) and indirectly political heft, there was different capital to be gained by promoting a voluntary, "friendly" form of dependence, removed from political business and standard clients' duties.[101] Lucullus, Pollio and Messalla also eventually withdrew from politics, which invites the idea that literary circles were alternative versions of society, even if the tension between equality and hierarchy did not go away. As Horace says to the rival suitor ("Pest") who tries to break into Maecenas's coterie: "I swear, it doesn't bother me that one man's richer or cleverer than me; there's a place for everyone" (*Sat.* 1.9.50–52). The Pest, to give him credit, is sceptical: "You don't say" (Vix credibile).[102]

Another difference matters still more. Unlike Pollio (patron to the bucolic Virgil and neoterics Gallus and Cinna), or Messalla (whose associates were largely elegists: Tibullus, Lygdamus, Sulpicia, Valgius and later Ovid), Maecenas fostered a far more comprehensive range of poetic genres. His writers became the supreme literary group of ancient Rome for two reasons: first, because Horace's poetry survived, providing a plausible account of his relations with his protégés, and secondly, because those protégés configured a new literary canon

---

97. On Philodemus's Epicurean connections to the circle, see Gigante and Capasso (1989).

98. Dalzell 1956: 161: Augustan literary activity cannot be reduced to three "neat coteries"; Chillet (2016: 468–69) prefers "networks" to "circles".

99. Anderson 2010; White 1993: 38.

100. As an *otium*-loving exception, Atticus was Maecenas's forerunner; Graverini 2006: 64–66.

101. Netz 2020: 523.

102. Speaking for everyone on the outside: Labate 2005: 56.

in Latin.[103] Given Horace's later activities as literary historian of the Augustan Age in *Epistles* 2 and the *Ars poetica*, the two are probably connected. Maecenas's pre-eminence coincides with Horace's narrative of his own redemption and successful career following the civil wars, along with Augustus's rise to power. The making of Horace, in other words, was also the making of Maecenas.

The notion of canonicity creeps up on us in *Satires* 1. On the Journey to Brundisium, Horace maps his life's significant encounters in reverse: first Maecenas, then Virgil and Varius, whom he greets as long-lost soulmates (*Sat.* 1.5.40–42). Next comes the backstory of his introduction to this "group of friends" (*Sat.* 1.6.62). The encounter with the "Pest" (*Sat.* 1.9), is a blatant public relations exercise to whitewash Maecenas's pure establishment and clear it of inferior talents. Finally, in *Satires* 1.10, Horace unveils a roster of contemporary poets, each ready to surpass the Greeks in a different genre: Fundanius in comedy, Pollio tragedy, Varius epic and Virgil pastoral (42–45). Modestly confining his own ambitions to satire (that uncanonical ragbag), he strategically omits genres yet to be tackled (iambic, lyric and epistle among them).[104] The implication is that this new canon overlaps with the informal friendship group radiating outwards from Maecenas, in the audience among Horace's appreciative fans (*fautores*). In a poem that is polemical about not polluting Latin with Greek, it is worth noting that he is not associated with a single Greek poet.[105]

As Pollio's presence in various lists so far indicates, the perimeters of such "circles" were fluid. Virgil wrote the *Eclogues* for Pollio; Messalla is present at Maecenas's fictional *Symposium*; Pollio was among Julius Caesar's close friends.[106] All three fish in the same talent pool at Seneca's declamation contests. "Circle", which suggests closure and equality, is not in any case the ancient metaphor. Horace prefers *numerus*, "number", "group", or *domus*, "house", a welcoming hierarchy of residents.[107] "Pyramid" might be a better image, or "concentric circles". The charmed trio (Horace nestling below Virgil and Varius) made the inner core, while Maecenas's other associates occupied peripheral tiers.[108] Further out were minor literati: grammarian Aristius Fuscus, the Viscus brothers,

---

103. Labate 2012: 405; cf. Citroni 2005.

104. His subsequent literary trajectory. Propertius will spot a further vacancy, for an elegist.

105. Whitmarsh (2013: 139) rehabilitates Greek poets in Rome as "witty, mobile, proud, and surprising".

106. Horace also beckons Pollio and Messalla to join his supporters at *Sat.* 1.10.85 (insurance?).

107. White 1993: 35–63.

108. Virgil and Horace: Jer. *Chron.* 189.2; Serv. *ad Ecl.* 3.90; *ad G.* 2.41; *ad Aen.* 8.310. Virgil and Varius: Donat. *Vit. Verg.* 37–42; *Vita Probi* 12. Virgil, Horace and Varius: *Laus Pisonis* 230–48; Mart. 12.3[4].1–2, 1.107.3–6; Jer. *Chron.* 190.4; Serv. *ad Ecl.* 9.35. Mart. 12.3[4].1–2, 1.107.3–6; Byrne 2004.

comedian Fundanius, Virgil's executor Plotius Tucca, epigrammatist Domitius Marsus and elegist Valgius Rufus.[109] There was fluidity across time, with a second generation arriving as doyens of a particular genre moved onwards and upwards: Valgius replaced Virgil in bucolic, Varius succeeded Pollio in tragedy, Virgil turned to epic, Propertius arrived to cover elegy. The tectonic plates of *amicitia* and patronage slid about. Maecenas was apparently Virgil's *amicus* when he published the *Eclogues*, but he is not the patron of that work. Similarly, there is no record of Maecenas's involvement with the *Aeneid* (not that it was traditional for an epic poet to acknowledge a patron).[110]

Lowest in the hierarchy, if physically close, are the freeloaders (*scurrae*) and hangers-on (*parasitae, umbrae*) onto whom Horace offloads his parasitic reputation. Servilius Balatro ("Slavish Buffoon", probably fictional) and Vibidius are cushioned next to Maecenas at Nasidienus's dinner (*Sat.* 2.8).[111] Sarmentus, a freedman perhaps acquired from Favonius, along with his Esquiline park, is mentioned as an upwardly mobile *scriba* turned performing clown, a *scurra* (*Sat.* 1.5.51–69) and Augustus's pet (Plut. *Ant.* 59.4).[112] Inscriptions record the names of plastic artists: C. Iunius Thalatio, a freedman maker of seals (*flaturarius sigillarius*), and Agrypnus, later responsible for imperial statues (*in statuis*).[113] Licymnia, a woman mentioned by Horace (*Carm.* 2.12) and conveniently equated by the scholiasts with Terentia, is probably fictional. Out on a limb is the beloved pantomime actor, Bathyllus.[114] The names are becoming Greek . . .

Finally, after Maecenas's death, another category comes into view: technical prose writers, who were often also his freedmen (so activating his role as *patronus* in the usual sense). Maecenas Licinius wrote on wine storage and agricultural produce and C. Melissus on animals, physiology and bees.[115] Sabinius Tiro, whose name suggests a perfect splicing of Horace's farm and Cicero's amanuensis, supplied the material on gardening Virgil regretfully postpones in *Georgics* 4. Rather than responding to Maecenas's personal interest in scientific and

109. Fuscus: *Sat.* 1.9.61, *Epist.* 1.10.1; Visci: *Sat.* 1.10.83, 2.8.20; Fundanius: *Sat.* 1.10.42, 2.8.19; Plotius Tucca: *Sat.* 1.5.40, 1.10.81; Domitius Marsus: Mart. 7.29.8; Valgius (also associated with Messalla): Hor. *Carm.* 2.9.5, *Panegyricus Messallae* 179–80.

110. True also of comedy (Fundanius) and tragedy (Varius); though patrons are acknowledged at Ter. *Ad.*, prol. 15–21.

111. *Sat.* 2.8.20–22. Horace, uninvited, does not reveal his place in the pecking order.

112. See also Juv. 5.3–4, Quint. 6.3.58. Other *scurrae* include Iortios and Gabba (see above p. 43).

113. Agrypnus: *CIL* VI 4032 (a funerary tablet in Livia's household columbarium).

114. Licymnia: ps.-Acro *ad* Hor. *Carm.* 2.12. Bathyllus as *Maecenatis libertus*: schol. *ad* Pers. 5.123.

115. Maecenas Licinius: Columella, *Rust.* 12.4.2. C. Melissus: Plin. *HN* 1 ind. 9–1, 1 ind. 7; cf. 28.62; Serv. *ad Aen.* 7.66; Ov. *Pont.* 4.16.30. Sabinius Tiro: Plin. *HN* 19.177.

agricultural writing, they are far more likely to be conscious supplements to Virgil. Finally, a "parasitic" literature of codification spread cultural models associated with the circle. The same C. Melissus wrote *Iocorum siue ineptiarum libri* (Books of jokes and nonsense), and Domitius Marsus *De urbanitate* (On urban wit).[116] Alternatively, these are works dreamed up by imperial literary historians to fill imagined gaps. Martial may even have invented the connection between Domitius Marsus and Maecenas to dignify epigram and exaggerate his need for a patron of his own.[117] Not so much a "pure house", then, as one plastered with later accretions.

## The Omnivorous Reader

A further corollary of the range of his protégés' interests was that Maecenas could be assumed to be an unusually catholic reader. When Horace complains about the difficulties of catering to audiences with different tastes, it is not his long-term patron that he has in mind:

> denique non omnes eadem mirantur amantque;
> carmine tu gaudes, hic delectatur iambis,
> ille Bioneis sermonibus et sale nigro.
> tres mihi conuiuae prope dissentire uidentur,
> poscentes uario multum diuersa palato.
>
> (*EPIST.* 2.2.58–62)

In short, not everyone admires or likes the same things: one likes lyric, another adores iambics, while a third prefers salty black satire in the style of Bion. I think they are almost like three guests with different tastes, who ask for various flavours to suit their very different palates.

Maecenas, by contrast, is imagined as omnivorous, greedy for a wide variety of literary production: not just lyric, iambic and satire, but also epic, tragedy, comedy, didactic, epistle and elegy, as well as less pretentious genres like epigram, pantomime and technical prose writing.[118] On each occasion, this adventurous diner can be counted on to sample whatever is on offer, from

---

116. Quint. 6.3.102–3. Three cookery books (*Baking*, *Cooking* and *Pickling*) for urban dinner parties (Col. 12.46) attributed to Augustus's associate C. Matius suggest an impulse to codify the recipes of Hor. *Sat.* 2.4. Heindorf (1815: 337) alone identifies Maecenas as the hidden *auctor* (*Sat.* 2.4.11).

117. Byrne 2004: 265. Marsus: Mart. 8.56[55].21–24; Ov. *Pont.* 4.16.5.

118. Reckford 1959: 207: "Undoubtedly, Maecenas always appreciated Horace's poetry."

humble Sabine wine in a Greek jar (Hor. *Carm.* 1.20) to Thyestean tragic feasts (Varius's *Thyestes*; *Sat.* 2.8), even a blast of garlicky breath (*Epodes* 3).

On the other hand, satisfying his high standards remains a challenge. This is a fastidious, mood-driven connoisseur, irritated by jagged fingernails and wracked by morbid worries, whose attention must be grabbed and held despite urgent distractions: "abandon serious matters" (*Carm.* 3.8.28); "leave behind your embarrassment of riches" (*Carm.* 3.29.10); "let go your worries about the city" (*Carm.* 3.29.16).[119] "We have Alban and Falernian wine for you if you don't like what's on the table," says anxious host Nasidienus in *Satires* 2.8. So, too, the town mouse anticipates his guests' boredom (*fastidia*) with a variety of dishes ("uaria . . . cena"; *Sat.* 2.6.86). Like the other guests, Maecenas will reject pretentious food but batten first on the host's discomfort, then on comedian Fundanius's digested recollection.[120] Poets contort themselves to avoid long-windedness (*ambages*), while evidently expecting their patron's indulgence of whatever lengths they demand.[121] If each of Maecenas's sympathetic faces is imagined as flexing towards different modes of writing and different worldviews, that only enhances his reputation as eclectic canon maker, choosy reader and split personality.

## Poetry and Play

It is no coincidence that several supporters of poets in the late Republic, not just Maecenas but also Piso (with Philodemus) and Lucullus (Archias)—are "paradoxical" characters, united by "a biographical tradition that stresses a pleasure-oriented way of life".[122] Perhaps the default Maecenas model looks something like this: poet(s) as chosen extension of the patron's leisure activities; propping up a symposium; taken in tow as a travelling companion; inspecting a rural estate or installed in a garden; a source of refreshment, provocation, play and wisdom. One primal scene for Horatian lyric is Herodotus's account of Polycrates of Samos, who ignored an embassy from the Persian king Oroetes (his future murderer) in favour of his favourite poet, Anacreon:

> The herald found Polycrates lying in the men's apartments, in the company of Anacreon of Teos; and, whether to show deliberate contempt for

---

119. Cf. Sharlet (2011: 36) on irritability as a "default setting" for patrons.

120. Hor. *Sat.* 2.8.16–18; inverted by Horace's refusal to offer Falernian or Formian wine at *Carm.* 1.20.10–12.

121. E.g., Verg. *G.* 2.46; Hor. *Sat.* 1.1.14, *Epist.* 1.7.82.

122. Damon 1997: 272.

Oroetes, or by mere chance, when Oroetes' herald entered and addressed him, Polycrates, lying with his face to the wall, never turned or answered him. (Hdt. 3.121)

Another is Theocritus's relaxed portrait of Ptolemy II of Egypt in *Idyll* 14, "a cultured *bon viveur*" who is "'one of us', but for the fact that he holds the purse strings":[123]

> Aischinas: What sort of man is he in other ways? Thyonichus: The very best—humane, a friend of the arts, knows about love, is charming in every way; he knows his friends, and his enemies even better; he's generous to many, doesn't refuse when asked, just as you would expect from a king— but you shouldn't ask on any pretext, Aischinas. (Theoc. *Id.* 14.60–65, trans. Hunter 2003: 35)

Ennius's "Good Companion", the confidant who provided comfort and acted as a safe repository for the residual anxieties of the working day, was better tailored to the Roman man of affairs, strung between soldiering and pleasure, responsibility and exhaustion.[124] Just so, Cicero credits Archias, Rome's poet at large, with "supplying us with refreshment for the mind after the noise of the forum and rest for ears wearied by the sound of abuse".[125] These ancestors are critical, as the poets create in Maecenas needs for entertainment, debate and solace that only their poetry can answer.[126]

The end result: Maecenas emerges as a flexible alternative both to other patrons and to a monolithic-seeming emperor. While his surviving poetry hints at a taste for the ludic (a taste Augustus shared with him in his limited time off), the recreations and retreats associated with him come to suggest more than that. In retrospect, they look like uncoerced rehearsal time (*praeludium*) or playgrounds for the poets before more serious engagement with the *princeps* and his *res gestae*. Horace's images of an *otium*-focused fraternity update the "Scipionic Circle", as Cicero had pictured it. He opens a further

---

123. Hunter 2003: 35. Demetrius of Phalerum, *philos* and possibly librarian to Ptolemy Soter, with an influence over artistic activities, may have been an Alexandrian model for Maecenas (so Richard Hunter suggests to me). See Herman (1980–81) on *philoi* at the Ptolemaic court; Habinek (2005) on play as Roman aristocratic performance.

124. He offered "salves, reliefs, and consolations for lessening the cares of life . . . in a man superior in birth and fortune" (Gell. *NA* 12.4).

125. Cic. *Arch.* 12.

126. Horace responds to an imagined need on Maecenas's part, then appeals to their fellow feeling to extricate himself; McDermott 1982: 217–18.

window on the off-duty activities of politicians by recalling Scipio Aemilianus, dressing down and fooling about in private with best friend Laelius and satirist Lucilius:

quin ubi se a uulgo et scaena in secreta remorant
uirtus Scipiadae et mitis sapientia Laeli,
nugari cum illo et discincti ludere, donec
decoqueretur holus, soliti.

(SAT. 2.1.71–74)

In fact, when the virtuous scion of the Scipios and gentle, wise Laelius left the public stage for a private place, they used to fool around and play with [Lucilius] in casual clothes, until the cabbage was cooked.

But while Scipio and Laelius were outward-looking partners in the satirist's clean-up of the city's morals, Maecenas remained in the private sphere, detached from the all-too-visible emperor: "a constant point of reference, irreplaceable but also abstract and remote".[127] He "allowed poets a loophole whereby they could construct a rhetoric of independence", even as they faced larger commitments beyond their self-sufficient domains.[128] Still, the interactions between an unelected *amicus Caesaris*, descendant of Etruscan kings, and his poets, a dispossessed Mantuan (Virgil), a freedman's son from the South (Horace) and an Umbrian equestrian (Propertius), *were* obliquely political, in that the internal virtues of the coterie (restraint, tolerance, quietism) provided second-degree propaganda for the emerging Augustan regime.[129] Shadowing imperial clemency and the "voluntary" self-effacement of imperial subjects, the poets' give-and-take banter with Maecenas was bromide in a revolution.

## Fictions of Demand and Refusal

It should come as no surprise that Maecenas, who rose to power despite refusing office, is a regular sounding board for the literary performance known as *recusatio* (refusal).[130] He also attracts priamels ("some do this, some do that, and I do something else") that justify unconventional life choices (Hor. *Sat.* 1.1.1–19;

127. Labate 2005: 60. Cf. schol. *ad Sat.* 2.1.7: Lucilius chasing Scipio round the dinner table with a rolled-up napkin; Gruen 1992: 280. Scipio and Laelius collected seashells "for fun and relaxation" (Cic. *De or.* 2.23).

128. Roman 2014: 320; see also La Penna 1963; Fowler 1995.

129. DuQuesnay 1984.

130. Zetzel 1982: 97.

*Epod.* 2; *Carm.* 1.1; Prop. 3.9), and questions, too. En route to Brundisium, Virgil and Horace produce sick notes for Maecenas's ball game (indigestion and sore eyes, respectively), face-saving excuses all round. Just so, the author of a *recusatio* tended to excuse himself politely from fulfilling a commission, usually for poetry on a grander plane, on grounds of physical weakness or mental incapacity.[131] On a pragmatic level, staging a response to an external request could showcase the author's impressive connections and indicate that he was "worth the effort of coaxing".[132] More significantly, it gave him a pretext for justifying an alternative poetic trajectory.

Typically, the topic waved in front of Augustan poets and resisted by them is an epic on the leader's military successes (a poet rarely rejects a minor task in favour of a major one).[133] Horace learned to give pat responses: "Much as I'd like to take it on . . . I'm just not capable" (*Sat.* 2.1.12–13); "Modesty prevents me from attempting such a feat, for which I don't have the energy" (*Epist.* 2.1.258–59). The fact that Virgil went on to produce the *Aeneid* only helps to support the idea of some concerted strategy for a great Augustan epic, fulfilled after many false starts (including Virgil's own). In fact, a human patron's intervention is just one choice among several scenarios. He replaces the deus ex machina (Apollo in *Eclogues* 6, who allows pastoral to continue, enlarged, or Cupid in Ovid, *Amores* 1.1, who hijacks tedious-sounding epic and diverts it to love elegy).[134] He also replaces the wayward muse who lures a barely resisting poet in new directions.[135] As a poet's alibi, Maecenas stands somewhere between divine authorization and feminine whimsy. Whenever he is accused of exercising force or being in league with the overlord whose stern orders or unsubtle hints he is conveying, he is also suspected of secret sympathy with his victim. An unconvincing stooge, he is less a direct conduit for another's wishes than a potentially divertible one.[136]

131. E.g., Verg. *Ecl.* 6; Hor. *Sat.* 2.1, *Carm.* 1.6; Prop. 3.3; Wimmel 1960; Citroni 1995: 87–88. Other patrons also receive *recusatio*: Verg. *Ecl.* 6.9 ("non iniussa cano"); Hor. *Sat.* 2.1.12–13, *Epist.* 2.1.258–59; Graverini 2006: 67n46.

132. White 1993: 70; cf. 64–91 (on the vocabulary of request).

133. Verg. *G.* 3.46–47 ("pugnas / Caesaris"); Hor. *Carm.* 2.12.10 ("proelia Caesaris"); Prop. 3.9.3: "the open sea", "uastum . . . aequor".

134. Callim. *Aetia* fr. 1 is the archetype.

135. Hor. *Carm.* 2.1.36 ("Musa procax"), cf. *Carm.* 2.12.13–14; *Carm.* 3.3.70. See Buchheit (1972: 18–31, 1977: 78–82) on patrons as muses: Verg. *G.* 2.39 (Maecenas), 1.40 (Octavian), *Ecl.* 8.11 (Pollio); cf. White 1993: 20.

136. Wallis 2018: 63–74. Islamic poets' resistance to alleged coercion allows them to define the relationship, stress the flexibility of patronage, and signal a move to "bigger and better things"; Sharlet 2011: 28–34.

In short, Maecenas's schemes usually end in failure.[137] After cursing him for unreasonable pressure (*Epod.* 14.5), Horace reveals that both men are equally weakened by lovesickness, a common cause that diverts the book's promised ending into "feebler", more elegiac iambics. In the *Odes*, he teasingly offloads an uncongenial subject onto a messenger complicit with his distaste for it: "Surely you don't think they are best fitted to the tunes of the lyre. . . . You yourself, Maecenas, will be better at telling prose histories of Caesar's battles" (*Carm.* 2.12. 1–4, 9–10). Propertius more actively calls Maecenas out on his hypocrisy in launching poets on the open sea of epic while keeping his own sails furled and lurking in the shadows (3.9.1–4, 30). Each of these dramas ignites, then immobilizes the patron's threats, allowing the poetry to go where the poet wants.[138] Even in antiquity, a patron's request was recognized as a convenient fiction. When one imperial elegist began a recitation with "Prisce, iubes . . ." (Priscus, you ask me . . .), his patron indignantly interrupted, "ego uero non iubeo" (But I didn't ask you!), making everyone laugh (Pliny, *Ep.* 6.15.2). Instead, Maecenas is invoked to witness and silently authorize a poet's own decision-making at an internal crossroads.[139] The motives he is ascribed—inclination, cruelty, flirtation, complaint, weakness, fear, desire—allow him to be distracted, seduced, cajoled, teased, soothed and fobbed off.[140] Such negotiations dramatize the voluntarism, sympathy and elasticity that patron and poet prize in the relationship. By contrast, Horace's fantasy of an interested emperor is of someone who flatteringly "forces" one to write (*Epist.* 2.1.228; "scribere cogas"), in a situation where one cannot (or would not want to) say no.[141]

## Fictions of Surprise and Wonder

Poems addressed to Maecenas often start with a question, negation or injunction to marvel. Is this, again, because this eccentric figure was peculiarly sympathetic to unorthodox viewpoints, refusals and quizzical reflections? Horace starts talking to Maecenas before we know anything about their relationship, slipping his name into his opening line: "Qui fit, Maecenas?" (*Sat.* 1.1.1). The name makes a crucial difference to the question Horace goes on to ask: "How come, Maecenas, people always think the grass is greener?" Underlying the

137. *Georgics* 3 is an exception (see chapter 3).
138. Henderson 1996: 131 = 1998a: 156.
139. Volk 2002: 136–38.
140. E.g., Hor. *Epod.* 14.5 ("occidis rogando"); *Carm.* 2.17.1 ("exanimas querelis").
141. J. Griffin (1984: 190) reads this ironically. Contrast Julius Caesar's unrefusable invitation to mime actor Laberius (Macrob. *Sat.* 2.7.2): "Power does compel, not only if it invites but even if it beseeches."

generalization is a more immediate question: How come Horace is speaking to Maecenas, seemingly as his equal? That should make the grass green enough for now. This motif—an opening question, plus Maecenas's name—became a token of allegiance.[142] The *Georgics* opens with four questions about the mysteries of agriculture, which Maecenas is called on to witness, if not answer. In the *Odes*, the queries have a sympotic flavour (*quaestiones conuiuales*), touching on mortality or time or details of ritual. One poem is prompted by Maecenas's anxiety about death (*Carm.* 2.17.1; "Cur me querelis . . . ?"). Another begins with Horace assuming that Maecenas is puzzled by his unlikely involvement in a married women's festival (*Carm.* 3.8.1–3).

Starting with a question not only attracted the listener's attention. It revealed a distance to be negotiated, helping poets to think around the relationship without presuming its straightforwardness. Conventionally, the patron asked the first questions. King Antigonus's interrogation of Bion began with a Homeric formula, framing patronage as an act of transition from one allegiance to another: "Who among men are you, and where are you from? What is your city and who your parents?"[143] A poet could equally use questions to assert his independence. Propertius seals his Monobiblos with genealogical queries focused on himself: "You ask, Tullus, who I am and where I come from" (22.1). Immediately Book 2 starts, he reframes his opening gambit as a question about the origins of his poetry: "Do you [plural] wonder what makes me write so many love poems, how my book comes softly on the lips?" (Prop. 2.1.1–2). The aetiology of poetic inspiration that follows credits the mistress above all and the patron only obliquely. Curiosity continues as the expected response to much of Propertius's third book (10.1 ["Mirabar"], 14.1 ["miramur"]), which repeatedly requires his addressee's bewilderment: "Quid mirare . . . ?" (Why are you amazed?; 3.11.1) (at the poet's enslavement to a woman); "Quid mirare . . . ?" (Why are you amazed?; 4.2.1) (at the shape-changing power of Vertumnus).

The question marks over Maecenas's own life choices made these questions entail "an open-ended approach to the possibilities of patronage".[144] Diverging towards esoteric topics flattered someone open to experiment and encouraged both parties to reflect on the elasticity of the relationship. Poets take for granted Maecenas's wide-ranging interest in matters religious, agricultural, etymological and ethical because this is where their own intellectual enquiries

---

142. Cf. Verg. *G.* 1.1; Prop. 3.9.1.

143. Diog. Laert. 4.7 = Hom. *Od.* 10.325; cf. Hor. *Epist.* 1.7.53–54. Horace anticipates, then shuts down Maecenas's expected questions about his philosophical (or patronal) allegiances: *Epist.* 1.1.13–14 ("ne forte roges, quo me duce, quo lare tuter: / nullius addictus iurare in verba magistri").

144. Sharlet 2011: 72.

take them. His curiosity is a fantasy they invent so that they can say whatever they feel like saying. "Surprise me," he seems to ask, and his poets oblige.[145]

## Between Patrons: Maecenas and Augustus

Personal qualities and canon formation aside, a unique aspect of Maecenas for the history of patronage is his role as mediator between the members of this new canon and Augustus.[146] What Virgil and Varius did for Horace, he, it is assumed, would do for all three with the emperor. But the broker who took his protégés to the next level is left behind, textually at least, at the midpoint of their careers.[147] As Virgil moved from Pollio (*Eclogues*) to Maecenas (*Georgics*) to Augustus (*Aeneid*), and Varius from Maecenas to Augustus, so Propertius left Tullus (*if* he is the patron of the Monobiblos) for Maecenas (Books 2 and 3) before becoming patron-free, or Augustus- and Rome-oriented, in *Elegies* 4. Horace swears loyalty unto death to Maecenas in *Epodes* 1 and celebrates their friendship in the *Satires*, before rehearsing a long string of farewells (*Carm.* 3.29, *Epist.* 1.1, 1.7, 1.14, *Carm.* 4.1, 4.11), accepting a state commission (*Carmen Saeculare,* 17 BCE) and addressing Augustus "face to face" in *Epistles* 2.1 (*c.* 11 BCE). There is one more ghostly appearance, in *Odes* 4.11 ("meus Maecenas"). Speculations about Maecenas's disgrace or retirement aside, the poets lived through a time of seismic political change. Superimposed on the networks of association and obligation that characterized Republican Rome was a new figure, the emperor, overarching patron to everyone.[148] As his presence becomes more sharply defined in poetry, so Maecenas's stature appears to diminish:

> But always behind Maecenas, never absent, though only most exceptionally addressed, there is the figure of Octavian and later of Augustus. He is always signified and represented as something beyond the ordinary level of humanity, like the mysterious young man of *Eclogue* 1or the god-to-be or the victorious leader of the *Georgics* or the heroic warrior of *Epode* 1 and 9 or the god in human disguise of *Odes* 1.2 or the victor whose accomplishments

145. See Gruendler (2005: 69–74) on surprise, self-satire and self-praise as ploys of Abbasīd poets.

146. Citroni 1992: 135. See Gibbon and Higgins (1974) on the Irish "gombeenman", a broker who shielded patrons and clients from direct encounters. More relevant are the chamberlains, viziers and scribes who interceded between poets and caliphs in Abbasīd Persia: Gruendler 2005: 64–65.

147. Zetzel 1982: 96; Citroni 1992: 385.

148. NB: Eilers 2002: 185: "The idea that the emperor was a universal *patronus* . . . is not found in any ancient source." But Augustus is visible, e.g., behind Antipater's loyal expressions to his patron Piso (*Anth. Pal.* 10.25.5-6 = GP 40.5–6): "And make my powerful ruler kind to him and kind to my verses."

elude the grasp of the puny poet in Propertius 2.1. This is a figuration unique to this period, and it has the special and very important significance that thereby these writers acknowledge a greater [*sic*] than Maecenas, who is at least as relevant to their poetry and to whom, in some sense, their writing is directed. (Gordon Williams 1990: 265)

How to interpret this watershed and this absent presence in relation to the poetry is far from simple. Many anecdotes fill the gap by supplying practical incentives for the poets' upward progress: Augustus's rejected offer to Horace of a bureaucratic post; his letter angling for inclusion in Horace's *Epistles*, which neutralized the boldness of *Epistle* 2.1; his intervention to stop the burning of the *Aeneid*; rumours of Maecenas falling out with either emperor or poets. Even after abandoning the idea of Maecenas's disgrace, Gordon Williams maintains that there had always been a long-term strategy for him to yield to Augustus, once the emperor had more time, to make way for a national programme of literature.[149] Other scholars speak of "Maecenas's plan", extrapolating from later assumptions about joined-up thinking between counsellor and emperor, or assuming a conscious strategy to assemble a new Latin literary canon.[150] Alternatively, the poets' growing autonomy was independently determined by broader ideological changes.[151]

Whatever motivated the transition, Maecenas's legacy remains that of an in-between figure, suspended not just between poets and emperor but also between two kinds of writing: one associated with pleasure, learning and countercultural independence, the other apparently dictated by a higher authority to reinforce imperial ideology. It is when Horace confronts the problems of dynastic ambition and imperial panegyric in *Epistle* 2.1 and *Odes* 4 that Maecenas recedes and worldlier forebears start to appear in his poetry: Simonides, Pindar, Theocritus, Choerilus and Ennius.[152] Augustus is recorded as giving quantifiable financial rewards (allegedly one million sesterces for Varius's *Thyestes*, performed at his triple triumph in 29 BCE, ten million to Virgil, and several donations to Horace).[153] The emperor actively intervenes in areas where Maecenas held back, a lonely figure fearful of missing out on the group's textual

---

149. Perhaps extrapolating from *Epist.* 2.1: Horace invites Augustus to postpone cares of state and attend to literary history.

150. Le Doze 2014: 115–32: "Le dessein de Mécène", 131: "une stratégie de promotion des lettres latines"; *contra* White 1993: 110–55. Le Doze (2019) draws on Republican historians' theories of prime conditions for a canonical era.

151. Roman 2014: 165.

152. Barchiesi 1996.

153. According to Donat. *Vita Verg.* 13, Suet. *Vita Hor.*, ps.-Acro *ad* Hor. *Epist.* 2.1.245–47 and the *didascalia* to Varius's *Thyestes*.

and social interactions. His "creeping invasion of . . . privacy" equally lapped at the edges of this friendship group.[154] Like the Pest, he plays enfant terrible, embarrassing Horace by exposing the motives and quid pro quos of patronage (whether inviting him to leave a parasite's table for a king's or begging for inclusion in his letters). He can partly be excused as a public, not a private commissioner, associated with the poetry of festivals and triumphs and forging a nation's collective memory. But while force was the prerogative of an autocrat ("Caesar, qui cogere posset" [Caesar, who could use force if he wanted to]; *Sat.* 1.3.4), it was never seriously laid at Maecenas's door.[155]

## Metaphors and Scenes of Patronage

At the poets' disposal was a rich image bank of inherited metaphors, from which their choices can tell us much about where they placed Maecenas on the historical spectrum of patron–poet relations. That said, using metaphors is always less a matter of straight correspondence and more one of approximation, of testing the water and trying to establish which analogies work and how exact or inexact they are.[156] Metaphors may be wishful descriptors for a passing infatuation on either side—or, worse, a patron's indifference.

The *Laus Pisonis*, our earliest source for "Maecenas" as a generic noun, is also a treasure house of images for the potential benefactor:

> I will travel higher if you open for me the path of fame, if you remove the shadow of obscurity. What use is a hidden vein of precious metal if it lacks a miner? What use is a ship becalmed in a harbour if it lacks a captain, even if it is equipped with all its tackle and could loosen the flapping sails on its well-turned mast with a slackened rope? *Laus Pisonis* 223–29)

In the space of a few lines, Piso is cast as welcoming host, excavator of hidden treasure, ship's captain, companion and pathbreaker; he is sunlight and food for dry soil. The poet credits Maecenas with miraculous powers to rescue, protect, open up, draw out, elevate, sustain and blast light onto the hidden talent of his protégés.[157] But if such metaphors suggest openness and wish-fulfilment—darkness becoming light, doors opening, skies clearing and hidden plants rising to the surface—another of their functions is to obscure. Figurative language,

154. Pandey 2018: 88. Cf. Donat. *Vita Verg.* 41: the *Aeneid* was published "auctore Augusto" (on Augustus's authority).

155. Suetonius suggests that Augustus coerced Horace (*cogere, iniungere, exprimere*). J. Griffin 1984: 203: "We are not in the world of Stalin and the Writers' Union."

156. Lakoff and Johnson 1980.

157. *erexit, eruit, patefecit*; Bellandi 1995: 89: "a kind of miracle-worker [taumaturgo]".

in short, is useful for capturing uncertainties in a relationship, sublimating its mechanics and negotiating change.[158]

Protesting his sincerity in *Epistles* 1, Horace declares to Maecenas: "You have heard me call you king and father to your face, and no less behind your back."[159] As often, he is being disingenuous; *rex* and *pater* never feature in his textual approaches, direct or indirect.[160] Most ancient poets, for all the volatility of their real-life relationships, favour stable or patriarchal analogies: god, parent, master, ruler, bulwark, guardian.[161] By contrast, Horace (the *Odes* aside) rejects imposing metaphors and shapes a patron who is informal, egalitarian, flexible and forgiving. When Maecenas's poets use divine, paternal or regal images, they do so to calibrate his distance and tie him to the long history of patronage. But they are equally drawn to analogies that suggest the versatility and even the precariousness of the relationship, female as well as male, surrogate as well as patriarchal. As ever, their selection is genre-specific: travel, play, chitchat and grooming in the sociable *Satires*; poison and witchcraft in the vicious *Epodes*; medicine and harvesting in the mature, philosophical *Epistles*; wine, flowers, fountains, hair, soothing lyres and seasonal change in the *Odes*; fertilization, grafting and transplantation in Virgil's *Georgics*. Metaphors, like the patron himself, are tied to a poet's chosen allegiances and value systems.

## Patron as God

To appreciate just how informal Horace's portrait of Maecenas is and how restricted his praise, it is worth looking back just a few years to Virgil's *Eclogues* (39 BCE), where the language of Hellenistic ruler cult is applied to its multiple patrons (Varus is promised a swan chariot to bear his name to the stars; Pollio's baby will herald a miraculous Golden Age). In *Eclogues* 1, set against the triumviral land reassignments, a rural smallholder, Tityrus, reports that a divine figure identified since antiquity with Octavian has granted him the right to remain on his farm: "A god has given me these peaceful conditions [otia]" (*Ecl.* 1.6). The direct equation of man and god is quickly excused as rustic hyperbole; Virgil teeters on the brink of saying that Octavian is a god, then covers himself, using inarticulate Tityrus as his alias.

---

158. Sharlet 2011: 94–124; Kurke 1991: 9–11 (Pindar); Gruendler 2005.

159. *Epist.* 1.7.37–38. See Nauta 2002: 16n51; Cucchiarelli (2019, *ad loc.*) sees the irony.

160. Martial pinpoints such titles as servile: "If I call you by your name now, when I used to call you king and master [regem et dominum], don't call me cheeky" (2.68).

161. Stevenson 1992.

Such manoeuvres belong to a venerable Greco-Roman tradition of lavish but usually backtracking comparisons between patrons and gods. The analogy with a patron is obvious enough.[162] But divine comparisons can equally be symptoms of doubt, pitting longed-for presence (*Ecl.* 1.41: "tam praesentis . . . diuos" [such ready-and-present deities]) against potential unavailability, the fantasy of lifelong protection against the likelihood of indifference. Bewildered language for coming face to face with the numinous suggests the patron's inaccessibility and provides a platform to express the inadequacy of the poet's praise.

In his approaches to Ptolemy II, Virgil's bucolic predecessor Theocritus had covered the full spectrum. In *Idyll* 17: Ptolemy is "like Zeus and Apollo", but also "like Achilles and Agamemnon". At a loss where to swing his axe in the forest of his numberless blessings, Theocritus finally resorts to simile: Ptolemy is "very like a god".[163] By contrast, in *Idyll* 14, he emphasizes Ptolemy's humanity and approachability.[164] The latter portrait is the one in which we are more likely to recognize Maecenas, whose mortality (in the form of brushes with death, or fear of death) is actively stressed.[165] In the background of all Maecenas-related poetry stands Augustus, Tityrus's young "god", whose genuine prospects of deification are steadily suggested.[166] When poets do try out divine analogies for Maecenas, they settle for lesser, more volatile gods: Mercury, Bacchus and Vertumnus.[167]

Horace is allergic to such extravagant comparisons, as is clear when he mocks an Asian tax collector's oriental-style abasement (*proskunesis*) before his Roman governor: "He praises Brutus, he praises his followers, and calls him 'sun of Asia' and his companions 'stars of salvation'" (*Sat.* 1.7.22–24)."[168] His own use of "god" always comes with a layer of irony; Maecenas and his friends are never sun or stars. Yet it has been argued that Horace's satirical language, normally an instrument of demystification, succeeded in making the new "ruler cult" of Augustus seem both sacralized and mysterious.[169] In that case,

---

162. Hunter 2006: 138.

163. Hunter 1996: 81. Cf. Thgn. 68–103 (the good king as godlike).

164. Hunter 2003: 35.

165. See Hor. *Carm.* 1.20, 2.17. Antipater praises Piso as "like a god" (*Anth. Pal.* 9.428.51.5 = *GP* 1.5; Whitmarsh 2013: 140–42). See Sharlet (2011: 16) on Islamic confrontations with the patron's death.

166. E.g. Verg. *G.* 1.24–25; Hor. *Carm.* 1.2.45–46, 1.12.1–3, 3.5.2–3, 3.25.4–6. Augustus joked about his future apotheosis (Suet. *Aug.* 71.3).

167. *Eleg. in Maec.* 1: Hercules and Bacchus; Messalla is compared to Osiris in Tib. 1.7; Bowditch 2011. Hymnic language for patrons: Tib. 2.1.35–36; Verg. *G.* 2.39–44; Ov. *Fast.* 1.3–26, *Laus Pisonis* 216–18.

168. Cf. Curt. 8.5 on flatterers' addresses to Alexander.

169. See Dufallo (2015: 318) on the interplay.

did he also create a "cult" of Maecenas? The first interview (*Sat.* 1.6.56–62) does more than mystify with its gaps and silences. It reads as an initiation scene that taps into the very source of the "mystery" metaphor in the hidden rituals of Greek cults.[170] The tongue-tied recruit (*infans*), for example, resembles the first-time initiand (*protomystes*, literally one who first closes his lips and/or eyes), with Virgil and Varius as the *mystagogoi* who induct him into the presence (*Sat.* 1.6.56; *coram*) of a higher *telestes/epoptes* (Maecenas).[171] Further characteristics of the ritual (secrecy, purity, set intervals between stages and transcendent "rebirth") suggest a context for Horace's muffled reportage. Even the biannual celebrations that followed each initiation, in February and September (Plut. *Dem.* 26), help explain the nine-month lag before his acceptance and entry into a new kind of speech.

What's more, this "mysterious" interview mirrors the larger plot of *Satires* 1: from blindness to clarity, exclusion to inclusion, silence to speech to silence again.[172] On the Journey to Brundisium, a night on the canal disturbed by croaking from the Pomptine marshes (*Sat.* 1.5.14–15) cues memories of Aristophanes's *Frogs* and its humorous treatment of eschatological initiation: road trip as *katabasis*, complete with enforced fasting and descents into mud.[173] Maecenas's arrival at Terracina is a mundane version of a blinding encounter.[174] Against the temple's gleaming marble, he comes into view as a pale afterthought, while Horace's momentary bedazzlement is banalized by the medical explanation (conjunctivitis) that stands in for a moment of epiphany:

hic oculis ego nigra meis collyria lippus
illinere. interea Maecenas aduenit . . .

(SAT. 1.5.30–31)

Here I put some black ointment on my sore eyes. Meanwhile, Maecenas arrived . . .

The expected *telete* or final stage of the journey is also anticlimactic: "Brundisium finis erat" (Brundisium was the terminus; 104). Parodying Virgil's messianic *Eclogue* 4 and adding a dose of Lucretian scepticism, Horace dismisses

170. Dufallo (2015) refers to "Horace's initiation" (317), "perhaps evocative of religious mystery" (324).

171. 56 *coram*: cf. Apul. *Met.* 11.23 (encounter with Isis): "accessi coram . . . de proximo adoraui".

172. See Zetzel (1980) on the direction inwards in *Satires* 1.

173. Cucchiarelli 2001: 25–29, 47–48.

174. See Sharlet (2011: 131) on blinding encounters with patrons.

a local miracle: "For I have learned that the gods lead lives without care, and if nature performs something extraordinary, it's not that the gods are angry and blasting it down from their penthouse in the sky" (*Sat.* 1.5.101–3).[175] Downplay it as he might, he himself is emerging from mud (95) into an equivalent worldly sanctum.[176] Three poems later, he is installed as a minor god on the Esquiline Hill: a block of wood serendipitously hacked into a statue of Priapus (*Sat.* 1.8.3: "deus inde ego" [Lo and behold, I was a god]), whose apotropaic gestures with his jutting red pole extend by implication to Maecenas's exclusive nearby park.

The book's other journey, Horace's wild goose chase through Rome to avoid the Pest (*Sat.* 1.9), is equally marked by mock religiosity. The street where he is accosted, Via Sacra, is not just a historic Roman thoroughfare: it is also a Latinized version of Hiera Hodos (Ἱερὰ Ὁδός), the "sacred road" that led pilgrims from Athens to Eleusis. Subliminally, this reinforces the idea of Horace as the superior initiate who guards a great man's unstained threshold against profane intruders (*Sat.* 1.9.48–52), while the Pest's failed attempt to demystify the operations of patronage reinstates the inviolacy of Maecenas and those allowed near him. Horace will eventually be "rescued" by a chance collision near the lawcourts cast mockingly as special treatment by the god of justice: "sic me seruauit Apollo" (98), a Homeric/Lucilian tag that displaces a thunderclap revelation but hints obliquely at a quasi-divine process of selection.[177] The Pest, by contrast, is summoned to court, reabsorbed into the forensic support system that underpinned routine *clientela*.

In *Satires* 2, gods and men move in a tighter constellation. Horace's thanks for his beloved farm are teasingly deflected from Maecenas to *Maia nate* (Mercury, god of good fortune; *Sat.* 2.6.5).[178] Rustic dinners of beans and bacon are hailed as "cenae deum" (dinners of the gods), a far cry from the notorious "Banquet of the Twelve Gods" staged by the emperor and his cronies.[179] Back in the city, Horace's proximity to divinity is confirmed, even when anaesthetized as slang in a lobbyist's mouth: "deos quoniam propius contingis" (since you are nearer to the gods [i.e., the emperor's court]; 52).[180] The metaphor

175. Cf. Verg. *Ecl.* 4.7 ("iam noua progenies caelo demittitur alto").

176. Pl. *Phd.* 69c; Plut. fr. 178 Sandbach.

177. Realized in Horace the poetic wunderkind in *Carm.* 3.4 ("animosus infans" [inspired infant]; 20); G. Davis 1991: 192.

178. Oliensis: 1998: 48.

179. Suet. *Aug.* 70. Did Maecenas play Bacchus?

180. Bowditch (2001: 24) brilliantly observes that the lobbyist's question concerns land settlements, so restoring "god" to the *Eclogues'* code for "military benefactor" and implying that all gifts of farms to poets fall in the same category.

hides real danger: were he to spill state secrets, the gods (or "the gods"?) would strike him down (54). The book ends with the sacrifice of ill-fated host Nasidienus, not just to cruel Fortune but also to the "Maecenas cult", along with his burnt offerings. Metaphor and humour allow the outrageous to be spoken without commitment.

## Patron as King

The most extravagant marker of Maecenas's difference from his protégés is his (alleged) kingly ancestry.[181] As we will see, this equips him to play an oriental tyrant in the *Odes* and a Persian gardener-king in the *Georgics*. Horace invokes the title only in the higher register of lyric. In *Satires* 1.6, Maecenas is merely the descendant of Republican generals, and even that grand lineage is immediately minimized when Horace hints at the Lydians behind his Etruscan forebears, many of whom are now slaves in Rome.[182] King Antigonus, recalled in the central interview, was the most democratic and satirical of autocrats: when a man called him "Child of the Sun", he replied, "The man who empties my chamber-pot doesn't think so" (Plut. *Mor.* 182c).[183] The gap in birth stimulates a bridging debate between clashing value systems— traditional nobility versus meritocracy—where slippery words are up for negotiation, like *liberalis*, "freeborn" or "gentlemanly in manner", *generosus*, "of good family" or "noble in behaviour", and *ingenuus*, "freeborn" or "innately good".[184]

In satire, *rex*, like *deus*, has more than one meaning: a (usually foreign) king characterized by disdain, grandiloquence and wealth, or any rich and powerful Roman, especially in his capacity as host to hungry parasites.[185] Both types frequent comedy, where the kings to whom parasites bow and scrape could be contemporary monarchs from the edges of the Greco-Roman world or legendary icons of wealth and power, like Croesus or Attalus. A taboo figure in Roman political memory, the king flourished in contemporary myth: "a figure of Roman daily speech with a hint of the fairy tale".[186] Foreign kings loom large in Augustan poetry because their historic dialogues with outspoken subjects

---

181. *Carm.* 1.1.1, 3.29.1; Prop. 3.9.1.

182. Cf. Cic. *Flac.* 65.

183. Diog. Laert. 7.1.36: King Antigonus teased the Stoic Persaeus about his supposed indifference to wealth.

184. See Wiseman (1971: 107–16) on new men's interests in redefining virtue as inner worth.

185. Nauta 2002: 16. *Rex*: e.g. *Sat.* 1.2.86, 1.3.12–13, 1.3.136; *Epist.* 17.43.

186. Fraenkel 2007: 133. Richlin 2016; cf. Ma 2003.

tested the limits of speaking truth to power.[187] But like human gods, they were becoming a possibility closer to home. A well-known conversation in Terence's *Eunuch*, between a parasite (Gnatho) and a soldier (Thraso) who boasts of his witty jokes and influence with a choosy offstage king, suddenly became topical:

> THR. What's more, when he'd had enough company and was tired of work, when he wanted a break, you know, as if . . . GNA. Sure: as if he wanted to spit out all his worries from his mind. THR. Exactly. Then he would take me aside as his sole companion. GNA. Goodness! You're talking about a most discriminating king. THR. No, that's how he is. He's a man of very few friends. GNA. (aside) None at all, if he spends his life with you. THR. They were all jealous, and bitched about me behind my back. I didn't give a damn. (Ter. *Eun.* 403–12)

This dialogue flickers through the *Satires*: Horace is envied as "Fortune's child" (*Sat.* 1.6.45–52, 2.6.49) and the tyrannicide Brutus is stymied with a killer pun about a man called Rex (*Sat.* 1.7). Even Horace's defence of Maecenas as "a man of few associates" (*Sat.* 1.9.44; paucorum hominum) recalls the Terentian soldier's smug reflection on his *rex* as "a man of ultra-few associates" (perpaucorum hominum; *Eun.* 409).[188] The echo activates a comic scenario where the Pest who boasts of storming Maecenas's palace plays bumptious *miles gloriosus* to Horace's possessive *parasitus*.

Other kings are invoked where they engage in conversation with frank commoners. Horace plays Bion to Maecenas's Antigonus, Solon to his Croesus (discussing the limitations of wealth in *Sat.* 1.1). With the return to hexameter in *Epistles* 1, the tables are turned and value systems clash again.[189] Patron-king (cf. *Epist.* 1.17.20, rex; 43–44 rege suo) has a new rival: philosopher-king. Horace will crown himself as the legendary king of playground chants ("The one who does right will be king") and live in happy frugality away from "regal Rome" (regia Roma): "I live and reign; Shun greatness; in a poor cottage you can rule and live better than kings and the best friend of kings."[190] But the poet who sends a volume of his work to Augustus (*Epist.* 1.13) and composes a recommendation letter for the eyes of his heir Tiberius (*Epist.* 1.9) is becoming closer to kings, not more distant.

187. Whitmarsh 2000: 306–8. Richlin 2016: 87.

188. Di Benedetto 1960.

189. Plato's letters from Sicily are a model here: see *Epist.* 2.311A–B.

190. *Epist.* 1.1.59–60, 7.44, 10.8; 10.32–33. See Gold (1987: 129) on philosophers who use kings at *Epist.* 1.17.13–15.

## Patron as Master

As a self-professed freedman's son, hypersensitive to social stratification, Horace pushes relentlessly at potential similarities between patronage and slavery (rooted in the original concept of *patrocinium*).[191] The first state was voluntary, the second forced, but both were undignified conditions from which escape was one day possible. In the *Satires*, Horace speaks in Aesopic fables to Maecenas's Xanthus (conservative ones where risk, desire and ambition are punished: a man drowns getting a jug of water from a big river; farmers envy their neighbour's goat; the frugal ant outlasts the feckless grasshopper; the town mouse is rejected by the country mouse). More explicit trickle-down analogies emerge when Horace allows a slave-cum-philosopher, Davus, Saturnalian freedom to expose him as a puppet "enslaved" to sex, food and status:

> For if someone who obeys a slave is an underslave, as your class is accustomed to name him, or a fellow-slave, what am I in respect of you? Why, you, who lord it over me, are the miserable slave of another master, and you are moved like a wooden puppet on strings that others pull. (*Sat.* 2.7.78–82)

Horace tolerates only so much free speech before apoplectically silencing Davus and threatening him with the chain gang on his Sabine Farm. But the humiliating portrait has been unleashed. As busy go-between for lobbyists, Horace has already evoked the *seruus currens*, the running slave of comedy. It has been suggested that freeborn Romans sometimes derived masochistic pleasure from imagining themselves as indispensable to a patron.[192] Yet one reason Horace so emphatically repeats the taunt about his birth ("libertino patre natum" [son of a freedman]) is to stress that he is at least freeborn: this, after all, is what qualifies him for Maecenas's friendship (*Sat.* 1.6.8: "dum ingenuus" [as long as one is freeborn]). Slaves beneath him in the pecking order remain mute or outrageously jumped up, like the freed Syrians allowed to vote for the death penalty for Roman citizens or to occupy good seats in the theatre.[193] When Horace sneers, "He is what my father used to be" (*Sat.* 1.6.41; namque est ille, pater quod erat meus), he draws attention to the social fluidity that brings him closer to his (Lydian) patron. Much has been written on *Epistles* 1 as Horace's most sustained plea for freedom, both philosophical and

---

191. W. Fitzgerald 2000: 71–77.

192. W. Fitzgerald 2000: 73–74; Tibullus's list of a poor man's loyal services to his mistress (1.5.61–66) corresponds to a slave's duties (and to a client's).

193. Gowers 2009: 308–9.

personal.[194] Perhaps his negotiations here are so effortful because, unlike a slave, a protégé who wanted to loosen ties with a patron had no formal process equivalent to manumission.

## Patron as Host

The house (Greek *oikos* or Roman *domus*) is a favourite site of patronage in Greco-Roman literature; the outer gate or threshold marks the critical boundary between acceptance and non-acceptance.[195] This is where Pindar stands triumphantly: "And I have taken my stand at the courtyard gates of a generous host as I sing of noble deeds" (*Nem.* 1.19–21). Horace trains a would-be client to cross "the marble threshold of the friend who is to be venerated" (*Epist.* 1.18.73). The Pest is left wondering how to storm the difficult outworks (*Sat.* 1.9.56) to Maecenas's hiding places: gardens, carriages, studies, arbours.

Among these, the dining room was a place of privileged access. From Homer's Demodocus on, hospitality was the most socially cohesive alternative to financial maintenance. Indeed, the shared meal, which underpinned the patronage system at all levels of society, barely counts as a metaphor. Civic or private, it was an arena for both shared celebration and humiliating competition between poets and run-of-the-mill clients. Pindar at the palace gates had awaited "a fitting feast" (*Nem.* 1.22), while Timon of Phlius satirizes Ptolemy's poets as kept chickens, squawking for food: "In fertile Egypt are fed many bookish scribblers, fenced-in, constantly squabbling in the Muses' hen-coop."[196] Greek *sumbioun* ("live with") and its Latin equivalent *conuiuere* (conflating living and victuals) were standard euphemisms for poet–patron relations. Horace acknowledges that he is Maecenas's *conuictor* (*Sat.* 1.6.47) and, looking back, that he has "consorted [or: eaten] with the great" (*Sat.* 2.1.76; cum magnis uixisse). Transcendent friendship became the only valid excuse for outstaying one's welcome; Cicero raises eyebrows at Philodemus's permanent residency with Piso (*Pis.* 68).

Even with money removed from the equation (the meal, then as now, fulfilled the "misrecognition agreement"), satirists reduce dinner parties to debasing exchanges of fodder for compliance ("fructus amicitiae magnae cibus" [the profit of friendship with the great is food]; Juv. 5.14). As with patronage in

---

194. W. Ralph Johnson 1993; McCarter 2015. Philosophical eclecticism frees Horace from patronage conceived as slavery: *Epist.* 1.1.13–14.

195. Hunter 1996: 44–45. Thresholds: Theoc. *Id.* 16.5; Hor. *Epod.* 2.7–8; Mart. 10.19.12–21, 10.58.11–12.

196. *Suppl. Hell.* 786. Hunter 2003: 33; Cameron 1995: 31–32.

general, the tension between social stratification and sympotic ideals of equality was insoluble.[197] Unlike the slave, the parasite had no ambition to move
on, unless the food was better elsewhere; a barnacle or shadow, he clung to his
master's side.[198] This is another of the humiliating roles that Horace pre-
emptively assumes, extending the homology to his leech-like underlings. As
ever, Augustus speaks the unspeakable, inviting Horace to leave Maecenas's
"parasite's table" and join the king's table instead (Suet. *Vita Hor.*: "ueniet ergo
ab ista parasitica mensa ad hanc regiam"), exercising his rights as though he
were already his *conuictor*.[199] The riskiest word in his jovial letter is *regiam*,
"royal", alluding to the old comic duo of parasite and *rex* but also a taboo de-
scriptor for dinner on the Palatine.

Dinner with Maecenas, meanwhile, remains firmly under wraps. The patron
is almost always shown dining out: chez Nasidienus (*Sat.* 2.8), Cocceius (*Sat.*
1.5.50) and Horace himself (*Carm.* 1.20, 3.8, 4.11). Exceptions include the post-
Actian celebration in his "lofty house" (*Epod.* 9.3; sub alta . . . domo), the meal
at which he fed Horace garlic (an inoculation against the charge of meaningful
sustenance at the patron's board?), and the scandalous reveal by slave Davus
of Horace's dependence on Maecenas's last-minute invitations (*Sat.* 2.7). Brief
glimpses of Maecenas's dining room emerge from Plutarchan anecdotes about
*scurrae*: dozing Gabba, and Iortios, who praised the roundness of an undeniably
rectangular table.[200] Tables rectangular and round nail the uneasy combination of hierarchy and equality in Maecenas's establishment—a circle Horace
finds it hard to square in his publicity exercise in *Satires* 1.9.[201]

Playing host himself (*Epist.* 1.5), Horace leaves sparing traces of the master-
formula.[202] The style of his own dinner apes his patron's elegant simplicity as
surely as the sparkling plates reflect the guests' faces. Maecenas's "clean house"
is recreated with spotless napkins that "should not wrinkle the nose" (22–23),
a nose we have seen before. The open-house invitation similarly comes with a
firm cut-off: room for Torquatus and his coterie, plus some hangers-on (28;
"pluribus umbris"), but after that, "It's too much of a squash for smelly she-goats"
(29). This prescription for a hermetically sealed, socially stratified gathering
of "equals" (26) is as near as we get to dinner chez Maecenas. Or rather, to a

---

197. Hunter 2003: 34–35.

198. Damon 1997; Tylawksy 2002.

199. Suet. *Vita Hor.*: "sume tibi aliquid iuris apud me, tamquam si conuictor mihi fueris".

200. Plut. fr. 180 Sandbach. See above p. 43 on Gabba.

201. Thanks to Keith Thomas for pointing this out.

202. In his defensive account of dining alone in *Sat.*1.6, verbs of attending on a patron (116–18:
"ministratur . . . sustinet . . . adstat") describe simple tableware and a trio of slaves.

miniature, displaced version of it (no baby donkeys here). It is later that the gastronomic rumours start to leak out.

## Journeys to and with the Patron

An epic stranger, washed up on a foreign shore; mercantile lyric poets; the wandering poet in Aristophanes' *Birds*; poets picked up on Mediterranean campaign: attempts to find a patron were often literalized as a physical journey.[203] Classic examples include Tityrus's journey to Rome in Virgil's first *Eclogue* and Gorgo and Praxinea's trip to Ptolemy's crowded Alexandrian palace in Theocritus's *Idyll* 15. Normally, the protégé made the running.[204] Horace's low-mileage investment in Maecenas collapses extravagant journeys like the virtual voyage around the world (*periplous*) that precedes Pseudo-Scymnus's "meeting" with King Nicomedes of Bithynia.[205] He slyly postpones, until just *after* his account of the "surprise" interview, the longer-haul journey he made to Rome as a schoolboy (*Sat.* 1.6.76). Travel with the patron (among the duties of a *cliens*, or *comes*, "companion") was a metaphor for faithful service. Antipater of Thessaloniki speaks of following the long ship of L. Calpurnius Piso Frugi (consul in 15 BCE) to Asia.[206] According to legend, Ennius, "picked up" by Cato in Sardinia, accompanied Fulvius Nobilior abroad to play *praeco* for some distinctly dubious achievements at the Battle of Ambracia, for which Cato christened him Nobilior Mobilior (Cic. *De or.* 2.255).

Maecenas's movements are positively erratic, and often destination-free. On the journey to Brundisium, he comes and goes somewhere in the middle distance, out of the corner of Horace's sore eyes. If he is the saviour who later sweeps Horace up in his carriage (*Sat.* 1.5.86; "rapimur raedis"), he is not named; Horace only years later reveals his familiarity with this office on wheels ("raeda . . . iter faciens"; *Sat.* 2.6.41–43). A patron on the move suggested transience as well as dependency. Horace tethers Maecenas as his stable prop (*Carm.* 2.17.3–4; "mearum . . . columen rerum" [pillar of my existence]), confronting the nightmare that he might die too soon (5–6; "if a premature force snatches you away, part of my soul"). The dream of catching up will be realized only in death: "We will go, we will go, wherever you lead, ready to cover the final journey as companions together" (*Carm.* 2.17.10–12). Yet the devoted

203. Hunter 2003: 31; Hunter and Rutherford 2009.

204. See Netz (2020: 521–22) on first-century BCE Roman patrons who found Greek protégés in the eastern Mediterranean.

205. Hunter 2006.

206. *Anth. Pal.* 10.25 = GP 40; Cf. Hor. *Epod.* 1; Tib. 1.3.55–56.

protégé who once followed Maecenas into battle (*Epod.* 1.1; "Ibis Liburnis," "You will go in your nimble ships") is the first to take leave, speeding away in his own little boat (*Carm.* 3.29.62–64).

Most of the time, then, patron and protégé are deliberately un-synchronized, physical distance standing in for a psychological distance that needs bridging.[207] Equestrian Propertius urges a galloping Maecenas to slow down to peruse the poet's roadside tomb (2.1.75–76), then to speed up to guide his talent forward: "Gentle patron, take the reins of my launched career, and give the signal with your right hand when my wheels are released" (3.9.57–58).[208] Images of sea voyages, long associated with epic, commit Maecenas to vicarious wavering on his poets' behalf: sailing forth or hugging the shore (Verg. *G.* 2.41, 45; Prop. 3.9.3–4, 30). Not simply a prop or bulwark, he is also an agile traveller, hard to pin down as he makes off in the speedboat of *Epodes* 1, the limousine of *Satires* 2.6 or the jeep of Propertius 2.1.[209] His mobility reflects the precariousness of any non-contractual relationship, which could be to the poet's advantage, too.

## Patron as Mistress

When the word "patron" evokes normative masculine roles, why ever would a male poet want to cast himself or his patron as female? Yet this is a surprisingly common phenomenon, from Han China (second century BCE to second century CE) to the Italian Renaissance.[210] Among Greco-Roman patrons, gender-queer Maecenas is almost uniquely susceptible to being cast in female roles or juxtaposed with female figures.[211] He brushes shoulders with mistresses and courtesans and shares a platform with muses, sometimes even blurs into his female others. This is partly because he is a reflector of the soft poetry (lyric, elegy, iambic), which may have fed his effeminate reputation as much as deriving from it.[212] But poets also stress their softness in relation to

207. E.g., Tib. 1.3.1: "Ibitis Aegaeas sine me, Messalla, per undas."

208. In Abbāsid Persia (tenth century CE), patrons are intercepted on the open road: Gruendler 2005: 62.

209. Modernizing the vehicles at *Epod.* 1.1 ("Liburni"), *Sat.* 2.6.42 ("raeda") and Prop. 2.1.76 ("esseda").

210. See Kelly (1984) on the Italian Renaissance; Rouzer (2001) on Chinese poets who impersonated women abandoned by men.

211. See Gambato (2000) on effeminate oriental kings in Athenaeus; Sharlet 2011: 137: Islamic patrons concealed "as if in the women's quarters"; Plin. *Pan.* 48: Domitian's "womanly pallor" as he lurks in his palace.

212. See chapters 4 and 5. Cf. Messalla in Tib 1.7.

him, as courtiers and lovers who minister to the emotional needs of an unwar-like, pampered and vulnerable patron.

The Roman threshold, as Ellen Oliensis has shown, did double duty for two kinds of harsh service: *amor* and *amicitia*. No sooner had the poet finished his sobbing nocturne at his mistress's door than he rose to greet an indifferent patron at the morning *salutatio*.[213] If a male patron was more "knowable" in terms of honour codes and reciprocal bonds than any fickle female, then the out-rageous fantasy of temporary enslavement to a woman might compensate for the harsh reality of long-term dependence on a man.[214] Recasting daytime allegiances in erotic terms, poets could plead irrationality on both sides as an excuse for rejection and exploit a perceived gulf between patrons and lovers in terms of moral and emotional predictability. By reinforcing the patron's weakness, they enhanced their own protective power.

Elsewhere, an extra female is introduced to triangulate the relationship be-tween poet and patron, solidifying their comradeship through shared erotic suffering or stimulating enmity and productive competition.[215] A special con-flict of loyalties erupts when master and mistress collide—for example, in the idyll-gone-wrong when Tibullus invites Messalla to visit his country estate and ends up pimping Delia to his overlord (1.5).[216] In *Epodes* 3, a female surrogate is dragged into a malevolent exchange: Horace prays that Maecenas's girlfriend will shrink from his garlicky kisses and retreat to the far edge of their bed, so performing an allowably petulant version of his own fantasy rebellion.[217] In *Odes* 2.12, Licymnia is dangled in front of Maecenas as shareable prey, her sexy gestures mirroring Horace's coy will-he-won't-he defiance of his patron's half-hearted request for dull military history.[218] Disputed females act as passive, face-saving mediators, modelling flexibility and resistance on both sides of the relationship. They allow a poet to melt existing hierarchies, seize the initiative, trade in desirable objects and even achieve imaginary revenge.

Patron and protégé dance around other female roles, too. Maecenas, sealed in his house, is as unattainable (at least to an *exclusus amator* like the Pest) as the aristocratic wives for whom he had such a soft spot:

> "accendis quare cupiam magis illi
> proximus esse." "uelis tantummodo: quae tua uirtus,
> expugnabis: et est qui uinci possit eoque

---

213. See Oliensis (1997) on "the erotics of *amicitia*"; Labate (1984) on courtship and *clientela*.
214. McCarthy 1998.
215. C. Williams 2012: 143–48; Gallus and Propertius.
216. Oliensis 1997: 156.
217. The implication is that she might be coaxed back.
218. Oliensis 1997: 163–64.

difficilis aditus primos habet." "haud mihi deero:
muneribus servos corrumpam; non, hodie si
exclusus fuero, desistam"

(SAT. 1.9.53–58)

"You fire me up all the more with longing to get close to him." "You only
have to want it; such is your valour, you'll storm the citadel; and he's the
sort that can be overcome, and to that end he makes the outer approaches
difficult." "I shan't be wanting; I'll bribe his slaves with gifts; and if I don't
get in today, I'll stand my ground"

si interdicta petes, uallo circumdata—nam te
hoc facit insanum—multae tibi tum officient res,
custodes, lectica, ciniflones, parasitae,
ad talos stola demissa et circumdata palla,
plurima, quae inuideant pure apparere tibi rem.

(SAT. 1.2.96–100)

If it's forbidden fruit you're after, ring-fenced (if that's what drives you
crazy)—then all kinds of obstacles will stand in your way: bodyguards,
covered litters, hairdressers, hangers-on—a gown down to the ankles and a
swathing cloak—and all the other things that begrudge you a sight of the real
thing.

Dispensing frank advice to social climbers in *Epistles* 1, Horace switches the
focus, comparing a grumpy client or freeloader (*scurra*) to a grasping prostitute (*meretrix*; *Epist.* 1.17.55), while a true *amicus* is like a wife (*matrona*; *Epist.*
1.18.1–4). Indirectly, these analogies hint at sexual exploitation as part of the
duty (*officium*) required of an inferior male by a superior one.[219] Literary success was often troped as sexual favouritism: Terence's biography hints that his
looks gave him a leg up with Scipio and Laelius; Horace's *Epistles* 1 is sent to
sell itself like a pretty slave boy.[220] So when Horace bleaches poetry from his
first interview, he risks conjuring a less savoury scenario of how he "pleased"
his patron, one that all his emphasis on his own purity and that of Maecenas's
house fails to suppress.[221]

219. Oliensis 1997: 153–54.

220. Suet. *Vita Terenti*; Hor. *Epist.* 1.20.10–12.

221. The patron's cool appraisal recalls sheikhs (*reges*) who judge horseflesh by covering the
attractive parts (*Sat.* 1.2.8). Purity: *Sat.* 1.6.57, 82; 1.9.49. "Pleasing": *Sat.* 1.6.62–63; cf. *Epist.* 1.20.23
with Bowditch (2001: 227); cf. Ter. *Ad.*, prol. 18–19.

Reflecting a time when homosocial relations were far more effusive than now, intimate erotic language colours textual interactions between male protégés and patrons: soulmates for life, inseparable halves of the same whole, united in death.[222] The ditty that opens "If I do not love you, my Horace, more than my own vitals" (2L = 3C = 186H) revealed, according to the *Vita*, "how much Maecenas loved Horace" (Maecenas quantopere eum dilexerit satis testatur); on his deathbed, he allegedly begged Augustus: "Don't let poor Horace starve." When Augustus enters the game, he gleefully inhabits the role of rich rival lover, traditional bugbear for the elegiac couple: "I'm longing to steal our friend Horace away from you." Triangulation, again: Augustus waives his rights to coercion, creating a temporary space for vulnerability and teasing, with Horace the prey contested by two men.

## Mothers, Midwives and Witches

When *patronus* evoked a surrogate "parent", and "birth" was an equally time-honoured metaphor for poetic production, sooner or later that stimulated questions about authorship.[223] Patronage is often explained as a voluntary societal advance on the stranglehold of kinship relations.[224] Horace's narrative in *Satires* 1 pivots on such a transition between real and metaphorical parents, from genetic and generic originals (freedman birth father and satirical forefather, Lucilius) to the surrogate care of the patron.[225] Understandable as an adoptive or foster father, Maecenas is sometimes more surprisingly cast as a mother.[226] At their first encounter, Horace the mute child (*Sat.* 1.6.57; *infans*, "speechless", also suggests "infant") makes Virgil and Varius virtual midwives to Maecenas's nine-month "gestation".[227]

Horace himself takes the maternal role in *Epodes* 1. Pledging undying loyalty to the patron departing for Actium, he plays mother bird to Maecenas's fledgling: "just as a bird brooding on her nest of featherless chicks fears the slinking serpent's approach more when she's left them behind" (1.19–22).[228] Why? Because asserting his right to be primary carer helps him resist the default status

222. E.g., Hor. *Carm.* 2.17; see C. Williams 2012: 116–73. Cf. Algazi and Drory (2000) on court erotics under the Abbasīds.

223. Friedman 1987; cf. Pind. *Ol.* 10.9 (*tokos*); Longinus, *Peri hupsous* 9.

224. T. Johnson and Dandeker 1989.

225. Schlegel 2000.

226. Horace's mother never features in his own genealogy.

227. The normal term for fostering, *excipere*, is avoided.

228. Oliensis (1998: 80–84) draws out the implications of the allusion to Hom. *Il.* 9.323–24 (Achilles as mother bird).

of hungry dependant or homebody to a soldier-husband and a correspondingly caring role for deputy Maecenas towards "absent husband" Augustus. Horace suggests that the two men are united in fragility: "soft men" (molles uiros; 10), "unwarlike and less than hard" (imbellis ac firmus parum; 16). He knows that iambic, most aggressive and macho of genres, is compromised by its female associations. The grotesque foremothers of Greek iambus, Iambe, Baubo, Empusa, associated with midwifery and childbirth, are reborn in his enemy-muse, the witch Canidia, who enables his malevolent poetry while sapping his strength.[229]

Yet if Canidia is the obvious scapegoat for the contagion of impotence afflicting the poet and his cronies, the circle around which Horace weaves his protective magic is being equally sabotaged from inside. The witch's other doppelgänger is her Esquiline neighbour, Maecenas, whose shot of garlic induces quasi-sorcerous pain and fantasies of parricidal revenge.[230] The patron's demands also align him with the erotic urging of two other old women so repulsive that they, too, are blamed for Horace's impotence.[231] In another uncanny symmetry, Maecenas's fragmentary hendecasyllables supplement the conversation, magically soothing Horace and turning hate to love by making the dyspeptic belly of *Epodes* 3 a maternal one:

> ni te uisceribus meis, Horati,
> plus iam diligo, tu tuum sodalem
> hinnulo uideas strigosiorem
>
> (2L = 3C = 186H; H PRINTED HERE)

> If I do not love you more than my own vitals, may you see your comrade scraggier than a mule

The pun on *uiscera*, "vital organs", "womb" or "children", reclaims Horace as not just an adult friend (*sodalem*) but also the adoptive child of a very fond mother figure.

Towards the end of the *Epodes*, Horace stages a genre-appropriate *recusatio*:

> candide Maecenas, occidis saepe rogando.
>    deus, deus nam me uetat
> inceptos olim, promissum carmen, iambos
>    ad umbilicum adducere
>
> (EPOD. 14.5–8)

229. W. Fitzgerald 1988; Oliensis 1998: 68–101; Barchiesi 2009a: 245.
230. Oliensis 1998: 89–90.
231. Gowers 2016a: 117–30.

Well-meaning Maecenas, you're killing me with your insistent demands. The god, the god prevents me from bringing to completion my once started iambics, the promised poem.

His inability to deliver the promised collection of poems is framed as obstetric complication (so *umbilicus*, originally "navel" or "umbilical cord", suggests).[232] This homage to iambic midwife figures also exploits fantasies of male pregnancy going back to Hesiod, Aristophanes and Plato, party to the long debate between *phusis* ("nature") and *techne* ("art"). Impregnated by the muse, the poet claims to carry his work to term by himself.[233] Horace may cast Maecenas as merciless midwife or sterile enabler to the poetic process because this allows him to credit his patron's support while maintaining his hard-won authorial rights.[234] It is even worth prolonging the birth pangs. After all, once he delivers for the patron, agent of completion, the poetry will dry up.[235]

Around this time, Maecenas the midwife had his hands full with two litters of ill-matched twins: *Satires* 2 and *Epodes*, 30 BCE; *Georgics* and *Thyestes*, 29 BCE. His nurturing influence would soon be hijacked by the enemies of favouritism. Vipsanius Agrippa would claim that Virgil was Maecenas's foster child (*a Maecenate suppositum*), corrupted by his bad style (*cacozelia*).[236] A similarly pejorative metaphor of "insinuation"—literally, being enfolded in the lap or bosom of a protector—colours the Horatian *Vita's* brisk account of the poet as arriviste:

> ac primo Maecenati, mox Augusto insinuatus non mediocrem in amborum amicitia locum tenuit. (Suet. *Vita Hor.* 44.9)

> First he insinuated himself with Maecenas, then with Augustus, and found a not insignificant place in the friendship of both men.

This vertiginous ascent ("First . . . then") is not so different from Suetonius's narrative about a lesser member of Maecenas's household, C. Melissus, exposed as an infant, then enslaved and trained as a grammarian.[237] When his birth mother tried to reclaim him, he chose to stay with his "foster-father":

232. The metaphor here is usually taken as bookish ("up to the book-knob"—i.e., complete; *OLD* s.v. *umbilicus* 2e). This section summarizes Gowers (2016a: 106–17).

233. Leitao 2012: esp. 120–27.

234. Leitao 2012: 20; Sedley 2004.

235. Tib. 1.7.9: "non sine me est tibi partus honos" (Your honour has not come to birth without me) makes the poet midwife to the patron's glory.

236. Donat. *Vit. Verg.* 44. See *OLD*, s.v. *suppono* 3, 7b. Persius casts his intellectual foster parent, the Stoic Cornutus, as a tender protector: 5.36–37; Bartalucci 1979.

237. Kaster 1995: 214–22.

Seeing that Maecenas found him pleasing and treated him as though he were a friend [in modum amici], he chose to remain a slave despite his mother's attempt to claim him as free, since he preferred his current condition to the true status he had by birth. In due course, he was given his freedom and also installed in the good graces of Augustus [Augusto etiam insinuatus est], who chose him for the job of organizing the libraries in the Portico of Octavia. (Suet. *Gram. et rhet.* 21.1–3, trans. Kaster)

The phrase "as though he were a friend" reveals a systemic paradox in Roman patronage. A slave could never be a real *amicus*, yet for Melissus voluntary service with Maecenas was preferable to other relationships.[238] Once freed, "Bee" was drawn to the imperial honeypot and took up the kind of bureaucratic post Horace had declined.[239] In both stories, the word *insinuatus*, "installed in the good graces of", makes imperial service a natural sequel to a patron's capacious embrace (*sinus*, "bosom, lap, fold", implying extreme cosseting, quasi-maternal or sexual).[240] Generally, though, the poets' physical contact with Maecenas, far from abject genuflection, embraces or handshakes, tends to be hands-off. While the Pest grabs Horace's hand, ("arrepta . . . manu"; *Sat.* 1.9.4) and voices a vulgar desire to be close to Maecenas (*Sat.* 1.9.54), Horace imagines himself as merely skimmed by the edge of a discerning nail or suspended (or not) from a haughty nose.

## Wealth

In Maecenas's case, the *sinus* metaphor is inextricable from bountiful generosity (the folds of a Roman toga did duty as a purse) and the poetic conflict between deep-sea adventure and shore hugging (*sinus* is also a bay and a ship's sail).[241] As Pindar sang in *Pythian* 1: "If you want to go on hearing your name sounded in tones of praise, go on being generous, unfurl your sails" (91–94). Propertius, too, puns on both meanings of *sinus* when he pits the largesse Maecenas receives from Caesar against his inspirational withdrawal from mainstream political life, absolving his patron (and himself) of being in Caesar's pocket:

And even if Caesar gives you resources to achieve things and at all times <u>wealth flows so easily into your purse</u> [tam faciles insinuentur opes] you hold back

238. Kaster 1995: 217.

239. On *insinuari* as a Suetonian verb, see Jones (1986).

240. Mart. 3.2.6: a slave-like book is installed *in Faustini sinu* and promoted.

241. Hor. *Sat.* 1.6.5, Cf. *Laus Pisonis* 228–29: "fluentia . . . uela"; *Eleg. in Maec.* 1.26: "uentosi . . . sinus".

and crouch low in the flimsy shadows. <u>You are the one who draws in the full
billow of your sails</u> [uelorum plenos subtrahis ipse sinus]. (Prop. 3.9.27–30)

Behind all dealings with Maecenas lies the hint of legendary wealth, oiling
the wheels of poetic productivity. In any speculation about why he was so
valued by his followers, this hint fills a perceived gap in the testimony: the dark
secret that held the happy coterie together. As with sex, though, just about any
patronage metaphor can be interpreted as a cover for riches. For all its substitutes (fertility, sunshine, warmth, protection, shade, a beneficent smile, nebulous "benefits" or "bounty"), the whiff of money can be made to emanate from
the noblest transactions. We saw how crucial metaphors were for concealing
the mechanics of Greek lyric poets' dealings with their patrons (terms for
"rewards" or "gifts", *misthos, xenia, kudos*, sliding between material and figurative senses) and for conveying the "perfect interconvertibility" of economic
and symbolic capital.[242] Metaphors of gifts, bounty, service and goodness are
so familiar from this mystifying discourse that they come equipped with the
key to their own unlocking. Despite the goal of transcendence, they risk being
cashed out, reduced to code for material transactions. A late Horatian ode,
*Odes* 8, is filled with financial terms (*pretium*, "price"; *munus*, "service", "gift")
that barely preserve their metaphorical status in a poem addressed to a rich
man.[243] Peter White even interprets ancient prop words associated with Maecenas (*praesidium*, "bulwark"; *columen*, "keystone"; and *tutela*, "protection")
as euphemisms for financial support.[244]

From another perspective, wealth is a state that will always separate poet
and patron, soulmates though they may be. In that sense, like birth, it is an
unending stimulus to the protégé to level up, or to interpose an alternative
value system. Hence the strong philosophical element in Horace's poetry, with
its store of accumulated wisdom about the negative impact of riches (*Epist.*
1.2.47–49: "Houses and farms, piles of bronze and gold, have never freed their
owner's sick body from fever or his mind from care").[245] Piling up images of
wealth, only to disavow it, Horace indicates that poetry has an equivalent
value. Tibullus similarly opens his love elegies by foregrounding the riches he
is disclaiming: "<u>Diuitias</u> alius fuluo sibi congerat auro" (<u>Riches</u> let another

242. See Kurke (1991: 246) on ambivalent money metaphors in Pind. *Isthm.* 2.

243. Barchiesi 1996: 24.

244. White 1993: 17. Such metaphors have a long history, from Pind. *Ol.* 2.90 to William
Cecil, Lord Burghley's *Ten Precepts*, no. 7, on life without a patron: "Thou shalt remain like a
hop without a pole; live in obscurity and be made a football for every insulting companion to
spurn at."

245. Cf. Schork 1971.

man heap up in a golden mound; 1.1.1). Yet just like *Arma*, "weapons", in the first line of Ovid's *Amores*, by the end of this poem "riches" will have transferred its meaning to its semantic opposite, or metaphorical other: "wealth" conceived differently, as devotion to the mistress and rural self-sufficiency.

## Patron as Co-creator

A literary patron's ability to draw out a protégé's innate talents finds many expressions: the fertilization of a seed, an architectural or agricultural prop, or the smoothing of an uneven surface. Often, the desired partnership is mapped onto a bipartite explanation of creativity: *ingenium*, the protégé's innate talent, enhanced by *ars*, the patron's art or artifice. As the goal of Horace's finishing process, Maecenas is particularly associated with refinement and polishing.[246] A pervasive image is the fingernail (*unguis*), both an index of completion in an artistic work and a tool of connoisseurship (running the nails over a work to test its smoothness).[247] A fastidious patron and a panoply of grooming tools (nail clippers, curling tongs, files, razors and currycombs) underpin Horace's story of cultural progress and unlocked potential: "ingenium ingens / inculto latet hoc sub corpore" (a huge talent lurks beneath this ill-groomed body; *Sat.* 1.3.33–34). When Horace reverts in *Epistles* 1 to an unkempt Diogenes, outwardly shaggy and seedy but inwardly self-sufficient, Maecenas's derision is the price for wriggling out from his clutches:

> If I meet you after having a lop-sided haircut, you laugh; if the edge of my ironed tunic happens to be worn, or if my toga is wonky, you laugh . . . since you are my protector in all things and wince if you see a badly cut nail on the friend who depends on you, always looks to you. (*Epist.* 1.1.94–97, 103–5)

It is relatively rare for poets to concede that they are entirely their patron's handiwork.[248] Unusually, Ovid writes to Sextus Pompeius from exile:

> sic ego sum rerum non ultima, Sexte, tuarum
>     tutelaeque feror munus opusque tuae.
>
> (*PONT.* 4.1.35–36)

Thus am I held to be not the least of your possessions and the reward and creation of your protection.

---

246. Gowers 2003: 85–86.
247. D'Angour 1999.
248. White (1993: 18) reads *munus* and *opus* as euphemisms for financial support.

More often, a patron is enlisted as a creative partner, whether adjunct or essential. In this role (as in *recusatio*), he faced off other rivals: gods and muses.[249] The language of divine presence is heavy in these reiterations of the *kleos*-bargain. Tibullus invites Messalla to "draw near and breathe on me" (huc ades adspiraque mihi; 2.1.35). Ovid quakes with terror when he invites Augustus's grandson Germanicus to look kindly on his *Fasti* (*Fast.* 1.15–18, 23–25).[250]

Maecenas's poets tend to avoid such tremulous self-abasement. When they use the language of divine inspiration (Verg. *G.* 3.42: "te sine nil altum mens incohat" [I cannot produce anything lofty without you]; *G.* 2.41: "ades" [be present]), it is in the context of a more equal partnership. Virgil hails his patron as "deservedly the greatest part of my fame" (o famae merito pars maxima nostrae; *G.* 2.40—thus conveniently displacing Pollio, patron of the *Eclogues*), while Horace uses the language of passionate affection: "part of my soul" (meae . . . partem animae; *Carm.* 2.17.5). Propertius enlists Maecenas (2.1) only to inform him that his poetry is parthenogenic. Muses often appear as capricious alternatives to the patron, who sweep the poet in new directions and have the power to override all other parties' desires. In *Odes* 2.12, while Maecenas dithers whether to withdraw his stern request, Horace turns to an irresistible Muse whose firm decision is final ("me dulcis . . . Musa . . . me <u>uoluit</u> dicere" [The sweet Muse <u>has willed</u> that I speak]). At the end of *Odes* 3, Maecenas is displaced by Melpomene, a more transcendent, more neutral guarantor of Horace's immortality.[251] Or rather: Maecenas is in debt to *him* for his posterity.[252]

## Sunshine and Shade

It was also common to couch a patron's interventions in metaphors from the natural world. Ever since Servius interpreted the canopy of Tityrus's beech tree (*Ecl.* 1.1: "sub tegmine fagi"): "allegorice sub tutela Imp[eratoris] Aug[usti]" (allegorically, under the protection of the emperor Augustus), a tree's shade was a favourite metaphor for patronal protection.[253] Lying replete

---

249. Fowler 2002: 151.

250. Hesiodic invocations of Zeus (*Op.* 1–8) or Zeus, Muses, kings and poets (*Theog.* 36–93) are often transferred to imperial patrons: e.g. Ov. *Fast.* 1.3–6, 15–20; Manilius 1.10; German., *Arat.* 1–4; Rosati 2002: 239–45.

251. Zetzel 1982: 96. For his name anagrammatized with *Camena* (muse) at *Epist.* 1.1.1–2, see Oberhelman and Armstrong (1995: 241n42). Cf. Suet. *Gram. et rhet.* 6: "sub clientela . . . Musarum"; Pseudo-Sulpicia 11: "precibus descende clientis et audi". Horace is loyal to the Camenae at *Carm.* 3.4.21: "uester, Camenae, uester . . .".

252. Bowditch 2001: 171.

253. Cf. Hor. *Epist.* 1.1.103: *tutela*.

under a tree is another euphemism for financial support: "per te secura saturi recubamus in umbra" (Thanks to you, we lie well-fed in the shade; Calp. *Ecl.* 4.37). But shade has further associations that fit well with what Maecenas offered the poets: cloistered semi-withdrawal from the world, Epicurean *ataraxia* and *otium*. This was his own preference, both actually—the bosky garden of *Eleg. in Maec.* 1.33—and metaphorically—when Propertius pictures him curled in the shadows (3.9.29), an image on which he models his own recumbent posture as a Callimachean poet (3.3.1). For Piso's poet, hungry for worldly success, shade equates to obscurity: "I will travel higher if you open for me the path of fame, if you remove the shadow" (sublimior ibo, / si famae mihi pandis iter, si detrahis umbram; *Laus Pisonis* 223–24). If the patron could withdraw his protective canopy at any point, he might conversely obstruct or overshadow the poet's development.[254]

Fertilization is another favourite metaphor. The patron takes a dormant "germ" or "seed" of talent, nourishes it and enriches it, enhancing the productivity of promising soil:

> et uiris dabit ipse fauor, dabit ipsa <u>feracem</u>
> spes animum
>
> (*LAUS PISONIS* 216–18)

Your very support will give me strength and hope itself give me <u>fruitful</u> inspiration.

Both *laetus*, "joyful", "fertile" (e.g., Verg. *G.* 1.1), and *ferax*, "fruitful", are originally agricultural adjectives.[255] Again, fertilization was yet another hands-off euphemism to mask the scandal of monetary recompense.[256] The concept of the great man as cultivator of his people originates in a Homeric simile comparing Penelope to a king whose crops and subjects thrive:[257] "The people prosper under his leadership, the dark soil yields wheat and barley, the trees

---

254. Suckers are destroyed by their mother's shade at Verg. *G.* 2.55–56. Aaron Hill wrote to James Thomson in *On his asking my advice to what patron he should address his poem, called "Winter"* (1726): "He who stoops safe beneath a patron's shade, / Shines, like the moon, by but a borrowed aid."

255. Cf. Greek *gonimos*.

256. In *Epodes* 2, the joke about a usurer (*faenerator*) who turns farmer relies on the double meaning of *faenus* (4), "dividend" and "harvest".

257. Patronage as fertilization: Bowditch 2001: 116–60, 210–46 (Horace and Virgil); Sharlet 2011: 182 (Arabic and Persian poetry). Islamic poets, writing for dry climates, use images of rain on parched soil; Sharlet 2011: 166, 181–82.

are heavy with fruit, the ewes never fail to bear, and the sea is full of fish" (Hom. *Od.* 19.111–13). Theocritus's extravagant "Encomium of Ptolemy", likewise, attributes the fertility of Egypt to the ruler's generosity (*Id.* 17.77–80).

As we will see in the next chapter, Virgil's *Georgics* makes an obvious context for casting the Maecenas relationship in agricultural terms. But *Epistles* 1, the product of Horace's riper years and a stock-taking moment in his career, also takes shape against a background of real-life and propagandistic bounty: the contained productivity of the Sabine Farm (*Epist.* 1.16), the overflowing granaries of Sicily and Asia (*Epist.* 1.11) and the return of the Golden Age in Augustus's cornucopia of peace (*Epist.* 1.12.28–29). The book is framed as a late-stage harvest, not just of wisdom but also of the patronal investment and the overload of debt that weighs it down: "haec seges ingratos tulit et ferret omnibus annis" (The field thus sown has always yielded and always will yield a crop of ingratitude; *Epist.* 1.7.21). Horace offers to repay Maecenas's attempts to refine his outer appearance with a hoard of philosophical understanding: "No one is so wild that he cannot be tamed [or: grow ripe, mitescere], if only he bend his ear to receive cultivation [culturae]" (*Epist.* 1.1.39–40). The burden of gratitude, as he later puts it, delicately reversing landlord and tenant, is like a farmer's unwelcome guest gift: "I am as obliged by your gift as if I were departing weighed down [with pears]" (*Epist.* 1.7.18). It is as though he himself had become a tree laden with fruit, clipped and rooted on his patron's plantation, or an over-cultivated farm, tied up in strings of obligation to a possessive landlord.

## Cutting Ties

I end with a closer look at *Epistle* 1.7, a poem rich with agricultural metaphors that also activates and intertwines many other familiar patronal images—slavery, shade, wealth, grooming—at a particularly fraught moment in the textual performance of the Maecenas relationship. Horace's most open expression of his need to break the stifling ties of dependency would become formative in the Renaissance discourse of patronage.[258] In line with the book's medical preoccupations, *recusatio* is initially presented as a sick note: "Your bard [uates tuus]", Horace writes, is quarantined in the country, and has broken his promise ("pollicitus . . . mendax"; 1–2) to return to Rome (so heralding an honest reckoning, which ends with Horace offering to return all Maecenas's gifts to preserve his independence).

Maecenas is indirectly rebuffed via two farming parables, one of a fattened vixen who cannot squeeze out after a binge in a grain bin and the other of Volteius Mena, an ordinary salesman with a perfect work–life balance. It starts

258. Burrow 1993: 31–33.

when Mena is taken up as an amusing project by a curious man of affairs. Philippus is stopped in his tracks on his way home from a busy day at the courts by the sight of a man "gently cleaning his own nails with a file in the carefree shade of a barber's shop" (50–51).[259] Intrigued by this moment of urban Zen and self-care, Philippus makes overtures. Mena plays hard to get but is eventually enticed, dined, uprooted from his city life and transplanted to a rural farm. Following a series of bad harvests and infestations, which leave him as scabby and unshaven as his sheep, he begs Philippus to return him to the city: "obsecro et obtestor, uitae me redde priori" (I beg and beseech you, give me back my old life; *Epist.* 1.7.95). Later writers like Ariosto would draw out the bitter undertones of this thinly veiled reproach.[260] Indeed, the fable "sheds more darkness than light on Horace's immediate situation".[261] It points to the vulnerabilities of the current relationship and tests its elasticity enough to "risk snapping the connection".[262] Much about the protagonists shouts "Horace and Maecenas": Mena is a freedman (socially below Horace) and a *praeco* (auctioneer, Horace's road not taken; *Sat.* 1.6.86); even a "Sabine farm" is named in all its specificity. Philippus, like Maecenas, is restlessly active (*strenuus*; 46), looking for "relaxation and laughter" (requiem . . . risus; 79). But there the similarities end.[263] Horace's farm is not an unwelcome gift but his life's solace; Maecenas took his time when pursuing him. Above all, this is a tale not of literary patronage but of mainstream *patrocinium*. The word *patronus*, usually suppressed, is mouthed by both Philippus (enquiring about the freedman's pre-existing obligations) and Mena (addressing his new "govern'r").[264] Conversely, the dinner at which this tiddler is hooked (*maena* = "sprat") is the start of suffocating commitment for a newly hired *cliens*:

> hic ubi saepe
> occultum uisus decurrere piscis ad hamum,
> mane <u>cliens</u> et iam certus conuiua . . .

(EPIST. 1.7.73–75)

Like fish that are often seen rushing to a hidden hook, by morning he was already <u>a client</u> and a reliable dinner guest.

---

259. Oliensis 1998: 162. Her reading of this poem's complexities (157–65) is still the best.

260. Oliensis 1998: 157: "polite rudeness or amicable hostility". Ariosto and Horace: see below p. 377.

261. Oliensis 1998: 162–63; *contra* McGann 1969: 54–55. See also W. Ralph Johnson 1993: 43–44.

262. Oliensis 1998: 157.

263. White 2007: 205.

264. *Epist.* 1.7.53–54, 92–93.

As for the farm, while Maecenas's gift conforms to the "misrecognition agreement", Philippus enables Mena to *buy* his farm with two instalments (one a loan, *mutua*) of seven thousand sesterces, a coin reintroduced to Rome only three years before. It must be significant that a *philippus* (named after Philip of Macedon) was a heavy gold coin (in which his son Alexander paid the untalented poet Choerilus; *Epist.* 2.1.234) and a *mina* a middling silver one. As the supreme paradigm of patronage and power misaligned, Alexander hovers as analogue for Augustus in much of Horace's later poetry.[265] Even the slave Demetrius who snaps to attention (*Epist.* 1.7.52–3) has the name of another Macedonian king. Words of getting and spending (*et quaerere et uti*), profit and loss (*rem strenuus auge, damnis*), lay bare the cycles of calculation common to patronage, farming and ethics.[266]

At the same time, Mena debases the ideal of Ennius's Good Companion: blurting too much ("dicenda tacenda locutus"; 72), too heavy on the praise ("non cessat laudare"; 78).[267] A lowly auctioneer who talks up scrap goods, he updates Ennius's ambivalent associations with *praeconium*, bigging up one's superiors. Even Philippus's genial "pile it high" (rem strenuus auge; 71) refers to profits, not fame; this will be a poor investment for him, despite its brief entertainment value. Through Mena, happily wedded to "the ties of trade" (mercennaria uincla; 67) but resistant to slavery, Horace lives out a freedman's fantasy of attracting, then rudely (*improbus*; 63) defying a superior who is the first to say hello. The most freighted word of the poem is *benigne*, the polite "No, thanks" with which Mena initially rebuffs Philippus, echoing the earlier fable of the farmer's unwanted gifts ("at tu, quantum uis, tolle." "benigne" [Go on, help yourself. No, thanks]; 16).[268] What if Horace had said no to Maecenas's original invitation? Would he now be a humble auctioneer sitting contentedly in a barber's shade, absorbed in self-care? The tranquil rhythms of Mena's life stir nostalgia as much in Horace as in Philippus. But there is no going back to his youth or his anonymous urban routines.

It is often assumed that what started as an unequal relationship developed over the years into true friendship.[269] All we can say for sure is that if *Epistles* 1 negotiates the "tense dialectic between *amicitia* and clientship", this is the poem where Horace attempts to commute the second decisively into the first.[270] He lets Maecenas down gently: anticipating hurt, cutting to the chase (82–83),

265. On Augustus and Alexander in *Epist.* 2.1, see Spencer (2003).

266. Cf. *Epist.* 1.1.80: "multis occulto crescit res faenore".

267. P. Hardie 2007b. Like the Pest: *Sat.* 1.9.13 ("uicos, urbem laudaret").

268. Also retracing Horace's attempt to limit Maecenas' *benignitas* 'generosity' in *Epodes* 1.

269. E.g., Bowditch 2001: 161–210.

270. Konstan 1995: 341; cf. Oliensis 1998: 155n2.

calling him "dulcis amice" (sweet friend; 12), taking for granted that his unflappable patron is a mellow observer of patronage relations more crudely defined and understands a subtly oblique fable. The quid pro quo of long intimacy is that a true friend should be able to weather the unspeakable (*tacenda*) as well as the speakable (*dicenda*). But something of the initial mystery has finally been broken: Maecenas's flexible friendship is given its ultimate test.

## Coda

One of the most devastating assaults on the Roman patronage system (*On Salaried Posts in Great Houses*) was written some 150 years later, by a Greek (predictably), Lucian, on behalf of paid retainers and teachers (also Greek), humiliated by their cohabitation with the Roman elite. Relaying his conversations with educated men whose experience of *philia* (= *amicitia*) Roman-style is tantamount to slavery, Lucian plays havoc with some familiar patronage metaphors. He turns voyages steered by the patron into shipwrecks from which drowning men are rescued by a saviour god.[271] Clients attracted over the threshold or hooked like gaping fish by the glitter of gold and the promise of "millions and farms" have become bottom feeders, beneath even Syrian doorkeepers and Alexandrian dwarves in the pecking order. Interestingly for our reading of Horace's first interview, privileged access to a great house is figured as initiation into the various stages of a cult (*telete*), from which brainwashed victims emerge blinking into the light.[272] In his poets' hands, Maecenas, as we have seen, escapes many of the more hierarchical, masculine, patriarchal and distant analogies for a patron's protection. But all we have is the written experience of those inside a relationship with him (or aspiring to it). Except for Horace, we hear nothing from the survivors who lived to tell the tale.

---

271. *On Salaried Posts* 1–2. The opposite of *Laus Pisonis* 253 ("tu nanti protende manum"); cf. Samuel Johnson's much-quoted words to Lord Chesterfield: "Is not a patron, my lord, one who looks with unconcern on a man struggling for life in the water, and, when he has reached ground, encumbers him with help?" (letter, February 7, 1755; Redford 1992–94: 1.96).

272. *On Salaried Posts* 1. In the apologetic sequel, the author is himself compared to someone flogging cough medicine with a hacking cough (*Apology* 7).

# 3

# Maecenas the Landlord

## VIRGIL'S *GEORGICS*

They have taken the gable from the roof of clay
On the long swede pile. They have let in the sun
To the white and gold and purple of curled fronds
Unsunned. It is a sight more tender-gorgeous
At the wood-corner where Winter moans and drips
Than when, in the Valley of the Tombs of Kings,
A boy crawls down into a Pharaoh's tomb
And, first of Christian men, beholds the mummy,
God and monkey, chariot and throne and vase,
Blue pottery, alabaster, and gold.

But dreamless long-dead Amen-hotep lies.
This is a dream of Winter, sweet as Spring.

—EDWARD THOMAS, *SWEDES* (1915)

VIRGIL'S MIDDLE WORK saw the light in 29 BCE: four books of hexameter poetry on crops, trees and vines, animals, and bees, with a sidelong glance at gardens. This literary hybrid of many moods and faces looks back to Hesiod's rugged almanac (*Works and Days*), Lucretius's poem on nature (*De rerum natura*), Varro's book on country matters (*De re rustica*), the antiquarian and astronomical works of Callimachus and Aratus, and universal Homer.[1] It also looks closely at itself. At the centre of a tripartite career (*Eclogues–Georgics–Aeneid*), the poem feels transitional, suspended in the chrysalis stage

---

1. P. Hardie 1998: 50: "pronounced mood-swings".

between pastoral and epic, watching itself come into being along with the plants.[2] Virgil celebrates diversification, seasonality and fertility, differences of scale and size; he encourages loving scrutiny of soil types, tiny insects, grafting and hoeing techniques. But the poem's scope is also hugely ambitious: beyond the narrow horizons of Italian farmland stretch the wastes of Scythia, the African desert, the realms of myth and history, the rise of Augustus and the celestial starscape.

Most attempts to extract the poem's meaning have ended, unsurprisingly, in uncertainty.[3] Hard-pressed analogies between human and plant and human and animal encourage us to allegorize farming, while opening up further problems of interpretation. Are trees and flocks ever just trees and flocks? Are there symbolic aspects to clearing, planting, grafting, organic succession, and spontaneity versus intervention? Does nature exist only to provide anthropomorphic models for the human community? What do we learn about the pursuit and usefulness of knowledge? In the most intellectually honest discussion of the poem's uninterpretability, William Batstone has warned of the hopelessness of all models (the commonwealth of bees is not exactly like human society), the failure of didaxis (too much overload to learn anything) and the fantasy of allegory (the correspondences never quite work). Seductive as they are, the implied parallels between trees, animals and human society must be approached with caution.[4]

The poem also features four of the most enigmatic and bodiless of Maecenas's appearances in Augustan literature. In one, Virgil describes him as "the greatest part of my glory" (G. 2.41), but he provides no details of their first meeting or any other aspect of their friendship. Instead, it is left to Donatus's *Life of Virgil* to supply background and motive. Just as the *Eclogues* was written (ten years earlier) for those who had saved Virgil's fortunes during the proscriptions (Pollio, Varus and Gallus), so the *Georgics* was written for Maecenas because he had intervened to stop a soldier killing Virgil in a violent agricultural dispute.[5] The territorial crisis dramatized in *Eclogues* 1.6, 70–72, and *Eclogues* 9.2–4 (reprieve at the hands of an unknown god or dispossession by

2. C. Hardie 1971; Thomas 1988b *ad* 1.2; Horsfall 1995: 72–73. Lucretian "process" verbs abound: *inolescere, rubescere, incanescere, trudere, splendescere*. See Jenkyns 1998: 317–20: a fluctuation between "ample" and "slender". Macrob. *Sat.* 5.1.15 praises the stylistic balance of G. 1.84–93 in soil metaphors: "neither abrupt compression, nor absurd flow, nor thin dryness, nor rich fertility".

3. E.g., Perkell 1989: 13–16; Batstone 1997: 143–44; Gale 2000: 1.

4. Batstone 1997. This paragraph and much of the section on *Georgics* 2 are adapted from Gowers (2016b).

5. Donat. *Vit. Verg.* 19–20.

his military veterans) is averted in Virgil's favour: his secure enclosure stands for poetic independence, salvaged, if potentially compromised, by a benevolent superior. The *Georgics* is imagined as a thank offering for benefits already received, the fruits of peace grown from once-contested soil.[6]

In addition, the anecdote offers a practical answer to an age-old puzzle: why did Virgil make Maecenas the dedicatee of an agricultural poem? With his name dropped into the poem's second line, we might expect him to be its foremost addressee. Yet he is soon eclipsed by rival patrons: first the rural gods, Liber and Ceres, Pan and the Nymphs, and then Octavian himself. For the rest of the poem, there is a far more consistent audience for the poet's practical advice: the hardy farmers (*duri agricolae*) of post-war Italy. To complicate matters, Virgil frequently uses a singular *tu*, "you", generic since Hesiod for the didactic addressee. Servius, for one, equates this with the "you" of Hesiod's pupil Perses, confident that Maecenas represents the equivalent in Virgil's "teacher-student constellation":[7] "These books are didactic, meaning that they have to be addressed to someone; for didactic requires knowledge to be imparted and the characters of a sage and a pupil; thus Virgil wrote to Maecenas as Hesiod wrote to Perses, and Lucretius to Memmius" (Serv. *ad* Verg. *G. praef.* 1). As we will see, the didactic tradition does provide Virgil with models for Maecenas, but these are neither Hesiod's Perseus nor Lucretius's Memmius.

By contrast, Richard Thomas notes the patterned occurrences of Maecenas's name, once per book (1.2, 2.41, 3.41, 4.1), but concludes: "He seems otherwise to have little to do with the poem."[8] Statistically speaking, this is true. Thomas's claim is as understated as Servius's is overstated. His enigmatic "seems" encourages us to think again about Maecenas's role.[9] Even in antiquity, it was clear that the farmers were not the poem's primary focus. Seneca deduces that Virgil wrote "not to teach farmers but to delight readers"; Columella claims that the *Georgics* will be appreciated more "by students of literature who could read at leisure [in otio legentibus] than by busy farmers [negotiosis agricolis]".[10] One solution has been to blend Maecenas and farmers together, making him their representative and understanding *agricolae* as "urban landowners", rather

---

6. Dio 55.7.1: because Octavian had received benefits from Maecenas, he was obliged to give him power over the city.

7. Volk's term: 2002: 37–39; cf. Thibodeau 2011: 8. See Schiesaro (1993: 133–35), Volk (2002: 122–39) and Cowan (2018) for more nuanced discussion of Virgil's addressees.

8. Thomas 1988b *ad* 1.2.

9. Octavian is addressed only three times (1.25, 503; 2.170).

10. Sen. *Ep.* 86.15; Columella, *Rust.* 9.2.5. Cic. *De or.* 1.69 defends Nicander for writing "with a poet's facility, not a farmer's".

than actual tillers of the soil.[11] Elite Romans retreating to country estates from fear or political disaffection might well be receptive to a poet's attempt to dignify a necessary upheaval. For the aristocrat who thought of agriculture as a dubious activity (traditional and honourable, but smelly and rustic as well), the *Georgics* held out a fantasy of hands-on contact with the native earth, uncompromised by the presence of surrogate managers or bailiffs and entirely concealing the invisible armies of enslaved workers who dealt with the heavier tasks.[12]

In any case, Maecenas was no average landlord. Until Octavian returned from Greece in 29, he was charged with the administration of Rome and Italy: a vast province of "care" that included but stretched far beyond the confines of any single estate. Perhaps he himself expected to be put out to pasture soon; perhaps he needed to be persuaded that country life was worth his trouble. Still persistent in some quarters is the idea that he was instrumental in brokering Octavian's request for a propaganda poem to praise the revival of traditional Italian agriculture. When Virgil folds the notion of "orders" into his text (3.41), they are often assumed to be instructions passed down from on high.[13] But that is to discount how differently Virgil represents Octavian's and Maecenas's wishes—as we will see.

In the crisp words of L. P. Wilkinson: "Nothing that we know of Maecenas suggests that he would have initiated a campaign for hardiness and simplicity."[14] He could rejoice with Gwendolen in *The Importance of Being Earnest*: "I am glad to say that I have never seen a spade."[15] It was Agrippa who was described as "closer to rusticity than self-indulgence [*deliciis*]".[16] Delicate Maecenas should be more of a soft foil to the rustic farmers. An anecdote about the Stoic Cleanthes, who insisted that outward appearance determined inner character, recounts how he was confronted by an effeminate *cinaedus*, hardened from working in the fields, and initially flummoxed—until a tell-tale sneeze revealed the man to be *malakos*, "cissy", after all.[17] Menander's *Dyskolos* dramatizes a more successful outcome: a delicate young suitor proves he is

---

11. Thibodeau 2011.

12. Thibodeau 2011: 86–100, 41–47. See Geue (2018) on Virgil's displacement of interhuman violence to the plant and animal worlds.

13. See White (1993: 99–109) on the evolution of the idea in post-Renaissance Europe.

14. Wilkinson 1969: 163.

15. Wilde 2019: 818 (*The Importance of Being Earnest*, act 2, lines 583–84).

16. Plin. *HN* 35.9.26. For Agrippa as "a huge bumpkin who would appear more at ease tramping a furrow, either before or after the plough, than walking in a drawing room", see J. Williams ([1972] 2014: 31).

17. Diog. Laert. 7.173.

worthy of a farmer's daughter by getting his hands dirty. Maecenas should have to be dragged reluctantly into the world of mud and manure, no less than Virgil himself, a delicate poet according to his biographers, who openly claims to be unequal to the task ahead of him. We might ask: what are two *malakoi*, or "soft" men, doing in the hard sphere of agriculture?

Even without Maecenas, the hard–soft dichotomy is crucial in a poem negotiating both how to live up to "hard" Hesiod and how to "harden off" the softness of the *Eclogues*.[18] Like agriculture, georgic poetry is a task that needs iron tools and an iron voice. Like crops and animals, farmers must be trained, curbed and broken in, in parallel with the poet's own acculturation from pastoral *Eclogues* to agricultural *Georgics*. Maecenas's own hard–soft qualities are famously condensed in the litotes "haud mollia iussa" (not un-tough orders; G. 3.41), which seems to cast him as the torturer who stretches Virgil's feeble capacity. But elsewhere he is invoked as sympathetic witness to the poet's doubts about writing in an unfamiliar milieu, his nostalgia for the softness and spontaneity of pastoral (its wandering beasts, self-seeded plants and wayward enchanter, Orpheus), and his aspirations to the cosmic sublimity of epic. Maecenas allows Virgil to devolve the burden of an inappropriate task back onto that task's imagined commissioner, the townie in a sunhat who plays at rural life but is urban at heart.

Short as they are, the four addresses to Maecenas stand out as highly marked sidings in the "didactic plot".[19] Separate from the folkloric "you" of the rest of the poem, the "Maecenas discourse" offers a contemplative interlude or outer frame in which Virgil can reflect on his progress and make Maecenas witness to his poetic decision-making.[20] The addresses are cryptic, sometimes highly metaphorical. But what happens when plain agricultural advice resumes? Does Maecenas just fade into the background?[21] Michael Putnam, for one, has argued for his overarching importance to the didactic plot: "The name of Maecenas is an ordering principle of the words themselves . . . a spirit of coalescence, imposed as intellectual pattern on materials often chaotic and returning us finally whence we started."[22]

This intuition, that Maecenas has a dynamic role to play in the entire economy of the *Georgics*, is vital. So, too, is the sense that he is aligned with a higher

18. "Hard" (χαλεπός) is repeated at Hes. *Op.* 557–58; Hor. *Sat.* 1.10.44 calls the *Eclogues* "molle atque facetum".

19. Didactic plot: Fowler 2004; Schiesaro 1994: 81.

20. Volk 2002: 138, 151.

21. Volk 2002: 131: it would be absurd for Maecenas to be actively engaged in building ploughs or tying vines to elm trees.

22. Putnam 1979: 18.

poetic intelligence than the farmers and a zeal for knowledge that goes beyond practicality. But there is equally a case for seeing Maecenas as a force for disruption and deviation, in a way that conveniently suits the poet's own sweet will. He has been seen as the conventional didactic student, a representative of the (elite) *agricolae* or someone on the outside of the poem, along with Virgil himself—even a broader poetic principle altogether. In the end, it may be the sheer vagueness of his representation that makes Maecenas so versatile an addressee:

> No particular aspect of his life or influence is specified. He is Virgil's moral support and the force that gives the project depth and breadth (3.42, 2.41), but his presence also suggests the poem's vulnerable position before other powers. He seems to mediate between Caesar's heroic accomplishments and the tenuis labor of Virgil's Callimachean project (2.41, 44). Because he straddles so many worlds and yet is not precisely defined, he becomes part of the fullness which inhabits both Virgil's subject and his audience. (Batstone 1997: 132–33)

## Reading to Augustus

Another anecdote in the *Vita* offers a second primal scene for the poem's production: Virgil read the *Georgics* aloud, soon after its composition, to the future emperor when he stopped at Atella on his way back to Rome after Actium. The reading took four days (so aligning Virgil's "works" with his "days"). Only when his voice gave out did the poet stop reading, at which point Maecenas took over:

> Georgica reuerso post Actiacam uictoriam Augusto atque Atellae reficiendarum faucium causa commoranti per continuum quadriduum legit, suscipiente Maecenate legendi uicem quotiens interpellaretur ipse uocis offensione. (Donat. *Vita Verg.* 27)

> He read the Georgics to Augustus when he returned after victory at Actium and had stopped at Atella for the sake of resting his throat. This took a continuous period of four days, with Maecenas taking it in turn to read for Virgil whenever he was interrupted by strain on his voice.

Christopher Nappa uses this anecdote to justify his emperor-focused reading of the poem: "Octavian is not the poet's only student in the *Georgics*, and at times he is not always the principal one, but he is always there."[23] Aware that any

---

23. Nappa 2005: 8.

Augustan reading risks straitjacketing the poem into some dogmatic, dutiful replica of a regime's values, Nappa frames the poem as a set of puzzles for the imperial reader to solve. True, the anecdote makes Octavian and Virgil the obvious protagonists: resting emperor and exercised poet exchange the roles Virgil gives them in the famous final *sphragis*, of active emperor and recumbent poet.[24] Both have voices that are under strain.[25] The author of the *Life* has been described as "an insightful reader of Virgil who saw with absolute clarity the connections between Actium, Octavian's triple triumph, and the *Georgics*".[26] Even so, it is hard to prove that Virgil has Octavian in mind in every line of the poem.

By contrast, Maecenas hovers in the background. Yet the *Life* is equally insightful about his role in the production process. Unlike Augustus—and unlike Octavia, who during Virgil's recital of three books of the *Aeneid* famously fainted at the mention of her dead son Marcellus (Donat. *Vita Verg.* 32)—he is no passive audience member but a reader in a more active, performative sense, almost an auxiliary voice. In other words, the anecdote captures something distinctive about his function in Virgil's poem. Maecenas's emergency interventions nod to his timely appearances at points where the *Georgics* text dramatizes its own interruption. He is the understudy, ready to take over (*suscipiente . . . legendi uicem*) when the poet's spirit fails.[27]

As it happens, the *Life* provides a follow-up account of Maecenas as proxy reader:

> But his [Virgil's] reading aloud had <u>a remarkably sweet and seductive quality</u> [cum suauitate et lenociniis miris]. According to Seneca, the poet Julius Montanus used to say that he would have managed to steal something from Virgil, if he could steal his voice, his face and his dramatic skill. For the same verses, if recited by Virgil, sounded wonderful, but if recited by someone else, just <u>flat and unmusical</u> [inanes . . . mutosque]. (Donat. *Vita Verg.* 28–29)

Once an adequate substitute for Virgil, Maecenas now, like everyone else, serves to offset the unique qualities of the poet's voice. This confirms another intuition: his appearances in the *Georgics* are, above all, "Virgil-focused"; his simulated coaxing fosters and reflects Virgil's own literary goals. Maecenas is not there to claim equal credit for the enterprise but as backing or reserve. In

24. G. 4.560–64: "Caesar dum magnus ad altum / fulminat . . . Vergilium . . . studiis florentem ignobilis oti . . ."

25. Unless the repaired *fauces* are not the emperor's voice passages but some narrow local defile.

26. Nelis 2013: 248.

27. Naumann (1981: 11–12) suspects the influence of G. 2.39—"tuque, Maecenas, ades . . . et lege" (where *lege* has the sense "grasp", "skim"—not "read").

short, he plays the same role in relation to Virgil that he played in real life for the absent Octavian.[28]

Is it necessary, though, to confine his "presence" to the four addresses? Elsewhere, it often seems as if Maecenas is being beckoned specifically by Virgil's *tus* and *tibis*, exhorted to scrutinize, hold his nose, take action or simply appreciate the intricacy of the poet's natural descriptions.[29] A more daring reading would presume that Maecenas, like Octavian, is "always there": "an equally congenial recipient of political allegory, philosophical allegory, Hellenistic poetasting, or agricultural practicality".[30] What difference to the *Georgics* would such a Maecenas-focused reading make? For a start, it would identify the poem as less regimented and more focused on pleasure. As sympathetic reader and ever-present foil to the rustic farmers, Maecenas is shaped in the poet's own image. At the same time, his distinctive personality feeds Virgil's representation both of him and of the poetry. Aestheticizing passages and moralizing ones that contrast urban effeteness with rural simplicity seem to be destined for his ears. Conversely, aspects of Maecenas's own split identity and unexpected choices are uniquely useful to Virgil in dramatizing his moments of indecision.

In short, Maecenas functions as a softer, more flexible alternative to Octavian, his rival in the *Georgics* as taskmaster, benefactor and identifiable student. Far in the future looms the epic Virgil plans to write on Caesar's military exploits, previewed in Book 3 but deferred for now; also the prospect of his deification.[31] Philip Hardie has argued that the *Georgics* offers the young emperor allegorical training, preparing him for future political responsibilities.[32] For as long as Octavian's destiny was under wraps, his temporary deputy, the turbaned Etruscan pretender, made a safer alternative ruler, a play king through whom to revive key moments in the long history of educating princes through agriculture. Virgil casts Maecenas as different versions, Greek, Roman and Persian, of the "great lord" in relation to the land: the urban owner who visits his estate to hunt or celebrate a festival, a tutelary nature god and a king prepared to get his hands dirty by touching the soil or planting trees, one who understands the analogies between governance and estate management.[33]

28. Nappa 2005: 25. Cf. Tac. *Ann.* 6.6.11 on Maecenas as temporary deputy in Italy.

29. Schiesaro 1993: 138: the poem is addressed to "a public of Maecenases". Sharrock 1997: 113: "descriptive-prescriptives" and "*tu*-directives" bind together "Maecenas, the *coloni*, and us".

30. Batstone 1997: 133.

31. Batstone (1997: 132) notes Octavian's "polyvalent and precarious potential"; hinted at by placeholders *mox*, "soon" (1.24), and *iam nunc*, "already now" (1.42); Nelis 2013: 254.

32. P. Hardie 2004.

33. Agricultural metaphors for education in antiquity: P. Hardie 2004: 84–86. Estate as kingdom: Verg. *Ecl.* 1.69, Cic. *De or.* 1.41.

My reading of the *Georgics* through its opening dedicatee will be partial, in both senses of the word: no Augustan temple of song (3.10–48), no Orpheus and Aristaeus (4.317–558). Beyond the four addresses, I will assume that Maecenas remains loosely "present" throughout the poem and that there are parts of the text where that presence is particularly worth bearing in mind. The addresses tell us little: he is a mere parenthesis in Book 1, a witness to indecision in Book 2, a sluggish hunting companion in Book 3 and a microscopic observer in Book 4. But for the *Georgics* "Maecenas" may represent something broader altogether: a principle of constant changeability, a barometer of poetic mood, a fellow-consciousness, a fish out of agricultural water—which is much the same thing as saying that he is a constructed reflection of the poet and the poem.

## *Georgics* 1

Maecenas first appears in parenthesis in the poem's opening period, a five-line table of contents or paratextual frontispiece to match the eight-line *sphragis* at its end:[34]

> Quid faciat laetas segetes, quo sidere terram
> uertere, Maecenas, ulmisque adiungere uitis
> conueniat, quae cura boum, qui cultus habendo
> sit pecori, apibus quanta experientia parcis,
> hinc canere incipiam.

(1.1–5)

> What makes the crops flourish, by what star it's fit to turn the soil, Maecenas, or tie the vines to elms, how to care for cattle and tend the flocks, and what skill's required to keep thrifty bees: from this point I begin my song.

His role, behind the scenes of the poem proper, appears collusive, even editorial. But the questions with which Virgil lays out his prospectus are ambiguous: it is actually unclear until line 5 ("hinc canere incipiam") that they are indirect rather than direct.[35] For just a moment, Virgil's "Quid faciat", "What (might) make(s)", recalls Horace's first satire, which also opens with a question and enlists the same mystery friend to reflect with him: "How come, Maecenas [*Sat.* 1.1.1; Qui fit, Maecenas] . . . our fellow men are universally restless?"[36] The

34. Carolyn MacDonald first described this to me as paratextual.

35. Batstone 1988: 230–32.

36. On intertextuality between *Satires* and *Georgics*, see Putnam (1995–96) and Freudenburg (2001: 35–38, 40–42, 77–82). G. 1.1–2 ("terram / uertere"), for example, is close to Hor. *Sat.* 1.1.28 ("ille grauem duro terram qui uertit aratro").

Horatian Maecenas looks similarly parenthetical, but turns out to be nothing less than the implied reason for the speaker's unusual contentment: why's all the world dissatisfied?—except for me—because of you.[37]

Did Horace's allusive thank you inspire Virgil? The quiet insertion of the proper name prompts us to make "Maecenas" the answer to these new questions, too. When the topic is not human restlessness but the bounty of nature, and if a patron, across cultures, is like a fertility god—especially relevant to an agricultural poem—then it should be Maecenas who makes the crops fertile and brings joy to the poet or the farmer.[38] He is the lodestar that guides the turning of soil and the propping of vines on elms, the one who generates care (*cura*), cultivation (*cultus*) and empirical know-how (*experientia*). The song could even be said to begin from him (*hinc canere incipiam*).[39]

What Virgil's wording indicates is that this is not simply a list of topics to be covered. It involves what Michael Putnam has called "a series of interrelationships, demands, and dependencies", including the connection between "singer and patron, teacher and the everyman 'you' who might understand" (even if "everyman" is not quite the right word for Maecenas).[40] In particular, his name is embedded just before an image of vines tied to elms for support. These training devices, a common sight on Italian farms and an established image for marriage, equally suggest the shelter and stability a patron gives to a developing protégé.[41] If Maecenas is fertilizing agent, protective prop or benign star, that makes his poets cultivars or tender saplings. Rather than corresponding to Lucretius's reluctant philosophy student Memmius (as Servius thought), Maecenas would seem to have more in common with Lucretius's nourishing patron goddess: *alma Venus*.[42] Like Liber (Bacchus), he is *liber(alis)*; like Ceres, he is *almus*.

This brief greeting is just the start of a long, almost overdetermined appeal for supporters. The bountiful patron yields his tutelary role, first to the gods of nature who nourish the crops and send the rain (21–23), then, by the end of the list, to Octavian himself ("bringer of fruits and lord of the seasons"; 27), soon, but not too soon, to join their ranks.[43] By lines 28–30, Virgil has made Octavian the earthly epiphany of Ceres, while Jupiter is surprisingly

37. Gowers 2012, *ad loc.*

38. Patronage as fertilization: see above, pp. 101–102.

39. On the range of *cultus* (growing crops, tending and civilizing), see Miles (1980: 64).

40. Putnam 1979: 17–18.

41. E.g., Catull. 62.49–50; Verg. G. 2.302.

42. So Dan-el Padilla Peralta once suggested to me.

43. Nelis (2013: 261) sees *Augustus* encrypted in line 27: "AUctorem fruGUm tempeSTatUMque potentem".

absent.[44] Thomas comments: "At times he seems to have been *supplanted* by Octavian."[45] This replanting idea holds good for Maecenas in reverse, modified as he is within a few lines into the gods of earthly fruits. Despite his low-key presence, he is the one aligned with ample generosity: pouring out (13), supporting (18), nourishing (22) and bestowing (23). Caesar is "bringer of fruits" (27) but operates more remotely: blessing (40), pitying (41), preparing to be invoked (42). In short, Virgil is hedging his bets. By the end of the first forty lines, not only has he enlisted two human patrons and many more divine ones but his Octavian has hijacked most of Maecenas's functions.[46] Along with a protective aura, he takes a more explicitly active role in the economy of the poem: to speed and bless the poet's enterprise ("give me an easy passage and bless my ambitious start"; 40) and proceed with him (41–42) to help the ignorant farmers.[47] He also reclaims the authority ceded to Maecenas during his absence in Greece and Egypt, indeed extends it outwards to the entire world: "urbis . . . terrarumque . . . curam" (24–25).[48] Maecenas will recover some of his powers in Books 2 and 3, but it is with Octavian that the poem will end.

From this point Maecenas seems to disappear, as if already superfluous. But we cannot entirely exclude him from what follows. For one thing, his ethnicity is instrumental. Thomas undervalues *Maecenas* as a textual element, but he does grant the omnipresence of the very un-Callimachean adjective *pinguis*, "plump", "rich", "full to the brim", which first appears at line 8, then a further twenty-plus times in the poem, used of plants, animals, soil ("enriched" by civilian blood at 1.492, "sanguine pinguescere campos"), manure, even the beehive.[49] Like the spirit of Autumn in Keats's *Ode*, conspiring to "fill all fruit with ripeness to the core, / To swell the gourd, and plump the hazel shells / With a sweet kernel" (6–8), Maecenas is a genius of brimming fertility throughout the poem—not just because that is what Virgil requires of him as tutelary spirit but also because he hails from Etruria, known for its rich clods of earth and plump sacrificial flautists ("pinguis . . . Tyrrhenus"; 2.193).[50] Environmental determinism and political expediency play their part in his incorporation into Virgil's vision of rustic Italy as much as into Augustus's ideological *tota Italia*. And

---

44. In 31 BCE, Athenian citizens erected two statues at Eleusis to Augustus, grain-giving "saviour and benefactor" of the cities of Greece; Vanderpool 1968.

45. Thomas 1988b: 61, emphasis added.

46. Schiesaro 1993: 135.

47. Schiesaro 1993: 134.

48. Cf. Tac. *Ann.* 6.6.11. *terrarum . . . curam* suggests both "care of (all) lands" and "care of the land".

49. See Thomas 1988b *ad* 1.4; Serv. *ad* 1.80: "pingui fimo uel umido uel fertili".

50. Diod. Sic. 5.40.3–5. Macfarlane 1996.

when Maecenas claimed descent from the Etruscans' ancestors, the Lydians, then some salient royal figures in the history of Middle-Eastern agriculture—Xerxes and Cyrus, who stooped to planting paradises with their bare hands—are at Virgil's disposal, too.[51]

From the first sinking of the gleaming plough into the unfrozen earth, heavy-duty work and tireless attention to external "signs", like oncoming rain or setting stars, are the solution to the farmers' battle for survival. By implication, the current Age of Iron imposes a newer, tougher model of patronage—fair rewards in return for hard labour—on the spontaneous bounty of the Golden Age, when "the earth bore everything more freely, unasked" (127–28). Human beings, especially Italians, are an innately "hard race" (durum genus; 63),[52] but, like the earth, need steering away from idleness (cf. 72: "harden a fallow field"). For Virgil himself, moving from Golden Age pastoral to Iron Age agricultural didactic is also an uphill struggle. Unlike the "unordered grass" (iniussa . . . gramina; 55–56) which spreads with abandon, he feels dragooned into strict time and space.

Hesiodic grimness overshadows much of *Georgics* 1, with the farmer imagined as shivering ploughman, frustrated oarsman and unwilling archaeologist, unearthing rusty helmets and other civil war relics from his fields. An anthropomorphized Earth threatens to revert to sloth, sterility and uselessness, like lazy tillers of her soil. Meanwhile, the farmer's responsibilities are only intermittently relieved by the different busyness involved in winter festivals:

> frigoribus parto agricolae plerumque fruuntur
> mutuaque inter se laeti conuiuia curant.
> inuitat genialis hiems curasque resoluit.

> (1.300–302)

In the cold season, the farmers mostly enjoy the fruits of their harvest and busy themselves in a round of feasts. Merry winter entices them and soothes their cares.

But if work is the only answer, why, in that case, does Virgil dwell so lyrically on wasted time and material, in lingering descriptions of weightless chaff or the playful whirling of feathers on the surface of water?[53]

---

51. Xen. *Oec.* 4.20–25: Cyrus plants trees. *Esther* 1: 5 Xerxes plants trees (Vulgate: "of the garden and woods, which had been planted by the royal hands with royal care"). See Briant (2002: 232–34) on Persian kings as gardeners.

52. Cf. Verg. *Aen.* 9.603.

53. Cf. 321: "culmum leuem stipulasque uolantis".

saepe leuem paleam et frondes uolitare caducas
aut summa nantis in aqua conludere plumas.

(1.368–69)

light chaff and falling leaves fly about or floating feathers frolic on the water's
surface.

Why does he spend time cataloguing the useless weeds that exhaust the soil?

urit enim lini campum seges, urit auenae,
urunt Lethaeo perfusa papauera somno?

(1.77–78)

For the flax crop drains the field dry, so do oats, so does the poppy drenched
in Lethaean slumber.

The agricultural landscape may offer Octavian a moral lesson in the advantages
of ruthless extermination.[54] But it also reveals something like an open conflict
of sympathy in Virgil's display of fellow feeling with the useless and the un-
hardy. This is a poem about aesthetics as well as the hard grind—the pleasures
of looking, touching, tasting and translating into poetry. While it is too simple
to claim that the *Georgics* associates success with Octavian and failure with
Maecenas, the fact that Maecenas already exists in the poem as an individualized alternative addressee aligns him with its "further voices". It is to him that
these slow descriptions of idle things are directed, which in turn reinforces his
enduring role as Octavian's foil: delicate, lazy and effete.

Book 1 illustrates how ambiguous Maecenas's role in the poem remains:
both *with* the farmers and supplementary to them.[55] Explaining how soil
types determine a nation's product, the poet urges the listener to use his eyes:
"nonne uides . . . ?" (1.56). Servius comments: "He is speaking to either Maecenas or the farmer [rustico]."[56] His doubts are reasonable, given the objects
in question: exotic imports, mostly from the East (Lydian saffron, Indian
ivory, Pontine musk and incense from the "soft Arabs"; 1.56–59), all unlikely
commodities for the farmer who goes to town to barter fruit and olives for
agricultural tools (1.273–75) and far closer to the delicate sensory world of
Maecenas.[57] Virgil is again pitching his words to a reader of wider experience
and greater sensibility. This exotic Maecenas is a missing link between Italy

54. P. Hardie 2004.
55. Schiesaro 1993: 138; Volk 2002: 138.
56. NB: Octavian, the most recent addressee, has been eliminated as too remote.
57. E.g., Hor. *Carm.* 3.29.3–4 (roses and nard); *Eleg. in Maec.* 1.131–32 (balsam).

and the "miraculous" fertility boasted by Asia (1.102–3). Octavian is known to have visited Eleusis in 31 BCE to experience the mysteries of Demeter and Persephone.[58] But the religious aura that Virgil attaches even to banal farm tools initiates his reader into mysteries closer to home:[59]

tardaque Eleusinae matris uoluentia plaustra,
tribulaque traheaeque et iniquo pondere rastri;
uirgea praeterea Celei uilisque supellex,
arbuteae crates et mystica uannus Iacchi.

(1.163–66)

And the slow lumbering wagons of the Eleusinian Mother, the threshing sledge and drags, the unduly heavy rakes; besides, the humble wickerwork tools of Celeus, the arbute hurdle and the mystical winnowing fan of Iacchus.

What follows—a compendium of ancient (Hesiodic, agronomic) farming lore—presents a greater challenge to the poet's seductive powers:

Possum multa tibi ueterum praecepta referre,
ni refugis tenuisque piget cognoscere curas.

(1.176–77)

I can repeat many ancient maxims to you, if you do not recoil with boredom or distaste for trivial concerns.

Again, the context inspires Servius's doubts: "*tibi* ('to you') [means] either 'o Maecenas' or 'o farmer'". Maecenas's boredom is predicted: "While the farmers hardly have a choice to disdain *tenuis curas*, Maecenas might be the one uninterested in the subject's triviality."[60] On the other hand, it may be precisely because he is invested with more serious cares (*urbis et Italiae*) that he needs steering towards more microscopic worries, persuaded that visual attention to detail, especially hidden detail, will be rewarded, whether he is looking up (*suspiciens*; 1.376), like the snorting heifer who sniffs the oncoming rain, or back ("si . . . respicies"; 1.424–25), to spot the allusive acrostic of the poet's name hidden in the moon's calendar.[61]

---

58. Suet. *Aug.* 93; Dio 51.4.1.

59. Nappa 2005: 45. Mystery cults and the *Georgics*: A. Hardie 2002; Johnston 2009.

60. Volk 2002: 138.

61. Cf. Virgil's direct address at *G.* 4.2: "hanc etiam, Maecenas, adspice partem . . . in tenui labor"; at 4.59 *suspexeris* is used of looking at a swarm of bees. Acrostic: MA–VE–PU at 1.429–33; Brown 1963. Virgil uses a term from (Etruscan) augury, *contemplator* (1.187, 4.61), to invite scrutiny of nut trees and bees.

From another point of view, Virgil's apologies are disingenuous. The witty and delightful catalogue that follows—miniature "monsters" of the threshing floor—is if anything designed for the ludic patron. Along with the Callimachean label *tenuis* ("refined" and "subtle" as well as "trivial"), the verb *inludere* ("elude", "get the better of") is also programmatic for the poet's playful juxtaposition of small and large, animal and human, as he fashions a tiny doll's house or comic stage of insect misers and parasites:[62]

> tum uariae inludunt pestes: saepe exiguus mus
> sub terris posuitque domos atque horrea fecit,
> aut oculis capti fodere cubilia talpae,
> inuentusque cauis bufo et quae plurima terrae
> monstra ferunt, populatque ingentem farris aceruum
> curculio atque inopi metuens formica senectae.

(1.181–86)

That is when a multitude of pests mock your efforts: the miniature mouse has built his house and granary beneath the earth, partially sighted moles have dug their chambers, a toad is found lurking in a crack, and all the other monsters that the earth produces, the weevil who plunders a colossal heap of flour, the ant who lays up stores against an indigent old age.

Not only do Eleusinian wagons and hoes contain mystery. So, too, do miniature things, especially hidden ones like the creatures that live unseen, in crevices, underground warrens or vast heaps of grain, through their power to defeat the human eye (cf. "oculis capti", of the mole). As John Mack writes: "Small things also 'get under your skin'. They are potent, irritating, sometimes malevolent."[63] Virgil's burrowing turns up unexpected menaces, like the toad hiding in the cracks (184), while even the subterranean mouse encrypts the word "mysteries" (*mysteria*): "mus . . . sub terris" (mouse . . . under the ground; 1.181–82).

> arida tantum
> ne saturare fimo pingui pudeat sola neue
> effetos cinerem immundum iactare per agros.

(1.79–81)

---

62. Quintilian 8.3.20 notes the self-conscious *exiguus* and the dramatic monosyllable *mus*. Thomas (1988b, *ad loc.*) rejects mock heroics, blaming Horace's *ridiculus mus*; *contra* Klingner 1963: 42. See Porph. *ad Hor. Ars P.* 47 on *curculio* as a "low word", saved by embellishment.

63. Mack 2007: 163. S. Stewart (1984: 44–53) connects the miniature with excessive description, Squire (2011: 8) with an ideology of containment.

Do not be ashamed to saturate the dry soil with rich manure or scatter filthy ashes over tired fields.

Servius glosses: "You should not blush [*non erubescas*] to load the sterile field with rich manure," the implication being that only gentlemanly readers would blush.[64] Defending the humble lentil is an equally delicate matter: "and you will not despise [nec . . . aspernabere] the cultivation of the Egyptian lentil" (227–28). Such phrases have been thought to reveal Virgil's attitude to the farm as "consistently urban", in that they "put a clear distance between the reader and the subject".[65] Equally, Virgil may be trying to close that distance, beckoning his squeamish or suspicious reader to come nearer, invest care at a more local level, and appreciate natural mysteries, great and small.

## *Georgics* 2

Next up is the book of trees, which gives a starring role to vines and their products. Virgil's progress through dense thickets of material ("densissima silua"; 17) is wildly uneven. Digressions sprawl, panoramas and catalogues unfold and close down, and step-by-step instructions are thin on the ground. He repeatedly expresses defeat about the subject in his grasp ("in manibus"; 45); enthusiastic forays are routinely followed by collapse. At 2.42–44, he says he will not list all the trees, not even if he had a hundred mouths and an iron voice. At 2.103–8 comes another admission of defeat: "It is not my brief to cover all the species and names of vines; there are as many types as grains of sand on the shore or waves in the sea."[66]

Why these openly paraded claims of failure? Surely not just because they are traditional in epic poetry. In this book, above all, Virgil rubs up against the encyclopaedic tradition. Theophrastus's *Historia plantarum,* a key source, comprised nine books about plant anatomy, propagation, wild trees, exotic trees, timber and its uses, shrubs, sub-shrubs, herbaceous plants, cereals, and plant juices, divided into local and exotic, wild and cultivated, simple and complex, natural and artificial, and subdivided within these categories by ever more minute distinctions, eventually necessitating a sequel, the *De causis plantarum,* with a further splintering of plant types and behaviours.[67] A good Aristotelian, Theophrastus starts with relationships between "parts" and "wholes"; he finds correspondences between plant parts and animal parts—heart, marrow, limbs,

---

64. Kaster 1997, 2005: 23–24.

65. Dalzell 1997: 123–24.

66. Cf. G. 3.284–85, 4.116–48.

67. Varro's Agrius (*Rust.* 1.5.2) complains about Theophrastus's "innumerable subdivisions".

veins, muscles, hair, male and female, parent and child (Virgil's anthropomor-
phizing is hardly original); he puzzles over what makes a tree different from
other plants; and he acknowledges, as Virgil does here, the marvellous and the
portentous in plant development.

It is to Theophrastus that Virgil's paragraph headings nod: "In the first place,
trees grow naturally in different ways"; "Learn cultivation, type by type"; "Nor
is the method of grafting or budding one and the same"; "Not just one type";
"Different soils bear different fruits."[68] But Virgil's lists are shorter and their
emphases different.[69] The sheer range of trees, from tiny seedlings to the great
mother laurel and the oak tree of Jupiter, is swallowed into a hasty etcetera:
"There flourishes the entire range of woods and orchards and sacred groves"
(genus omne / siluarum fruticumque uiret nemorumque sacrorum; 2.19–20). An
Aristotelian ideal of comprehensiveness is decisively rejected in favour of
selectivity.[70]

This is the context in which to consider Maecenas in Georgics 2, along with the
other tutelary figure Virgil enlists to send him off track. Bacchus is not just
the book's opening sentinel and the tutelary deity of trees but also its principle
of deranged behaviour, right down to the final hoedown of drunken farmers.
He presides over a book steeped from beginning to end in Bacchic frenzy
(given the focus on intoxicating vines).[71] Maecenas is his human counterpart.
A case of divided loyalties, perhaps, were it not that the two figures have much
in common in their respective spheres and a similar function in relation to the
poet.[72] Maecenas's legendary fancy dress of mitra (turban) and flowing robes
is also the regalia of Lydian Bacchus.[73] Yet the connections go beyond mere
outfits and career choices. In the implied hierarchy of authority figures in the
Georgics, human and divine, Maecenas and Bacchus are virtual equivalents.

68. 2.9: "principio arboribus uaria est natura creandis"; 2.35: "generatim discite cultus"; 2.73:
"nec modus inserere atque oculos imponere simplex"; 2.83: "genus haud unum"; 2.109: "nec uero
terrae ferre omnes omnia possunt".

69. Thomas 1987.

70. Muecke 1979: 92. Thibodeau (2011: 116–51) sees the selectivity as intellectually motivated,
to increase the prestige of what is included, pique curiosity and elevate agronomy among the
liberal arts. But Ford (1992: 67–89) regards incomplete epic catalogues as apotropaic. Plin. HN
14.7 is wistful about Virgil's self-exemption from encyclopaedic completeness.

71. The olive, heralded at 2.3, has only six lines (420–25).

72. Similarities made explicit at Eleg. in Maec. 1.57–69.

73. G. 4.380 ("Maeonii . . . Bacchi"). Prop. 4.2.31 (Bacchus): "mitra . . . Iacchi"; Sen. Ep. 114.4
(Maecenas): solutis tunicis and head-wrapping; Eleg. in Maec. 1.25 (Maecenas) = 59 (Bacchus):
"tunicae . . . solutae" (with Schoonhoven 1980: 51–54). See Mac Góráin (2009b, 2014) on Bacchus in Augustan literature and culture.

Neither is the boss, like Caesar and Jupiter; instead, each plays enabler, mediator and boon companion. Back in the dedication of *Georgics* 1, the two figures shared a billing: Maecenas and the heavenly stars, followed by Liber (Bacchus) and Ceres. There, Virgil hinted at similar functions for the gods of fertility and the bountiful patron: both bestow *cura* and *cultus*, make a farm flourish and poetry grow at the same time. Now, they are interchangeable: a god portrayed as a patron, a patron as a god.

Bacchus is invoked first, and Virgil's words can be unpacked to reveal the workings of a small Dionysiac miracle:

> Hactenus aruorum cultus et sidera caeli;
> nunc te, Bacche, canam, nec non siluestria tecum
> uirgulta et prolem tarde crescentis oliuae.
> huc, pater o Lenaee (tuis hic omnia plena
> muneribus, tibi pampineo grauidus autumno
> floret ager, spumat plenis uindemia labris),
> huc, pater o Lenaee, ueni, nudataque musto
> tinge nouo mecum dereptis crura coturnis.
>
> (2.1–8)

So far I have sung of the cultivation of the soil, and heavenly stars: now, Bacchus, I sing of you, and with you the woody thickets and the offspring of the slow-growing olive. Come, Lord of the winepress—everything here is teeming thanks to your largesse, for you the field is burgeoning with autumn fruits, the vintage foams in overflowing vats—come then, Lord of the wine press, pull off your boots and paddle bare-legged with me and dye your shins purple in the grape juice!

Virgil urges Bacchus to come and join in the vintage, like some urban lord invited to visit his villa (Dionysophanes in *Daphnis and Chloe*, for example),[74] urging him to rip off his boots (*cothurni*) and get down and dirty treading the grapes.

Bacchus is traditionally an ambiguous deity: a conquering hero who lays down his weapons to carouse with his celebrants, a farouche god whose lurking malevolence can be dispelled by a gentle welcome.[75] Virgil's greeting is, then, "partly . . . apotropaic".[76] The god is hailed as Dionysus Lenaeus (*pater o*

---

74. Longus, *Daphnis and Chloe* 4.1; at 4.13, the arrival of Dionysophanes (= Dionysus manifest) stirs a quasi-Dionysiac *thorubos*; Cioffi 2014: 25.

75. Eur. *Bacch.* 861: "most terrible to mortals and most gentle"; cf. Hor. *Carm.* 2.19.27–28: "sed idem / pacis eras mediusque belli"; *Eleg. in Maec.* 1.57–69.

76. Mac Góráin 2013: 145.

*Lenaee*), lord of the Lenaea festival, traditionally etymologized from Greek *lēnos*, "wine press". Thomas reads the address metapoetically: "Remove the buskins [of tragedy], Bacchus, and join me in soaking your naked legs in the new wine [of Virgilian poetry]."[77] High boots are indeed a traditional metonym for tragedy, but that is partly because they are already the regalia of Lydian Bacchus.[78] War and peace have been seen as another contrast: the Dionysiac frenzy of Mark Antony, exemplified in the discordant ending of Book 1, domesticated into controlled Augustan fertility.[79] Yet this is less one state of affairs giving way to another than a double vision (tragedy *and* comedy, war *and* peace, high *and* low, exuberance *and* taming), one that remembers the god's roles in each sphere at once. Bacchus is not just the presiding god of wine: he is also the god of freedom, epiphany, inspiration excess and metamorphosis.[80] He is not here to be toned down in line with moderate poetry: he is here to keep things ambitious and plentiful (with all the dangers that entails—witness the caution against heavy drinking at 2.455–57).[81]

The appeal to Bacchus is, in short, the first of Book 2's tales of the unexpected, which will include the ripped-off tunics of injected trees (75), the wonders of the Indian banyan (122–24), farmers' naked wrestling (531) and above all the identity crisis of the tree that looks with disbelief at its adopted fruit, *non sua poma* (82). The local miracles start here. Bacchus sheds one kind of boots, his traditional buskins, only to acquire another. Knee-deep in the purple juice, he and the other grape treaders will look down at their bare legs to see *non sua crura*, their shins stained with purple juicy boots where the old ones used to be.[82] Under the sign of Bacchus, this book will be transformative and defamiliarizing. "New must" (*nouo musto*) is almost "new mystery", as celebrated by mystic Dionysus.[83] Arboriculture is not always about taming: it is sometimes about Promethean daring, the production of civilization, education and discipline out of violence and torture. Grafting takes place "unchecked" (*impune*; 32), as though it might invite punishment; the pruner "barely hesitates" (*haud dubitat*; 29), as though he might have second thoughts. But he who dares wins.

77. Thomas 1988b *ad* 1.7–8.

78. Fraenkel (1957: 204) attributes the detail to a hymn's traditional focus on a god's footwear.

79. R. Smith 2007.

80. Bacchic epiphany: see Henrichs 1993: 17; Spineto 1998; inspiration: Gale 2000: 74.

81. R. Nisbet and Hubbard (1970: 13) identify Bacchus with "lighter genres". But in *Carm.* 3.25, he leads Horace into "perilous terrain"; Batinski 1990–91: 373.

82. *Cothurni* are always purple in Virgil: *Ecl.* 7.32 ("puniceo ... cothurno"); *Aen.* 1.337 ("purpureoque ... cothurno".

83. Cf. 1.166: "mystica uannus Iacchi".

Immediately following this gorgeous opening splurge, Virgil sobers up for Lucretian didactic: "principio" (In the first place; 9). Now, he is openly torn between two ways of describing trees: the sublime, alchemical way or the plodding, prosy way. The invocations that follow reflect this division. First, Virgil tells the *agricolae* to get moving, along with their idle terrain:

Quare agite o proprios generatim discite cultus,
agricolae, fructusque feros mollite colendo,
neu segnes iaceant terrae.

(2.35–37)

Get to, farmers, learn agriculture, category by category, soften the wild fruits through cultivation, and don't let the soil lie idle.

Then he turns to offer Maecenas a bizarre extravaganza of poetic apprehensiveness:

tuque ades inceptumque una decurre laborem,
o decus, o famae merito pars maxima nostrae,
Maecenas, pelagoque uolans da uela patenti.
non ego cuncta meis amplecti uersibus opto,
non, mihi si linguae centum sint oraque centum,
ferrea uox. ades et primi lege litoris oram;
in manibus terrae: non hic te carmine ficto
atque per ambages et longa exorsa tenebo.

(2.39–46)

And you, be at hand, and help me complete the task I've begun—Maecenas my pride, who rightfully possesses the chief part of my fame, and unfurl your flying sails, for the sea lies open. I cannot hope to embrace everything in my poem, no, not if I'd a hundred tongues, a hundred mouths and a voice like iron. But come and skim the shore: dry land is at hand. I'll not detain you with poetic fiction or with long preambles and digressions.

While Bacchus was invoked as a worldly patron, Maecenas is now summoned as a god, recouping the divine aura accorded to Octavian in Book 1 (2.39, "tuque ades" ~ 1.24, "tu adeo"), as well as the invitation to accompany the poet on a journey already launched.[84] He is cast as Virgil's necessary prop and travelling

---

84. 2.39: "inceptumque una decurre laborem" ~ 1.40–42: "da facilem cursum . . . uiae mecum . . . ingredere". Schiesaro (1993: 136) sees Maecenas as a travelling companion to new realms of knowledge; cf. Volk 2002: 133n21.

companion ("ades . . . decurre"), his ornament ("o decus") and his promoter ("o famae merito pars maxima nostrae").

From now on, the address is a messy patchwork of poetic indirection, which is what makes its disavowal of *carmen fictum* and *ambages*—"digressions" (Thomas) or "riddling" (Nappa)—so disingenuous. Virgil waves a full panoply of tropes from the epic and anti-epic catalogue tradition: many mouths, armoured voices, flying at full sail into the open sea and bringing a task to shore. This is poetic overkill. Virgil has been judged "broadly humorous", in appealing for a hundred mouths and an iron voice to equip him for nothing scarier than the various branches of arboriculture.[85] As Thomas rightly notes, the word *opto* turns the usual protest of incapacity ("I can't do it") into one of choice ("I won't do it").[86] But the choice here is not so much between tasteful Callimachean restraint and epic ambition as between comprehensiveness and skimming: "primi lege litoris oram" (skim the edge of the shore) means not "keep to your small orbit" but "skirt the very edge of the subject". So Venus, she of the purple boots in *Aeneid* 1, promises to cut a long story short with her pocket tragedy of Dido:

> longa est iniuria, longae
> ambages; sed summa sequar fastigia rerum.

> (AEN. 1.341–42)

It is a long tale of wrong, with many windings; but I will trace the main headings of the story.

Epic goddess and georgic poet share an instinct for compendiousness.

Why, we might ask, is sailing the predominant metaphor here (2.41, 44–45: "pelagoque uolans da uela patenti . . . primi lege litoris oram; / in manibus terrae")? Perhaps to recall the original catalogue, the one about ships in *Iliad* 2, or Hesiod's juxtaposition of farming and sailing.[87] Or to draw on Pindar's "off-course" images for swerving poetic digression:[88]

> Hold the oar! Quick, let the anchor down from the prow to touch the bottom, to protect us from the rocky reef. The choicest hymn of praise flits from theme to theme, like a bee. (Pind. *Pyth.* 10.49–55)

---

85. Farrell 1991: 233. See Hinds (1998: 34–47) for sparkling discussion of the "many mouths" topos in Latin literature.

86. Thomas 1988b *ad* 2.42–44.

87. See M. West (1978: 313) on seafaring at Hes. *Op.* 618–94: "not an alternative way of life to farming". Rosen 1990: Hesiodic sailing is a metaphor for irrational, grandiose desires.

88. Farrell 1991: 246n85.

My friends, I was whirled off the track at a shifting fork in the road, although I had been travelling on a straight path before. Or did some wind throw me off course, like a skiff on the sea? (Pind. *Pyth.* 11.39–43)

Virgil continues to equate flat farmland with flat sea (2.54, 4.117: *aequor*), perhaps nodding to the strange mannerisms and mixed metaphors of Maecenas's own prose, where sea and shore are interchanged. Seneca will dismiss Maecenas's fragment "they plough the seabed with boats and, upturning the waves, leave gardens behind" as "the eloquence of a drunkard—twisted, wayward and full of licence" (*Ep.* 114.4). He also reuses Virgil's metaphors to label a man stylistically and ethically far out: "hic te exitus manet, nisi iam contrahes uela, nisi, quod ille sero uoluit, terram leges" (This end awaits you, unless you shorten your sails and hug the shore—as [Maecenas] refused to do until it was too late; *Ep.* 19.9).[89]

Haphazard and "drunken" as they seem, Virgil's clichés are closely tailored to his subject matter. Servius claims that he replaced Lucretius's *aerea uox*, "voice of bronze", Homer's metal of choice, with *ferrea uox*, "voice of iron", Ennius's metal of choice. Why? Because the "bronze age" is now Virgil's Iron Age, which needs iron tools for digging and pruning (cf. 2.220, 301: *ferrum*). Virgil's *amplecti* is also used of vines "embracing" elms at 2.367.[90] As for *lege*, it means "pluck" (cf. 2.152, of fruit-picking) and "read", as well as "skim". The phrase "in manibus terrae" (the land is in (y)our grasp) elides reachable shore with the soil itself, suggesting both proximity and actual touch. In Book 2, Maecenas will encounter earth of all kinds—rich, thin, friable, claggy. He will sample it with his hands (249), stamp it with his feet (232) and spit out its bitterness (246–47): "The hand is ... at once the measure and the container of the miniature."[91] Equipped with Virgil's handbook, he will touch dry soil and hold a sampler of its possibilities in his palm.

All the while, this stockpile of epic clichés and mixed metaphors looks like a joke about avoiding the most appropriate metaphor of all: not seeing the wood for the trees. Horace had already written of the hopelessness of bringing Roman wood to the vast forest of Greek literature:[92]

"in siluam non ligna feras insanius ac si
magnas Graecorum malis inplere cateruas."

(SAT. 1.10.34–35)

---

89. Cf. Prop. 3.9.3–4.
90. Cf. 1.2: "Maecenas, ulmisque adiungere uitis".
91. Mack 2007: 5.
92. Cf. Cic. *De or.* 2.65: "infinita silua".

Carrying timber to a forest would be no crazier than your choosing to swell the packed ranks of the Greeks.

Before him Theocritus, despairing about where to begin praising Ptolemy Philadelphus, had used the image of a woodcutter confronted by innumerable trees on Mount Ida:

> When the woodcutter goes to richly forested Ida, he looks round to see where to start his task in the midst of such plenty; what shall I first record, for inexpressibly many are the honours that the gods have bestowed upon the best of kings? (*Id.* 17.9–12)

No more obvious trope could describe cutting a path through dense arboricultural lore. But if Virgil is mobilizing Theocritus on Ptolemy, Maecenas will be disappointed when a purely poetic agenda emerges, in lieu of the expected meed of praise.[93] Or will he? This should be *recusatio* after his own heart.

It is here that Hesiod sheds light on Maecenas's role. His *Works and Days* offers an obvious precedent for the doubled addresses.[94] While the farmers, recipients of practical didactic advice, recall the stolid brother Perses, Maecenas is closer to Hesiod's "kings", the privileged listeners to whom he addresses the fable of the hawk and the nightingale because he credits them with "having deeper intelligence".[95] They are the ones who understand high-level allegory and solve riddles—in effect, who understand poetics.[96] Just so, Maecenas appears in the *Georgics* whenever Virgil is talking about how his poem is coming into being. Unlike farmers, kings do not need full or straightforward accounts. They are there to drink in poetic description appreciatively, for its own sake. Both Maecenas and Bacchus liberate Virgil from the duty of completeness.

When Virgil turns to spontaneously seeded plants, we see how imperceptibly the "Maecenas discourse" overflows into the main "plot" of the poem:

> <u>Sponte sua</u> quae se tollunt in luminis oras,
> infecunda quidem, sed laeta et fortia surgunt;
> quippe solo natura subest.

(2.47–49)

---

93. For Hunter (2003: 103), Theocritus's praise of "the best of kings" (*Id.* 17.12) recalls Hesiod *Theog.* 81–103, the passage on "reverend kings". See below on Book 4.

94. Volk 2002: 136.

95. Hes. *Op.* 202–11.

96. *Op.* 202; cf. *Theog.* 80–103, with Stoddard (2003) on Hesiod's kings and singers. Serv. *ad G.* 2.41: "constat Maecenatem fuisse litterarum peritum et plura composuisse carmina".

Plants that lift themselves <u>spontaneously</u> into the shores of light spring up infertile but joyful and strong; for there is a natural power in the soil.

Not only does *sponte* look back to 2.10–11—"Other plants, <u>spontaneously</u>, with no one forcing them" (aliae nullis hominum cogentibus ipsae / <u>sponte sua</u>)—it also suggests a parallel with the liberty Maecenas has supposedly just granted Virgil. Plants, like favoured poets, can do their own sweet thing. As he describes them pushing into the edges of light (cf. Lucr. 1.22: "in luminis oras"), Virgil simultaneously describes his own freedom to test limits (*oram*). From now on, beyond sticking to the main headings, he will do as he pleases and, he assumes, as Maecenas pleases, that reader with a short attention span.

All this negotiation takes place against three strands of narrative or metanarrative: plant life, the poet's career and the history of civilization through agriculture. Virgil's broad classification of trees into wild and cultivated makes his natural world into a simultaneous version of Hesiod's Five Ages; a Golden Age of spontaneous growth exists side by side with his Iron Age, where everything is forced into furrows (2.61–62: "omnes cogendae in sulcum"). Virgil is strikingly inconsistent about the role of agriculture in human and plant history. Sometimes, it is a process of softening what was once hard: "fructusque feros mollite colendo" (soften wild fruits by cultivating them; 36).[97] Elsewhere, it is a process of hardening off what is soft: planted hazels outlive self-seeded river plants (*molle siler*; 12) because they are hardy (*edurae*; 65), worked on by the harsh regime (*dura imperia*; 369) of the farmer. Pleasure in spontaneity goes together with the assumption that self-seeded plants are degenerate, slow and unviable in the modern world, while goldenness is recreated in the artificial experiments that produce many-fruited miracle trees.

Also hidden in the plants' life is a history of Virgil's own poetic development:

> tamen haec quoque, si quis
> inserat aut scrobibus mandet mutata subactis,
> exuerint siluestrem animum, cultuque frequenti
> in quascumque uoles artis haud tarda sequentur.

> (2.49–52)

Yet these, too, if grafted or transplanted in dug-out trenches, will slough off their woodland nature and with persistent cultivation not be slow to follow whatever pattern you wish.

---

97. Cf. the "hard to soft" civilizing process of Lucretius 5.368–69.

Growing into the *Georgics*, he, too, needs to lose *mollitia* and become robust for practical agriculture, shake off the "woodland nature" of his pastoral persona and be fast-tracked into other people's *artes* through "persistent cultivation".[98] Still, floppy poplars and willows transplanted from the "soft" *Eclogues* keep him nostalgic for his bucolic past.[99] Sometimes, he prefers instant gardening: "haud dubitat" (2.29), "haud tarda" (2.52), "nec longum tempus" (80). Then again, he warns that speedy plants die young. Like the plants, he fights different impulses: be spontaneous or forced; be eclectic or exhaustive.

Take the list of grape types at 2.89–102, an attempt at a "catalogue raisonné" that rapidly collapses, despite its range of textures and savours—*pinguis* to *leuis*, shrivelled to bosomy. Both system and poetics are hard to extract here, when *pinguis*, "rich", a quality distanced in the *Eclogues* but positive in the *Georgics*, is every bit as good in a grapey context as *tenuis* or *rarus*, "thin", "fine".[100] What this aborted list tells us is that under the aegis of Maecenas, connoisseur of grapes and literature, didactic is licensed to be purple, allusive and selective.[101] Or take the description of exotic trees at 2.114–35. Despite the *laudes Italiae* to come, Italy is not world enough for Maecenas or for the poet. It has been argued that this catalogue, taken wholesale, embodies negative metapoetics: Virgil pushes away the East, identifying Alexander the Great, the muddy Ganges and Medea's poison with anti-Callimachean pomposity.[102] But there is plenty of orientalizing here, even so: Virgil positively lingers on the precious by-products—ebony, silk, cotton, balsam—that find their way to Roman dressing tables. In particular, the rhetorical question "Why do I need to mention balsams to you, sweating through their scented bark?" (quid tibi odorato referam sudantia ligno / balsama . . . ; 2.118–19), looks like a meaningful aside to the perfumed patron.[103]

As the products of the East are brought closer to home, so domestic plants become more exotic.[104] Virgil's neoteric twistedness culminates in the list of so-called "impossible" grafts at 2.69–82. Why does he put into didactic poetry what appear to be plain "lies", botanical impossibilities that contravene the

---

98. Cf. Thomas 1988b *ad* 2.51; Putnam 1979: 91.

99. Bucolic Virgil's "soft" or "delicate" plants include *Ecl.* 6.53 ("molli . . . hyacintho"), *Ecl.* 2.50 ("mollia . . . uaccinia"), *Ecl.* 5.38 ("molli uiola").

100. Thomas 1988b *ad* 1.8.

101. Serv. *ad G.* 2.95–96 sees a recherché contrast between Cato's tastes and Catullus's and Calvus's. See Serv. *ad Aen.* 8.310 for the medicinal benefits of wine discussed at Maecenas's *Symposium*.

102. Harrison 2007: 137–48.

103. Maecenas's acolytes are encouraged to bring balsams and other Eastern spices to his tomb (*Eleg. in Maec.* 1.131–32).

104. See Macaulay-Lewis (2008) on plants imported to Rome through conquest.

basic principle that plants only take to each other if they are from the same genus (only two of Virgil's six grafts being plausible)?[105] The bewildered tree staring at its grafted offspring looks like a "chilling characterization of man's distortion of the natural world".[106] But while Virgil inspired poetic grafters after him to describe ever more fantastical transplants, there is no evidence that before his time grafting presented any kind of serious moral or religious problem. It was "at best a blessing and at worst a curiosity".[107]

Whatever it means (arbori-)culturally speaking, Virgilian grafting is special and miraculous: genetic engineering as science fiction.[108] The explicit disavowal of fiction and metaphor earlier suggests reading the technique allegorically, whether as a model for intertextuality and Roman cultural hybridity or as the master emblem for Virgilian poetics: an amalgam of nature and art that takes Greek material, softens it, educates it and strips it down into an ideal form, reversing poetic belatedness through technical innovation.[109] Teaching a bud to "take" in wet bark ("udo . . . libro"; 2.77) may tell us something about implanting didactic in book form, an impression helped by Lucretian word blending, as *includunt* soaks through *udo* into *inolescere*:[110]

> huc aliena ex arbore germen
> includunt udoque docent inolescere libro.
>
> (2.76–77)

It's here that you enclose a bud from another tree and train it to grow in the sappy rind.

Planting also suggests metaphors for Virgil's relationship with Maecenas: the poet as tender slip transplanted into the patron's care or grafted onto his stock. Biological relationships in the arboreal world are not always nurturing; witness the shocking image of baby suckers smothered by their mother's shade:

> nunc altae frondes et rami matris opacant
> crescentique adimunt fetus uruntque ferentem.
>
> (2.55–56)

105. Ross 1980, 1987; Thomas 1988a.

106. Thomas 1988a: 271. Coo 2007: Virgil applies crown-grafting techniques (*obtruncatio*) to describe plant spears burrowing into Polydorus's flesh.

107. Lowe 2010: 467.

108. Plut. *Quaest. conv.* 2.6.1: a tree with many different fruits, "more monstrous than the poets' sphinxes and chimaeras".

109. Nappa 2005: 73; Pucci 1998: 102–6; Clément-Tarantino 2006.

110. Putnam 1979: 93; Henkel 2009: 245.

Now its mother's lofty foliage and branches overshadow it, withering its fruit and nipping it in the bud.

The representation of adoption, on the other hand, is more benign. Vigilant farmers are told to acclimatize transplanted vine slips, even to the point of marking their original orientation on their bark, since "habit is so important in our tender years" (adeo in teneris consuescere multum est; 2.272).[111] Virgil is talking about botany and acculturation at the same time, and the violent transformations each inflicts on fragile shoots.[112] Even the "mighty shade of branches" (ingenti ramorum ... umbra; 489) suggests a human protector's care.[113] Maecenas himself is no less of a transplant, a Lydian-Etruscan hybrid incorporated into greater Italy along with the plump flautist ("pinguis ... Tyrrhenus"; 193) and the tidal Tiber ("Tyrrhenus ... aestus"; 164) feeding artificially into Agrippa's technological marvel, Lake Avernus.[114] His Etruria is recalled not in decline but in its sturdy heyday (533), the acorn from which Rome grew into "most beautiful city in the world" (534).

Only towards the end of the book does the poet start to adopt a "sour grapes" attitude to urban civilization, one that also seems directed specifically at the luxurious patron. Rural Italy, the ideal land that stands in for both Octavian and Maecenas as a dispenser of bounty ("Hail, land of Saturn, great mother of fruits and men"; 2.173–74), offers "the quiet of broad estates" (latis otia fundis; 468) and "sweet sleep under a tree" (molles ... sub arbore somni; 470), away from the daily round of clientela (461–62) and the deceptive delights of conspicuous consumption—tortoiseshell inlays, dyed wool and cinnamon oil (463–66). Virgil pits "golden" rus against "iron" urbs, speaking of the happy man who gathers the fruits that his estates have spontaneously produced (500–501), while in dystopian Rome men observe "iron laws" (ferrea iura; 501) and haunt "the courts and thresholds of kings" (504), drinking from jewelled goblets and sleeping on purple sheets.[115]

Rustication, meanwhile, holds out a bracing alternative: hard graft mixed with leisure. Virgil's country almanac blends workdays with holidays, rural ways of looking combining the functional with the aesthetic, the microscopic

---

111. Cf. fragile seedlings at 2.63–64, 343–45. See P. Hardie (2004: 94) for educational parallels at Quint. 1.120, 1.3.17.

112. The story of ripping infant slips (germen = "embryo") from their mother's body and inserting them into another plant draws on the violence of Bacchus's double birth.

113. As Talitha Kearey reminds me, protegat echoes Ecl. 1.1 = G. 4.566: tegmine.

114. Putnam 2008.

115. Putnam 2008.

with the synoptic. Maecenas's presence not only frees Virgil to express a purely aesthetic delight in the plenitude of uncultivated landscape:[116]

et iuuat undantem buxo spectare Cytorum
Naryciaeque picis lucos, iuuat arua uidere
non rastris, hominum non ulli obnoxia curae.

(2.437–39)

and it is a delight to view Cytorus's undulating boxwood, or groves of Narycian pitch pine, a delight to see fields that owe nothing to men or hoes.

It also allows him to escape from the challenge of writing scientific or cosmogonic epic (475–89) by hurling himself into an imaginary far-off glade that bears little relation to Italian farm landscape and casting himself as a maenad, running wild but guarded by an invisible protector:[117]

rura mihi et rigui placeant in uallibus amnes,
flumina amem siluasque inglorius. o ubi campi
Spercheosque et uirginibus bacchata Lacaenis
Taygeta! o qui me gelidis conuallibus Haemi
sistat, et ingenti ramorum protegat umbra!

(2.485–89)

Let the country and the liquid streams in the valleys give me pleasure, let me love the rivers and the woods, unknown. O for the plains of Spercheus and Mount Taÿgetus, where Spartan girls run wild! O for someone to transport me to the cool valleys of the Haemus and protect me with the shadows of mighty branches!

In return, arboriculture offers pleasure for the eyes as well as plain instruction. The geometric plantation of trees known as the quincunx is extolled both as a practical design that allows trees to breathe and as a form of visual nourishment for "an unoccupied mind":[118]

116. "Boxwood to Cytorus" was an ancient variant on "coals to Newcastle" (taking something to a place where it is already in abundant supply).

117. Bacchic imagery (476: "ingenti percussus amore"; 487: "bacchata") is imported from Lucretius on poetic digression/inspiration: 1.922–23 ("sed acri / percussit thyrso laudis spes magna meum cor").

118. More obviously directed to leisured Maecenas than to the busy farmers: Volk 2002: 146–47. Beauty as well as utility in planting: cf. Xen. Oec. 4.21. Cf. Plin. HN 17.78 ("aspectu grata"); Quint. 8.3.9 ("speciosus").

omnia sint paribus numeris dimensa uiarum;
non animum modo uti pascat prospectus inanem,
sed quia non aliter uiris dabit omnibus aequas
terra, neque in uacuum poterunt se extendere rami.

(2.284–87)

So let all your paths be laid out equal in size: not just so that the view might nourish an unoccupied mind, but because only like this will the earth grant equal vigour to all plants, and the branches be able to extend into free air.

Virgil's quincunx also recalls a more exotic legend, freely reimagined by Cicero in *De senectute* (17.59) after a scene in Xenophon's *Oeconomicus* (4.20–21). On a visit to Cyrus, Lysander praised the designer of the beautiful ornamental garden and arboretum. Cyrus replied that he had designed the garden and planted many of the trees with his own hands. Seeing the gardener-prince in his Persian garb—purple, gold and jewels—Lysander pronounced him blessed among men, since his good fortune was inseparable from his virtue. This purple-clad tree planter looks very like an ancestor for Virgil's georgic patron. Maecenas's luxurious aura is reflected in the descriptive glitter and mystery of the world of plants, his contradictions in their changing scale. But he also gives Virgil a powerful reason to sing the praises of country life, to entice a careworn politician away from urban responsibility to a different kind of care, one with a dignified royal pedigree. Like the good kings of antiquity, he will refresh his mind, or fill it up again, by plunging his hands into his adoptive soil.[119]

## Georgics 3

The book of animals is so dominated by its frontispiece, the magnificent "temple of song" destined for Caesar, that the address to Maecenas (postponed until verse 41, as in Book 2) comes almost as an afterthought—if also a release. In the previous lines, Virgil sketches the epic he will one day write about Octavian's military victories out of Pindaric, Callimachean and Ennian images of the poet as royal bard and promoter of immortality. Planning the pageant sucks most of the oxygen from this part of the poem.[120] Maecenas is

---

119. Cf. App. *B Civ.* 1.104 on Sulla: "Because he was fed up with war and fed up with power, he finally fell in love [erasthēnai] with rural life."

120. Scholarly oxygen, too: Wilkinson 1969: 165–72; P. Hardie 1986: 48–51; Thomas 1983; Horsfall 1995: 63–100; Conte 1992.

a latecomer to the planned celebration, waiting in the wings.[121] He is summoned only once Virgil has decided to retreat from a task beyond his current capacity and explore instead a different terrain:

> interea Dryadum siluas saltusque sequamur
> intactos, tua, Maecenas, haud mollia iussa.
> te sine nil altum mens incohat: en age segnis
> rumpe moras; uocat ingenti clamore Cithaeron
> Taygetique canes domitrixque Epidaurus equorum,
> et uox adsensu nemorum ingeminata remugit.
> mox tamen ardentis accingar dicere pugnas
> Caesaris et nomen fama tot ferre per annos,
> Tithoni prima quot abest ab origine Caesar.

(3.40–48)

In the meantime, let us pursue the virgin woods and glades, Maecenas—orders far from soft: without you, nothing lofty can be launched by my imagination. Come, then, end your slow delay: Cithaeron calls with a loud shout, so do the hounds of Taygetus and Epidaurus, tamer of horses, and the sound bellows back from the resounding woods. Next, though, I will brace myself to tell of fiery Caesar's battles and bear his renowned name down as many years as separate Caesar from the birthdate of Tithonus.

The meaning of "haud mollia iussa" and its significance for real-life patronage relationships have long been disputed.[122] Are the orders insistent or harsh? Are they just difficult to follow? What are they? And who, ultimately, is giving them?[123] The verb *iubere*, "order", and its close synonyms are standard terminology for the fiction of a patron's request (polite or otherwise): the harder the urging, the more momentous the writer's task, enhancing the prestige of patron and literary enterprise alike.[124] But far from involving the promised poem on Caesar's battles, the "orders" here are nothing more than Virgil's chosen theme for *Georgics* 3 (farmyard and hunting animals), autonomously selected but represented as being imposed by a no less exacting taskmaster (hence the lingering assumption that we are still dealing with top-down demands for an Augustan

---

121. "Meanwhile" (interea; 40), heralding his entrance here, is also used of his sudden appearance at Terracina (Hor. *Sat.* 1.5.31).

122. Graverini 2006: 68–71.

123. E.g., Horsfall 1995: 97: "Maecenas' *iussa* are . . . not so much insistent as difficult of fulfilment and different from the *mollitia* inherent in bucolic."

124. White 1993: 136, 266–68.

propaganda poem).[125] For Virgil the substituted enterprise, a journey "into virgin woods and glades", is "far from soft" itself.[126] It is equally pioneering (*intactos*), dressed up with seductive alliterative language (*siluas saltusque sequamur*), mythical colour (*Dryadum*) and an expectant audience (Maecenas).

In any case, why soften the edge of "orders" here? Human patronage is often modelled on traditional modes of divine inspiration, translated into the language of human command.[127] "Without you, nothing lofty can be launched by my imagination": the animal theme demands grandeur, even sublimity, no less than the postponed epic.[128] Here, Maecenas is less Octavian's executive than the muse of an independent task. In this respect, the patron is again closer to Lucretius's Venus than he is to his Memmius:

> nec sine te quicquam dias in luminis oras
> exoritur neque fit laetum neque amabile quicquam,
> te sociam studeo scribendis versibus esse

> (LUCR. 1.22–24)

Nor does anything rise into the shining shores of light without you [Venus], nothing is joyful or lovely. I yearn for you as my companion while I write these verses.

Yet none of this explains why Maecenas is aligned not with mediating Caesar's will (in the shape of the postponed epic) but with supporting Virgil's partial *recusatio*, in other words his deviation towards the chosen theme of *Georgics* 3. Apollo's orders in *Eclogues* 6 (9: "non iniussa cano" [I sing a task wished upon me]) happened to coincide with the poet's wish to reject epic themes in favour of softer ones. But the strained litotes, "haud mollia" (far from soft), is far more nuanced than a simple *dura*, "hard". Not only does it indicate the seriousness of what lies ahead, it also draws attention, defensively so, to the questionable dignity of any branch of farming activity as poetic subject matter, so marking the poet's limbo between the delicate bucolic he has left behind and the

---

125. Talitha Kearey reminds me of the tension between force and mock force in the image of Augustus as commissioner of the *Aeneid*: Donat. *Vit. Verg.* 31 ("supplicibus atque etiam minacibus per iocum litteris efflagitaret").

126. Fantham 2013: 99. See Préaux (1959: 100) on unforced plants (2.10: "nullis . . . cogentibus"; 1.55–56: "iniussa . . . gramina"); cf. Prop. 3.9.52: "crescet et ingenium sub tua iussa meum".

127. Cf. Verg. *Ecl.* 8.11–12 ("accipe iussis / carmina coepta tuis"); Marangoni 2002–3: 82–90.

128. Graverini 2006: 69. On *sine te*, see Mynors (1990, *ad loc.*); Coleman (1988, *ad* Stat. *Silv.* 4.7.21).

magnificent epic of the future.[129] Virgil may also be teasing a patron notorious for his dissolute habits, a hypocritical taskmaster who is namby-pamby (*mollis*) himself.[130] But the variable Maecenas, imprinted with the changing moods and textures of poetry, is never more fluctuating than in the *Georgics*.[131] In the next line, the "soft" patron is identified with far-reaching aspiration ("te sine nil altum"): with him, cattle poetry will reach new heights.[132]

Maecenas also prompts Virgil's decision to pitch his animal book via the most seductive context for a visiting aristocrat: hunting.[133] In Xenophon's view, this ennobling pastime helped to divert the competitive impulses of the Greek elite away from politics.[134] But hunting was more than just a sport: it was also a metaphor for the shared search for knowledge.[135] In this new undertaking, Maecenas is as much Virgil's companion as he is his taskmaster, so the poet's urgent tally-ho seems to suggest. Hierarchies dissolve in the commotion. If Maecenas is the addressee of the brisk call that follows—"en segnis / rumpe moras!" (Come, put an end to slow delay!; 3.42–43)—Virgil in his enthusiasm seems to usurp his master's voice. With similar calls, epic gods rouse mortals to action.[136]

Escaping to the legendary mountains and glades of Greece is a far cry from the reality of Roman herding. Towering above Thebes, Mount Cithaeron (43) was celebrated not just for sheep pasturing and hunting but also for blind wandering and irrational slaughter: Oedipus's exile, the Bacchantes's *sparagmos* of Pentheus and the dismemberment of Actaeon by his own dogs, a place of defection and madness.[137] In short, it was a tragic place. As a lost fable of Aesop puts it: "There are misfortunes and troubles on Cithaeron, and the praises of Cithaeron are a source of tragedy. I make poets out of shepherds, but Cithaeron turns those who are shepherds into crazed beings."[138] The

---

129. See R. Tarrant (2012) on *Aen.* 12.25: *haud mollia fatu* (Latinus), "underscoring L[atinus]'s awareness that T[urnus] will not like what he has to say"; cf. *Aen.* 9.804 (Jupiter with Juno).

130. Makowski 1985.

131. Jenkyns 1998: 317–20.

132. Graverini 2006: 69.

133. E.g., Longus, *Daphnis and Chloe* 1, proem.

134. Johnstone 1994; Vilatte 1986: 274; Green 1996.

135. Green 1996; Henderson 2001a: 3; Whitlatch (2013, 2014), on Lucr. 1.402–11 and its antecedents; cf. Schiesaro (1997) on knowledge in the *Georgics*.

136. E.g., Verg. *Aen.* 4.569, 9.12–13. A patron's hunting plans are called "soft orders" at Hor. *Epist.* 1.18.45: "lenibus imperiis" perhaps glosses "haud mollia iussa". Cf. Sen. *Med.* 54 ("rumpe iam segnes moras"); Trinacty 2014: 188–90.

137. Fowler 2002: 156–57.

138. In Himerius's summary: Penella 2007: 96.

speaker here is a rival, Mount Helicon, and the context a singing contest between the two for the favour of the nymphs, who are threatening to stray to
Cithaeron from the home they share with Apollo and the Muses.

As it happens, Mount Helicon has already appeared in *Georgics* 3:

> primus ego in patriam mecum, modo uita supersit,
> <u>Aonio</u> rediens deducam <u>uertice</u> Musas
>
> (3.10–11)

> If my life lasts, I will be first to return to my country, leading the Muses <u>from
> the Aonian peak</u>.

Virgil promises to introduce Greek-influenced poetry to Italy and add his
name to the roll call of poetic initiates (Hesiod, Pindar and Callimachus) associated with the mountain's slopes. Helicon is an Apolline foil to Cithaeron,
its darker Bacchic rival.[139] Thus Virgil the hunter's voice is that of Euripides's
Dionysus, "And I will go to the glens of Cithaeron, where the bacchantes are,
and join them in their dances", or his Agave, "calling on Dionysus her fellow-
hunter, her accomplice in the chase".[140] In the legendary past, the mountain's
slopes ("uocat ingenti clamore Cithaeron"; 3.43) had resounded not just with
hunters' yelps but also with Oedipus's howls and the wailing of bacchantes.[141]
Poetic deviation is again framed as divine possession.[142]

To summon Maecenas in connection with the animal plot, rather than with
Caesarian epic, and to represent it as wayward passion and offbeat challenge to
a more dutiful imperial tribute, is to recruit a sympathizer with irrationality and
tragic error, one open to risk-taking and self-feminizing abandonment. As Don
Fowler says of poetic scenes of Bacchic overpowering: "Set free to wander over
the untrodden wastes that lesser men avoid, [poets] gain access to the wild
power of the satyr, but are simultaneously themselves pursued and enraptured
like Bacchants and nymphs."[143] Far from Putnam's "ordering principle", Maecenas is an incentive to dangerous chaos, a gadfly to send the poet spinning.[144]
Nor is hunting itself "definitely *haud mollis*".[145] Xenophon ennobled it to defend

139. For Mynors (1990, *ad loc.*) any Bacchic resonance is "entirely out of place".

140. Eur. *Bacch.* 62–63, 1145–46.

141. Soph. *OT* 421; cf. Verg. *Aen.* 4.303, Ov. *Met.* 3.702–3; Taplin 2010.

142. Cf. Verg. *G.* 2.485–89; Hom. *Od.* 5.102, Callim. *Hymn to Diana* 188. See Fowler (2002:
147–55) on poetic inspiration as feminized Dionysiac *thiasos* (Lucr. 1.921–30; Hor. *Carm.* 3.25).

143. Fowler 2002: 159.

144. Putnam 1979: 18. Bacchic possession and gadflies: cf. Eur. *Bacch.* 660.

145. Volk 2002: 135.

it from accusations of effeteness, while Astylus the urbanite in *Daphnis and Chloe* arrives "to hunt the hares, like a wealthy young man who had nothing to do but amuse himself, and was visiting the country in search of some fresh diversion".[146] It may be the ambivalent combination of sublime ambition and loss of (masculine) dignity entailed in such a crazed adventure that the peculiar phrase captures: "soft", compared with military panegyric; "hard", in terms of poetic risk-taking.

Casting the patron as a god or muse of Bacchic inspiration is not, of course, to presume anything about the real Maecenas's tastes or wishes—except that he enjoyed the sport of kings.[147] He is constructed merely as companion for the poet's own impulses. Something of this is hinted at in the booming sounds that frame the hunting scene. The overpowering "shout" (ingenti clamore) of Cithaeron, Taygetus and Epidaurus drowns out human orders, even divests humans of responsibility for the siren call, an anthropomorphized echo of the hunters' cries, reduplicated ("mooed back", even) by the surrounding woods: "et uox adsensu nemorum ingeminata remugit" (3.45).[148] This succession of reactive voices brings us back to the anecdote about the first reading of the *Georgics*, where Maecenas took over when the poet's voice failed. Both contexts, in fact, reinforce the idea that Maecenas is neither a normal listener nor a co-composer of the poem. Instead, like the woods, he is there to supply the author with approbation (*adsensu*), to be the involuntary, reduplicating echo (*uox ingeminata*) to Virgil's own voice, and to stand by when that voice fails. A fantasy of sympathetic nature resonates through Book 3: the woods bellow back the groans of fighting bulls, the buzzing air is thick with the moos of maddened cows, Saturn fills Mount Pelion with his whinnying, and the sea crashes in harmony with the thunder during Leander's last swim.[149] Against this background of natural responses, Virgil suggests a similar fantasy: the ringing endorsement of a sympathetic patron.

A new context—choosing cattle- and horseflesh—replicates the hard–soft alternation of the plant world. Animals become metapoetic: *mollitia* is rejected in favour of toughness and magnitude (*fortis, longus, asper, arduus*). Cows are

---

146. See Johnstone (1994: 228–29) on Xen. *Cyn.*; Longus, *Daphnis and Chloe* 4.11.

147. Polyb. 31.29.1–12: Scipio Aemilianus was educated in the royal Macedonian game preserves, "regarding himself as if he were a king". See Briant (2002: 230–32) on Persian kings as hunters: e.g., Cyrus in Xen. *Cyr.*; Green 1996: 244–54.

148. Cf. 3.371–75, 411–14.

149. 3.223: "reboant siluaeque et longus Olympus" (punning on *bos*, "ox", and Greek *boein*, "shout": Thomas 1988b, *ad loc.*); 150–51 (gadfly): "mugitibus"; 93–94 (Saturn): "hinnitu . . . acuto"; 260–61 (crashing sea): "inlisa reclamant / aequora"; cf. Verg. *Aen.* 12.928–29: "totusque remugit / mons circum et uocem late nemora alta remittunt".

preferred when they are heavy-set (54, 58), foals considered more promising when they risk crossing unfamiliar rivers (77–79). Sluggishness in old horses is intolerable (95–96); mares are denied pampering (*luxu*) as they prepare for mating (135); the defeated bull undergoes training "among harsh rocks" (229–30) to restore his former strength. The selection and training of a pedigree warhorse is grounded in the Roman civic ideal, which curbs natural vigour through strict training.[150] Where Maecenas is concerned, horses are an enthusiasm that unites knights (*equites*) and kings alike.[151] And when the pedigree horse snorts at distant battle sounds (83–85) and champion bulls stage their epic showdown (220–41), Virgil is already writing the promised Olympian triumph poem in another guise. This is sublime poetry, nowhere more so than in the description of charioteers who defy gravity like acrobats (108–9).

The Dionysiac hunt sets the stage for a consciously tragic book, from the Sophoclean "black sand" raked up from the seabed (241; in a simile for the bullfight) to Io stung by the gadfly and propelled across the world (152–53) and Leander's fateful swim (258–63). The emotional focus is less on victory than on bereavement and failure: the recalcitrant loser in the battle of the bulls, or the partner left behind when the dead ox is cut from the plough, humanoid and inconsolable. Gods disguised as beasts (Saturn, Pan), humans converted into beasts (Io) and beasts described in human terms invest the book with a tragic blurring of categories familiar from Euripides.[152] Destructive forces drive the narrative: blind love (210: "caeci . . . amoris"), succeeded by all-consuming disease (the insatiable plague that grows every day, like Virgil's Fama).[153] All this suggests a model for a poet who is more than a little out of control. The love call that summons him into the deep dark woods exposes him to beguiling adventure that may also be entrapment, as the parable of the Moon captured by Pan in sheep's clothing foretells.[154] Yet it is equally a warning to the patron Virgil beckons along with him that he, too, is entering uncharted territory.

By contrast, the second half of the book reverts to praise for *mollitia*. Another self-conscious pause lifts the poet abruptly away from the weirdness (or, in Mynors's view, the "entrancing subject") of *hippomanes*, the mythical

---

150. P. Hardie 2004: 96. See Xen. *Eq.* for a similar Greek ethos.

151. Horace calls the practice of covering deceptively attractive parts of a horse to aid judgment "the custom of kings": *Sat.* 1.2.86 ("regibus . . . mos").

152. Putnam 1979: 191–201; Miles 1980: 199–200; Gale 1991, 2000: 88–112.

153. 3.553 ~ *Aen.* 4.176–77.

154. 3.392–93: "captam te, Luna, fefellit / in nemora alta uocans". The description of trapped woodland beasts at 1.140–41 suggests an analogy between knowledge, conquest, deceit and hunting.

secretion that makes mares in heat nymphomaniac.[155] The care of sheep and goats offers a serious challenge to epic dignity, if also a more open field for poetic exploration:

> Sed fugit interea, fugit inreparabile tempus,
> singula dum capti circumuectamur amore.
> hoc satis armentis. superat pars altera curae,
> lanigeros agitare greges hirtasque capellas.

$$(3.284-87)$$

But time, irrecoverable time, flies past meanwhile, as I flit round everything in turn, possessed by love. Enough of cattle: there remains the other part of my care, how to drive along the woolly sheep and hairy goats . . .

Maecenas is not invited to this second stocktaking moment. But Virgil reuses some of the language of his earlier addresses, starting with the signature *interea*, "meanwhile". Time flies, says the poet, as he flits love-struck around his subject matter, a maenad or gadfly infected with the same crazed emotions as his passionate bulls and mares.[156] It is hard, he admits, to dignify humble topics like smaller farm animals, but "sweet love", again, is the force that snatches a helpless poet away over untrodden mountain terrain (291–93).[157] This time, however, the steep climb is rewarded by a softer descent.[158]

The notion of time's tyranny at this point is of course a fiction, designed to suggest that the georgic poet is under pressure to divide up his poem, like a farm, into appropriate domains. But it is worth pausing to reflect on where Maecenas belongs in this hierarchy of "care". The phrases "meanwhile" and "the other part of my care" (286) might more accurately describe him than "the chief part of my [poetic] fame" (o famae merito pars maxima nostrae; 2.40) does.[159] Just as with the range of farming topics, where major yields to minor in a dwindling economy of ramifications and sub-headings, and each book and section act as postscripts to the last, Virgil divides his attention differently between his patrons—Octavian (official priority) and Maecenas (beloved afterthought)—in a way that reflects the split between duty and free will in his

---

155. Mynors 1994 *ad* 3.284–94.

156. Thomas 1988b: *ad* 3.285; Gale 1991: 421.

157. Cf. 3.293 ("diuertitur"), 2.476–77 ("ingenti percussus amore / Musarum"); Gale 2000: 190–92. Fowler (2002: 151n22) calls Virgil's passion "similar to that of the animals in heat".

158. See Putnam (1979: 203) on 295 ("stabulis mollibus") and 299 ("molle pecus").

159. Cf. Prop. 2.1.25–26 ("et tu / Caesare sub magno cura secunda fores"). Putnam (1979: 211) notes the interchangeability of *cura* and *amor* at 384–413.

poetic progress. Didactic (unlike lyric) is designed to replace civic responsibilities with other cares; it seizes an "unoccupied mind" only to fill it up again. Indeed, Maecenas's later biographical associations with misdirected or enfeebling passion may stem partly from his complicity with these poetic deviations. Perhaps he was recruited for the Epicureans because of his forced exposure here to the plague narrative, so reminiscent of Lucretius 6. The "untouched glades" promised at the start of Book 3 (intactos . . . saltus; 40–41) become the clammy contagion of its ending ("contactos artus" [touched limbs]; 566).

Maecenas's presence may be especially required at the point where the plague's undiscriminating slaughter prompts pessimistic moralizing (525–30). Humans and anthropomorphized beasts split back again into their respective ethical categories: unworthy and worthy, respectively (525–30). Innocent cattle, who live like simple old Italians on plants and spring water, deserve their deaths, Virgil says, so much less than corrupt humans who wallow in unending feasts:

> quid labor aut benefacta iuuant? quid uomere terras
> inuertisse grauis? atqui non Massica Bacchi
> munera, non illis epulae nocuere repostae:
> frondibus et uictu pascuntur simplicis herbae,
> pocula sunt fontes liquidi atque exercita cursu
> flumina, nec somnos abrumpit cura salubris.

> (3.525–30)

What use are his work and his service now? What does it matter that he turned the heavy soil with the plough? Yet no gifts of Massic wine or repeated banquets harmed these beasts: they graze on leaves and simple grass, their drinks are clear springs and racing rivers, and no cares disturb their healthy sleep.

The quid pro quo of labour and benefits in the relationship of working animal to owner evokes the reciprocal relations of poet and patron, just as both parties confront a desolate scene where the very basis of such a relationship has been annihilated. Scaliger famously declared that he would rather have written these lines than have had the favour of Croesus or Cyrus.[160] It is no coincidence that he names two of the richest but most self-aware rulers of antiquity, given how tempting it is to feed Maecenas into these lines: the feasting insomniac, distraught with care. Conversely, for sceptics of Maecenas's ancient biography, this passage with its image of disturbed sleep looks like a source for Seneca's

---

160. Scaliger, *Poetics* 5.1: "malim a me excogitata atque conlecta quam aut Croesum uel Cyrum ipsum dicto habere audientem".

portrait of the sleepless sybarite at *De providentia* 3.10, whom wine, a far-off orchestra and a thousand other pleasures fail to distract. When *cura* in Virgil denotes both the anxiety that interrupts sleep and the loving attention of the georgic poet, that suggests that didactic poetry has a very different charge from soothing lyric: always an urgent disruption or distraction, an exhilarating gallop to fresh woods and pastures new.[161]

## Georgics 4

Protinus aerii mellis caelestia dona
exsequar: hanc etiam, Maecenas, aspice partem.
admiranda tibi leuium spectacula rerum
magnanimosque duces totiusque ordine gentis
mores et studia et populos et proelia dicam.
in tenui labor; at tenuis non gloria, si quem
numina laeua sinunt auditque uocatus Apollo.

(4.1–7)

Let me at once pursue the celestial gift of ethereal honey: Maecenas, give this section, too, your full attention. I'll tell in sequence of a sight you'll wonder at: of trivial things, great-hearted leaders and a whole nation's customs and pursuits, their tribes and battles. Small-scale work, but no small glory, if benign powers allow and Apollo listens to my prayer.

Out of the putrid ending of *Georgics* 3 comes forth the sweetness of honey, as Virgil beckons Maecenas to squint at the miniature world of the humming hive. For a moment, Virgil treats his patron as if he were his only audience ("admiranda tibi . . . dicam" [I shall say things to make you marvel]; 2–5) and had been following the poem closely all along (cf. 4.2: "hanc etiam . . . adspice partem" [take a look at even this section]).[162] At the same time, the book demands a narrowing of Maecenas's synoptic vision. He is invited to peer at the tiniest, if most entrancing, of supplementary topics ("leuium spectacula rerum"; 3), greeted as a special sympathizer with topsy-turvy values where scale has no correlation with importance. Once again, he is placed in opposition to the simpler relationship of size to power associated with the emperor-to-be.[163]

161. Macrob. *Sat.* 5.16.5 includes the plague in a list of "restorative" Virgilian passages: "ut legentis animum uel auditum nouaret".

162. Volk 2002: 135.

163. Verg. *G.* 1.27 ("auctorem"), 2.170 ("maxime Caesar"), 4.560 ("Caesar magnus").

The opening phrase, "the celestial gift of ethereal honey", hangs in the air not just as the book's subject but also as a potential analogue for poetry and the gifts of patronage, the poet's tithe of honey-tongued song exchanged for a sugar daddy's divine, sustaining bounty. It is programmatic of the sweet verse to come.[164] But Virgil's suppression of the age-old link between honey and poetry is striking.[165] The sterile, fascist world of his hive defeats the creative fertility of the poet's ideal society: "Virgil did not want to connect his bees, inspired though they are, with poetry and song."[166] The honeycomb itself, though, is described in terms of plastic art: the bees "re-mould their waxy kingdoms" (cerea regna refingunt; 202), "mould intricate dwellings" (daedala fingere tecta; 179) and "hammer out fresh wax and shape sticky honey with skill" (hinc arte recentis / excudunt ceras et mella tenacia fingunt; 56–57). It is artistry, as much as industry, that they share with the giants who manufacture divine armour under Mount Etna (170–79).[167] The busy hive, on the other hand, evokes Maecenas's house, that hermetically sealed hierarchy of happy workers Horace describes in Satires 1.9 to the excluded Pest.[168] There are shades of Roman clientela in Virgil's description of the bee king and his adoring, thronging subjects:

ille operum custos, illum admirantur et omnes
circumstant fremitu denso stipantque frequentes

(4.215–16)

He is the overseer of their labours, they do reverence to him, and cluster round him with thick buzzing and surround him in a dense crowd.

Even so, if Virgil means to allegorize either poetry or patronage through the bees, we are not being helped to see it. Maecenas's role here is far more that of fellow viewer, so the strikingly visual language (aspice, admiranda, spectacula) suggests. The quasi-ethnographic description of the bee community inspires the book's main diversion: a mythical retelling of the miraculous bugonia, spontaneous generation of bees from a dead ox's carcass. Replacing putrescence with celestial honey, Georgics 4 is an imagined De rerum natura 7, following the pattern of light and dark in the Lucretian original, which ended so depressingly with the aftermath of the Athenian plague. But nothing prepares us for the derailment

164. Thomas 1988b: 2.148 .

165. Varro Rust. 3.16.7: "Musarum . . . uolucres"; Lucr. 4.22: "Musaeo melle".

166. J. Griffin 1979: 231.

167. Cf. Verg. Aen. 6.847: excudent (Greek sculptors).

168. Hor. Sat. 1.9.49–52. Horace's association with Maecenas is "honey" (melli est; Sat. 2.6.32). Hes. Theog. 81–84, 91–97 allows both princes and poets a share of "honeyed speech".

that follows: a fable about Aristaeus the master beekeeper and Orpheus the mysterious singer and his lost Eurydice, which opens in Egypt, land of marvels—a tale and a setting that could appeal to Maecenas for its Arabian Nights quality as much as to Augustus for its reminders of Actium and Cleopatra.[169]

For now, Virgil's discussion of the bees is every bit as rooted in wonder.[170] When Columella identifies the designated audience of the *Georgics* as leisured students of literature, not working farmers, it is the poet's interest in arcane bee lore that decides him (Columella, *Rust.* 9.2.4–5). The bees offer a "model" kingdom in two senses, not just a miraculous non-human community, blessed by efficiency and longevity, but also a miniature one.[171] Susan Stewart writes: "Whereas the miniature represents closure, interiority, the domestic, and the overly cultural, the gigantic represents infinity, exteriority, the public, and the overly natural."[172] In fact, where nature and culture are concerned, the bees cut across these binary distinctions: both a natural phenomenon and a mysterious analogue for human culture in its highest form, the functioning polis (*urbis*; 154, 193).

Many readers have seen in the two warring kings, one splendid and vigorous, the other squalid and corpulent, an allegory of Octavian and Antony.[173] True, there is a strong pointer to Rome in "paruos . . . Quirites" (tiny [Roman] citizens; 200). But this city with walls is hermetically sealed and totalitarian, like a foreign state.[174] Its kings belong to the realms of history, geography and fantasy.[175] The bees' scaly, gold-threaded armour, eunuch-like workforce, unshakable loyalty to a single monarch, glue "stickier than pitch from Phrygia", responsiveness to Cybele's cymbals and regal designation (*rex, regnum*) all speak of foreign absolutism, not Roman oligarchy. The hive's gummed exterior ("propolis", after all, is an architectural metaphor) and labyrinthine interior recall an Eastern palace, like Priam's house in *Aeneid* 2, visible in cross-section when Pyrrhus rips off its side, exposing hidden quarters and receding passages.[176] Normally, the beehive is an inaccessible place. Virgil must rely on second-hand report

---

169. Cf. Plin. *Ep.* 8.202: "miraculorum ferax commendatrixque terra" (a land fertile in and boastful of its wonders).

170. Gale 2000: 227–31; Deremetz 2009.

171. Cf. August. *De civ. D.* 22.24.648: "We are more struck by the achievements of ants and bees than by the vast bulk of whales." See Pease (1926: 31–32) on rhetorical magnification of small creatures; Squire (2011) on the aesthetics of tininess.

172. S. Stewart 1984: 70.

173. Cf. bee similes for citizens at Verg. *Aen.* 1.430–36, 12.587–92.

174. Thomas 1982: 70–92.

175. Cf. Hor. *Epist.* 1.1.

176. Latinus's city is smoked out like a hive at Verg. *Aen.* 12.587–92.

(natural-historical and wonder writing) to make it yield its secrets.[177] According to Pliny, an ex-consul once made a beehive with walls of translucent horn, to see its hidden workings.[178]

The bees receive the same loving scrutiny as the minuscule pests in Book 1.[179] They, too, are playful, in their youthful limbering up ("ludet . . . iuuentus"; 22) and their idle swarming ("ludo . . . inani"; 105).[180] Yet this tiny play world is also a serious training ground for the student of politics, as the book's opening motto implies.[181] It provides delight and civic teaching in equal measure. We might think anachronistically of Indian or Persian kings' pleasure in miniature paintings, or in chess, with its symbolic wars between two kings, where the "vizier" (the original name for what we call the queen) is the more powerful token. Closer to Virgil's time are emperors' *naumachiae* with toy boats or the draughts (*latrunculi*) that the author of the *Laus Pisonis* justifies as semi-serious activity for his patron. As a spectacle, the bee kingdom is like a toy farm, its battlefield like a gaming board.

Off-duty Maecenas is invited to inspect a wonderful theatre of activity, to imbibe theoretical training as an involved observer of political systems.[182] This "prince" can inspect (*conspexeris*; 59) and wonder at (*mirabere*; 60, 197) miniature kings, who are in turn wondered at by their subjects (*admirantur*; 210), so that the wonder redounds harmlessly to him. In another theatre of ideas, Dio will assign Maecenas a speech outlining a vision of Augustan Rome as absolute monarchy and opposing Agrippa's traditional oligarchy. Sure enough, an explicit comparison to Eastern autocracies emerges from the bees' unquestioning obedience to their leader:

praeterea regem non sic Aegyptus et ingens
Lydia nec populi Parthorum aut Medus Hydaspes
obseruant.

(4.210–12)

Besides, neither the Egyptians and vast Lydia, not even the Parthian peoples or the Medes revere their king in this way.

177. Cf. Sylvia Plath, "The Arrival of the Bee Box" (1965): The box is locked, it is dangerous. / I have to live with it overnight / And I can't keep away from it. / There are no windows, so I can't see what is in there. / There is only a little grid, no exit (st. 2).

178. *HN* 11.16.

179. 4.61 ~ 1.187: *contemplator*.

180. Plato allegorizes drones at *Resp.* 8.552b.

181. Dahlmann 1954.

182. Nappa 2005: 183: "a good laboratory for Octavian and Maecenas"; La Penna 1977: 65: "un modello etico-politico augusteo".

As Mynors declares, Virgil's parallels "are not historical: Lydia had not been a kingdom for centuries . . . but every schoolboy had heard of Croesus".[183] This is exactly the point: to recall the glory days of Maecenas's own ancestors, the Lydians, and the great Kings of Persia and vast kingdoms that had long been obliterated. Eastern-style kingship, a sensitive subject to raise directly with Octavian, can be directed far less controversially to this spurious descendant of foreign despots.

One phrase, overlooked by commentators, cements the links between the miniature and the political. "Kingdoms of wax" (cerea regna; 202), is usually interpreted straightforwardly as a description of the fragile bee dwellings that must be repaired when disaster strikes. But wax is also a modelling material for human artists.[184] If the bee community's links with the idealized political "hive" in *Republic* 7 and 8 are familiar, kingdoms of wax specifically recall another Platonic fantasy city, in the *Laws*: "almost as if he [the hypothetical lawgiver] were telling his dreams *or, as it were, modelling a city and citizens out of wax*".[185] This joins the bees to a long tradition of philosophical utopias.[186] All human beekeepers are gigantically empowered, able to wipe away the little creatures' "passionate emotions and vital battles" (86) with handfuls of dust (87) or crush a king by stripping off his wings (106–7). As the mock-heroic comparison to Cyclopes (170–79) suggests, we are all ogres to the bees.[187] Virgil endows every viewer with a sublime perspective on the natural world, the kind Seneca would give Lucilius in the *Natural Questions* or Lucian his Menippean aeronauts, peering down on the insect-like populations of the earth.[188]

Natural history draws not only on bird's-eye views for its metaphors but also on the idea of deep penetration into hidden places: "haec enim et his similia magis scrutantium rerum naturae latebras quam rusticorum est inquirere" (Matters of this kind are more the hunting ground of those who investigate the hidden places of nature than of country folk).[189] Columella's phrase, "hidden places of nature", comes directly from the winding crannies of Virgil's

---

183. Mynors 1994 *ad* 210–11. Ambrose, *Hexameron* 5.21 (68) compares mutinous bees who kill themselves by their own stings to Persians, who "even today are said to observe this custom".

184. Lucian, *Somnium* 2; *SHA Elagabalus* 25.9; Diog. Laert. 7.177.

185. Pl. *Leg.* 5.746a, emphasis added.

186. Plato's bee imagery (e.g. *Resp.* 7.520b, 8.554b): see D. Tarrant 1946; Pelletier 1948; R. Liebert 2010. Wax-moulding metaphors: Pl. *Leg.* 4.712b, 789e2.

187. See Mac Góráin (2009a) on Virgil's microcosms in relation to his poetic career; Giusti (2014) on bees and Cyclopes.

188. On Sen. *QNat.*, see Gareth Williams (2012) and Gunderson (2015). Luc. *Icaromenippus* 19.

189. Columella, *Rust.* 9.2.5.

beehive, so forging a closer link between Maecenas and the intellectuals to whom he believes Virgil's poem is directed:[190]

> saepe etiam effossis, si uera est fama, <u>latebris</u>
> sub terra fouere larem, <u>penitusque repertae</u>
> pumicibusque cauis exesaeque arboris antro.
>
> (4.42–44)

Often, if reports are accurate, they even make their homes in tunnelled subterranean <u>hiding places,</u> or are <u>discovered deep</u> in hollow pumice or the caverns of decaying trees.

In short, the bees' homes reveal hidden natural-historical secrets to an engaged reader. Poised above this miniature realm, a worldly king and a latter-day singer inspect its workings from a godlike metaphysical perspective, contemplating a diorama bounded in a nutshell: sound and fury followed by eternal quiet.[191]

Bypassing the most complex digression of the *Georgics*, the story of Aristaeus and Orpheus, let us end with an equally mysterious interlude in Book 4: the so-called "Old Man in the Garden" (116–48). It is prompted by a crisis: the need to restore an inactive hive to productivity by planting new flowers. Sidetracked, Virgil voices his regrets about having no time or space to write a fifth georgic, on gardening—which he then writes, compressed into twenty lines.[192] He begins by conjuring a "memory" of a garden he once saw ("memini ... uidisse"; 125–27), a little plot of abandoned land ("pauca relicti / iugera ruris"; 127–28) clinging to the slopes of Tarentum and farmed by a retired soldier:

> nec fertilis illa iuuencis
> nec pecori opportuna seges nec commoda Baccho.
>
> (4.128–29)

not fertile ground for ploughing, no good for pasture and unsuitable for vines.

For bees, however, this plot is a paradise. What has been planted is another miniature, a mise en abyme of *Georgics* 4 so far, on soil untilled by the other three books. But the description of the teeming garden and its tireless custodian

---

190. Lucr. 1.401–2: Memmius is compared to a hunting dog rootling in underground burrows (*caecasque latebras*). See Rimell (2015: 236) on the bees as underworld creatures.

191. Thibodeau (2011: 189–201) sees Book 4 as therapy for the passions of Book 3.

192. Gowers 2000: 127–32.

is framed by editorial apologies. Like the garden, the poet is hemmed in by time and space:

> Atque <u>equidem</u>, extremo ni iam sub fine laborum
> uela traham et terris festinem aduertere proram,
> forsitan et pingues hortos quae cura colendi
> ornaret canerem
>
> (4.116–19)

And <u>for my own part</u>, if I were not already near the end of my labours, drawing in my sails and hurrying to turn my prow to shore, perhaps I would be singing of the careful cultivation that decks out productive gardens . . .

> uerum haec ipse <u>equidem</u> spatiis exclusus iniquis
> praetereo atque aliis post me memoranda relinquo.
>
> (4.147–48)

<u>For my own part</u>, I pass on from this theme, confined within narrow limits, and leave it for others after me to speak of.

As a *praeteritio*, this is both literal (Virgil might almost be on a voyage around Italy, sailing past Tarentum on a boat) and deceptive. Far from being abandoned or unclaimed (*relicti*; cf. 148: *relinquo*), the garden is laid out (or versified) with a poet's care: 144 "He planted even adult elms <u>into lines</u> [or verses]" (ille etiam seras <u>in uersum</u> distulit ulmos).[193]

One explanation for Virgil's brevity is generic: he is bowing to the internal hierarchy of agricultural writing, where gardening occupied a very minor place.[194] But the imagery of deep sea and safe shore here is already familiar from the poet's display of indecision to Maecenas in Book 2. Unlike the bee community, the old man prefers self-determination and self-sufficiency over obedience to others.[195] By contrast, the word *equidem*, "for my own part", which frames the passage (116, 147), indicates that Virgil has been forced to abandon his preferred topic against his will. Strikingly, it is the only time in the poem this happens. Normally, Maecenas and Virgil see eye to eye.

---

193. Plin. *HN* 14.7: avoiding the bounty of gardens ("hortorum dotes fugisse"), Virgil "has plucked only the flowers of his subject matter [flores modo rerum decerpsisse]".

194. Gowers 2000; Thibodeau 2001. See Horsfall (1995: 72) for Virgil's other omissions: asses, donkeys, mules, poultry, pigs and dogs (the last incorrect: see 3.404–13).

195. La Penna 1977; Clay 1981; Perkell 1981.

Indeed, this very passage will inspire a later portrait of the patron:

maluit umbrosam quercum nymphasque cadentes
paucaque pomosi iugera certa soli;
Pieridas Phoebumque colens in mollibus hortis
sederat argutas garrulus inter aues.

(ELEG. IN MAEC. 1.33–36)

He preferred a shady oak and waterfalls and a few secure acres of fruitful soil; cultivating the Muses and Phoebus in his luxurious park, he would sit chattering among the chirping birds.

Maecenas sits not in a labourer's cabbage patch but in a pleasure park, cultivating Apollo and the Muses (and nymphs, as "nymphas . . . cadentes", waterfalls, suggests).[196] At ease in a *locus amoenus*, he plays at country life in the city, his park reduced to the old man's "few acres of ground", fruitful (*pomosi*) and guaranteed (*certa*). Not for him the well-spaced vegetables of the old man's plot; instead, he chatters with a chorus of birds, who might be his poets.[197] The scenario builds on a contrast already embedded in Virgil's miniature garden poem: packing his beds with flowers, the old man "used to equate his wealth with that of kings" (132). The *Elegiae* show us a king in a garden: no worker, like Xerxes or Cyrus, but a man of leisure holding court, in an "anti-georgic" poem that defends idleness as deserved retirement or part of a rounded aristocratic life.[198]

Why, then, does Virgil leave out the material for which we have the greatest evidence of Maecenas's interest, among all the branches of agriculture? Curiously many of the lost gardening writers of the Augustan Age (Sabinius Tiro, Maecenas Licinus, Melissus) have connections to him.[199] Does Virgil's *praeteritio* defer to an overlord, or relegate to an understudy? The immediate context for the garden excursus is a list of measures to take if bees turn unproductive. Strip the kings of their wings so the rest will not stray, tempt them with flowers, guard them with a statue of Priapus and make their enclosure a pleasant place of safety, not a claustrophobic cage. Virgil is usually thought to be addressing some generic beekeeper:

---

196. See Schoonhoven 1980: 47–49; Schmidt (1972: 191n12) on the metapoetics of *sedere / considere*; Bellandi (1995: 79n3) on the ethics, comparing the lazy Epicurean at Cic. *De or.* 3.63: "in hortulis quiescet suis . . . recubans molliter et delicate".

197. Della Corte 1974–75: 1.44; 2.114–15; *contra* Bellandi 1995: 80n6.

198. On retirement and gardening, see Cic. *Sen.* 52–60.

199. Thibodeau 2011: 220–21. See pp. 70–71 above.

ipse thymum tinosque ferens de montibus altis
tecta serat late circum, cui talia curae;
ipse labore manum duro terat, ipse feraces
figat humo plantas et amicos inriget imbris.

(4.112–15)

Let the man who has these concerns bring thyme and laurestines down
from the high mountains himself and plant them all around the hive; let
him wear out his own hands with hard labour, let him embed fruitful plants
in the soil himself and water them with kindly rain.

But the repetition of *ipse* also suggests a lazy master, who, if he cares about
these things ("cui talia curae"), should take on the heavy work.[200] This unspecified person is also urged to play fertilizing agent, producing fruitful plants
with kindly (lit. "friendly") rain. If *ipse* is understood as the patron, the lines
become a metapoetic prelude to the *praeteritio*: get a move on, Maecenas, and
write that gardening poem yourself.

The puzzle of identification here is the larger problem of the poem's ambiguous addressees *in nuce*. Is Maecenas ever expected to help out in the *Georgics*,
or is he just there to be entertained while others do the spadework?[201] When
the poet of the *Elegiae* writes so defensively on Maecenas's behalf, he contrib-
utes to a larger debate about the place of work and leisure in the make-up of an
aristocratic life. It is tempting to think that his ad hominem defence was partly
launched by the *Georgics*, which takes as a central theme the stand-off between
*labor* and *otium* and is so unclear about where the patron stands in all this.

With the bees' miraculous rebirth ("mirabile monstrum"; 554), the poem
comes to an abrupt stop. The reader's gaze is directed upwards towards the
grape-like swarm ("uuam"; 558) hanging from the branches of a tree; meanwhile, Virgil seals Book 4 with his celebrated *sphragis*. Summarizing his earlier
subject matter—crops, trees and herds—he pits his own "ignoble leisure"
(displacing bucolic Tityrus, under the same shady tree) against Octavian's
thunderous exploits at the epic river Euphrates:

Haec super aruorum cultu pecorumque canebam
et super arboribus, Caesar dum magnus ad altum
fulminat Euphraten bello uictorque uolentis
per populos dat iura uiamque adfectat Olympo.
illo Vergilium me tempore dulcis alebat

200. *OLD*, s.v. *ipse* 12. Cf. *ipse* as "master" at Verg. *G.* 2.536.
201. Geue 2018.

Parthenope studiis florentem ignobilis oti,
carmina qui lusi pastorum audaxque iuuenta,
Tityre, te patulae cecini sub tegmine fagi.

(4.559–66)

These things I've sung till now, about the care of fields and herds and trees,
while mighty Caesar thunders in battle by the deep Euphrates and in victory
dispenses his laws to willing peoples and takes the path up to Olympus. Meanwhile, I, Virgil, was nursed by sweet Parthenope and flourished in the pursuits
of inglorious idleness; I played around with shepherds' songs and in my bold
youth I sang of you, Tityrus, under the shade of a spreading beech tree.

There are new answers, now, to the opening questions of *Georgics* 1. Virgil
credits his career to the joint protection of Octavian and an adopted nurse, the
city of Naples (Parthenope), not to Maecenas. While Caesar fights wars to
secure the poet's peace, Naples has sustained ("alebat") Virgil's intellectual
development and made him flourish like a joyful plant ("florentem").[202] Celebrating Caesar's onward journey to the stars and his own transplantation to
a place where he can write about work because he is at leisure, the poet abandons his companion on the road so far, still staring at the miracle cluster suspended from its adoptive tree.

Maecenas has served his purpose as far as the didactic plot is concerned.
But his presumed unreceptiveness to agricultural training has been a crucial
stimulus. A comparison in one of Virgil's sources, Xenophon's *Oeconomicus*,
suggests how this works. Two types of farmer, hard-working or knowledge-
able, are like two kinds of traveller: one sets out cheerfully and makes rapid
progress towards his goal, while the other stops every so often to rest by a
fountain or under a shady tree and look around him, "chasing the soft
breezes".[203] Where the journey of the *Georgics* is concerned, Virgil needs to be
both travellers at once. But his two patrons represent two different reading
speeds: while Octavian forges ahead, Maecenas lingers in the interstices. He
joins Virgil in chasing the breezes. Whether indulging his poet's disobedience
or being chastised for his own sluggishness, he is the most responsive of team-
mates in the poem's stop-start progress.

202. Cf. parental imagery in the "Ille ego" variant sphragis: "Mantua me genuit, Calabri
rapuere, tenet nunc Parthenope" (Mantua bore me, Calabria made off with me, now Parthenope
keeps me). Virgil's flourishing is suggested by two legends in Donat. *Vit. Verg.*: a poplar cutting
planted after his birth outgrew the other trees (5); a transplanted laurel branch in his mother's
pregnancy dream bore fruits and flowers (3).

203. Xen. *Oec.* 20.18, cited by Batstone (1988: 239n28).

# 4

# Maecenas the Lyric Tyrant

## HORACE'S *ODES*

Plerumque gratae principibus [sic] vices. Continuous eloquence wearies.
Princes and kings sometimes play. They are not always on their thrones. They
weary there. Grandeur must be abandoned to be appreciated. Continuity in
everything is unpleasant. Cold is agreeable, that we may get warm.

—BLAISE PASCAL, *PENSÉES* 6.354–55

I rather like bad wine; one gets so bored with good wine.

—BENJAMIN DISRAELI, *SYBIL*, CHAPTER 1

IN 23 BCE, the poet who had made his name writing down-to-earth satires and
love–hate iambics launched his masterpiece: three books of lyric poems that
pitched their author's claim to be included as a tenth great among the Alexandrian canon of nine Greek lyricists, by subsuming all their features into one
volume. In Denis Feeney's words: "The audacity is marvelous."[1] Horace's finished product not only crystallized one man's imagined memory of the Greek
lyric tradition, it built on it, too, bringing into the present day the elements he
found significant in a body of work that far exceeded the fragments that we
have now. For all the urgent topicality of the *Odes*, and their hope that the pax
Augusta will break the endless cycle of civil war, Horatian lyric soars above
pedestrian concerns, embracing a fantasy world of Bacchic delirium, heart-
rending music and orientalized languor. In reading the *Odes* as an exotic, hedo-
nistic excursus from the here and now of masculine-centred Roman politics, I
find I have an ally in Don Fowler, who long ago saw the potential they offered

1. Feeney 1993: 41 = Lowrie 2009: 203.

for a queer or camp reading. After all, as he put it, the *Odes* contain "no short-age of queens, divas and sequins".[2] If Cleopatra in *Odes* 1.37 springs immediately to mind, then the greatest diva of them all is Maecenas, transformed for purpose here into a glittering, stately, melancholy figure.

Along with intense engagement with points further east, Horace's Greek forebears offered him glorious confidence in the power of lyric to create long-term fame, for both its author and chosen others.[3] Where Maecenas's fame is concerned, the *Odes* carry far more weight than he could ever have imagined—and partly because Horace's praise is so light-touch. As always, the patron is the opening dedicatee of the collection, his name wrapped around the first three books, from *Odes* 1.1 to *Odes* 3.29, minus the final poem. He is addressed seven times across eighty-eight poems, more than any other individual, and mentioned one more time, perhaps posthumously, in *Odes* 4.11. By turns, he plays ruler, drinking partner, surrogate lover, critical audience and intimate friend. Some of these roles are familiar from the *Satires* and *Epodes*, but the lyric context brings new traits into focus: kingly ancestry and uncomfortable wealth, morbid neuroses and political anxiety, a fear of death and a love of wine, perfume and luxurious purple clothes.

Even so, this remains a portrait in fragments. The usual way of fleshing it out has been to appeal to external testimony, much of which is itself extrapolated from the *Odes*, by Seneca, Pliny, Suetonius, the scholiasts and others. Where the text becomes impressionistic, commentators tend to plug the gaps by importing a rounded personality, along with predictable tastes and responses for Horace to pique or humour. A passing rejection of purple-dyed cloth (*Carm.* 3.29.15: *ostro*), for example, prompts the comment: "Maecenas the dandy seems to have had a liking for the colour."[4] Maecenas is blamed for Horace's deficiencies: the curiously affected language of *Odes* 3.8 is interpreted as a parody of his style, rather than an experiment of Horace's own making.[5] Horace's sympotic scenes are indeed so synaesthetically vivid that it is hard not to imagine his patron there, reacting to the poet's teasing. Oliver Lyne writes of *Odes* 2.18: "Maecenas must have been of quite extraordinary temper to rise above these

2. Fowler 2008: 103: "One could do a tour-de-force reading of the *Odes* based on the crucial queer theory notion of camp."

3. Barchiesi 2000: 176 = Lowrie 2009: 432: "[Horace's] lyric forestalls the process by which important people of the past become dependent on literature for their long-distance public image. This is, after all, what time had done to Polycrates in Ibycus and to Hieron in Pindar."

4. R. Nisbet and Hubbard (1970, *ad loc.*) citing Juv. 12.38–39: "uestem/purpuream teneris quoque Maecenatibus aptam" (which may well have been extrapolated from the *Odes*).

5. Bradshaw 1970: 45–50. Oliensis (2002: 99) cites Seneca's critique of Maecenas to explain the fluid syntax in the tail-ends of some Horatian odes.

sorts of insinuations and digs." *Odes* 2.12, similarly, "conveys a pleasing complicity between poet and grand patron". On the condemnation of wealth in *Odes* 2.18: "One point to get clear is that Maecenas evidently had a sense of humour, and could take a joke against himself. He was a big man, big enough to tolerate tolerable ribbing by his inferiors. This gives vital context to, and possible explanation of, odes which may otherwise seem to us too close to the bone."[6]

Another scenario is equally resilient: Maecenas the neurotic and Horace the therapist. In Kenneth Reckford's words: "Horace offers advice for the psychological problems of Maecenas, his need for extravagant luxury and his preoccupation with death, just as he counsels Dellius, Plancus, Licinius and his other neurotic friends and contemporaries."[7] Francis Cairns agrees: "Maecenas, although fond of luxury, was obsessed with illness and death."[8] To bring the terminology up to date, it has even been suggested, again on the basis of the *Odes*, that Maecenas suffered from bipolar disorder and had a major depressive episode after his divorce from Terentia.[9]

In short, many Horatian commentators tend to feed back into the poems biographical facts that come out of those poems in the first place. Yet there is scope for an alternative reading that makes no assumptions at all about Maecenas's real-life habits or responses: Horace is simply constructing his patron as an appropriate recipient of lyric poetry. This distinctively "lyric" portrait of Maecenas is less a depiction of a historical personality than a tissue of textual memories from Greek poetry and historiography of those tyrants whose cares were sung away by lyric poets. In other words, Horace invents a need in Maecenas that only lyric can meet: hence the pauper's disdain for the grandee's pomp and wealth, the gentle humour, as opposed to iambic vitriol and satiric digging, and the offerings of wine, perfume and fast-moving poems. Some of the most persistent features of Maecenas's biography originate in the *Odes*: his Tower, his royal ancestry, even the Sabine Farm. Yet, as we will see, there is no secure factual basis for any of them. They are simply there to equip Horace with a suitable addressee.

Accepting just how artificial the portrait is makes it possible, at the same time, to integrate Maecenas more fully into the world of the *Odes*, to appreciate how his hard-soft, male-female, Roman-Etruscan personality infuses the entire collection, reflecting the core of Horace's lyric identity, not just in the poems where he is named but among the femmes fatales, tyrants and queens who

---

6. Lyne 1995: 131, 104, 102.

7. Reckford 1959: 204.

8. Cairns 2007: 105 = 2012: 238.

9. A. Watson 1991. See above all André 1967, ch. 1.

populate other poems, too. As with the *Satires*, *Epodes* and *Georgics*, the sheer discontinuity of the lyric corpus presents familiar problems of interpretation. Do we hold Maecenas in our heads as supreme addressee throughout, or is he lost among all the other names and overshadowed by the patron of all, Augustus? How distinct are the addresses to Maecenas anyway, when other friends are counselled against the lure of wealth, the pull of destiny and the need to live for the moment, even told they are the twin half of Horace's soul?[10] Is it just that the familiar dedication and the sheer number of appearances tempt us to extract from the *Odes* the coherent history of a relationship?

This is exactly what Matthew Santirocco does in his pioneering reading of what he calls the "Maecenas Odes", treating the poems addressed to Maecenas (*Carm.* 1.1, 1.20, 2.12, 2.17, [2.18], 2.20, 3.8, 3.16, 3.29) as a mini-narrative that charts Horace's growing independence from one end of the collection to the other.[11] The net result is a satisfying role reversal. Horace begins as devoted client to Maecenas and ends up as his independent "spiritual patron".[12] J. E. G. Zetzel, similarly, has noted how Horace, loyal to Maecenas for three books, signs him off in *Odes* 3.29 because he no longer needs him for ascent to the throne of lyric *princeps* in *Odes* 3.30.[13] I will also follow the "Maecenas trail", starting with *Odes* 1.1 and ending with *Odes* 3.29 (with a glance at his reappearance in *Odes* 4.11), but as just one of many that can be tracked through the *Odes*. I appreciate that there is a built-in danger in trying to pin down any kind of dichotomy or exclusion in this slippery work, which so often collapses binary oppositions. This leaves me open to the possibility that a non-Maecenas poem is as much infused with (or directed at, or reminiscent of) Maecenas as one that contains his name. Frequent deviations from the obvious path will test my suspicion that he is present in a much broader sense.

## Horatian Lyric

Generalizing about the *Odes*, and lyric poetry overall, is notoriously difficult.[14] Horace's aim of impersonating all the lyric poets in one volume involves him in rapid switches of subject, metre, personality, outlook—gender, even: "At

---

10. Citroni 2009.

11. Santirocco 1984. Cf. Fraenkel (1957: 214–33) and Lyne (1995: 102–31) on poems taken out of order.

12. Bradshaw 1989: 186: "Horace proved to be the great patron and Maecenas the fortunate recipient of a priceless gift—immortality"; cf. Reckford 1959: 204: "The client now supplies the spiritual patronage."

13. Zetzel 1982: 96. Maecenas of course returns as distanced patron of the *Epistles*.

14. Lowrie 1997: 11.

moments the poet can get intoxicated like Anacreon, can be proud like Pindar, negotiate patronage like Simonides, and then step back and assert control."[15] The absence of obvious thematic or metrical coherence challenges us to bind the poems into a united whole but also guarantees the failure of that attempt. The flowers in this garland splay and drift; even individual poems wander far from their beginnings.[16] Horace's lyric world fans out from its notional centre (the sympotic pergola, with its flitting girls, fast-fading wreaths and warming wine) towards Augustus's border campaigns and the tribes whirling on the margins of the empire. In her definitive study of Horace's narrative odes, Michèle Lowrie speaks of "the central bothersome question of Horatian lyric: what keeps these poems together when they try so hard to drive themselves apart?"[17] A question that could equally be inverted: what keeps these poems apart when they so persistently blend together?[18]

One binding factor must be literary self-consciousness. Each poem is a performable lyric specimen that demonstrates its elasticity, its ability to embrace themes that heavier genres like epic, tragedy and historiography cover at greater length, its ambition and maturity compared to other light genres like elegy and epigram, and, through images such as fountains, wine and garlands, its essentially fluid and fleeting nature.[19] Time and desire have also been identified as central themes, with the male poet charting a triumphant progress over the passage of the years and the mortality of his conquests alike.[20] Horace's choice to thematize occasion was, in Alessandro Barchiesi's view, another stroke of genius.[21] Not only is carpe diem or "gather ye rosebuds" a typical theme of Greek sympotic poetry. On a secondary level, it helps later readers process the gap between (supposedly) spontaneous outburst (Greek) and bookish specimen or replica (Roman); the "there and then" versus the "here and now".

For Lowrie, the main thread is the poet's autobiography, specifically the myth of his lyric vocation: "This narrative tells a story about the role of the poet in relation to the ruler, society, friendship, eroticism, and, in large part, to poetry

---

15. Barchiesi 2000: 169 = Lowrie 2009: 421.

16. See William R. Johnson (1982: 127) on lyric open-endedness; Oliensis (2002) on hair as a closural/anti-closural device in the *Odes*; Eidinow (2009) on the influence of the Hellenistic scriptural end-twirl, the *coronis*.

17. Lowrie 1997: 3.

18. Metre, for one thing, but Griffiths (2002) argues that adjacent odes in the same metre can be joined together, so producing a neater total of poems.

19. Commager 1962, G. Davis 1991, Lowrie 1995.

20. Ancona 1994.

21. Barchiesi 2000: 170 = Lowrie 2009: 421–22: when Horace hails Venus to come from Cyprus in *Carm.* 1.30, these days she has further to travel.

itself."[22] The two rhetorical categories into which she divides the terrain of the *Odes* have helped shape my reading here: "essential" lyric discourse, exemplified by one-on-one, of-the-moment speech acts, and "supplementary" narrative, incorporating time-specific historical events.[23] The former continually redefines itself in relation to other forms of generic interference (especially those associated with anger, violence or panegyric), while the latter is kept at bay until it becomes an accessory to the hymnic praise of Augustus and his family in *Odes* 4.[24]

Where does Maecenas fit in such a scheme? Many recent studies barely mention him (including Lowrie's, even though he is relevant to each one of the external relationships that she lists). At first sight, the Maecenas poems should belong squarely to "essential" lyric, in that they occur in the present moment (a moment that embraces a timeless past and future as well) and lack the historical digressions of narrative. Alternatively, they could be thought to stand outside either category, readable, as in the *Georgics*, as meta-commentary on the other poems, especially when they revisit past events like Maecenas's sickness or Horace's escape from a falling tree; anniversary celebrations give the collection its own layers of internal time. As for the notional (and unstable) binaries into which Horace's rhetorical world is disposed (male and female, Western and Eastern, Roman and barbarian, hard and soft, historical and immediate, important and trivial, fixed and fugitive, military and sympotic), Maecenas clearly straddles each pair of opposites, as much a boundary crosser in this regard as Horace's magnificent Cleopatra.[25] Not only does the kaleidoscopic configuration of the *Odes* simulate Pindaric bee-like flight from mode to mode: it is also custom-made to relieve a patron's boredom and chase his moods. Like the seasons, the poems offer *gratae uices*, "pleasant changes", for the easily sated mind.[26]

For all Horace's aspirations to grandeur and solemnity, his "essential" lyric allegiances lie at the light, soft, smooth, sweet, fugitive and sympotic end of

22. Lowrie 1997: 3–4.

23. Lowrie 1997: 26.

24. This is to over-simplify Lowrie's subtle deconstruction of lyric and narrative as opposites (1997: 1–48). But the following brief summary is helpful (45): "The excurses into epic, the high style, narrative, myth, and history depart from a center that is lyric, *tenue*, discourse, sympotic."

25. Sappho fr. 16 Voigt. See Lowrie (1997: 138–64) on *Carm.* 1.37; Oliensis (1998: 144) on Maecenas as invisible paradigm for this poem: "The virile hardness that was once the signature of Rome's imperial identity comes to signify subjection, while effeminate softness—as embodied, to take one well-known example, in a figure such as Maecenas—functions as an index of power."

26. Cf. Arist. *Rh.* 1371a: "Change also is pleasant, since change is in the order of nature; for perpetual sameness creates an excess of the normal condition; whence it was said: 'Change in all things is sweet.'"

the spectrum, where the ethereal is prized over the apparently weighty and the combined heft of power, fame, riches and military strength downplayed in favour of delicacy, charm, modesty and unique allure (Sappho's choice of her darling's body over the entire Lydian army being the template). While Maecenas has a strong extra-textual identity as a historical figure (powerful, wealthy and a magnet for praise), and while, as a knight (*eques*) of Lydian ancestry, he is akin to both Lydian cavalryman and Pindaric charioteer, his other characteristics predispose him to the softer, more lyrical end of things; or rather, he is repeatedly invited by Horace to cross the boundary between hard things and soft ones. More approachable, more malleable than Augustus (male, Western, Roman, hard and historical), his desired transitions help Horace to settle the core identity of his lyric enterprise—whether Maecenas's softness is a genuine characteristic or partly fabricated to suit the poetry.

## Lyric Patrons

A singular aspect of Maecenas, as opposed to any other human addressee, is that he is enlisted to create Horace's posterity. His appearance in the *Odes* is not simply a matter of recording a personal bond or marking continuity with Horace's previous poetic ventures. He has a new role to play. At first sight, the presence of a patron at all might seem odd: the lyric "I", from a Romantic viewpoint at least, should be quintessentially autonomous. What need of a Maecenas to inspire lyric flights of fancy? The patron figure was not just a marker of continuity with Horace's earlier poetry. It was also a distinctive element in his "memory" of Greek lyric, a generic marker folded into his collection along with drinking, the changing seasons, love, sailing and playing the lyre. Patrons were central to the archaic world that Horace is at pains to conjure up, a world that spans two hundred years from Alcman to Pindar, but one that emerges in his hands as a somewhat timeless zone of Greek past-ness that embraces the Hellenistic period and the present day as well. Crucial exceptions are the Lesbian poets, Alcaeus and Sappho—as it happens, the primary models for Horatian lyric—who appear to have existed in a patron-free zone.

What might Horace's cumulative "memory" of patronage in early Greek lyric have been? A first assumption would be that its patrons were always also rulers: "Powerful individual autocrats and lyric poets go together."[27] Among these were the tyrants of Syracuse (Hieron I), Acragas (Theron), Athens

---

27. Hornblower 2009: 49; he notes that autocrat-patrons were not exclusive to the archaic or classical periods (e.g. Dionysius of Syracuse also collected writers: Philoxenus, Xenarchus, Antiphon, Aristippus and possibly Plato; Morgan 2013).

(Peisistratus), Corinth (Periander) and Samos (Polycrates). Secondly, these rulers were known for fostering several different poets (Polycrates, for example, attracted Ibycus and Anacreon; Peisistratus, Anacreon and Simonides; Hieron, Simonides, Pindar and Bacchylides). Thirdly, lyric poets were correspondingly promiscuous: Simonides, Pindar and Anacreon all had several different patrons during their careers. The biographies suggest a flurry of activity: poets sailing around the Mediterranean, washing up in one foreign city and suing for support from the local autocrat, before moving on to the next one.[28] There was always an underlying contract, one that Richard Martin has termed the "*kleos*-bargain": you give me fame and I'll give it back to you (most explicit in Ibycus's praise of Polycrates in fr. S151, where the tyrant is offered fame tied to that of the poet).[29] As we have already seen, there was only partial openness in talking about exchange, whether this consisted in actual rewards (*misthos*), guest gifts (*xenia*), or a more ethereal surplus of *kudos* or *kleos*.[30] Social bonds were hazily defined, too: autocrats and their social inferiors are often portrayed as equal *philoi* at the symposium.

Just how easy or desirable was it to reproduce any of these aspects of archaic Greek lyric patronage in Rome? Like his lyric precursors, Maecenas is known as the patron of a circle of poets. Like *his* lyric precursors, Horace is a poet who wanders between many different addressees, eventually using Maecenas as jumping-off point for a more august relationship, which first looms as a possibility as early as *Odes* 1.2. Looking back, Horace could see what the archaic poets could not: they had survived posterity better than their patrons. But what about the traffic in praise, particularly praise of a ruler? Thanks to a penumbra of biographical gossip around the ancient reception of Greek lyric, especially where the canny Simonides was involved, the high-mindedness of those early exchanges had long been called into question.[31] As we have already seen, Horace's memory of the archaic period was mediated through Hellenistic reassessments of the poet–patron relationship; by his time, ancient lyric was perceived as the place where praise first became problematic.[32] Pindar's question, "Whom should I praise: man, hero or god?" (*Ol.* 2.1–2), became especially pointed when the current autocrat had not decided to which category he belonged:

28. Hunter and Rutherford 2009: introduction.

29. Ibycus fr. S151.47–48; Martin 2009: 90.

30. Bowie 2009.

31. Barchiesi 1996; see also Hunter (1996) on Theoc. *Id.* 16, where Simonides is an anti-model for poet–patron relationships.

32. Barchiesi 1996, 2009b: 327–28.

Quem uirum aut heroa lyra uel acri
tibia sumis celebrare, Clio?
quem deum?

(CARM. 1.12.1–3)

Which man or hero do you choose to celebrate, Clio, on the lyre or the
shrill flute? Which god?

The problem of whom and how to praise swells with the aggrandizement of
Horace's patrons and the growing spectre of dynastic monarchy in the gap between *Odes* 1–3 and *Odes* 4, where the precedent of Pindaric panegyric is at last
confronted head-on.[33] The poet's efforts to present his voice as genuine and
independent mean that he has to tone down compliments and gratitude to the
more faceable patron Maecenas, or even avoid them altogether. As we have
seen, too, Horace has a habit of screening out direct links between poetry and
rewards, expressing his thanks for Maecenas's generosity, but with the utmost
delicacy.[34]

At the heart of this conundrum is the "Sabine Farm", the gift often assumed
to underlie all these gestures. As Arnold Bradshaw has exhilaratingly demon-
strated, there is no evidence, from the text or otherwise, that it had any connection to Maecenas.[35] For readers, the farm can be made to occupy many
different levels of reality: it is a substantial entity with a specific site, a dis-
creetly veiled generator of surplus gratitude that in turn generates the poet's
exchanges with his patron, a literary symbol of Horace's lyric enclosure that
floats above any act of exchange, or, most radically, a rugged retreat Horace
bought with his own savings in order to establish his autonomy.[36] If the *Odes*
construct Maecenas as a new version of the lyric tyrant, as I will argue they do,
then important freedoms for Horace are built into the arrangement.[37]

33. See Kurke (1991: 246) on money and its metaphors in Pind. *Isthm.* 2. Barchiesi 1996: 23:
"Horace is writing lyrical encomia in a world that has no shared conventions about money and
poetry. His interest in Pindar, Simonides, and Theocritus must have something to do with the
difficulty of reenacting 'the economy of praise' in Augustan Rome."

34. Lyne 1995: 102.

35. Bradshaw 1989. The legend was launched by Porphyrio *ad* Hor. *Epod.* 1.31, *Carm.* 2.18.12–
14 and pseudo-Acro *ad Carm.* 2.18.12.

36. Positivist: Frischer et al. 2006; Cairns 2007: 107–9 = 2012: 241–43. Sceptical: Bradshaw
1989. Agnostic: Bowditch 2001: 5; G. Davis 1991: 199–205, Leach 1993; Roman 2014: 112–13.

37. Barchiesi 2009b: 328: Maecenas is "an ambiguous figure, one who could provoke dependence but paradoxically guarantees autonomy".

# A New Lyric Contract?

The launch poem of the collection is often dismissed as a wrapper, "mechanical and gratuitous", assumed to have been tacked on at some late stage.[38] This is to overlook its central function: to strike a new contract between poet and patron.[39] A familiar name from the *Satires*, *Epodes* and *Georgics* opens the collection: here comes another "Maecenas production". Goodbye, now, to the hypocritical, irritable patron of the *Satires* and the edgy drinking partner of the *Epodes*. Enter, now, the lyric tyrant, "scion of kings" (atauis edite regibus; *Carm.* 1.1.1) and conduit of the Muses' desires, addressed in the language of archaic prestige as "my protection and sweet ornament" (praesidium et dulce decus meum; 2), assimilated to city walls and prize possessions. The opening *o*-apostrophe labels the poem "essential" lyric, defined by Lowrie as the poetry of "fictitious utterance".[40] A "signature" priamel follows, detangling the negative list of Horace's *Satires* 1.1: no longer "One man grumbles about such and such", but "One man likes this, one likes that—and/but I like composing lyric." Everyone agrees that Pindar is in the air. The priamel form itself and its first example, an Olympic charioteer, shout *Olympian* 1; the memory of Pindar (*Pyth.* 6 and *Ol.* 6) resounds again in *Odes* 3.30.[41] Solid defensive structures already associated with Maecenas—the ship's towers (propugnacula) of *Epodes* 1 and the escarpment (agger) of *Satires* 1.8—are sublimated into metaphor. Horace's *praesidium* recalls in particular the Sicilian tyrant Theron of *Olympian* 2, whose protective powers were aligned with those of his city: "Bulwark of Acragas, choicest flower of illustrious ancestors, whose city towers on high."[42]

Signals such as these enable us both to recognize the lyric heritage of the poem and identify it as a bona fide sequel. Yet it is striking how far, by the end, Horace has deviated from Pindar. Stringing together a list of alternative human delights and ambitions (charioteering, politics, farming, seafaring, hunting, lying by a country stream), he reserves for himself a privileged place in the cool grove (gelidum nemus) of the Muses, putting devotion to poetry on a par with other obsessions, but rejecting the merchant's greed and the hot ambition of

---

38. Santirocco 1984 243, defending it. The stichic *Carm.* 1.1 and *Carm.* 3.30 are paratextual bookends.

39. William R. Johnson (1982: 129) alone sees a "suave satirist" replaced by "an arrogant, affected stranger". On continuity with Hor. *Sat.* 1.1, see Shey 1971: 190–93; Santirocco 1984: 16–17.

40. Lowrie 1997: 14.

41. Barchiesi 2000: 172 = Lowrie 2009: 425: "The king of the lyric canon for the king of patrons, Maecenas."

42. Pind. *Ol.* 2.2.6–7. Cf. Verg. *Aen.* 5.262: "decus et tutamen". On *praesidium*, see Gelzer (1969: 65–66).

the racetrack.[43] Having set up *Olympian* 1 as intertext, he swerves conspicuously away from its finale, which runs: "May you walk on high for the time that
is yours, and may I join victors whenever they win and be foremost in wisdom
among Hellenes everywhere" (Pind. *Ol.* 115–16). If Horace's anticipated Pindaric duty is to "shoot arrows of fame" at Maecenas, the end of the poem yields
an unexpected twist.

Instead, the patron is invested with a different kind of power: to insert his
poet into the prestigious list of Greek lyric poets, in other words to canonize
him as their successor. "Insert" suggests many different metaphors: twisting
garlands, grafting plants, filing books or setting jewels. But all of them conjure
up Hellenistic concepts: connoisseurship, taxonomy and publishing (cf.
"edite" [issued]; Hor. *Carm.* 1.1.1).[44] If jewels, then here, perhaps, lies the germ
of the legend that Maecenas was a gem collector. If books, then that suggests
a bibliophile or canon maker. If flowers, then Horace may envisage as his prototype the "Garland of Meleager", Greek epigrams pressed into a collection in
the first century BCE.[45] Whatever kind of assemblage is being troped—and
it may be several at once—Maecenas's roles are recognizably Alexandrian:
editor, canonizer and anthologist. In *Odes* 3.25, Horace is ready to insert Augustus as a perpetual ornament among the constellations ("aeternum meditans
decus / stellis inserere"; 5–6).[46] In retrospect, this reveals Maecenas, not Horace, in the role of panegyrist here, the one who names a new star. Not only is
Horace asking to be "inset" along with the other poets, he is also putting his
collection on display, like gems or flowers, to be treasured, sorted, gazed at,
examined for patterns—rearranged, even.

If we do not appreciate the delicacy of this tribute and the special role it ac-
cords Maecenas as ideal reader, it is easy to think that he is being let down.[47] The
quid pro quo for his cooperation, in line with the archaic "praise economy",

43. Gold (1992: 183) identifies the "priamel to Maecenas" as a Horatian *sphragis* (cf. also
*Epist.* 1.1; Zetzel 1982). On the man by the stream as Horatian surrogate, see Dunn (1989); cf.
Gold (1992: 182). Barchiesi (2000: 177 = Lowrie 2009: 433) calls the poet "(Callimachus-wise)
separated and insulated from his audience".

44. "Insero" is often thought to gloss Greek ἐγκρίνειν (include in the canon), following
second-century BCE grammarians Aristophanes of Byzantium and Aristarchus of Samothrace
(though Kovacs [2010] argues that *insero* is not otherwise used of canonizing). Grafting: Mayer
2012: 63.

45. Leigh 2010. In *Carm.* 2.5, Horace's androgynous Gyges is the anomaly "entwined" (inseres) into a chorus of girls.

46. G. Davis 1991: 112. Cf. *Carm.* 4.3.14–15: "dignatur suboles inter amabilis / uatum ponere
me choros".

47. E.g., Mayer 2012.

should be a corresponding promise of fame. Yet no such promise is forthcoming.[48] Instead of praising Maecenas to the stars (so Virgil had promised Varus at *Ecl.* 9.29: "singing swans will bear [your name] aloft to the stars" [cantantes sublime ferent ad sidera cycni]), Horace undertakes the journey himself, bumping the stars with his own head. Instead of *feram*, "I shall bear [your name]", we hear *feriam*, "I shall strike", an action specific to lyre playing. It is the lyric poet who will walk on high; his addressee is not invited along for the ride. Just so, in *Odes* 2.20, Maecenas is left on the ground to witness the soaring swan's flight.[49]

Many readers regard the opening address as fulsome enough, especially when Maecenas's claims to noble birth may have been phony anyway. Everyone has marvelled at the hubris of Horace's self-crowning (whether it signifies ecstatic happiness or an implied assault on the firmament). Less acknowledged is the gap where the reciprocal gesture of praise should be. To save Horace's reputation, it is worth comparing a celebrated but very different negotiation: the preface to Tacitus's *Histories* 1, where the author indefinitely defers his plans to write contemporary history. Tacitus's evasion has been explained as a necessary move to exempt both himself and the emperor of the time, Trajan, from the collaboration or reciprocal backscratching that vitiates true history.[50] When Horace swerves past the expected praise of Maecenas, that moves them both beyond the *kleos*-bargain Pindar and Simonides had with their tyrants, exposing only the poet to further risks of envy and downfall. Instead, the patron is granted a more refined Hellenistic role, that of collector or connoisseur.

This is just one example of how Horace summons up the world of archaic lyric to signal difference. Geography is another. *Odes* 1.1 opens up the Rome-centric world of the *Satires* to embrace not just Olympia and Cyprus but Libya, Attalid Turkey and Africa as well. Rome is in the picture, too. In the first of many bird's-eye views in the *Odes*, Horace looks down on his electorally fickle fellow Romans ("mobilium turba Quiritium"; 7)—not just to reject their herd mentality but also to add his city to the old lyric map, extending its horizons westwards. Here is the first of many hints that Horace identifies mobility as a supremely lyric trope.[51] The archaic model of the "wandering poet"

48. *Contra* G. Davis (1991: 112): "the *laudandus* is Maecenas and the *laudator* shares the honor of deification"; Lyne (1995: 71): "a magnificent and startling tribute to the great man".

49. Woodman (2002: 54) sees a boastful inversion of Sappho fr. 52 Voigt "I do not expect to touch the sky", reinforced by "Lesboum . . . barbiton" (34) and the subsequent turn to Sapphics in *Carm.* 1.2.

50. Sailor 2008: 121–63.

51. Cf. *Carm.* 1.7.14 ("mobilibus . . . riuis"); 1.15.10 ("moues"); 1.25.5 ("mouebat"); 1.23.5–6 ("mobilibus . . . foliis"); 2.1.1 ("Motum"); 3.8.10 ("dimouebit"); 3.5.51 ("dimouit"); 3.29.1 ("uerso"); 4.1.2 ("moues"); 4.10.5 ("mutatus. . . . uerterit"). Henderson (1996: 121 = 1998a: 151: 151) joins the first

is useful for poetry that moves from addressee to addressee, place to place and mode to mode.[52] Richard Martin bases a tongue-in-cheek checklist of aims for a successful wanderer on the parody version in Aristophanes's *Birds*: (1) praise the place and let the people come later; (2) make yourself the voice of tradition; (3) for success, don't dress (hint at how cold you are feeling); (4) inflate your worth; (5) handle many genres (*polyeideia*); and (6) practice makes perfect.[53] In many respects, from self-inflation and show-off range to traditional tropes and underdressing, Horace fits the Greek model well. But far from praising Rome to get an entrée to Maecenas, he is already sure of him (he is "mine" [*meum*]). With his band of followers, in his chilly grove, Horace is not asking for a place to come out of the cold, except insofar as the canon is concerned. Everyone else can have lineage (*atauis edite regibus*; *nobilis*) and ancestral property (*proprio . . . horreo*; *patrios . . . agros*) and carve out distinctive paths (*euitatis metis*; *findere*; *secet*; *partem . . . demere*). But the lyric Horace positions himself as free-floating, choosing for himself a very undefined resting place and a correspondingly infinite trajectory.

Towards the end of the poem, Horace puts a further screen between himself and his patron, delegating his functions to surrogates. Ivy wreaths promote the poet from human to divine sphere (*dis miscent superis*), while a grove and choruses of nymphs and satyrs, not the patron in his exclusive townhouse, separate him from the crowd (*secernunt populo*). Horace hails Maecenas as *meum* (2) but there is no answering *tuus*. Instead, an insistent *me . . . me . . . me* pounds its hymnic beat, while strains of a corresponding *tibi* and *te* are swallowed up in *tibi-as* and *te-ndere*. Maecenas's function is no longer to inspire praise or enrich or protect his poet, only to slot Horace quietly into his collection.

## The Mobile Patron

The first *Ode* seems to relegate the patron to a still point in the poet's moving world, aligning Maecenas with the poem's passive observers—war-hating mother, tender spouse and even faithful hound (with Horace the careering charioteer, callous soldier, intent hunter and springing boar). But in later encounters he will become less predictable. This is partly because he needs to reflect key features of Horace's lyric poetry and persona: mobility and transience.

---

word of *Carm.* 2.1, *Motum*, to its last, *plectro*, to conjure lyric performance (*plectrum mouere*) in a new mode. W. Ralph Johnson (1982: 2) illustrates lyric's shifting identity via Tertullian's description of the peacock (*De pallio* 3.1–2): "changeable with every step he takes" (*totiens denique mutanda quotiens mouenda*).

52. See Gold (1982b: 185) on "shifting changes of address".

53. Martin 2009.

Strikingly often, Maecenas appears in a suspended state. For all the impression of lingering sympotic dialogue (meta-lyric commentary or pillow talk between two *philoi* on their couches, sparked by some trivial conundrum), he is never quite with Horace in the *Odes*: encouraged to join him, but rarely actually there.[54] There are hints of friendly banter on intellectual subjects, literary decisions, calendrical puzzles and astrological lore, with anything abstruse usually interpreted as an in-joke. The traditional fluctuation we have seen between intimacy and detachment, sameness and difference, means that the addresses that knit Maecenas into the fabric of the poems cover the full range from genuflection to endearment.[55] A crux at *Odes* 1.20.5, "care eques" (dear knight) or "clare eques" (famous knight), requires us to judge the underlying relationship quite presumptuously.[56] "Maecenas meus" (my Maecenas; *Carm.* 4.11.19) might be loving or possessive. Does *dilecte* (*Carm.* 2.20.6) mean "beloved" or "selected"?[57] Across the spectrum of the *Odes*, either interpretation is possible.

In *Odes* 1.20, Horace hosts a party, enticing Maecenas with "cheap Sabine wine" in a Greek jar, laid down personally (*ego ipse*) on the occasion of a public celebration (unspecified; the scholiasts claim that Maecenas had recovered from illness). The wine is usually presumed to be a token tithe from the Sabine Farm, or more imaginatively a metaphorical offering of Romanized Greek poetry (specifically modest and Sapphic), a sign of Horace's refusal to offer Maecenas grand encomium.[58] Instead, he must be beguiled and refreshed with the only plonk on offer:[59]

> Vile potabis modicis Sabinum
> cantharis, Graeca quod ego ipse testa
> conditum leui, datus in theatro
>     cum tibi plausus,

54. Spencer (2006: 269): "As we have come to expect in the Odes, [Maecenas's] advent is prospective (even speculative) and always imminent."

55. See C. Williams (2012) on the language of Roman male friendship.

56. R. Nisbet and Hubbard (1970, *ad loc.*) prefer *clare* (Bentley), as more respectful with *eques*. Murray (1985: 45n20) defends *care* as a virtual oxymoron, like "dulce decus" (*Carm.* 1.1.2); Philodemus uses "φίλτατε Πείσων" (dearest Piso), in an invitation (*Anth. Pal.* 11.44).

57. Oliensis (2002: 98) compares *dilecta*, of Lalage, the chosen one at *Carm.* 2.5.16.

58. Commager 1962: 326. Cf. 327 on *Carm.* 1.26: the garland for Lamia is the poem. R. Nisbet and Hubbard (1970, *ad loc.*) are implacable: "This kind of interpretation ought to be rejected without hesitation." Cf. Bacchylides fr. 21M (a modest feast with "Boeotian cups"), Xenophanes fr. 1DK (an evening that excludes epic accompaniments) and Anacreon *eleg.* 2 West (sweet love poetry substituted for military themes); Race 1978.

59. The *grands vins* offered to Maecenas at Nasidienus's dinner (Hor. *Sat.* 2.8.14–17) are an embarrassment of riches ( "diuitiae miserae"; 18).

clare Maecenas eques, ut paterni
fluminis ripae simul et iocosa
redderet laudes tibi Vaticani
    montis imago.

Caecubum et prelo domitam Caleno
tu bibes uuam: mea nec Falernae
temperant uites neque Formiani
    pocula colles.

(CARM. 1.20)

You will drink cheap Sabine wine in modest cups, famed knight, Maecenas, which I myself sealed and laid down in a Greek jar when the theatre resounded with your applause, while at the same time the banks of your ancestral river and the joyful echo of the Vatican hill ring with your praise. You may drink Caecuban wine, and the grape crushed by a Calenian press; neither Falernian vines nor Formian hills flavour my drink-offerings.

We are never told *why* Maecenas was being celebrated, and it is left to the crowds in Pompey's theatre to offer applause and the banks of Maecenas's ancestral Tiber and the nearby Vatican Hill (*Vaticanus*, an Etruscan name, also suggests *uates*, "bard" and *cano*, "sing") to echo back his praise ("reddere laudes tibi" [7] being the operative phrase missing from *Carm.* 1.1).[60] A cluster of words briefly equates Maecenas with the charioteer in a Pindaric *epinikion* (*theatro, plausus, eques*), suggesting a contrast between worldly one-off plaudits and Horace's less resounding but more permanent gesture of commemoration.[61] But direct exchanges of praise for gifts (and more prestigious wine, inviting further favours) are off the agenda. It is other aspects of the relationship (appreciation, sympotic compatibility and literary intuition) that Horace puts on display.[62]

At the poem's sonic centre is the merry echo ("iocosa ... imago"; 6–7) of praise bouncing off the Vatican Hill.[63] Like the patron in Roman poetry, it reflects

---

60. Commager (1962: 326) considers *Carm.* 1.20 "a pleasant or humorous echo of the applause M. received". *Contra* Cairns 2007: 85–86 = 2012: 215: the people's encomium of Maecenas "complements and confirms the ode's *explicit praise of him*" (emphasis added).

61. *Vin ordinaire*: Cairns 2007: 87–88 = 2012: 218; "Château Horace": Bradshaw 2002: 6 (on *Carm.* 3.21).

62. D. West (1995, *ad loc.*) contrasts the "real friendship" shown here with *Anth. Pal.* 11.44, where Philodemus asks Piso to turn his eyes on him. Macleod (1983: 229) sees in the wine terms *temperant* and *domitam* signs that Maecenas "dominates, and is dominated, by his wealth or fame; the poet is simply free".

63. Echoing the "iocosa ... imago" of echoed praise at *Carm.* 1.12.3–4.

whatever the poet wants it to. *Odes* 1.1 had contained *six* occurrences of the word *si /seu*, before culminating in the final bargain ("si me inseres").[64] Horace is parading not just his own hard-to-get-ness but contingency on both sides of the relationship. Here, Maecenas is poised between different halves of his life: public duty and private pleasure; care and ease; even, retrospectively, life and death.

This lyric mobility, physical and mental, will go on to shape the composite "Maecenas portrait" of the ancient biographies: the feline and efficient political operator who sinks back into effeminate indolence in his private life, often accompanied by restless dissatisfaction and morbid hypochondria.[65] In Seneca's famous sketch in *Epistulae* 114, it is an aspect of locomotion—a louche walk—that betrays Maecenas's character.[66] Horace's lyric portrait drives it home just how circular arguments from externals are. If Maecenas's fear of death, his possible Epicureanism and his neuroses are traits distinctive to the *Odes*, his character may develop out of a specific need for restlessness to match that of the flitting poet—rather like the *puella* in elegy, who has to evade permanent capture so that she can generate more elegy.

In other words, Horace conjures up needs in his patron that lyric poetry, specifically, is able to meet.[67] He plucks essential traits of the genre from the Greek tradition, clustered around the emotional effects of lyre playing on its audience.[68] Paramount are ideas of sweet, soothing consolation and the power to banish care, as indicated in the address to the instrument in *Odes* 1.32, "o laborum dulce lenimen" (o sweet softener of care), and in the pleasing sound of Orpheus's lyre: "blandum" (*Odes* 1.12.11).[69] Generic demands, as much as any real-life schedule, explain why Horace so often pictures his patron weighed down by anxiety, so that music and the wine that is its liquid equivalent can

64. N-H 1970 *ad Carm.* 1.1.32: "the conditional clause expresses cautiously a hope for continuing inspiration"; *contra* Syndikus 1972: 1.34.

65. See McDermott 1982: 212–14. David West (1991) robustly dismisses all claims of hypochondria as fictional.

66. Degl'Innocenti Pierini 2013: "a portrait on the move".

67. McDermott 1982: 217–18.

68. See G. Davis (1991: 114–44) on garlands, fountains and modest meals as metapoetic symbols of lyric.

69. Cf. *Carm.* 1.24.13 ("blandius"); 1.16.25 ("mitibus"; lyric as opposed to iambic); 2.1.40 ("leuiore plectro"); 2.12.13–14 ("dulces ... cantus"); 2.13.38 ("dulci sono"); 3.4.41 ("lene consilium"); 4.3.18 ("dulcem ... strepitum"). See L. Watson (2003: 436) for Greek sympotic parallels for the consoling powers of lyric: Alc. fr. 335, 346 L-P; Thgn. 879–83; *Anacreontea* 38.1, 15–18 West; Giangrande 1967: grander powers are claimed for the lyre at Pind. *Pyth.* 1.5–13; *Nem.* 4.1–5.

work their distracting magic.[70] In *Odes* 2.12, Horace reminds Maecenas that he would not want the harsh themes of battle set to the soft strains of the lyre, *mollibus citharae modis*. Of course not: he has been primed to know that sweetness or softness is the supreme quality of lyric; *nolis*, "you would not want", apparently indicating the patron's hardness to please, is rather an expression of trust in his shared sense of decorum (cf. 4: *aptari*).

Lyric's functions in the *Odes* cover a broad spectrum: slowing down time, seducing, being unwarlike, pleasing, babbling, sanctifying, placating, restoring, soothing, enabling release, stopping lamentation, spreading joy, putting to sleep, moving (literally or emotionally), being sociable. Sometimes, its powers are metaphorical extensions of musical technique: tuning or tempering, modulating or trying out different modes and measures.[71] Many of these effects are conveniently catalogued in the responses of the underworld inhabitants to the music of Sappho and Alcaeus in *Odes* 2.13 (including torture victims like Prometheus and Tantalus): wonder ("mirantur"; 30), disarmament ("demittit [auris]"; 34–35), restoration ("recreantur"; 36), beguilement ("decipitur"; 38) and relief from care ("nec curat [agitare]"; 39).[72]

---

70. *Carm.* 1.24.3–4 ("liquidam ... / uocem cum cithara"); 1.7.17–19 ("finire memento / tristitiam uitaeque labores / molli ... mero"); 1.7.31 ("nunc uino pellite curas"); 2.11.17–18 ("dissipat Euhius curas edacis"); 2.7.21 ("obliuioso ... Massico"); 3.13.2 ("dulci ... mero"); 3.21.13–18 ("tu lene tormentum ingenio admoues / plerumque duro; tu sapientium / curas et Arcanum iocoso / consilium retegis Lycaeo"); 3.29.2 ("lene merum"); cf. *Epod.* 13.17 ("omne malum uino cantuque leuato").

71. Slowing time: *Carm.* 1.12.9–10 ("rapidos morantem / fluminum lapsus celerisque uentos"); 3.11.14 ("et riuos celeris morari"). Seducing: *Carm.* 1.12.11–12 ("blandum et auritas fidibus canoris / ducere quercus"); 3.9.10 (the rival Chloe is "dulcis docta modos et citharae sciens"; cf. 1.15); 3.11.13–14 ("tu potes tigris comitesque siluas / ducere"). Being unwarlike: *Carm.* 1.15.15 ("imbelli cithara"). Pleasing: *Carm.* 1.15.18–19 ("grataque feminis ... carmina"); 3.11.5 ("grata"); 3.11.23–24 ("grato ... carmine"); 4.1.23 ("delectabere"). Babbling: Orpheus *Carm.* 3.11.5 ("loquax"; cf. Lalage, *Fons Bandusiae*). Sanctifying: *Carm.* 1.26.11 ("sacrare"). Placating: *Carm.* 1.26.2 ("placare"). Restoring: *Carm.* 3.4.40 ("recreatis"; cf. 2.13.36). Soothing: *Carm.* 3.11.23–24 ("mulces"); Hypermestra is not violent like her sisters: *Carm.* 3.11.42–44 ("ego illis / mollior nec te feriam neque intra / claustra tenebo"). Releasing: *Carm.* 3.11.49 ("i pedes quo te rapiunt et aurae"). Stopping lamentation: *Carm.* 2.9.17–18 ("desine mollium / tandem querelarum"; cf. 3.7.30: "querulae ... tibiae"). Spreading joy: *Carm.* 3.3.69 ("iocosae ... lyrae"). Putting to sleep: *Carm.* 3.1.20–21 ("non auium citharaeque cantus / somnum reducent"). Moving: *Carm.* 3.11.1–2 ("Mercuri—nam te docilis magistro / mouit Amphion lapides canendo"). Being sociable: *Carm.* 3.11.6 ("diuitum mensis et amica templis"). Music: *Carm.* 4.3.18 ("temperas"), 1.32.5 ("modulate"), 2.1.40 ("modos").

72. Cf. Lowrie 1997: 218. In *Carm.* 213, Horace sings his way out of "iambic" anger against the lethal tree.

The same effects are conjured up in the various addresses to the patron. Horace presents a Maecenas worn out by hard work or boredom, needing to be whisked away by enchanting poetry.[73] In *Odes* 2.17, he is accused of being exhaustingly anxious: "Cur me querelis exanimas tuis?" (Why do you kill me with your moaning?). In *Odes* 2.20, Horace answers an imagined summons ("ego quem uocas" [I, whom you call]; 6). In *Odes* 3, Maecenas remains invested with morbid fears and worries. Only Horace's music has the power to un- furrow his worried brow and persuade him to escape the demands of (external, public, time-specific) history for the oblivion of (interior, private, timeless) lyric.[74] Again, his role as the careworn patient of Horatian lyric continues to account for some of the hoariest features of Maecenas's biography, ancient and modern, while the notoriously "split" personality may have arisen from Hor- ace's repeated appeals to the man of affairs to leave behind the long-term cares of state for the mindful ease of a private individual:

> neglegens ne qua populus laboret
> parce priuatus nimium cauere et
> dona praesentis cape laetus horae ac
>     linque seuera
>
> (CARM. 3.8.25–28)

Relax, take time out, stop caring too much about the nation's suffering: gladly accept the here and now and leave behind what's serious.

The battle for Maecenas's soul is staged and restaged. Torn between different spheres and weary of sameness, he is repeatedly co-opted for the lyric world of wine and love. Meanwhile, Horace fashions new roles for himself, less as the grateful recipient of financial support and singer of praise than as soother of the cares and opponent of the troublesome wealth that together create the patron's limitless need for him.

We have already found suggestive parallels in the Islamic world for the per- ceived instability of poet–patron relations.[75] There, as in Horatian lyric, the passing of time was a delicate topic. Patron and client could be portrayed as immune, or as vulnerable as everyone else: hence Horace's pledge of loyalty above and beyond Maecenas's inevitable death (*Carm.* 2.17). If the restless

---

73. *Carm.* 2.13.30 ("mirantur") ~ 3.8.2–3 ("quid . . . miraris"); 2.13.34–35 ("demittit [auris]") ~ 3.8.17 ("mitte ciuilis super urbe curas"); the two verbs are combined at 3.29.11: ("omitte mirari").

74. *Carm.* 3.29.16 ("sollicitam explicuere frontem"); cf. *Epod.* 13.5 ("obducta soluatur fronte senectus").

75. Sharlet 2011: 2.

Maecenas is less a unique historical character than a figment of the transhistorical representation of patronage, the generic expectations of lyric—fleeting and mobile—only intensify the characterization. For Horace, the patron reflects back the uncertainty of the human condition, which looms large in lyric poetry. If Maecenas's commitment to their transactions is fluid, then so can Horace's be. Ultimately, it is the unaccountability of both figures that enables the poet to bypass traditional conditions and achieve the lyric freedom of movement he requires.

## Maecenas the Lyric Tyrant

Anachronistic though the Islamic analogy is (out by a thousand years or more), it may not be so inappropriate considering the prominent role that Horace's lyric world gives to Eastern rulers in general. Maecenas, scion of Republican generals in *Satires* 1, is reintroduced in *Odes* 1.1 as the descendant of kings (nationality unspecified). He and Horace will later be cast as soul brothers, but for now the social gulf is magnified, appropriately for a higher-status genre. Until his descent is narrowed down to "Etruscan" at *Odes* 3.8.1 ("Tyrrhena regum progenies" [Offspring of Etruscan kings]), the range of Maecenas's royal forebears remains infinite. The *Odes*, bluntly, are awash with tyrants: the Attalids of Pergamon, the Mermnads of Lydia, the Persian Achaemenids, the Parthian dynasties, Sicilian tyrants, the Ptolemies of Egypt . . . also, thanks to tragic choral lyric, mythical tyrants like Thyestes and Tantalus (the latter originally a Lydian king).[76] Indeed, "tyrant" was originally a Lydian word; extreme paradigms of tyranny were found east of Greece and among Westerners drawn towards these paradigms. Horatian tyrants function as exemplary figures, as they had done in tragedy and historiography: they warn of the dangers of flying too high, excessive greed and the sudden flux of Fortune (feared by "tyrants in purple" in *Carm.* 1.35: "purpurei . . . tyranni" [12]).[77]

While these tyrants are ascribed to distinct eras and nationalities, Horace, in true orientalist fashion, tends to blur Persia, Lydia, Egypt, Arabia and mythical

76. *Carm.* 1.1.12 ("Attalicis condicionibus"); 1.16.16–17 ("irae Thyesten exitio graui / strauere"); 1.29.1–2 ("Arabum inuides / gazis"); 2.18.5–6 ("Attali / ignotus heres"); 2.18.36–38 ("superbum / Tantalum atque Tantali / genus"); 1.35.9–12 ("te [Fortunam]. . . . purpurei metuunt tyranni"); 3.1.16–21 ("districtus ensis cui super impia / ceruice pendet, non Siculae dapes / dulcem elaboratum saporem, / non auium citharaeque cantus / somnum reducent"); 3.16.41–42 ("si Mygdoniis regnum Alyattei / campis continuem").

77. Herodotus's narratives of Croesus, Cyrus, Cambyses, Darius and Xerxes reinforce the despotic template: all five monarchs overreach themselves and end unhappily (though Dewald [2003] notes a bifurcation between Greek and Eastern despots).

Troy together across place and time into one ethical representation of a luxurious, corrupt, absolutist, un-Roman world.[78] This lack of differentiation was widespread in Greco-Roman antiquity. For example, Athenaeus's compendium of Greek writing about tyrants (*Deipnosophistae* 12) presents luxury/*truphē* as a contagion that spread continuously from East to West: "Eastern effeminacy first conquers the Persians, then the Lydians, the Etruscans, the Sybarites and the Ionian peoples, either because of geographical contiguity or as a result of cultural influence, bringing about the decay and the destruction of empires and powerful cities."[79] Out of many fragments across many centuries emerges something resembling a universal typology of "soft" tyrannical behaviour: lolling in exotic palaces or gardens in the shade, grazing erotically on one's concubines and eunuchs, trailing purple robes and wearing make-up, feasting to the sound of music, and so on. The lack of specificity gives us leeway to generalize about tyrants in Horace.[80]

It is uncontroversial to call the *Odes* "orientalist" poems, with their stereotypical images of captured kings walking in Roman triumphs (*Carm.* 2.12) and enslaved princes and princesses harnessed to Roman desires (*Carm.* 1.19.2–10). But "orientalizing", in the sense of drawing culturally and aesthetically on the East, is less common. True, Horatian lyric spans the whole of the Roman Empire and beyond: Scythians, Britons and chilly Hyperboreans are as much part of its world as Persians; Italian places like Bandusia and Tibur are pinned on the lyric map.[81] Still, there remains something particularly potent for the *Odes* about Eastern despots and luxury.[82] Giuseppe La Bua has argued that "the East" enables Horace to reconcile his private concerns with simplicity and small-scale aesthetics with the demands of Augustan propaganda (in particular, the campaign to recover the Roman standards lost to the Parthians at Carrhae in 53 BCE).[83] Again, Horace's aesthetic refusal of Persian

78. Parker 2011: 9.

79. Gambato 2000: 228. See also Nenci 1983.

80. S. Morris (2003: 1) speaks of "a serious flirtation with autonomous rule(rs) in practice and rhetoric, myth and tragedy", noting (17) the influence of Persia on Greek artistic representations of mythical kings (Midas, Priam, Busiris) and on elite education (e.g., Xen. *Cyr.*). See Heckster and Fowler (2005: 21) on the progressive "basilization" of Roman generals Sulla, Pompey and Julius Caesar; and (35–36) the influence of the Achaemenid model on Hellenistic monarchs and Roman aristocrats and emperors—despite a Greco-Roman rhetoric of "Persian decadence" and "oriental despotism".

81. Feeney 1993: 57 = Lowrie 2009: 227.

82. Omrani 2014; Paratore 1966. Roman images of the Parthians: Wisseman 1982; Lerouge 2007; Schneider 1998.

83. La Bua 2013: 268.

paraphernalia in *Odes* 1.38 is compatible with support for Augustan foreign policy.[84] At first sight, this seems plausible: Horace helps ward the slippery, violent Parthians away from Roman frontiers and the boundaries of his poems (either zealously: let's fight this war; or nonchalantly: let's forget them for now).[85] Border campaigns would appear to belong to the "non-lyric" world of historical or real-time narrative, with Horace patrolling lyric boundaries as Augustus polices the wider empire.[86] Barbarian drunkenness and excess are symbolically excluded from moderate symposia (*Carm.* 1.27, 1.38) and Maecenas is distracted from crises of foreign policy over Eastern frontiers (*Carm.* 3.29.37–38).[87] In *Odes* 1.19, even Venus sweeps in from Cyprus to banish Scythians and Persians from Horace's poetry.

Even so, to categorize the Parthians as both contemporary and demonized ("the ethical representation of a 'negative' world") is an oversimplification.[88] First, every bit as important as present-day Parthia for the *Odes* is Horace's memory of Persia and the East in Greek lyric, in particular. Two timeframes ("now" and a generalized "then") overlap when he refers to the Parthians as "Persians" or "Medes", speaks of Bactria as "reigned over by Cyrus" or of King Phraates as "restored to Cyrus' throne".[89] Thinking of lyric as Greek, it is easy to forget that Lesbians Alcaeus and Sappho lived only ten kilometres from the coast of modern Turkey, that Anacreon was from Teos in Ionia, Alcman perhaps from Sardis in Lydia. In the sixth century, Greeks had engaged in extended flirtation, diplomatic, mercantile and cultural, with kingdoms further east. Beyond Anatolia fluttered the silk curtain of the Persian Empire, which dominated Lesbos and overran Lydia in the mid-sixth century, and whose remote "King of Kings" became good to think with in Greek political thought, both as the pinnacle of human wealth and happiness and as an object of pity, thanks to his

---

84. La Bua 2013: 275–76.

85. *Carm.* 1.2.22 ("graues Persae"); 1.12.53–56 ("ille seu Parthos Latio imminentis / egerit iusto domitos triumpho, / siue subiectos Orientis orae / Seras et Indos"); 1.19.11–12 ("animosum . . . Parthum"); 1.21.14–15 ("in / Persas atque Britannos"); 1.29.4 ("horribilique Medo"); 2.13.18 ("Parthi . . . Parthus"); 2.16.6 ("Medi . . . decori"); 3.2.3 ("Parthos feroces"); 3.5.4 ("grauibus Persis"); 3.8.19 ("Medus infestus"); 4.15.23 ("infidique Persae").

86. Lowrie 1997: 261–62; Oliensis 1998: 107–27.

87. See La Bua (2013: 276–80) on Persians in Horatian *recusatio*: *Carm.* 2.16 (*otium* cannot be bought by Eastern treasures); 2.18 (denouncing Eastern materialism); 3.24 (against luxurious Arabs and Indians).

88. La Bua 2013: 268.

89. *Carm.* 1.2.51 ("Medos"); 1.21.14 ("Persas"); 1.2.22 ("Persae"); 3.29.27–28 ("regnata Cyro"/"Bactra"); 2.2.17 ("redditum Cyri solio"). David West (1995: 93) is wrong to say: "The Parthians were a burning issue in the mid-20s. But not here for Horace."

enslavement to wealth and paranoid fear of his subjects.[90] Aeschylus imagines entering the minds of the enemy in *Persians*, while his Agamemnon trails fantasies of obeisance home from Troy. Kathryn Morgan puts it well when she speaks of Athens's "complicated . . . love-hate relationship with the trappings of tyrannical eastern power".[91]

Secondly, the element of seduction in Western encounters with the East, ancient as well as modern, should not be underplayed. Horace may try to ward off the Persians, as Augustus does the Parthians, but he also nests them in his poetry. Behind the image of any perfume-drenched Roman patron wearing purple at a feast lies a story about conquest, commerce and Western desire.[92] Horace's symposia are heavy with Eastern perfumes, his guests lured by whiffs of Achaemenid and Syrian nard, Arabian incense and myrrh, and Persian roses.[93] If the *Odes* had a scent, it would be muskily oriental; Horace's Latin is spiced with words like *acinaces*, a Persian dagger, and *gaza*, Persian for "treasure".[94] Delicate living, *truphē*, was "an ideological agenda in which power, by sharing pleasure, seduces as well as compels obedience".[95] If Horace declares his hatred of Persian paraphernalia, it is also what equips and refines his poems.[96] In *Odes* 1.38, the late rose in the tyrant's paradise is both a rejected trimming and the appended poem itself.[97]

Where does Maecenas fit into this picture? In the *Satires*, Horace had credited him with descent not only from the Etruscans, the glamorous royal losers of early Roman history, but also, further back in time, their ancestors, the Lydians.[98] "Lydian" may be a slightly more exotic variant on "Trojan" at a time when many of the Roman elite were claiming descent from Aeneas and his followers.[99] But it becomes particularly useful to Horace when Lydianizing

---

90. See R. Nisbet and Hubbard (1978, *ad Carm.* 2.2.18) on the proverbial blessedness of the Persian king: e.g. Pl. *Ap.* 40d, *Euthyd.* 274a; *contra* Pl. *Grg.* 470, Xen. *Mem.* 4.4.6, Cic. *Tusc.* 5.35.

91. Morgan 2003: xv.

92. As Phiroze Vasunia reminds me.

93. R. Nisbet and Rudd (2004, *ad Carm.* 3.29.3–5) *ad Carm.* 3.29.3–5. Perfumes in the *Odes*: *Carm.* 2.7.7–8, 2.11.14–17, 3.1.44, 3.29.3–4; cf. *Epod.* 13.8–9 (Achaemenio . . . nardo"). Balsam for Maecenas's hair: cf. Verg. *G.* 2.118–19; *Eleg. in Maec.* 1.131–32. Plin. *HN* 13.1.3 traces the invention of perfume to Persia; *HN* 13.2.17 records the "royal unguent" made for Parthian kings from Eastern perfumes.

94. Xerxes dedicated an *acinaces* to the sea before invading Europe (Hdt. 7.54).

95. Kuttner 2005: 144.

96. Contrast "I hate holding back", also in a sympotic context: *Carm.* 3.19.21–22 ("parcentis ego dexteras / odi").

97. Commager 1962: 118; G. Davis 1991: 123–24, 228–33; Lowrie 1997: 171–72.

98. *Sat.* 1.6.1–2: "Non quia, Maecenas, Lydorum quidquid Etruscos / incoluit finis nemo generosior est te".

99. Erskine 2001: 15–23.

played such a specific role in the history of archaic Greek lyric. For Sappho and Anacreon, in particular, Lydia was a geographically and culturally close temptation, halfway to being engulfed by Persia (in their time, it was already a Persian satrapy).

Greek poets disguised their ambivalence in stark love–hate terms: "I hate the dangerous lifestyle of tyrants" (Pind. *Pyth.* 11.53); "My darling Cleis, for who I would not trade all of Lydia" (Sappho fr. 132.2–3 Voigt); "I would rather see my beloved's lovely walk and sparkling face than the Lydians' chariots and armed infantry" (fr. 16.17–20 Voigt); "She outshines the ladies of Lydia" (fr. 96.6–8 Voigt); "I have no interest in the affairs of gold-rich Gyges [king of Lydia]" (Archilochus fr. 19 West). These comparisons echo through the *Odes*: "nec Babylonios / temptaris numeros" (Don't try Babylonian calculations [i.e., Eastern astrology]; *Carm.* 1.11.2–3); "Arabum inuides / gazis" (You have your eye on the treasures of Arabia; *Carm.* 1.29.1–2); "Persicos odi, puer, apparatus" (I hate Persian paraphernalia; *Carm.* 1.38.1); Maecenas should prefer a single lock of Licymnia's hair to "all the wealth of Persia, Lydia and Arabia" (*Carm.* 2.12.21–23); "[While you loved me, Lydia,] I lived more happily than the Persian king" (Persarum uigui rege beatior; *Carm.* 3.9.4).[100] But Sappho (fr. 98 Voigt) hankered after an embroidered headband that was the essence of Lydian luxury, and said wistfully (fr. 58 Voigt), "I love delicate living [*habrosunē*]."[101] Horace's lyric identity takes its energy from this push-pull between disapproval and allure, which reflects similar contradictions in early Greek lyric.

Within a century of the Odes, biographers were constructing Maecenas as a full-blown fantasy tyrant: turban-wearing, flanked by eunuchs, torn apart by love, sleepless despite the distractions of music and flowing water. His associations with heated swimming pools, gardens and even baby donkey meat can be traced back directly to portraits of Persian kings in Herodotus and Xenophon.[102] Herodotus's Persian courtier Otanes is eloquent about the anxieties that attend absolute power and the need for balance between inadequate praise and excessive flattery in dealing with a capricious tyrant:

> And yet a tyrant ought to be free of envy, having all good things; but he becomes the opposite of this towards his citizens; he envies those who live

---

100. Cf. Hor. *Epist.*1.7.35–36: "nor would I exchange peace and freedom for all the riches of Arabia". See R. Nisbet and Hubbard (1978, *ad Carm.* 2.12.2) for other rejections of Eastern magnificence.

101. Kurke (1992) tracks the word, originally shorthand for Eastern luxury in the sixth century, then more negatively associated with degenerate *truphē*.

102. Maecenas: Dio Cass. 55.7.6; Plin. *HN* 8.170; Tac. *Ann.* 15.39. Persian baths: Xen. *Cyr.* 8.7.4 (cf. 8.8.20); Plut. *Alex.* 20.12–13. Gardens: Xen. *An.* 1.2.7: a *paradeisos* of Cyrus the Younger in Celeanae, Phrygia; Arrian 6.29.5: Alexander visits Cyrus's garden tomb at Pasargadae. Persian donkeys as food: Hdt. 1.133.

most successfully, and is pleased by the worst of his citizens; and he is the best at receiving slander. Of all men he is the most inconsistent; for if you admire him modestly, he gets angry that you do not give him excessive attention, but if you give him excessive attention he is angry because you are a flatterer. (Hdt. 3.80.3)

In Xenophon's *Hiero*, an imaginary dialogue between Simonides and Hiero (a fourth-century fantasy of a fifth-century encounter), the poet plays devil's advocate, arguing with Socratic irony that a tyrant has every sensory advantage over a private citizen, while Hiero is left to point out that plenty only ruins enjoyment:[103]

> Tyranny displays its apparently valuable treasures unfurled before the world's gaze: but its troubles it keeps concealed in the tyrant's heart, in the place where human happiness and unhappiness are hidden away. (Xen. *Hier.* 2.4)

And around 100 CE, Dio Chrysostom provides a script for Persian royal paranoia that looks extraordinarily like an expanded biography of Horace's Maecenas:

> For these reasons he [Diogenes] refused to compare himself any farther with the king of the Persians, since there was a great difference between them. In fact, the king was, he said, the most miserable man alive, fearing poverty in spite of all his gold, fearing sickness and yet unable to keep away from the things that cause it, in great dread of death and imagining that everybody was plotting against him, even his own sons and his brothers. So the despot could neither eat with pleasure, though the most tempting dishes were placed before him, nor drown his troubles in wine. Not a day did he pass "at ease" in which he looked about without suffering torments. When sober, he longed for intoxication in the belief that he would then have relief from his misfortunes, and when drunk, he imagined himself to be ruined just because he was unable to help himself. And further, when awake, he prayed for sleep that he might forget his fears, but when asleep he would immediately leap up, imagining that his very dreams were killing him; and neither the golden plane-tree, nor the mansions of Semiramis, nor the walls of Babylon were of any help to him. . . . Yet, difficult and grievous as the position of monarch was, he never wanted to get rid of it, nor could he. (Dio Chrys. *Or.* 6.35–39; Loeb translation)

Maecenas was, of course, no real tyrant: that was his advantage over Augustus as lyric interlocutor. But no one at this time, least of all Augustus himself,

103. Gray 1986.

knew where the die would fall. Horace, meanwhile, casts his lyric patron as an imaginary king, draped at a feast with garlands and anointed with perfume: sometimes a Persian shah, anxious about palace plots; sometimes a Lydian satrap or Greek tyrant, torn between Eastern luxury and more restrained Greco-Roman values.[104]

Horace, in turn, models himself on itinerant purveyors of wisdom: poets, wise men, astrologers, musicians and doctors.[105] The Greek history of East–West relations often focuses on personal encounters between monarchs and frank-speaking wise men (Solon with Croesus of Lydia in Herodotus, for example) or Greek political traitors ("Medizers" like Themistocles, Pausanias, Alcibiades and Alexander).[106] For instance, the power of lyric insouciance over imperial aggression is exemplified in the tale of Polycrates of Samos, lying in his men's quarters with Anacreon and responding to the visit of the Persian ambassador by turning his head to the wall, "either because he happened to be facing that way or as a sign of not caring" (Hdt. 3.121). Just so, the Greek doctor Democedes cured Persian Darius of a sore foot with "gentle" remedies, where the "violent" ones of his Egyptian competitors had failed (Hdt. 3.130). Arion the citharode was protected by Periander of Corinth and by the musicality of his playing (Hdt. 1.23). Plato's second letter to Dionysius of Syracuse captures both the versatility of ruler–subject friendship across several centuries and the tensions between antagonism and intimacy, distance and closeness, in these encounters:

> When men talk about Hiero or Pausanias the Lacedaemonian, they love to bring in Simonides' meetings with them and what he did and said to them. And they regularly celebrate Periander of Corinth and Thales of Miletus in the same breath, and Pericles and Anaxagoras, and Croesus and Solon, too, as wise men, with Cyrus as ruler. And the poets follow their example and bring together Creon and Teiresias, and Polyeidos and Minos, Agamemnon and Nestor, Odysseus and Palamedes—it seems to me that the earliest men also linked Prometheus with Zeus in this sort of way—and some of these men they depict in conflict, and others as friends, others still friends at first, then in conflict, and sometimes in agreement, but at other times in conflict. (Pl. *Letter* 2, 311a–311b)

---

104. Ath. 12.540e: Polycrates, tyrant of Samos, aspired to Lydian softness, building a red-light district to imitate the "Sweet Embrace" street in Sardis and weaving "Samian flowers" (i.e., collecting beautiful men and women) to match "Lydian flowers".

105. On the Herodotean "tragic warner", see Bischoff (1932), Lattimore (1939) and Gray (1986).

106. Adaptations of Herodotean encounters: e.g., Diod. Sic. 9.2.1–4, 9.12.2, 9.26–27 (Croesus); 15.6–7 (Dionysius and Philoxenus and Plato).

It is from this web of myths about encounters between tyrants and those who succeeded in soothing, teaching and persuading them—and in the process maintained (or failed to maintain) their independence—that Horace invents his lyric friendship with Maecenas.

In *Odes* 2.17, Horace adopts another role associated with closeness to Eastern kings: private astrologer.[107] Consoling Maecenas, he observes a miracle of horoscopic coincidence: since his and his patron's ascendant signs are in alignment, they will die on the same day. The details here are abstruse for a modern (probably also for an ancient) reader to understand.[108] But whatever is being claimed here, and however serious its intent, horoscopic or genethlialogical (birthdate) astrology was highly topical. It had strong connections with late-Republican dynastic ambitions and increased interest in individual cosmic destiny, propelled by renewed contact with the East: "Astrology belonged with the sole ruler, as state diviners belonged with the Republic."[109] According to ancient tradition, astrology originated in Mesopotamia, among the Babylonians (Chaldaeans) and the Zoroastrians (magi), and was practised first by kings (closest to the secrets of the heavens), then by priests; it reached Rome around the mid-third century BCE. Horace's mock caution to Leuconoe, "Don't try out Babylonian calculations" (nec Babylonios / temptaris numeros; *Carm.* 1.11.2–3), is more in line with official Roman suspicion towards the art (Agrippa banished astrologers, with sorcerers, from Rome in 33 BCE) than with his indulgence here of himself and Maecenas.

The same poem sets Maecenas up as a king in a private court, twinned with his resident magus and given a parallel personal myth of miraculous escape, followed by popular celebration (his Jupiter pulls rank over Horace's Faunus). The projected thanksgiving at the end pulls us back to the world of social difference: Maecenas will supply the bulk of the victims and a votive shrine, Horace only a humble lamb. But it is Horace's escape that is transcendental in its lyrical weightlessness ("ictum . . . leuasset"; 28–29), while for Maecenas airborne Fate only temporarily slows her wings ("tardauit alas"; 25):

> te Iouis impio
> tutela Saturno refulgens
>    eripuit uolucrisque Fati

107. See Parker 2008: 251–307: the mystique of barbarian wisdom was "most readily conceived at the edges of the known world".

108. Inspiring the biographical legend that Horace's death and Maecenas's coincided; Bradshaw 2002: 14.

109. T. Barton 1994a: 38, 1994b: 36–37. Augustus's pet astrologers: see Suet. *Aug.* 94.12 (Theogenes); Schmid 2005: 355–57 (Thrasyllus); Volk 2009: 131–32 on personal diviners.

tardauit alas, cum populus frequens
laetum theatris ter crepuit sonum;
   me truncus inlapsus cerebro
     sustulerat, nisi Faunus ictum

dextra leuasset, Mercurialium
custos uirorum. reddere uictimas
   aedemque uotiuam memento;
     nos humilem feriemus agnam.

(CARM. 2.17.22–32)

The protection of Jupiter, outshining impious Saturn, snatched you away
and slowed the fluttering wings of Fate, while the crowds in the theatre
cheered three times with a joyful shout. As for me, a tree-trunk falling on
my head would have carried me off, had not Faunus, guardian of Mercurial
poets, relieved the blow with his right hand. Remember to offer victims and
a shrine of thanks. I'll sacrifice a humble lamb.

## Diues Maecenas

If there is one area of unwavering confidence in Maecenas's biographical residue, it is the assumption that he was endowed with legendary wealth and that
from this Horace received his due share. Nisbet and Hubbard, for example,
break all their own rules by reading Maecenas into a poem where his name does
not even appear. Although *Odes* 2.18 is addressed to an ambiguous *tu*, they argue
that it implicates the patron himself (last addressed by name in the previous
poem), in an attack on luxury that features Attalid (i.e., Lydian) wealth, Tantalus
(originally a Lydian king) and Etruscan clients trailing purple robes.[110] Horace,
meanwhile, disavows opulent display ("No ivory or gold ceiling shines in my
house"; 1–2) and sets himself up as self-sufficient, paradoxically courted by
others ("pauperemque diues me petit" [a/the rich man seeks me out, a poor
man]; 10–11) and financially independent of any (or "my"?) powerful patron
("nec potentem amicum / largiora flagito" [nor do I make extravagant demands
on a powerful friend]; 12–13).

   The clinching element would seem to be Horace's declaration here that he
is content with the Sabine Farm. But Arnold Bradshaw, who translates *unicis
Sabinis* as "in Sabine country alone", points to the danger of circular arguments: "the *potens amicus* is Maecenas because Maecenas gave Horace his

---

110. R. Nisbet and Hubbard 1978: 290.

farm: Maecenas gave Horace his farm because he was the *potens amicus*".[111] "Sabine country", he points out, was used proverbially of any unfashionable address, and "Sabine farm" of disputed territory in a legal context.[112] Instead, the farm may be an Italianized focus for tragic/Herodotean warners' homilies to great rulers. The lyric poet can assert his independence without regard for his patron's feelings—as if Pharaoh Amasis were speaking frankly to Polycrates, or (given the Lydian colouring) Solon to Croesus.

Maecenas does appear explicitly in *Odes* 3.16, another anti-wealth poem, as an ambiguous fifth exemplum in a list of powerful men ruined by bribes. Again, Horace expresses satisfaction with his estate: "[I am] more splendid as the owner of property that others despise than if I hid away all the produce of the Apulian's plough." Again, this is an austere kind of thank you, if thank you it is.[113] Maecenas stands out from the other rich men by virtue of his knightly rank and the integrity of his client, but the juxtaposition is telling. It has been suggested that it is "not too far-fetched to visualize the wealthy *eques* as having investment interests in African *latifundia* and in Lydian-Phrygian gold deposits. . . . [H]is antique lineage and exotic tastes might conjure up in Horace's eyes, twinkling in Tiburtine sun, the image of an Eastern potentate."[114] Again, these are circular assumptions, reflecting the analogies the *Odes* themselves make between Maecenas and Eastern tyrants.

## Therapy for Maecenas

In *Odes* 2.17, Maecenas is thinking about death: if he dies first, Horace will not mourn him adequately.[115] Some external reality (such as morbid hypochondria) is usually adduced, to which this poem is regarded as the response.[116]

---

111. Bradshaw 1989: 170–73.

112. Catull. 44: "o funde noster seu Sabine seu Tiburs" (curiously close to the Horatian Vita's phrasing: "uixit plurimum in secessu ruris sui Sabini aut Tiburtini"); Cic. *Mur.* 26 ("fundus Sabinus meus est"), with Skinner 2001.

113. Lyne 1995: 123: "This says 'thank you' and lauds the Sabine estate after a fashion. But it *is* after a fashion and indeed austere"; Bradshaw 1989: 179: "*Inclusam Danaen* is a statement about H's personal philosophy; it is not a way of saying either 'Thank you' or, as some have more tortuously argued, 'Please.'"

114. Schork 1971: 536.

115. Mörland 1965, Syndikus 1972: 1.455–63.

116. E.g., Lyne 1995: 116: "Apparently he is ill, and in fear for his life. The Ode is Horace's response"; 117: "[*querela*] was therefore a risky word to use unless Maecenas' laments about his health were something of a shared joke among his circle, a joke which even Maecenas shared, possibly rather queasily".

Once again, this puts the cart before the horse. Rather, it is the poet who first dreams up a need in Maecenas, then constructs himself as lifeline to the patron whom he describes in another breath as his glory and support ("mearum grande decus / columenque rerum"; 3–4). Manly sentiments all round, but there is an unexpected intimacy in Horace's tetchy opening complaint, "Why are you wearing me out with your moaning?", and a "swooning" sensuality in the sigh at 5–6, "Ah! If a premature force snatches away part of my soul." All this spices up the more conventional vow of comradeship that follows: "ibimus, ibimus, / utcumque praecedes, supremum / carpere iter comites parati" (We'll go, we'll go, wherever you lead, ready to tackle the supreme journey together; 10–12).[117] Horace feminizes Maecenas, first as the passive victim of rapacious death ("rapit" [snatches]; 5), then as a damsel in distress, rescued by a god ("eripuit" [snatched away]; 24).[118]

The opening *querelis*, "laments", prime marker of elegiac poetry, sets the scene for romantic visions of symmetrical affection, same-starred destiny and union in death.[119] Horace stages a classic display of similarity and difference between poet and patron.[120] Alternatively, the contest for Maecenas's soul reads as a generic tussle. Elegy, a key rival for non-epic, non-narrative space against which Horace defines lyric, is associated with endless lamentation, lyric with a more mature acceptance of the flow of time.[121] Lyric lightness assuages elegiac dejection, cast here as the premature and excessive mourning of a needy patron.[122] Thus therapy for Maecenas dramatizes the poet's promotion of one genre over another.

## Love for Lydia

At first sight, the gap between the war poems and the erotic ones is one of the most unbridgeable divides in the *Odes*. Yet even this turns out to be something of an illusion.[123] For Horace, the *Iliad* is a place where erotic and military

117. Oliensis 1997: 167. McDermott (1982) reads the poem as homosocial literary play, recalling Calvus and Catullus (Catull. 50).

118. Also, briefly, himself ("altera [uis]"; 6); Oliensis 1997: 168.

119. Equally evoking lovers' devotion (cf. Prop. 2.20.18; Syndikus 1972: 1.458) and a proconsul going to his province with his *comites*; Lyne 1995: 121.

120. McDermott 1982: 227: the poem's "protestation of intertwining fates is paradoxically filled with humorous allusions to the two men's differences".

121. Lowrie 1997: 271–74, 277–97.

122. In *Carm.* 1.24, the lyre and lyric acquiescence are cures for grief; cf. *Carm.* 2.9 (Valgius), 1.33 (Tibullus); G. Davis 1991: 145–88.

123. Lowrie 1997: 122–23.

conquest were always already intertwined. He marks out his lyric assault on epic by recalling the centrality of erotic pairings to primeval war narrative: Paris and Helen (*Carm.* 1.15), Achilles and Briseis (*Carm.* 2.4.3–4), Agamemnon and Cassandra (*Carm.* 2.4.7–8).[124] Conversely, the lyric-erotic sphere is sharpened by violence: "nos conuiuia, nos proelia uirginum / sectis in iuuenes unguibus acrium / cantamus" (We sing of banquets, of battles carried on by maidens attacking young men with their sharply cut nails; *Carm.* 1.6.17–18). The immorality of the East and its charisma converge above all in *Odes* 1.15, where Horace chooses to approach Homer through the Lydianized figure of Paris, whose seduction of Helen launched ten years of East–West war. For all his curls and perfume and destructive liaison, Paris is depicted holding a lyre, as much of a "lyric" ancestor, then, as Orpheus or Arion:[125]

nequiquam Veneris praesidio ferox
pectes caesariem grataque feminis
imbelli cithara carmina diuides . . .

(CARM. 1.15.13–15)

In vain will you play the warrior under Venus's protection, comb your hair, and pluck out songs that women love on your unwarlike lyre.

Bad influence he may be, but Paris represents the contradictions in Horace's androgynous persona: a scented intruder into epic, an effeminate straying into essentially masculine territory, like epic characters Nastes, girlish leader of the Carians in *Iliad* 2, or transvestite Achilles, reincarnated in the deserter Sybaris of *Odes* 1.8 and the girlish Gyges of *Odes* 2.5.[126] This flexibility in matters of gender is nothing if not appropriate for lyric, which, like elegy, marks itself stylistically as "soft" or "gentle" and whose line-up of nine Greek luminaries contains a unique, if mannish female: "mascula Sappho" (masculine Sappho; *Epist.* 1.19.28).[127]

---

124. On the traditional "intrusion" of *eros* into epic: Hinds 2000; in Horace: G. Davis 1991: 27; Lowrie 1997: 133–34. The *Iliad* is often represented in lighter *recusatio* poems by its effeminate elements: Ibyc. fr. S282a.10–12 (Paris "deceiver of his host" and "slim-ankled" Cassandra); Theoc. *Id.* 16.48–50 (the Lycian chiefs, Priam's long-haired sons and Cycnus with his girlish skin).

125. La Bua 2013: 284; Kraggerud 1987; cf. *Carm.* 1.6.10: Horace's own muse is "imbellis . . . lyrae . . . potens".

126. Hom. *Il.* 2.870–75. Cf. G. Davis 1991: 27–28.

127. Sappho and Horace: Barchiesi 2000: 169 = Lowrie 2009: 421; Woodman 2002. Alcaeus, whose themes stretched from warfare and seafaring to boys with black eyes and hair (*Carm.* 1.32.5–12), makes an elastic model for the *biformis uates*; Lowrie 1997: 85–86.

As for the desired boys and girls of the *Odes*, many of their names could be pinned on a map of the East–West flow of luxury and tyranny: Cyrus (Median King of Persia), Gyges (King of Lydia), Lydia, Lyde, Telephus (a Greek who went east, to Mysia, to become the ancestor of Lydian and Etruscan kings), Sybaris (a Greek colony in Southern Italy, known for *truphē*), Tyndaris (also in Sicily)—now all deracinated slaves, prostitutes and sexual objects. Their names tease us with their allegorical potential. Are we meant to plot the erotic onto the geopolitical, as in *Odes* 1.8, where Lydia seduces Sybaris, or in *Odes* 1.17, where one Cyrus disrupts an Anacreontic drinking party with Persian-style violence, or in *Odes* 1.23, where "Cyri torret amor" (love of Cyrus bakes me) neatly translates Greek *philocyros*, "lover of Cyrus" (Strabo's name for the Medizing Alexander), while assimilating Cyrus's allure to desert heat?[128] Is the androgynous Gyges in *Odes* 2.5 the same as the wealthy Gyges, loyal to Asterie, in *Odes* 3.7, and what is their relationship to the Gyges of Herodotus and the "hundred-handed" giant Gyges?[129] Ingenious arguments have been made for seeing Liguria in Horace's Ligurinus and Galatia in his Galatea, but the imperial correspondences seldom work so well.[130] Cyrus is both a random lover boy and a Persian king in the *Odes*, Lydia both a femme fatale and a distant land. It is easier to make imaginative links between two different kinds of tricky negotiation with the seductive but treacherous East than press the names into the service of Augustus and his various campaigns.

Remarkably many of these once-illustrious names are associated with Maecenas's putative Lydian ancestors, another hint that he colours even those poems where he does not obviously appear. Of these significant names, "Lydia", Horace's long-term on-off lover, is especially resonant.[131] Beyond topographical associations with the Anatolian satrapy of that name, she may also evoke Lydian modes of lyre playing (which Plato calls "soft" or "effeminate").[132] More than that, Lydia stands out among the many girl musicians of the *Odes*—Chloe, Phyllis and others—as the recurrent "muse" of Horatian erotic lyric: tyrannical, fickle and subject to decay, but always a match

---

128. On Cyrus at *Carm.* 1.17.25 and 3.29.27, see Putnam (2000: 21–22). *Philocyros*: Strabo 11.11.4. Sybaris: Jaeger 1995: 184–85.

129. On *Carm.* 3.7, see Harrison (1988), Mutschler (1978: 113n9), Cairns (2012: 362–63), R. Nisbet and Rudd (2004, *ad loc.*). Gyges and Asterie are also Titans' names: Cairns 2012: 368–71; Ancona 1994: 38–43; Lowrie 1997: 268.

130. Mitchell 2010.

131. On Lydia's close namesake Lyde and her associations with Lydian modes and Antimachean mourning, see Lowrie (1997: 275–97). Lyde then blends into Lyce (= *lupa*, prostitute?) in *Carm.* 4.13.

132. Pl. *Resp.* 398e9–10. Cf. Lydian flutes in the last stanza of *Carm.* 4.15.

for the poet and endlessly renewable in his poetry. Her orientalized name not only suggests Horace's lyric aspirations to Eastern luxury, it also echoes Maecenas's Etruscan-Lydian origins. There are further reasons to connect her with the patron. After Maecenas, Lydia is the character addressed most often in the *Odes* (four times to his seven). A narrative of a relationship has taken shape around her poems, too. Indeed, perhaps the reason that Maecenas's Lydian, as distinct from Etruscan, roots are omitted from the *Odes* is because Horace preferred not to make the link too obvious between his two most frequent lyric addressees.

As we have seen, imaginative connections between a poet's enslavement to a patron and his enslavement to a long-term mistress are common across Roman elegy, satire and lyric, despite differences in honour codes, social practice, and historical versus fictional status. To restate this distinction in Lowrie's terms, if the patron is drawn to "supplementary" narrative, the mistress belongs firmly to "essential" lyric discourse. Yet Maecenas, we appreciate, has a foot in both worlds. He is repeatedly being enticed over the threshold into the poet's enclosure and urged to submit to lyric devices and desires. We have also seen how commonly erotic language overflows into poetic interactions between male clients and patrons, allowing a poet to negotiate the dynamics of the relationship more expressively or playfully. In *Odes* 2.12, Horace casts both Maecenas and himself as "feminine" or "passive", while a *hetaera* or muse, Licymnia, triangulates the alternating relations of poet and patron, persuading Maecenas to prefer her fluttering eyelashes to all the wealth of the East and permitting Horatian lyric to invest more firmly in erotic (Sapphic) values. In *Odes* 2.17, meanwhile, Maecenas plays the querulous "mistress" whose fears are allayed by her stouter-hearted lover.

The harsh abuse of Horace's addresses to Lydia is a far cry from these soothing or playful poems. Yet the "Lydia cycle" (*Carm.* 1.8, 1.13, 1.25, 3.9) plays a special role as a piquant, out-of-sync parallel to the Maecenas odes, enabling Horace to enlarge more frankly on the hazards of the client–patron relationship by recasting it in erotic, antagonistic male-to-female terms. Lydia allows him to speak about his fear of rivals and the patron's unreliability and waning power.[133] In *Odes* 1.8, the femme fatale is scolded for diverting a young recruit, Sybaris, from his military vocation and turning him "soft" in the process. The geopolitical referentiality of Horatian names is typically imprecise, but there is a clear allusion here to the traditional drift of *truphē*, luxury, from Lydia

---

133. Oliensis (1997: 157–58, 164) sees "mollis Ionia" (delicate Ionia; Prop. 1.6.31) and "Lydia . . . arata" (arable Lydia; 1.6.32) as the "other women" who seduce Tullus on his Eastern travels; she does not explicitly equate Maecenas and Lydia.

(East) to Sybaris (West). In the last line of the poem, Horace pointedly evokes the presence of luxurious elements in the *Iliad*: his "Lycias cateruas" (Lycian cohorts) recall the Lycians' neighbour in the Trojan catalogue, Homer's effeminate Carian Nastes, who went to war "dressed in gold, like a girl, fool that he was" (*Il.* 2.872–73). If Horace casts himself as the spokesman for hard military values, outraged by Lydia's effrontery in diverting Sybaris from his epic mission, his "I"-figure is rather a sham drill sergeant.[134] His lyric sympathies should lie at least partly with the "soft" world of orientalized erotics and Lydia as its presiding muse.

This conflict is deepened in *Odes* 1.13, where Horace plays a jealous rival and Lydia in her turn is seduced by a "barbarian" suitor, Telephus, with dangerous kisses. All Horace has as counterforce are lyric powers of persuasion, as he despairingly reminds his mistress that lasting happiness can come only from the eternal bond of quasi-married love:[135]

> felices ter et amplius
> quos irrupta tenet copula nec malis
>     diuulsus querimoniis
> suprema citius soluet amor die.
>
> (*CARM.* 1.13.17–20)

Thrice happy and more are those whom an uninterrupted bond holds together and whom a love torn apart by serious quarrels will not loosen sooner than the day of death.

Given that the same model of undying love will be applied to relations between Maecenas and Horace in *Odes* 2.17, it is worth considering the alternative translation suggested by Ronnie Ancona: *irrupta copula* (18) as not "uninterrupted bond" but "interrupted bond".[136] The best Horace could then envisage for his relationship with Lydia would be not utopian, seamless love but one that survives frequent hiatuses: "Lover and beloved have a new possibility: rather than accepting or rejecting an idealized love that denies change and exists unproblematically over time, they can choose a love that continues but which must

---

134. Draft dodging, as with Achilles on Scyros, signals *recusatio* of epic; also, since Horace lingers on Sybaris's abandoned military training (dressage, discus, javelin, heat and dust), *recusatio* of Pindaric epinician. Lowrie (1997: 29) points to the difficulty of characterizing the speaker: rivalrous or detached and avuncular?

135. Ancona 1994: 123: Horace's list of the afflictions of the lovestruck, from Sappho on, omits loss of voice (contrast *Epod.* 11.9–10: "amantem languor et silentium / arguit").

136. Ancona 1994: 125–27.

be continually renewed."[137] A love, in other words, that reflects the very disjunction and moodiness of lyric erotics. Just so, the relationship with Maecenas is vulnerable to interruption and betrayal (the *Odes*, after all, flit between multiple addressees and stop only for occasional reunions), while still being renewable for as long as Horace needs his patron.

But it is *Odes* 1.25, "the crudest and nastiest poem in Horace's lyrics", that offers the darkest warning to a patron who spreads his favours.[138] One day, Horace predicts, the incorrigibly promiscuous Lydia will age and the lovers now crowding her doors will fade away:

Parcius iunctas quatiunt fenestras
iactibus crebris iuuenes proterui
nec tibi somnos adimunt, amatque
    ianua limen,

quae prius multum facilis mouebat
cardines; audis minus et minus iam
"me tuo longas pereunte noctes,
    Lydia, dormis?"

(CARM 1.25.1–8)

The boisterous young men knock your closed shutters less frequently now. They no longer rob you of sleep, and the door whose hinges once moved easily now hugs its threshold. You hear this less and less these days: "Are you sleeping, Lydia, while I endure long wakeful nights?"

Thresholds are the haunts of both clients and erotic suitors in Rome, and it is no strain to see an analogy between Lydia's admirers ("iuuenes proterui" [boisterous young men]) and a great man's clients.[139] But there is still a crucial erotic difference: "gendered distinctions between male lover and female beloved".[140] While young men are noisy, sleep-depriving indicators of Lydia's current desires and desirability, her appeal as a woman is fragile and time-bound. In the suspended moment that the poem captures, Lydia's once-busy door begins to swing less frequently: "the door whose hinges once moved

---

137. R. Nisbet and Hubbard (1970, *ad loc.*) firmly explain *irruptus* as a calque on Greek ἄρρηκτος, "unbroken".

138. Ancona 1994: 127. Cf. Collinge 1961: 52.

139. On the erotics of the threshold, see Oliensis (1997: 151). With *faciles cardines*, compare the Pest's "faint heart never won fair lady" tactics for overcoming Maecenas's *difficilis aditus primos* (Hor. *Sat.* 1.9.56–58).

140. Ancona 1994: 23.

easily now hugs its threshold" (3–6). Here, "moved" (*mouebat*), marker of lyric's mobility, speaks of successful two-way traffic, rhetorical and physical; it was the lovers' *moving* laments that persuaded Lydia's door to *stir*. The pivotal word here is *inuicem*, "in turn", which launches a fantasy of reversal between desirer and desired object.[141] Soon, the disappointed speaker warns, Lydia will grow old and be the one locked out—sleepless, discarded like a withered leaf by disdainful lovers, roaming the streets at night and possessed by naked desire like a bacchante or a mare in heat. Horace would never have spoken directly to a male friend like this: his attack on a moribund but unseasonably libidinous object is all too gender-specific.[142] In his lyric world, male desire and desirability, as well as male bonds, are permitted to last longer. But even the "affair" with the patron is not exempt from time's onward movement.[143]

Lydia fades until Book 3, when she and Maecenas share the stage again following the Roman *Odes*; they are in fact uniquely juxtaposed, in *Odes* 3.8 (Maecenas) and 3.9 (Lydia). The first of these poems is a sympotic invitation (like *Carm.* 1.20, 3.29 and 4.11) with Maecenas summoned as the ideal witness of the feats of Horace the wunderkind, planted to elicit the aetiological explanation that follows and equipped with the necessary bilingual expertise ("docte sermones utriusque linguae" [expert in the parlance of either language]; 5) to appreciate Horace's learning. This time, his appetite for wonder (3: *miraris*) is whetted by a bizarre convivial puzzle—the prospect of a transvestite Horace, a bachelor (*caelebs*) apparently infiltrating today's women's festival, the Matronalia—before he is reassured: this is in fact the anniversary of his lucky escape from a falling tree. Mars ("Martiis [. . . Kalendis]") at the start of the poem is a red herring: not the masculine god of war, but his month, March, in a poem that celebrates domesticity and survival against a foreign backdrop of long-haul self-combustion ("Medus infestus sibi luctuosis / dissidet armis" [the Medes are at war with each other, divided by battles with many losses]; 19–20).[144] In a familiar move, the patron is urged to forget worldly cares, be first intrigued by, then involved in the mythical history of divinely sanctioned emergence that Horace has progressively created for himself.[145] Horace's decision to celebrate a private, rather than a public festival makes him "a model for his patron to emulate".[146]

---

141. Ancona 1994: 28. Cf. G. Davis 1991: 216.

142. Ancona 1994: 128–39; Putnam 1982.

143. See Mitchell (2012) on aging coevals Augustus and Horace in *Odes* 4; Gowers (2016a) on Horace's attack on the aging *hetaera* Lyce (*Carm.* 4.13) as displaced frankness to Augustus.

144. Putnam 1996: 38n.20.

145. See G. Davis (1991: 78–114) and Lowrie (1997: 187–223) on Horace's personal myth.

146. Santirocco 1984: 249. See Feeney (2007: 148–60) on the power of Roman anniversaries, especially birthdays, following Julian reform of the calendar.

The poem that follows (*Carm.* 3.9) smacks more of the universal than the occasional and gives Horace a different kind of sparring partner. In elegantly patterned amoebean verses, he and Lydia symmetrically vow and disavow their on-off entanglement. The hierarchical distinction between male lover and (usually) female beloved is replaced by a knowing reciprocity. Each partner is now open to the "contingent separateness" of the other, recognizing that the relationship on both sides is subject to the passage of time, which offers a paradoxical kind of immunity.[147] The relentless conditionals ("As long as", "What if . . .", "Although") indicate that "alternatives are already present".[148]

What's more, the contrast in Odes 3.8 between feuding Medes and housebound matron acquires an almost erotic charge. The exchanges expressed in alternating stanzas reflect the traditional lyric trade-off between Eastern wealth and unique love object. Horace's words, "I flourished more blessed than the King of Persia" (Persarum uigui rege beatior; cf. Sappho frr. 16, 96, 132 Voigt), remind us that the Persian king was an erotic super-rival who traditionally attracted the most beautiful women, thanks to his legendary riches. The values implicit in the priamel of Odes 1.1 and its contingent (*si /seu*) bargains with the patron anticipate the "lyric" evaluation Maecenas is spurred to make in Odes 2.12 between Eastern wealth and Licymnia's charms. Lydia counters unexpectedly by comparing herself to an archetypal Roman matron.[149] The pair are enchanted not just by each other's renewed devotion despite the alternatives available, but by the game of capping and persuasion itself—typically lyrical, perhaps, as the standby muse Chloe with her lyre suggests. In any case, the acknowledged mobility of lovers here is a permanent marker of fugitive lyric. Lydia ends breezily, but gratifyingly:

> "tu leuior cortice et improbo
>   iracundior Hadria,
> tecum uiuere amem, tecum obeam lubens."

> (CARM. 3.9.22–24)

"You are more unstable than a cork and more temperamental than the unruly Adriatic, but I would gladly live with you, gladly die with you."

This is the last we see of Lydia in the Odes. The imagined reunion of separated lovers in their "bronze yoke" ("iugo . . . aeneo"; 18) foreshadows the poetic

147. Ancona 1994: 129–30.
148. Commager 1962: 57.
149. Putnam 1982: 111n6: "deliberate shock". Lowrie (1997: 351) challenges Ancona's conclusion that Horace's amours are superficial because they do not end in marriage: "not a traditional inspiration for good poetry".

monument of *Odes* 3.30: it freezes *sub specie aeternitatis* a love that accepts uncertainty and flourishes not on constancy but on rival threats.[150] Already, the snapshot of two survivors, Horace and Maecenas, in *Odes* 3.8 has started to look provisional. Read alongside the Lydia poems, the episodic representation of their relationship seems less like a solid marriage and more like a sporadic renewal of vows by volatile lovers.[151]

By contrast, the threat of Horace's poetic rivals is dealt with more resoundingly. Fellow poets commemorated elsewhere as part of the "circle" (*Sat.* 1.5, 1.10) are presented in the *Odes* only as Horace's friends, not as Maecenas's. They are given solicitous send-offs (Virgil, *Carm.* 1.3, in the guise of a kindly send-off to Greece via the high seas of epic), mourned as lost (Virgil, *Carm.* 4.3), assigned secondary, non-lyric roles (in *Carm.* 1.6, Varius is given the dull task of an epic on Agrippa's military exploits) and conspicuously excluded from Horace's symposia. In other words, they are tactfully removed from the lyric domain. Meanwhile, Horace embeds his own stunning miniatures of *Iliad*, *Aeneid* and tragedy in the brief compass of lyric. Oliensis sees the philandering Jupiter who pays for access to Danaë in *Odes* 3.16 as Augustus, a new and invincible rival on the lyric scene who threatens to seduce Horace with his dangerous wealth.[152] Yet *Odes* 3.9 has already suggested that not only Maecenas has other options. Horace's own door may lie open for a returning lover: "si flaua excutitur Chloe / reiectaeque patet ianua Lydiae?" (If blonde Chloe is cast off, does your door lie open for rejected Lydia?; 19–20).

By the time of *Epistles* 2.1, Horace is the only one left alive to cast a literary-historical eye back over the Age of Augustus (or Age of Horace?). Challenging the emperor to smile on a new era of major poets, he pours scorn on the one-word value judgments and facile comparisons (*synkrises*) typical of Greek literary histories. Horace is usually heavy with the special pleading here for his contemporaries:

> at neque dedecorant tua de se iudicia atque
> munera, quae multa dantis cum laude tulerunt,
> dilecti tibi Vergilius Variusque poetae
>
> (*EPIST.* 2.1.245–47)

---

150. Bronze signals durability: pseudo-Acro *ad loc.* But see Oliensis (1997: 177) on *Carm.* 1.38: "lyric perfection depends on nonfruition".

151. Cf. the legend of Maecenas's on-off relationship with Terentia. See Martini (1995) on their prenups and divorce; Dio Cass. 54.19; Plut. *Mor.* 760a; Sen. *Ep.* 114.6, *Prov.* 1.3.10: "morosae uxoris cotidiana repudia".

152. Oliensis 1997: 166.

But your beloved poets Virgil and Varius do no discredit both to your judgment and to the gifts they have received which give back great honour to the giver.

Denis Feeney concludes: "Virgil and Varius are *not* Choerilus, at the end of the poem, as Augustus is *not* Alexander (229–47)."[153] Yet with comparisons on the brain, it is hard to rule out a modicum of similarity between the bad Greek epic poet who took cash from his ruler and the good Roman epic poets who are alleged to have done the same.[154] The poem that "clinches Horace's right to rank with Virgil and Varius" does this precisely by co-opting their chosen genres—panegyrical epic and drama—for its literary overview.[155]

## Valedictions

*Odes* 3.29, the penultimate poem of its book, is the last addressed to Maecenas before Horace completes his lyric monument, more enduring than all the mausolea and pyramids of earthly rulers. This is itself a monumental poem, with its superb iconic image of the erratic, onward-flowing Tiber, and Horace's gravest statement yet about the vulnerability of great men to Fortune (and his own invulnerability). It panders to a restless patron's need for changing scenery, but this time anticipates a parting of the ways. In the opening appeal to Maecenas to tear himself away from the rival world of civic cares and beat it to his summer residence, Santirocco detects new signs of impatience; the wine has been waiting for hours:[156]

> Tyrrhena regum progenies, tibi
> non ante uerso lene merum cado
>     cum flore, Maecenas, rosarum et
>         pressa tuis balanus capillis
>
> iamdudum apud me est. eripe te morae,
> ne semper udum Tibur et Aefulae
>     decliue contempleris aruum et
>         Telegoni iuga parricidae.

---

153. Feeney 2002b: 179.

154. White (2007: 198) (surprisingly) finds it odd that Horace does not recall his own grants from Augustus (Suet. *Vita Hor.*).

155. Feeney 2002b: 179. NB: these are two genres in which one does not traditionally credit a patron.

156. Santirocco 1984: 250: Horace "implies that previous invitations have gone unheeded".

fastidiosam desere copiam et
molem propinquam nubibus arduis;
   omitte mirari beatae
     fumum et opes strepitumque Romae.

plerumque gratae diuitibus uices
mundaeque paruo sub lare pauperum
   cenae sine aulaeis et ostro
     sollicitam explicuere frontem.

(CARM. 3.29.1–16)

Scion of Etruscan kings, smooth wine awaits you at my house, from a cask never opened before, and rose petals along with ointment squeezed for your hair. Tear yourself away from what keeps you, and do not stand forever staring out at damp Tivoli, and the slopes of Aefula, and the heights of Telegonus who killed his father. Leave behind your irksome wealth and the steep palace that scrapes the clouds. Stop gawping at the smoke and riches and noise of Rome. Rich men have liked to ring the changes: neat dinners in poor men's little houses, free from tapestries and purple, tend to unknit their worried frowns.

There are, of course, other ways of reading "impatience": as a symptom of lyric urgency, a marker of how the occasion needs to be endlessly renewed, or a polite presumption that Maecenas is about to reject Horace, just at the point when Horace's own need is diminishing. Santirocco calls Maecenas "unreconstructed" here. It seems to me that he is more than usually "constructed"—as someone who will always need rescuing.[157] Recalling the anxious complaints of *Odes* 2.17, Nisbet and Rudd note: "Maecenas was an inveterate worrier."[158] As usual, Horace needs Maecenas to be incurable, endlessly in need of words of wisdom, washed down by the smooth wine ("lene merum"; 2) of consolatory lyric. As the seductive voice of sympotic oblivion, it is Horace who has the power now to insert Maecenas (as the word order reflects) into a fug of perfume and rose petals. He is the sage who plays down worldly government and empire in favour of self-control ("potens sui"; 41). Borrowing Eastern roles for his new function as "spiritual patron", he plays court astrologer or wise warner, whispering in the ear of the tyrant over whom a sword hangs.[159]

---

157. Santirocco 1984: 250.

158. R. Nisbet and Rudd 2004, *ad Carm.* 3.29.16. Cf. Citroni 2009: 89: "The anxious and passionate tone cannot be fully understood if we neglect Maecenas' anxious character, known from Seneca and the elder Pliny."

159. Reckford 1959: 204; Santirocco 1984: 253. Cf. Sharlet 2011: 32: "Poets can reject a patron for a spiritual hermit-like existence."

It may be perverse to see an orientalizing aspect to this poem when Maecenas is so clearly positioned in Rome (perhaps on the Esquiline), looking out
(*contempleris* [7], a term from Etruscan augury) over the Campagna. But his
*political* gaze is fixed much further east. In short, he has two fields of vision:
one close-range (essential, lyric) towards sites of quiet retreat (Tibur, Aefulae
and Tusculum), the other far-range (supplementary, narrative) towards the
borders of the empire (China, Parthia and Scythia), where a contested river
("Tanais . . . discors" [war-torn Don]) figures his divided heart:[160]

> tu ciuitatem quis deceat status
> curas et Vrbi sollicitus times
>     quid Seres et regnata Cyro
>         Bactra parent Tanaisque discors.

(CARM. 3.29.25–28)

You worry about the state of the nation and, concerned for Rome, fear
what's rumbling in China, or Persia, which Cyrus once ruled, and war-torn
Don (i.e., Scythia).

The poem is also thought to contain an allusion to Maecenas's famous Esquiline lookout point, his skyscraper palace:[161]

> fastidiosam desere copiam et
> molem propinquam nubibus arduis

(CARM. 3.29.9–10)

Leave behind your irksome wealth and the steep mass that scrapes the clouds.

As we will see (chapter 9), this nebulous figment has been specifically identified with the legendary "Tower of Maecenas". But a more plausible explanation
is that it is a traditional symbol of tyranny riding for a fall.[162] The generic advice of Artabanus to Xerxes not to overreach himself by invading Greece (Hdt.
7.10: "You see how it is always onto the highest buildings and the tallest trees
that God hurls his bolts") has been seen behind the tragic counsel of *Odes*
2.10.9–12:[163]

---

160. Cf. the ominous "Medes fighting among themselves" of *Carm.* 3.8.19. The Tusculan idyll
is disturbed (8) by gratuitous mention of its founder Telegonus, murderer of Ulysses.

161. Flimsier than the stars banged by Horace's head in *Carm.* 1.1; cf. 30: "caliginosa nocte".

162. Bizarrely dismissed by R. Nisbet and Rudd (2004, *ad Carm.* 3.29.9–10): "It goes too far
to see an allusion, however humorously, to the perils of greatness."

163. See R. Nisbet and Hubbard 1978, *ad loc.*

saepius uentis agitatur ingens
pinus et celsae grauiore casu
decidunt turres feriuntque summos
    fulgura montis.

Tall pine trees bend more often in the wind and high towers fall with greater calamity and lightning always strikes mountain peaks.

The same speech, along with Artabanus's earlier fruitless advice to Xerxes's father Darius not to invade Scythia (4.83), may well lurk in the background of *Odes* 3.29, too, explaining the inclusion of Persia ("ruled by Cyrus") and Scythia among the foreign trouble spots listed at 27–28. In rejecting palace halls, purple robes and irksome wealth, the poem also anticipates Seneca's choral lyrics, which draw on a long tradition of Greek tragic images, filtered through Horace.[164] Indeed, the first ode of *Agamemnon* "restores" Horatian images to a tragic context: cloud-scraping towers, blasted trees, sleepless princes and a self-preserving sage who sails away in a tiny boat.[165]

Towards the end of *Odes* 3.29, the figure of Fortune appears, generous and fickle by turns:

Fortuna saeuo laeta negotio et
ludum insolentem ludere pertinax
    transmutat incertos honores,
        nunc mihi, nunc alii benigna.

(CARM. 3.29.49–52)

Fortune delights in her cruel activity and is relentless when she plays her outrageous games. But she likes to transfer her passing attentions: first she's kind to me, then she's kind to someone else.

Not only is she worlds away from the providential benefactress of Augustus in *Odes* 1.30. She is also the divine equivalent of the unpredictable Etruscan Tiber (33–41) and a shadow figure for its compatriot, who may at any time shift his own "passing attentions" to rivals—just when the poet himself is en route to a closer encounter with Augustus.[166] Horace flaunts inconstancy as a necessary response, praising Fortune while she lasts ("laudo manentem"; 53) but renouncing her

---

164. R. Tarrant 1976: 180–84.

165. Sen. *Agamemnon* 92–107.

166. Both are changeable: "nunc . . . cum pace . . . nunc . . . cum fera diluuies quietos / irritat amnis" (34–41) ~ "nunc mihi, nunc alii benigna" (52). See Santirocco 1984: 244–45, 251. "Incertos honores" (51) recalls the "superuacuos honores" of the tomb in *Carm.* 2.20.

gifts when she flies away ("si celeris quatit / pennas, resigno quae dedit" [if she shakes her swift wings, I renounce all she gave me]; 53–54). The image screens his own imminent departure.[167] In *Odes* 1.1, Horace had called Maecenas his *praesidium*: now he steers his little boat under his own *praesidio* (62).[168] In *Odes* 2.17, he had called him his great support ("grande columen rerum"; 4): now he is his patron's prop. The wandering poet of *Odes* 1.1 does not even stay to host his own party. As if pre-empting his guest's refusal, he gracefully jettisons his winnings, cloaks himself with virtue and makes off in his little boat, going with the flow.[169] The words of the Islamic thinker Al-Mawardi seem particularly appropriate for Horace's lyric universe: "There are three things with which there is no security: the ruler, the sea and time."[170]

Maecenas makes one more appearance in the *Odes*, a ghostly one, in *Odes* 4.11. Horace's last symposium is a waiting game, with the lost patron figured as a late arrival or an empty chair. Now the poet adopts a less threatening symbiotic model: the master and his docile geisha, Phyllis, "green shoot" but also "last of my loves" (meorum finis amorum), trained to echo back his voice—a rare sign of spring in a book where everyone is dead or aging. Horace's "memory" of Greek lyric symposia is overlaid by his memory of happier parties in *Odes* 1–3; the simple arbour of earlier days is replaced by a bustling establishment with its own "smoke, wealth and noise". In between, the scholarly argument goes, Maecenas disappeared from the political scene, either through disgrace or voluntary retirement.[171] Somehow, we know that he will not show for this occasion, even though it celebrates his birthday, more sacred to Horace than his own; the Ides of April is a day that splits ("findit"; 16) the month in two, from which "Maecenas meus" disposes ("ordinat"; 20) his flowing years.[172] Feeney notes the tension between the precision of the new Roman calendar, which so clearly fixes anniversaries, and the "watery immeasurability of the natural flow of years" (affluentis ... annos), which harks back to the magnificent river image ("fluminis ritu ...") for the passing of time in *Odes* 3.29.[173]

167. Echoed at *Epist.* 1.7.34: "hac ego si compellor imagine, cuncta resigno"; cf. Sen. *Dial.* 9.11.2–3.

168. Santirocco 1984: 252.

169. Cf. Hunter 1996: 97: "Poet and patron need each other, and are in much the same boat; that at least is the theory"; Feeney 2002b: 185 (on *Epist.* 2.1, but surely remembering *Carm.* 3.29): "The boat will carry poet and patron down the river of time together, as objects of reverence, envy, or ridicule."

170. Cited by Sharlet 2011: 35.

171. Gordon Williams 1990.

172. *Idus* was etymologized from Etruscan *iduare = diuidere* (Macrob. *Sat.* 1.15.17): Putnam 1982: 191; Feeney 1993: 63n77 = Lowrie 2009: 230n78.

173. Feeney 1993: 59 = Lowrie 2009: 230.

The condemnation of worldly wealth in earlier poems now contracts to fit Phyllis's erotic horizons. A rich female rival ("puella / diues"; 22–23) holds her beloved Telephus in chains; her only solace will come from singing with Horace (35–36). From this point, Maecenas appears tangential to the business of the poem. But two pieces of mythical machinery wheeled out to illustrate the perils of overreaching, Phaethon and Bellerophon, seem almost too heavy for the erotic context. The second story, in particular—Bellerophon thrown by Pegasus after aspiring to Olympus ("exemplum graue" [a serious (lit. heavy) example]; 26)—might recall the absent knight. Wherever he is, Maecenas will remain grounded, his inspired horse weighed down by its earthly rider ("terrenum equitem grauatus"; 27), while Horace launches himself into orbit and looks back pityingly over his shoulder.[174]

Appropriately, then, the last image of Maecenas in Horatian lyric is one that crystallizes his associations with dividedness and fluidity, along with a strong gravitational pull from worldly things (Roman politics, the Parthians, friendship with the great) that only lyric poetry can lighten.[175] For all his protestations of sameness, "twinned souls", Horace manipulates Maecenas however he requires, to enhance his own identity: he is light to Maecenas's heavy, clear to his cloudy, poor to his rich, free to his troubled. That Horace's most frequent addressees are Lydian Maecenas and a woman called Lydia suggests that the entire collection is written under the influence of an orientalizing muse. Mirroring Horace's own androgynous, luxurious, changeable lyric persona, Maecenas sits wherever Horace needs him, on either side of Sappho's seesaw comparison: as "othered" King of Persia, Lydian cavalryman or seductive, ungraspable love object (Gyges, Telephus).[176] We know him for his neuroses and changeable moods, his wealth, his regal ancestry, and his signature equestrian status (*eques*). But so many of these associations arise from Horace's need to cast him as witness of his lyric ascent: a "bipolar" patron consorted with, then abandoned by a *biformis uates*.

174. Lightened like Pindar the Dircaean swan: *Carm.* 4.2.25: "multa Dircaeum leuat aura cycnum". Horace probably derived the Bellerophon story and its moral from Pind. *Isthm.* 7.44–48; Thomas 2011: 223.

175. *Carm.* 1.2.5–6 ("graue . . . saeculum"); 1.2.22 ("graues Persae"); 2.1.3–4 ("grauisque / principum amicitias"); 2.10.10 ("grauiore casu" [*feriunt*]).

176. At *Carm.* 1.7.9, an echo of *Maecenas eques* can be heard among the legendary cities ripe for epic praise: "aptum dicet equis Argos ditesque Mycenas".

# 5

# Maecenas the Pacemaker

PROPERTIUS'S *ELEGIES*

IN THE MID-TWENTIES BCE, a young poet from Umbria made a bid to break into the "circle" of Maecenas and incorporate the great patron into his poetry. This is how posterity has characterized Propertius: as the immature upstart or outsider, waiting by the door of a potential patron as he bewails his exclusion from his mistress's house. One tradition even has it that Propertius is the brash "Pest" of Horace's *Satires* 1.9, who plans to mount an assault on Maecenas's fortress by bribing his slaves; another that he lies behind the unnamed elegiac poet, the self-appointed Roman Callimachus and Mimnermus, satirized by Horace in *Epistles* 2.2.[1] He is never otherwise mentioned in the poetry of Virgil and Horace, nor in any later portrait of Maecenas's circle. All the work that survives in his name is in elegiac couplets, the metre of love and lament, which in its un-epic alternation between hexameter and pentameter configures the idea of shortfall or unmanly feebleness.[2]

But Propertius, like Catullus before him, is also associated with extreme defiance of authority. In his first poem, he confesses that his enslavement to the dominating Cynthia has swept him far away from the traditional career path of an elite Roman male (war, the *cursus honorum* and worldly success).[3] Bewilderment and humiliation follow, yet the decision to write elegy—an impulse attributed variously to Cynthia, the muses and the gods—is often interpreted as an indirect form of protest; the "Augustan"/"anti-Augustan" debate thunders around Propertius as much as any Roman poet.[4] "Soft" (*mollis*) love is not just

---

1. Butrica 1996: 133–34n101. Text used is Heyworth (2007c), with alternatives from Barber (1960) and Fedeli (2005) noted where used.

2. Wyke 1987; Kennedy 1993; Keith 1999.

3. 1.1.6: "nullo uiuere consilio"; 18: "nec meminit notas, ut prius, ire uias"; 26: "non sani pectoris"; 30: "qua non ulla meum femina norit iter".

4. Stahl 1985, Kennedy 1992.

an abject experience for a young man but also an alternative way of life, which paradoxically involves harsher pains than war. Lounging in his mistress's lap, as he passively observes Augustus's triumphs, the poet is also launching a countercultural assault on old ethical models.[5] For this Roman, losing his way is nothing short of a vocation.

Maecenas is much more than simply a patron figure in Propertius's poetry.[6] He is also an authoritative role model, as the poet explicitly indicates, as well as a mirror for the ambidextrous relationship of elegiac poetry to the (notionally) separate worlds of love and war. In the two poems addressed to him (2.1 and 3.9), Propertius emphasizes Maecenas's links to Augustus and his campaigns: for better or worse, he is presented as his second-in-command, one sign of his devoted service being that he is charged with delivering the usual Augustan request for an epic about the emperor's *res gestae*—a request that is initially, at least, anathema to the poet (and also, it is hinted, to the patron). Yet it is also clear that, thanks to his own decision to remain an equestrian and turn his back on high office, Maecenas straddles both value systems at once. He is a figure through whom the poet can meditate on what appears to be an unbridgeable gap: between the elegiac lifestyle of love and leisure, on the one hand, and involvement at the political centre, at the other.[7] Maecenas, indeed, plays a role not unlike that of the elegiac couplet itself, alternating between major and minor, hard and soft, powerful and weak, giving form to unclassifiable contradictions and ambitions, both in the poet himself and in elegiac poetry.[8]

But what does it mean to speak of Maecenas as Propertius's "patron" anyway? He is not addressed until Book 2 of the elegies, and how we interpret his presence there depends to a large extent on the ground laid in Book 1 and what we want to insert in the interval that elapses before Book 2.[9] Already in the Monobiblos, Propertius puts himself at the centre of a quasi-social network of other male addressees, a network that Maecenas will in due course displace while facing competition from the primary and enduring magnet of the poet's inspiration and the first word of his poetry: his love object and muse, Cynthia. A longstanding assumption is that Propertius transferred his loyalties between Books 1 and 2 from one patron, Umbrian Tullus (nephew of L. Volcacius L. f. Tullus, who had

5. Rosati 2005.

6. On Propertius's Maecenas, see Cairns 2006: 250–319.

7. No surprise that elegy, a self-consciously "alternative" genre, hosts this debate; Rosati 2005: 139. See Gibson (2011) on equestrians and love elegy.

8. Wiggers 1977: 341 (on 2.1): "Propertius remakes Maecenas in his own image"; Wallis 2018: 73 (on 3.9): Maecenas as "an authoritative rationale that explains and justifies the poet's aesthetic choices". Cf. Comber 1998: 47; Gold 1982b. On elegiac patronage, see Gold (2012).

9. See Rothstein 1920: 2.308.

defected from Antony to Octavian, was consul with him in 33 BCE and proconsul of Asia in 28–27 BCE), to Maecenas, Etruscan pillar of the Augustan
regime.[10] That either of them was actually Propertius's patron has recently
been questioned by Stephen Heyworth, in a provocation that is worth taking
seriously.[11] To test it, we must first consider the claims of the rival dedicatee,
Tullus, notional "patron" of Book 1.

As addressee of Propertius's first poem and named in three more, Tullus
seems to qualify well enough for a patron's marked status. At the same time,
he is just one among many Propertian *amici* in a collection which resembles
the interactions of a homosocial coterie, talking to each other over the largely
mute form of the mistress. Like the other males addressed in Book 1 (apart
from Gallus, the poet-lover who is first Propertius's student, then appears to
overtake him as a kind of double), Tullus functions primarily as a foil, serving
to define the poet's life choices as unconventional, if not to say entirely crazed.
For example, as a soldier or delegate travelling to Asia in 1.6 (presumably on
his uncle's staff), he offsets Propertius's devotion to the life of love and leisure.
He also helps him pitch a further, paradoxical opposition: between the seductive
*mollitia* of the East—corollary to Tullus's military or diplomatic exploits—and
the greater harshness of domestic subjection to a tyrannical mistress ("duro
sidere"; 36). In 1.14, the image of Tullus lying by the Tiber and drinking wine
out of antique cups sets the scene for an angry denunciation of wealth. In 1.22,
Tullus is enlisted to enquire about Propertius's origins, just at the point where
the two, as we learn retrospectively, are about to part forever (such questions
about lineage had been, more naturally, the starting point of Horace's adoption
by Maecenas in *Satires* 1.6).

To complicate matters, the two closing poems of Book 1 suddenly disclose
what might in retrospect be seen as its "true" agenda. All the focus on unhappy
love and intense rivalry is displaced by a deeper sorrow, caused by the recent civil
war.[12] In Elegy 21, Gallus the erotic sparring partner (1.5, 10, 13, 20) is transformed
into a soldier slain at Perusia, who appeals to a comrade to identify his bones,
now scattered over the mountains of Etruria. Elegy 22, again addressed to Tullus,
functions as a *sphragis*, or seal, a blazon of mutual friendship in which Propertius
embeds his own name ("PRO nostra semPER amiciTIa"; 2).[13] The poem's final
image of adjacent terrain—Umbria and Etruria ("proxima suppositos contingens

---

10. Cairns 2006: 250–319. DuQuesnay (1992: 78–83) makes the patronage of the Volacii
crucial to Propertius's career.

11. Heyworth 2007b; for the history of the debate, see 102n27. *Contra* Cairns 2006: 250: "It
is thus made abundantly clear that Propertius has entered the new patronage of Maecenas, and
so indirectly of Augustus."

12. Breed 2009, 2010.

13. Heyworth 2007a: 100–101.

Vmbria campos / me genuit terris fertilis uberibus" [Umbria rich in fertile soil
bore me, on the border where it touches the nestled plains]; 9–10)—masks the
probable allegiance of Tullus's family to Antony with the suggestion of a mutually cherishing fraternal or parent–child relationship. In retrospect, it also suggests the poet's shift between two geographically contiguous *amici*, Umbrian
Tullus and Etruscan Maecenas.[14] Political differences notwithstanding, Propertius seems to bury the hatchet, though "tombs of Perusia" (Perusina . . . sepulcra;
1.22.3) starkly identify that massacre as a defining moment.[15]

Despite the frequency and the marked positioning of Tullus's name, which
rivals Cynthia's own as "beginning and end" of the Monobiblos, Heyworth
remains adamant: nothing suggests that Tullus and Propertius were close.
There is, in his words, "No warmth . . . no jocularity . . . no sense of obligation
to do what the patron expects".[16] Tullus is instead "a poetic tool, used to exploit the poetic potential of patronage, rather than a reflection of a real-life
relationship". In 3.22, Tullus returns (along with other elements from the
Monobiblos), and here, instead of praising his Eastern exploits, Propertius
appears to satirize even more harshly the time he spent "enjoying the tourist
spots of Asia". Heyworth sees the relationship as characterized by "distance
and contrast, not intimacy and respect", and concludes contentiously that Tullus is nothing more than a "poetic imitation" of a patron.

If jocularity, intimacy and warmth are textual indicators of authentic patron–
poet relations at this point in Roman literary history, this only shows how Horace's representation of his relationship with Maecenas in the *Satires*, *Epodes* and
*Odes* had become *the* model for a friendship that cuts across social hierarchies
and career differences. In Tullus's favour, 1.6, the poem that satirizes his pursuit
of Eastern fleshpots in the guise of provincial administration, opens with a lavish display of loyalty quite reminiscent of Horace's to Maecenas in *Epodes* 1:

> Non ego nunc Hadriae uereor mare noscere tecum,
> > Tulle, neque Aegaeo ducere uela salo,
> cum quo Rhipaeos possim conscendere montes
> > ulteriusque domos uadere Memnonias.

(1.6.1–4)

I do not fear now to know the Adriatic together with you, Tullus, and hoist
my sails on the Aegean sea. With you I could climb the Rhiphaean mountains and travel beyond the dwellings of the Memnonians.

14. NB: 1.21.4: "pars ego sum uestrae proxima militiae".
15. Suet. *Aug.* 15.1; Stahl 1985: 99–110; DuQuesnay 1992.
16. Heyworth 2007b: 96. Cf. J. Griffin 1994: 57.

Tullus is invoked to sympathize with Propertius over the manipulative erotic demands that keep a lover safely land-bound, as well as witness his polite regret at missing out on the cultural wealth of Athens and material riches of Asia. Again, when Tullus parties by the Tiber, the poet rejects wealth in favour of amorous attachment, concluding:

> quae mihi dum placata aderit, non Lyda uerebor
> regna uel Alcinoi munera despicere.

(1.14.23–24)

As long as she [Cynthia] comes to me appeased, I shall not be afraid to spurn Lydian kingdoms or gifts of Alcinous.

Such a pointed critique of Eastern luxury (which offers no immunity to love) is familiar from Horace's addresses to Maecenas in the *Odes*. There, too, the patron figure was urged to endorse value systems that breached ideological divides, so allowing the presumed basis of the relationship—a crude transfer of wealth from one party to the other—to be confronted and vigorously disavowed.[17] To conclude: there is no way, based on what we know of Horace's textual approaches to Maecenas, to decide retrospectively whether Tullus is just a friend or specifically a patron. In particular, Heyworth's assumption that "distance and contrast" are incompatible with "intimacy and respect" where a patron is concerned is misleading. As we have seen, it tends to be precisely the oscillation between these attributes that identifies a patron.[18] Conversely, the suspicion that Tullus is hierarchically Propertius's equal but spiritually his opposite might incline us to disqualify him. All we can be sure of is that "Maecenas" had become synonymous with "patron" for a literary audience: once named, he would overshadow any rival for that role (save, of course, an emperor).

Poem 2.1

Maecenas enters Propertian elegy in the opening poem of Book 2, displacing Tullus as he had displaced Virgil's bucolic patron Pollio at the start of the *Georgics*—just after the killing fields of Umbria have been brought into uncomfortable focus. Questions about Maecenas's involvement in that campaign hang in the air, and a hostile tone can undoubtedly be drawn out of this poem.[19]

---

17. Heyworth (2007a: 65) defends Markland's conjecture of *Lyda* over *ulla*.

18. See pp. 54–55 above.

19. Heyworth 2007b; *contra* Cairns 2006: 262–63. Colaizzi 1993: 135–36: "Elegiac poetry at this stage of Propertius' career seems like a coiled spring. . . . [I]t threatens at any time to unwind into something stinging and timely."

Among its hostages to fortune, as Propertius points out, is the poetic commission Maecenas is alleged to be handling: an epic on Augustus's military exploits. The poem shares its fictionalized pressure with Horace's *Odes* 2.12; we are primed to expect the *recusatio* that follows, with its accompanying protests of elegiac feebleness.[20] Yet instead of naming honourable *foreign* wars among the discarded subject matter, Propertius wickedly inscribes epic into elegy in the form of an unwelcome list of reminders of the most shameful *civil-war* battles in Maecenas's and Augustus's past: Perusia, Mutina, Sicily . . . This is patronage relations with an edge, such as we have not seen before, even in late Horace.

After questioning Tullus's role in Book 1, Heyworth is equally sceptical whether Propertius's displays of independence in Book 2 are compatible with having anyone, let alone Maecenas, as a patron. It is true that Propertius is never included in Maecenas's cluster of poets, either in Horace's and Virgil's works or in imperial memories of the charmed circle. For Heyworth, stories about Maecenas taking over from Virgil to recite the *Georgics* or remembering Horace in his will confirm that the relationships involved were "engaged and serious". Although he concedes that Virgil mentions Maecenas only in the *Georgics*— and minimally so—his view is that "didactic and epic leave [Virgil] less opportunity than a more personal poet might have for effusive demonstration of his affection; and there is the exquisite patterning of the addresses (1.2, 2.41, 3.41, 4.2), and a thoroughness to the commitment".[21]

Again, much of this is contentious, but it needs to be taken seriously, not just on its own terms, but also to reflect on the responsibility Horace's intense tracking of his relationship with Maecenas bears for conditioning responses to the merest mention of his name in another author's poem. Horace has single-handedly set the standard of what a Roman patron–poet relationship should be and how it should be represented. As Heyworth puts it:

> Horace's poetry addressed to or concerned with Maecenas gives us a picture of a lively, complex and affectionate friendship, in which the personal remembrance of honours paid by the public (*Carm.* 1.21 [*sic*: actually, 1.20]) is set beside teasing (*Carm.* 2.12, 17) and thoughtful examination of their model roles as *patronus* and *cliens* for the education of readers (*Serm.* 1.9, *Epist.* 1.7).[22]

Maecenas does not appear until the seventeenth line of 2.1, where an address to "the Über-patron of Roman culture" comes as something of a surprise.[23] Before then, it is all about the girl (unnamed but assumed to be Cynthia) and

20. See above p. 184 on Hor. *Carm.* 2.12; Wallis 2018: 72.

21. Heyworth 2007b: 102.

22. Heyworth 2007b: 102–3.

23. Heyworth 2007b: 101.

love poetry.[24] Propertius starts by responding to a plural audience, presumably his readers, who are conveniently curious about the origins ("quaeritis . . . unde") of his elegies, marked as aetiological poetry (long before Book 4).[25] These questions displace the requests for information about the poet's own origins in the previous poem: "quaeritis unde" (2.1.1) ~ "qualis et unde . . . / quaeris" (1.22.1–2).[26] Rather than play the shared "Etruscan" card again with a new candidate, Propertius asserts, for now, that his poems originate uniquely from his beloved erotic object, in a kind of inverted parthenogenesis (*ingenium* might be expected to produce a *puella*, but the process is figured as being the other way around):[27]

> Quaeritis unde mihi totiens scribantur amores,
>     unde meus ueniat mollis in ora liber.
> non haec Calliope, non haec mihi cantat Apollo:
>     ingenium nobis ipsa puella facit.
> siue illam Cois fulgentem incedere †cogis†,
>     totum de Coa ueste uolumen erit;
> seu uidi ad frontem sparsos errare capillos,
>     gaudet laudatis ire superba comis;
> siue lyrae carmen digitis percussit eburnis,
>     miramur faciles ut premat arte manus;
> seu cum poscentes somnum declinat ocellos,
>     inuenio causas mille poeta nouas;
> seu nuda erepto mecum luctatur amictu,
>     tum uero longas condimus Iliadas;
> seu quicquid fecit, siue est quodcumque locuta,
>     maxima de nihilo nascitur historia.

> (2.1.1–16)

You ask how I come to write so often about love, and from where my book comes softly on the lips. It is not Calliope, not Apollo, who sings these songs to me. My beloved herself is the source of my inspiration. If you make her glide along, gleaming in Coan silks, this whole volume will be spun of Coan silk; or if I have watched how her hair strays over her brow, she rejoices to

---

24. Breed 2009: 38: "The plot of the Monobiblos is retroactively fixed as a story about love told with the language of war ([45] *uersamus proelia*)".

25. Heyworth 2007a: 104.

26. Heyworth 2007a: 101.

27. At 2.1.5 I print the disputed MS reading *cogis*, obelized by Fedeli (2005).

walk proudly with her hair praised. Or if she has struck out a lyric song with her ivory fingers, I marvel at how easily and artfully she applies her hands. Or if sleep closes her weary eyes, I find a thousand new reasons for my poems; or if she rips off her clothes and wrestles with me naked, then we compose long Iliads; whatever she does and whatever she says, the greatest of narratives is born out of nothing.

As in 1.1, gleaming, gliding Cynthia appears from the start to trump any earthly patron for the role of supreme generator of variegated (*totiens*) Propertian poetry. Yet the list of her attributes and the ways they are given life in the poems indicates that the process is a reciprocal one: *she* inspires *his* powers of creation; *he* creates *her* posterity in return (it is his praise of her hair, for example, that leads her to walk tall in triumph); *together*, they fashion a delicate elegiac book, imagined with silk covers and straying tendrils, one that "comes softly [*mollis* the emphatic word] on the lips".[28] Elegy, the poet stresses, is his destined metier (when he lacks the *praecordia*, "guts" [41], necessary for hard epic, "duro . . . uersu").[29] It is also a self-contained world, one that encompasses encomium, aetiology, epic and history all at once.[30] After this declaration of independence—or rather, of co-dependency with the mistress—we might wonder, not for the first time: what need of a patron anyway?

Maecenas's relatively late entry as addressee has precedents in contemporary Roman poetry (including Propertius's own).[31] But at this point in literary history his name is magnetic enough to suggest that he is the dedicatee not just of this poem but also of the entire book.[32] As often, a rhetorical approach to a great man is a sounding board for a poet's renewed self-definition. Maecenas is entreated first to accept a poetic refusal that pits elegy, eroticism, *otium* and a circle of two against the din of epic, war and empire, then to mediate between poet and emperor. Purposely co-opted from another sphere, he is transformed from supporter of military epic and war veteran to elegiac mourner and witness to the tough erotic suffering of elegy's practitioners. He is an especially soft target,

---

28. Heyworth (2007a: 104) justifies *in ora* (not *ore*), understanding "before the public gaze" or (more likely) "on to people's lips" (cf. 3.1.24: "maius ab exsequiis nomen in ora uenit"). P. A. Miller (2001: 138–39) prefers the sensual feel of "on the lips".

29. An elegiac formula since Tib. 1.1.63–64: "non tua sunt duro praecordia ferro / uincta, nec in tenero stat tibi corde silex" (your innards are not bound with hard iron, nor is your tender heart composed of flint).

30. Zetzel 1982.

31. E.g., Prop. 1.5: Gallus named in the penultimate line 8.

32. Fedeli 2005: 41. Apart from Cynthia, and Lynceus in the final poem, no other individual is addressed in Book 2.

Propertius implies, for conversion, given that he, too, prefers peace to war and could well be touched by the experience of Octavian's massacres at Mutina and Perusia, the seats (as the poet pointedly puts it, later in the poem, and again in 3.9) of Maecenas's Etruscan ancestors. In this respect, Maecenas is every bit the conflicted mediator he is in Horace's and Virgil's poetry.

What is less clear is the role he is being given in the generation of Propertian elegy. Is he the subject of the disputed singular verb *cogis*, a patronal verb if any were, in line 5: "whether *you force* her to walk in Coan robes . . ."? If Maecenas is involved in Cynthia's creation, then the agency is triangular: the written "Cynthia" is styled by patron and poet alike, with the *puella* creating the poet's talent and the poet (through his muse surrogate, *mea Musa*) weaving the patron into his verse (*contexeret*). The worldly patron then acts as conduit for the solitary poet's words, broadcasting his obscure name (*breue nomen*) publicly (*in ora*). But all these assumptions hang on a doubtful manuscript reading.[33] More likely, Maecenas is entirely excluded from the creative process. As in Horace, immortality in return is not explicitly offered; that will come in 3.9, where the patron is promised his own version of the fame shared here between Cynthia and the poet: "uenies tu quoque in ora uirum" (you too will come upon the lips of men; 32).[34] Instead, his role here is ancillary. Straddling both worlds—adjunct to war but associated with peace (as reiterated in 3.9)—he is useful to push against, both as servant to authority and slave to wealth and luxury. He is enlisted to witness the poet's defiance as much as to create a safe environment for poetic production.

If we consider how this poem operates in terms of the "erotics of *amicitia*", Propertius is doing some particularly fluid things with mistress and patron.[35] Even before he officially swims into view and while she still holds sway, Maecenas and Cynthia leak into each other in curious ways. Propertius proclaims, for example, in lines 3–4 that Cynthia's sartorial tastes determine the texture of his book: a silken, diaphanous series of folds or loops that make a winding *uolumen*, just like her sinuous gossamer robes.[36] Although Stahl dismisses the opening catalogue as a provocatively "silly" indicator of Propertius's poetic

33. See Heyworth (2007a: 105) on the crux (he favours Leo's *cerno*); *cogis* recalls Hor. *Sat.* 1.3.4: "Caesar qui cogere posset".

34. Recalling the poet and the Scipios in Ennius's epitaph (Enn. *min.* 46 Courtney; "uolito uiuos per ora uirum").

35. Oliensis 1997.

36. Verg. *Aen.* 2.208: *uolumen* of a snake's folds; cf. *Aen.* 7.350: *uoluere* of a snake creeping through a queen's garments. Heyworth (2007a: 105–6) prefers *totum de Coa* (*hoc/hac* omitted): the roll is both "made of" and "about" Coan cloth.

concerns, Coan silk has been redeemed in recent years as a metapoetic symbol: we see through this see-through tissue ("Cois tibi paene uidere est / ut nudam"; Hor. *Sat.* 1.2.101–2) to Philetas of Cos, elegiac contemporary of Callimachus, and the familiar poetics of fine-spun textiles.[37] Cynthia's preferred clothes are thus compatible with Propertius's preferred aesthetic texture. Housman expostulates: "Imagine Maecenas, or, if you prefer it, the gentle reader . . . insisting that Cynthia should parade in Coan stuffs."[38] Yet this is not so hard to imagine, considering Maecenas's later reputation. The image of the book as the body of the beloved as she goes walking, spun from Coan silk inside and out, may be exactly what sowed the seeds of Seneca's portrait of the effeminate statesman who sauntered through Roman streets in flowing robes (Sen. *Ep.* 114.5: "solutis tunicis") and Velleius's description of the statesman as "overflowing with more than womanly softness" (2.88.2). In other words, the interweaving of patron and mistress here may have had unforeseen biographical consequences: Propertius's scorn for his mistress's silken robes fed later critiques of Maecenas's sartorial tastes.[39]

Set sharply against this portrait of Cynthia, a "walking book" of elegiac poetry, is a rival poetic agenda, one attributed to a hypocritical patron.[40] Despite the poem's "new start" following the Monobiblos, the memory of Perusia lingers. Propertius makes Maecenas's hypothetical rejection of mythological and historical epic, from the Gigantomachy to Marius, in favour of a poem on Augustus's civil war victories first into a barbed compliment, then into a threat:

> bellaque resque tui memorarem Caesaris, et tu
>  Caesare sub magno cura secunda fores.

$$(2.1.25–26)$$

I would record the campaigns and achievements of your friend Caesar, and you would be my second care below great Caesar.

For a moment, the privileged wars in prospect look like Maecenas's own ("bellaque resque tui"), before they are credited to "great Caesar" alone and Maecenas is relegated to an afterthought ("et tu") and a subordinate place. But even secondary, pentameter association with Augustus comes at a cost. Propertius

---

37. Prop. 1.2.2 scorns Cynthia's Coan robes.

38. Housman 1972: 2.581.

39. See Keith (2008: 145–46) on the elegists' lavish catalogues of luxury goods.

40. Colaizzi 1993: 131–32.

cracks open the bandaged wounds of civil war, exposing Maecenas as party to sacrilegious Caesarian bloodshed and traitor to his own people:

> nam quotiens Mutinam aut, ciuilia busta, Philippos
>     aut canerem Siculae classica bella fugae
> euersosque focos <u>antiquae gentis Etruscae</u>

$$(2.1.27-29)$$

For whenever I sing of Mutina, or Philippi, the graveyard of the civil war or the Sicilian naval defeat and the ruined hearths <u>of the ancient Etruscan race</u>.[41]

The promise of privileged inclusion in some grander version of Propertian elegy starts to look like a threat that needs dispelling. Pressure grows on Maecenas to admit that the self-contained narratives of elegy ("maxima de nihilo nascitur historia" [an important story is born out of nothing]; 16) and battles "fought in a narrow bed" (angusto . . . proelia lecto; 45) might be a safer kind of poetry to support. While Propertius proposes that his muse weave ("contexeret"; 35) Maecenas into the poetic texture of those (notorious) battle scenes,[42] the homosocial loyalty ("fidele caput"; 36) normally prized over "fickle girlfriends" (leues . . . puellas [49–50], above all Helen in the *Iliad*, in Cynthia's oddly censorious reading, bracketed by Heyworth) emerges as a risky kind of commitment.[43] If Theseus and Achilles were guarantors of their best friends' eternal fame (37–38), then Maecenas's incorporation into Augustan epic as Octavian's number two may tarnish his record permanently.[44]

But this is not the end of Propertius's edgy manipulation of Maecenas. The blurring of patron and mistress we saw at the start of the poem has logical consequences for its finale, too. Worn down by erotic pain and eventually succumbing to *Liebestod*, Propertius morbidly imagines his funeral cortège issuing from Cynthia's house (56). The lone mourner at his tomb turns out not to be his long-standing beloved but the new acquaintance, Maecenas, to whom Propertius is bound in a reciprocal relationship, just as Maecenas is

---

41. Umbrian Perusia had been one of the twelve confederate cities of Etruria.

42. Fedeli 2005: 71–72.

43. See Keith 2008: 134: Propertius manipulates Cynthia in 2.34 to consolidate his homosocial relations with "Lynceus" (possibly Varius Rufus), Virgil and rival love poets.

44. Another couplet bracketed by Heyworth (2007c). Keith (2008: 132) is more positive: "By describing Maecenas' relations with Augustus as friendship, rather than patronage, Propertius tropes his own relations with Maecenas under this figure."

bound to Augustus. The simple explanation is that male fidelity and compassion have, once again, trumped female instability:[45]

> Maecenas, nostrae spes inuidiosa iuuentae,
>     et uitae et morti gloria iusta meae,
> si te forte meo ducet uia proxima busto,
>     esseda caelatis siste Britanna iugis,
> taliaque illacrimans mutae iace uerba fauillae:
>     "Huic misero fatum dura puella fuit."

$$(2.1.73-78)$$

> Maecenas, hope and envy of our youth, rightful pride of my life and death, if your travels ever take you near my tomb, halt your British chariot with its engraved yokes, and, weeping, lay these words on my silent ashes: "A hard girl was the death of this unhappy man."

Not just a mourner here, Maecenas is also recognizable as the random ("forte") wayfaring addressee of a funerary epigram, hailed away down some byroad from important worldly business to attend to the poet's last rites.[46] This looks like a very Callimachean coup: the patron diverted from mainstream to recherché, from trite to offbeat.[47] That Heyworth finds "inuidiosa" (envied) sarcastic and the rest almost parodically hyperbolic ("vague . . . in what sense is M 'rightful glory for the poet's life and death'?") is a residue of the barbed and bitter tone he detects earlier in the poem and in 1.21–22.[48] We are, indeed, back in the very scenario with which Book 1 ended: an address to the patron in the voice of the (soon to be) dead poet, with Maecenas urged to pay his respects to another casualty, at another kind of civil war burial ("ciuile bustum" ~ "meo . . . busto" [2.1.75]).[49]

To some observers, Maecenas in his chariot is simply a proud warrior diverted from the highroad of epic to observe the poet's last rites in some obscure elegiac cul-de-sac: "The image of Maecenas proclaiming over the speaker's ashes in his chariot of conquest imparts an air of epic grandiosity to

45. Keith 2008: 132–33.

46. On Propertius and the tropes of funerary epigram, see Fedeli (2005: 100).

47. Cf. 3.16.25–26, 30, for burial on a busy road; Houghton 2011: 62–64.

48. Heyworth 2007a: 106–8. Fedeli (2005: 100–101) takes "nostrae" as a virtual *meae*: Propertius refers not to rivals for Maecenas's attention but only to his own aspirations.

49. Cf. Colaizzi 1993: 142. Breed (2009: 38) sees the "plot" of the Monobiblos condensed here, from *Cynthia prima* to epigrammatic epitaph.

the scene of death imagined by the speaker."[50] But an *essedum* is as often a lady's carriage as it is a war vehicle; Cynthia herself favours such a "chick-chariot"
(2.32.5).[51] To be sure, the adjective *Britanna* trails associations with military
conquest, but this Celtic vehicle is positively "gaudy", adorned with an embroidered yoke ("caelatis . . . iugis") recalling the golden chains ("auratis circumdata colla catenis"; 33) that draped conquered kings in a Via Sacra triumph.[52] True, the patron appears to have fallen hard for the soft elegiac mode
(his epitaph is restricted to the distinctively weaker pentameter); true, he
looks like an ideal reader of Propertian elegy, who obligingly supplies a sympathetic answer to the opening question, "unde . . . scribantur amores": it is
*indeed* your cruel mistress who has caused this pain.[53] The proud charioteer
appears to respond to a poet's solipsistic desire for an abject end, while the
elegiac poet wins victory in death—in a reversal of the traditional hierarchy
of poet and patron, or at least a demonstration of noblesse oblige.[54]

But Propertius's imagined victory in death may be yet more resounding.
When the poem has already attuned us to slipperiness in matters of gender as
well as politics, its final stand-off between militantly soft *mollitia* and the conventional pressure to make war and/or write encomiastic epic invites us to
question the identity of the harsh mistress (*dura puella*). Is it really Cynthia
who has finished the poet off? Might it instead be the hypocritical patron, who
persists in barking harsh orders from his girlish vehicle, despite being no war
hero?[55] The pretence of masculine sympathy between poet and patron is
more precarious than it seems. It is not without irony that the epitaph Maecenas so tearfully recites commemorates a "hard girl" responsible for Propertius's
death. At the very moment when the poet seems to be deflecting hostility onto
a female third party, the vulnerable patron ends up condemning himself.

## Poem 3.9

In Book 3, following the model of Horace's *Odes* 3, the poet's self-anointing as
high priest of poetry continues apace.[56] As in the Roman *Odes*, Maecenas is not
addressed in the opening poems, where Propertius's pride swells with increasing

---

50. Greene 2000: 258.

51. P. A. Miller 2001: 137: "not a vehicle of machismo." Cf. Cic. *Att.* 6.1.25, *Phil.* 2.24; Ov. *Am.*
2.16.49–50.

52. Colaizzi 1993: 140. Cf. Sen. fr. 48 Haase; Suet. *Claud.* 16.4.

53. Colaizzi 1993: 140.

54. E.g., Colaizzi 1993: 140: "Maecenas has . . . become an elegiac spokesman."

55. Cf. the ambiguous "cloaked lady-friend" (lacernatae . . . amicae) of Juv. 1.62.

56. Assuming that this is a true third book and Book 2 is not split into two halves.

confidence.[57] In 3.1, he crowns himself a Callimachean *uates* in a ceremony where the patron's place is taken by the muses; in 3.3 he takes his anti-epic orders from a god, Apollo, whose divine instructions contradict and supersede those of any earthly benefactor. When Maecenas finally glides in, in 3.9, after yet another dogfight with Cynthia in 3.8, something of the poet's apotheosis rubs off onto him: he is addressed in quasi-divine terms.[58] In other ways, Propertius continues to push at the patron's ambiguous loyalties. Aligned with Augustan imperialism, but also marked by his signature rejection of worldly glory, Maecenas is again challenged to practise what he preaches. If he leads the way in writing the kind of epic he appears to be demanding, or alternatively, in leading armies or assuming high office, Propertius will automatically follow. As one who succeeded in achieving power while appearing to be modest, Maecenas is enlisted as an apt model for Propertian poetry, slim and small-scale, but mighty nonetheless:

> at tua, Maecenas, uitae praecepta recepi,
> cogor et exemplis te superare tuis.

$$(3.9.21–22)$$

But I have learned your advice for living, and am constrained to surpass you by your own example.

Heyworth, again, is sceptical whether this poem gives any better evidence of a genuine relationship between the two men: "The two poems that mention Maecenas do so only to refuse what he is presented as requesting: Augustan epic."[59] Yet refusal may be the very opposite of a negative indicator. As Jonathan Wallis has argued, Propertius is using the *recusatio* form here because it had already been "canonized" in connection with Maecenas's name—not just in *Georgics* 2 and 3, but also in Horace's *Odes* 2.12, a poem with which Propertius especially engages.[60] There, Maecenas was teased for conveying Augustus's request for a historical epic and challenged to write it himself, in narrative prose (inimical to his neoteric tastes), thus co-opted to the poet's aesthetic viewpoint.[61] Yet, however "copycat" the *recusatio*, Propertius adapts it by promoting

---

57. See Wallis 2018: Propertius imitates Horace's addresses to Maecenas in the middles of books: *Carm.* 1.20, 2.12, 3.16.

58. Bennett 1967.

59. Heyworth and Morwood 2011: 183. Cf. Heyworth 2007b: 105: "A relationship that consists only of refusals can hardly be characterized as *amicitia* or patronage." *Contra*: Cairns 2006: 260–69; Stahl 1985: 162–71.

60. Wallis 2008, 2018: 69–72.

61. See above p. 100, and Wallis 2018: 72.

an elegiac (not lyric or didactic) alternative to epic. He also takes it in a new direction by meditating on the topic of models in general (anticipated in 2.1's *spes inuidiosa*): artists' models, artists as models, exemplarity and imitation. The tussle with the patron conceals a simultaneous attempt to compete with Horace and Virgil, whom Propertius emulates to situate elegy among the other refusenik genres and claim to be its representative.

The early appearance of Maecenas's name appropriates what is by now a Horatian model—the first-line address—while the reuse of the priamel form recalls *Satires* 1.1.1 and *Odes* 1.1.[62] Too sensitive to mention in 2.1, Maecenas's Etruscan ancestry is back on parade: "Etrusco de sanguine regum" (from the blood of Etruscan kings [lit. from the Etruscan blood of kings]; 1—varying Hor. *Carm.* 3.29.1: "Tyrrhena regum progenies")—where *sanguine* suggests "bloodshed" as well as "bloodline". The elegiac pentameter shows Maecenas choosing to undercut his status ("intra fortunam qui cupis esse tuam" [who prefer to stay within your rank]; 2). He is a compatriot and fellow equestrian, distanced by his lineage and his role in the Augustan regime. This combination of likeness and difference will be crucial to the poem's dynamics. On the one hand, Maecenas is co-opted as a sympathizer with self-limiting, modest poetry. On the other, he remains a foil and unreachable model for the poet, spurring him on to greater things.

Elegiacs suit these contradictions well, with aspirational hexameter and straitened pentameter framing Maecenas's antithetical aspects:

> Maecenas, eques Etrusco de sanguine regum,
>    intra fortunam qui cupis esse tuam

$$(3.9.1-2)$$

> Maecenas, knight born from the blood of Etruscan kings, you who prefer to stay within your rank.

Another uneven couplet pits the grandiose demands of the patron against Propertius's own shrinking reluctance:

> quid me scribendi tam uastum mittis in aequor?
>    non sunt apta meae grandia uela rati.

$$(3.9.3-4)$$

> Why do you send me into such a vast ocean of writing? Huge sails do not fit my (small) boat.

---

62. Gold 1982b: 112–13.

Later, it is Maecenas who appears in the secondary role, his fame derived from loyalty to his overlord Caesar:[63]

> Caesaris et famae uestigia iuncta tenebis:
>    Maecenatis erunt uera tropaea fides.

(3.9.33–34)

> You will follow in the footsteps of Caesar's fame: Maecenas's loyalty will be his true memorial.

The undulating form of the elegiac couplet registers an uneasy equilibrium between aesthetic difference and generous coexistence.

At the same time, Propertius's appeal to Maecenas reads as a bid for inclusion in a precise literary "moment", as represented by the cluster of poets already associated with him. As the priamel gains momentum, the poet intervenes in a long tradition of *synkrisis*, competitive comparison, among the great painters and sculptors of fifth- and fourth-century BCE Greece.[64] By implication, a further *synkrisis* is being made between those artists and the Augustan poets, so parading a similar high point in artistic history and enabling an elegiac poet to claim a modest but integral place in the contemporary pantheon.[65] Little attention has been given to these lists, except to note the frequent but not entirely consistent fit between hexameters and grandiose aspiration and pentameters and small-scale finesse.[66] Thus Lysippus, personal sculptor to Alexander the Great, who is said to have derived glory from naturalistic sculptures (like the Zeus of Tarentum and possibly the archetype of the giant "Farnese" Hercules), occupies a hexameter, while Calamis's prowess, limited to equestrian sculpture, is reserved for the pentameter:

> gloria Lysippo est animosa effingere signa;
>    exactis Calamis se mihi iactat equis.

(3.9.9–10)

> Lysippus's glory lies in fashioning lifelike statues; Calamis's specialty is making horses.

---

63. Cf. 2.1.25–26 above.

64. First classified by the Pergamenes but embryonic already in Homer. See Feeney (2002a: 8–9) on the *synkrisis* mentality as fundamental to Roman culture; see further Vardi 1996.

65. Keith (2008: 134–35) sees him appealing to Maecenas's interests as a collector.

66. E.g., Heyworth and Morwood 2011: 185.

Apelles, similarly, demanded the highest crown for his Coan Aphrodite (hexameter), while Parrhasius claimed a modest place for himself by virtue of his miniature or domestic art (pentameter):[67]

> in Veneris tabula summam sibi poscit Apelles;
>   Parrhasius parua uindicat arte locum

$$(3.9.11-12)$$

Apelles demands the prize for his painting of Venus; Parrhasius claims a place through his small-scale art.

Another couplet pits the grand narrative plots of Mentor against the delicate marginal tendrils of Mys ("Mouse"):[68]

> argumenta magis sunt Mentoris addita formae;
>   at Myos exiguum flectit acanthus iter.

$$(3.9.13-14)$$

Narrative scenes were often added to Mentor's mould, while Mys's acanthus winds its tiny path.

It might seem natural for Propertius the elegist to identify with the humbler artists in the pentameters. But the distinction between hexameter and pentameter does not always apply.[69] Lysippus and Calamis, for example, both produced finished works ("effingere" ~ "exactis") and lifelike ("animosa") sculptures.[70] Propertius is as much the poet of Venus as he is a small-scale artist. In a poem where he ends up promising Maecenas the earth, his affinity may be as much with ambitious artists as it is with humble ones.

Such a catholic approach to talent would be typical of the *synkrisis* tradition in general. In *Brutus*, Cicero had plotted the steady progress of Greek sculpture towards a naturalistic ideal, offering generous concessions along the way:[71]

---

67. Cf. Plin. *HN* 35.36.67. I interpret *summam* as "top prize", not "supreme woman", and prefer Barber's *poscit* to Heyworth's *ponit*. I also prefer the MS *locum* to Heyworth's favoured *iocum*, the point being that Parrhasius finds a "place" in the pantheon despite being a "small" artist.

68. Acanthus shoots are associated with Corinthian (girlish and graceful) columns at Vitr. 4.1.8–10.

69. *Contra* Bennett 1967: Propertius's point is that only those who play to their strengths become immortal; Maecenas has misassigned epic poetry to an elegiac poet.

70. Heyworth 2007a: 319–20.

71. Strabo 8.372 and Quint. 12.10.7 are similarly even-handed.

Quis enim eorum qui haec minora animaduertunt non intellegit Canachi signa rigidiora esse quam ut imitentur ueritatem; Calamidis dura illa quidem, sed tamen molliora quam Canachi; nondum Myronis satis ad ueritatem ad-ducta, iam tamen quae non dubites pulchra dicere; pulchriora etiam Polycliti et iam plane perfecta, ut mihi quidem uideri solent? (Cic. *Brut.* 18.70)

What critic who attends to the minor arts does not recognize that Cana-chus's statues are too stiff to be naturalistic; that Calamis's, too, are rigid, but suppler than Canachus's; that Myron's are not so naturalistic, though one would not hesitate to call them beautiful; and that Polyclitus's are even more beautiful, and indeed to my mind quite perfect?

Behind Propertius's reminiscences of *synkrisis* in the plastic arts lie further layers of comparison: parallels and equivalences between canons of artists and sculptors and canons of orators and poets, and between Greeks and Romans in their various spheres.[72] Dionysius of Halicarnassus, for example, pronounces the speeches of Isocrates, dignified, grand and sublime, equivalent to the art of Polyclitus and Phidias, and those of Lysias, delicate and graceful, equal to those of Calamis and Callimachus.[73] Quintilian (10.1.85) calls Virgil "the Roman Homer" and Sallust "the Roman Thucydides" (10.1.101).[74] By two syncritical removes, then, Propertius's list of Greek artists invites com-parisons with contemporary Roman poets. To make his contrasts easily transferable to the literary sphere, he contrasts majestic, politically impor-tant, large-scale representations of gods and humans with humble, small-scale depictions of animals, flowers and everyday life. To read "Propertius" into both halves of each couplet is to recognize the paradoxical coexistence of important plots (*maxima historia*) and Callimachean delicacy in his elegies.

Sure enough, Propertius glides from artists' personal preoccupations to their involvement in civic life, claiming a politically ambitious, almost Pindaric role even for secondary figures. Thus, while Phidias was celebrated for his Olympian Zeus, Praxiteles's signature marble was the pride of his city, Athens, and equally illustrious; the running races of Olympia offered prizes (*palma*) and public renown (*gloria*), no less than grander chariot races (15–18). Prop-ertius's catalogue also has strikingly little regard for chronology.[75] Mixing

---

72. Hinds (1998: 64–69) points to the interestedness of these comparisons.

73. Dion. Hal. *Isoc.* 3.542.

74. On Horace's disdain in *Epist.* 2.1.50–62 for knee-jerk comparisons (i.e., the Varronian tradition), see Feeney (2002a) and Brink (1982: 83–91).

75. Greek "antiquity" becomes a conglomerate, with style rather than temporality the motor of change.

fifth-century BCE democratic Athens and fourth-century BCE autocratic Macedon has interesting consequences for his concept of the Augustan Age and its relationship to art. In particular, one might ask why he starts with a latecomer in the historical scheme: Lysippus, whose relationship with his ruler, Alexander, has been seen as "a major turning-point in the history of western art",[76] and who was known for his lifelike and unashamedly heroic sculptures.[77] Hellenistic epigrammatists, including Posidippus, had used him as an analogue for their status as poetic innovators.[78] Above all, mobility was the shared characteristic:[79]

> Opting decisively for mobility Lysippos has beaten Polykleitos at his own game, just as the handsome, ever watchful, ever-active Alexander saw himself as surpassing Achilles. Such genre-mixing is characteristic of Lysippos, suggesting that his subjects transcend the clear-cut categories of the classic; with Alexander in particular, traditional modes of behaviour, and thus of mimesis, are now obsolete, as are traditional notions of function. He is now the new ideal, a hero on earth and an exemplar to follow, even (eventually) to worship.[80]

It should be clear why such a comparison works in Propertius's favour. Later in *Brutus*, Cicero adds a postscript to his catalogue of sculptor–orator comparisons: Atticus will vicariously anoint none other than Cicero as the Roman Lysippus to Crassus's Polyclitus. Propertius's agenda may be similar. As plotted in *Brutus*, sculpture progressed from hard to soft, rigid to lifelike: "rigidiora . . . dura . . . sed tamen molliora . . . pulchra . . . pulchriora . . . perfecta".[81] By this measure, "soft", flexible elegy might also claim to be the acme of artistic evolution. When Horace laid out his new Roman canon in *Satires* 1.10, silently reserving slots in iambic, lyric and epistle for an as yet undesignated occupant, his scheme also left elegy conveniently vacant. Propertius appears to be staking his claim to this slot, along with a place in the canon.[82]

76. Beard and Henderson 2001: 226, citing Plin. *HN* 34.63.

77. Plin. *HN* 34.65; Plut. *Mor.* 335A–B, 360D; A. Stewart 1990: 1.186–91.

78. See, e.g., AB 62.4–6, with Gutzwiller 2002 and A. Stewart 2005: 185–88.

79. Cf. A. Stewart 1990: 1.188: "comprehensive but flexible".

80. A. Stewart 1990: 1.189.

81. A typical art-historical narrative: A. Stewart 2005: 186; cf. Quint. 12.10.9, Luc. *Rhetorum Praeceptor* 9; Pollitt 1974: 82–83.

82. Cairns (2006: 255) puts the cart before the horse: "Presumably [Maecenas] can be credited with Propertius' gradual move away from purely personal erotic elegy to elegies embracing moral, social, and political themes."

Priamel and *recusatio* intertwine in the final element of the list. Propertius seems to imply that he is innately unsuited to war, and, by implication, to its portrayal in epic:[83]

> hic satus ad pacem, hic castrensibus utilis armis:
>     naturae sequitur semina quisque suae.

(3.9.19–20)

One man is born for peace, another is designed for military campaigning. Each man follows the talents implanted in him at birth.

It is at this point, not surprisingly, that Maecenas returns, as climax of the catalogue:

> at tua, Maecenas, uitae praecepta recepi,
>     cogor et exemplis te superare tuis.

(3.9.21–22)

But I have followed your template for living, Maecenas, and I am forced to surpass you by your own example.

As the single most compelling example of the principle being promoted ("solitary, select, and indigenous"), he supplants everyone.[84] Not just outstanding in one field, he embraces stark opposites in one person, excelling in peace and, less plausibly, war, so prominent and yet so modest that any attempt to surpass him will logically result in further expansion and further contraction. While Propertius goes on to note Maecenas's receipt of unstinting largesse ("et omni / tempore tam faciles insinuentur opes" [and at all times let wealth flow so easily into your purse]; 3.9.27–28), in the next breath he characterizes him as constricted and self-effacing:

> parcis et in tenues humilem te colligis umbras;
>     uelorum <u>plenos subtrahis</u> ipse <u>sinus</u>.

(3.9.29–30)

You hold back and crouch low in the flimsy shadows. You yourself <u>draw in the full billow</u> of your sails.

---

83. Bennett (1968: 319) notes the emphasis on innateness: *semina, nata, satus*.

84. Bennett 1967: 231. Heyworth (2007a) transposes the couplet to after 34 (on the grounds that this gives a clear progression from the artists' fame in 9–16 to Maecenas's fame in 23–34).

Cynthia's robes, symbol of delicate and fluid poetry (1.2.2: "tenues Coa ueste mouere sinus"), have become the billowing sails and gaping purses of poetic and political mobility, opening and shutting by turns.[85] Maecenas's life choices offer Propertius a supremely flexible template, contradictory in a way that is essential to this poet's self-definition.[86]

Propertius's choice of metaphors here recalls another moment of indecision witnessed by Maecenas.[87] Caught midcourse in his didactic enterprise in *Georgics* 2, Virgil had debated whether to sail further into the deep or hug the shore (40–41, 44–45), a dilemma between comprehensiveness and selectivity. Propertius redirects this to reflect on a hypocrite who has apparently commissioned a grand epic but opted out of grandeur himself. Why send an inadequate poet onto the high seas, against the commands of Apollo in 3.3, as well as against his own lived example? Just as Maecenas is content to live in the shadow of Caesar (memorialized for his loyalty, above all: "Maecenatis erunt uera tropaea fides"; 34), so Propertius is justified in sticking to an inland stream ("exiguo flumine"; 36) rather than launching into the swollen sea of epic ("tumidum mare"; 35).

So far, so conventional. But a catalogue of rejected epic topics (the usual Thebaids and Iliads) is followed by a sudden volte-face. Enlisting Maecenas as quasi-god, guide, leader or muse ("te duce"; 47), Propertius promises to launch into even more ambitious waters—gigantomachy and the history of Rome, from Romulus and Remus to the triumphs of Caesar and suicide of Antony (47–56)—all the more disconcerting when these alternatives had been lumped together, and rejected, along with mythical epic themes, in 2.1 (19–24).[88] No amount of textual manipulation can explain away this "fundamental change of tack".[89] And no face-saving return to a smaller orbit follows. The poet is irrevocably launched on higher themes, with the patron on board.[90]

Perhaps we should accept Propertius's stated intentions at face value, recalling as they do Virgil's abrupt changes of tack in *Georgics* 2. There, Maecenas

---

85. Butrica 1996: 143. Seneca takes up the sailing image to describe Maecenas's own style (*Ep.* 19.9).

86. See Wallis (2008: 88) on Maecenas as a thematically complicated figure like Propertius.

87. Another nautical image at 3.3.21–24 recommends compromise: "Let one oar cleave the ocean, the other the shore"; cf. 3.3.15, 3.9.3–43; see Heyworth and Morwood 2011, *ad loc*; Bennett 1968.

88. For Bennett (1968), *te duce* recalls kletic hymn; for Wallis (2018: 67–68), Lucretius's Calliope (6.94–95).

89. Heyworth and Morwood 2011: 193. Heyworth (2007a: 326–27) replaces the *hoc* of 59 with *nunc*, "as things stand": Propertius puts forward this condition (if Maecenas changes his way of life, then Propertius will aim correspondingly higher) only because he knows it is an impossible one.

90. Wallis 2008: 91–92.

was credited with the flexibility to bless any kind of poetic decision; Propertius now appropriates that blessing for his own work. Logically speaking, if Maecenas is constructed as an infinitely variable figure, one who is enlisted to endorse changes of poetic direction, Propertius *must* be open in the future to undertaking more ambitious poetry and extending his "elegiac horizons". As Umbria nourished his childhood (1.22.10), as Virgil grew to engender a poem "bigger than the *Iliad*" (2.34.66) and as the Roman twins were nourished by the she-wolf, so this poet's talents and scope will expand organically when fostered by Maecenas's "commissions":

> eductosque pares <u>siluestri ex ubere</u> reges,
>     <u>crescet</u> et ingenium <u>sub tua iussa</u> meum.

(3.9.51–52)

[I will sing of] the twin kings reared <u>on a woodland teat</u>, and may my talent <u>grow under your direction</u>.

In short, the thematic disparity in 3.9 between beginning and end accurately reflects the wider plot of this "intermediate" book, which returns to amatory themes and small-scale poetry, then bids a notional farewell to erotic elegy (3.24–25).[91] In such a context, the figure of Maecenas marks a turning point. A "proem in the middle", 3.9 appoints him to succeed Cynthia as developer of the poet's *ingenium*.[92]

The poem ends by taking up the racing imagery that marked the opening priamel with Pindaric resonances (8–10, 17–18), "restoring" Maecenas the *eques* to his original function:[93]

> mollia tu coeptae fautor cape lora iuuentae,
>     dexteraque immissis da mihi signa rotis.
> nunc mihi, Maecenas, laudes concedis, et a te est
>     quod ferar in partes ipse fuisse tuas.

(3.9.57–60)

As my supporter, take up soft reins to guide my youthful career, and grant me propitious signs when my wheels have hit the road. Now, Maecenas, you grant me praise, and it is thanks to you that I will be said to have been on your team.

---

91. Wallis 2008: 90.

92. Keith 2008: 136. Ov., *Pont.* 4.1.29–36 adapts Propertius's *synkrisis*, culminating with a portrait of himself as Sextus Pompeius's masterpiece (35–36).

93. I print the lines in their traditional order, with *nunc* instead of Heyworth's *hoc* (Heyworth 2007c transposes lines 57–58 to between 46 and 47).

The reins lodged here with Maecenas, as in the tomb scene in 2.1, may be "soft" (mollia), but the poet's career is already galloping into the future.[94] Where is he going? Heyworth has argued that Propertius deploys Maecenas's unconventional career choices to justify immobility in his elegiac vocation: "The programmatic poems . . . provide an assertion of stasis, not a route map for a career."[95] Yet the chariot here is so evidently in motion (*immissis rotis*), spurred on by its adopted driver, almost a metaphorical version of the sculpted chariot groups of the poem's opening; just so, an earlier image of the poet, knees buckling under the great burden placed on his head (5–6), suggests Lysippus's Farnese Hercules.[96] In a sculptural context, Cicero's *Brutus* tells us, *mollis* means "flexible" or "lithe" as much as "feeble" or "soft". Propertius credits Maecenas not just with providing the prototype for his own stylistic decisions and directing his future course but also with being a discriminating connoisseur who apportions praise across different literary spheres ("hoc mihi . . . laudes concedis" [this share of praise you grant me]; 59) and spurs his protégés on to more ambitious performances. But where posterity is concerned, the elegist appears to claim only a modest place as a team player—wisely, perhaps, given that Lysippus's and Apelles's poetic equivalent at Alexander's court was Choerilus, a notorious sycophant.[97]

In the event, however, no independent memory survives of Propertius's adoption by Maecenas. Nor does he even fare well in posthumous *synkrises* among the Latin elegists. Velleius (2.36.3), for example, canonizes Tibullus and Ovid but omits Propertius. Quintilian grudgingly allows him a few supporters:

> elegia quoque Graecos prouocamus, cuius mihi tersus atque elegans maxime uidetur auctor Tibullus. sunt qui Propertium malint. Ouidius utroque lasciuior, sicut durior Gallus. (Quint. 10.1.93)

> We give the Greeks a run for their money in elegy, where to my mind Tibullus seems the neatest and most elegant author. Some people prefer Propertius. Ovid is more playful than either, just as Gallus is tougher.

Reflecting on Propertius's interaction with Horace, Virgil and Varius, Butrica concludes that it would best be described as "an amicable and creative

---

94. Latent confusions of *curriculum*, "course of action", "race track", "chariot", are in play. Comber (1998: 47) notes that the eques is the controlling image of the poem.

95. Heyworth 2010: 99.

96. The Farnese (or "Weary") Hercules, holding up the earth for Atlas, is thought to be based on a Lysippan original. Lysippus's chariot groups were relocated to Rome; Vell. Pat. 1.11.3–4.

97. Cf. Hor. *Epist.* 2.1.232–44: Alexander had no poets to match Lysippus and Apelles; Virgil and Varius are marked out (245–50) as the paid artists of Horace's own era.

*aemulatio*; as Virgil aspired to be the Roman Theocritus, Hesiod, and Homer, as Horace aspired to be the Roman Alcaeus, so Propertius would become the Roman Callimachus".[98] But just how amicable and creative was it? Virgil never mentions the younger poet; Horace, it seems, satirically dismisses his claims along with all neat Greco-Roman *synkrises*.[99] Propertius, meanwhile, lower down in the hierarchy, engages with both respectfully, on the surface. He takes pains to emulate Virgil's pre-epic procrastination.[100] He pays lip service to Horace's humble assessment of his place in Maecenas's house (*Sat.* 1.9.52): "Everyone has his place."[101] Like the Greek artist Parrhasius, all that Propertius appears to be claiming is a niche based on supremacy in a minor sphere (cf. "parua uindicat arte locum" [claims a place through his small-scale art]; 3.9.12). Yet he cannot but set his sights on future grandeur.

## Bacchus and Vertumnus

To cast Maecenas as *dux* and *fautor* in the *recusatio* poems is almost to grant him the status of a beneficent god.[102] Conversely, two poems that focus on gods endow them with the role of patrons. Propertius's first experiment in hymnic mode, 3.17 (a specimen of the very generic elasticity Maecenas was called on to license), is addressed to Bacchus. There is clear water between this poem and the Apolline *recusatio* of 3.3: no rational orders, this time, but drift—suction, even—towards the god of irrational inspiration ("aduoluimur"; 3.17.1).[103] Propertius incorporates many conventional features of Bacchic hymns, but John F. Miller argues for the poem's engagement with Horace's two Bacchus odes in particular, a relationship he regards as "fundamentally agonistic".[104] Horace had set a precedent for treating the god as an irresistible incentive to stray towards wilder or sublime poetic themes, and Propertius undeniably echoes the end of *Odes* 3.25 ("nil paruum aut humili modo, / nil mortale loquor" [I speak of nothing small, or in humble mode, or mortal]; 16–17) in his "haec ego non humili referam memoranda coturno,/ qualis Pindarico spiritus ore tonat" (I report these things that should not be

98. Butrica 1996: 133–34.

99. Horace parades his friendship with two other elegists, C. Valgius Rufus (*Carm.* 2.9) and Albius Tibullus (*Carm.* 1.33 and *Epist.* 1.4).

100. Bennett 1968. Cf. Wallis 2008: 96.

101. If the Lynceus addressed in 2.34 is Varius Rufus, as Boucher (1958) argued, then Propertius is hustling a rival friend of Maecenas away from elegiac territory.

102. Bennett 1968.

103. See now Wallis (2018: 131–63, esp. 155–56) on the poet's suspended loyalties.

104. J. Miller 1991: 80.

recalled in a low buskin, the kind of breath that thunders in a Pindaric mouth; 3.17.39–40).

So striking is this departure from the Callimachean norm that Miller concludes that the poem is actually humorous.[105] But that is to discount the negotiations of 3.9 and Propertius's promise there to expand his "elegiac horizons"—not to mention his ongoing transformation in this very poem from humble suppliant ("humiles"; 1) to arrogant Pindaric mouthpiece ("non humili"; 39).[106] For Horace, Bacchus had been a launching pad, first (in *Carm.* 2.19) for his metamorphosis into a swan in *Odes* 2.20, then for tackling the dangerously unimaginable topic of Caesar's praise, in *Odes* 3.25: "egregii Caesaris . . . / aeternum meditans decus / stellis inserere et consilio Iouis" (studying to set the eternal glory of outstanding Caesar among the stars and the council of Jupiter; 4–6).[107] Yet, as Miller points out, Propertius's *laudandus* here is "only" the god himself, which suggests that, although he has now explicitly praised Maecenas, he is still not ready to praise Caesar.[108] In his view, the elegiac poet is equally preoccupied with echoing a consciously "delicate" forebear, Tibullus, alluding (in his final prayer) to the rustic lover's call for soporific wine at 3.17.42: "atque hoc sollicitum uince sopore caput" (and wrap this anxious head in sleep).[109]

For all the competitive sparring with a poetic contemporary, some equally important intertexts are in play. Shortly before Virgil called on Maecenas to witness his poetic indecision in *Georgics* 2, he had called on Bacchus, god of many levels, to bless his book of trees (2.1–9). The parallel addresses, we saw, suggested a special sympathy between the mediating poetics of god and patron—a sympathy later exploited by the poet of the *Elegiae in Maecenatem*, who uses Liber to vindicate Maecenas. Propertius is as attentive a reader of Virgil's Bacchus as he is as of his Maecenas. When he decrees, "if only my vats froth with purple must and the new grapes stain the feet that press them" (dum modo purpureo spument mihi dolia musto / et noua pressantes inquinet uua

---

105. Cf. 2.1.39–40: "sed neque Phlegraeos Iouis Enceladique tumultus / intonat angusto pectore Callimachus". Apollo's Callimachean prohibitions in 3.3 will be reiterated by Horus, if not heeded by the poet, in 4.1.

106. J. Miller 1991: 79n. 10: in Book 3, Propertius is already "flirting with Augustan or national themes".

107. See Schiesaro (2009) on Horace's Bacchic poetics.

108. J. Miller 1991: 79–80.

109. Cf. Tib. 1.2.1–2: "adde merum uinoque nouos compesce dolores, / occupet ut fessi lumina uicta sopor" (Bring more neat wine and soothe unfamiliar sorrows with the grape, so that sleep steals over my weary eyes.) J. Miller (1991: 81–83n23) points to Propertius's use of *compescere* in the same line position at 3.17.3.

pedes; 3.17.17–18), he is clarifying the mystery of Virgil's Bacchic hymn, where the grape treaders rip off their purple boots only to replace them with wine-stained shins (G. 2.7–8).[110] Down on the farm, there was no need to shed the metaphorical buskins of high style, as Propertius's "non humili coturno" (39) makes explicit.

What is more, the dialogue with Tibullus extends well beyond that second elegy. Bacchus is not only prominent but even elided with the patron in Tibullus's birthday celebration for Messalla (1.7), as he returns triumphantly from Aquitaine in 27 BCE. Lowell Bowditch has drawn out the ways in which Tibullus aligns a hyper-masculine Roman general with orientalized wine gods Bacchus and Osiris, so assimilating him to the effeminate frame of elegy: the builder of a hard gravel road, the Via Latina ("glarea dura"; 59), is draped with soft garlands ("mollia . . . serta"; 52).[111] By contrast, the perfumed, long-robed, mitra-clad Bacchus of Propertius 3.17 (29–32) is no enemy to grandiose poetry: he will stretch Propertius's powers of song to Pindaric stature and urge him to produce the very songs he had promised Maecenas in 3.9. Meanwhile, the poet vows to be hailed as "a poet who sang of Bacchus's worth" (uirtutisque tuae, Bacche, poeta ferar; 20), just as he had hoped for eternal alignment with his patron's values: "et a te est / quod ferar in partes ipse fuisse tuas" (and it is thanks to you that I will be said to have been on your team; 3.9.59–60).

But this is not the final bow of Maecenas, or of the poetics identified with his name. I end with a riskier experiment in reading "Maecenas" into Augustan literature, in a book where he is never even mentioned.[112] Propertius's fourth book, published around 17 BCE, largely delivers on his earlier promise to extend elegy beyond the purely personal or erotic. The ancient origins of Augustan Rome are excavated in a modern reconstruction of Callimachus's *Aetia*, with overt Augustan panegyric on the agenda (4.6, 4.10, 4.11), for all that the poet never addresses Augustus directly. Yet the confused programmatic pointers of 4.1 (where the astrologer Horus appears to counter the poet's poetic ambitions by relaying the usual advice from Apollo) leave us in limbo.[113] Nor is there any real farewell to gender or generic experimentation: themes from Rome's

110. Gowers 2016b; Bowditch 2011: 118. See pp. 123–24 above.

111. Prop. 3.1.19–20 pits the "soft garlands" (mollia . . . serta) of Callimachus against the "hard crown" (dura corona) of the *triumphator*; Bowditch 2011: 114n57. Messalla and wine: Gaisser 1971: 228.

112. Cairns (2006: 279) suggests that he actively supplied Propertius with Etruscan material.

113. See Lowrie (2011) on Horus as orientalized "enemy within", in whose "alienating voice with Eastern overtones" Propertius expresses his relationship to imperial power; cf. Lee-Stecum 2006.

legendary past include the transvestite Hercules of 4.9 and the lovestruck Vestal Tarpeia caught in the firing line in 4.4. Repressed eros returns in 4.7 and 4.8 in the shape of a resurgent Cynthia. The former poem may even leave a trace of Maecenas. When she returns from the grave to berate her faithless lover, Cynthia's clothes are burned by the funeral pyre, her skin is worn away and she wears just one jewel, a flame-tarnished beryl:

> eosdem habuit secum quibus est elata capillos,
>     eosdem oculos; lateri uestis adusta fuit,
> et solitum digito beryllon adederat ignis,
>     summaque Lethaeus triuerat ora liquor.

(4.7.7–10)

She wore her hair as at her burial, her eyes, too: her dress was burned to her body and the fire had eaten at the usual beryl on her finger. The water of Lethe had worn down the surface of her face.

Coincidence or not, this is also the signature jewel that glints at the centre of Maecenas's gem collection, as imagined by his posthumous admirers.[114] If Propertius is haunted by past allegiances to both *puella* and patron, the beryl is the silent token that knits the pair together.

Among Book 4's antiquarian subjects is a speaking statue of Vertumnus, Etruscan god of the changing seasons.[115] Once a wooden statue, now cased in bronze, he relates how he became a fixture in the Vicus Tuscus and thus an imported oddity at the heart of Rome. He boasts of his name's disputed etymology (9–12: *uertere* plus *amnis* or *uertere* plus *annus?*) and his manifold powers of transformation—into woman, man, horseman, fisherman, harvester, gardener, Bacchus with a *mitra*, Apollo with a lyre:

> Qui mirare meas tot in uno corpore formas,
>     accipe Vertumni signa paterna dei.
> Tuscus ego, et Tuscis orior, nec paenitet inter
>     proelia Volsinios deseruisse focos.
>
> . . .

---

114. 3L = 2C = 185H = Isid. *Etym.* 19.32.6 ("beryllos . . . nitentes"); *Eleg. in Maec.* 1.19 ("uincit beryllus [MSS beritus] harenas"); Augustus *ap.* Macrob. *Sat.* 2.4.12 ("berylle Porsennae"). See pp. 327–28 below.

115. Varro *Ling.* 5.46. See Hutchinson (2006: 87–88) on speaking statues in inscriptions, epigrams and Callimachus's *Aetia*; he notes the suggestiveness of the metre: "medium and mobility interact".

opportuna mea est cunctis natura figuris:
  in quamcumque uoles uerte, decorus ero.
indue me Cois: fiam non dura puella;
  meque uirum sumpta quis neget esse toga?
da falcem et torto frontem mihi comprime faeno:
  iurabis nostra gramina secta manu.
arma tuli quondam et, memini, laudabar in illis.
  corbis in imposito pondere messor eram.
sobrius ad lites; at cum est imposta corona,
  clamabis capiti uina subisse meo.
cinge caput mitra: speciem furabor Iacchi;
  furabor Phoebi, si modo plectra dabis.

(4.2.1–4, 21–32)

Why do you marvel that I have so many shapes in one body? Listen to the ancestry of the god Vertumnus. I am Etruscan and descended from Etruscans; I do not regret leaving Volscian hearths in a time of war. . . . My nature is capable of every kind of transformation: turn me into whatever shape you want, I will be appropriate. Put me in Coan silks, I will become a yielding mistress: when I put on a toga, who would deny that I am a man? Give me a sickle and bind my temples with twisted straw: you will swear that my hands have been cutting hay. Once I bore arms, and, I remember, I was praised in that arena; wearing a heavy basket, I became a reaper. In the lawcourts I was sober; but when I put on a garland, you will declare that wine has gone to my head. Surround that head with a turban, and I will rave in the image of Bacchus; yet I will also rave like Apollo, if you only give me a lyre.

According to modern orthodoxy, this is a poem about the versatility of Propertian elegy, above all in this experimental book that showcases its ability to move from *mollitia* to *militia* and all points between.[116] Vertumnus speaks not just as a specimen of Rome's ethnic hybridity but also as a self-conscious mediator between amatory and aetiological poetry.[117] Many of his varied changes span past and future Propertian topics.[118] Most obviously, the first pair of transformations, into a girl, then into a man, acknowledge elegy's

---

116. Fox (1996: 158) notes "his versatility, his changes of *persona*, his interest in aetiology, and his concurrent natural tendency to refer to early Roman history". See also Marquis 1974: 500; Pinotti 1983: 95–96; Shea 1985; Deremetz 1986: 141–49; DeBrohun 1994; Newman 1997: 276; O'Neill 2000: 273.

117. Cf. the grafting image of 17–18; Lee-Stecum 2006: 34.

118. Deremetz 1986.

fluctuating gender boundaries, while Vertumnus's passivity as a mannequin who undergoes multiple costume changes—*indue, comprime, imposito, imposta*—reminds us of the malleability of all elegiac characters.[119] While the *puella* in Coan silks clearly recalls Cynthia, her abnormally yielding character (*non dura*) and diaphanous garments may also, some have argued, suggest easy virtue, in line with the Vicus Tuscus's long associations with prostitution.[120] Indeed, the subsequent transformation into a man in a toga may play off a further case of gendered ambivalence in Roman dress: a toga was respectable costume for a man, but the mark of an adulteress or prostitute when worn by a woman.[121] As fisher (37) or fowler (33), the god revives the protean transformations of Horace's Vertumnus,[122] while commemorating his fluid incarnations as a male-female Etruscan god before his identity calcified as Roman and masculine.[123] Bacchus and Apollo (31–32) are more obviously recognizable as the two divine overseers of Propertian elegy, responsible for mixed generic messages, the one inspiring grandiosity, the other urging restraint. Vertumnus's epigraphic signature, "VNVM OPVS EST, OPERI NON DATVR VNVS HONOS" (The work is unique, but the honour given it is not; 64), has been seized on as a slogan for the fame of Propertian elegy.[124]

Such metapoetic and metacultural interpretations satisfy most modern readers. But a different view is presented in two articles, published simultaneously but now largely forgotten.[125] Pierre Grimal and Robert Lucot both argue that the multiform Etruscan god is nothing less than an encrypted enigma of (the otherwise forgotten) patron Maecenas—indeed, that the god's learned discussion of his name's etymology was just the sort of conundrum that would have amused him.[126] After all, Maecenas was a knight, *eques*, but not always a warlike one, a *desultor* (35–36) with a foot in both private and

---

119. By contrast, Ovid's Vertumnus retains his underlying identity as the masculine (desiring) subject; Lindheim 1998.

120. O'Neill 2000.

121. McGinn 1998: 156–71; Olson 2006.

122. Hor. *Sat.* 2.3.227.

123. Varro, *Res divinae* fr. 119 Cardauns: "deae Volumnae". On Etruscan Veltha/Veltune/Voltumna as "a god with strange and contrasting attributes", see Pallottino (1975: 141). Other androgynous gods are latent in the poem: Messor (cf. *messor* [28]; Corbeill 2015: 105); Fauor (33), the MS reading at 33 reinstated by Cairns (2006: 282–83), the name (also Favor Pastor; cf. *pastor* [39]) of an Etruscan god related to Thufltha, a fowler god (cf. *aucupio*) linked with Pales, also gender-ambiguous; De Grummond 2005.

124. By, e.g., Pinotti (1983: 95–96).

125. Le Doze (2012) is the exception.

126. Grimal 1953; Lucot 1953.

public camps, an Etruscan interested in Etruscan antiquarianism who had left his roots for the city of Rome. The first of the god's transformations—into a soft girl in Coan silks, then back into a man in a toga—should remind us of not just the clothing that fashions an elegiac poetry book but also the trademark flowing robes of a patron who, like a mistress, could be both *durus* and *mollis*.[127] The *mitra* worn by Bacchus (31) is a woman's headdress (Cynthia's at 2.29a.15), but also the national male headdress of Maecenas's chosen ancestors, the Lydians.[128] Once an androgynous (or even female) god, Vertumnus is not ashamed to alternate feminine and masculine attire.

*Poésie à clef* is out of fashion these days, and I do not suggest decrypting Vertumnus as Maecenas.[129] At least one artist did, though: in a striking portrait called *Vertumnus*, Giuseppe Arcimboldo (1526/27–1593) depicted the face of his eccentric patron Rudolph II as a collage of fruit, vegetables and flowers. The striking correspondences here suggest a more nuanced approach to the affinities between the Augustan patron and the lasting residue of Propertian elegy.[130] While the defiant tone of this cross-dressing deity goes some way to normalize both the gender slippage of silk-robed Book 2 and the consciously transvestite project of Book 4, Vertumnus's easy ambidextrousness also masks the full range of misunderstandings that the cultural scapegoat Maecenas provoked by pursuing novel (or archaizing) modes of aesthetic pleasure. My point is not to have us decide between the two interpretations of the poem: Propertius/Propertian elegy/Propertian cultural hybridity on the one hand and "Maecenas" on the other. What interests me is that they are both good readings: they both let us discover an encoded figure for Augustan *uarietas* or, rather, the shocking confusion of norms that is as much part of that culture as Augustan classicism is. To decide to read "Vertumnus", even tentatively, as "Maecenas" makes this poem an early chapter in the history of his reception—Propertius's reflection on the multiformity not just of Augustan poetry but also of its now-submerged patron as muse and generator of poetic themes.[131] Maecenas may have made Augustan poetry various, and the poem can be read as a tribute to that, but Augustan poetry made *him* various as well.

127. See Rosati (2005: 139) on the ideological applicability of Maecenas's "soft" elegiac lifestyle.

128. See Cairns (2006: 278–79) on Lydians in Propertius who invoke Maecenas: e.g., Hercules's emasculating enslavement to Lydian Omphale in 4.9; Bacchus suggests his love of wine and luxury, Ganymede his love of Bathyllus.

129. With the exception of Heslin (2011).

130. Cf. Nigro 1998.

131. The opening *Qui mirare* evokes the opening of 3.11; cf. Hor. *Carm.* 3.8.2–3 (addressed to Maecenas).

# 6

# Maecenas as a Figure of Style

### THE TWO SENECAS

> Seneca's Letter 114 to Lucilius
> Is all about style,
> About the questions of words
> And about the questions of shirts,
> The colors and the jewelry you choose,
> A wife, a friend,
> The slaves in your care,
> How the sun passes through
> The eye of your home.
>
> —C. PERRICONE, *FOOTNOTES* (2018)

"THE WAY MAECENAS lived his life is too notorious to need narrating." So Seneca the Younger introduces his famous character assassination in *Epistles* 114.[1] The Romans evidently knew more than we do. For us, Maecenas's last years are a gaping void that hypothesis after hypothesis has attempted to fill.[2] Did he die of natural causes on his Esquiline estate, enjoying a well-deserved retirement? Or did the once-discreet diplomat fall into disgrace after abetting Murena's conspiracy? All the Suetonian *Vita Horati* reveals is that Maecenas died sixty days before Horace in 8 BCE, they were buried side by side on the Esquiline, and Maecenas left all his property to Augustus. Virgil had predeceased him in 19 BCE, Propertius in 15 BCE; whether Varius survived him is unknown. What at least is clear is that the poets' textual representations of their

---

1. *Ep.* 114.4: "Quomodo Maecenas uixerit notius est quam ut narrari nunc debeat".
2. Gordon Williams 1990; White 1991.

relationship with Maecenas established a lasting image bank of poet–patron relations that could be plundered and manipulated by anyone in search of a sympathetic supporter.[3]

In the chapter that follows this one, I explore what happened to Maecenas's posthumous reputation as imperial favourite and supreme protector of poets. Here, I consider a different but related aspect of his personality: Maecenas as a figure of style. Mysterious figure that he was, everyone agrees that he had a distinctive way of being and moving in the world, a set of embodied dispositions such as trailing robes, lofty stare and mincing walk. The Younger Seneca calls it "habitus, uultus, incessus" (appearance, expression, gait; *Ep.* 114.22); Pierre Bourdieu, following Aristotle, might call it *hexis* (how one carries or comports oneself). According to Seneca, Maecenas was equally notorious for his eccentric *literary* style (*oratio*). For all his internal contradictions, he offered an object lesson in Boileau's principle "Le style, c'est l'homme même," or, as Seneca puts it, "talis hominibus fuit oratio qualis uita" (The way men speak is the way they live; *Ep.* 114.1), two aphorisms that characterize style not just as some trivial ornament but, for better or worse, as a way of life and essential bearer of human identity. The etymology of English "style" (from Latin *stilus*, a writing instrument) puts the literary cart before the behavioural horse. Montblanc's Maecenas pen, we saw, tries to condense both aspects in the same format.

Yet the precise qualities of Maecenas's style—or, for that matter, anyone's style—remain hard to pinpoint. Theoreticians invariably run into paradoxes when attempting to define the concept. What is style, after all, but something specific yet indefinable, a set of uniquely distinctive traits or tics captured, or rather approximated, through laborious paraphrase or exaggerated parody, and measurable only as deviation from some bland norm? In a recent discussion, Jeff Dolven has pondered these contradictions epigrammatically.[4] Is style a rightness or a wrongness? Is it ineffable perfection? Is it a tic, fault or blemish, something that jars or seeks attention, the proverbial pearl in the oyster? Is it imitable or inimitable? Is it separate from substance, an outer skin that can be put on and off? Or a giveaway symptom of an underlying personality? Is it unique, or a contagion that can spread?

The problem with Maecenas is that he answers to all these definitions in different contexts. If the secrets of his style remain elusive, it is not just because most of its traces, bodily and textual, are lost. It is also because reports of it vary so strikingly, which suggests that style is less a settled residue than something pinpointed and re-evaluated by its observers. During his lifetime,

3. Bellandi 1995: 78. See also Labate 2012; Graverini 2006.
4. Dolven 2018.

Maecenas's followers kept him under wraps, an exclusive model to which they aspired. For Horace, he was the unattainable end goal of a civilizing process: goodbye to broken fingernails, bad haircuts and messy togas (which in itself feeds the lingering idea that Maecenas was personally fastidious). Yet his style was more than just a look. As philosopher Jenefer Robinson puts it: "A literary style is a way of *doing* certain things."[5] Horace anticipates this, noting of their first encounter: "respondes, <u>ut tuus est mos</u>, / pauca" (You replied briefly, <u>as is your manner</u>; *Sat.* 6.60–61). A few poems later, style (low-key, nonchalant) and its expression have become the poet's own: "<u>sicut meus est mos</u>, / nescioquid meditans" (Mulling over some bit of nothing, <u>as is my manner</u>; 9.1–2).

Within two generations, this exemplary Maecenas would become a sacrificial victim on the altar of his poets' reputations and a role model for later dandies and decadents. The bland façade built by his protégés cracked, releasing a spate of behavioural details and habits, many of which conform to traditional Roman stereotypes of effeminacy, luxury and affectation. He was identified as *mollis* across all areas of his life, whether this was understood as effeminate, metrosexual, counterculturally queer, or fond of a certain kind of "weak" language or word arrangement.[6] The idea Seneca presents as a truism in *Epistles* 114—that literary style is a symptom of lifestyle, and vice versa—is, it has been noted, the least original aspect of that letter.[7] This was just the latest fundamentalist attempt to counter a long tradition—most crisply exemplified by Catullus 16, but going back to the effete orator Hortensius and Aristophanes's preening Agathon in *Thesmophoriazousae*—of defending one's speech or verses as unrepresentative of one's real-life habits, usually against accusations of unmanliness or sexual depravity.[8]

These defences were not helped by another venerable rhetorical tradition: the use of metaphors of adornment to characterize literary style.[9] Maecenas's written affectations are typically described in the language of sartorial or cosmetic excess. His first critic and parodist, we have seen, was Augustus, whose catalogue of bon mots in his "jewel" letter captures his friend's weaknesses as faux Etruscan, gem fancier and flowery penman. Other damning phrases include Augustus's "myrrh-drenched ringlets" (myrobrechis cincinnos) and Tacitus's "curling tongs" (calamistros) and "dyed whorish garments" (fucatis et meretriciis uestibus).[10] Seneca, too, knits extravagant written style together with excessive

5. Robinson 1985: 227.
6. Edwards 1993: 63–97.
7. Sklénář 2017: 5.
8. Möller 2004.
9. Bramble 1974: 38–41.
10. Macrob. *Sat.* 2.4.12; Tac. *Dial.* 26.1.

grooming to make a memorable equation between stylistic metaphors and behavioural traits. The effect is to make his conclusions irrefutable:

> Quod uides istos sequi qui aut uellunt barbam aut interuellunt, qui labra pressius tondent et adradunt seruata et summissa cetera parte, qui lacernas coloris inprobi sumunt, qui perlucentem togam, qui nolunt facere quicquam quod hominum oculis transire licent; inritant illos et in se auertunt, uolunt uel reprehendi dum conspici. talis erat oratio Maecenatis omniumque aliorum qui non casu errant sed scientes uolentesque. hoc a magno animi malo oritur. (Sen. *Ep.* 114.21–22)

> You observe this practice [matching speech to demeanour] in those who either pluck or thin out their beards, or who closely clip and shave the upper lip while preserving the rest of the hair and allowing it to grow, or in those who wear cloaks of shamelessly gaudy colour or see-through togas, and who wish to do nothing that will escape the eyes of humanity; they provoke and attract people's attention, and they wish even to be censured, so long as they are the centre of attention. That is the style of Maecenas and everyone else who strays, not by chance, but knowingly and voluntarily. This arises from great evil in the soul.

A generation later, Quintilian, too, would turn to Maecenas for examples of literary *transgressiones*, "changes in natural word-order" (a term with its own moral dimension):

> Quaedam uero transgressiones et longae sunt nimis . . . et interim etiam compositione uitiosae, quae in hoc ipsum petuntur, ut exultent atque lasciuiant, quales illae Maecenatis: "sole et aurora rubent plurima"; "inter sacra mouit aqua fraxinos"; "ne exsequias quidem unus inter miserrimos uiderem meas" (quod inter haec pessimum est, quia in re tristi ludit compositio). (Quint. 9.4.28)

> Some transpositions, indeed, are too long . . . and at times they even involve structural abnormalities deliberately designed to frolic and flirt, like these phrases of Maecenas: "They blush in the sun and the fullness of dawn"; "Sacred among the ash trees moves the water"; "May I never funeral rites my own see among the mourners" (this is the worst of all, because the expression is playful in a mournful context).

For both authors, Maecenas's writing is outrage on the page: playful deviation from bland conformity towards syntactic license and broader exhibitionist tendencies—symptoms of "great evil in the soul".

Criticisms like these, as we have seen, have a historicizing dimension. Post-Augustan writers tend to reinvent Maecenas as a scapegoat for Augustan decline. Perhaps it was hard to categorize him in any other way. There were no obvious res gestae to record; his out-of-town trips, as depicted by Horace (*Sat.* 1.5, 2.6), had no visible end point. He represented friendship for friendship's sake, imperial indulgence, *otium* (by the end, permanent) or purposeless pleasure-seeking. From the outside, his habits made him a classic instance of style without substance, a mere surface, coating an inner void, or, worse, inner corruption. It cannot have helped that he belonged to a race that had reached the end of the line and was going nowhere: Virgil's "always inert Etruscans" (*Aen.* 11.732–33). Like dandies in all periods, he was "an anachronism that refuses to go away . . . and makes a point of being out of step with its context".[11] Nonetheless, as Jeff Dolven says of Oscar Wilde: "Who needs *what* if you have enough *how*?"[12] Or, put differently: "Style can be a way without a destination."[13]

Unlike Agathon, Catullus and Hortensius, Maecenas never had the chance to defend himself. The legend that he wrote his own style manifesto stems from four tantalizing words—"MAECENAS DE CVLTV SVO"—posted ahead of a catalogue of scandalous literary faux pas in the surviving text of Seneca's *Epistles* 114 (3). "Maecenas on His Own Style" suggests a lost context or organizing principle for the literary excerpts that follow (even if *cultus* normally refers to behavioural, not rhetorical, attributes). But while Seneca does occasionally embed titles in his writing, there is nothing obviously autobiographical about these fragments.[14] Disappointingly, the phrase is more likely to be a marginal gloss.[15] The scribe who inserted it may have been referring to the previous section of the letter, where the word *cultus* is applied to Maecenas's personal style: "Were his words not as distinctive as his style [cultus], his retinue, his house, his wife?"[16] For all its flimsy authority, the style manifesto, or *apologia pro vita sua* (recalling Mark Antony's "On His Drunkenness") is still regularly listed among Maecenas's collected titles, along with his *Symposium* and *Prometheus*.[17] This is partly because it provides such a convenient container for the miscellaneous snippets of literary style and lifestyle that dovetail in Seneca's letter and are crystallized in its overarching motto.

11. Gelder 2007: 123.

12. Dolven 2018: 53. Hor. *Sat.* 1.1.1—"Qui fit, Maecenas" (How come, Maecenas . . . ?)—sounds initially like the story of Maecenas's coming to be, not just Horace's; Gowers 2012, *ad loc.*

13. Dolven 2018: 7.

14. Berti 2014: 225–29.

15. Reynolds 1965, *ad loc.*

16. *Ep.* 114.4: "non tam insignita illius uerba sunt quam cultus, quam comitatus, quam domus, quam uxor?" Cf. Berti 2014: 228–29.

17. On Maecenas's other titles, see Bardon (1949: 166–67, 1952: 2.16–17) and André (1967: 105).

A glance at the small corpus of Maecenas's fragments at least suggests where his reputation came from. In these short samples, the prose is so self-consciously metrical that it is often hard to see any distinction from the poetry.[18] Several of the poetic fragments have a ludic feel to them, suggesting a "party animal" in a habitat of sympotic extemporizing or homosocial flirtation, one prone to mawkishness or even ghoulishness. There is also a certain shock value. One oddly ordered prose phrase, "ne exsequias quidem unus inter miserrimos uiderem meas" (may I never funeral rites my own see among the mourners; 16L), is censored by Quintilian for its inappropriate frivolity: "The expression is playful in a mournful context" (in re tristi ludit compositio; 9.4.28). Some verses, at least superficially, confirm the impression of *mollitia*. Among these are two intimate hendecasyllabic poems addressed to Horace, both exaggeratedly intense: the jewel poem (3L=2C=185H) and the one declaring his undying love ("If I didn't love you, Horace, more than my own guts, you'd see me scraggier" . . . and here the text is corrupt: "than a castrated mule" (2L=3C=186H). Another droll ditty, in Priapeans, is cheerily voiced by a victim of anal impalement (1L=4C=187H). Scraps of a hymn to Cybele speak of tossing heads and self-flagellation (4–5L=5–7C=188–90H).

Other fragments suggest that nonchalance (*sprezzatura*) was a signature pose. A stray hexameter (6L=8C=191H) runs: "I don't care for a grave. For nature gives outcast bodies burial" (nec tumulum curo; sepelit natura relictos). The impaled victim (1L=4C=187H) claims: "While life remains, all's good" (dum uita superest, benest). The jewel poem (3L=2C=185H) protests satisfaction with little: "Nor do I want" (nec . . . quaero). As for the precious vocabulary and word order, they strongly evoke neoterism (i.e., "modernism"), fashionable in the mid-first century BCE but by now long outdated. The metres (galliambics, priapeans and hendecasyllables), too, recall Catullus above all, suggesting explicit and/or unconventional sexuality. The vocabulary is often prissy, diminutive or overtly affectionate (*anellos, lapillus, percandida, perpoliuit* in the jewel poem, for example); word order is elaborately patterned.[19]

---

18. All fragments are preserved in Lunderstedt (1911; L); verse only in Courtney (2003: 276–81; C) and Hollis (2007: fragments 183–93; H). Prose fragments: Sen. *Ep.* 19.9, 114.5, Quint. 9.4.28. Sometimes single words are recorded for their grammatical or transgender quirks: 3L=2C=185H (*Thynica*); 9L=10C=193 *dub.* H (*Quiritem* as an unusual singular; a confusion with Hor. *Carm.* 2.7.37; cf. 19L: a confusion with Prop. 3.8.37); 7L=1C=184H (*catinus* as masculine); 8L=9C (*cardo* as m., which it usually is; the text must be corrupt); or for unusual metre: 4–5L=5–7C=188–90H (galliambics). The second poem to Horace is included in Suet. *Vita Hor.* (2L=3C=186H); the hexameter is found at Sen. *Ep.* 92.25 and the victim of impalement at Sen. *Ep.* 101.10 (see below). The corpus also includes scattered sayings, jokes and anecdotes; 29–30L.

19. See 26–27L for examples.

So far, the criticisms seem fair enough. But Maecenas has also been made to shoulder the blame for anything outré in his poets' works. For example, one fragment attributed to him (19L) is actually identical to Propertius 3.8.37: "nexisti retia lecto" (you have stretched nets over the bed).[20] Stylistic oddities in Horace in *Odes* 3.8, a poem addressed to Maecenas, have been blamed on the patron's bad influence: a man "funeralled by a tree" (funeratus; 7), a day that "will uncork" wine (dies . . . corticem . . . dimouebit; 9–10) and a wine jar "taught to drink smoke" (amphorae fumum bibere institutae; 11).[21] Virgil's *cacozelia*, too, was excused on the grounds that it was influenced by Maecenas (more on this later). Moreover, the ancient tendency to use grooming metaphors for Maecenas's style, knitting together *oratio* and *habitus* just as Seneca wanted, has continued to influence modern critics. Paul Lunderstedt, who first collected Maecenas's work, detects an "Asianic" pathology: invented words, crimped clauses (*sententiolae*) and excessive use of affectedly metrical prose.[22] Yet if this writing were assigned to one of Maecenas's poets instead, ways would doubtless be found to praise its imaginative use of chiasmus, iconic word order, metre and neologism.

Recent editors (Courtney and Hollis) have collated and discussed Maecenas's literary fragments as a self-standing but depleted corpus. Here, I prefer to examine them in their original settings, as exhibits embedded in new contexts and serving specific agendas. The works of the two Senecas, combined in this chapter, conveniently plot the downturn in his fortunes. If the Elder (54 BCE–*c.* 39 CE) shows us Maecenas at work as a critic or judge, defending Virgil's lapses in style, then the Younger's moralizing tirades, ironically our best source for the surviving fragments, treat him as a stylistic abomination in his own right. Behind the son's *Epistles* 114 lie his father's prejudices about the decline of post-Ciceronian rhetoric:

> Everything that Roman oratory has to set against or even above the arrogant Greeks blossomed in Cicero's day: all the talents who have illuminated our subject were born then. Since then, things have got worse every day. (Sen. *Controv.* 1, *praef.* 6–7)

---

20. Diom. 1.369. Misassigned, perhaps, because it immediately precedes the poet's address to Maecenas in 3.9.

21. Bradshaw 1970: 148–49.

22. Cf. Petron. *Sat.* 1.2. See also Sklénář 2017: 4: "Seneca's assertion of a link between Maecenas's character and his literary style implicitly stamps as 'oriental,' hence anti-Roman, this impresario of high classicism under whose patronage Horace inveighed against *Persici apparatus.*"

Peace, luxury and having more time for the arts of care had made affectation a cultural norm:

> cantandi saltandique obscena studia effeminatos tenent, [et] capillum frangere et ad muliebres blanditias extenuare uocem, mollitia corporis certare cum feminis et inmundissimis se excolere munditiis nostrorum <u>adulescentium specimen est</u>. quis aequalium uestrorum quid dicam satis ingeniosus, satis studiosus, immo quis satis uir est? emolliti eneruesque quod nati sunt in uita manent, expugnatores alienae pudicitiae, neglegentes suae.

> Disgusting delight in song and dance obsesses these effeminate men. Braiding the hair, refining the voice till it is as seductive as a woman's, competing with women in bodily softness, adorning themselves with filthy fineries— <u>this is the pattern our youths set themselves</u>. Which of your contemporaries— however adequate his talent and diligence—is adequate as a man? Born feeble and spineless, they remain that way throughout their lives: assailing others' chastity, neglectful of their own. (Sen. *Controv.* 1, *praef.* 8–9; Loeb translation, adapted)

"This is the pattern our youths set themselves." Maecenas's unique and eccentric style was not just imitable, it is implied, it was positively contagious. Just so, Seneca *père* sets a template for Seneca *fils* to follow.

## Maecenas and Controversy

Velleius's even-handed Tiberian character sketch (2.88) holds Maecenas in the balance, but after that his reputation begins to slide. His next posthumous appearances are in the *Controversiae* and *Suasoriae*, two collections of highlights from memorable declamations compiled by the Elder Seneca. These staged debates make an oddly apt setting for Maecenas: after all, he was as controversial as he was persuasive. His appearances as a critic (*iudex*) weighing in on Virgil's posthumous behalf make sense against a broader backdrop of forensic appearances. If a crucial aspect of Maecenas's character was his flair for soothing other people's disputes, disputes equally often revolved around him, as several anecdotes attest. Once, when he lent his support to the plaintiff in an adultery trial, tensions rose so high that Augustus had to step in to protect him and his fellow advocate.[23] Similarly, the landmark divorce case *Terentia v. Maecenas* has been called "a controversy between two personalities".[24] Riots erupted over the celebrity actors at the Ludi Augustales, at which Maecenas backed his adored

---

23. Dio 54.30.4.
24. Martini 1995: 184; cf. Guarino 1992: 145n38. *Dig.* 24.1.65.

Bathyllus.[25] And when Seneca the Elder's younger son Gallio gave an oration "on behalf of Bathyllus", he raised the hackles of a rival, Labienus. Gallio's lost apology for a controversial favourite may be a by-product of the continuing debate over Maecenas himself, praised in the *Elegiae* and pilloried in Seneca's *Epistles*.[26] Meanwhile, the images of torture and sexual deviance that surround Maecenas in the Younger Seneca's writings suggest either a history of active involvement in declamation or, more likely, an overflow of the fantasies of declamation into his biography.[27]

## The World of Declamation

Declamation, the practice of making imaginary speeches on legal or historical dilemmas, was a central element in late-Republican and imperial rhetorical education—and a strange and fascinating phenomenon.[28] Flashy orations by teenage speakers on far-fetched questions—should a man be rewarded for tyrannicide after being found in bed with the tyrant's wife? should a father let his daughter be executed after she helped her mother to poison her half-brother? should Alexander the Great enter Babylon after a bad omen?—would seem to have little to do with either real-life experience or wider political activity. Yet the declamation hall, once considered a curious backroom in Latin literature, has been reclaimed as a central space for cultural formation and social advancement.[29] Here, after all, ambiguous limit cases in Roman ethics were thrashed out and conflicts of family loyalty confronted; here, rivals old and young fought for the intellectual high ground; this was the crucible of Roman mythology.[30]

The declaimers themselves do surprisingly little to disabuse us of the artificiality of their world. Seneca himself compares their speeches to shadow boxing, dreaming, kindergarten and sailing a toy boat on a small pond, promoting a narrative of social and stylistic decline that casts modern speakers as

25. Tac. *Ann.* 1.54.

26. *Controv.* 10 *praef.* 8. See Fairweather (1981: 110) on speeches *ad imitationem fori* (replying to a famous orator's speech): e.g., Cestius's *In Milonem* (*Controv.* 3 *praef.* 16) and Latro's *Pro Pythodoro Messalae* (about another patron's favourite; *Controv.* 2.4.8).

27. Torture and declamation: Bernstein 2012; Morales 1996; Pagán 2007–8.

28. Bonner 1949; Fairweather 1981: 104–31.

29. Sinclair 1995: 103; Bloomer 1997a: 201; Gunderson 2003: 13–14, 102: "parvenus and social climbers".

30. Ethics: Roller 1997. Fathers and sons: Sinclair 1995; Bloomer 2007: 304. Declamation as surrogate mythology: Beard 1993.

effete pygmies next to great orators like Cicero.[31] Even so, it is hard to account for these lurid panoramas of father–son conflict, evil stepmothers, inheritance, rape, torture, madness and mutilation. Were they rehearsals for the future dispensation of justice? Did they teach and reproduce Roman masculine norms by advocating for society's most marginal figures, women, orphans, slaves and the disabled?[32] Or did they experiment gratuitously with melodrama and horror by simulating human suffering, even dredging up the unspeakable obsessions of the Roman unconscious?[33]

Maecenas appears a handful of times in Seneca's collection, both as an authoritative member of the audience and as a promoter of poetic and rhetorical champions. Rival patrons Asinius Pollio and Messalla Corvinus are there on the ground as well, scouting for talent, rooting from the sidelines and ruling between contestants (here, at last, patron and *patronus* are the same thing). The briefest of Maecenas's interventions is a scholarly quip. When one Claudius Sabinus chose to orate in both Latin and Greek (*Controv.* 9.3.14), Maecenas is said to have joined in the mocking chorus by muttering an aside from Homer: "You could not tell which side the son of Tydeus [Diomedes] was fighting for" (*Il.* 5.85–86; supply: "whether for the Trojans or the Achaeans"; i.e., Greek speakers or the ancestors of Latin speakers).[34] In the end, another man's joke won the day. But the Homeric tag in question went on to have a rich afterlife. In Erasmus's *Adages*, it is cited to illustrate *diuersarum partium*, conflicting loyalties.[35] And already in its declamatory context it prompts larger questions about critical impartiality, not just in Homer (often regarded as laudably evenhanded) but also in Maecenas himself.[36] Just whose side was he on?

The resonances between Maecenas's background presence and the fictional world over which he presides are striking. In this venue for intergenerational struggle, up-and-coming speakers flex their rhetorical muscles and strain their emotional nerves in front of critics who praise, flay, endorse or censor them. Central to all declamation was the theme of the family, an "argument magnet" but equally a hostage to fortune in this alternative setting to the traditional

31. *Controv.* 3. *praef.* 13–14; *Suas.* 2.10. Narratives of decline: J. Walker 2000: 94–109; Gunderson 2003: 13. Declamatory training as mollycoddling: *Controv.* 9 *praef.* 4–5.

32. Sinclair 1995; Kaster 2001; Bloomer 1997a, b; Gunderson 2003.

33. Suffering: Connolly 2016. Declamatory fathers: Gunderson 2003 (esp. 18, 22, 59–89); Sussman 1995; Bloomer 1997b; Lentano 2005. Rhetorical teachers as "fathers": Kaster 1988: 68.

34. Maecenas ("equally at home in both languages": Hor. *Carm.* 3.8.5) quotes the original Greek.

35. On the survival of Homeric tags in Renaissance rhetoric, see Wolfe (2015).

36. The Doloneia episode (*Il.* 10) was suspected in antiquity of being interpolated because it was unusually pro-Greek; Casali 2004. On Homeric commentary and ancient education, see Nünlist (2012).

biological unit.[37] While blood ties were being supplemented offstage by intellectual and rhetorical mentors, declaimers fixated not just on biological relationships between fathers and sons but also on Roman society's usual contingency
measure: adoption.[38] The literary phenomenon of "outfathering" (Erik Gunderson's term) takes its primary inspiration from literary patronage. Horace had
already pictured himself as Maecenas's foster child and Virgil had been called his
"surrogate son".[39] Familial language equally infuses Seneca's account of declamation as the site of social and literary progress. Where Maecenas is concerned,
metaphors of adoption and grafting, its plant equivalent, abound, trailing with
them double-edged associations with favouritism, interloping and excess.[40]

If "declamation is . . . about authority", this applies to its critics as much as
to its practitioners.[41] Seneca lets us eavesdrop not just on the students' fraught
auditions but also on the stylistic wrangling of the literary establishment over
its protégés, where taste was as much a matter of dispute as any *controversia*.[42]
Two generations after his death, Virgil was largely exempt from the narrative of
decline, and Maecenas, custodian of his shrine, had all the clout needed to fend
off big-headed rivals. But the newly canonized poet was regularly lambasted by
the younger generation (the *obtrectatores Vergilii*).[43] "Upstarts" pillaged his
poems to lend their own speeches dignity.[44] They pulled him down from his
pedestal, making insinuations about his personal relationship to Maecenas and
holding Maecenas responsible for his direst lapses in taste, especially his *cacozelia* (immoderate affectation, or trying too hard).[45] Seneca's Maecenas struggles
to uphold Virgil's mastery of due proportion and defends him for having sometimes gone just a little too far. Against his paler rivals, Virgil will emerge "even
more exalted".[46] In other words, Maecenas actively fulfils the roles he was urged

37. Bloomer 2007: 304.

38. Sen. *Controv.* 2.1.13, 2.4; Calpurnius Flaccus, *Declamations* 11 and 30; Bernstein 2009, 2013.
Suet. *Gram. et rhet.* 16: Q. Caecilius Epirota as "tenellorum nutricula uatum" (the nanny of
tender young poets).

39. Gunderson 2003: 59. Hor. *Sat.* 1.6.56–62; Donat. *Vit. Verg.* 44.

40. See Gowers 2011: 90n12, 114n99) on adoption/grafting metaphors. Adoption as a symptom of luxury: Bernstein 2009: 339–42.

41. Gunderson 2003: 21.

42. Gunderson 2003: 17, 22.

43. Donat. *Vit. Verg.* 43–46.

44. On Seneca's defence of potential plagiarists, including Virgil, see McGill (2012:
147–209).

45. Jocelyn (1979: 94) speaks of the "thin line" between affectation and using language fe-
licitously and boldly. See P. Hardie (2009b) on Virgil as paradoxical poet.

46. *Vita Vergilii Donati aucti* 70: "Maro uero exaltatior"; McGill 2012: 218–19.

to play in the *Georgics*: virtual confidant and passive champion. But in safe-guarding Virgil's reputation he puts his own on the line.

## Maecenas the Critic

Two passages in the *Suasoriae* show Maecenas acting for the defence. In one, he supports Virgil's relatively restrained handling of sublime topics; in the other, he condones his long-windedness. *Suasoriae* 1 collects exercises on a favourite theme of declaimers, whether Alexander should sail the ocean to conquer the Far East, one guaranteed to bring out the most bombastic rhetoric. Virgil's rational litotes is bound to compare well with the insane hyperbole of Greek orator Dorion:

> corruptissimam rem omnium, quae umquam dictae sunt ex quo homines diserti insanire coeperunt, putabant Dorionis esse in metaphrasi dictam Homeri, cum excaecatus Cyclops saxum in mare deiecit: haec quomodo ex corruptis eo peruenant, ut et magna et tamen sana sint, aiebat Maecenas apud Vergilium intellegi posse. tumidum est ὄρους ὄρος ἀποσπᾶται. Vergilius quid ait? rapit
>
> > haud partem exiguam montis. [*Aen.* 10.128]
>
> ita magnitudini studet, <ut>[47] non imprudenter discedat a fide. est inflatum καὶ χειρία βάλλεται νῆσος. Vergilius quid ait [qui] de nauibus?
>
> > credas innare reuolsas
> > Cycladas. [*Aen.* 8.691–92]
>
> non dicit hoc fieri sed uideri. propitiis auribus accipitur, quamuis incredibile sit, quod excusatur antequam dicitur. (Sen. *Suas.* 1.12)

They used to think that the most decadent thing said since speakers started to go mad was a phrase of Dorion translating Homer, where the blinded Cyclops throws a rock into the sea. Maecenas used to say that you could tell from Virgil how this, instead of being decadent, could be made grand and yet sane at the same time. It is bombastic to say, "A mountain is torn from a mountain." So what does Virgil say? His character seizes "No small part of a mountain". Thus he keeps size in mind without ill-judged departure from the truth. It is overblown to say "and an island is picked up and thrown". What does Virgil say of ships? "You might suppose there floated the upturned Cyclades." He

---

47. <>, here and elsewhere, indicate an editor's supplement to make sense. Latin text used is Winterbottom (1974).

doesn't say it happens—but that it seems to happen. However incredible it may be, anything excused before it is uttered is received favourably. (Loeb translation, adapted)

This is esoteric territory, but a basic assumption is that the Cyclops theme had always been a magnet for outsized expression.[48] What Seneca omits to say is that, compared with Dorion, Homer had been relatively restrained: "He broke off the top of a great mountain and threw it" (*Od.* 9.481).[49] Maecenas, meanwhile, cleverly chooses a passage from *Aeneid* 10, distracting the critics from Virgil's bombastic adaptation of the equivalent Homeric episode in *Aeneid* 3: his Etna "licks the stars" (sidera lambit; 3.574); his man-mountain Polyphemus "assails the lofty stars" (altaque pulsat / sidera; 3.619–20).[50] In short, Maecenas has fixed the evidence to prove that Virgil produced phrases that were "wholesome" (sanus) and un-corrupt while also being "grand" (magnus)—the very qualities we will see Seneca the Younger deny Maecenas.

In another passage, Maecenas defends Virgil from rival patron Messalla, who has suggested that most of a line from *Aeneid* 11 is superfluous:[51]

sed ut sciatis sensum bene dictum dici tamen posse melius, notate prae ceteris quanto decentius Vergilius dixerit hoc, quod ualde erat celebre, "belli mora concidit Hector":

quidquid ad aduersae cessatum est moenia Troiae,
Hectoris Aeneaeque manu uictoria Graium
haesit. [*Aen.* 11.288–90]

Messala aiebat hic Vergilium debuisse desinere; quod sequitur

et in decimum uestigia rettulit annum

explementum esse. Maecenas hoc etiam priori comparabat. (Sen. *Suas.* 2.20)

But, to let you see that a well-expressed idea can find an even better expression, notice particularly how much more fittingly Virgil put the celebrated phrase: "Hector, brake on war, has fallen" [a line earlier attributed to

48. Berti 2007.

49. The verdict of Hermog. *Inv.* 4.2.

50. P. Hardie (1986: 263–67, 241–92) defends Virgilian hyperbole. But *sidera lambit* is criticized by Favorinus at Gell. *NA* 17.10.17: "uacanter hoc etiam," inquit, "accumulauit et inaniter."

51. Zwierlein (1999: 134–35) regards the anecdote as invented, either by Virgil's advocates or to reflect early philological criticism of his works.

Silo][52]: "Whatever delay there was by the walls of hostile Troy, it was by Hector's hand and Aeneas's that victory was put on hold for the Greeks." Messala used to say that Virgil should have stopped here, and that what follows "and retreated till the tenth year" is merely a stopgap. Maecenas thought this as good as what goes before. (Loeb translation, adapted)

This time, Maecenas defends the completed line against the charge of redundancy or in-filling (*explementum*, "padding"). Curiously, given his earlier quip about Homer's "son of Tydeus", the original Virgilian speaker here is none other than the veteran Greek warrior Diomedes, reluctantly approached in retirement in *Aeneid* 11 to reprise the duel with Aeneas aborted by Aphrodite in *Iliad* 5. A serene and apparently impartial observer, he forms a bridge between two epics.[53] But another function of his refusal speech is to give Aeneas after-the-fact military glory and equal credit with Hector for the Trojan resistance. As it happens, the words quoted here are not just intertextually but also *intra*textually significant. They correct Turnus's version of events at *Aeneid* 9.155: "decimum quos [Danaos] distulit Hector in annum" ([the Greeks] whom Hector [alone] delayed till the tenth year).[54] Diomedes's re-evaluation shows that he rates Aeneas on a par with Hector. Just so, another peaceable judge, Maecenas, rates the excessive Virgilian line on a par with its predecessors, putting his pet poet Virgil on a level with Homer.

On the other hand, Maecenas never gives his reasons. The suspicion will always be that he is acting simply out of blind loyalty in endorsing Virgil's words as integral, not tacked on. Like Diomedes, he is out of the ring himself. But in playing "indulgent father" he lays himself open to charges of corruption. Seneca's larger point is to contrast Virgil with the flowery excesses of a contemporary orator, Arellius Fuscus, who incidentally seems to have had much in common with Maecenas. Janet Fairweather writes: "It is in the fragments of Maecenas' prose, which Suetonius mentions as exemplifying *cacozelia* in the time of Augustus, that we find writing most closely comparable with the Fuscine manner."[55] Maecenas's biased indulgence of one prodigal favourite, Virgil, is halfway to indulgence of another, the spoilt pantomime star Bathyllus.

---

52. McGill 2012: 167–73.

53. Hinds 1998: 116–20, Papaioannou 2000.

54. Horsfall 2003, *ad loc.*

55. Fairweather 1981: 149. Cf. *Suas.* 2.23 on Fuscus: "Their excessive elegance and limp rhythm [nimius cultus et fracta compositio] may offend you when you reach my age." Seneca criticizes Musa's affectations in similar terms to his son's critique of Maecenas: *Controv.* 10 *praef.* 9: "quis enim ferat hominem de siphonibus dicentem 'caelo repluunt' et de sparsionibus 'odoratos imbres' et in cultum uiridarium 'caelatas siluas' et in <pictura> 'nemora surgentia'" (For who could bear a man saying of siphons that "they rain back at the sky" and of sprinklers that they

As for the less fortunate orators who won't stand the test of time, the critics not only nail their crude textual insertions, they also expose their social aspirations. The verb *inserere*, "graft", appears in loose connection with Maecenas when Arellius Fuscus, again, is arguing that it is not worth sacrificing Iphigenia to avenge Helen's adultery (a textbook dilemma that pits family loyalty against political expediency and divine will). At a critical moment, he goes off at a tangent to paraphrase Virgil on weather signs, his point being that the Greeks' shipping forecast is determined by nature, not by angry gods:

> In ea descriptione <quam> primam in hac suasoria posui, Fuscus Arellius Vergilii uersus uoluit imitari. ualde autem longe petit et paene repugnante materia, certe non desiderante, inseruit. ait enim de luna: quae siue plena lucis suae est splendensque pariter assurgit in cornua, imbres prohibet, siue occupata nubilo sordidiorem ostendit orbem suum, non ante finit quam <in> lucem redit. at Vergilius haec quanto et simplicius et beatius dixit:

> luna reuertentes cum primum colligit ignes,
> si nigrum obscuro comprenderit aera cornu,
> maximus agricolis pelagoque parabitur imber. [G. 1.427–29]

> et rursus:

> sin . . .
> pura nec obtunsis per caelum cornibus ibit. [G. 1.432–33]
>   (Sen. *Suas*. 3.4–5)

> In the description that I put first in this *suasoria*, Arellius Fuscus wanted to imitate some lines of Virgil. But they were far from his point, and he put them in [lit. grafted in] almost against the interests of his topic, which certainly had no need of them. For he says of the moon: "If her light is undimmed, and she rises with equally shining horns, she prevents rain; if she shows a duller orb because she is covered by cloud, she does not end the rain until she restores the light." How much simpler and more successful are Virgil's words: "When first the moon gathers her returning fires, If she grasps black air in her dark horns, The heaviest rain will be in store for farmers and sailors. And again: "But if . . . she travels clearly through the sky with unblunted horns" . . . (Loeb translation, adapted)

Seneca points out that Fuscus did not simply imitate Virgil: he committed a literary faux pas by grafting on (*inseruit*) Virgilianisms where they were "far from his point" and "against the interests of his topic". Virgil's original was both "simpler and more successful". Elsewhere, Seneca describes Fuscus's style as "soft" and

---

are "scented rains" and of ornamental gardens that they are "engraved woods" and of a picture "springing groves"?).

"limp", either too thin or too diffuse.[56] The plagiarist reveals himself by the lack of seamlessness in his graft. Dark Fuscus fails to steal Virgil's brilliant glow.[57]

But Fuscus is also credited with an ulterior motive. Allegedly, he used the irrelevant Virgilian paraphrase because he wanted to win credit from Maecenas, to "get in with him":

> solebat autem Fuscus ex Vergilio multa trahere, ut Maecenati imputaret. totiens enim pro beneficio narrabat in aliqua se Vergiliana descriptione placuisse, sicut in hac ipsa suasoria dixit: cur iste <in> interpretis ministerium placuit? cur hoc os deus elegit? cur hoc sortitur potissimum pectus, quod tanto numine impleat? aiebat se imitatum esse Vergilianum "plena deo". (Sen. *Suas.* 3.5)

> Fuscus was in the habit of borrowing many passages from Virgil, in order to win favour with Maecenas. For he was always telling how as a service to Maecenas he had given pleasure with some Virgilian usage, such as in this very *suasoria*, where he said: "Why did this man [Calchas the priest] find favour for the role of mediator? Why did the god choose him as mouthpiece? Why did he light on this heart above all to fill with such divine power?" He said he had imitated the Virgilian *plena deo* [lit. "she, full of the god"].

The verb in question, *imputare*, usually means "to store up credit with someone" or "to boast".[58] In the post-classical period, it came to be used of grafting (by analogy with Greek *emphuein*). Fuscus's act of textual insertion (*inseruit*) thus looks like effrontery on several levels (the English noun "imp" comes from a verb that means "to tack on a young shoot"). His attempt to "latch onto" or "suck up to" an important member of the audience smacks of social as well as literary insinuation; he wants to be "adopted" by Maecenas (as a mediator of the divine mouth of Virgil). As the phrase *pro beneficio*, "by way of a service", indicates in the next sentence, the scene of declamation is a blatant extension of patron–client relations and the *suasoria* a ploy to convince on quite another plane, beyond the immediate argument.

Fuscus effectively replays the upstart in another narrative about trying to get in with Maecenas, Horace's *Satires* 1.9, where the boastful Pest boasts that he will dislodge stalwarts like Varius and Viscus from their perches:[59]

---

56. *Controv.* 2 *praef.* 1 ("mollis"); *Suas.* 2.23 ("fractus"); *Controv.* 2 *praef.* 1 ("summa inaequalitas orationis, quae modo exilis erat, modo nimia licentia uaga et effusa"). Cf. *Controv.* 9.1.13: "He said, 'I strive to compete with the best epigrams, and try not to plagiarize [lit. steal] them but compete with them.'" See McGill 2012: 147–50.

57. Contrast the "murky" declamation hall: "umbroso et obscuro . . . loco" (*Controv.* 9 *praef.* 5).

58. *TLL*, s.v. *imputare*.

59. Cf. Hor. *Sat.* 1.9.45–46: "haberes / magnum adiutorem" (You would have [in me] a great supporter).

"si bene me noui non Viscum pluris amicum,
non Varium facies: nam quis me scribere pluris
aut citius possit uersus?"

(HOR. SAT. 1.9.22–24)

"If I know myself well, you will not value Viscus more as a friend, nor Varius. For who could write more verses than me, or faster?"

In this little street drama, another Fuscus, Aristius Fuscus, plays a cameo part.
And Horace smugly recalls his own experience with Maecenas in terms that suggest a more successful case of "getting in with" and finding favour: "It means a
lot to me that I met with your approval" (magnum hoc ego duco, / quod placui
tibi; *Sat.* 1.6.62–63).

Grafting imagery recurs, finally, in connection with Maecenas in a well-
known scandal of the declamation hall, where fathers natural and adoptive
play a more than fictional role. In the presence of some special guests, the
emperor Augustus and his son-in-law Agrippa, Seneca's old friend Latro com-
mits a blunder so awkward as to override the fiction of the declamation plot:[60]

> in hac controuersia Latro contrariam rem <non> controuersiae dixit sed sibi.
> declamabat illam Caesare Augusto audiente et M. Agrippa, cuius filios, ne-
> potes suos, Caesar [Lucium et Gaium] adoptaturus diebus illis uidebatur. erat
> M. Agrippa inter eos qui non nati sunt nobiles sed facti. cum diceret partem
> adulescentis Latro et tractaret adoptionis locum, dixit: iam iste ex imo per
> adoptionem nobilitati inseritur <et> alia in hanc summam alia in hanc sum-
> mam. Maecenas innuit Latroni festinare Caesarem; finiret declamationem.
> quidam putabant hanc malignitatem Maecenatis esse; effecisse enim illum, non
> ne audiret quae dicta erant Caesar, sed ut notaret. (Sen. *Controv.* 2.4.13)

In this *controversia*, Latro said something that was contrary not to the *controversia* but to himself. Latro was speaking this case in the presence of
Caesar Augustus and Agrippa. At the time, it looked as if Augustus was going
to adopt Agrippa's sons, his own grandsons [Lucius and Gaius]. M. Agrippa
was one of those men who was not born an aristocrat but made one. Latro
was speaking on the young man's behalf, and when he got to the part about
adoption, he said, "Now adoption grafts this child from the lowest class onto
the nobility." And he made other remarks to this effect. Maecenas nodded to
Latro that Caesar was in a hurry; could he finish his speech? Some people

---

60. Bartsch 1994: 82–83. See Gunderson (2003: 101) on the declamatory audience's appetite
for political allegory.

thought that this was spiteful of Maecenas; he had made sure not that Caesar failed to hear what was said but that he noticed it.

The legal conundrum under discussion, whether the son of a prostitute should inherit the fortune of his rich noble grandfather, is a typically perverse hypothesis, which takes ad absurdum some standard conflicts in Roman elite life between family and rank, blood and adoption:[61]

> *A man disinherits his son. The son moves in with a prostitute and they have a child. When the son falls ill, he sends for his father, and when his father arrives he entrusts his own son to him and then dies. The father adopts the boy; he is accused of insanity by his other son.* (Sen. *Controv.* 2.4 *praef.*)

What causes this declaimer to score an own goal ("something . . . contrary not to the *controversia* but to himself") is the fact that a significant family in the audience happens to be artificially engineering its future. Latro's unintended implication is that the low-born Agrippa had corrupted a noble line through his royal marriage and that Agrippa's children were mothered by a prostitute (the empress Julia).[62] Speaking in this session on behalf of the un-prodigal son, he turns to a horticultural metaphor:[63]

> iam iste ex imo per adoptionem nobilitati inseritur

> Now adoption grafts this child from the lowest class onto the nobility.

As the son's representative, Latro argues that madness lies with the father whose charity exceeds the proper bounds of class: adoption is a kind of adulteration that threatens the family's status and inheritance. His censoriousness reflects badly on the imperial family. In a society where adoption was a normal solution for aristocratic childlessness, there were two sides to the debate over biology versus expediency.[64] Maecenas himself reduced the Augustan succession to a shocking *controversia*: "You [Augustus] have made him [Agrippa] so great that he must either become your son-in-law or be slain" (Dio Cass. 54.6).

Thinking on his feet, Maecenas gestures to Latro that it is time to bring the speech to a close; the emperor is in a hurry ("festinare Caesarem"). The scene unfolds in slow motion: Caesar hurries slowly. Mediating between actor and audience, the mandarin's inscrutable nod (*innuit*), far from hiding the gaffe, draws attention to it. Maecenas, in short, proves himself a master of

61. Bernstein 2009.

62. Bernstein 2009: 342: Sen. *Controv.* 2.4 and Calpurnius Flaccus, *Declamations* 30 both concern a grandfather's adoption of his grandchild, the son of a prostitute.

63. Cf. Sen. *Octavia* 249: Nero as *insitiuus*, "grafted on".

64. Corbier 1991a, b.

proto-Tacitean innuendo.[65] In relation to the two families concerned (the messy royals and the three-generation clan in the declaimer's fantasy), he occupies an interesting position: an alternative to Agrippa, without the family ties, but an adoptive parent to the young speakers who scramble for his attention. He is the compère of the situation and its evil godfather.[66] Known for his generosity (*benignitas*), he is labelled *malignus*, "mean" (from *malus*, "bad", and *gigno*, "give birth"), a quality of bad seeds and mean critics alike.[67] He kills off young sprigs as well as fertilizing their talent.

Summing up, Seneca gives credit where it is due: praise for Augustus for letting the misstep pass (*notare* is "to censure" as well as "to notice") and pity for Latro for being unable to apologize without making things worse. Only Maecenas's motives remain shrouded in doubt. In the context of a rhetorical debate, he has in effect become an unresolved *controversia* (which is roughly where he will remain for the rest of post-Augustan literature). "Some people thought . . ." (quidam putabant).[68] Is he a skilled dissimulator or an innocent? Like Diomedes, is he fighting with the Greeks or the Trojans?

These sketches of Maecenas, transmitted by Seneca to his sons, mark a halfway stage on his downward trajectory, a tipping point for his critical standing. As an Augustan throwback, he staunchly backs his protégés, whatever their faults; thanks to his authority and vigilance, the moral and stylistic integrity of Virgil, his adopted "son", is preserved intact. As a forerunner of Neronian decadence, he is a slippery manipulator between actors and audience.[69] The father's description of Fuscus's style sets a precedent for the son's description of Maecenas's style.[70] In the Younger Seneca's writings, he will take the entire burden of suspect taste on himself. As for the interlopers who smuggle in their ersatz imitations, their sense of exclusion is palpable. In retrospect, they make Horace's request to Maecenas, "But if you *insert* me into the lyric poets" (quodsi me lyricis uatibus inseres; *Carm.* 1.1.35), sound like a brash social climber's appeal to a literary kingmaker.

<hr />

65. Plass 1988: 123, 98–102, 126.

66. Old French *compère* means "godfather" (Medieval Latin *compater*).

67. Hor. *Epod.* 1.31: "benignitas tua". For *malignitas* in plants: Columella 3.10.18; Van Den Berg 2008: 400. *Malignus*, "spiteful", is used of plagiarism spotters in Terence's prologues: McGill 2012: 173–74.

68. Diana's cruelty provokes a *controversia* at Ov. *Met.* 3.255: "pars inuenit utraque causas".

69. See also Bartsch 1994: 82–84.

70. Sen. *Controv.* 2 *praef.* 1: "his ornament too contrived [cultus nimis adquisitus], his word arrangement more effeminate [mollior] than could be tolerated by a mind in training for such chaste and rigorous precepts". Pollio on playful Fuscus (*Suas.* 2.10: "non est suadere, sed ludere") sounds like Quintilian on playful Maecenas (9.4.28: "in re tristi ludit compositio"). See Fairweather 1981: 249–50.

## Maecenas in Seneca's Letters

A generation on, the Maecenas who appears in the Younger Seneca's letters and treatises is virtually unrecognizable. The esteemed patron has become a decadent rake, a spineless, abject figure—in short, a "broken" man.[71] This new Maecenas is a frail composite of flesh, blood and nerves, a loose-belted dandy parading in the streets of Rome, a debauchee tossing and turning on his feather bed, a tortured failure with Promethean aspirations. Was there some personal vendetta? It is easy to conclude that it suited Seneca to present him in this way. After all, Maecenas had been his more successful equivalent as advisor and close confidant to an emperor. Seneca could best safeguard his posthumous identity as the morally compromised philosopher at Nero's court by condemning the "too easy" life of his predecessor.[72] Another theory is that Maecenas was deployed as a weapon to attack Nero's affectations and those of his style consultant Petronius at a safe distance.[73]

Perhaps the most plausible explanation is that Seneca was manipulating a cardboard figure already deployed in the rhetorical schools, one heavily dependent on stereotypes from Republican invective (which had always worked to maintain the integrity of the elite by ritually excluding its misfits).[74] His portrait stands on one side of an old debate about Roman masculine identity answered (or generated, depending on chronology) by the staunch defence of Maecenas in the *Elegiae*. Populist figures like Julius Caesar had used louche dress as a symbol of political change and succeeded in being regarded as effeminate and masculine at the same time.[75] Still, this was risky behaviour. "Maecenas" had become a walking controversy in which the reputation of the Augustan Age was at stake, and Seneca makes the Augustan poets complicit in the overthrow of their master.

Above all, Seneca's attack on Maecenas's style needs to be understood as just one element in a larger philosophical project. Here was a subject who pursued, with exceptional consistency across all areas of his life (deportment and desires, as well as writing), a trajectory directly opposite to that of the Stoic *proficiens*. Whereas philosophers aspired to a state of perfect, manly *uirtus*, Maecenas was dragged from the heights by urges towards "softness", both

---

71. Gunderson (2015: 94) pairs him with Hostius Quadra (*QNat* 1.16): "two broken men".

72. Avallone [1962/63]: 136n5: "vendetta di grande scrittore contro il mediocre dilettante, di stoico contro l'epicureo, di sfortunato ministro di Nerone contro il fortunato ministro di Augusto"; Le Doze 2012, 2014: 213–27.

73. Byrne 2006.

74. Peirano 2012: 220–33.

75. See Dio's portrait of Julius Caesar at 43.43.1–4 (flowing clothes, high heels, loose belt); Edwards 1993: 90; Corbeill 1996: 194–98.

physical and mental.[76] Seneca characterizes abstractions like the soul or human morality in graphically material terms, making his languid Maecenas a corporealized version of the deteriorating soul:[77]

> male mihi esse malo quam molliter—<"male"> nunc sic excipe quemadmodum a populo solet dici: dure, aspere, laboriose. audire solemus sic quorundam uitam laudari quibus inuidetur: "molliter uiuit"; hoc dicunt, "mollis est". paulatim enim effeminatur animus atque in similitudinem otii sui et pigritiae in qua iacet soluitur. (Sen. *Ep.* 82.2)

> I would rather lead a bad life than a soft life. Understand "bad" in the popular sense: hard, harsh, arduous. We often hear other people's lives praised by those who envy them: "So and so lives a soft life." By this they mean: "He is soft." For the soul is slowly made womanish, and is weakened until it matches the ease and idleness in which it lies.

The hard-soft sinner is too inured by vice to be malleable, too flabby to be rectified:

> sed ualde durus capitur; immo, quod est molestius, ualde mollis capitur et consuetudine mala ac diutina fractus . . . simul et emarcuit et induruit; non potest recipere rationem, non potest nutrire. (Sen. *Ep.* 112.1, 3)

> But he is caught in a really hardened state; or, what is more intractable, he is caught in a soft state, long broken down by bad habits . . . he has rotted away and hardened at the same time; he cannot take in reason, he cannot feed it.

In other words, the main function of this decadent Maecenas—loose, lax, castrated, even—is as a teaching aid in Senecan metaphysics.[78] Notions of enervation and flux inform contrasts between two types of soul: one wholesome, robust and virile, the other decaying, fluid and soft.[79] If the perfect Stoic is self-contained, his boundaries with the outside world rigorously defined, surface hard and impenetrable, Maecenas is made of all too porous stuff. In his case, the thinnest membrane separates inside and outside, soul and body, action and writing. As pleasure "flows" (influat) into his weak soul, so unnecessary indulgences "seep into his marrow and muscles" (in medullas neruosque descendere deliciae).[80] Conversely, his garments, desires and words spill beyond their proper limits: "si non etiam oratione diffluetet" (if he

---

76. Graver (1998: 611n11) urges against translating *mollis* as "effeminate" (though the word subsumes that idea).

77. On Senecan imagery, see Armisen-Marchetti (1989).

78. Cf. Gareth Williams 2016: 141.

79. E.g., Sen. *Ep.* 114.22–23. See Bartsch (2005: 81–82) on the Stoic sage as impenetrable.

80. Sen. *De vita beata* 5.4; *Ep.* 114.25.

had not overflowed even in his speech; *Ep.* 114.4), "delicati [oratio] tenera et fluxa" (the speech of a pampered man is delicate and fluid; *Ep.* 114.20).[81] In short, these osmotic tendencies make him a philosophical antitype, a negative tool in the service of Stoic formation.

As for Maecenas's political career and dealings with his friends, the Augustan legacy has largely been swept away. Seneca associates him not with deft political mediation and the exclusive bonds of the *convivium* but with indiscretion, extravagance and showing off. Ideas of leakage and laxity apply here, too. Friendship, dinners and wealth are liberally dispersed, private habits flow into public duties. Yielding to the weaker vessels who surround him—his wife and eunuch attendants—Maecenas sinks in rank and gender, a forerunner for the devious hangers-on of the imperial court: empress, pantomime, slave.

A passage in *De providentia*, for example, contrasts Regulus, the martyr who made light of being tortured and crucified by the Carthaginians, with Maecenas, the sleepless voluptuary whose insatiable desires and lack of moral purpose exposed him to far greater pain (the torment recorded by Cicero, *Pis.* 43, keeping Regulus awake by removing his eyelids, sharpens the comparison):

> feliciorem ergo tu Maecenatem putas, cui amoribus anxio et morosae uxoris cotidiana repudia deflenti somnus per symphoniarum cantum ex longinquo lene resonantium quaeritur? mero se licet sopiat et aquarum fragoribus auocet et mille uoluptatibus mentem anxiam fallat, tam uigilabit in pluma quam ille in cruce; sed illi solacium est pro honesto dura tolerare et ad causam a patientia respicit, hunc uoluptatibus marcidum et felicitate nimia laborantem magis iis quae patitur uexat causa patiendi. (Sen. *Prov.* 3.10)

> Do you really think you would be happier being Maecenas than being Regulus, when Maecenas, exhausted by lovesickness and tearful at his daily rejection by his sulky wife, couldn't get to sleep unless he had an orchestra playing quietly and far off? Even if he was drugged by wine and distracted by the splashing of water and a thousand other pleasures to divert his anxious mood, he still slept in his feather bed as badly as Regulus on his cross. Regulus was at least consoled by the fact that he was enduring a hard fate for an honourable cause and could turn from his suffering to contemplate its cause, whereas Maecenas, wasted by pleasure and stressed by too much good fortune, was more troubled by the cause of his suffering than by the suffering itself.

One way to understand this passage is as a wilful misreading of Horace's *Odes* as a Stoic text. Two of Horatian lyric's most memorable figures (the heroic martyr

---

81. Stoicism as virile and hard: Sen. *Constant.* 1.1 (other philosophers treat pupils *molliter et blande*); *De vita beata* 7.3 (pleasure as *mollis* and *eneruis*).

who sacrificed his life for the Roman state and the orientalized fop entreated by a poet to forget his cares and enjoy the moment) are pitted at opposite poles of virtue and vice.[82] Seneca isolates morbid Maecenas from his poets, downplays their respectful tributes and exaggerates his need for their poetry into deep-seated psychic deficiency. While Virgil is elevated to the status of a sage whose wisdom fell on deaf ears (Ep. 101.13), Maecenas shoulders the blame for Augustan poetry—above all its inconsistency, in gender, genre and style.

Even so, this repellent, unassimilable alien with something of the sublime about him could almost pass for an abject version of Seneca himself. But for the grace of Stoicism, Seneca might have succumbed to the same decadent desires. Hence his sympathetic sighs of regret at Maecenas's unfulfilled potential and grudging praise of his better literary efforts, before their paths utterly diverge. Maecenas must be kept down, irredeemably soft, for Seneca to progress towards toughness. Yet some of their distinguishing literary tics are dangerously similar, as the following summary of Senecan style suggests: "The metaphorical potential of words is exploited to the limit. Personification abounds. Paradox jolts the reader's attention; *emphasis* accentuates significance; antithesis contrasts ideas or things superficially similar; *sententiae* distil from particular circumstances general principles and suspend, by way of their finality, continuity."[83] No less than Maecenas's lost "Style Notes", Seneca's *Letters* are a self-portrait: "To reveal his philosophy requires that he reveal himself as a moral being, reveal how his mind works, reveal his 'manner of life' (*qualis uita*), which is, in turn, mirrored in his style (*talis oratio*)."[84] As we know, style can often best be defined through what it is not—or does not want to be.[85]

Maecenas first enters the *Letters* in *Epistulae* 19, where Seneca considers the pursuit of *otium* and its relationship to friendship and personal integrity. As his addressee Lucilius contemplates withdrawal from public life, Seneca advises him on image management: retirement, once achieved, should be "neither paraded nor concealed".[86] Morally speaking, a return to the old simple ways is preferable to the life Lucilius now leads as a victim of his own fame, surrounded by flatterers and consumed by insatiable desires. But to attain a change of scene needs courage and stealth. Later, Tacitus would make his

---

82. Cic. *Fin.* 2.65 contrasts Regulus with Thorius, "potantem in rosa".

83. Wilson 1987: 108

84. Wilson 1987: 108. Cf. Dem. *On Style* 227: a letter as an image of the writer's soul.

85. Graver (1998: 614) notes the difficulty of extracting a formula for "good style" from Sen. *Ep.* 114. Sen. *Ep.* 46, praising Lucilius's vigorous but sweet writing, offers some guidance.

86. Sen. *Ep.* 19.2 ("non emineat sed appareat"); cf. *Ep.* 5.1.

Seneca explicitly cite the precedent of Maecenas and his easy retirement as he failed to escape the toils of Nero's court.[87]

These glimpses of a worldly backdrop frame a quotation from Maecenas's *Prometheus*, a work mentioned only here and represented for posterity only by this single line of prose.[88] Images of Lucilius's life at the centre, enslaved to the glow of publicity and flattering clients, have already coloured Maecenas's brief entry with memories of "friends in high places". In particular, Lucilius's meteoric social rise throws a spotlight on Maecenas as author and courtier, one that ultimately mirrors Seneca's own identity: "Your brilliant talent, the elegance of your writing and your noble friendships have thrust you into the centre of things" (Sen. *Ep.* 19.3). Even the Prometheus story is foreshadowed in the metaphors of exposure and rapaciousness Seneca attaches to the idea of the prominent individual and his hangers-on: "Prosperity is both greedy and exposed [exposita] to others' greed" (*Ep.* 19.7). If Prometheus stands for audacity punished, a spirit of daring is needed not just to achieve worldly power but, paradoxically, to shed it, too.

At this point, Maecenas appears, a surrogate philosopher voicing a sublime motto, even under torture:

> uolo tibi hoc loco referre dictum Maecenatis uera in ipso eculeo elocuti: "ipsa enim altitudo attonat summa." si quaeris in quo libro dixerit, in eo qui Prometheus inscribitur. (*Ep.* 19.9)

> I want at this point to bring in a quotation from Maecenas, who spoke the truth even when on the rack: "Even the high place blasts with thunder at the top." If you want to know what book this line comes from, it is the one entitled *Prometheus*.

The quoted line suggests: "There is a risk of thunder even (or, particularly) on the highest peaks."[89] This is no casual allusion; Seneca reveals both author and source.[90] Just for a moment, though, it is not clear who is speaking: Prometheus or Maecenas? In a tragic world that puts eminent men at risk, archaic trickster and modern statesman are conflated. The rack, *ipso eculeo*, mirrors the rock, *ipsa . . . altitudo*: two poles of fortune contained in the same view.[91]

---

87. Tac. *Ann.* 14.53–56.

88. Perhaps a Menippean satire, on the lines of Varro's *Prometheus*: Rossbach 1920; Avallone [1962/63]: 227.

89. Taking *summa* as accusative neuter plural, rather than nominative feminine singular, agreeing with *altitudo*.

90. Rare for him; but cf. *Ep.* 22.5: "Epicuri epistulam".

91. Cf. Soldo 2021: 242.

In *Prometheus Bound*, thunder and high places were associated with the punitive powers of Zeus (Aesch. *PV* 1080–93). Here, Lucilius's plan to retire gives the motto a contemporary charge. It suggests Maecenas's experience of court politics: "It's tough at the top" or "If you don't like the heat, get out of the kitchen."[92] Did the heights of Augustan power send overreaching citizens crashing?[93] So Maecenas, courtier-cum-tragic-hero, seems ruefully to conclude, now that it is too late (*sero*).[94] Or is he counselling Augustus to limit his own power?[95] There are shades of wise warners here from Herodotus, Horace's *Odes* and Greek tragic choruses, even the imagery of Seneca's own choral admonitions against wealth and prominence: "While I stood high in power, I never ceased to fear, to dread the sword at my own side. . . . The humble citizen fears no house built high and threatening on a mountaintop."[96] Nor does the confusion between author and speaker stop here. The *eculeus* (a "horse"-like rack on which a victim was pinioned and possibly impaled) is a plausible term for the punishment of a Titan exposed to an eagle's constant pecking. Equally, it suggests the equestrian who underwent exquisite mental torment even in the lap of luxury.[97] Throughout his works, Seneca dwells on "the paradox of adversity", the idea that good fortune is even more damaging than bad.[98] Pitted against torture victim Regulus, the sybarite emerges still more miserable, thanks to the pointlessness of his suffering.

This example is typical of Seneca's almost pathological interest in the relationship between bodily and psychic pain. While no one would actively wish to be tortured, he says elsewhere, the highest aim is to face the rack with Stoic equanimity (*Ep.* 67.4). But his engagement with physical agony is often gratuitously intense. In *Epistles* 101, he quotes with contempt a poem by Maecenas that speaks of "sitting on a sharp cross", presumably being anally impaled:[99]

---

92. Echoing Seneca on Lucilius's ascent: "nec te in altum fortuna misisset" (and would that Fortune had not raised you to the heights; *Ep.* 19.5).

93. In the Regulus Ode (Hor. *Carm.* 3.5.1–2), Jupiter's thunder is an analogue for Augustan power.

94. Costa (2014: 245) sees Maecenas/Prometheus as a tragic late learner (*opsimathēs*).

95. André 1967: 82. See Courtil (2014: 194–205) on torture in Seneca as an "unnatural" index of tyranny.

96. Sen. *Thyestes* 447–49, 455–56. Cf. Sen. *Ag.* 59–63; Sen. *Oedipus* 8–11; Hor. *Carm.* 2.10.11–12, Ov. *Rem. am.* 270; Makowksi 1991: 30n18.

97. Sen. *Prov.* 3.10. For music as relief for Prometheus, cf. Hor. *Carm.* 2.13.37–38 ("Prometheus . . . dulci laborem decipitur sono").

98. Motto and Clark 1985.

99. Sometimes also ascribed to his *Prometheus*: Mazzoli 1968.

inde illud Maecenatis turpissimum uotum quo et debilitatem non recusat et deformitatem et nouissime acutam crucem, dummodo inter haec mala spiritus prorogetur:

debilem facito manu,
   debilem pede coxo,
tuber adstrue gibberum,
   lubricos quate dentes:
uita dum superest, benest;
   hanc mihi, uel acuta
si sedeam cruce, sustine. [4C = 1L = 187H]

. . . quid sibi uult ista carminis effeminati turpitudo? quid timoris dementis-simi pactio? quid tam foeda uitae mendicatio? huic putes umquam recitasse Vergilium:

usque adeone mori miserum est? [= Turnus at Verg. *Aen.* 12.646]

optat ultima malorum et quae pati grauissimum est extendi ac sustineri cupit: qua mercede? scilicet uitae longioris. quod autem uiuere est diu mori? (*Ep.* 101.10–13)

That is the origin of that most debased of prayers, in which Maecenas says he is willing to suffer weakness, deformity and finally the pain of impale-ment, provided that he can prolong the breath of life during his suffering:

Cripple my hands,
   Cripple and lame my feet;
Heap up a crooked hump on my back,
   Shake my teeth till they rattle.
All is well, if my life remains.
   String it out, I beg you,
Though I sit on the piercing cross!

. . . What does he mean by such indecently effeminate verse? What does he mean by making a contract with utterly demented fear? What does he mean by begging so shamefully for life? He can never have heard Virgil read the words:

Tell me, is Death so wretched as that?

He asks for the climax of suffering, and—this is the hardest thing to bear—he wants his suffering to be prolonged and extended. And what does he gain from this? Merely the gain of a longer existence. Isn't that simply a lingering death?

Whatever its original context (quite possibly ludic), Seneca takes the ditty, with its grotesque images and thumping metre, seriously enough.[100] Instead of praising Maecenas for cheerful endurance, he sneers at him for feebly avoiding death and finds something wilfully languid in his preferred alternative: a protracted end. Seneca's language here anticipates his description of a complex period of Ciceronian prose: "illa in exitu lenta . . . deuexa et molliter detinens" (that lingering cadence . . . long drawn out and listlessly delaying; *Ep.* 114.16). It also looks ahead to suicidal Petronius's dreamy bandaging and un-bandaging of his slit veins (Tac. *Ann.* 16.19). The limp victim of luxury blurs with the victim of torture; French *roué* suggests "deserving to be broken on the wheel" (*roue*) or "already broken on the wheel".[101] Libertine and impaled victim share spineless, useless bodies (*corpus fractum et inutile*), distorted (*distorto*) and feminized (*effeminati*) by passivity, endlessly strung out (*districtum*). In praying for weakness (*me debilites licet*) and preferring protracted pain, Maecenas lays himself open to a suspicion Seneca seizes on, that he must hanker sadomasochistically after agony: "He asks for the climax of suffering, and—this is the hardest thing to bear—he wants his suffering to be prolonged and extended" (*Ep.* 101.13).

For all that, almost the most painful thing for Seneca about Maecenas's thunderous motto in *Epistles* 19 is its weak Latinity: a unique use of *attonare* in the active voice (Seneca is fonder of the passive participle, *attonitus*).[102] If *eculeo* is correct, Seneca skews his case by inserting some "out of control" anagrammatizing of his own—*e-c-u-l-e-o e-l-o-c-uti*—as if Maecenas's "tortured" diction were a side effect of the rack.[103] Offering to play interpreter, he glosses and rationalizes the metaphorical leap: "hoc uoluit dicere, attonita habet summa" (He meant by this, "The summit [or high places] has/have thunderstorms"— or, "The summit [or high places] hold(s) the high places thunderstruck"). Whether he is belittling Maecenas or trying to unlock a Heraclitan proverb for a literal-minded layman, his own version is hardly less obscure.

Worse is to come. Maecenas is presented as a sad parable for today's aspirants:

> est ergo tanti ulla potentia ut sit tibi tam ebrius sermo? ingeniosus ille uir fuit, magnum exemplum Romanae eloquentiae daturus nisi illum eneruasset felicitas, immo castrasset. (Sen. *Ep.* 19.9)

---

100. Makowski 1991; D. West 1991: 47.

101. Derrida (2005: 19–21) hears notes of derailment and seduction: going off *la rue*.

102. E.g., *Ep.* 110.5: "uana sunt ista quae nos mouent, quae attonitos habent" (All those things that stir us and leave us thunderstruck are empty). Costa 2014: 165: *attonare* is a calque on Greek *embrontan*.

103. Cf. the verbal churning of Atreus at Sen. *Thyestes* 176: "ignaue, iners, eneruis".

Was any power worth the price of making your style so drunken? He was a man of talent, who could have provided a great model of Roman eloquence had good fortune not enervated him, even castrated him.

Here begins the correspondence between rhetorical metaphor and physical debauchery that will flower in *Epistles* 114.[104] "Drunken style" (*ebrius sermo*) is more than just confused syntax or isolated personal tic: it becomes a direct consequence of political power. If the speaker offers a model to posterity, it will be a cautionary one: "hic te exitus manet nisi iam contrahes uela, nisi, quod ille sero uoluit, terram leges" (This end awaits you if you do not furl your sails and make for the shore—something he wished for too late; *Ep.* 19.9).

Maecenas thus offers one answer to the overall question of the letter: how to get out, of a way of life, of a career ("quis exitus erit?" [5]; "'quomodo' inquis 'exibo?'" [8]). But what *was* the "fortune" that had such a grave effect? Did his "soft" end come about thanks to his retirement or to continued life at court, entailing decadence or disgrace? It is no clearer whether this end was plain disaster (as *sero*, "too late", suggests) or further entrapment, "sticking around", even an enviable case of "getting away with it". Is Prometheus a role model, or just an example of a tragic end thankfully avoided?

If Seneca's voyage metaphors seem familiar, it is not just because they return us to the "safe haven" imagery used earlier in the letter.[105] They also recall Maecenas's most familiar literary appearances, as silent witness to Virgil, Horace and Propertius as they couched metapoetic decision-making in nautical tropes.[106] In the *Georgics*, as we saw, he was a sounding board for a poetic dilemma (*G.* 2.41–45: "Maecenas, expand your sails and fly across the open sea . . . come near and seize the edge of the shore; the land is in your grasp").[107] Seneca offloads Virgil's hesitation onto Maecenas, identifying him for posterity with poetic choices that he only passively endorsed. In Propertius 3.9, by contrast, Maecenas is accused of hypocrisy in sending the poet onto the high seas (3: "tam uastum . . . aequor") while keeping his own sails furled (30: "uelorum plenos subtrahis ipse sinus"). Seneca builds on the elegist's "suspicious" reading of Virgil's inconsistent and arbitrary Maecenas by extending the notion of wavering to his entire career. Fashioned as soft by virtue of his poets' literary preferences, he is left behind by them, suspended between sublimity and failure, as they sail

104. Climactic correction with *immo* as a Senecan tic: Traina 1995: 96–97.

105. 2: "in freto uiximus, moriamur in portu". Cf. Sen. *Tranq.* 5.5: retreat from political corruption as touching shore after a perilous voyage; a digression at *Ben.* 6.7.1 recalls Verg. *Aen.* 5.162–63. Seneca's shipwreck imagery: Armisen-Marchetti 1989: 141–42.

106. Seafaring imagery: Curtius 1953: 128–30.

107. Soldo 2021: 245. Harbours signifying closure or retirement: Verg. *G.* 2.541, 4.116–18.

further out. Seneca concedes that Maecenas started out with admirable innate talent (*ingeniosus*)—like Lucilius (*ingeni uigor*)—only to lose it with his decline into soft living and bad style. Both life and style are presented as virtual emasculation ("eneruasset . . . castrasset") for which good fortune is to blame.[108] Seneca divides Maecenas from his poets, claiming Virgil as common property ("Vergilius noster") while devaluing the patron and rejecting him as a purveyor of truth.[109]

Maecenas's next appearance is in a more explicitly metaphysical context, in a letter on the nature of the good life. Seneca dwells on the body's natural weakness and the soul's potential to rise above its ignoble desires. The soul is divided into a stronger, more rational half and a weaker, less rational one, which is then subdivided into two parts, one ambitious and uncontrolled (with its seat in the passions) and the other sluggish and devoted to pleasure:

> inrationalis pars animi duas habet partes, alteram animosam, ambitiosam, inpotentem, positam in adfectionibus, alteram humilem, languidam, uoluptatibus deditam: illam effrenatam, meliorem tamen, certe fortiorem ac digniorem uiro, reliquerunt, hanc necessariam beatae uitae putauerunt, eneruem et abiectam. (Sen. *Ep.* 92.8)

> The irrational part of the soul has two parts. One is spirited, ambitious, uninhibited, based in the emotions; the other is lowly, feeble, given over to pleasure: Philosophers have abandoned the uncontrolled part, which is still the better one, bolder and more worthy of a man, and considered the other part, listless and feeble, essential to the good life.

The Platonic origins of this division between reason and passion are clear enough.[110] Also Platonic are the images of good and bad sovereignty that characterize the soul as governor of the body. But Seneca's brand of Stoicism is focused less on the unchanging nature of the ruling consciousness than on its instability.[111] His division between appetitive ambition and weak sensuality also calls to mind stereotypical Senecan tyrants: Atreus and Thyestes, for example, who between them embrace the monomaniac and self-indulgent aspects of tyranny. Here, Maecenas embodies in one person the soul that wavers between tyrannical great-heartedness and tyrannical flaccidity.

---

108. Cf. *Ep.* 114.8 ("eneruati"); Möller 2004: 205–6.

109. Epicurus replaces him: *Ep.* 19.10. For Epicureans as only superficially soft, cf. *Vit. Beat.* 13.3 and *Ep.* 33.2 (with Edwards 2019: 159); see Edwards (2005: 84–86) and Schiesaro (2015) on Seneca's attraction to Epicurus.

110. Star 2012: 180.

111. Star 2012: 182.

At first, though, another striking image swims into view. Anyone who subordinates his reason to the soul's irrational and lustful parts will turn the Supreme Good into a grotesque hybrid, like Virgil's Scylla, a woman above the waist, a monster below:

> prima hominis facies et pulchro pectore uirgo
> pube tenus, postrema immani corpore pistrix
> delphinium caudas utero commissa luporum

(VERG. AEN. 3.426–28)

Above, a human face and a maiden's beautiful body, down to the waist; below, the huge bulk of a sea-monster, with a dolphin's tail joined to a wolf's belly.

The soul's sensual part is conceived as a "lazy, flaccid animal" (animal iners ac marcidum), broken down and softened by pleasure ("dissoluit et omne robur emolliit"): "It is a fragile thing, whose strength may easily fail at the top of the climb" (in summo deficit cliuo). By contrast, the invincible philosopher at the start of the letter is Nietzschean in his certainty: "He occupies the heights, supported by himself alone: for anyone who is held up by another's strength may fall."[112] With ideas of Promethean aspiration echoing from *Epistles* 19, it is unsurprising that images of female-animal hybridity and material decomposition are followed by another one-line quotation from none other than Maecenas:

> diserte Maecenas ait,
>     nec tumulum curo: sepelit natura relictos.

> alte cinctum putes dixisse; habuit enim ingenium et grande et uirile, nisi illud secunda discinxissent. (Sen. *Ep.* 92.35)

As Maecenas eloquently put it, "I don't care for a grave. For nature gives outcast bodies burial." You would think this was said by a man of principle [lit. one with a high belt]; for he had a noble and virile intellect, had prosperity not slackened it [lit. loosened its belt].

Once again, the author is weighed in the balance.[113] First, grudging admiration, then something more equivocal. Pilfering another line from Virgil, "his canibus data praeda Latinis" (prey given to these Latin dogs; *Aen.* 9.485), and tweaking it into "canibus data praeda marinis" (prey given to marine dogs), Seneca sets it in a new relationship to the earlier quotation: human bodies are thrown

---

112. Sen. *Ep.* 92.2.

113. See Graver (1998: 613, 628) on the convenient slippage of *ingenium* between literary and psychological meanings in *Ep.* 114.

straight to ... Scylla's dogs.[114] Maecenas, then, emerges from poetic or Epicu-rean therapy to utter the defiant riposte *non curo*, "I don't care", before succumb-ing again to moral collapse. As the anti-type of the striving Stoic, Maecenas represents ambition and luxury in counterpoise, soul and body conflicted in the same organism. Like Scylla, he is a different creature below the waist. Like a soft tyrant or the weaker part of the soul, he gives in to temptation. Maecenas's bodily desires are characterized as "a moody and pampered dominion" (moro-sum imperium delicatumque; 33), recalling his sulky wife (*morosa*, "moody", at *Prov.* 3.10). Poetico-biographical "facts"—in other words, those signs of need or weakness or forced allegiance to poetic softness that Maecenas's poets conve-niently created in him—are recycled in the service of ethics and psychology. So crystallizes the "mini-biography" that lasts to the present day.

## *Epistles 114*

The loose belt plays a larger part in the climactic example of Senecan critique, celebrated for its venomous "symphony of grievances". Here enters a mincing figure hard to recognize from his portraits in Augustan poetry but all too easy to align with the victims of Republican invective.[115] Ironically, *Epistles* 114 is also our best source for Maecenas's prose writing, thanks to the catalogue of contemptible fragments dredged up as symptoms of a life badly lived. Seneca starts with generalities and returns to them at the end, but the singular per-sonality of Maecenas as vilified object is central.

In her lucid analysis, Margaret Graver concludes that this specimen of physi-cal and mental fluidity, with his trailing robes (*tunicis solutis*) and loose belt (*dis-cinctus*), inverts wholesale the Stoic principle of *tenor*/Greek *tonos*, the combina-tion of physical and mental control that is the binding proof of *uirtus*.[116] Seneca moves from his sermon on "Le style, c'est l'homme", illustrated by Maecenas's laxity across all areas of his life, to a metaphysical discussion of self-control versus weakness in the human soul, and ends with a satirical extravaganza on the absurdity of gastronomic excess. Connecting the various themes is a funda-mentalist belief in a comfortingly simple interrelationship between moral, physi-cal and stylistic traits: "Intoxication, effeminacy, moral weakness, and bad prose ... interentail in a strange chain of equivalences."[117] But the driving force

---

114. On Seneca's Virgilian quotations: Auvray 1987, Mannering 2008: 186–201.

115. André 1967: 19: "orchestration de tous les griefs". Invective against the effeminate: Glea-son 1995; Edwards 1993: 63–97; Corbeill 1996: 128–73; 1997.

116. Graver 1998: 620–24.

117. Graver 1998: 614. Often challenged in antiquity: cf. Catull. 16, Ov. *Tr.* 2.323–60, Mart. 1.35. See Bramble 1974: 23–25; Möller 2004.

of the letter is more than just philosophical. Seneca is satirical and prurient beyond the call of duty. Again, the corpus he plunders above all is Horatian satire,
which enables him to hoist an Augustan patron with his own petard.

Starting as it does with a question about time, 1 "Quare quibusdam tempo-
ribus . . . quaeris" (You ask for what reason and at what periods of history; *Ep.*
114.1), the letter proposes a tendentious literary-historical framework. It marks
the Augustan Age as the start of decline, not the apex of Roman culture, turning Maecenas into a forerunner of Neronian decadence, on which this is one
of the great contemporary assaults (along with Petron. *Sat.* 1–3 and Persius's
first satire).[118] To this day, "decadence" has many applications: "from the decline of bodily health and the loss of social cohesion to the increasing linguistic
complexity of modern poetry."[119] Maecenas's descent—synchronic (the lower
parts of his body follow the dictates of the "lower" part of his soul) and dia-
chronic (his career defaults on its early promise)—stands for a larger picture
of societal and cultural decay, which begins with the Augustan court and
reaches its nadir under Nero. A few counterfactual concessions are made to
the potential genius dragged down by self-indulgence:

> magni uir ingenii fuerat si illud egisset uia rectiore, si non uitasset intellegi,
> si non etiam in oratione difflueret. uidebis itaque eloquentiam ebrii homi-
> nis inuolutam et errantem et licentiae plenam. [Maecenas de cultu suo.]
> (*Ep.* 114.4)

> He would have been a man of great talent, if he had followed a straighter
> path, if he had not avoided being understood, if he had not been so effusive
> in his language. Thus you will find that his expression is that of a drunkard—
> involved, rambling and uninhibited. [Maecenas on His Style]

But when his reputation as a political dove is reassessed, the trademark clemency (*mansuetudo*) is renamed as "softness": "apparet enim mollem fuisse, non
mitem" (He appears to have been not mild but soft; 7).[120]

Seneca introduces Maecenas by proclaiming that the way he lived—his
walk, his pampered softness, his exhibitionism—needs no introduction:

> Quomodo Maecenas uixerit notius est quam ut narrari nunc debeat quo-
> modo ambulauerit, quam delicatus fuerit, quam cupierit uideri, quam uitia
> sua latere noluerit. (*Ep.* 114.4)

---

118. All three brim with bodily metaphors: Bramble 1974. For decline as an explanation in
imperial rhetorical theory, see Sen. *Controv.* 1 *praef.* 7–8, Vell. Pat. 1.17, Tac. *Dial.* 28–32, Longinus, *Peri Hupsous* 44; Summers 1910: 338–40.

119. Potolsky 2004: vi.

120. Seneca conceived as mild in relation to Nero: Ps.-Sen. *Octavia* 445: "praecipere mitem
conuenit pueris senem".

> How Maecenas led his life is too notorious for me to need to relate: how he walked, how pampered he was, how much he wanted to be seen, how he refused to cover up his vices.

This is *praeteritio* that lingers unnecessarily on its scandalous subject matter.[121] As Seneca sees it, Maecenas's notoriety is not just a consequence of historical memory, it is aided by his exhibitionist tendencies, his public flaunting of his vices in the streets of Rome as a loafer performing *otium*.[122] Whatever the historical basis, Seneca has other motives. By stressing Maecenas's glaring visibility, he compensates for the poets' hermetic protection of their patron and their mystifying strategies of representation. As with other post-Augustan writers, Seneca's "manhandling" (Graver's term) is an overreaction to his teasingly guarded charisma. Maecenas's attendants, two eunuchs, "more men than he was", even suggest sidekicks Horace and Virgil. The patron's sympathy is reworked as passive inattention; Seneca has already accused Maecenas of being deaf to Virgil's "Stoic" advice (*Ep.* 101.13).

The compulsion to spill what was once contained may also explain why this section contains so many echoes from the ur-text of mystification in the Roman streetscape: Horace, *Satires* 1.9, where the satirist successfully deflects a brash outsider from Maecenas's house. One of Horace's ploys to fend off his pushy new acquaintance is to claim that he is on his way to visit "someone you don't know" (non tibi notum; 17). The Pest's desired destination, Maecenas's house, is equally under wraps. Horace is "pulling up the draw-bridge after himself". His Maecenas is not to be known, except by a precious few ("paucorum hominum"; 44).[123] Now, suddenly, his life lies open. It has become public property: "too notorious to need narrating".

As for the phrase that introduces this section, "quomodo Maecenas uixerit" (how Maecenas lived his life), it reads like a knowing answer to the impudent question posed by the same enfant terrible: "Quomodo Maecenas tecum?" (What's life like with Maecenas?; Hor. *Sat.* 1.9.43). Horace had responded by stonewalling, stressing the moral stainlessness, altruism and common purpose of the charmed circle, only increasing the Pest's longing for access to it. Seneca dislodges the patron from his pedestal and pins him at one extreme on a scale of eccentricities, stylistic and sartorial, inspired by Horace's own variations on deviancy, inconsistency and behavioural excess in *Satires* 1.1–3. The rough-diamond narrator of the *Satires* (thinly disguised at *Sat.* 1.3.33–35) is vindicated, while smooth, flashy Maecenas becomes a moral antitype. Another

121. Möller 2004: 182–83.
122. Möller 2004: 182.
123. Henderson 1999: 223.

opposition, from *Satires* 1.2, informs Seneca's "portrait on the move" of Maecenas the mincing statesman:[124]

> Maltinus tunicis demissis ambulat, est qui
> inguen ad obscenum subductis usque.
>
> (HOR. SAT. 1.2.25–26)

Maltinus walks the streets in flowing robes; another man has his pulled
right up to show his indecent groin.

The idea that the louche Maltinus is a cover for Maecenas (cf. *ambulauerit,
solutis tunicis*) is usually credited to later scholiasts, but it may have been Seneca who initiated the connection.[125]

Even Horace's paradigmatically inconsistent diva, Tigellius, with his seedy
band of parasites, mime actresses and clowns ("quippe benignus erat" [After
all, he *was* generous]; *Sat.* 1.2.4), begins to look like a caricature of Maecenas
as unstinting patron and unappreciated artist. In the same poem, Horace had
hinted at similarities between jealously guarded matrons and the desired patron,
hidden in his sealed house. Seneca's countermove is even more sensational. His
exhibitionist Maecenas recalls the prim matrons' opposites, prostitutes who
flaunt their wares beneath see-through Coan silks:

> altera, nil obstat: Cois tibi paene uidere est
> ut nudam, ne crure malo, ne sit pede turpi;
> metiri possis oculo latus.
>
> (HOR. SAT. 1.2.101–3)

The other type leaves no holds barred: you can see her nude through Coan
silks and check her legs aren't crooked, her feet aren't ugly; you can size up
her figure at a glance.

More accurately, he squeezes him into an unhappy middle, as practitioner of a
"now you see it, now you don't" striptease (cf. 21: "perlucentem togam"), somewhere between the matrons' prudery and the prostitutes' honest nakedness:

> adde huc, quod mercem sine fucis gestat, aperte
> quod uenale habet ostendit nec, si quid honesti est,
> iactat habetque palam, quaerit, quo turpia celet.
>
> (SAT. 1.2.83–85)

124. Degl'Innocenti Pierini 2013: 55–57; cf. Corbeill 1996: 128–73.
125. Porph. *ad* Hor. *Sat.* 1.2.25; Tischer 2006: 134–35.

Add the fact that she struts her stuff without cosmetics, and shows her wares openly, won't boast and flaunt the charms she has while hiding her bad points.

Unlike Tigellius, Maecenas could hardly be more consistent (*compositus*) across all aspects of his behaviour. Seneca thus finds a satirical pedigree for both philosophical inconstancy and faulty literary technique; departures from the behavioural mean, as in Horace, illustrate a range of rhetorical solecisms, from awkward archaism to over-smooth fluidity.[126] Maecenas is just the salient figure in a panorama of deviancy that spans the full Republican repertoire of sartorial and rhetorical markers, from men who shave their legs to those who leave their armpits hairy, from brusque admirers of the Twelve Tables to lovers of Ciceronian smoothness.[127]

Other oppositions, ethnic and cultural, are in play. Maecenas's riskiest mistake was letting his private luxury overflow into public routine, and here one detail seems oddly specific. He dared to appear on official business wearing a cloak wrapped around his head:

sic apparuerit ut pallio uelaretur caput exclusis utrimque auribus, non aliter quam in mimi fugitiui diuitis solent (Sen. *Ep.* 114.6)

This was the man who appeared with his head covered in a cloak with only his ears showing, like a rich man's runaway slaves in a mime

Slaves in Greco-Roman comedy did indeed often elude their masters by wrapping their heads in the *pallium* or cloak that gave *fabula palliata* its name.[128] But far from hiding from view, this Maecenas flaunts his presence. His makeshift head covering looks suspiciously like a xenophobic version of the Lydian turban or *mitra*, which King Midas, for example, wrapped around his head to conceal his donkey's ears (Ov. *Met.* 11.180–81) but which normally left the ears exposed, as in vase paintings of fifth-century "Lydianizing" turban-wearing sodalities.[129] Seneca proceeds to explain this headgear according to a very different semiotics, making Maecenas a "Lydian" in another sense, not an aristocrat or a king, but a shifty comic slave.[130] The giveaway word here is

---

126. For Freudenburg (1993: 193–98), the adulterer in his *discincta tunica* (Hor. *Sat.* 1.2.132) represents dishevelled style.

127. Gesture in Republican invective: Corbeill 2004: 107–39. Hairstyle and dress as indexes of character: Edwards 1993: 63, 90–92; Corbeill 1996: 151–68; Gell. *NA* 6.12.5. Depilation and style: Edwards 1993: 68–69.

128. Cf. Plaut. *Curc.* 288; *Poen.* 976.

129. See chapter 1.

130. Cic. *Flac.* 65: all comic slaves are Lydian (or called Lydus).

*diuitis*, which epitomizes the downgrade from Roman millionaire to Plautine "towelhead", or from Midas to mime actor and fugitive.

Continuing to make Roman absurdity out of Eastern absolutism and retrospectively orientalize the Augustan court, Seneca turns to sex:

> hunc esse cui tunc maxime ciuilibus bellis strepentibus et sollicita urbe et armata comitatus hic fuerit in publico, spadones duo, magis tamen uiri quam ipse; hunc esse qui uxorem milliens duxit, cum unam habuerit? (*Ep.* 114.6)

> Was this the man who, in the raging din of civil strife, when Rome was in a state of emergency under martial law, appeared in public flanked by two eunuchs, more men than he was; was this the man who had but one wife but married her a thousand times?

If the servants who flanked Maecenas were "more men than he was", this makes him an imperial eunuch avant la lettre. If his wife enslaved and rejected him, such that he remarried her a thousand times (*milliens*), he is a Persian polygamist—or even a wife himself, a military man's housekeeper:[131] "nam etiam cum absentis Caesaris partibus fungeretur, signum a discincto petebatur" (Even when he stood in for the absent Caesar, the password was requested from a man in pyjamas; *Ep.* 114.6).

Finally, Maecenas's passivity as poetic addressee is recast as passivity in the sphere of pleasure, which culminates in impotence and voyeurism.[132] A man overcome by morbid passion who can no longer perform will end up enjoying his favourite delights only vicariously:

> cum uero magis ac magis uires morbus exedit et in medullas neruosque descendere deliciae, conspectu eorum quibus se nimia auiditate inutilem reddidit laetus, pro suis uoluptatibus habet alienarum spectaculum, sumministrator libidinum testisque, quarum usum sibi ingerendo abstulit. nec illi tam gratum est abundare iucundis quam acerbum quod non omnem illum apparatum per gulam uentremque transmittit, quod non cum omni exoletorum feminarumque turba conuolutatur, maeretque quod magna pars suae felicitatis exclusa corporis angustiis cessat. (*Ep.* 114.25)

> But when the disease by degrees has eaten away the body's strength, and luxurious habits have descended into the marrow and the sinews, a soul like this rejoices at the sight of bodies which, through excessive greed, it has

---

131. Cf. Luc. *Bellum ciuile* 8.401 on the Parthians' "thousand brides". For a more mundane possibility, divorce and remarriage, see above, pp. 2–3.

132. See Kaster (2002) and Bartsch (2006: 81–83) on *patientia* as both Stoic virtue and mark of deviancy.

made useless; instead of its own pleasures, it views those of others; it becomes the supplier and witness of the lusts which, as the result of over-gratification, it can no longer satisfy. Wallowing in pleasure is less delicious to that soul than bitter, because it cannot send all the whole menu down its throat and stomach, because it can no longer spin in a crowd of male and female prostitutes, and it is miserable because a large part of its happiness is ruled out by the limitations of the body.

By implication, Augustus's minister is no better than a pimp ("sumministrator libidinum"), blurred with the crowds of superannuated male prostitutes and women ("omni exoletorum feminarumque turba") he used to enjoy.[133] His susceptibility to *deliciae* remains consistent, whether these are sensory treats, stylistic self-indulgence or human favourites ("se in delicias dedit" [*Ep*. 114.2]; "delicatus" [4]; "istis orationis portentosissimae deliciis" [7]; "deliciae" [25]), and this will become the lasting residue of his personality ("deliciis"; *Ep*. 120.19).

As for Maecenas's incriminating literary fragments, why does Seneca object to them so much? Bold metaphors and neologisms are indeed combined with bizarre and choppy syntax, so that the snippets fall short of a literary ideal that, like the perfect human, is *compositus*, put together in a controlled way. But the way Seneca arranges them is maximally wild and experimental. Strung together out of context, first interlarded with shocked intakes of breath (*quid; uide ut; quid*), then swimming unbroken into each other, they are almost impossible to translate without rationalizing the syntax and doing violence to the word order:[134]

quid turpius "amne siluisque ripa comantibus"? uide ut "alueum lyntribus arent uersoque uado remittant hortos". quid? si quis "feminae cinno crispat et labris columbatur incipitque suspirans, ut ceruice lassa fanantur nemoris tyranni". "inremediabilis factio rimantur epulis lagonaque temptant domos et spe mortem exigunt." "genium festo uix suo testem." "tenuisue cerei fila et crepacem molam." "focum mater aut uxor inuestiunt." (*Ep*. 114.5)

What could be more shocking than "On the river and among the woods be-tressing the bank"? Look at "They plough the seabed with skiffs and upturning the shallows rake up gardens in their wake." How about "He curls his mouth with a feminine pout and pigeons up his lips, sighing, like the tyrants of the grove who sway with languid necks"? "The unregenerate

---

133. "Over-age male prostitutes", *exoleti*, recall *uerba exoleta*, the "obsolete words" (10) loved by antiquarians; cf. *Ep*. 122.7.

134. Avallone [1962/63]: 219–36; André 1983; Bardon 1952: 2.13–19; Makowski 1991; Mattiacci 1995.

conspirators rummage through feasts and make trial palaces with flagons and exact death by means of hope." "The spirit is barely witness to his own feast." "The slender thread of wax and the clattering grinder." "Mothers or wives enrobe the hearth."

Maecenas had evidently become a "proverbial goldmine of *mala exempla*".[135] On the other hand, it is entirely possible that these are parodies made up by Seneca himself.[136] If they are genuine, what is really striking (and suspicious) is how cleverly selected they are. Not only do they illustrate aspects of style considered limp, attention-seeking or perversely novel: irrational metaphors and syntax, neologisms (*cinnus, columbari, fanari, inremediabilis, crepax*), deponent verbs (active in sense but appearing passive) and pathetic fallacy (e.g. *comantibus, columbatur, fanantur, rimantur, inuestiunt*).[137] They also pack in images redolent of the decadent life that the letter condemns: woman(liness) (*feminae*), hair and crimping (*comantibus, crispat*), erotics (*labris columbatur*), gardens (*hortos*), tyrants (*tyranni*), floppy necks (*ceruice lassa*), feasts (*epulis*), wine (*lagona*), wives (*uxor*), clothes (*inuestiunt*), Bacchic mania (*fanantur*).[138] Churned-up seas and long-haired riverbanks foreground fluidity.[139] Verbal affectations are imagined as crimped hair or ringlets, surface tricks described as rouge or slinky garments.[140]

135. Avallone [1962/63]: 266, cited by Makowski 1991: 30n21.

136. Cf. Quintilian's similar list at 9.4.28.

137. Sklénář (2017: 5) observes how the excerpts illustrate the stylistic vices of *Ep.* 114.1.

138. Women: "effeminatus", "mollitiam" (3); "uirilis" (22); "feminarumque turba" (25). Hair: "qui aut uellunt barbam aut interuellunt" (21); Berti (2014: 231) compares the seductive pastoral of Apul. *Met.* 5.25.3 ("proxime ripam uago pastu lasciuiunt comam fluuii tondentes capellae"); cf. Auson. *Mos.* 189–99. Erotics: "libidinum" (25). Floppiness: "eneruati . . . motum illi felicitate nimia caput"(8); "marcent . . . ex languido fluidoque" (23). Feasts: "conuiuiorum luxuria" (11); "culinas nostras et concursantis inter tot ignes cocos" (26). Wine: "eloquentiam ebrii hominis" (4); "in uino . . . titubat . . . ebrietas" (22). Wives: "uxor" (4). Clothes: "perlucentem togam" (21); Lunderstedt (1911: 73) cites Plin. *Ep.* 8.8.4: "ripae fraxino multa, multa populo uestiuntur".

139. Cf. "effluxit" (15); "et omnis ex languido fluidoque conatus est" (23). I read "rake up gardens" (remittant hortos) as picking up *arent*, "plough" (cf. Cat. 64.12: "proscidit aequor"): churned up, the water sprouts plant-like foam.

140. Summers (1908: 171) suspects "ringlets" (printing *concinnos* for *cinno*). Gell. *NA* 20.9.2 quotes Matius's "sinuque amicam refice frigidam caldo columbatim labra conserens labris" (Revive your cold sweetheart in your warm embrace, stitching lip to lip like doves); Antonius Julianus adds an extract from Matius's mimiambi: "iam tonsiles tapetes ebrii fuco quos concha purpura imbuens uenenauit" (The shorn rugs are now drunk on the purple with which the shell has drenched and imbued them).

In one sense, then, the scribal interpolator is right: this *is* Maecenas "on his personal style". The fragments exaggerate the notorious personal and stylistic traits listed earlier, magnifying the reader's disapproval. Translated back into rhetorical metaphors later in the letter, they bolster the identification of world view and style for which Seneca is arguing.[141] Maecenas can even be dismissed as inadequate in relation to the poetic genres he fostered: georgic poetry ("tenuisue cerei fila et crepacem molam") and comedy or love poetry ("labris columbatur"). He can be convicted of the very indirections that Virgil claims to avoid in his address to him at *Georgics* 2.46, so that the wayward Pindaric imagery for which the poet was responsible can now be conveniently offloaded onto the patron.

This concerted flaying of Maecenas chimes with an anecdote about Virgil, accused by one Vipsanius/Vipranius (possibly Agrippa) of a specific kind of *cacozelia*:

> M. Vipranius [Vipsanius edd.] a Maecenate eum suppositum appellabat nouae cacozeliae repertorem, non tumidae nec exilis, sed ex communibus uerbis atque ideo latentis. (Donat. *Vit. Verg.* 44)

> M. Vipranius [Vipsanius] called Virgil Maecenas's substitute son and "inventor" of a new kind of affected style, not the swollen or the thin kind, but one composed of ordinary words and therefore less obtrusive.

Behind this cryptic sentence lies an ancient typology of styles couched in bodily metaphors, "as if a writer's style resembled the flesh on the bones of an animal".[142] A close study of rhetorical definitions concludes that between the "bloated" and "windy" style and the "thin" and "moistureless" one lay a middle style, characterized by "lack of muscle, flabbiness, vagueness and ambiguity".[143] This sounds very like the metaphorical basis of Seneca's attacks on Maecenas's writing, as scapegoat for the "flaccid" style.[144] In his defence, one of Maecenas's objectionable metaphors, "rimantur epulis" (rummage for a feast), draws directly on Virgil's "rimaturque epulis" (and gropes for his feast; of a vulture pecking at Tityus).[145] But Seneca roundly condemns Maecenas as corrupt:

---

141. Gunderson 2015: 161n42: "One can and should read bi-directionally, and that is just what happens to Maecenas in this letter."

142. Jocelyn 1979: 71.

143. See *Rhet. Her.* 4.15 with Jocelyn (1979: 67–142). Cf. Varro ap. Gell. *NA* 6.14.5.

144. *Contra* Mattiacci 1995: Maecenas's writings are both *tumidum* and *exile*; Sklénář 2017: 4–5: both "drunken" and over-styled. Cf. Macrob. *Sat.* 2.4.12: "stilo . . . remisso, molli et dissoluto".

145. Verg. *Aen.* 6.600. Berti 2014: 235–36.

If the soul is strong and well [sano ac ualente], speech is also robust, tough and virile [robusta, fortis, uirilis] . . . when it has yielded to pleasure, the soul's functions and actions grow feeble and each effort comes from a limp and wavering source [ex languido fluidoque] (114.22–23).

This is the very language Seneca the Elder's Maecenas had used to defend Virgil: "et magna et tamen sana" (both grand and wholesome; *Suas.* 1.12).

Virgil will stay in Seneca's mind for the rest of the letter, as he turns from Maecenas and literary style to more general assertions about conflicts in the human soul, framed in terms of good governance and tyranny. The mentality of a ruler connects the microcosm of soul with the macrocosm of empire: "Seneca is concerned with the language (*oratio*) of a potentate and how this externalizes the workings of his soul."[146] Drawing on the exotic titles the poets bestowed on him, he continues to stain Maecenas with Eastern tyranny, adapting Virgil's warring king bees to develop analogies between *imperium* and mental control:

> rege incolumi mens omnibus una est,
> amisso rupere fidem

(SEN. *EP.* 114.23 = VERG. G. 4.212–13)

While the king is safe, everyone acts with one mind; when he is lost, their obligations are broken.

It is the presence of the word *mens*, "mind", in Virgil's original that makes it so adaptable to a metaphysical context: "animus noster modo rex est, modo tyrannus" (Our mind is sometimes a king, sometimes a tyrant; *Ep.* 114.24).[147] Incidentally, Seneca's use of the quotation reinforces my earlier suggestion that Maecenas, not Augustus, is the implied addressee of Virgil's bee politics in *Georgics* 4, the man with kingly fantasies who is also a theorist of monarchy.[148]

But it is not just political analogies that the quotation activates. The picture of a leader who unites his people suggests Maecenas's "circle", which held together with one mind as long as he headed it (cf. Hor. *Sat.* 1.9.47–51) but which without him fell apart. Seneca sometimes draws on past eras for epistolary company, reviving idealized circles from the lost middle Republic, the "Scipionic Circle" in particular.[149] He does not celebrate Maecenas's coterie in the

---

146. Star 2012: 177.

147. More bee quotations at *Apocol.* 3, *Clem.* 1.4.2.

148. See above p. 146. See also Sklénář 2017: 13–15.

149. Gowers 2011a: 173.

same way. Instead, he deliberately isolates the patron from his special group and undoes its cohesive work: "'Quid ergo? beneficia non parant amicitias?' parant, si accepturos licuit eligere, si collocata, non sparsa sunt . . ." ("What," you say, "do not kindnesses establish friendships?" They do, if one has had the privilege of choosing those who are to receive them, and if they are placed judiciously, instead of being scattered broadcast . . . ; *Ep*. 19.12). Nor can the *convivium* sustain its integrity in an era of decadence. The binding power of food and wine dissolves: courses are served in the wrong order, recherché ingredients are poured wholesale down the gullet, wine produces tottering drunkards. Seneca's "pornographic" treatment of Maecenas's style—its shameless metaphors, its drunken rambling—hints at off-stage scandals.[150] Instead of a closed circle, there is *turba cultiore* ("the arty crowd"), where *turba* is the normal word for diluting the prestige of any self-proclaimed exclusive group and *cultiore* suggests elegance taken to extremes.[151] So the tight-knit clique of Maecenas leaks and seeps beyond its confines, infected retrospectively by Neronian corruption. The ideal poetic circle that Horace so carefully fashioned in his *Satires* had seemed unassailable because it was so unspecific. The Maecenas so hazily sketched there practised a fetishized lifestyle (*mos*) to which few had access; his household upheld the proper hierarchies (*Sat.* 1.9.51–52). Seneca undoes all this prudent work. His Maecenas is as promiscuous and perverse as his flamboyant style: "So improperly arranged, so carelessly thrown in, so unconventionally placed, these words show that his character [mores] was no less novel, depraved and idiosyncratic" (*Ep.* 114.7).

## Maecenas the Decadent

There is one saving grace. Seneca's composite is one of Western culture's earliest portraits of the libertine or decadent. His Maecenas is a forerunner not just of Tacitus's Petronius but also of Casanova, the Marquis de Sade, Aubrey Beardsley and Oscar Wilde.[152] The "tortured inconstant soul" recalled by Syme, a hybrid of Horatian lyric longing and Senecan metaphysical analogy, will have a long afterlife in the sphere of aesthetics.[153] Hypersensitivity unites the insomniac Maecenas of Horatian lyric and Senecan sermon with the fastidious Maecenas of Horace's *Epistles*, wincing at a jagged fingernail (*Epist.*

150. Gunderson 2015: 167n59.

151. Cf. Sen. *Ep*. 114.25: "omni exoletorum feminarumque turba".

152. Sklénář 2017: 4: "a sort of proto-Aubrey Beardsley figure whose perfumed style matched his dandyish dress and libertine habits".

153. Syme 1939: 341. Decadence: Gilman 1979; Potolsky 2004.

1.1.104). A direct line stretches from these portraits to another neurotically refined fictional aristocrat, Jean Des Esseintes:

> Ever since his early youth, he had been tormented by inexplicable feelings of revulsion, by shuddering spasms which left him chilled to the marrow, his teeth on edge, whenever, for instance, he saw wet laundry being wrung out by a servant; these reactions still persisted; even today it actually made him suffer to hear someone tearing up a cloth, or to rub his finger over a bit of chalk or run his hand over a piece of watered silk.[154]

Like Des Esseintes, Maecenas is a deviant who fashions a life *à rebours*, in contraflow to Seneca's project of moral progress.[155] So the metaphors of *Epistles* 122 suggest:[156]

> ideo, Lucili, tenenda nobis uia est quam natura praescripsit, nec ab illa declinandum: illam sequentibus omnia facilia, expedita sunt, contra illam nitentibus non alia uita est quam contra aquam remigantibus. (Sen. *Ep.* 122.19)

> And so, Lucilius, we should stick to the path that nature has ordained for us, not deviate from it: if we follow it, everything is easy and straightforward; if we struggle against it, it is a life that constantly rows against the current.

---

154. Huysmans (1891) 1998: 70.
155. Sen. *Ep.* 114.10 speaks of style swinging between novelty and archaism.
156. Makowski 1991: 27: "épater la bourgeoisie"; cf. Sklénář 2017: 6.

# 7

# Missing Maecenas

POST-AUGUSTAN APPEARANCES

laudatur ab his, culpatur ab illis
He is praised by some, deplored by others
—HORACE, *SATIRES* 1.2.11

But ah, Maecenas is yclad in clay,
And great Augustus long ago is dead:
And all the Worthies liggen wrapp'd in lead,
That matter made for Poets on to play.
—EDMUND SPENSER, *THE SHEPHEARDES CALENDAR*

FOR THE CENTURY and a half following his death, Maecenas remained an absent presence in Latin literature, invoked and mourned against the towering development of that era: the consolidation of the emperor as Rome's most visible benefactor. Beneath the overarching imperial umbrella, however, some things did not change. Local networks of elite and other patrons continued to operate; parochial ties of *amicitia* and *officium* continued to be exercised.[1] From exile in the early first century CE, Ovid writes to both Augustus and lesser patrons Paulus Fabius Maximus, Cotta Maximus and Sextus Pompeius, as well as to various anonymized benefactors, as if to withhold their identity signalled the breakdown of the *kleos*-bargain under such dire circumstances.[2]

For all that, some significant changes affected literary production at Rome. Encomium and panegyric developed as rhetorical modes, from hesitant and

---

1. On imperial patronage, literary and otherwise, see Saller (1982a, b) and Nauta (2002).
2. Oliensis 1997: 178.

problematic to routine—and still problematic. While emperors went on refusing to be named as divine, divinity became a standard element in the discourse that surrounded them.[3] Court culture took hold, with its networks of favourites, dissidents and spies; imperial spectacle, victories and favourites became predictable poetic topics; *otium* supplanted *res gestae* as an arena for elite self-fashioning.[4] In particular, a new term came into effect, perhaps inspired by Maecenas's bidirectional relationships: "indulgence" (*indulgentia*), a euphemism for whatever special favours a powerful patron bestowed on a client or an emperor on a subject.[5] Successful freedmen, actors, provincials and immigrants were perceived as displacing what Juvenal deplores as the "half-eaten nobility" (nobilitate comesa; Juv. 1.34). For all the lavish dinners and public feasts on offer, not everyone, it seems, found space at the imperial table.

Maecenas's uniqueness and good fortune were commemorated from different angles. He came to exemplify the generous, civilized nobleman, a patron in his own right, but just as importantly the necessary barrier or conduit between an independent-minded poet and a demanding higher patron, the emperor. His posthumous reputation splits drastically in ethical terms too: "He is praised by some, deplored by others" (laudatur ab his, culpatur ab illis), as Horace said of another paradigm of inconsistency, the diva-benefactor Tigellius (Hor. *Sat.* 1.2.11). As we have seen, the debating habit, preserved in the Elder Seneca's declamatory collections, helped to shape a controversial character, while the Younger Seneca leaves us with the most devastating of critiques. Works that spar over Maecenas's memory run the full gamut from encomium and funeral elegy to satire, philosophical epistle to ironic historiography. Their authors are swayed by different concepts of periodization—whether they see the Augustan Age as the apogee of artistic fulfilment or as the first chapter in the history of imperial decline—and by their views on *otium*, social exclusivity, and the benefits of entwining private and public patronage. Some celebrate Maecenas as the archetype of the ideal patron, who presided over a paradise where potential was fully realized and money flowed like milk and honey. Others cast him as a slimy dissimulator, prototype of the imperial courtier, not only surrounded by pantomimes, freedmen, parasites, eunuchs, courtesans and favourites but tending towards

---

3. See M. Griffin (2000) on the source of Domitian's title *dominus ac deus*. Citizens offered to devise a genealogy from Hercules for Vespasian, who laughed them away; Suet. *Vesp.* 12.1.

4. La Penna 1981, Leppin 1992.

5. Courtney 1980 *ad* Juv. 7.21. An inscription (*AE* 1973: 137) commends Domitian's *indulgentia* to the citizens of Puteoli; Flower 2001. Cf. Stat. *Silv.* 1 *praef.* ("indulgentissimo imperatori"), ibid. 5.2.125; *Eleg. in Maec.* 1.105; Calp. *Ecl.* 4.33, 7.73; *Laus Pisonis* 111. Cf. Tac. *Dial.* 9 (Vespasian's gift of half a million sesterces to the poet Saleius Bassus was "indulgentiam principis"; cf. Juv. 7.80); Suet. *Iul.* 69 ("indulgentia ducis" of Julius Caesar).

all those roles in his own right. The sense of exclusion forcefully imposed by Horace intensifies. Everyone is a Pest now, shut out of a charmed circle.

No sooner does the individual Maecenas fade from view than he resurfaces as generic *Maecenas* or splinters into plural *Maecenates,* a receding train of reincarnated dandies and sluggish statesmen—pale imitations and distorted caricatures of the original. The Younger Seneca's writing had already pierced the membrane that once made him impenetrable to the world and allowed unpalatable things to leak out. At the same time, perceived gaps in Maecenas's life story begin to be filled by creative fictions (*pseudepigrapha*): a missing funeral lament, narratives of the poets' first approaches, and details of the gifts he really gave them.[6] Once-valued qualities tip easily into their negative versions: nonchalance (*neglegentia*) is reinterpreted as idleness, mildness as softness, generosity as overflow.[7] The shadowy figure in the background of Augustan poetry gains a fleshier corpus—unctuous, corrupt, dripping, even. Care for his poets is recast as pampering and exposed as a quid pro quo of cash, food or sex in return for forced praise.[8]

At its least subtle, Maecenas's upright character dissolves into a fatty stew of humidity, nakedness and corruption. In Juvenal's first satire, for example, among a parade of unspeakables who justify his critique of modern Rome, a millionaire leans out of his carriage window flashing a gaudy ring, sparking memories of "supine Maecenas":

> cum iam sexta ceruice feratur
> hinc atque inde patens ac nuda paene cathedra
> et multum referens de Maecenate supino
> signator falsi, qui se lautum atque beatum
> exiguis tabulis et gemma fecerit uda?
>
> (JUV. 1.64–68)

When a signatory to fake wills is carried on six [slaves'] necks in a litter that is gaping open here and there and almost indecently exposed, strongly reminiscent of lounging Maecenas—a man who has made himself prosperous through little codicils and a moist signet ring.

The famous executive ring is here repurposed for will tampering and unpleasantly moistened for use. Far from sealing, it positively enables the flow of

---

6. Peirano 2012: 10.

7. See, e.g., Bellandi (1995: 83) on *mollitia* as nonchalance "misunderstood". Cf. Sen. *Ep.* 114.7: "mollem . . . non mitem" (not mild but soft).

8. Damon 1997.

favours. The effeminate vehicle (*cathedra*) with twitching curtains stands in for its lolling, exhibitionist passenger, while the relaxed posture of *otium* is portrayed as indolence (*supino*), maintained on the backs of others. Elsewhere in Juvenal, what survives of Maecenas is the luxurious dress that attracts copy-cat dandies: "uestem / purpuream teneris quoque Maecenatibus aptam" (a purple robe suitable for delicate/young Maecenases; 12.39–40).[9]

Similarly diminished or warped reminders of his singularity abound in imperial fictions or semi-fictions (Petronius's Trimalchio, Tacitus's Petronius and other imperial statesmen) and in the real freedmen and freedwomen who preserve his name in imperial *columbaria*: Delphus Maecenatianus, C. Maecenas Nicia(s), Maecenatia Trophime. The adjective *Maecenatianus*, "derived from, possessed by, or characteristic of Maecenas", not only labelled his ex-slaves and categorized by-products of his estates, such as wine (*uina Maecenatiana*) and the Tower (*turris Maecenatiana*), but also suggested his aura and the contagiousness of his habits, in an era where simulation was a hallmark. When Tiberius asked Postumus Agrippa's impersonator how he became Agrippa, Clemens replied, "the same way you became Caesar" (quo modo tu Caesar; Tac. *Ann.* 2.40.3).[10]

The residue of Maecenas in post-Augustan literature offers a broad spectrum of responses to his absence: longing, mourning, emulation, caricature, revulsion, like-minded boredom and wholesale resentment. Some leeway with chronology may perhaps be tolerated when the texts concerned are so hard to date and the relationships between them so hard to define.[11] Scholars have found it convenient and productive to put authors into clusters, Nero's reign being a favourite magnet.[12] For authors like Petronius and Calpurnius Siculus, a Neronian date is periodically challenged, but to little effect.[13] Key texts like the *Elegiae in Maecenatem* and the *Laus Pisonis* float without date or identifiable author. Double layers of distance are a further complication: Trajanic writers Suetonius and Tacitus refract Maecenas through the lens of Nero, Domitian, Nerva, Trajan and Hadrian; Cassius Dio, third-century CE Greek historian, imagines rival policy proposals by Maecenas and Agrippa, which plainly address concerns of his own time.[14] It has sometimes been argued that

---

9. Cf. Mart. 10.73.4: "Ausoniae . . . togae qua . . . uti uellet Maecenas".

10. Syme 1958: 1.92 calls Titinius Capito, an equestrian who aped senators, "a document of social mimicry".

11. Bellandi 1995: 78n2: the *Laus Pisonis* postdates and engages with the *Elegiae*; cf. Nicastri 1980; La Penna 1981.

12. Gowers 1994; Vout 2009.

13. E.g., Champlin 1989 (Calpurnius); Flobert 2003 (Petronius).

14. I do not discuss the two speeches (Dio Cass. 52.2–40) here. For a variety of approaches, see P. Meyer (1891), R. Meyer (1986), Smyshlyayev (1991), Kulhmann (2010) and Adler (2012).

dates don't matter, given that rhetorical solutions to addressing an emperor or imperial patron are timeless events.[15] There is some truth to this, yet individual emperors will have had different potential relationships to any hypothetical "Maecenas", depending on their level of interest in the arts and the harshness of their regimes. At any rate, post-Augustan Maecenas emerges as strangely lopsided. Neither the *Elegiae*, the most appreciative imperial tribute, nor Seneca's coruscating *Epistles* 114 refers to his activities as a patron, only to those of a statesman and devotee of leisure. Maecenas's posthumous memory is sifted to suit the divergent needs and perspectives of his observers.

## Maecenas Indulged

How do you solve a problem like Maecenas? The case for the defence is refreshingly put in the *Elegiae in Maecenatem*, a poetic diptych that supplies the need for a memorial for Augustus's "right-hand man" (Caesaris . . . dextera; 1.13–14). This *pseudepigraphon* or "chronological fake" purports to be a timely response to his death (8 BCE), but was almost certainly written sometime in the first century CE.[16] It remains unclear whether it pre- or postdates Seneca's epistle 114 (60s CE), with which it shares certain features (its focus on loose robes and its silence about Maecenas's role as patron).[17] The twin poems were first separated by Scaliger and are traditionally included in the *Appendix Vergiliana*, the spurious "collected works" of the young Virgil.[18] They evoke Maecenas's other poets, too: Horace (one Lollius is the poems' commissioner) and Propertius (imitating his choice of elegiacs) are implicitly reproached for not writing any lament themselves.[19] The first poem praises Maecenas's career as Augustus's caretaker in Rome and (less plausibly) as his aide-de-camp at Actium, excusing his early retirement as honourable and harmless. In the shorter second poem, a dying Maecenas clings onto speech, devising a succession policy for Augustus while predicting his apotheosis.

Read together, the two poems offer a sentimental retrospective on the Augustan Age from the imagined viewpoint of an imperial favourite.[20] They

15. Ov. *Tr.* 1.1 and 2 and Hor. *Epist.* 2.1 are primary influences.

16. On the date: Schoonhoven 1980: 39–66; Della Corte 1974–75: 2.118, Nigro 1998: 148; Le Doze 2012.

17. See Bickel 1950; Peirano 2012: 230.

18. See Schoonhoven (1980: 1–6) on the textual tradition; for further commentary, see Fraschetti and Ursini (2016).

19. Suet. *Vita Hor.* records seeing bogus elegies ascribed to Horace.

20. Maecenas as a challenging rhetorical topic: Peirano 2012: 225; cf. Pease 1926. See Fairweather (1981: 110) on imperial imitations of poems on Augustan favourites: Gallio's *Rescriptum*

celebrate a trendsetting courtier as something rare and precious: a beryl among common grains of sand (*Eleg. in Maec.* 1.19), "unique Maecenas" (unus Maecenas; 2.25).[21] In so doing, they configure, then mourn, a special coincidence of individual choice and political climate. Not only did the pax Augusta enable Maecenas's life of *otium* in a tranquil garden:

> maluit umbrosam quercum lymphasque cadentes
>     paucaque pomosi iugera certa soli:
> Pieridas Phoebumque colens in mollibus hortis
>     sederat argutas garrulus inter aues.

(ELEG. IN MAEC. 1.33–36)

He chose instead a shady oak and falling waters, a few sure acres of fruitful soil. Cultivating the Muses and Apollo in luxurious gardens, he reclined, chattering with the shrill birds.

In hindsight, the lifestyle dictated the tone for the era, with nonchalance becoming a self-fulfilling prophecy. As Maecenas is made to say: "Thanks to you [Caesar], I was the only Maecenas. I did it my way; I wanted whatever would be" (unus Maecenas teque ego propter eram. / arbiter ipse fui; uolui, quod contigit esse; *Eleg. in Maec.* 2.26–27).

Ironically, this portrait of a one-off dates from a time when "Maecenas" as a type was beginning to multiply. Both the elegies and the Senecan letter probably respond to an imperial vogue for redeploying Augustan characters as ethical exempla.[22] Along with Velleius's sketch of Maecenas's career as balancing act, they suggest that there was already a live debate focused on his unconventional life choices.[23] While the first poem's manifesto for an easy life fills the need for further information about Maecenas's *cultus*, the second ventriloquizes his lost conversations with Augustus. The poet is self-conscious about his twice-removed distance from the Augustan centre, both temporal and spatial: he never knew Maecenas as a friend but claims a secondary link to the inner circle via Lollius, along with solid elegiac credentials (the lament, *triste carmen*, he has already composed for the prematurely dead Drusus). The name Lollius immediately frames the *Elegiae* as a defence, specifically an unlikely or

---

*Labieno pro Bathyllo Maecenatis* (Sen. *Controv.* 3 *praef.* 6) and Latro's oration *Pro Pythodoro Messalae* (Sen. *Controv.* 2.4.8).

    21. Cf. Maecenas 3L = 2C = 185H (line 2: "beryllos . . . nitentes"); Augustus *ap.* Macrob. *Sat.* 2.4.12: "beryllus Porsennae".

    22. Peirano 2012: 230.

    23. Le Doze 2012.

unconvincing one.[24] In *Odes* 4.9, Horace had addressed a humiliated general of that name in a poem full of negatives and indirection, shielding him against hostility (*Livor*) and stressing poetry's capacity for forgetting and suppressing as much as remembering and celebrating.[25] Our poet is intent on remembering or misremembering Maecenas, to the point of giving him a distinguished war record and a poetic legacy equal to Homer's.[26]

Along the way, this apology for loose robes and indolence makes further claims for its unlikely hero: openness ("simplicitate"; *Eleg. in Maec.* 1.22), guilelessness ("candidus", "candoris"; 1.3, 135) and merit ("merito"; 1.2).[27] The choice of elegiacs already gestures to libertine values: Lollius's commission demands "softness", both ethically and metrically. Like Propertius before him, the poet makes self-conscious epigrams from the coexistence of lightness and weightiness in his subject's life: "It was greater to have had the power and not want triumphs; it was a greater thing to reject greatness" (1.31–32); "In those days he was not delicate [tener]: he was a fearsome [grauis] opponent" (1.44).[28] When he finally speaks, Maecenas boasts of being an "exemplum . . . molle"—a lesson in softness—or even "an elegiac template" (2.23), so endorsing Propertius's earlier conflation of metre and model:

> at tua, Maecenas, uitae praecepta recepi,
>     cogor et exemplis te superare tuis.

> (PROP. 3.9.21–22)

But I have taken on your mode of life, Maecenas, and am driven to surpass your own standards of behaviour.

Meanwhile, images of warmth, sensuality, ornament and delicious ease flood the poem with material softness: flowers, amber and cinnamon, shining robes, saffron and rose bedsheets, rare jewels and shady nooks (all staving off chilly, shadowy death: "frigidus", "umbris"; *Eleg. in Maec.* 2.2, 1.135). Instead of standing or marching, characters sit, recline and sleep—posture embodying peace.[29] Familiar ambidextrous figures offer role models for work–life balance and

---

24. Peirano 2012: 220.

25. *Eleg. in Maec.* 1.23 ("liuide") and 1.21 ("carpitur") ~ Hor. *Carm.* 4.9.34 ("carpere liuidas obliuiones"); Peirano 2012: 219.

26. "Maeonii libelli" (1.37) confuses Maecenas and Homer, two Lydians; Scaliger preferred *Aeonii*. The war record is excavated from the "suppressed" memories of Prop. 2.1; Nigro 1998: 146.

27. "candide Maecenas" was Horace's term of address in *Epod.* 14.

28. Cf. Prop. 3.9.29–30.

29. *Eleg. in Maec.* 1.36 ("sederat"), 50 ("sedente"), 88 ("percubuisse"), 93 ("dormiat"), 96 ("membra . . . sternere"), 99 ("requiescat").

devotion to luxury: Apollo (sounding the lyre after Actium), Hercules (in drag, enslaved to Omphale, an elegiac *tenera puella*), Tithonus (pampered geriatric husband of Aurora) and Antony (whose infatuation with Cleopatra nearly cost the Romans their city). Bacchus is the outstanding figure, decked in gold, silver and precious stones after conquering India, a vision in fancy dress that is almost a supplementary "memory" ("sum memor et certe memini") of Maecenas's sartorial extravagance:

> et tibi securo tunicae fluxere solutae,
> > te puto purpureas tunc habuisse duas.
> sum memor et certe memini sic ducere thyrsos
> > bracchia purpurea candidiora niue,
> et tibi thyrsus erat gemmis ornatus et auro,
> > serpentes hederae uix habuere locum;
> argentata tuos etiam sandalia talos
> > uinxerunt . . .

> (*ELEG. IN MAEC.* 1.59–66)

And in your carefree state your tunics flowed—I think you were then wearing two shining ones. If memory serves, I recall that your arms, whiter than the gleaming snow, were holding thyrsi, and your thyrsus was adorned with jewels and gold; the snaking ivy barely had space; and silver sandals bound your feet. . . .

As often, the elegist views the world through rosy erotic spectacles. Why else would Rome's interior minister have made the streets safe, if not to facilitate nocturnal love affairs (1.29)? Surely a stellar war record equips a soldier to conquer in bed, too?

> sic est: uictor amet, uictor potiatur in umbra,
> > uictor odorata dormiat inque rosa.

> (1.93–94)

So it goes: the winner can make love, the winner can have his way in the shade, the winner can sleep in a sweet-smelling bed of roses.

In this seductive atmosphere, even the most aggressive critic is set up to be mollified:

> liuide, quid tandem tunicae nocuere solutae?
> > aut tibi uentosi quid nocuere sinus.

> (1.25–26)

Mean-spirited man, what harm did his loose robes ever do you? What harm did his billowing folds do you?

Demonized (sooner or later) by Seneca, Maecenas's unhitched robes float through the poem as its dominant symbol, inviting everyone to unwind, hang loose or go with the flow (*uiuere solute*), as if harking back to some pre-lapsarian "naturist" era:[30]

> quod discinctus eras, animo quoque, carpitur unum:
>     diluitur nimia simplicitate tua.
> sic illi uixere quibus fuit aurea Virgo,
>     quae bene praecinctos postmodo pulsa fuit.
>
> (1.21–24)

The fact that you wore your robes loose, mentally speaking, too, is the only gripe against you. But that is dissolved by your all too uncomplicated way of being. That's how people lived in the time of the golden Virgin, who was driven away when men started to wear formal clothes.

Even Augustus is credited with a "tender" regard for his friend ("mollibus . . . oculis"; 2.13) and praised for his good judgment in sponsoring a life of ease, one justified by the natural rhythm of the seasons and the pax Augusta, a golden age where peace and partying naturally follow war:

> pax erat: haec illos laxarant otia cultus,
>     omnia uictores Marte sedente decent
>
> (1.49–50)

Peace came: this quiet time had relaxed the way of being. Everything is fitting for the victors once Mars sits back.

Yet for all the poet's ingenious appeals to nature, divine will and historical determinacy, the defence remains firmly ad hominem:

> Caesar amicus erat, poterat uixisse solute
> . . .
> indulsit merito
>
> (1.103, 105)

---

30. Cf. *Eleg. in Maec.* 1.25 ("uentosi . . . sinus"), 1.59 ("et tibi securo tunicae fluxere solutae" [But thanks to peace your robes flowed loose] [Bacchus]), 1.77 ("tunicas . . . fluentes" [flowing robes] [Hercules]). Loose-beltedness: Schoonhoven 1980: 40–42, C. Barton 1994: 88; cf. Cic. *Brut.* 262 on Caesar's "undressed" style.

Caesar was his friend: he was allowed a life of relaxation . . . he deserved to be indulged.

The little garden where Maecenas sits in the shade communing with the birds (sometimes understood as his poets)[31] is a secure space ("certi . . . soli") enabled by an exceptional friendship. As Carlin Barton writes: "That [Maecenas's] behavior is intrinsically something *needing* indulgence is never questioned."[32] In a poem that credits its subject with the gifts of the muses but never overtly remembers him as a literary patron, it is Augustus who plays patron and Maecenas the pet or protégé whose leisure he protects.

In general, the poem takes a skewed look at power and its paradoxical workings: "Maecenas was a very soft man. He was also a powerful man."[33] The voluntary renunciation of office for which he was celebrated (1.31–34) confers a different kind of transcendence, a kind of Olympian serenity:

maius erat potuisse tamen nec uelle triumphos,
    maior res magnis abstinuisse fuit

(1.31–32)

It was greater to have had the power and not want triumphs; it was a greater thing to reject greatness

omnia cum posses tanto tam carus amico,
    te sensit nemo posse nocere tamen.

(1.15–16)

While you had all the power in being close to such an important friend, no one ever thought you would be capable of doing harm.

Far from being a deficiency of the weak, gender fluidity is reinstated as the prerogative of the invincible (after all, it was Julius Caesar who inspired Sulla's warning never to trust a man in a trailing skirt).[34] The sexual mastery of the winners after Actium (getting their way in the shade) coexists equally with the idea of male helplessness in the face of seduction. Maecenas is not just Hercules and Antony: he is also Omphale (*tenera puella* and fellow Lydian)

31. Birds ("argutas . . . aues"; 1.36) as poets: Della Corte 1974–75.

32. C. Williams 2012: 176.

33. C. Barton 1994: 89.

34. C. Barton 1994: 88–89: "Maecenas, like Hercules, can 'play'—even at being enslaved and emasculated—*because* he is the victorious warrior."

and Cleopatra.[35] In fact, all this special pleading risks casting him as imperial favourite or "pretty boy", forerunner to Nero's Sporus or Hadrian's Antinous.[36] If Jupiter is remembered, post-gigantomachy, for his "gentle" possession of Ganymede (*Eleg. in Maec.* 1.92: "presso molliter ungue rapit" [gently seized him in his squeezing talons]), how then should we understand the sentimental relationship between Augustus and Maecenas, or take the final words of the poem, where Maecenas predicts that Augustus will be received into Jupiter's bosom or lap ("patrio ... sinu"; 2.34)?[37] Capricious queen and humiliated slave; besotted master and pampered toy boy: models of sexual symbiosis and inverted power stain the memory of Maecenas's relationships with his associates.

For all their soft-focus sweetness and artfully woven lines, the two *Elegies* have been criticized for choppy structure, vague ordering and illogical non sequiturs. But an analogue for their internally plaited but externally disjointed couplets suggests itself in the garlands of flowers (*Eleg. in Maec.* 1.143–44) and exotic spices (saffron, cinnamon, balsam) offered at Maecenas's tomb (1.133–34). Like these cult offerings, the poems' mottoes are units that perpetuate Maecenas's memory, often by excerpting and adapting his various appearances in Augustan poetry. Already aligned by Virgil and Propertius, Maecenas and Bacchus nudge closer together here. When Bacchus speaks "novel words" (uerba ... noua; 1.68), "more softly than usual" (mollius ... solito; 1.67), he could be mimicking Maecenas's silky tones.[38] Virgil is remembered at his most elegiac (mourning Daphnis in the *Eclogues*), most exotic (conjuring up scented balsam and cinnamon in the *Georgics*) and most Epicurean (remembering the old man in *Georgics* 4, whose garden is improbably recreated here in Maecenas's "few modest acres" of orchard).[39]

Among the many allusions to Augustan elegy threaded into the poem, most compelling are the reminiscences of prophetic visitors in Propertius's Book 4, when dying Maecenas declares his undying love for Augustus (*Elegiae* 2). But which of Propertius's ghostly females is remembered above all? Arethusa, faithful to her husband, away at the wars? Cynthia, enraged and flashing a signature

35. C. Barton (2007: 65) compares Maecenas to Cleopatra.

36. See Vout (2007: 21) on the exceptionality of emperors' toy boys: "There *is* power in being passive."

37. Augustus's effeminacy: Suet. *Aug.* 68; Hallett 1977. See Nigro (1998: 139) on Jupiter and Ganymede as Maecenas and Bathyllus. Cf. Vout 2007: 13: "Can one contemplate an emperor and boy-love and not think of Jupiter and Ganymede?"

38. Cf. Hor. *Carm.* 4.2.10–11: Bacchic dithyrambs as noua uerba; cf. Sen. *Ep.* 114.7: Maecenas's uerba compared to his "mores ... nouos".

39. See Nigro 1998: 140–41. Balsam and cinnamon: Verg. *G.* 2.118–19, 213, 466. Small plot: Verg. *G.* 4.127–28 ("cui pauca relicti / iugera ruris erant").

beryl?[40] Or the matron Cornelia (Prop. 4.11), bringing reassurance about the family's future? The third is probably the dominant model, given Maecenas's preoccupation with Augustus's succession (*Eleg. in Maec.* 2.3–6, 29–32) and the shadowy presence of two wives, Terentia (2.10) and Livia (2.31), who suggest conjugality as a template for the friends' relationship.[41] There is something erotic in Maecenas's expression of his bond with the emperor as *amor* (2.19), his prediction of Augustus's tears (2.13) and his formulation of their love: "I was truly the heart of your heart" (pectus eram uere pectoris ipse tui; 2.26). Despite his frustrated longing for Terentia ("dying, he sought the embrace, kisses, words and hands of his beloved wife" [moriens quaerebat amatae / coniugis amplexus oscula uerba manus]; 2.9–10), his final loyalties are to the other partner for whom he tactfully suppresses the memory of a painful "rupture" (discidio; 2.7), whether this indicates the civil war, the divorce from Terentia or the rift caused by sexual rivalry.[42] With imperial conflicts telescoped into this elegiac love triangle (or rectangle), it is hard to tell how many women the poem contains. The gender play in *Elegiae* 1, which made Maecenas the emperor's soft-mannered, long-skirted favourite, has made it impossible to decide.

## Tacitus, Maecenas and Boredom

Assessing Maecenas a hundred years after his death, the historian Tacitus is far less inclined to indulge him. Instead, he makes him the prototype for a relentless parade of over-powerful imperial advisers, starting with the sinister Sejanus of *Annals* 3–4, a fellow Etruscan and relative who rose from the praetorian guard that Maecenas had helped to found.[43] Sejanus develops into a nightmare version of the "emperor's friend", an individual who took unprecedented liberties with the equestrian-courtier model and went overboard in his aspirations:

> uidebatur suspectumque iam nimiae spei Seianum ultra extulisse. (Tac. *Ann.* 3.29.4)

> [Tiberius] appeared to have over-promoted Sejanus, who even then was suspected of excessive ambition.

---

40. See below, pp. 327–28.

41. Prop. 4.11.58 ("gemitu Caesaris"), 60 ("lacrimas") ~ *Eleg. in Maec.* 2.13–14; Prop. 4.11.91 ("seu memor ille mea contentus manserit umbra") ~ *Eleg. in Maec.* 2.16–18; Prop. 4.11.69 ("et serie fulcite genus") ~ *Eleg. in Maec.* 2.30 ("et tradant porro Caesaris usque genus").

42. Schoonhoven (1980, *ad loc.*) prefers the idea of a rift between friends.

43. Tac. *Ann.* 1.24. Terentia was Sejanus's great-aunt; Woodman and Martin 1996: 272. The two men's routes to and from power became a topic for political and ethical rumination (*la fable du favori*) among Tacitists in seventeenth-century France; Amstutz 2011. See below, p. 385.

uis tu quidem istum intra locum sistere: sed illi magistratus et primores, qui te inuitum perrumpunt omnibusque de rebus consulunt, excessisse iam pridem equestre fastigium longeque antisse patris mei amicitias non occulti ferunt perque inuidiam tui me quoque incusant. (*Ann.* 4.40.5)

[Tiberius to Sejanus] You for your part wish to remain within that station. But those magistrates and prominent figures who assail you against your will and consult you on every topic make no secret of their view that you have long since transcended the heights of the equestrian order and left my father's friendship behind, and in resenting you, they accuse me too.

Still, there is something in the refined discretion of the original that Tacitus finds hard to fault. Against the exponential rise of Sejanus, the Tiberian regime finds a closer Maecenas lookalike in Sallustius Crispus Passienus, great-nephew of the historian Sallust. Crispus actively modelled himself on Maecenas, reincarnating the court pussycat sketched by Velleius Paterculus (2.88):

> Though he soon gained access to offices, he emulated Maecenas [Maecenatem aemulatus], and without rising to a senator's rank overtook in power many who had won triumphs and consulships. He differed from old school manners in his elegance and refinement, and in his wealth and affluence he verged on luxury [diuersus a ueterum instituto per cultum et munditias copiaque et affluentia luxu propior]. But beneath all this was a vigorous mind, equal to important business, all the sharper for looking somnolent and apathetic. So it was that next to Maecenas, while Maecenas kept his influence, and later in the top place, he carried the burden of imperial secrets [cui secreta imperatorum inniterentur]. (Tac. *Ann.* 3.30)

Maecenas and his paler Tiberian shadow have three things in common: each dropped out of the *cursus honorum* but leapfrogged over those who climbed up the ranks; each balanced a decadent private life with professional efficiency; and each eventually fell out of love with his ruler.[44] Both men's power derived from privileged access to the emperors' secrets.[45] The fluctuation between watertight security and outward flow is never better expressed than here. Crispus is both a reliable repository for imperial confidences and an over-lavish distributor of personal largesse. Maecenas had become the Roman imperial archetype of the unelected "friend".[46] As Seneca wrote, had he been Nero's contemporary, he

---

44. On Tacitus's Maecenas and Sallustius, see Byrne (1999b).

45. Kehoe 1985: 253–54: Tacitus promoted secrecy as the fundamental characteristic of the Tiberian principate. Cf. *Ann.* 1.6 ("particeps secretorum").

46. Enn. fr. 285 Sk. Sallustius Crispus as *amicus principis*: Crook 1955: 31, 34, 182n290. Imperial institutionalization of *amicitia*: Winterling 1999.

"would have been among the dissimulators".[47] It was Crispus's son, who served under Caligula and became Nero's stepfather, who fully inhabited that role. When asked by the emperor if he had slept with his own sister, he was cunning enough to reply: "Not yet" (Suet. *Vita Crispi*). That "not yet" (*nondum*) finds its way into many narratives we now think of as Neronian.[48] It helps cast Nero's rushed reign as time out of joint, compared with the steady maturing of Augustus: not enough time, or sometimes too much.

Even so, Maecenas's diligent but languid-seeming personality inflects Tacitus's own response to the longueurs of imperial history. In his diagnosis of the end of imperial friendships, he picks out an unusual symptom among all the violent deaths of the *Annals*: boredom. The submarine energy ("suberat . . . uigor animi") of apparently sluggish courtiers dissipated into exhaustion and pretence, caused by nothing more sensational than the cessation of desire, either because the emperor withdrew his favour or because both sides lost their appetites. The calculus of pleasure that regulated their private lives informed their careers, too, as dynamic imperial relations slid uneventfully into mere routines and appearances:

> He had been privy to the murder of Agrippa Postumus. But with advancing years [Crispus] retained more the appearance than the reality of the emperor's friendship. The same lot had fallen to Maecenas—<u>whether influence, which is rarely permanent, comes to an end, or there comes a loss of appetite, sometimes to those who have no more to give, sometimes to those with no more to desire</u> [fato potentiae raro sempiternae, an satias capiat aut illos cum omnia tribuerunt aut hos cum iam nihil reliquuum est quod cupiant]. (Tac. *Ann.* 3.30; Loeb translation, adapted)

Such anticlimactic motives, typical of Tacitus's cynical style of analysis, take on an extra edge when read against his own metahistorical ruminations. Repetitive patterns are equally a feature of the larger monotony (*taedium*) he disingenuously ascribes to his material, as his work approaches its end:[49]

> meque ipsum satias cepisset aliorumque taedium expectarem . . . at nunc patientia seruilis tantumque sanguinis domi perditum fatigant animum et maestitia restringunt. (*Ann.* 16.16)

> [Had I been narrating foreign wars] I would myself have lost appetite for the task and would expect the tedium of others . . . As it is, our slavish impassivity

47. Sen. *Ben.* 6.32.4.

48. Gowers 1994: 138–39.

49. Cf. Tac. *Ann.* 4.32–33. See B. Walker (1960: 204–34) on Tacitus's use of type-characters.

and the vast amount of wasted blood at home exhaust my mind and constrict it with sadness.

Here, the numbing or draining effects of imperial history on its chroniclers and readers sound very like its interpersonal equivalent, the mutual fatigue of courtier and ruler. Maecenas's political career, subject to mood swings and fading desires, mirrors the longue durée of Tacitean history: impermanent ("raro sempiternae") but also enervated and enervating. As Seneca wrote: "There comes upon some people a surfeit of doing and seeing the same things, not a hatred [odium] of life so much as boredom [fastidium] with it" (*Ep.* 24.26). Or, to paraphrase Cicero: it is hard to tell why the things that initially give us the greatest pleasure eventually tire or disgust us the most.[50]

This idea of a sickening fullness recurs in Tacitus's dramatization of Seneca's mistimed appeal to Nero for permission to retire (*Ann.* 14.53–56). Feeling the heat, Seneca grasps at parallels with Maecenas and Agrippa, two Augustan counsellors who managed to withdraw from court with their ruler's blessing:

> Augustus, your great-great-grandfather, allowed Marcus Agrippa a hidden retirement on Mytilene, and <u>to Gaius Maecenas, a quasi-foreign retirement in the city itself</u> [C. Maecenati urbe in ipsa uelut peregrinum otium]. The first had been his co-commander in war, the second had been involved in numerous activities in Rome, and both had received rewards, generous ones, in proportion to their immense merit. (Tac. *Ann.* 14.53)

On the surface, the two men's labours have come to a natural and mutually acceptable fruition ("[he] allowed . . . [they] received"). Seneca euphemizes the events of 23 BCE, when Agrippa was bundled out of the way to support the interests of rival heir Marcellus, and Maecenas's indiscretion over Murena's conspiracy made him at least a liability.[51] In both cases, *otium*, "retirement", covers a face-saving solution: voluntary effacement in Agrippa's case, veiled disgrace in Maecenas's. In other words, Tacitus embeds in Seneca's desperate rhetoric two earlier charades that foretell, rather than contrast with, the present specimen of imperial play-acting.

Seneca goes on to plead that Nero's bounty—villas, gardens and investments—have become an overwhelming burden, one that interferes with his proper mission, spiritual contentment. The time is ripe, he says, using an image of physical satiety: "We have both filled up the measure: you, of what a prince may give to his friend; and I, of what a friend may take from his prince" (sed uterque

---

50. Cic. *De or.* 3.98. See Kaster (2005: 104–33) on *fastidium*; W. Fitzgerald (2016: 48–51, 57–64) on *fastidium* and *satietas* as antonyms of *uarietas*.

51. Bastomsky 1972.

mensuram impleuimus, et [tu], quantum princeps tribuere amico posset, et ego, quantum amicus a principe accipere; Tac. *Ann.* 14.54). But Nero, an apt pupil, plays him at his own game. As a young prince, he lacks the seniority and authority of Augustus, who knew the right time to let his adjuncts go, once they had fulfilled their necessary duties to him: "My great-grandfather Augustus allowed Agrippa and Maecenas <u>to take retirement after their years of service</u>" (usurpare otium post labores; *Ann.* 14.55).

So rapid, indeed, is the onset of Nero's reign that he has not yet ("nondum"; *Ann.* 1.4.55) finished giving (or taking). Thanks to his relative youth and the conventions of gift exchange, his easy benefactions can continue to run his friend through a Danaid sieve of endless debt and gratitude.[52] What is more, he is canny enough to know how any retirement would be interpreted, as a sign of his own greed and cruelty (in other words, he sees through the bromide "Augustan" version of Agrippa's and Maecenas's withdrawal). The two end the charade by going through the usual courtly motions, with Seneca trapped as ever by his own hypocrisy, down among the dissimulators:

> He followed his words with an embrace and kisses—nature had fashioned him and use had trained him to veil his hatred under insidious caresses. Seneca—such is the end of all dialogues with an autocrat—expressed his gratitude: but he changed the established routine of his former power, banished the crowds from his antechambers, shunned his attendants, and appeared in the city with a rareness ascribed to his detention at home by adverse health or philosophic studies. (Tac. *Ann.* 14.56; Loeb translation)

Shortly after the imagined time of this dialogue, in an epistle to Lucilius, Seneca himself wrestles with a related paradox: the high visibility of retirement under an emperor: "One man hides away in Tarentum, another is holed up in Naples, another hasn't left the house for years: whoever makes a drama out of his retirement attracts a crowd" (Sen. *Ep.* 68.5). Even if the pursuit of *otium* was proof that one did not want to become emperor, it remained suspicious in other ways. Where did this leave Maecenas? Did he, as Seneca suggests, seize some optimal sweet spot for retirement? Or was he caught in a living death on the Esquiline, "foreign exile in the city"? Was "productive leisure" a euphemism for forced withdrawal to gardens and villas? The move attracted scrutiny, but Seneca's representation of it remains opaque. Maecenas's end can be read as a positive story of gracious concession and natural ripeness or as a trailer for Neronian speciousness, mistiming and ennui: "no longer" fighting with "not yet". Think back to the *Epistles* and Horace's attempts to return his patron's gifts (*Epist.*

---

52. Seneca conceives of the unthinking consumer as a wine filter: *Ep.* 77.16 ("saccus es").

1.7.34: "cuncta resigno"), around the period to which Seneca refers. On the receiving end of the appeal, Maecenas has no power to talk back.

Another striking feature of the negotiation is how comprehensively Tacitus feeds the notion of tiredness, his own and others', into its construction. Some scholars have been harsh:

> smoothly Ciceronian speeches abounding in trope and cliché, in language which for Tacitus is unusually dead . . . as though Tacitus, feeling compelled to allow Seneca a proper appearance, had in the event been defeated by boredom. Stale similes, stale and conventional phrasing make Seneca's last attempt to escape the mesh a matter of indifference to writer and reader alike.[53]

More generously, one could give Tacitus credit for actively simulating tedium on the page and tying it consciously to his own weary generalizations ("such is the end of all dialogues with an autocrat"). Even his performance of choked dejection ("maestitia constringunt") in his apology for being boring responds to a series of deaths by constriction or beheading, accompanied by the usual thanks to the gods. As the end approaches, he says he is inclined to report them only if there is some interesting or extreme variation to break the monotony.[54]

## Petronius and Maecenas

One such variation is a joyful performance of nonchalance in the face of mortal danger: the suicide of T. Petronius.[55] This dapper figure, Nero's aristocratic friend and "style consultant" (arbiter elegantiae), is still regarded as the most plausible author of *Satyrica*, the fragmentary picaresque novel that has the Cena Trimalchionis, a rich freedman's dinner party, at its centre. Petronius's suicide is the last in a Tacitean trio of Neronian authors' deaths, each one freestyle (*uoluntaria*) but forced (*coacta*), each one a generic summation of its protagonist's life and work, each one controlled, hands-off, by an imperial "patron". This light-hearted death is the parody version, the satyr-play or Epicurean light relief to the botched tragedies and martyr scripts of Lucan and Seneca in *Annals* 15; it also makes a diptych with the Stoic martyrdom of Thrasea Paetus that follows in *Annals* 16.[56] How far the novel feeds into the death and the

---

53. Henry and Walker 1963: 105n1.

54. Tac. *Ann.* 14.64. For being bored (*fastidiosus*) as one cause of imperial death, cf. Sen. *Epist.* 77.6.

55. Rankin (1971: 2) calls the death "cool". See Dinerstein (2017: 4–5, 11) on "cool" as insouciance in the face of suffering or torture.

56. Connors 1994: 228–30; O'Gorman 2000: 156–58. Binding and loosening imagery links Petronius's and Thrasea's deaths, each claiming liberation from Nero; Santoro L'Hoir 2006: 107–8.

death into the novel is endlessly debated, since Trimalchio rehearses his own end at the dinner table, complete with mourners and showy monument.[57] But this gem of a portrait is a far cry from Trimalchio's vulgar and macabre dinner-theatre, a hyper-refined variation on the old "paradoxical" clichés that turns suffering into cool and boredom into an art form:[58]

> De C. Petronio pauca supra repetenda sunt. nam illi dies per somnum, nox officiis et oblectamentis uitae transigebatur; utque alios industria, ita hunc ignauia ad famam protulerat, habebaturque non ganeo et profligator, ut plerique sua haurientium, sed erudito luxu. ac dicta factaque eius quanto solutiora et quandam sui neglegentiam praeferentia, tanto gratius in speciem simplicitatis accipiebantur. proconsul tamen Bithyniae et mox consul uigentem se ac parem negotiis ostendit. dein reuolutus ad uitia seu uitiorum imitatione inter paucos familiarium Neroni adsumptus est, elegantiae arbiter, dum nihil amoenum et molle adfluentia putat, nisi quod ei Petronius adprobauisset. unde inuidia Tigellini quasi aduersus aemulum et scientia uoluptatum potiorem. (Tac. *Ann.* 16.18)

In Petronius's case, some brief background must first be given. He used to spend his days asleep and his nights doing business and pursuing pleasure. And just as others are shot to fame by their hard work, he was by his laziness. He was not considered a glutton and a spendthrift, like many people who drain their resources, but someone of educated luxuriousness. And the more relaxed and apparently careless his words and actions were, the more indulgently they were received as a sign of authenticity. Yet as governor of Bithynia and then consul, he proved himself energetic and equal to the job. Then, thanks to his loose living, or at least the appearance of it, he was taken up by Nero among his closest friends, as his style consultant, inasmuch as Nero thought nothing beautiful or luxurious unless Petronius had given it his stamp of approval. This caused Tigellinus to be jealous of him as a rival, more influential than himself in the science of pleasure.

Once again, Tacitus is inspired by his subject, even threatened by it (just as Tigellinus was). His introductory sketch matches Petronius in its restraint ("pauca"), thoughtful nuance ("quandam; nihil . . . nisi quod"; "quasi") and ability to sift appearance from reality ("speciem simplicitatis"; "ad uitia seu uitiorum imitatione"). The account is studded with epigrams, echoes, paradoxes and oxymorons: "erudito luxu", "scientia uoluptatum", "officiis et oblectamentis",

---

57. Holmes 2008: 50n32.

58. Scaevinus, accessory to Petronius's downfall, "overflows" with luxury ("dissoluta luxu mens") and blathers ("uagis sermonibus") under pressure (Tac. *Ann.* 15.49).

"industria . . . ignauia", "adfluentia . . . adprobauisset", "quanto solutiora . . . tanto gratius".[59] Even the syntax suggests Petronian indolence: passive verbs for the effortless rise to power (*transigebatur, habebatur, accipiebantur*), with the subject relegated to the dative or accusative case (*illi, hunc*), then an active verb for the brief spell of service as proconsul in Bithynia and suffect consul in Rome (*se . . . ostendit*), before passivity resumes (*reuolutus, adsumptus est*). He didn't have to lift a finger until he did. Yet he ruled Nero's style choices as Nero ruled the world: "I am the arbiter of life and death for all peoples," as Seneca has him say in *De clementia*.[60]

As for the death scene, it replicates the ebb and flow of the biography:

> Forte illis diebus Campaniam petiuerat Caesar, et Cumas usque progressus Petronius illic attinebatur; nec tulit ultra timoris aut spei moras. neque tamen praeceps uitam expulit, sed incisas uenas, ut libitum, obligatas aperire rursum et adloqui amicos, non per seria aut quibus gloriam constantiae peteret. audiebatque referentis nihil de immortalitate animae et sapientium placitis, sed leuia carmina et facilis uersus. seruorum alios largitione, quosdam uerberibus adfecit. iniit epulas, somno indulsit, ut quamquam coacta mors fortuitae similis esset. ne codicillis quidem, quod plerique pereuntium, Neronem aut Tigellinum aut quem alium potentium adulatus est, sed flagitia principis sub nominibus exoletorum feminarumque et nouitatem cuiusque stupri perscripsit atque obsignata misit Neroni. fregitque anulum ne mox usui esset ad facienda pericula. (Tac. Ann. 16.19)

> As it happened, at that time Caesar was on his way to Campania, where Petronius, who had got as far as Cumae, was detained. He refused to prolong the suspense that fear or hope would entail. Yet he did not rush to take leave of life, but having cut his veins, bound them up or reopened them at will. He conversed with his friends, not on serious subjects or those that might rouse them to endurance. And he listened to people reading to him, not about the immortality of the soul and the wisdom of philosophy but singing light songs and frivolous poems. He treated some of his slaves with generosity, others with the lash. He started feasting, then indulged in sleep, so that although his death was forced it would look like an accident. In his will, he did not flatter Nero or Tigellinus, as many dying men used to do, but wrote down the emperor's crimes under the names of his male and female lovers and specified the novelty of each sexual act and sent this

59. Bertrand-Dagenbach 1992: 602–3; Rudich 1997: 188.
60. Sen. *Clem.* 1.1.2: "ego uitae necisque gentibus arbiter."

under seal to Nero. He broke his seal-ring so that it could not subsequently be used to cause danger.

Here, the veins are the all-important feature. Slit, bandaged up, then opened again, they key the life as well as the death: binding and dissolution alternate like *negotium* and *otium* in imperial service ("obligatas aperire rursum" [16.19] ~ "solutiora . . . parem negotiis . . . dein reuolutus" [16.18]).[61] Actions are suspended, going nowhere: "He got as far as . . . he was detained"; "He refused to prolong the delay . . . yet he did not rush." This is a poised death, a libertine's death ("ut libitum"), light and easy ("leuia", "facilis"), neither serious ("seria") nor effortful ("peteret"). Not a philosopher's death (although its levity recalls Socrates's final hours), but philosophical in its equivalent control and autonomy.[62] Nor an emperor's death, though it mocks imperial quirks with its arbitrary mood swings (expressed through zeugma—"alios largitione, quosdam uerberibus adfecit"—and chiasmus—"iniit epulas, somno indulsit").[63] The parting shot, a will fired off to Nero cataloguing his sexual partners and positions, is Petronius's signature act, quite literally.[64] The author breaks the mould along with his seal ring.[65]

Can we also read the death as homage to Maecenas, that other pleasure lover? He, too, did it his way (*Eleg. in Maec.* 2.27: "arbiter fui"); he, too, was implausibly praised for *simplicitas* and compromised by *neglegentia* and *affluentia*. Both figures were innovators: Maecenas in life and style, Petronius in life, style and death (*talis mors qualis uita*). Is this how Maecenas would have ended his life, had he lived under Nero and not been allowed to die in his bed? Is this how he did die, faking a natural, easy end? The dinner-party setting suggests the gracious withdrawal of a satisfied Epicurean from life's feast, or the perfectly happy death of the actor M. Ofilius Hilaris, according to Pliny the Elder, who returned home to a birthday feast after winning a dramatic prize and who died while gazing at the comic mask on which he had draped his victory wreath, only to be discovered when someone tapped him on the shoulder to tell him his drink was getting cold.[66]

---

61. Bertrand-Dagenbach 1992: 604.

62. Rankin 1971: 2; Connors 1994: 230–31; Hill 2004: 250.

63. Haynes 2010: 73: "The *arbiter elegantiae* literally becomes the arbiter of life itself." Cf. Barthes (1982: 165) on suspension and liberation in Tacitean death scenes.

64. "sub nominibus" makes the sexual partners joint "authors" of the document.

65. Plin. *HN* 37.20: Petronius smashed an expensive ladle to stop Nero inheriting it. But his suicide had its imitators: e.g., Sir Hercules Occam in Aldous Huxley's *Crome Yellow* (1921, London).

66. Plin. *HN* 7.54.

Yet the Petronian context equally suggests fullness, even disgust: life as ennui, sleep to pass the time of day, and languorous autoerotic delaying tactics to stave off the end. Seneca records how another courter, Tullius Marcellinus, starved himself, gave gifts to his slaves, as if distributing the leftovers from life's feast, then had hot water slowly poured over him, "not without a certain pleasure, which a gentle letting go [lenis dissolutio] often induces, familiar to those of us who have occasionally fainted" (*Ep.* 77.5–9). Presumably Petronius devised the same sexual pleasures for jaded palates (*exoletorum*; *nouitatem cuiusce stupri*) that he went on to satirize, once the novelty wore off for both partners. The death fixes the end of imperial friendship at the point where a courtier-confidant symbolically spills a ruler's trusted secrets. But it is also a fantasy for Tacitus of authorial control, of being able to ration, even eroticize the steady drip of imperial bloodshed—not to mention a retrospective lesson to Maecenas about the fine art of calibrating pleasure.

## Trimalchio and Maecenas

If Petronius preserves the spirit of Maecenas, bored but infinitely restrained, how is it that his supreme fictional creation and antitype, the dinner tyrant and vulgar, boastful freedman Trimalchio, also reads as an offshoot of the Augustan courtier? The interlaced connections between Seneca, Petronius and Maecenas and their masters Nero and Augustus are hard to disentangle. It has been argued, for example, that Seneca's attack on Maecenas in *Epistles* 114 is a hidden attack on Petronius, Maecenas's equivalent at Nero's court, and that Petronius endowed Trimalchio with the very qualities that Seneca had reviled in Maecenas.[67] Parallels between Trimalchio and Maecenas are indeed glaring: a morbid obsession with time and death (however hard to substantiate in Maecenas's case); unruly wives; and passion for ball games, jewel poems, opulent dress and eunuch attendants.[68] Far more telling, though, are the differences between the hermetically sealed Augustan original and the gabbling, megalomaniac Neronian imitator. Victoria Rimell has detected a crucial link between the two social bubbles of the *Satyrica*—freedmen, on the one hand, and poet-intellectuals, on the other—in the ubiquitous verb *effundere* "pour out", which suggests metaphorical porosity in both spheres between inside and outside (from "eviscerated" dinner pig to poetic Trojan Horse) and a similar two-way churning, regurgitating

---

67. Byrne 2006; *contra* Labate 2012: 416. Interactions between Seneca and Petronius: see Star 2012; between Nero and Petronius: Vout 2009.

68. D'Arms 1981; Baldwin 1984; Byrne 2006; Labate 2012: 418–19. See Crum (1952) and Bartsch (1994: 199) on Trimalchio's similarities to Nero.

engagement with the world, via material consumption or literary production.[69] This word also makes a good basis for thinking about the distinction between Trimalchio and Maecenas: Trimalchio "pours out" what Maecenas's poets had kept under wraps, not just the menu at his dinners but also his philosophy of life. Yet Seneca in *Epistles* 114, around the same time, had created a very leaky Maecenas. Perhaps it makes more sense to think of Maecenas as a moveable cursor on the dial of permeability.

When Trimalchio reveals plans for the showy epitaph on his tomb, he indicates that he is in some sense inspired by Maecenas:

> C. Pompeius Trimalchio Maecenatianus hic requiescit. huic seuiratus absenti decretus est. cum posset in omnibus decuriis Romae esse, tamen noluit. pius, fortis, fidelis, ex paruo creuit, sestertium reliquit trecenties, nec umquam philosophum audiuit. uale: et tu. (Petron. *Sat.* 71.12)

> Here lies C. Pompeius Trimalchio Maecenatianus. The priesthood of Augustus was granted to him in his absence. He could have joined any guild in Rome but he turned it down. Pious, brave, loyal, he grew from very little and left thirty million. He never listened to a philosopher. Farewell, Trimalchio; and you, passer-by.

The final name here, *Maecenatianus*, is an *agnomen*, traditionally a marker of distinction (like Scipio *Africanus*) and a conspicuous add-on to the names given on an earlier inscription: "C. Pompeio Trimalchioni, seuiro Augustali, Cinnamus dispensator" (To C. Pompeius Trimalchio, priest of Augustus, from his steward Cinnamus; *Sat.* 30.1–2). What does it mean, then, to call oneself *Maecenatianus*? What is at stake in this late-stage and presumably bogus claim to an association?[70] Some epigraphers regard the name as a synonym for a freedman of the imperial house (*Augusti libertus*), given that Maecenas left all his human property to Augustus: such a distinguished but superannuated name would not threaten powerful freedmen at Nero's court, like Pallas and Narcissus.[71] But does *Maecenatianus* add charisma or at least a snobbish veneer? The name-dropping has been judged rhetorically clumsy, "an aristocratic flourish that risks rebounding", especially when Maecenas evoked effeminacy as much as he did regal descent, equestrian distinction and artistic patronage, and when the anachronistic binding of his name with Pompey's speaks of a typically manic imperial conflation of exemplary

---

69. Rimell 2002: 26, 203–5.

70. *Agnomina* were commonly adopted by ex-slaves, though their use waned in the early second century CE; Schmeling 2011 *ad Sat.* 71.12.. See Priuli 1975: 43–45.

71. Tarpin 1995.

figures.[72] True, there is something "Maecenas-ish" in Trimalchio's cool refusal of office and boast of honours in absentia.[73] At the same time, his instructions evoke models of euergetism or Saturnalian release quite alien to any Maecenas: dinners at two denarii a head; a dining room big enough to hold the entire *populus*; large-scale public largesse; freedom for all slaves.[74]

A few chapters later, Trimalchio's autobiography, the story of a slave's rise to world domination (or at least the fantasy of it), suggests further comparisons. The iconography of naval victory and imperial expansion is adapted to triumphs in the shipping trade (which may also explain the name *Pompeius*, after the "great" admiral). Clearly, more than one kind of commerce was involved:[75]

> tam magnus ex Asia ueni quam hic candelabrus est. ad summam, quotidie me solebam ad illum metiri, et ut celerius rostrum barbatum haberem, labra de lucerna ungebam. tamen ad delicias ipsimi annos quattuordecim fui. nec turpe est, quod dominus iubet. ego tamen et ipsimae satis faciebam. scitis quid dicam: taceo, quia non sum de gloriosis. ceterum, quemadmodum di uolunt, dominus in domo factus sum . . . (Petron. *Sat.* 75.10–76.1)

> I arrived from Asia when I was as tall as this candlestick. In fact, I used to measure myself against it every day, and wiped my lips from the lamp so that my moustache would grow faster. But I was my master's pet till my fourteenth year. And it's not dirty, if the master asks for it. And I kept her indoors happy too. You know what I mean; I'll shut up, I'm not big-headed. Anyway, the way things went, I became master of the house.

Symbiosis through mutual satisfaction (*satis facere*)—that is, sex as a route to freedom—was evidently not enough for Trimalchio (*nemini tamen nihil satis est* ), who would expand his operations on an imperial scale, ending up with astronomical wealth, a palace with many rooms, slaves, parasites and a toy boy of his own—even a pet astrologer, who knew his insides better than he did. In short, the frog became a prince.[76]

Whereas Horace's frog fable in *Satires* 2.3 cautions against trying to live up to Maecenas, Trimalchio throws to the winds the restrained "Maecenatianus"

---

72. Beard 1997: 97–98.

73. D'Arms 1981: 112; Labate 2012: 418. D'Arms 1981: 113: both Trimalchio and Maecenas prefer *honestum otium*, engaging in trade rather than seeking honours.

74. Whitehead (1993: 311) compares funerary depictions of communal banquets.

75. Often the size and shape of a pubescent boy, the *candelabrus* exemplified the fate Trimalchio escaped by growing up and resisting his own objectification; Bielfeldt 2018; Lenski 2013. On the sexual function of *deliciae*, see Bodel (1989) and Richlin (2015), *contra* Pomeroy (1992).

76. Petron. *Sat.* 77.6.

model to which he has nominally subscribed. He "pours it all out", burbling on about his unstinting benefactions ("nummos in publico de sacculo effundentem" [pouring out sacks of money to the public]; Petron. *Sat.* 71.9), naked ambition, embarrassing physical ailments and mercenary values ("bene emo, bene uendo" [I buy well, I sell well]; 75.9). His every move, along with the overload of information, offends against the restraint of the privileged "circle", at least when seen through the eyes of a fastidious, even sickened observer, the freeloader-intellectual Encolpius. Still, is this really such a misreading of a famous name? Trimalchio can't help casting Maecenas and his followers by association in a more lurid light. Wasn't Maecenas also consumed by luxury and the endless search for novelty? Weren't his friends eunuchs, pets or aging catamites, like Trimalchio's drip-eyed Croesus (the "boy", *puer*, who never grew up), or spoiled puppy, Pearl?[77] Wasn't he also an indulged favourite who sprang from nowhere? And what was the quid pro quo for *his* favours? All told, Trimalchio's story might start to colour our reading of a late first-century BCE tombstone that commemorates an Eros Senecio ("Old Lover-Boy")—shared slave of one C. Maecenas and his wife Terentia.[78]

## The Missing Patron

At Trimalchio's dinner, the joke is that all the seats, not only the token "freedman's place" (libertini locus; Petron. *Sat.* 38.11), are occupied by ex-slaves. There is no room for poets. Nor are there patrons in this miniature society, now that Trimalchio has ditched the master who gave him his first leg-up.[79] Instead, we have "a Maecenas without poets and a poet without a Maecenas".[80] This dislocated condition is one many imperial writers bemoan, among them Calpurnius Siculus, the *Laus Pisonis* poet, Martial and Juvenal. The first two, like Petronius, are traditionally assigned a Neronian date, challenged unsuccessfully from time to time; Martial and Juvenal belong some fifty years later, in the period spanning Domitian, last of the Flavians, and the reigns of Nerva, Trajan and Hadrian. The emperor, whichever one is being addressed, is considered the supreme patron, whether or not he has proclaimed an interest in the arts. There is a new euphemism for his attention, *ducis indulgentia*, "the emperor's indulgence", a term applied to Maecenas as Augustus's protégé in the *Elegiae* (1.105).

77. *Margarita* is also the name of a *delicatus* at Petron. *Sat.* 63.2; cf. Augustus's nickname for Maecenas, *Tiberinum margaritum* (Macrob. *Sat.* 2.4.12).

78. Hammond 1980.

79. Mouritsen 2011: 291.

80. Labate 2012: 422.

With private patronage still a steady undercurrent, ambitions to reach the "empty ears" of the *princeps* are more directly stated, and "face-to-face" appeals to patrons brasher. Horatian restraint is swept away in favour of cruder demands: sustenance for starving poets, whether they are rural shepherds or the inhabitants of urban garrets, in return for offerings of praise. Still, when many of these poets are unknown, undatable or anonymous, and when their patrons have such unspecific, often allegorical or symbolic type-names—Meliboeus, Piso, your imperial majesty—it is hard to feel any closer to a direct or authentic approach. These may instead be empty or timeless exercises on the theme of finding a patron, ones that fill in gaps in the Horatian record while leaning on Horace's own story of his success.[81] An important alternative model is Ovid, a poet with no consistent patron, whose appeals to elite friends and the emperor Augustus are generated by the greater isolation of exile.

Posthumous memories of Maecenas's interventions in Augustan poetry involve some curious distortions. While the original dedications had tied him to poets' transitional or "middle" periods—Horatian satire, epistle, iambic and lyric; Virgilian didactic; Propertius's central books of elegy—literary history becomes retrospectively compressed so that the middle drops out.[82] Maecenas's support for Virgil is extended to the beginning (*Eclogues*) and the end (*Aeneid*) of his career. He is credited with commissioning sublime works (epic, and tragedy, in Varius's case) as much as with blessing *recusatio* and small-scale poetry. This can be partly explained by the new appetite for panegyric—unstinting praise of the emperor—always a suspect mode of writing but one that now served a distinct purpose regarding an earthly god and for which responsibility could be conveniently shed onto the mediator who took a naïve poet's talent to unforeseen heights. That is why the *Eclogues* (associated with spontaneous bounty and miracle working) are preferred as a scene of patronage to the *Georgics* (where concepts such as *labor* and *cura* suggest longer-term obligation).

Both pastoral and satire hold their ground as the places where patronage is discussed; the two genres offer prototypes of the transformative journey from rude beginnings to tentative engagement with higher spheres. The main models, as ever, are Virgilian Tityrus's memory of his visit to Octavian in Rome and Horace's accounts of his progress from stammering schoolboy to poet laureate, enabled first by Maecenas, then by Augustus.[83] Now that book distribution has reached an international scale (Martial imagines a soldier thumbing his epigrams on the edges of the empire, 11.3.3–4), and the *princeps* has global reach, the tranquil shade once prized (Tityrus's rural shelter, Mena's barber shop or Horace's

---

81. Peirano 2012: 170.
82. Bellandi 1995: 87.
83. Henderson 1998b: 169–71.

Sabine Farm) is devalued as pointless obscurity.[84] Instead, rural origins are seen as a launching pad from which to aim at the encomiastic genres that triumviral and Augustan poetry had so programmatically rejected. Maecenas is reintroduced not just as the archetypal mediator between rustic origins and urban fulfilment but as the proof that private and imperial patronage might coexist, or at least flow smoothly into each other. His absence enables a new kind of *recusatio* in his name: poets still excuse themselves from approaching the higher genres, not because he colludes with them but because he is no longer there.

Calpurnius Siculus's neo-Virgilian *Eclogues* are traditionally assigned to the literary revival associated with Nero's reign, which began with the promise of a return to the Augustan "golden age" and a corresponding renewal of the Augustan literary canon. Nothing is known about the writer beyond his name, which suggests a link with the noble Calpurnii Pisones as well as the bucolic ancestor Theocritus.[85] This is an overheated version of Virgil's pastoral world: seething noonday heat, with the foaming wine presses at boiling point.[86] The first word, "Nondum" (Not yet), compresses two different ideas: staving off the ever-imminent end of the pastoral world and expanding the potential of a contracted genre.[87] Times are changing and the patron-god, the emperor, is a novel entity: "non eadem nobis sunt tempora, non deus idem" (Our times are not the same, our god is not the same; Calp. *Ecl.* 1.30).

While names and scenes remain Virgilian, the boundaries of the pastoral landscape have expanded. Tityrus is in the past, overlaid on Virgil as a musical ancestor of modern bucolic; enter a new hero, Corydon, the lovelorn rustic of Virgil's second eclogue, and a new patron, Meliboeus, Tityrus's less lucky but more enterprising and world-worn counterpart in his first. Tityrus's journey to Rome in search of a patron becomes Corydon's, transferred to a climactic position at the end of the poetry book (Calp. *Ecl.* 7), so fulfilling the trajectory of bucolic towards panegyric arrested in Virgil's sixth eclogue. Awestruck by the Roman amphitheatre with its stage forests and far-off glimpse of the beneficent emperor ("indulgente deo"; *Ecl.* 7.75), naïve Corydon is "hard to pull away" from the city's magnetic attractions ("lentus ab urbe" [7.1] is a stickier version of Virgil's "lentus in umbra"). Meanwhile, Meliboeus's banishment (only as far as Rome, not Britain, as it turns out) is treated as a stroke of luck from which those left behind can reap dividends, as they struggle not just to write the fine-spun poems Apollo required from "Virgil" in *Eclogues* 6 but also to carry out the more basic task of feeding the flocks.

84. Though the retreat of Juvenal's Umbr-icius (*Satires* 3) counters this.
85. Newlands 1987.
86. See Gowers (1994) on Neronian literature as overheated.
87. Gowers 1994: 133.

The equation between Meliboeus and Maecenas takes time to emerge. His essential role as mediator between emperors and poets is briefly hinted at the end of *Eclogues* 1:

carmina, quae nobis deus obtulit ipse canenda,
dicamus teretique sonum modulemur auena:
forsitan augustas ferret hunc Meliboeus ad aures.

(CALP. ECL. 1.92–94)

Let us sing the songs that the god himself gave us to sing, and measure the sound on a smooth pipe: perhaps Meliboeus will carry these songs to royal ears.

In *Eclogues* 4, Meliboeus is directly addressed, thanked for his *indulgentia* (33; again, the imperial word for patronage) and for his immediate help in sustaining the pastoral environment:[88]

ecce nihil querulum per te, Meliboee, sonamus
per te secura saturi recubamus in umbra
et fruimur siluis Amaryllidos

(ECL. 4.35–37)

Lo, it is by your grace, Meliboeus, that we sing no complaint; it is by your grace that we recline well-fed in carefree shade and enjoy the woods of Amaryllis.

Euphemisms for a life of ease bankrolled by a patron ("nihil querulum", "per te", "secura", "saturi recubamus in umbra" and "fruimur") are thick on the ground. Yet pastoral is perceptibly on the move. Meliboeus is equally praised for his help as the critic (his pricked-up ears, *acutae aures,* and polishing file, *lima,* straddle the oral and the bookish) who preps bucolic panegyric for its ultimate destination, Palatine Apollo (and his library) and the open ears (*uacuae aures*) of the emperor. In this respect, too, he is another Maecenas, an equation encoded at the end of the poem for those in the know:[89]

tum mihi talis eris, qualis qui dulce sonantem
Tityron e siluis dominam deduxit in urbem
ostenditque deos et "spreto" dixit "ouili,
Tityre, rura prius, sed post cantabimus arma."

(ECL. 4.160–63)

---

88. *saturi,* "well fed", rematerializes the metapoetic *satis/satur* from *Eclogues* 10.70, 77.
89. Maecenas, as opposed to Pollio: Bellandi 1995: 88n29; Byrne 2004.

Then you will be to me like that man who escorted Tityrus, sounding sweetly, out of the woods and towards the metropolis, and showed him the gods, and said, "We will turn our backs on the sheepfold and sing first the countryside and then the weapons of war."

In this context, the Virgilian career is reinterpreted as the holistic plan of a single overseer, who escorted ("deduxit") Virgil all the way from *Eclogues* to *Aeneid*: "incipe, nam faueo" (Begin, because I am on your side; *Ecl.* 4.73). Calpurnius takes a classic trope of Virgilian bucolic, emergence from the woods towards the city (both the physical trajectory of Virgil's *Ecl.* 9 and the generic evolution resisted in *Ecl.* 4 and 6), and fills it out using Horace's more complete autobiography.[90] Departure from the countryside, a source of fear, regret and genre annihilation in the original, is tied to the brighter prospect of attaining fame by polishing one's potential. Meliboeus is merely a more open conduit: "canales / exprime qui dignas cecinerunt consule siluas" (Widen the pipes which sang of woods worthy of a consul; *Ecl.* 4.76–77).[91] The end-goal for which his channelling influence remains essential is smoothly burnished verse ("tereti . . . uersu"; *Ecl.* 4.152), which falls easy on the emperor's ears, so meshing rural simplicity with urban sophistication, private with imperial patronage, and turning bucolic into a capacious, mobile and friction-free genre.[92]

The book culminates in an awestruck rustic's encomium of the Roman amphitheatre (*Ecl.* 7), complete with woods, animals and canopied shade, and presented in Corydon's naïve vision as a glittering, Orphic model of *rus in urbe*. Meanwhile, the emperor has taken root in the countryside in the form of an epiphanic rural god, no longer threatening its existence but breathing sympathy and inspiring growth and wonder:

> cui silua uocato
> densat odore comas, stupefacta regerminat arbos.
> illius ut primum senserunt numina terrae,
> coepit et uberior sulcis fallentibus olim
> luxuriare seges tandemque legumina plenis
> uix resonant siliquis.

(ECL. 4.110–15)

Call on him and in his honour the wood thickens its perfumed hair, and the awestruck tree breaks into bud again. When first the earth felt his aura, the

90. Henderson 1998b: 181.

91. Cf. *Ecl.* 4.3, 6.2.

92. Cf. *Ecl.* 1.93 "tereti . . . auena"; 5.67, 6.38, 7.51 (of well-made things). The Loeb translation "humble" does not seem right; this is an aspirational adjective.

crops began to spread more richly in once failing furrows and at last the beans can hardly rattle about, their pods are so full.

Now Meliboeus/Maecenas must share the role of fertilizing influence with this more distant figure. He is the conduit to an even higher sanctum ("sacra Palatini penetralia . . . Phoebi" [the sacred chamber of Palatine Apollo]; *Ecl.* 4.159). Like Virgil in the *Georgics*, Corydon hedges his bets while unfurling his ambitions. He continues to bargain, turning Apollo's ear-tugging caution in *Eclogues* 6 into a hint from "resentful Poverty" (inuida paupertas) to use the emperor's favour to upgrade to a proper farm (*Ecl.* 4.152–59). According to pessimistic readings, this distillation of bucolic poetry signals corruption: innocent shepherds have become shockingly rapacious.[93] From another perspective, Calpurnius is keeping faith with the original scope of pastoral, which originally extended to royal visits (the tour of Ptolemy's palace in Theocritus's *Idyll* 15) and the active pursuit of patrons (*Idylls* 16 and 17 embrace *reges* and even *proelia*, in the shape of Ptolemy and his wars in Sicily).[94] Theocritus had already incorporated encomium for a ruler into bucolic, envisaging it as not disturbing but actively guaranteeing the continuity of rural peace, suggesting in the process just how "natural" it was for panegyric to sweep up bucolic images of fertility:

> May they cultivate fields that flourish; may countless thousands of sheep, fattened on their pastures, bleat over the plain; may oxen heading for their byres hasten on his way the man traveling at dusk; may the fallow land be made ready for sowing, while high in the trees the cicada, keeping watch over the shepherds in the heat of the day, chirps up in the branches. (Theoc. *Id.* 16.90–96, trans. Hopkinson, Loeb)

## Laus Pisonis

The *Laus Pisonis*, a similarly floating text as to chronology, lacks an author's name but supplies a potential patron's instead. The Piso in question is probably C. Calpurnius Piso (consul in 41 CE), who conspired against Nero in 65 CE and whose ancestors also included Philodemus's patron, L. Calpurnius Piso (attacked by Cicero in *In Pisonem*), grandfather of the young dedicatees of Horace's *Ars poetica*.[95] It has been argued, however, that the poem is not a

---

93. P. Davis 1987: 47.

94. Magnelli (2006: 468–69) calls Calpurnius a true bucolic poet for overriding Virgil's generic limitations.

95. Piso is named as a patron at Mart. 12.36 (with Seneca, Memmius and Crispus) and Juv. 5.108–12 (with Seneca and Cotta). Other candidates for authorship include Virgil, Ovid, Lucan and Calpurnius Siculus; Amat 1991: 44n112; Di Brazzano 2004: 64.

"real" petition but another creative fiction, inspired by the Neronian Piso's reputation as a patron of the arts.[96] Along with other imperial fictions, like the *Panegyricus Messallae*, the *Ciris* and *Catalepton 9*, it aims to fill a gap left in the triumviral record of patronage, in this case the first stage of approaching a patron, muted by Horace because needing to "apply" was a sign of failure.[97] This poem "for and about Piso" is also an inversion of Cicero's *In Pisonem*, and perhaps also of the poem satirized in that speech as praise gone horribly wrong, an account of "all his lusts and immoralities, all his varied dinners and banquets, all his adulteries" forced out of a Greek "flatterer" (adsentator), Philodemus (Cic. *Pis.* 70). By contrast, the spontaneous-seeming *Laus Pisonis* attempts to restore high-mindedness to the patronage relationship, offering a sympathetic picture of the role of culture and leisure in imperial elite self-fashioning, an area in which Maecenas was a pioneer.[98]

The eager author, who claims to be no more than nineteen, has fewer inhibitions than Maecenas's poets. Prepared to negotiate the time-honoured *kleos*-bargain by offering a sampler of the praise withheld or stinted in Horace's *Odes*, he catalogues Piso's myriad talents—forensic, cultural and sporting: "Your virtue thrills me, your life which in every way inspires admiration" (5–6). While the effort brings on intermittent, melodramatic displays of helplessness (limp-necked, knee-capped exhaustion at 75–76), this is a game of catch-as-catch-can. The young desperado pitches enthusiasm in lieu of poetic talent ("animum, non carmina, iacto"; 214), his verse doing its utmost to "mirror" Piso's own dynamic versatility in parading "versatile/verse-y virtue" (cf. 137: "uirtus numerosa"), aiming, thrusting and parrying, whether his patron is launching javelins (178–84), oratorical blasts (57–58) or finely turned, metaphor-filled epigrams (95–96).[99] Like Piso, he shifts tack ("mille modos"; 197), sallies forth from new angles and goes in for the kill ("Now you strike his exposed flank with an unexpected thrust"; 184). Even Piso's pet game of *latrunculi*, checkers (190–208), supplies the interloper with a playtime analogy for gambits, retreat and eventual conquest, one that reduces patronage to a zero-sum game—winner takes all—whether seen from the poet's vantage point ("clausaque deiecto populetur moenia uallo" [when the rampart is

---

96. Peirano 2012: 120–47.

97. Peirano 2012: 86–87; 164–69 on the "job application" poem as a symptom of a poet's failure to be commissioned. Suet. *Vita Hor.* 20 recalls seeing a spurious Horatian application letter to Maecenas; Peirano 2012: 169–70.

98. Fairweather (1981: 110) discusses works *ad imitationem fori*—i.e., ripostes to famous speeches—e.g., Cestius's *In Milonem* (Sen. *Controv.* 3 *praef.* 6).

99. See also Geue 2019: 143–63. Cic. *Pis.* 71: Philodemus puts his Piso's life on show "as if in a mirror".

down, let him demolish the enclosing walls]; 204) or the patron's ("et tibi captiua resonat manus utraque turba" [and both your hands rattle with the crowd of pieces you have taken]; 208).

It is as if Horace's Pest had been allowed to put his case less ineptly and parade his versifying talent rather than just boasting about it. Having fired off his salvos of praise, the author moves stealthily towards Piso's threshold, assisted by an obliging muse instead of recalcitrant Horace ("limina Pisonis mecum pete"; 81) to breach the locked house and reveal the activities inside. Finally, on the brink of fulfilling the Pest's dream—storming the patron's walls and dislodging crowds of rivals—he plants his blatant request:[100]

> dignare aperire Penates
> hoc solum petimus.
>
> (218–19)

Just do me the favour of opening your home: this is my sole request.

History does not relate whether he succeeded in charming his way into the patron's heart, for all his earnest hopes ("mea uota / si mentem subiere tuam" [If my wishes have infiltrated your heart]; 246–47).

Such a display of bravado does not necessarily indicate that the poem is an "ironic parody of patron-poet relations".[101] For all his extravagance, the Piso author avails himself of Horatian-style disclaimers to separate himself from toadies and brash *scurrae* (disowned at 122–35), pleading pure soul, humble background and youthful fervour. He is spurred on by thoughts of fame, not hunger or greed (219–20)—even if Piso is a likely source of emergency funding ("subito . . . censu"; 111). The patron is no longer a man "of few companions" but surrounded by enormous crowds who follow him from lawcourts to salon to gaming board (134–35). All the more surprising, then, that while he is named, there is no corresponding signature by a youth so clearly out to make a name for himself.

Another name has been in the shadows all along: Maecenas, the hidden model not just for Piso's way of life, heavy on leisure pursuits (137–58), but also for the claims that he is discriminating and unsnobbish and tends a busy hive of differently talented artists (113–14, 117, 133). After two hundred lines, the late-lamented patron of patrons is finally named:

100. "summoto . . . uulgo" (dislodging the crowd; 136) ~ "summosses omnis" (I'm sure you'd dislodge everyone; Hor. *Sat.* 1.9.48).

101. Peirano 2012: 163.

ipse per Ausonias Aeneia carmina gentes
qui sonat, ingenti qui nomine pulsat Olympum
Maeoniumque senem Romano prouocat ore,
forsitan illius nemoris latuisset in umbra
quod canit, et sterili tantum cantasset auena                    235
ignotus populis, si Maecenate careret.
qui tamen haut uni patefecit limina uati
nec sua Vergilio permisit numina soli:
Maecenas tragico quatientem pulpita gestu
erexit Varium, Maecenas alta tonantis                            240
eruit et populis ostendit numina Graiis.
carmina Romanis etiam resonantia chordis,
Ausoniam chelyn gracilis patefecit Horati.
o decus, in totum merito uenerabilis aeuum,
Pierii tutela chori, quo praeside tuti                           245
non umquam uates inopi timuere senectae.

(*LAUS PISONIS* 231–46)

The very poet who makes his *Aeneid* resound through Italian peoples, the
poet who thumps Olympus with his mighty name and challenges old
Homer with his Roman accents, perhaps his songs might have lurked obscurely in the shadow of the grove and he might have sung on a sterile reed,
unknown to the nations, if he had lacked a Maecenas. But it was not just to
one poet that Maecenas opened his doors, not just to Virgil that he gave his
support: he also raised up Varius, who made the stage tremble with his
tragic bearing. Maecenas drew out the mightily thundering poet and
showed divine powers[102] to the peoples of Greece. He also introduced
songs that echoed on the Roman strings and Italian lyre of stripling Horace.
Glorious man, you who deserve fame for eternity, guardian of the Pierian
chorus, under whose protection no bard ever feared for an indigent old age.

Maecenas's "circle" crystallizes here into the trio Virgil, Varius and Horace,
with Virgil paramount.[103] While Piso's ancestor L. Calpurnius Piso had Epicurean associates like Philodemus, the poet nowhere mentions the family history
of patronage. It is Maecenas who is credited with single-handedly solidifying
the Roman canon while fostering each poet's career, particularly when embark-
ing on sublime themes ("qui . . . pulsat Olympum"; "alta tonantis"; "carmina . . .

102. Reading *numina*, not *nomina*: Bellandi 1995: 89n31.
103. Always the hierarchy: cf. Vell. Pat. 2.36; Bellandi 1995: 86.

resonantia").[104] He is a Promethean figure who raised his puppets to upright posture and higher ambitions. His poets supply his titles: *decus*, "glory", *tutela*, "protection", *praes*, "defence".[105] Calpurnius's themes are replicated, too: patronage as movement from the backwoods to the city; the need for poetry to be smooth and inoffensive and rustic innocence equivalent to poetic obscurity (*latuisset, latentem, caligine, celare*). But far from simply mediating between the poets and a higher power, Maecenas is organically tied to the imperial regime and outward-facing cultural responsibility.[106] Without him, Virgil would have lurked in the bucolic undergrowth, singing on his sterile reed; Varius would not have been elevated to the tragic stage; and stripling (*gracilis*) Horace would not have directed his lyre towards Greece.[107] The author is also explicit in promising what Horace was too delicate to promise in the *Odes*, immortal fame in return for the patron's support:

> quod si quis nostris precibus locus, et mea uota
> si mentem subiere tuam, memorabilis olim
> tu mihi Maecenas tereti cantabere uersu.
> possumus aeternae nomen committere famae          250
> . . .
> tu nanti protende manum: tu, Piso, latentem
> exsere. nos humilis domus, at sincera, parentum     255
> et tenuis fortuna sua caligine celat.
> possumus impositis caput exonerare tenebris
> et lucem spectare nouam, si quid modo laetus
> adnuis et nostris subscribis, candide, uotis.
> est mihi, crede, meis animus constantior annis,     260
> quamuis nunc iuuenile decus mihi pingere malas
> coeperit et nondum uicesima uenerit aestas.

But if there is any room for my appeals, if my prayers have reached your heart, then you will one day be sung in polished verse and enshrined in memory as my Maecenas. I have the power to commit a name to eternal fame . . . Stretch out your hand to a swimmer, Piso, bring a hidden man into the light. My ancestral home, humble but true, conceals me in its darkness.

---

104. Cf. Verg. *G.* 3.42: "te sine nil altum mens incohat"; Bellandi 1995: 86–87 and n24. There may also be an allusion to Maecenas's thunder fragment (Sen. *Ep.* 19.9).

105. Verg. *G.* 2.40 ("decus"); Hor. *Carm.* 1.1.2 ("praesidium"), 2.17.4 ("grande decus columenque rerum"); *Ep.* 1.1.103 ("tutela").

106. Bellandi 1995: 89n31.

107. Bellandi (1995: 88n33) traces *ostendi* to Hor. *Epist.* 1.19.24, where it suggests back-reflection from Italy to Greece; here, Maecenas takes over as his poets' publicist.

I can relieve my head of its shadowy burden, I can see new light, if only you nod joyfully and support my dreams, kindly one. I have a spirit more solid than my years, though youthful colour has only now begun to tinge my cheeks and my twentieth summer has not yet come.

Just as Horace had suppressed the Pest's name (*Sat.* 1.9.3: "known to me only by name"), so our poet hugs the riddle of his identity while focusing on other names, past and potential ("ingenti . . . nomine" [232], "ostendit nomina" [if not *numina*; 241], "nomen committere famae" [250]). In Piso's case, the job of commemoration is done and eternal fame guaranteed, for a gentleman with a portfolio of peacetime activities. Now, the ball is in his court: the nameless client waits for a matching invitation, a helping hand for a drowning man, an offer to push his germinating talent further into the light.[108] His foray into sports and board games may be just the youthful warm-up (cf. 87: "proludit") for some solemn (and unwanted?) epic Pisoneid of the future.[109] Just "not yet" (*nondum*) . . .

## Martial

Along with his contemporary Juvenal, epigrammatist Martial bewails the thin soil in which imperial poetry must take root. Mythical patrons are extinct in his world of callous philistines and starving poets.[110] At the same time, the two poets systematically vulgarize patronage as an exchange of verse for food or cash (following Persius, who had called the stomach "master of arts and bestower of talent"; prol. 10–11). They resuscitate the *rex* and parasite from comedy and the begging poets of archaic Greece.[111] As soon as modern *clientela* becomes an excuse for not writing poetry, it starts to generate poetry on this very topic.[112] Martial plays jack-of-all-trades, courting numerous minor patrons in minor verse, as well as paying respect indiscriminately to successive emperors Domitian, Nerva and Trajan. As Luke Roman writes: "If the poet were afforded the shelter of a great patron . . . he would be able to focus on an ambitious, integral work, rather than continuously pursuing many smaller gifts."[113] Yes, and no longer be Martial as we know him.

The lack of a permanent patron is something Martial turns to his advantage. It becomes his virtual alibi for not writing important poetry, allowing him to

108. The drowning metaphor recalls Ovid's exile poetry; e.g., *Tr.* 5.9.18, *Pont.* 2.6.14.
109. Cf. Stat. *Achil.* 1.19: "praeludit Achilles"—junior epic "limbers up" for the *Iliad*.
110. Labate 2012: 412.
111. Damon 1997: 4.
112. W. Fitzgerald 2007: 27.
113. Roman 2014: 318.

justify a relatively modest outlay of space and time with no prospect of reward, to remain in close contact, often uncomfortably so, with the full barrage of physical sensations on offer in smelly, hectic Rome. It also entitles him to offer his poems directly to the emperor (epigram-turned-panegyric is fast-tracked to the top) while hinting that patronage might come independently from that source. As Victoria Rimell writes: "It is the absence of a single rich patron, and hence the chronic lack of separation, of a protective intermediary figure between poet and world, and between poet and emperor, that provides the impulse, as Martial envisages it, for his project in merging poetry with world."[114] Martial's Maecenas is less a refined listener and expert critic than someone to provide a basic livelihood; not just a lost ideal or the defensive layer that insulates a poet from external reality, but a fall guy for any current emperor's inadequacy. Yet external reality is the stuff of Martial's writing. For all his complaints, he cherishes his freewheeling independence: "The epigram becomes the art of survival as Martial dishes the dirt, takes revenge, enlists allies, and solicits friends."[115]

Some of these paradoxes emerge in the small batch of poems where Martial alludes to Maecenas by name, remembering him as the bountiful protector of a legendary literary stable. If a poet needs *otium* to practise his art in peace, then spontaneous, occasional epigram might be thought of as leisure's quintessential product.[116] Yet Martial recasts himself as a begging Simonides at the rich man's gate.[117] Should he be careful what he asks for? *Otium* granted by a patron comes with strings attached: the more leisure, the more (and the grander) the poetry expected in return. That is why he usually casts Maecenas not as joined at the hip with Augustus but as an independent private patron.[118] Fitzgerald calls Martial "the poet of the *tamquam*" ("as if"), an experimenter with counterfactual fantasies in the small space of his poems.[119] Among these hypotheticals is Maecenas's miraculous reincarnation. What would the consequences really be for a career change? What prospects would be realistic for the lowest poet in the literary heap?

> saepe mihi dicis, Luci carissime Iuli,
>     "scribe aliquid magnum: desidiosus homo es."

---

114. Rimell 2009: 9. Roman (2014: 318) calls Martial a "journeyman" poet, citing his hint to Domitian: "A poor man pursues rewardless friendships" (5.19.8).

115. W. Fitzgerald 2007: 12.

116. Kay 1985: 63: "written by an *otiosus* for *otiosi*".

117. In his obituary for Martial, *Ep.* 3.21, Pliny claims to have helped him with a *uiaticum*, more a record of his generosity than evidence of Martial's neediness.

118. Bellandi 1995: 95n47.

119. W. Fitzgerald 2018: 111. See also Saller 1982a.

otia da nobis, sed qualia fecerat olim
    Maecenas Flacco Vergilioque suo:
condere uicturas temptem per saecula curas
    et nomen flammis eripuisse meum.
in steriles nolunt campos iuga ferre iuuenci:
    pingue solum lassat, sed iuuat ipse labor.

(MARTIAL 1.107)

You often say to me, dearest Lucius Julius, "Write something important: you're a lazybones." Give me downtime, then—the kind Maecenas once gave to his Horace and his Virgil—and I would try to write something that would last for centuries and snatch my name from the flames of the funeral pyre. Bullocks don't like carrying their yoke into barren fields. Rich soil brings on lassitude, but labouring in it is pleasant.

Playful but nagging ("saepe") pressure from "dearest" Lucius Julius cuts to the chase of a traditional patron's request.[120] The intimate context allows Martial to turn traditional *recusatio* on its head.[121] Rather than plead humility or feebleness, he retorts with a cynical demand: if you really want something important ("aliquid magnum"), then give me the *otium* Maecenas gave his poets, as though heroic inspiration were directly related to material security, euphemized here as "leisure" (*otium*). Maecenas stands in for Octavian in the primal scene of the *Eclogues* ("deus nobis haec otia fecit"; 1.6), while Martial ransacks the agricultural settings of both *Eclogues* (leisure) and *Georgics* (work), adding imagery from the *Aeneid* ("condere", "per saecula", "flammis eripuisse") to pinpoint the contradictions involved in ploughing another man's furrow. The consequences of receiving such a gift are weighed: centuries-long immortality versus expectations of "labor", whatever the terrain. It could be agreeable to wallow in the "rich soil" of patronage, however enervating or decadent; forbidden "fatness" makes labouring a pleasure, even under a yoke; protected working conditions blend sloth with activity, care with sinecure.[122] But Martial's fantasy is half-hearted: "It is as unlikely that he would ever write serious

---

120. "Often" (*saepe*) translates *pollaki*, the lost first word of Callim. *Aet.* 1, so activating a famous *recusatio*: Knox 2006. Latin text used is Shackleton Bailey (1993).

121. Citroni 1975: 326.

122. As if preferring the farmer's view of (desirable) fatness (cf. Verg. *G.* 1.64: "pingue solum"; *Aen.* 4.202) to the poet's (Callim. *Aet.* 1 prol. and Verg. *Ecl.* 6.4–5: "pinguis / pascere . . . ouis"). "Ploughing the sand" was proverbial for "wasting time writing": Ov. *Pont.* 4.2.15–16, Juv. 7.48–49, 103.

poetry as that he should ever find a real second Maecenas."[123] Away from the lotus eaters, he can claim his own version of active *otium*: busy epigram writing, stigmatized ironically as laziness (*desidia*).[124]

Martial renews the thought experiment in 8.55 (56), where he claims that only the existence of great patrons can guarantee the existence of great poets:

> Temporibus nostris aetas cum cedat auorum
>     creuerit et maior cum duce Roma suo,
> ingenium sacri miraris deesse Maronis
>     nec quemquam tanta bella sonare tuba.
> sint Maecenates, non deerunt, Flacce, Marones          5
>     Vergiliumque tibi uel tua rura dabunt.
> iugera perdiderat miserae uicina Cremonae
>     flebat et abductas Tityrus aeger oues:
> risit Tuscus eques paupertatemque malignam
>     reppulit et celeri iussit abire fuga.          10
> "accipe diuitias et uatum maximus esto;
>     tu licet et nostrum" dixit "Alexin ames."
> adstabat domini mensis pulcherrimus ille
>     marmorea fundens nigra Falerna manu,
> et libata dabat roseis carchesia labris          15
>     quae poterant ipsum sollicitare Iouem.
> excidit attonito pinguis Galatea poetae
>     Thestylis et rubras messibus usta genas
> protinus Italiam concepit et "arma uirumque",
>     qui modo uix Culicem fleuerat ore rudi.          20
> quid Varios Marsosque loquar ditataque uatum
>     nomina, magnus erit quos numerare labor?
> ergo ero Vergilius, si munera Maecenatis
>     des mihi? Vergilius non ero, Marsus ero.

As the age of our ancestors yields to our own, and as Rome has grown greater along with her ruler, you wonder that genius like divine Virgil's has disappeared, and that no poet thunders of wars with such a loud trumpet. Let there be Maecenases, Flaccus, and there will be no lack of Virgils; even your own country may provide you with a Maro. Tityrus had lost his acres in the neighbourhood of poor Cremona, and was sadly weeping for his lost

---

123. Howell 1980: 328.

124. Cic. *Brut.* 9 contrasts *inertia/desidia* with free time well spent ("oti moderati atque honesti"). Martial makes *desidia* synonymous with epigrammatic production: 8.3, 10.70.

sheep. The Tuscan knight smiled on him, drove spiteful poverty from his door, and ordered it to take flight. "Accept," said he "my wealth, and be the greatest of bards; what's more, you can have my Alexis to love." That most beautiful boy used to assist at his master's feasts, pouring dark Falernian with marble-white hand, and presented him with the cup just sipped with his rosy lips, lips which might have teased Jupiter himself. Plump Galatea and Thestylis with her red cheeks burned by harvesting vanished from the thoughts of the thunder-struck bard. At once, he was inspired by Italy, and "Arms and the man"—he whose inexperienced voice had only just been able to weep out a Gnat. Why need I mention the Varii and Marsi, and other poets who were enriched, to enumerate whom would be a long task? Shall I, then, be a Virgil, if you give me the gifts that Maecenas gave him? I shall not be Virgil: I shall be Marsus.

The Augustan age is again evoked as a cultural zenith: why is it that now, when Rome and its ruler are greater than ever, there are no great poets?[125] The equation looks simple enough: Maecenas plus Virgil equals great poetry. But "sacred" Virgil and his motives are questioned and the personalities of the *Eclogues* reconfigured. Maecenas the "Tuscan knight" is again overlaid on Virgil's Octavian, the smiling god who dries Tityrus's tears and drives away his poverty, guaranteeing literary greatness but now with a bonus gift thrown in: the rights to Maecenas's catamite, Alexis. Tityrus, meanwhile, is aligned with Virgil, making Corydon's yearning for Alexis in *Eclogues* 2 into a closeted author's confession and hinting at pederastic exchange in Maecenas's coterie.[126] Maecenas also channels the imperious Apollo who witnesses Ovidian *recusatio* in the *Amores*. With Alexis dangled as bait, his "accipe diuitias" (Take my wealth) clarifies the sexual undertones of the Ovidian "accipe . . . opus" (Take your task; *Am.* 1.1.24), while erotic distractions plump Galatea and tanned Thestylis (*Ecl.* 2) are dismissed as rustic fancies next to the allure of a marble-limbed waiter.[127] Still, "little" Martial finds it amusing to mock Augustan poetry's rejection of larger themes. Whereas in *Amores* 2.1 the "thunderbolt" (fulmen) of

125. Martial carefully detaches "Maecenases" from the current emperor, Domitian; Bellandi 1995: 96–97.

126. "iugera perdiderat miserae uicina Cremonae" (Mart. 8.55[56].7) ~ "Mantua uae miserae nimium uicina Cremonae" (Verg. *Ecl.* 9.28). Apollo had called Virgil "Tityrus" at *Ecl.* 6.4; cf. Serv. *ad Ecl.* 1.1: "et hoc loco Tityre sub persona Vergilium debemus accipere". Martial's Maecenas slots into Virgil's bucolic world as Iollas in *Ecl.* 2 (traditionally seen as a mask for Pollio); Bellandi 1995: 92n40.

127. "Revealing" the pretty boys of Hor. *Sat.* 2.8.13–15 as sex objects and extending Maecenas's wife-sharing lower down the chain.

the mistress's locked door had blasted all thoughts of gigantomachy ("excidit ingenio Iuppiter ipse meo" [I clean forgot the Jupiter theme]; 18), here the farm girls are thrown over in a flash at the prospect of sharing Ganymede.[128] So Virgil abandons youthful rusticity (*rudi ore*) and moves on up to more sophisticated sexual tastes and higher literary spheres.[129]

The narrative of patronage generated here blurs generic progression with wish fulfilment, sudden mood swings (tears to smiles), urbanization, and quick-grab money and sex, while the idea of a coup de foudre ("attonito"), accompanied by the instantaneous "conception" ("concepit") of *Georgics* ("Italiam") and *Aeneid* ("arma uirumque"), blots out with miracle-speak Horace's slow-burn gestation (*Sat.* 1.6.60–62).[130] Meanwhile, the quasi-elegiac "weepiness" that marks early Virgilian poetry, *Eclogues* and *Culex*, invokes sympathy between Virgil and his miniaturist counterpart, only to explode it with a surprise ending: if a Maecenas ever appeared ex machina, Martial would not be his Virgil—but his Domitius Marsus. Since Martial provides the only evidence we have for Marsus's connection with Maecenas, it has been suggested that he may have had a vested interest in incorporating epigram into the Augustan canon.[131] Even so, he shrinks from the *magnus labor* required of a great poet, preferring to remain lazy and grumbling. Those "various" people (*Varii*) and massed tribes of followers (*Marsi*) are "too much like hard work to enumerate" (22). All this is muttered in the ear of one Flaccus, "Floppy": not just the perfect sympathizer with *recusatio* but also a reminder of Horace, next-feeblest of Maecenas's poets in residence, the *homuncio* (mannikin) who had occupied the littlest niche, which Martial now claims for himself.

The lack of a Maecenas is also bemoaned in Book 11, a post-Domitianic "Saturnalian" collection dedicated with high hopes to good king Nerva. Martial's ambivalent relationship to rusticity emerges from a poem where he claims that his epigrams are not read only by sophisticated city folks ("urbana . . . otia") but by frozen centurions as far away as Ovid's Black Sea. Not-Rome is not just *rus* but the margins of the empire: this is a claim to world domination, shared with an emperor hailed as a new Augustus. But Martial, like Catullus, pleads an empty purse ("sacculus"; 6), again an alibi for not writing the kind of poetry

---

128. See W. Fitzgerald (2007: 364n53) on the sexual innuendo in Martial's *arma uirumque*.

129. Cf. Tac. *Agr.* 3: "incondita ac rudi uoce".

130. *risit* is the "effortless laughter of a god"; L. Watson and Watson 2003: *ad loc.* Bellandi (1995: 92n40) takes *Italiam* as the *Aeneid* (*Aen.* 1.2: "Italiam fato profugus Lauiniaque uenit"), with *Georgics* elided (cf. Calp. Sic. 4.163).

131. At 7.29.7–8, Virgil, Alexis and Maecenas, plus Marsus and Melaenis, form a *menage à cinq*, Marsus replacing Horace as the lowly friend with the inferior girl (cf. *Epodes* 14). Martial's addressee, Voconius Victor, wrote verses on a (bucolically transgendered) Thestylus.

that will last forever and suit the rigid military juggernaut that is Rome (cf. 3: "Martia signa"). As it is, he makes a good stab at panegyric in the tiny space of epigram. His other alibi is the absence of a Maecenas:

> at quam uicturas poteramus pangere chartas
> quantaque Pieria proelia flare tuba,
> cum pia reddiderint Augustum numina terris,
> et Maecenatem si tibi, Roma, darent!

(11.3.7–10)

But what immortal pages could I have written and what battles tooted on the Pierian trumpet if, when the holy gods restored Augustus to the earth, they had also given a Maecenas to you, Rome!

By focusing attention on the irrevocability of this legendary sidekick, Martial hints obliquely that Nerva might be prepared to play Augustus in the matter of patronage.[132] Fitzgerald writes: "Conveniently this figure of Maecenas allows Martial to detach this complaint from the emperor himself."[133] Yet Domitian's disappearance has another consequence: Maecenas and a beneficent emperor can once again be suggested as an effective unit (even if Maecenas the never-never patron allows Martial to skirt the question of serious collaboration).[134]

In the preface to Book 12, Martial writes from self-imposed exile in Spain to a new dedicatee, Priscus Terentius. A fish out of water, depressed by small-town politics, the urban poet restores his book from Spanish siesta time (*desidia*) to Roman ears and the pulsing inspiration that is the city (cf. *praef*.: "illud materiarum ingenium"). With Domitian and his rigid artistic monopoly consigned to the past, he loses no time in welcoming a new Maecenas, praising him for his brave generosity under the last emperor and hinting that he might carry on the good work:[135]

> Quod Flacco Varioque fuit summoque Maroni
> Maecenas, atauis regibus ortus eques,
> gentibus et populis hoc te mihi, Prisce Terenti,
> fama fuisse loquax chartaque dicet anus

---

132. Martial's appeals to emperors are vague enough (6.10, 6.87, 8.24, 8.82); Bellandi 1995: 97n51.

133. W. Fitzgerald 2007: 291. For *pia numina* as Virgilian, cf. *Aen*. 4.382.

134. Bellandi 1995: 98.

135. See Bellandi (1995: 95–96) on the additional problem of Domitian's own interest in the arts; Coleman 1986: 3088–89, Tandoi 1968: 134–35.

tu facis ingenium, tu, si quid posse uidemur;                    5
    tu das ingenuae ius mihi pigritiae.
...

largiri, praestare, breues extendere census,
    et dare quae faciles uix tribuere dei,                       10
nunc licet et fas est. sed tu sub principe duro
    temporibusque malis ausus es esse bonus.

(12.3.1–6, 12.6.9–12; LINES PRINTED TOGETHER<br>BY SHACKLETON BAILEY [1993: 3.94])

What Maecenas, the knight sprung of royal lineage, was to Horace and
Varius and supreme Virgil, many-tongued Fame, and a long-lived work,
shall proclaim to all people and nations that you, Priscus Terentius, have
been to me. You give me my facility, and whatever power I am thought to
have; you give me the right to enjoy the freedom of laziness . . . To be mu-
nificent, to provide, to increase slender means, and give what indulgent
gods have scarce bestowed is now permitted and lawful. But you dared to
be bountiful under a harsh emperor and in bad times.

The cluster of protégés from *Satires* 1 is reconstituted, while Horace's opening regal asclepiad (*Carm.* 1.1.1: "Maecenas ataus edite regibus") is cut down
to knight size (". . . eques") in the pentameter (2). Priscus is credited for having
fashioned the poet, such as he is, and granted him leisure, the very thing that
bored him in Spain.[136] The independent patron serves a purpose, ironically,
only once the emperor is removed as an object of fear. Roman subjects are
pictured as slaves released from an overthrown master, even as Priscus himself
has "freed" Martial to write, without strings, like some liberal Maecenas.[137] On
the other hand, the pun on *ingenium*, "innate talent", and *ingenuus*, "liberal,
innate, authentic", suggests that the freedom from labour (*desidia*) legally bestowed on a freed slave by his ex-master (*patronus*) is innate to both epigram
and an epigrammatist known for his "natural laziness" (*ingenua pigritia*).[138]
Another hexameter ("largiri, praestare, breues extendere census"; 9) displays
epigram's infinite capacity to accept whatever largesse (*largiri*) will allow it to
stay small (*breues*). Another consequence of manumission was that it entitled
a former slave to cast about for many different new patrons. From the start,
Martial reveals the global scale of his ambitions ("gentibus et populis"; 3),
equal to an emperor's reach. Sure enough, the next three poems are directed

---

136. Cf. Prop. 3.9; Ov. *Pont.* 4.1.35–36.
137. Cf. Tac. *Agr.* 2–3; Sen. *Apocol.* 12.
138. Cf. 12.18.10 ("pigri"; when retired in Spain).

to viable patrons Nerva and Trajan—quickfire proof of the link between epigrammatic brevity and poetic fickleness.[139]

## Juvenal

Like Martial, Juvenal survived authoritarian emperors. Like Martial, he de-
votes himself to prowling the streets of Rome, the city he loves and hates,
mining the rich seam of corruption he finds there. Even more so, Juvenal is the
poet of glass half-empty, with his vignettes of half-eaten chickens, threadbare
aristocrats, broken china and humiliated clients who take the leavings at two-
tier feasts. This is his Roman reality. But unlike Martial, he aspires to heroic
grandeur (billowing sails, war trumpets), to becoming an exceptional poet
outside the common herd ("uates egregius"; 7.53), along with writers of epic
and tragedy. Like Petronius's mad epic poet, Eumolpus (Petron. *Sat.* 83), greatness is an ambition for him, as it is not for Martial. He is less a gentleman in
search of preferment than an independent soul, intoxicated by resentment.
For him, Maecenas remains a comfortably elusive commodity, captured in
memorable caricatures (the lolling passenger of *Satires* 1.64–67 and the purple-
clad fashion icon at *Satires* 12.39). Meanwhile, Juvenal drags Maecenas's poets
down with him, in a sour-grapes attack on a more privileged age.

*Satires* 7 addresses the emperor directly as the only hope for the ragged artistic community at Rome—most probably Hadrian, though an argument can
equally be made for Domitian, to whose reign many events in the poem refer.[140]
A specific name may indeed be missing in order "to make the point that the
problem of patronage is systemic, not transient".[141] Depersonalized, on both
sides—unnamed emperor, anonymous satirist—the appeal is a general one on
behalf of the writerly condition, pitied as a state of permanent madness or incurable addiction.[142] The Muses are now as grim ("tristes"; 2) and starving ("esu-
riens"; 7) as their acolytes, who must prostitute their works and sell off their
household goods to write sublime poems in garrets, pursuing an unrewarding
profession into their twilight years ("facunda et nuda senectus" [eloquent but
threadbare old age]; 35).[143] Devotion to Mount Helicon is demystified and

---

139. In 12.36 Martial "forgets" Maecenas in a list of ideal patrons (Piso, Seneca, Memmius
and Crispus).

140. Bartsch 1994: 125–47. Earlier addresses to emperors, Ov. *Tr.* 1.1, *Tr.* 2 and Hor. *Epist.* 2.1,
lie behind this poem.

141. Geue 2018: 55; Bartsch (1994: 142–43) concludes that the indeterminacy is deliberate;
the *Historia Augusta* makes Hadrian as much of an artistic impresario as Domitian.

142. Cf. Hor. *Ars P.* 472 on Empedocles: "certe furit".

143. See Nauta (2002: 5–6) and Colton (1991: 283–302) on the shared motif in Juvenal and
Martial.

literary works reduced to bare materiality: mythical characters and themes find themselves becoming pledges at the pawnbroker's or librettos for pantomimes. In hard times, even pampered Statius is forced to pimp his "girlfriend", the *Thebaid*, and sell his "virgin" *Agave* to Paris, an imperial favourite who dispenses equestrian rings to the favoured few.

The poem's exhilarating rage is stoked by the scandalous mismatch between the original Dionysiac frenzy of these themes and characters and their banal endings as job lots at auctions, along with wardrobes and occasional tables (10–12). This literary crisis is partly laid at the door of unsympathetic private patrons (22–35), but if the emperor praised at the start is Domitian, then the portrait of patronage in his era is hardly flattering. Statius the court success is a self-defeating example of a neglected poet, and Paris at least a partial indictment of the imperial system of dispensing privileges.[144] The Juvenalian speaker is steeped in the language he despises: does his abrupt switch of tone, from conventional praise to abject complaining, reflect the doublespeak that he finds in the patronage system as a whole?[145]

Maecenas is mentioned once by name, at the head of a list of long-lost private patrons:

> quis tibi Maecenas, quis nunc erit aut Proculeius
> aut Fabius, quis Cotta iterum, quis Lentulus alter?

> (SATIRES 7.94–95)

> Who will now be your Maecenas, or your Proculeius, or Fabius, or Cotta, who a second Lentulus?

Both Paulus Fabius Maximus and Cotta Maximus were among Ovid's patrons, while Gaius Proculeius is a rich benefactor in Horace (*Carm.* 2.2).[146] Not only does the list dilute Maecenas's singular charisma and separate him from the Augustan regime, it is also a reminder that poets like Horace and Ovid were spoiled for choice and spread their loyalties. Maecenas's oblique presence has already infiltrated the poem: in receding vistas onto the life of ease that patronage enables (privately funded Lucan, supine in his marble gardens; poets lounging on beds in the shade; lawyers who rent sardonyx rings, litters and purple robes to impress their supporters) and in the glimpsed success of his poets, to whom he is partly an invisible but amusingly mundane source of board and lodging and partly the quasi-divine inspiration that promotes them to higher things.

---

144. Bartsch 1994: 133.
145. Townend 1973: 152; Bartsch 1994: 132.
146. Cf. Juv. 5.109: Cotta, Seneca and Piso as patrons.

Yet the legendary encounter with Maecenas retains its transformative cachet, as Juvenal raids the poets' own works for suitable metaphors:

> neque enim cantare sub antro
> Pierio thyrsumque potest contingere maesta
> paupertas atque aeris inops, quo nocte dieque
> corpus eget: satur est cum dicit Horatius "euhoe."

(*SATIRES* 7.59–62)

For miserable poverty cannot sing in the Pierian cave or hold a thyrsus without the means to meet the body's needs, night and day: Horace was well-fed when he cried "Io Bacchus".

Horace's satirical mantra "iam satis est" (*Sat.* 1.1.120) is converted into the smug sufficiency (*satur*, full) of a regular at Maecenas's symposia, superimposed on the whirling vision of Bacchus's cave in *Odes* 2.19: a career path from *satur* to satyr?[147]

Meanwhile, in Virgil's progress from *Eclogues* to *Aeneid*, Tityrus-like salvation is comically shrugged off as "a boy and tolerable digs" (puer et tolerabile hospitium), followed by epic transformation into a snake-haired Fury:

> magnae mentis opus nec de lodice paranda
> attonitae currus et equos faciesque deorum
> aspicere et qualis Rutulum confundat Erinys.
> nam si Vergilio puer et tolerabile desset
> hospitium, caderent omnes a crinibus hydri,    70
> surda nihil gemeret graue bucina.

(*SATIRES* 7.66–71)

An ambitious soul is needed, one not obsessed with buying a blanket but thunderstruck at the vision of horses and chariots and the faces of the gods and the looks of the Fury who struck fear into Turnus. For if Virgil had lacked a boy and adequate lodging, all the hydras would have fallen from his hair and his unheard bugle would not have blared anything of weight.

The scenario envisaged is Allecto's visit to Turnus in *Aeneid* 7, the book where a rural community's propulsion into war is bound up with grandiose poetic ambition ("maius opus moueo" [I put a greater task in motion]; Verg. *Aen.* 7.45). Virgil here plays both the astonished victim of inspiration (*attonitae*) and the Fury in all her horrible glory ("all the hydras would have fallen from

---

147. *Carm.* 2.19.5–7; cf. Lucr. 1.922; Ov. *Tr.* 4.1.43.

his hair"), while the carefully chosen *bucina* (cow horn, from *bos*) recalls the emergency reuse of that "pastorale signum" (pastoral signal; *Aen.* 7.513) to fast-track the birth of war (*Aen.* 7.520).[148]

From the *Georgics*, meanwhile, the Virgilian work in the middle, Juvenal gleans agricultural images and reapplies them to the thin soil of a modern literary career: "But we press on like this, driving furrows in thin dust and upturning the beach with an unproductive plough" (*Satires* 7.48–49); "Are your labours any more fertile, historians?" (7.98–99); "Will this produce a crop? What fruit will come from tilled soil?" (7.103).[149] Even the "genuine harvest" (ueram ... messem; 7.112) of the lawyers is not equal to a thousandth of a sports star's fee. It may be that Juvenal redirects Horace's and Virgil's career paths towards Bacchic frenzy to make them conform to his general diagnosis: that all poets tend to madness. December-long abstinence from wine (7.97–98) recalls Horace's *Satires* 2.3, where the poet goes dry for the Saturnalia (Hor. *Sat.* 2.3.4–5), only to conjure up a monstrous interlocutor, the mad Stoic Damasippus, "author" of his longest, maddest satire. The equivalent for Juvenal is the preceding poem, *Satires* 6, his tirade against women, which boasts of being outsized, tragic-scale poetry in a Sophoclean or Bacchic vein.[150] If Maecenas established the idea that the patron was a muse for the poetry sent in his direction, then what more appropriate addressee for a schizophrenic appeal on behalf of indigent poets than a crazed emperor?

The seventh satire is often discussed as a problem poem, thanks to its stark contradictions. Which emperor is being addressed and where does the first-person speaker stand? He is so devastating in his critique of pampered poets, corrupt courtiers and mean patrons, yet so obsequious to his imperial addressee, in language that ricochets back to Martial, Statius and Calpurnius. It has been suggested that the split is a symptom of the linguistic predicament faced by contemporary poets: "It is as if the speaker *were* a Domitianic court poet."[151] Or, for that matter, a Neronian or a Hadrianic court poet (since all three emperors were interested in the arts, found rivals hard to stomach and received the same flowery praise). "The leader's indulgence" (ducis indulgentia; 7.20–21) echoes Statius, Calpurnius and the *Laus Pisonis*, a term applicable to "any imperial ego, any imperial patronage".[152] But, as we have seen, it may go back specifically to Maecenas. Maecenas has set the mould not just for private patrons but

---

148. Verg. *Aen.* 7.446–48, 450. *attonitus* is also associated with Bacchic matrons (*Aen.* 7.580), mothers admiring Camilla (*Aen.* 7.813–14) and Latinus overcome (*Aen.* 12.610).

149. Verg. *G.* 1.64 ("pingue solum ..."), 70 ("sterilem ... harenam").

150. Juv. 6.636: "grande Sophocleo carmen bacchamur hiatu".

151. Bartsch 1994: 141.

152. Bartsch (1994: 134) considers the identity of the emperor "a non-question".

also for Domitian's favourite Paris, dispenser of favours in turn. If his absence makes him a scapegoat for an emperor's dereliction of duty, then his lingering presence, in the imperial courtiers or favourites who reincarnate him, has much the same effect.

## The Next Maecenas?

Pliny's *Letters*, written around the same time, are the textual record of an intricate web of social connections, with Pliny himself the spider at its centre. An establishment figure, he needs no patron to support his writing, financially speaking, and is all too eager to reveal his own activities in that area. But he has other reasons to offer a flattering portrait of one Titinius Capito, a sociable magnet for Roman writers and a plausible candidate for Maecenas *redivivus*:

> uir est optimus et inter praecipua saeculi ornamenta numerandus. colit studia, studiosos amat fouet prouehit, multorum qui aliqua componunt portus sinus gremium, omnium exemplum, ipsarum denique litterarum iam senescentium reductor ac reformator. domum suam recitantibus praebet, auditoria non apud se tantum benignitate mira frequentat; mihi certe, si modo in urbe, defuit numquam. (*Ep.* 8.12.1–2)

> He is an excellent person, to be counted among the chief ornaments of our era. He is devoted to literature and adores, fosters and enables literary types. He is a comfort and haven of refuge to all kinds of authors, an example to everyone, someone who has restored literature and given it a new life when it was already in decline. He lends his house for recitals and is wonderfully kind in attending readings elsewhere. He never failed to appear at my recitals if he was in Rome.

Capito seems almost too good to be true. Pliny packs in all the reassuring old images for ideal patrons (harbour, bosom, ornament). Even so, he sounds a melancholy note: this is culture imagined on the point of decline ("litterarum iam senescentium")—"no longer", rather than "not yet"—propped up by last-minute attempts to resuscitate idealized salon culture by replicating its traditional venues (*domum, auditoria*). Behind the rosy eulogy lie two men's anxieties about their complicity with an earlier regime (Capito had been Domitian's secretary *de epistulis*). Pliny duly reveals that he is taking the day off to hear Capito read not his latest light poetry but expiatory hagiographies of the Stoic martyrs.[153] Any illusion of a spontaneous gathering is soon banished by the stilted calculus of quid pro quos that pins a price on every urban foray:

---

153. On Pliny's and Capito's consciences, see Freudenburg (2001: 225–29).

quod si illi nullam uicem nulla quasi mutua officia deberem, sollicitarer tamen uel ingenio hominis pulcherrimo et maximo et in summa seueritate dulcissimo, uel honestate materiae. scribit exitus illustrium uirorum, in his quorundam mihi carissimorum. (*Ep.* 8.12.4)

But even if I didn't owe him any return or any kind of reciprocal duty, still I would be nagged into going by the man's exemplary talent, which is both limitless and sweet in its utmost seriousness, or by the worthiness of his subject-matter. He is writing the deaths of famous men, some of whom were very dear to me.

It is as if the stress-ridden Horace of *Satires* 2.6 were being superimposed on the wide-eyed neophyte (Horace or the Pest) of *Satires* 1.9. Despite the happy coincidence declared in this case between desire and duty ("I don't know whether I *want* to hear, or *ought* to hear him more"; *Ep.* 8.12.1), mutual literary kowtowing and public virtue signalling join the other services to be rendered and debts to be paid in Pliny's social calendar:

uideor ergo fungi pio munere, quorumque exsequias celebrare non licuit, horum quasi funebribus laudationibus seris quidem sed tanto magis ueris interesse. uale. (*Ep.* 8.12.5)

It's as though I were paying a dutiful tribute to those whose funerals I could not attend but whose funeral orations I seem to be witnessing, all the more authentic for being belated. Farewell.

Maecenas is nowhere mentioned in the letter. It is Syme who christens Capito "the Maecenas of his age".[154] This is because Pliny so clearly remakes him in this nostalgic, competitive image: "among the chief ornaments of this era", "an example to everyone".[155] Yet the new Maecenas is shown as the original one never was: obliging an audience to listen to his compositions as he had listened to theirs; implicated in the same belated praise ("laudationibus seris") as the martyrs; and inscribed as restorer and rebuilder ("reductor ac reformator") of culture, as though he were patching up a broken aqueduct. His soirée is a sombre publicity stunt, as is the letter. For all Pliny's assurances that voluntarism is alive and well and there is still sweetness to be plucked from a joyless occasion, this is payback time for all concerned.

---

154. Syme 1958: 1.93.
155. In a book concerned with exemplarity: cf. *Ep.* 8.13, 14.

# 8

# Jewels and Seals

DESPITE THE FACT that there is no reliable evidence for any personal gem collection, jewels and seal rings have long encrusted the textual memory of Maecenas. Not only have they played a disproportionately large part in the hunt for and creation of his identity,[1] they have also generated lasting claims in the process. Maecenas has often been assumed to be a jewel enthusiast, while even his writing style tends to attract the adjectives "jewelled" and "precious". His likeness, it was alleged for centuries, can be found in the profile of a high-browed beardless man found on certain engraved gems (amethyst, carnelian, sardonyx, garnet) now displayed in European museums.[2]

This is a context where biographical arguments have been especially circular. To be fair, if Maecenas the gem fancier has been extrapolated from a few scattered literary allusions, he must take some of the blame himself.[3] When Pliny cites him as an authority (*ex auctoribus*, *HN* 37, index) on gems, he may simply have had sight of the poem addressed to "my Horace" (mi Flacce), in which Maecenas claims to prize him above all the jewels in the world.[4] Preserved incomplete by Isidore (*Etym.* 19.32.6), this poem generated a playful dialogue with Augustus, who, when he wanted to tease Maecenas, reset those emeralds, beryls, pearls and jaspers in a parodic prose letter, exposing them as so much pseudo-Etruscan paste (fr. 31 Malcovati = Macrob. *Sat.* 2.4.12). We have already considered the two fragments for what they tell us about homosocial banter and Maecenas's softening influence on his ruler. My focus now is on the materials they evoke and what they suggest about their owner's relationship to the world.

1. Ridley 2020.

2. Bernoulli 1882: 1.239; Ball 1950; Ridley 2020.

3. Petrain (2005) considers Maecenas's poem (and the jewel poem at Petron. *Sat.* 55) an example of the "jewelled" style associated with late antiquity. On the gem portraits of Maecenas, see chapter 1.

4. fr. 3L = 2C = 185H.

Ring wearing in Rome, a habit adopted from Greece, had long been a marker of identity, signifying status—authentic or bogus (a ring being a marker of the equestrian order)—office, gender and, of course, taste.[5] Pliny notes the increasing complexity of the semiotics involved, tracing a swing towards luxurious ornaments over functional devices in line with broader patterns of moral decline.[6] In the previous century, Ateius Capito had lamented that men of old used to wear no more than one ring, not for decoration (*ornatus*) but for the simple purpose of sealing documents (*signandi causa*).[7] As habits became more luxurious (*luxuriantis aetatis*), costly ornamental rings came to be worn on the left hand (the hand of leisure, *otiosior*) to protect them from the routine operations of the right (*officio manus dexterae*).[8] When rings are involved in pinpointing Maecenas's identity, both hands, left and right, and two functions, administrative and decorative, are in play. Together, seal rings and ornamental jewels mark out a life split between connoisseurship and administration—the aesthetics of private collecting pitted against the pragmatics of executive authority. As imperial go-between, conduit of sentimentality and devotee of luxury, someone who floats between absence and presence in his poets' works, Maecenas becomes a magnet for these metonymic reminders of his various activities.

From antiquity, the personal signet ring was the token par excellence of the "memorable self".[9] Its impression offered a secure and replicable reminder of an individual's unique will, while at the same time compensating for their absence (one word for a ring was *sumbolon*, literally a token or substitute). Ancient seals were often engraved with clasped hands or the words "Remember" or "Remember me" in Greek.[10] These tiny objects contained enormous power: talismanic, binding and ideological.[11] The image they bore could be infinitely reproduced. As Verity Platt writes: "Self-replicatory power is intrinsic to the seal; without it, the object would be merely decorative, comparable to a cameo."[12]

Anecdotes in Pliny and Cassius Dio capture the importance of seal rings for Maecenas's bureaucratic activities. Among his most intimate possessions,

5. Hawley 2007.

6. Plin. *HN* 33.8–30.

7. Fr. 12 Strzelecki = Macrob. *Sat.* 7.13.11–15.

8. Hawley 2007: 107.

9. Fumerton 1991.

10. Platt 2006: 248.

11. Platt 2006: 237: "so much semiology in such a tiny element of matter"; cf. S. Stewart 1984: 14. Ancient seal rings: Boardman 1970; Henig 1994.

12. Platt 2006: 238; echoing Ateius Capito (see above).

we learn, was a signet ring bearing the image of a frog, an amusing little device whose stamp on tax bills excited dread in their recipients.[13] As Augustus's proxy, along with Agrippa, he was additionally entitled to use one of the emperor's rings.[14] In Dio's account, a miniature story unfolds about authority and surrogacy in the processes of imperial administration:

> He [Augustus] also gave to Agrippa and to Maecenas so great authority in all matters that they could even read beforehand the letters which he wrote to the senate and to others and then change whatever they wished in them. To this end they also received from him a ring, so that they might be able to seal the letters again. For he had caused to be made in duplicate the seal which he used most at that time, the design being a sphinx, the same on each copy; since it was not till later that he had his own likeness engraved upon his seal and sealed everything with that. (Dio Cass. 51.3.5–6, Loeb translation)

Pliny provides additional information: Augustus found two identical sphinx rings among his mother's relics (which conveniently explains how he was able to divide his signatory authority).[15] Augustus later replaced the ambiguous sphinx with a ring depicting Alexander the Great, and finally with his own portrait designed by Dioscorides, which made him undisputed author and signatory of every communication.[16] The ring was subsequently handed down to future emperors.[17] Again, the narrative tracks the evolution of imperial authority: originally shared and open to adjustment, then concentrated unalterably in the emperor's will and person.

As symbols of surrogacy, autonomy and dynastic succession, seals are crucial to our picture of Maecenas, not only as pioneering imperial bureaucrat but also as patron. His chosen image of a frog sitting on a lotus leaf turns out to be a common Egyptian motif (like Augustus's enigmatic sphinx), a symbol of the goddess Hekat, midwife and fertility goddess—two roles we have already seen associated with his patronal activities.[18] If this testimony is too flimsy in itself to suggest parallels between authorization and patronage, then Maecenas's administrative surrogacy can be seen to mirror his unobtrusive but essential literary role in other ways, as well. In the newly bureaucratic environment of Horace's *Satires* 2, for example, the seal operates as the physical instrument of political power. Horace complains that lobbyists implore him to get their documents sealed by

---

13. Plin. *HN* 37.4.10.

14. Plin. *HN* 37.4.10; Dio Cass. 51.3.6.

15. Plin. *HN* 37.4.10.

16. Plin. *HN* 37.4.10; Suet. *Aug.* 50.

17. Simpson 2005.

18. The leaf symbolized some large number.

Maecenas (*Sat.* 2.6.38: "imprimat his, cura, Maecenas signa tabellis"). In a literary context, the poets had already competed for his imprimatur: the casual but vital *Maecenas* inserted into the first line of *Satires* 1 and fourth line of *Epodes* 1 could be said to function textually as a preliminary editorial "seal", the patented stamp of a "Maecenas production", as it would do for Virgil (*G.* 1.2) and Propertius (3.9.1). In this respect, the opening name balances, or competes with, the poetic motif of the *sphragis*, the "seal" with which many Greco-Roman authors, starting with Theognis, signed their works: "Let the seal of the wise man, Cyrnus, be set upon these lines . . . Every man shall say, 'These are the lines of Theognis of Megara, famous throughout the world'" (Thgn. 1.19, 23).

Already in *Satires* 1, images of sealing and unsealing (pursed lips, words unsealed by drink) had marked the poet's resistance to "loose talk" (always ironic in the context of frank *sermones*, "conversation, gossip"), whether at a dinner party, alone in a portico, in the streets of Rome or in Maecenas's carriage.[19] At the end of *Satires* 2.3, the frog that explodes as it tries to emulate a calf (in a retelling of Aesop's fable) could even be said, given the patron's chosen symbol, to function as a kind of emergency seal, thumped down on a monstrously long poem at the moment when it threatens to spill unpalatable secrets about both parties. The seal is also a symbol of the mystery bound up in Maecenas's house; after his time, a broken seal becomes an image of secrets carelessly spilled.

Further connections emerge between the self-conscious materiality of epistolary writing and the written communications of poet-scribe, patron-signatory and emperor. In the interlude between the two volumes of Horace's poetic *Epistles*, one dedicated to Maecenas and the other starting with a direct address to the emperor, Augustus made a real-life approach to Horace, so the story goes, via a letter to Maecenas that Suetonius claims to have seen with his own eyes. A vacancy had arisen for an imperial secretary (*de epistulis*), but Horace apparently declined it, despite Augustus's attempt to outsource to this promising junior the letter-writing role previously shared by Maecenas and Agrippa:

> ante ipse sufficiebam scribendis epistulis amicorum, nunc occupatissimus et infirmus Horatium nostrum a te cupio abducere. ueniet ergo ab ista parasitica mensa ad hanc regiam, et nos in epistulis scribendis iuuabit. (Suet. *Vita Hor.*)

> Previously I could cope with my personal correspondence, but now I am extremely busy and my health is bad, and I want to entice our friend Horace away from you. Make him leave your parasitic table and come to this royal one and agree to help me with my letters.

---

19. Contrast Hor. *Sat.* 1.4.89 ("condita cum uerax aperit praecordia Liber") with 1.4.138 ("compressis . . . labris"), 1.9.14 ("nil respondebam") and 2.6.58 ("egregii . . . altique silenti").

Approaching Horace himself, the emperor adopted a different tack, hinting that he might care to mention him in his literary works:

> You should know that I am angry because you don't choose to converse with me in your many writings of that kind; or are you afraid of losing your reputation in the future, because you will be seen to be my friend [familiaris]? (Suet. *Vita Hor.*)

Augustus wants two kinds of writing from Horace: one practical and immediate (help with his correspondence) and one long-term and literary (a place in his *Letters*). The special attention Maecenas receives from his poets has become an object of desire and envy, not unlike his wife Terentia. From one viewpoint, Augustus comes across as naïve and literal in thinking that Horace, just because he writes literary epistles, would make an excellent secretary; from another, he is a master of realpolitik, inoculating himself in advance against charges of collusion between subject and *princeps*.[20] Authentic or not, the letters construct an imperial backstory for Horace's direct approach to the emperor in *Epistles* 2.1, the so-called "Letter to Augustus".[21]

The path to Augustus is paved more obliquely in *Epistles* 1, with its courtly letters of introduction: a recommendation on behalf of a young courtier to Tiberius (*Epist.* 1.9) and instructions to an emissary, Vinnius Asina, to deliver a bundle of papers to Augustus (*Epist.* 1.13), at a moment when the monarch is receptive to them. Other epistles offer outrageously close-to-the-bone disclosures (given that Maecenas is their over-reader) about how to unlock the social and financial potential of successful client–patron relationships (*Epist.* 1.17, 1.18). All this mediation unfolds against the backdrop of the chief diplomatic event of the times, the Parthians' restoration in 20 BCE of the Roman standards (*signa*) captured at Carrhae in 53 BCE (*Epist.* 1.18.56–57). Ellen Oliensis has brilliantly spotted a ghostly encryption of this larger event in Horace's instructions to Vinnius (*Epist.* 1.13.2): "Augusto reddes signata" can mean either "You will deliver [the volumes] sealed to Augustus" or "You will bring home the standards to Augustus."[22] The Parthian concession also underwrites Horace's voluntary offer in *Epistles* 1.7 to restore past gifts from Maecenas: "cuncta resigno" (I unwrite everything; 34).[23]

---

20. Oliensis 1998: 182.

21. Oliensis 1998: 191; cf. Oliensis 1997: 166–67. Surprisingly, the authenticity of the letter has never been doubted.

22. Cf. Hor. *Epist.* 1.12.37–38.

23. *Epist.* 1.7.9—"testamenta resignat" (unseals wills)—anticipates the story of Horace's last hours: unable to write, he could give only a verbal, not a written indication that he was making Augustus his heir (Suet. *Vita Hor.*).

International politics aside, however, the more obvious metaphor contained in *signata* and *resigno* is that of the seal (also *signum*).[24] In an epistolary volume this has a special charge, as Horace's close attention throughout to the physical aspects of signing, sealing and delivering letters makes clear. In *Epistles* 1.13, there is the obvious paradox that, in making us privy to his instructions to Vinnius, Horace is breaking the seal of his covering note, showing the effort that lies behind any performance of discreet compliance. Indeed, all the *Epistles* are in some sense opened letters, as if some moment of shared sympotic frankness had thrown caution and privacy to the winds: "quid non ebrietas dissignat? operta recludit" (What does drunkenness not unseal? It uncorks what's hidden; *Epist.* 1.5.16). It is Horace's barely suppressed hope that "the eyes and ears of Caesar" will deign to look in his direction, even that Vinnius will tell the crowds that he is on a mission to Augustus, or that he will stumble and accidentally break the package.

*Epistles* 1.13, in short, "displays the very overzealousness against which it warns and broadcasts the very information it purports to censor".[25] Yet for all the momentous iterations of the scolding author, we are none the wiser as to the contents of the parcel. The joke is that instead of being sealed dispatch boxes (*signata uolumina*)—correspondence prepared by the emperor's new clerk?—the package is finally revealed as the poet's own production ("carmina"; 17). Obvious possibilities include *Odes* 1–3 or, more amusingly, *Epistles* 1 itself.[26] In other words, Horace is responding to the emperor's second request, to give him a (tangential) appearance in his *Epistles*, and not to his first, to accept a job as his secretary.[27] Tactlessly, the writing he sends the emperor here is exactly what at the start of the book he had seemed to begrudge Maecenas, whose name is now replaced by a more ambitious imprimatur ("Augusto"; 2). If the Horace of the *Epistles* continues to censor himself, he will go on to reveal himself as an undercover exhibitionist. The book-cum-slave sent into the city streets in the final poem, *Epistles* 1.20, is credited with brazen contempt for locks and seals, which Horace, the model of discretion (*pudico*), disclaims: "odisti clauis et grata sigilla pudico" (You can't stand the locks and seals that discreet people like to use; *Epist.* 1.20.2). As he releases his book to the glare of publicity (a book that is a fantasy version of himself as free agent, emancipated from Maecenas's clutches), Horace's final *sphragis* or seal on his collection is an image not of Augustus, or of Maecenas, but of himself, a portrait signed and dated in his forty-fourth year.

24. Cf. Putnam 2006.

25. Oliensis 1998: 186.

26. Oliensis 1998: 190.

27. Oliensis (1998: 190) reads *Epist.* 1.13 as a displaced end poem promising Horace's inevitable transition from Maecenas's house to Augustus's.

# Jewels

The playful touch that seal rings lent to Roman imperial bureaucracy makes it somewhat artificial to separate their semiotics from those of ornamental jewels. Yet Pliny nicely sums up a fundamental distinction between the functional purpose of the one and the aesthetic appeal of the other: "Many people think it is sacrilege to violate gems with seal-designs, the very purpose for which they were made, so much do they value their variety, colours, material, beauty . . ." (*HN* 37.1). The symbolic charge of the "merely decorative" gemstone suggests a different aspect of Maecenas: aesthete, collector and connoisseur.

The great gem collections of antiquity were found above all in the Hellenistic courts, where collecting was tied to foreign conquest (especially in Persia and the East) and became a focal point in historiography, museology, diplomacy and courtly erotics.[28] Roman generals brought the taste westward: the first gem cabinet (*dactyl[i]otheca*) in Rome was owned by Sulla's stepson Scaurus, while Pompey dedicated the ring cabinet of Mithridates on the Capitol and Julius Caesar six cabinets of gems in the temple of Venus Genetrix.[29] When Empress Livia dedicated the fabled ring of Polycrates (recovered after he threw it into the sea) in the Temple of Concord—surely apocryphal—she conflated three golden ages of autocratic gem collecting: archaic, Hellenistic and Roman-imperial.[30] It may be that the cultural capital of gems heightened the prestige of the imperial house.[31] However, given the ring's alleged provenance—a tyrant's reluctant hand—the gesture looks more like one of public munificence and exemplary self-denial, not to say an insurance policy against unexpected reversals of fortune.[32]

History has made Maecenas into something more controversial: a private gem collector. A self-portrait of Pompey made entirely out of pearls provoked Pliny to jeer: sic pretiosum fieri? (Is this how to become precious?).[33] In a private context, jewels could be touched, polished, collected, inspected from many angles as marvels of nature and human artifice, gifted to enhance the prestige of the giver, prized as the possessions of their current and former owners, and worn to enhance the beauty of the wearer. Maecenas's alleged

28. Kuttner 2005. See Elsner (2014: 152–53) on Posidippus's *Lithika* as a meeting place of Hellenistic and Achaemenid cultures.

29. Plin. *HN* 37.11.

30. Plin. *HN* 37.4.

31. Petrain 2005: 348.

32. Hulme (2011) suspects that Augustus was the real dedicator (cf. Suet. *Aug.* 30). On Polycrates and his fateful ring: Hdt. 3.40–43. Jewels and envy: *Anth. Pal.* 6.329 = Leonides 8 Page.

33. Plin. *HN* 37.6.

obsession speaks of choice, curiosity and wonder, susceptibilities that the poets flatter when they direct his gaze to their works.[34] It also makes him a challenger to imperial values, monolithically conceived as all about public munificence, grandeur and the heaping up of power. Tiny but disproportionately precious, jewels disrupt conventional equivalences between size and value, quantity and worth, decoration and centrality.[35] As Pliny writes:

> aliquas uero extra pretia ulla taxationemque humanarum opum arbitrantes, ut plerisque ad summam absolutamque naturae rerum contemplationem satis sit una aliqua gemma. (*HN* 37.1)

> Some [unengraved jewels] they consider to be beyond price and classification in terms of human wealth, so that very many people find a single gemstone alone enough to provide them with the ultimate aesthetic experience of the wonders of Nature.

Such aesthetic equations of tininess with extreme value had had special force since the Hellenistic period, when poets like Callimachus and Aratus promoted delicacy and finesse over triteness and pomposity.[36] But the gem-focused poems of the *Lithika*, "Precious Stones", part of a papyrus collection rediscovered in 2001 and attributed to Posidippus (*c.* 310–*c.* 240 BCE), are otherwise unprecedented in that era. These exquisite epigrams aspire to be polished and sparkling substitutes for the stones they conjure up as well as fitting artefacts for the hands that have fingered them and the bodies they will adorn:[37]

> Timanthes carved it—this sparkling lapis lazuli
>     rayed in gold, this semi-precious Persian stone—
> for Demylus, and for a tender kiss the dark-haired
>     Coan Nicaea [owns it] now, a [lovely] gift.

> (LITHIKA AB 3, TRANS. NISETICH 2005: 18)

In Ann Kuttner's words: "The epigrams are mostly about pure pleasure."[38] This means the pleasure of refracted light, glamour, erotic promise and

---

34. Wonder in the *Lithika*: AB 13.2, 15.7, 17.2. Choice: AB 9.1.

35. Theophr., *De lapidibus* 33: rarity is as desirable as beauty.

36. Callim. *Aet.* fr. 1 Pfeiffer; *Hymn to Apollo* 105–12. The programmatic word λεπτός (*leptos*), "slender", features at *Lithika* AB 1.4. Yet Porter (2011) argues that "lithic aesthetics" equally celebrate bulk and sublimity.

37. The name for a gem cabinet, *dactyl(i)otheca*, literally "finger-ring depository", privileges touch and the multiple agency of hands: e.g., AB 4.2 ("Δαρείου δακτυλο["). Elsner (2014) speaks of "descriptive intimacy" (153) and "the loving connoisseurial caress of the expert gem-handler" (156).

38. Kuttner 2005: 142.

many-faceted identity: jewels as markers of empire and intimate gifts, products of nature and art, magnetic and anti-magnetic, gleaming and dull, physical and written, inanimate and animated. The poems speak of "synecdochic relation-ships between poem, gem, body-part, erotic object, patron".[39] Above all, they celebrate the ethos of delicate living (*truphē*), which we have seen characterize Maecenas's behaviour: "an ideological agenda in which power, by sharing pleasure, seduces as well as compels obedience".[40] Conversely, gem collect-ing provided an analogue both for artistically arranged poetry books and for the connoisseurship of the discerning patron:

> Hellenistic gem artistry gave Posidippus powerful metaphors. Gemmed ornament nests substances. To choose, embed, juxtapose a word, or an epi-gram, remade older metaphors of ποίησις. As intertext, other poets are gems to inlay, their lines, heirloom allusions—or plunderable δακτυλιοθῆκαι, exploitable mines! Object assemblage, as the gem and status sections cel-ebrate it, tropes editorship and anthology. Authors essay gems others will treasure, accumulate; editors who make one assemblage also anticipate reconstellation. (Kuttner 2005: 163)

The relationship between patron and poet receives its tightest instantiation in an epigram dedicated to the emerald seal ring Polycrates failed to sink in the sea (AB 9), here alleged to have borne the image of a lyre:

> [You chose] the lyre for your seal, Polycrates, the lyre
>    of the singer [who pl]ayed [at your] feet.
> . . . rays; and your hand [to]ok
>    . . . possession.
>
> (*LITHIKA* AB 9, TRANS. NISETICH 2005: 19)[41]

In the space of four lines, the tyrant's all-powerful hand is shown succumbing to the aesthetic pull of humble but manually dextrous artists: lyricist, jeweller and epigrammatist. Commemorating all parties, the poem offers a miniature ecphrasis of the primal scene where Anacreon's music seduced Polycrates (Hdt. 3.41) together with a re-enactment of the *kleos*-bargain struck by another of his poets, Ibycus (Page, *SLG* 151.47–48). It becomes Posidippus's *sphragis*, one that preserves the memorable self of Polycrates through the different layers of art-istry he supported.[42]

---

39. Elsner 2014: 164.
40. Kuttner 2005: 144.
41. Both ellipses are present in the original.
42. Bing 2005: 121.

The discovery of *Lithika* has only sharpened our understanding of the two fragments of Maecenas and Augustus that contain exuberant lists of jewels.[43] Both poem and letter read as written performances of *truphē*: Maecenas answers desire with desire, while Augustus flirts with his favourite courtier.[44] Abdicating real-life power over their addressees, both seduce by sharing the pleasures of language and feeling. It has been suggested that *Lithika* influences Roman literary culture in another way: not just in its metapoetic alignment of poet and jeweller as refined artists but also in its tentative questioning of the value of gems in relation to other commodities.[45]

Maecenas begins with just such a confrontation between different value systems, in what sounds very like a Horatian priamel:[46]

> lucentes, mea uita, nec smaragdos
> beryllos mihi, Flacce mi, nitentes
> nec percandida margarita quaero
> nec quod Thynica lima perpoliuit
> anellos neque iaspios lapillos

$$(3 \text{L} = 2 \text{C} = 185 \text{H})$$

Flaccus, love of my life, I do not seek out shining emeralds or sparkling beryls or gleaming pearls or rings that a Bithynian file has polished or jasper gems.

These five verses respond to Horace's anti-luxury poems, *Odes* 1.31 and 1.38, as well as to all those other priamels that, along with the name *Maecenas*, had become the stamp of "a Horatian opening". Now, it is Maecenas's turn to renounce the luxury with which Horace has reproached him. Stylistically, he recalls Catullus in his use of tender diminutives ("anellos", "lapillos") and endearments ("mea uita", "Flacce"), regard for polish ("nitentes", "percandida", "perpoliuit"; cf. Cat. 1.2: "libellum . . . arida modo pumice expolitum") and jaunty hendecasyllabic metre. The poem harnesses the competition between wealth and love that goes back to archaic Greece (Sappho's poetry, most memorably) and is updated in Roman love poetry, in the face of demanding mistresses and richer suitors.[47] An

---

43. Petrain (2005: 346) argues that the *Lithika* directly influenced Maecenas; see Hutchinson (2003) for its influence on Latin poetry in general.

44. McDermott 1982.

45. Petrain 2005: 340–43.

46. Petrain 2005: 340–9, focusing on *Lithika* AB 16, the first epigram on a non-precious stone. The sceptical tradition about the value of jewels includes choliambist Phoenix of Colophon (*Collectanea Alexandrina* 6), and the inserted poem at Petr. *Sat.* 55.6–9.

47. E.g., Prop. 2.22a.9–10; Tib. 1.1.51–52; Hor. *Carm.* 4.11.21–24.

anti-materialist ending could easily be supplied along conventional lyric or elegiac lines: forget those precious jewels, darling—all I want is you.[48]

But the catalogue of jewels does not simply disclaim material riches. With its seductive variations on sparkle and rarity, it positively savours them, adorning them with syntactical complexity.[49] Artful chiasmus ("lucentes . . . smaragdos / beryllos . . . nitentes") and rhyme ("anellos . . . lapillos") arrange the stones in patterns, while the jeweller's Bithynian file stands in for the finishing touch of the refining author ("Thynica lima perpoliuit"). The pleasure of polishing and setting almost exceeds the glow of the raw material: *quaero* here means "I seek out" (as in *exquisitus*, "recherché"), rather than simply "I want", while *per-candida* (trumping the *candide* of *Epodes* 14.5, addressed to Maecenas) and *per-poliuit* suggest the perfectionist or connoisseur.

Caught between these value systems—luxury and simplicity—where does Horace stand in relation to the jewels? At first sight, with the negative *nec* postponed, the opening lines make him a typically neoteric "inserted apposition": a parenthetical *mea uita*, "my life", is followed by another parenthetical *Flacce mi*, "my Flaccus [Horace]". Each phrase might then be taken as equivalent to what surrounds it: *lucentes . . . smaragdos*, "shining emeralds", and *beryllos . . . nitentes*, "sparkling beryls".[50] Yet unlike the jewels Horace is singular, a diamond in the rough in need of polishing.[51] Maecenas's pet, if not the most sparkling, is still the nonpareil in his collection.[52] The poem quivers with barely suppressed eroticism; written jewels stand in for real objects of desire and lubricants of courtship. Propertius uses the nickname *mea uita* when he tells his mistress she is most beautiful when jewel-free (1.2.1); Ovid uses it of Corinna when he fantasizes about becoming her licked and wetted ring at bath time (*Am.* 2.15.21). The jewels of Posidippus's *Lithika* had set off the beauty of queens and *hetaerae*, worn close to the skin, softened and animated by warmth and moisture.[53] Lacking its final seal, the poem suspends Maecenas between desires material and emotional. What Posidippus memorably calls the "wet glance" of the collector flickers away from "my life" and "my Flaccus" towards the unfinished list of glinting jewels.[54]

---

48. Oliensis 1997: 165.

49. Petrain 2005: 349.

50. Cf. Prop. 2.3.14: "oculi, geminae, sidera nostra, faces"; Ov. *Am.* 2.16.44: "perque oculos, sidera nostra, tuos" (eyes twinned with stars). The notions "two" and "twin" mark similarity and difference.

51. Fingernails: *Sat.* 1.10.71; *Epist.* 1.1.104, 1.7.51, 1.19.46. Figurative polishing: *Ars P.* 291 ("labor limae"), 292–94; cf. *Sat.* 1.10.65–66, Cic. *Fam.* 7.33.2.

52. See Petrain (2005: 332–33) on the hierarchy of precious and non-precious in *Lithika*.

53. Kuttner 2005; Elsner 2014.

54. Posidippus, *Lithika* AB 3.2.

By contrast, Augustus's letter is roundly humorous. His favourite's jewel fetish brings out a special twinkle in the emperor's eye, and it is tempting to read this as an imaginative response to Maecenas's poem, given the presence of many of the same stones (pearls, emeralds, jasper and beryls):[55]

> Idem Augustus quia Mecenatem suum nouerat stilo esse remisso, molli et dissoluto, talem se in epistulis quas ad eum scribebat saepius exhibebat, et contra castigationem loquendi, quam alias ille scribendo seruabat, in epistula ad Maecenatem familiari plura in iocos effusa subtexuit: "uale mel gentium †meculle†, ebur ex Etruria, lasar Arretinum, adamas Supernas, Tiberinum margaritum, Cilniorum smaragde, iaspi figulorum, berulle Porsenae, carbunculum †habeas†, ἵνα συντέμνω πάντα, μάλαγμα [Kaster: ἄλλαγμα] moecharum! (Macrob. Sat. 2.4.12 Kaster 2011: 349–50, adapted = Augustus, Epistles fr. 32 Malcovati)[56]

> Because he knew that Maecenas had a free-and-easy writing style given to extravagance and effeminacy, Augustus often adopted the same character in the letters he wrote to him, the opposite of the austere style he otherwise cultivated in his writing. He rounded off a personal letter to Maecenas with the following joking effusion: "Farewell, my honey of all the world, †poppy-juice?†, my ivory of Etruria, silphium-juice of Arretium, diamond of the Upper Sea [Adriatic], pearl of the Tiber, emerald of the Cilnii, potters' jasper, beryl of Porsenna, carbuncle—may you get one!—in short, you softener of married women!" (trans. Kaster)

Letting down his guard, Augustus teases his friend with a lucky dip of nicknames cobbled together from unlikely pairs of exotic luxuries (ivory, diamond, beryl) and Etruscan markers (Etruria, Tiber, Porsenna).[57] He pricks up his ears to the sound of Maecenas's name, from its beginning (me-li, me-culle . . . μάλαγμα moecharum) to its end. The words adamas and Supernas are not just here to mix Greek and Latin morphology.[58] They are here because they are Etruscan masculine nominatives with -as endings, like Maecenas.[59] Medicinal substances (honey, poppy juice and silphium) sit alongside precious stones, as if revealing the secrets of Maecenas's dressing room or medicine cabinet

---

55. Petrain 2005: 346: many jewels are common to both authors; both use n. margaritum, not f. margarita.

56. Dagger symbols (obeli) indicate disputed or spurious text.

57. The text is corrupt: see Gelsomino 1958; Kaster 2010: 41. The list recalls Augustus's Saturnalian tombolas: Suet. Aug. 75.

58. So Petrain (2005: 347) claims.

59. Varro lists Etruscan names at Ling. 8.41: "Lesas, Ufenas, Carrinas, Maecenas".

while topping up his syrupy poetic effusions (*effusa*).[60] Augustus harps on Maecenas's uncertain status: exotic rarity or homegrown fake? Finally, he pops the bubble of his friend's pretensions with an outrageous pun on two meanings of *carbunculus*, precious stone and embarrassing sore, before building to a bilingual, alliterative climax: "μάλαγμα [malagma] moecharum!" Who these adulterous women (*moechae*) are, or what a *malagma* is, other than a thing that softens, or what the relationship between the two is, is less clear.[61] Is Maecenas an emollient for "buttering up" matrons, "putty in their hands", or a mattress or medicinal poultice? Active or passive, he is undeniably "soft".

One jewel, the beryl, seems to have a special association with Maecenas. Featuring in both lists, it is also singled out in the *Elegiae* to mark his gem-like rarity:

> tu decus et laudes huius et huius eras,
> uincit uulgares, uincit beryllus harenas,
>     litore in extremo quas simul unda mouet.

(ELEG. IN MAEC. 1.18–20)

You were the ornament and glory of both [Apollo and Minerva], as the beryl surpasses the common sands when the sea stirs them both at the edge of the shore.

Normally found in granite rock, this sea-green relative of the emerald may have been chosen as foil to myriad grains of sand because its aquamarine hue is enhanced by seawater. Pliny writes: "The most valuable beryls are those that in colour resemble the pure green of the sea."[62] He adds that the stone is always cut hexagonally to multiply its facets; in isolation, it is dull, until the moment it reflects light (a suggestive image for Maecenas, the cipher illuminated by others' attention). Just so, the decadent Des Esseintes in Huysmans's *À rebours* weighs down his hapless tortoise not with precious jewels (diamonds, emeralds, rubies, topazes) but with murky semi-precious stones, those with "vitreous, morbid sparks, with feverish, piercing flashes of fire", stones "striped with concentric veins that constantly appear to stir and change position, depending

---

60. Gelsomino (1958: 149) takes *meculle* as a diminutive of *mecon*, poppy juice, and points (n166) to Augustus's fondness for medical metaphors. Silphium in a poultice (*cataplasma*): Hippoc., *De fistulis* 9.

61. Gelsomino (1958: 152) imagines a face mask: "non solum es mollis, sed ita molliens, ut iure te uti possint moechae ad molliendam molliculam cutem suam." A recent conjecture, *allagma*, "recompense" (Kaster 2010: 41–42) makes the climax less colourful.

62. Plin. *HN* 37.5.20: found mostly in India. Cf. Posidippus, *Lithika* 6.3 (a glittering beryl, if the text is correct).

on the way the light falls".[63] The beryl is already familiar from Propertius, where it cements the mysterious bond between Maecenas and Cynthia, sporting a sooty beryl when she returns as a ghost (4.7.9).

Like the jewel-poems of the *Lithika*, the two fragments stand as "emblems for a set of courtly social relations".[64] In the first, Maecenas plays Augustus's *deliciae* or *hetaera*; in the second, Horace's *domina* or *puella*. If Augustus collects Maecenas as a rarity, a multifaceted gem—fascinating even if fake—Maecenas in turn acquires Horace and embeds him among his more polished jewels ("mea uita"; "mi Flacce"). Indeed, Horace's lyric request to be "inserted" by Maecenas (*Carm.* 1.1.35: "me . . . inseres") has in a sense been granted, into the intimate folds of a private collection as much as into the poetic canon.[65] What is more, the jewel collection is one of many metaphors, along with the garden and the garland, for the poetic circle and the cultural transformation wrought by the patron's eye, hand or file on poetic raw material.[66] The circle itself has been likened to a *parure* (a matching set of jewels).[67] Another scholar spells it out: "Horace became Maecenas' friend because of that enormous poetic talent for which [Maecenas] seems to have had a jeweler's eye."[68] Maecenas's textual associations with gemstones tell us nothing about his real-life habits as a collector. Instead, they crystallize his identity as a private follower of pleasure and rarity, a discriminating curator and enabler who sought out "diamonds in the rough", chiselled them and held them up to the light.

63. Huysmans (1891) 1998: 37.

64. Elsner 2014: 167 (on Posidippus).

65. Cf. Hor. *Epist.* 1.1.3: "iterum antiquo me includere ludo". See above p. 163 on *inserere* in the *Odes*.

66. Cf. *Laus Pisonis* (225–26) on the patron as a miner of talent.

67. Le Doze 2014: 145.

68. W. Ralph Johnson 1993: 28. He adds: "His eye for what most people, then and now, would call rectitude seems to have been, as it were, not wholly trained".

# 9

# The Gardens, the Tower, the Auditorium

## The Gardens

*semper serta tibi dabimus, tibi semper odores,*
*non umquam sitiens, florida semper eris.*

—ELEG. IN MAEC. 1.143–44

[To the earth on Maecenas's grave] We will always give you garlands, we will always give you perfume. You will never go thirsty, you will always be decked with flowers.

Somewhere under Termini Station in modern-day Rome lies the ancient footprint of Maecenas's Esquiline estate. He is said to have acquired it from Favonius, supporter of Cato, from whom it was confiscated after Philippi.[1] On Maecenas's death it passed to the emperors, but the name, Horti Maecenatiani ("Maecenas Park"), stuck, ensuring that he remained a fixture in Roman topography for centuries to come.[2] This estate has played a crucial part in reinforcing aspects of Maecenas's biography: his Epicurean tendencies, his luxurious tastes, his halfway position between centre and margins, and his associations with morally suspect individuals—Republican pleasure lovers and rich imperial hangers-on. The *Elegiae* even picture him in a garden setting, supplying a virtual tomb for his acolytes to decorate with flowers, wine and spices.[3] But

---

1. Schol. *ad* Juv. 5.3; see also André 1967: 73 and n4; Osgood 2006: 263, 320.

2. Dio 55.7.5. See below on Fronto. Constantine donated a *possessio Micinas Augusti* to the Basilica San Lorenzo (Lugli 1930–38: 3.459).

3. See Suet. *Vita Hor.* 20 for the legend that he and Horace were buried side by side on the Esquiline. Rodríguez-Almeida 1987: 418n14; cf. Häuber 1990: 65; 2011; 2014: 330) wishfully identifies a late-Republican tomb, the Casa Tonda, destroyed during the construction of Piazza

the ephemeral nature of gardens in general adds an extra layer of melancholy: it suggests both Maecenas's fall from greatness and the transience of his circle.

For all their imaginative cachet, we know nothing about how these gardens originally looked. The *Elegiae* offer a stereotypically idyllic picture of shady oak trees, splashing fountains and chirping birds, all unrealistically minimized into one tiny plot:

> maluit umbrosam quercum nymphasque cadentes
>     paucaque pomosi iugera certa soli.
> Pieridas Phoebumque colens in mollibus hortis
>     sederat argutas garrulus inter aues.

(ELEG. IN MAEC. 1.33–36)

> He preferred a shady oak and falling water and a few secure acres of fruitful soil; cultivating the Muses and Phoebus in his luxurious park, he would sit chattering among the chirping birds.

Since then, wilder assertions have been made and tailored to fit other aspects of Maecenas's life. The gardens, it is claimed, were designed in the "Hellenistic-Persian style", with at least three "hanging" terraces and enough further space to accommodate the heated pool and fountains to soothe the insomniac owner—and even an enclosure for the notorious edible donkeys.[4]

One thing is clear: the Horti were on a much larger scale than the "few secure acres of fruitful soil" in the couplets above might suggest.[5] The park covered a vast area of the Esquiline Hill; its exact dimensions and boundaries continue to be debated.[6] Since the discovery of the so-called "Auditorium of Maecenas" in

---

Vittorio Emanuele, as Maecenas's *tumulus*. On *horti* and tombs, see Bodel (1997: 18–26) and Verzár-Bass (1998). Emperors buried in gardens: Hartswick 2004: 19.

4. Häuber 2011, 2014: 135); Wikipedia contributors, "Gardens of Maecenas", *Wikipedia, The Free Encyclopedia*, accessed May 8, 2023, https://en.wikipedia.org/w/index.php?title=Gardens_of_Maecenas&oldid=1148698406. Platner and Ashby 1929, s.v. *Horti Maecenatis*: "Maecenas is said to have been the first to construct a swimming bath of hot water in Rome which may have been in the gardens." Cianfriglia (1976–77: 70) identifies as the bath a round building depicted on fragment 593 of the Severan plan of Rome. Cassio (1757: 2.300–302) offers an outrageously detailed outline: tower on the left, swimming pool on the right and two concave orchestras to provide the *symphoniarum cantus* of Sen. *Prov.* 1.3.10. At p. 303, he craftily elides "quomodo Maecenas uixerit" (Sen. *Ep.* 114.4) with the passage on building and decoration at *Ep.* 114.9, suggesting that generalizations about luxury apply specifically to Maecenas.

5. The rhetoric of the settled veteran, not the profiteer.

6. Häuber 2011, 2014; Richardson 1992: 200–201; Coarelli 2004; Colini 1979.

1874, it is thought to have straddled the Servian Agger, or rampart, where it probably enclosed at least part of a former paupers' graveyard.[7] This made it the first substantial Roman garden estate to be located at least partly within the city boundary.[8] Sculptural finds in the vicinity are impressive—above all, the Laocoön, rediscovered in 1506.[9] Many of these have been arranged and rearranged to suggest a particular aesthetic programme and specific patterns of behaviour: drinking, dining and divinely inspired poetic recitation.[10] Two buildings associated with the gardens—the Tower of Maecenas (iconic but possibly imaginary) and the Auditorium (real but mysterious)—have been used to support the idea that the park was an exquisite site of artistic activity. Behind the idyll, however, may lie a very different reality: one of property speculation, cultural opportunism and preferential largesse.

The Horti Maecenatiani are the best known among a group of estates and pleasure grounds that ringed Rome on both sides of the city boundaries from the late Republic on. It was normal for them to keep the names of their original owners, names that trace the evolving history of garden ownership, from Republican trendsetters (Horti Luculliani, Sallustiani, Lamiani, Lolliani) to imperial freedmen (Horti Epaphroditiani).[11] They fronted a densely populated hinterland of market gardens and villas that stretched into the suburbs and beyond.[12] The story of Maecenas's park is a typical one. A private estate built on land partly reclaimed from burial pits and wasteland on the upper outskirts of Rome and possibly funded by shady means, it was "bequeathed to" (i.e., repossessed by) the emperor on the owner's death. Used by the imperial family as an alternative residence, it was revived in the form of pleasure gardens for Renaissance popes and aristocratic families, but later wiped out by the juggernaut of late nineteenth-century urban development.[13]

It is no accident that the earliest known creators of Roman *horti*—Lucullus and the two Sallusts—were, like Maecenas, associated with a new model of leisured behaviour, specifically retirement after active service at home or

---

7. Häuber (2014: 307–34) argues that they subsumed the area traditionally assigned to the Horti Lamiani.

8. Chillet 2011.

9. See the thrilling account of Barkan (1999: 2–17).

10. Häuber (2014: 109–10) insists that the shady oak and splashing fountains of *Eleg. in Maec.* 1.33 indicate a location close to the oak grove by the Porta Querquetulana, with its guardian nymphs (Querquetulanae Virae).

11. Beard 1998: 25–26.

12. Purcell 2007; Champlin 1982.

13. For other examples of imperial expropriation of private gardens, see Hartswick (2004: 11–12).

abroad. Military contact with the East brought a further wave of luxurious living to Rome, realized above all in Lucullus's *paradeisos* (enclosed pleasure garden).[14] The arcades and promontories at his country villa even inspired Pompey to give him the nickname "Xerxes in a toga" (Xerxen togatum).[15] In this, and in more positive ways—for example, his founding of a library in Rome—Lucullus provided an obvious model for the philhellenic or orientalizing Maecenas.[16] In neither case did owning *horti* in an elevated region of Rome entail wholesale "Epicurean" withdrawal from politics. From another perspective, it signified the encroachment on the centre of outlying ways of life. As Andrew Wallace-Hadrill observes: "Lucullus' gardens . . . ensured his continued prominence and conspicuousness at precisely the moment he had withdrawn from open political competition."[17] In turn, Maecenas transmitted a model of luxurious semi-retreat to his successor as imperial counsellor, Seneca the Younger. In Tacitus's *Annals* 14, Seneca begs Nero to let him retire, appealing in vain to the precedent of Augustus, who had granted Maecenas "peregrinum otium" (foreign retirement) in the city, a kind of blessed urban exile that may or may not have been tantamount to an abdication of his power.[18]

For the Julio-Claudian emperors who inherited them, the Horti Maecenatiani continued to function as a place of convenient withdrawal halfway from the bustle of the centre. It tells us something that Augustus chose to stay in the Esquiline park when he was unwell (Suet. *Aug.* 72) and Tiberius retreated there after exile on Rhodes (Suet. *Tib.* 15).[19] It was Nero who first linked the gardens to the Palatine by means of the Domus Transitoria, then swallowed them into the Domus Aurea.[20] In all cases, "gardens" are shorthand for some palace situated in the park. This made the *horti* the focus of business as well as pleasure, the suspicion being that both were conducted on a specifically monarchical or even tyrannical model, following the same Persian and Hellenistic dynasties that

14. Vell. Pat. 2.33.4; cf. Ath. 274e–f, 543a.

15. Vell. Pat. 2.33.4. Cf. Plin. *HN* 9.170. See P. Hardie (2007a) on "Roman Xerxes".

16. See Plut. *Luc.* 42.1 with Swain 1992: 313.

17. Wallace-Hadrill 1998: 3, and see 3–6.

18. Tac. *Ann.* 14.53–54.

19. Dio 65.10.4–5: Vespasian was accessible to his citizens from his home in the Horti Sallustiani.

20. Tac. *Ann.* 15.39.1: "qua Palatium et Maecenatis hortos continuauerat". Pliny reports (*HN* 36.37–38) seeing Laocoön in "Titus's house" (Titi . . . domo). Boatwright (1998) and Beard (1998: 26–27) note the Tacitean verb *inhiare*, "gape greedily after", used of emperors' and empresses' desire to possess gardens (e.g., *Ann.* 11.1.1, 12.59.1), often by engulfing their ground plans into larger estates.

inspired the terraces, pools and walkways.[21] Philo tells how Caligula led a team of Jewish ambassadors up the garden path in the Horti Maecenatiani and Lamiani, airily discussing improvements like translucent ceiling glass instead of attending to their demands.[22]

Many myths still cling to the Roman *horti*, partly because we tend to visualize ancient gardens in the image of the opulent villas built over them in later periods. In Nicholas Purcell's words, the *horti* have become "another set of topoi in the repertoire of Roman luxury" and "a foreword to a teleoscopic history which has its main fulcrum in the western Renaissance".[23] Rather than a narrative of continuous ownership—as the names of the larger *horti*, whether aristocratic or imperial, suggest—these estates tell a tale of flux. Partitioned, amalgamated, broken up, transferred, sold off or gifted in the interests of patronage, they were less coherent estates than patchworks of disparate lots. Plural *horti* (a grand park) might easily develop from or revert to a conglomeration of little *horti* (cabbage patches), since market gardens and tomb gardens often remained components of the sites in question. One Sabinus Tiro dedicated to Maecenas a gardening manual, *Cepourgica*, "On horticulture", from which Purcell deduces that "our equestrian magnate" was linked "with the speculative world of the dubious profits of the market-garden as well as with the more refined and voluptuary milieu of the suburban *horti*".[24] Such estates were associated, then, as much with big business as with contemplation in the shade. They were less "tranquil abodes of the gods" than sizeable transferable assets.[25]

Yet the mythical aspect of Maecenas's gardens—a calm and rarefied environment on the Esquiline heights—still holds sway. Our only strictly contemporary reference is in Horace's *Satires* 1.8, a tale of nocturnal witchcraft narrated by a statue of Priapus, nervous custodian of an Esquiline vegetable patch, whose brief is also to protect certain *nouis hortis*, "new gardens". Does this phrase refer obliquely to the new urban villa into which Priapus and his little tomb garden (*kēpotaphion*; or market garden or family cabbage patch)

21. See Beard (1998: 31–32) and Von Stackelberg (2009: 134–40) on *horti* as stages for imperial performance.

22. Philo, *Leg.* 349–66; Millar 1977: 22–23; Von Stackelberg 2009: 134–40. Cf. Phaedrus 2.5: Tiberius is chased around the flower beds at Misenum (once Lucullus's villa) by a pushy petitioner; Henderson 2001b: 9–31.

23. Purcell 2007: 374. Cf. Wallace-Hadrill 1998: 1.

24. Plin. *HN* 19.177. Purcell 2007: 367.

25. The title of Cima and La Rocca 1986. *Horti* could be conceived simultaneously as sybaritic retreats and investment opportunities—Tac. *Ann.* 14.53.5: "tantis agrorum spatiis, tam lato faenore exuberat".

have been absorbed, along with potteries, sandpits and shrines?[26] The poem
never actually mentions Maecenas.[27] We are left to guess which invisible philanthropist has cleared up a former communal burial ground of mass paupers'
graves (*puticuli*) and larger tombs (*monumenta*) and enabled the Roman public
to promenade along the sunny Agger, enjoying wholesome air and a pleasing
view:[28]

> nunc licet Esquiliis habitare salubribus atque
> aggere in aprico spatiari, quo modo tristes
> albis informem spectabant ossibus agrum

(HOR. SAT. 1.8.14–16)

> Now it is permitted to live on the healthy Esquiline and stroll on the sunny
> rampart, where until recently there was a gloomy view of land disfigured
> by white bones.

Nor does Horace imply that Maecenas opened his gardens to all comers.[29]
All he reveals is that people could walk along the Agger; they could not necessarily enter the gardens, only perhaps look into them. Maecenas is generally
associated with exclusivity. Better to imagine that his gardens were closed to
the public, unlike those of Agrippa, who disapproved of private property and
left his baths and at least part of his *horti* in the Circus Maximus to the Roman
people, as Julius Caesar did his gardens in Trastevere.[30] Maecenas's bouncer
Priapus is bent on warding away trespassers, at least avian ones; the waving
antenna on his head "prohibits upstart birds . . . from settling in the new gardens" (importunas uolucres . . . uetatque nouis considere in hortis; 6–7).
Other gardens had "keep out" signs.[31] Maecenas's guarded park is easily
thought of as a forerunner of those private Renaissance gardens of which

---

26. Porphyrio *ad* Hor. *Sat.* 1.8.7 detects an ambiguity: "potest nouis hortis accipi pro recens
satis"; Purcell 1987: 37; Boatwright 1998: 80–81; Edmunds 2009: 130. Gardens and tombs: Bodel
1997. Giraldi (1545: 452) conflates Horace's poem with Columella 10.32 and 108, claiming that
Maecenas's gardens housed a shrine to Priapus to which poets pinned the Priapea later attributed to Virgil.

27. *Contra* Ps.-Acro *ad* Hor. *Sat.* 1.8.7: "horti M<a>ecenatis"; cf. Porph. *ad loc.*: "primus
Maecenas [ad] salubritatem aeris ibi passus hortos constituit".

28. Gowers 2017b. Purcell (1987: 37) compares the Greek *proastion* (garden suburb).

29. Labate 2016: 84.

30. Dio 55.7.5: "as though presenting himself as a supreme friend to the people". Maecenas
made Augustus his heir: D'Arms 1998, Papi 1996.

31. *CIL* VI 31285 (*PR* for *priuatum*) with Wiseman 1992: 72. Cf. Ps.-Acro *ad* Hor. *Sat.* 1.8.8:
"nam sepulchra publica erant antea, nunc Maecenatis horti".

Werner Gundersheimer writes: "The *hortus conclusus*, the *locus amoenus*, the *giardino segreto* are fantasies (sometimes fulfilled) of exclusiveness."[32]

Why was Maecenas associated with the Esquiline Hill, in particular? True, much of the best land in Rome had already been occupied by other estates: Caesar's in Trastevere or Lucullus's on the Pincio overlooking the Campus Martius.[33] When Livy paints the highest of the original seven hills as a guerilla landscape during the Hannibalic War—"ravines, vegetable-gardens, tombs and sunken lanes everywhere"—he may well be imposing a contemporary impression on an earlier period.[34] He is also likely to have looked for symbolic continuity between Maecenas and his Etruscan forebears. Maecenas was not the first Etruscan grandee to settle on the Esquiline.[35] The hill had been occupied in the sixth century BCE, according to legend, by King Servius Tullius, who chose to move there from the city centre. According to Livy, Servius expanded the city to include the Viminal, Quirinal and Esquiline hills; more accurately, he "enlarged the Esquiline" and kept his seat there, "so that it acquired dignity".[36]

Was Maecenas modelling himself on Servius? Or does Livy emphasize the notion of an Esquiline dignified by Servius because he is thinking of Maecenas's current estate?[37] Just as Augustus built his Palatine house near the Casa Romuli, so Maecenas may have chosen to live on the hill where an ancient Etruscan king had lived, associating himself with local cults of Diana and Fortuna.[38] The garden's relatively central site allowed Augustus to make symbolic capital out of Rome's incorporation of an Etruscan outsider.[39] Maecenas's clean-up job looks like a benefaction to match Agrippa's overhauling of the city's waterworks. But there was probably more than a dash of self-interest. Again, Purcell is unsentimental: "Maecenas' own reclamation of the Esquiline cemeteries, and appropriation of the ancient walls of the city, explicitly stated that his

---

32. Gundersheimer 1981: 8.

33. Bodel 2014: 178.

34. Livy 26.10.5–6: "conualles tectaque hortorum et sepulcra et cauas undique uias". Purcell 2007: 364.

35. Porph. *ad* Hor. *Sat.* 1.8.7 calls him the first to build gardens there. A circular structure at the northwest corner of the *horti* has conveniently been identified as Servius Tullius's tomb: Häuber 2011. Tarquin is also said to have lived on the Esquiline: Solin. 1.26.

36. Livy 1.44 apparently draws on Varro's etymology of *Esquiliae*: "ab eo quod excultae a rege Tullio essent" (*Ling.* 5.49.1).

37. Ampolo 1996.

38. A slave's son identified by Emperor Claudius (author of a history of the Etruscans) with the condottiere Mastarna: *ILS* 212.

39. Chillet 2016.

development was about the growth and improvement of the city. Beneath the salutary ideologies lay a hard-headed financial logic."[40]

It was not just by covering over the *puticuli* that Maecenas brought lustre to the highest hill. Uniquely, he established his poets there, or so the ancient sources suggest. Was this colony an empyrean cluster of inspired minds, a Roman Helicon?[41] Or a scattering of grace-and-favour homes, dispensed by an active patron to an upwardly mobile client base?[42] Virgil is said to have lived near the gardens, while Propertius waves a virtual banner to announce his residence there: "Go, slave, and write that your master lives on the Esquiline."[43] Horace was allegedly buried there, by Maecenas's side. Later residents may have included Albinovanus Pedo, the poet to whom Scaliger optimistically attributed the *Elegiae*, and Pliny the Younger.[44] Martial describes the steep climb from the Subura to Pliny's house, past Pedo's more modest residence, and advises his reader not to disturb Pliny during the day but by lighting-up time instead:

> sed ne tempore non tuo disertam
> pulses ebria ianuam uideto . . .
> seras tutior ibis ad lucernas:
> haec hora est tua, cum furit Lyaeus,
> cum regnat rosa, cum madent capilli
>
> (MART. 10.20[19].12–13, 18–20)

But make sure you don't knock drunkenly on eloquent Pliny's door at an awkward time. It will be safer for you to go by lamplight: this is your hour, when Bacchus raves, when the rose rules, when hair is perfumed.

A hundred years on, the sympotic residue of the gardens (perfume, garlands, wine, plucked from Horace's *Odes*, in particular) has rubbed off on a new neighbour, along with the Esquiline's bookish cachet. Above Pliny's sanctum hangs a "do not disturb" sign; Martial plays doorkeeper, warding off pushy intruders.[45] These are images we see again and again in relation to Maecenas's

---

40. Purcell 2007: 370; Bodel 1994.

41. Keith 2008: 9–10. Häuber (2014: 109) envisages a *collegium poetarum* who drank from a sacred spring.

42. Purcell 2007: 373. Cairns (2010: 73) suggests a "rent-free" arrangement.

43. Donat. *Vit. Verg.* 13; Prop. 3.23.23–24.

44. On Pedo: Syme 1978: 88–90; White 1993: 240n2; Hollis 2007: 372–81.

45. Henderson 2001b: 27: "Seclusion *prompts* intrusion." By contrast, the rooftops of Julius Martialis's elevated villa on the Janiculum (Mart. 4.64.10: "celsae culmina delicata uillae") enjoy an open panorama of the seven hills (11–12), to which the owner's "open" hospitality responds ("tam comi patet hospitalitate"; 28); Fabbrini 2007: 29–32.

*horti*: trespassers versus the custodians of a rarefied inner circle; a sympotic core that encompasses both temporary pleasure-seeking and lasting inspiration. In the context of historical change, Purcell rightly warns: "It may be unhelpful to see the golden age of the *horti* as an end in itself."[46] At the same time, it is precisely this "golden age" that is upheld by today's outsiders, the scholars who labour to recreate an authentic setting for Maecenas and his poets.

## The Tower of Maecenas

La tanto ricercata torre di Mecenate somiglia un poco all'araba fenice, che vi sia ciascun lo dice, ove sia nessun lo sa.

—SABATINI, *LA TORRE DELLE MILIZIE ERRONEAMENTE DENOMINATA* (1914)

The much-sought Tower of Maecenas is rather like the Arabian phoenix: everyone says it exists, but no one knows where it is to be found.

At the back of the suntrap garden of Palazzo Colonna in Rome stands a dilapidated brick wall; on the ground some way off lie two heavy fragments of marble entablature. They are all that remains of a colossal Roman temple (third century CE), probably once dedicated to Serapis or the Sun. In the Renaissance, they formed the picturesque backdrop to a neoclassical shrine whose wall and loggia were lovingly embellished with antique sculptures by a humanist owner, Cardinal Prospero Colonna (1452–1523). Drawings from the period reveal a more coherent structure: a balustraded staircase leading to an elaborate halved pediment, with a slim tower to one side, now thought to be a medieval addition. Taken as a unity, the assemblage went by many names, several tower-related: Frontispizio di Nerone, Casa di Nerone, Torre di Nerone, Torre di Mecenate, Torre Mesa, Palazzo dei Cornuti, Tempio di Serapide, Tempio del Sole, Tempio di Giove and Palazzo di Mecenate.[47] Among these titles, two historical personalities stand out: Nero and Maecenas. This was by no means the only "Tower of Nero" or "Tower of Maecenas" in Renaissance Rome. The contest over the building's identity and location turns out to be part of a much larger fantasy of contact with ancient Rome, in which, not surprisingly, Nero's and Maecenas's self-appointed successors loom large.

The legendary "Tower of Maecenas" makes its first appearance in extant Latin literature at a charged historical moment. In 64 CE, much of central Rome was consumed by fire, leaving behind an iconic tableau of a narcissistic ruler who took callous pleasure in its destruction. Suetonius's *Life* tells how

46. Purcell 2007: 372.
47. Brothers 2002: 56.

Nero fiddled while Rome burned, or rather dressed up for the occasion in a special stage costume and recited a version of the *Sack of Troy*, accompanying it on the lyre. In a cruel parody of famous generals' laments at the destruction of their own or others' cities (Scipio at Carthage, Marcellus at Syracuse, Aeneas with the paintings of Troy in *Aeneid* 1), he chose to look out from a panoramic vantage point and reduce the inferno below to a tasteless aesthetic opportunity:[48]

> hoc incendium e turre Maecenatiana prospectans laetusque "flammae", ut aiebat, "pulchritudine" Halosin Ilii in illo suo scaenico habitu decantauit. (Suet. *Ner*. 38.2)

> Looking out at this fire from the Tower of Maecenas, and rejoicing in "the beauty of flame", as he put it, he recited The Sack of Troy wearing his stage costume.

Among the three surviving accounts of the fire, Suetonius's is the only one that represents the actor-emperor as singing from the Tower. It is also—and this is more surprising—almost the only ancient testimony for the existence of a tower at all.[49] While Tacitus's Nero strums on a "private stage" (domestica scaena), Cassius Dio dresses him in a citharode's costume and puts him on "the roof of his palace" or "on the roof of the [Palatine] palace".[50] Of the three, Tacitus is the kindest—initially, at least. He relates how, before the fire reached the Domus Transitoria (which connected the Palatine with the Gardens of Maecenas on the Esquiline), Nero opened his gardens to the destitute population and housed them in makeshift shelters (*Ann*. 15.39.1). Yet he cannot resist adding that this charitable act was sabotaged by a malicious but unverifiable rumour: Nero used the catastrophe as an excuse to climb onto his private stage and draw comparisons between past and present disasters.[51] By contrast, Dio flatly condemns the emperor's activities: he may have thought he was singing the *Sack of Troy*, but for the spectators it seemed more like the "Sack of Rome".

The phrase *turris Maecenatiana* in Suetonius's account is usually translated "Tower of Maecenas". However, it is vital to note that this Latin phrase does

---

48. Rossi 2000; O'Gorman 2000: 168–71.

49. Cf. ps.-Acro *ad* Hor. *Carm*. 3.29.7: "Turrim in hortis suis Maecenas construxisse dicebatur, unde haec omnia [the view to Tivoli, Aefulae and Tusculum] prospectaret"; cf. Porph. *ad* Hor. *Carm*. 3.29.6–8.

50. Tac. *Ann*. 15.39.3; Dio 62.18.1 probably refers to the Esquiline palace Augustus inherited from Maecenas, which remained intact, rather than the eponymous Palatine one, destroyed in the fire; Perrin 1996: 399).

51. Cf. Tac. *Ann*.15.38.1.

not involve a direct possessive: that would be *turris Maecenatis*. The adjective we have instead, "pertaining to Maecenas", may indicate nothing more than "the tower [or even *a* tower] that stood in the Horti Maecenatiani", an estate associated equally with its later imperial owners.[52] Likewise, *uina Maecenatiana* (Plin. *HN* 14.67) does not mean "the wines of Maecenas" but "wines in Maecenas's style" or "wines made on Maecenas's estates". A salutary parallel is the *turris Antonia*, "Antony's tower", built by Herod in Jerusalem and first named for Antony well after his death.[53]

If no material traces of Maecenas's tower survive, there are still plenty of imaginative ones. Though absent from Horace's sketch of Maecenas's gardens in *Satires* 1.8, the tower has had a rich afterlife, especially in the Italian Renaissance, and continues to have a solid presence in classical scholarship.[54] But why is it always taken for granted that it existed? The supporting evidence, drawn from two other Horatian poems, is thin. *Epodes* 9 refers briefly to Maecenas's "alta domus" (high-built house), as a site for post-Actian celebrations. This might indicate a hilltop estate; it might equally tell us nothing (a victor's house is always lofty).[55] More often cited is *Odes* 3.29, where Maecenas is encouraged to abandon life at Rome and share one more drink with Horace, just as the poet is on the brink of finishing his lyric collection and dispensing with his patron's services. The stanza in question speaks hyperbolically of a massive building (*molem*) that touches the steep-climbing clouds (*propinquam nubibus arduis*):[56]

> fastidiosam desere copiam et
> molem propinquam nubibus arduis,
>   omitte mirari beatae
>     fumum et opes strepitumque Romae.

(HOR. CARM. 3.29.9–12)

> Leave behind your burdensome possessions and the massive structure that touches the steep-climbing clouds, give up marvelling at the smoke, the riches and the noise of wealthy Rome.

---

52. The suffix -*(i)anus* in the names of imperial palaces normally invokes biological paternity: thus the *domus Augustiana* must by analogy have evolved from the original nucleus of the *domus Augusta*, the *domus Tiberiana* from the *domus Tiberii*, and so on; Carandini 2010: 279.

53. Tac. *Hist.* 5.11, Joseph. *BJ* 5.238.

54. Labate 2016: 79.

55. Hom. *Il.* 23.712–13: a high house built by a master builder; cf. *Il.* 16.212–13; Pind. *Ol.* 1.42: "highest hall of Zeus"; *Pyth.* 6.7–14; Sen. *Thyestes* 445–46.

56. R. Nisbet and Rudd 2004, *ad loc.*: "With *arduis* the clouds are perhaps visualized as heights that even Maecenas cannot quite reach."

This cloud-scraping abode might, for all we know, be a tall townhouse that Maecenas is urged to forsake along with the smoke and noise of the city centre. A striking parallel for the vista is Aeneas's panorama of Carthage from the hills above (which again includes its noise, *strepitus*):

> iamque ascendebant collem, qui plurimus urbi
> imminet, aduersasque aspectat desuper arces.
> miratur molem Aeneas, magalia quondam,
> miratur portas strepitumque et strata uiarum.

(VERG. AEN. 1.419–22)

And then they reached the top of a hill which loomed large over the city and looked out towards the citadel opposite. Aeneas marvelled at the massive conglomeration, once a collection of huts, marvelled at the gates, the noise and the layout of the streets.

By analogy, Horace's *moles* may even mean Rome itself. But the reference to height more likely indicates an elevated residence from which Maecenas looks down, marvelling ("mirari"), on the hubbub below.[57] In the previous stanza, he had been urged to stop gazing out (*contempleris*, a word from augury)[58] towards the Alban Hills:[59]

> eripe te morae,
> nec semper udum Tibur et Aefulae
> decliue contempleris aruum et
> Telegoni iuga parricidae.

(HOR. CARM. 3.29.5–8)

Don't wait: tear yourself away; don't always stare out at watery Tivoli and the slopes of Aefula and the terrain of Telegonus the parricide.

It is this image of some indefinite elevated mass, fictional or not, that generally serves to support both the existence of the tower and the idea of its eminent position.[60]

---

57. For *mirari* used of looking at panoramas, cf. Prop. 1.14.3; Fabbrini 2007: 6n5.

58. Cf. Verg. *G*. 1.187, 4.61.

59. Tibur, Praeneste and Tusculum were all visible from the city (Strabo 5.3.11–12).

60. E.g., Platner and Ashby 1929: s.v. *Horti Maecenatis*: "This turris was probably the molem propinquam nubibus arduis of Horace (Carm. iii.29.10)." R. Nisbet and Rudd (2004, *ad* Hor. *Carm.* 3.29.9–10) cite Porphyrio: "turrim Maecenas dicitur in hortis suis exstruxisse" (a likely extrapolation from this passage and from Suetonius).

Reassured by this nebulous parallel, historians turn to details: was the tower free-standing or a turret tacked onto a larger house?[61] Towers were components of both Hellenistic buildings (as in the fantastical architectural stage paintings found in houses on the Bay of Naples) and Italian fortified farmhouses (Seneca mentions defensive turrets as part of Scipio's humble cottage at Liternum; Pliny has several towers on his villa at Laurentum).[62] Thus the Tower of Maecenas could have been anything from military-style addition to garden gazebo to supplementary *diaeta* (living room or study). Particularly suggestive is the allusion to "observatories" in Plutarch's description of Lucullus's villa at Tusculum.[63] Another possibility, much discussed, is that the tower recognized Maecenas's Etruscan allegiances. A traditional etymology of "Tyrrhenian" linked it to Greek *tursis*, "tower", which, says Dionysius of Halicarnassus, "they were the first of the inhabitants of this country to build".[64] Add to this the legend that Servius Tullius, Etruscan king of Rome, moved his seat to the Esquiline and the tower starts to read as a statement of genetic identity.

It is equally likely, though, that "tower" is synecdoche for the lofty palace of which it formed a part.[65] In one of Martial's epigrams, the owner of a suburban villa looks out from a "high tower" (turre ab alta prospicis) over ornamental laurels:

> at tu sub urbe possides famem mundam
> et turre ab alta prospicis meras laurus,
> furem Priapo non timente securus.

(MART. 3.58.45–47)

But you are lord of an elegant insufficiency, and look out from your tall tower at mere laurel trees, resting assured that your Priapus fears no vegetable-thief.

Yves Perrin's convenient solution to the impasse is that the tower was both free-standing *and* part of a larger building, imitating a very specific model: the Pharos (lighthouse) at Alexandria, which is reconstructed as a tall detached tower in a rectangular courtyard, with a symmetrical shorter tower at each

---

61. See Colini 1979: 247; Perrin 1996, esp. 399.

62. Sen. *Ep.* 86.4; Plin. *Ep.* 2.17.12–13. Grimal (1943: 276–77) suggests the influence of hunting hides in Persian gardens.

63. See Davies (2010: 232) on "viewing stations" at Hadrian's Villa at Tivoli.

64. Dion. Hal. *Ant. Rom.* 1.26.2.

65. R. Nisbet and Rudd (2004: 346; cf. *ad* Hor. *Carm.* 3.29.9–10) prefer a "towering mansion on the Esquiline" to a simple tower.

corner of the surrounding wall.[66] Only the latest discussion of the Tower of Maecenas, by T. P. Wiseman, has dared to challenge the orthodoxy, asking simply: "Was there a tower?" (and concluding that there was, but that it was part of a larger palace).[67]

Tower building and tower dwelling in Rome had long been morally suspect. Tall buildings spoke of grandiose ambition, whether public or domestic.[68] This suggests a cultural mismatch between the tower and an owner who apparently lacked pretensions to worldly glory. Perrin speculates that some element of civic interest or imperial indulgence must have been invoked for Maecenas (famously a private citizen) to have passed current building regulations, or else that he put his tower to a less worldly use: to practise astronomy, for example.[69] In his history of towers from Babylon to the twentieth century, Theodore Ziolkowski oversimplifies in claiming that the Romans "lacked any appreciation for freestanding, functionless towers and built only structures that had a practical purpose, such as lighthouses or watchtowers on fortresses".[70] What all towers, defensive or ornamental, had in common, is that they were there to be looked out of. When Seneca says of the towers on the villas of Marius and Pompey that they are almost "military" (militare), the implication is that the dynasts carried this form of surveillance over into their leisure activities.[71] In Rome, statesmen who apparently retreated to the hills were all the better placed to survey the city from above and intimidate those below.[72] When Virgil's Dido looks out (prospiceres) from her high palace at the Trojans leaving Carthage, Servius thinks of Valerius Poplicola, forced to raze his grandiose house overlooking the Forum, which he wrongly but understandably transfers from Palatine to Esquiline.[73]

Should we be thinking, then, of Maecenas's tower as a philosopher's or misanthrope's turret, in a tradition that runs from Timon of Athens to Montaigne and Jung?[74] The lookout post of an imperial spy or that of a serene Epicurean? Tacitus (*Hist.* 3.38) neatly illustrates how towers and gardens could double as

66. Perrin 1996: 402. Colini (1979: 242–43) reconstructs the tower as an 18-metre-high edifice, with windows on all sides and a viewing terrace.

67. Wiseman 2016.

68. Amm. Marc. 22.16.10, for example, wrongly attributed the Pharos to Cleopatra.

69. Perrin 1996: 403. Ambitious architecture was frowned on long before the *Lex Iulia de modo aedificiorum urbis* (6 BCE); cf. Strabo 5.3.7; Nichols 2010: esp. 43–47.

70. Ziolkowski 1998: 14.

71. Sen. *Ep.* 51.11: "uidebatur hoc magis militare, ex edito speculari late longeque subiecta".

72. Wallace-Hadrill 1998.

73. Serv. *ad Aen.* 4.410.

74. Ziolkowsi 1998. See Gowers (2010) on Augustus's high bolthole, "Syracuse".

places in which to lurk and luxuriate, to see and be seen. One night, as the emperor Vitellius lay sick in the Horti Serviliani, he noticed a nearby tower, all lit up. On learning that his loyal subject Blaesus was dining there, the emperor was persuaded by his brother Lucius Vitellius that Blaesus was a threat to his power and should be put to death. Lucius exploits the contrast between low-lying emperor and elevated dinner guests for full rhetorical effect. Up in the tower, he says, a rival for the throne "surveys" (*prospectantem*) the emperor's misery from his dining room; just so, says Tacitus in an aside, courtiers survey (*speculantur*) their rulers' moods and weaknesses. The verb *speculari*, commonly used of military spying, especially from a great height, is the one used by Velleius Paterculus of Maecenas's activities at Augustus's court (2.88.3). What he had done at the centre of things, in other words, he continued to do at the margins.

To sum up: it is perfectly plausible that, like other Hellenizing and pleasure-loving Romans, Maecenas built an imposing hilltop palace, designed to imitate the Alexandrian Pharos or some other wondrous building. Whether it was a place of retreat or a place from which to survey the city and the Campagna is unclear.[75] Ultimately, the hybrid nature of Maecenas's activities as pleasure lover, court spy and semi-detached statesman dissolves the pressure to choose. There is no concrete evidence that the palace included anything that resembled a physical tower or, even if it did, that it was built by Maecenas himself, rather than by some later imperial owner.

## Tragic Towers

There is another way of approaching the parallels drawn between Horace's *Odes* 3.29 and Suetonius's account of the Great Fire. If, as we saw, Horace's *Odes* construct Maecenas as the ideal recipient of lyric poetry (an ambitious but careworn tyrant ready to be seduced or reformed by soothing or moralizing songs), the palace in the clouds, despite its localized orientation, is probably a convenient figment, a variation on traditional Greek symbols of tragic hubris, especially where a fall from a great height is involved. Take, for example, the chorus of Sophocles's *Oedipus Tyrannus* (873–80): "Insolence breeds the tyrant; insolence, bloated aimlessly on what is overripe and rich with ruin, scales the precipitous ramparts, then topples and falls in ruin, where it cannot find a

---

75. Horace hints at grandiosity in his patron's building projects—*Sat.* 2.3.307–9: "'accipe: primum / aedificas, hoc est longos imitaris, ab imo / ad summum totus moduli bipedalis'" ("Listen: first, you're a developer—I mean, you're imitating the high-rise boys—even though top to toe you're only two feet tall"; *aedificas* denotes specifically overambitious building: e.g., Plaut. *Mostell. passim*, Mart. 9.46).

viable foothold." Counsellor Artabanus gives similar advice to Xerxes: "You see, it is always onto the highest buildings and the tallest trees that God hurls his bolts" (Hdt. 7.10).[76] This is the pedigree of many precarious towers that appear in Horace's *Odes*: the "lofty towers" of 2.10.10–11, the "royal piles" of 2.15.1–2 and the "brazen tower" that opens another ode to Maecenas, 3.16, where Danaë's high prison is a metaphor for the false allure of wealth, so launching another Horatian negotiation of the relationship between poor poet and rich patron.[77] Horace prefers to keep his head below the parapet, but slips in a pointed address to Maecenas:

> iure perhorrui
> late conspicuum tollere uerticem,
>    Maecenas, equitum decus.

(CARM. 3.16.18–20)

With reason, Maecenas, glory of the equestrians, have I shrunk from raising my head where it can be seen far and wide.

In challenging the wealthy knight to keep his profile low, unlike Lydian kings with vast estates (*Carm.* 3.16.41–42), Horace forgets his own dream of bumping his head against the stars (*Carm.* 1.1.36). For all this, Nisbet and Rudd, invested as they are in the materiality of the tower, still deny that at *Odes* 3.29.9–10 Horace is making a generalized allusion to "the perils of greatness".[78] There are two possibilities: either Horace's lyric towers are introduced because Maecenas had a real tower, or—equally plausible—he is subsequently said to have had a real tower because he is so closely connected with moralized towers in the *Odes*.

By Nero's time, the conventionality of the topos was beyond doubt. Another tower features in the first choral ode of Seneca's *Agamemnon* (92–102). Wind-battered, head in the clouds, it, too, illustrates the dangers of overweening ambition:

> A tower with its head in the very clouds [nubibus ipsis inserta caput] is lashed by the rainy south wind and a grove that spreads thick shadows sees its venerable timber smashed; lightning strikes exposed hilltops, larger physiques are more prone to disease, and when common cattle run out to graze, it is the longest neck that is chosen for the axe. Whatever Fortune raises on high, she lifts in order to cast it down.

76. R. Nisbet and Hubbard (1978, *ad Carm.* 2.10.9) give this along with further Greek and Roman parallels.

77. The first time a tower is mentioned in relation to the Danaë myth.

78. Alluding to Lyne (1995: 112), whose "perils of greatness" cites R. Nisbet and Hubbard 1978 (*ad Carm.* 2.10.9; cf. *Carm.* 2.15.1–2 ["regiae moles", or "royal piles"]).

Seneca pays homage here to Greek tragic ancestors, filtered through Horatian lyric.[79] But between Horace and Seneca lies another tragic parallel. Climbing to the top of his father's house to watch the conflagration and collapse of Troy, Virgil's Aeneas singles out a beetling tower (*turrim*) that offers a panoramic view of the city:

euado ad summi fastigia culminis, unde
tela manu miseri iactabant inrita Teucri.
turrim in praecipiti stantem summisque sub astra
eductam tectis, unde omnis Troia uideri
et Danaum solitae naues et Achaica castra . . .

(VERG. AEN. 2.458–62)

I climbed up to the highest point of the roof, from where the unhappy Trojans were hurling their weapons in vain. A tower that stood on the sheer edge, projecting from the top of the roof to the stars, from where all of Troy could be seen and the Greek ships and camp . . .

Aeneas's viewpoint suggests the synoptic poetic vision needed to condense this long story into one book and one tragic night.[80] Meanwhile, the tower, about to fall with a resounding crash, is metonymic of the city's ruin.[81]

Virgil's rooftop panorama has further potential: it makes an obvious primal scene for Nero's Trojan reenactment.[82] The tragic components of *Aeneid* 2 (unity of time, place and action, an extended messenger speech) may even dictate Tacitus's decision to make Nero perform his extended Troy drama on a "private stage".[83] Nero's claim to Trojan ancestry may have inspired Dio to put him on the roof of the Esquiline palace, which, like Anchises's house in Troy, offered "the best general view of the greater part of the conflagration".[84] But why does Suetonius alone specify the "Tower of Maecenas" (*Nero* 38.2)? On reflection, this may also be an over-determined choice. Not only was this

79. Seneca's language binds together two over-reachers in the *Odes*: Horace in *Carm.* 1.1 ("nemus . . . inseres . . . uertice" ~ "inserta . . . caput . . . nemus") and Maecenas in *Carm.* 3.29 ("molem . . . nubibus" ~ "nubibus . . . turris"); cf. Sen. *Phaedra* 1128–29.

80. Verg. *Aen.* 2.11: "et breuiter Troiae supremum audire laborem" (cf. "longo . . . luctu" [2.26], "longo . . . bello" [109]).

81. On synecdochic towers at *Aen.* 9.530–66, 12.672–75, see P. Hardie (1995) and Rossi (2004: 171–96).

82. Dio Cass. 62.17.1, with Baxter 1968.

83. Tac. *Ann.* 15.39.3: "cecinisse Troianum excidium, praesentia mala uetustis cladibus adsimulantem".

84. Dio Cass. 62.18.1.

the tallest tower atop the highest hill in Rome.[85] It also stood in the area where Virgil, inspired poet of Troy, supposedly chose to live, near his patron's park. This may well of course be another convenient fiction.[86] But where better to picture Virgil standing to perform, on his patron's orders, Aeneas's first-person tale of a city's destruction?[87] Of all places, real or imaginary, the tower made the perfect dramatic setting for Nero to play two roles that he uniquely combined: Aeneas's descendant and Virgil's successor.[88]

Other affinities between Nero and Maecenas suggest themselves: their aesthetic stance (Nero's attraction to "the beauty of flame"); the panoramic view of the remote observer?[89] Or transgressive ambition and the spectacle of hubris about to be brought low? One of Nero's unrealized dreams, says Suetonius, was to play Virgil's losing hero Turnus; another was to abdicate and live as a citharode.[90] As a reader of tragic Virgil and lyric Horace (Hor. *Carm.* 2.10.10–12), Nero would know that tall towers are especially exposed to lightning strikes and general collapse.[91] If his own variation on the thunder theme ("ipsa enim altitudo attonat summa" = Sen. *Ep.* 19.19) is anything to go by, Maecenas, too, listened to Horace's warnings ("too late", Seneca says, in tragic vein). Suetonius saw the links and put them to work in what amounts to a meditation on the rise and fall of regimes through the symbolism of stricken towers.[92] Soon his Nero, retreating from the city to the humbler suburban *horti* of his freedman Phaos, will be blinded by an ominous flash (Suet. *Ner.* 48.2: "fulgure aduerso") and housed in a tomb built on the Collis Hortulorum (the Pincio) "because it is visible from the Campus Martius".[93] If Maecenas was a lightning rod for the Augustan Age, an angel who fell to earth despite the tragic warnings of his bards, then Nero, in trying to renew both the sorrows of Troy and the legacy of Augustan Rome from this unbeatably elevated place, was riding for a similar fall himself.

85. See Vout (2012: 194) for parallels with Homeric *teichoscopia*.

86. Donat. *Vit. Verg.* 13: "habuitque domum Romae Esquiliis iuxta hortos Maecenatianos"; plausible, in Purcell's view (2007: 373); cf. Rawson 1976.

87. Austin 1964 *ad Aen.* 2.5: "ipse . . . uidi".

88. Dio 62.18.3–4: "last of the Aeneadae and descendant of Augustus".

89. De Lacy 1964.

90. Turnus: Suet. *Ner.* 54.1; Connors 1998: 98: "In real life, Nero played the losing role." Citharode: Dio 63.27.2. Cf. Champlin 2003: 82: "In short, tragedy and citharody up to the end."

91. Lightning was a genuine risk for garden towers: Dio 42.26.3; Julius Obsequens 7. An inscription found in the Horti Sallustiani in 1883 (FVLGVR CONDITV) marked the area struck as a sacred *bidental* or *puteal*; Hartswick 2004: 19–20.

92. Cf. Kraus (1994) on Livy.

93. Suet. *Ner.* 50.1.

## Later Towers

Since antiquity, the quest to locate and visualize the tower has been driven by a strong element of fantasy. For some centuries, it disappears from the record, swallowed up in Nero's new Domus Aurea.[94] In the Middle Ages, however, Towers of Maecenas begin to spring up all over Rome. The Nero legend drew pilgrims to the sacked city in search of its true location, "among the fragmented columns, the shattered statues and the winding streets bristling with fortifications".[95] An early candidate was the so-called *turris militiarium* (Torre delle Milizie), a brutal medieval edifice jutting out from behind the cloister of Santa Caterina a Magnopoli, near Trajan's Markets. But others followed: Torre dei Capocci (or degli Arcioni), in Piazza di San Martino ai Monti, and—where we started—Torre Mesa, the thin brick tower attached to the so-called "Frontespizio di Nerone" in the gardens of Palazzo Colonna.[96]

A classical ruin with a tower attached, in the gardens of a prominent humanist: the coincidence was too good to be true. Prospero Colonna duly claimed that his gardens once housed the "Tower of Maecenas", even though his own modest tower was added in the late Middle Ages and stood on the Quirinal, not the Esquiline.[97] He could not have been a more fitting owner, celebrated as a "new Maecenas" by Flavio Biondo, author of *Roma instaurata* (1444–46), thanks to his learning, liberal virtues and circle of humanist friends (which included Poggio Bracciolini and Leon Battista Alberti).[98] This was not just blanket flattery but reflected Colonna's desire "to build on a circumstantial association by recreating his own *all'antica* garden with materials drawn from that of his illustrious predecessor".[99]

Most of the remaining structure was demolished in the 1630s by Duke Filippo Colonna, but earlier prints and drawings show how tenderly Prospero decorated his garden ruin using inlaid fragments and supports from his collection of classical marbles.[100] An anonymous sketch from the 1530s shows the balustrade and

94. Perrin 1996: 400.

95. Sabatini 1914: 13.

96. Falsely etymologized from *Maecenas*, *mesa* is probably from vernacular *miéza*, "halved"; Sabatini 1914: 16.

97. Scaglia 1992: 37.

98. Biondo [1444–46] 1954: 283–84: "alter nostri saeculi Maecenas summae humanitatis liberalitatisque vir et studiorum humanitatis apprime doctus cultorumque amantissimus". He confuses Quirinal and Esquiline, identifying the Quirinal temple as "hortorum Mecoenatis"; Brothers 2002: 58.

99. Brothers 2002: 58.

100. Christian 2010: 49, fig. 19; 52, fig. 23.

FIGURE 9.1 Anon. (sixteenth century), pen and ink drawing, loggia in garden of Palazzo Colonna, Rome, with "Temple of Serapis".
© Metropolitan Museum, New York

its pediment (figure 9.1).[101] Classical soirees were held in the loggia, where Flavio Biondo entertained the cardinal's guest Sigismondo Malatesta with discourses on ancient literature and Roman ruins. In Kathleen Wren Christian's words: "For the humanist circle Colonna sponsored, the parallel between Colonna's garden and the site where Maecenas had met the poets he sponsored, among them Virgil, Horace, and Propertius, was too perfect to resist."[102]

In turn, the Quirinal remains helped to inspire another residence, this time in the countryside and built for another Maecenas.[103] Around 1484, Giuliano da Sangallo pored over his drawings of the supposed remains of the "palazo Mecenate" at Palazzo Colonna and was inspired to design a country house for the most celebrated of all Renaissance patrons, Lorenzo de' Medici. Poliziano wrote to Ludovico Bolognino: "Lorenzo is the Maecenas of his age, and like the Roman Maecenas, assists men of genius and erudition with his advice, his wealth and his personal efforts."[104] Sangallo's antiquarian interest in the "palazo" produced a striking composite (figure 9.2). The façade of the Villa Medici

101. Christian 2010: 49, fig. 19; Scaglia 1992.
102. Christian 2010: 48.
103. Brothers 2002: 65–68; 2022: 242–44.
104. Brothers 2002: 72n46; 2022: 243.

FIGURE 9.2 Villa Medici, Giuliano da Sangallo (*c.* 1480), Poggio a Caiano. *Photo:* Ralph Lieberman (Ralph Lieberman Archive, Harvard University)

at Poggio a Caiano, outside Florence, features an innovative ensemble, never seen before in Tuscan villa design, of sweeping, curved, symmetrical steps, arched arcades and rustic central pediment.[105]

What's more, there even appeared to be an ancient precedent for such a design. Outside Tivoli lay the remains of a sanctuary of Hercules popularly known as the "Villa of Maecenas".[106] Piranesi's romantic engraving of 1763 gives it a distinctive arcade above a podium base (figure 9.3). The poet Naldo Naldi hailed Lorenzo as another Maecenas or Lucullus, alluding to the "large halls built on spacious porticoes" in Lucullus's villa and drawing parallels between Lucullus's introduction of the cherry tree from Pontus to Italy (Plin. *HN* 15.102) and Lorenzo's cultivation of the mulberry bush.[107] Another happy convergence of elements determined the unique design of the villa at Poggio a Caiano: Lorenzo's and Colonna's aspirations to reincarnate Maecenas, the suggestive remains of the temple in Palazzo Colonna and the sanctuary at Tivoli, and the sense that a villa fit for a new Maecenas or Lucullus required both an elevated site and a garden setting.[108]

105. Brothers 2002: 66. Foster (1978: 524–29n710) suggests that the villa was based on the Quirinal temple, so may have prompted the identification of the Quirinal site with the Palace of Maecenas.

106. Drawn by Antonio da Sangallo il Giovane and later by Pirro Ligorio; Brothers 2002: 67.

107. Naldi 1934: 4.

108. Brothers 2002: 67.

FIGURE 9.3 *Remains of the "Villa of Maecenas" at Tivoli*, engraving
by Giovanni Piranesi (1763).
© Fine Arts Museums of San Francisco, Achenbach Foundation
for the Graphic Arts

Back at Rome, even such a decisive act of appropriation as Colonna's failed
to dispel the controversy over the tower's original site, judging by the subsequent
manoeuvres of Roman antiquarians and cartographers. Andrea Fulvio (1588)
ignored Colonna's claims and moved the "Horti Mecenatis", together with their
multistorey palace, back to the Esquiline.[109] Leonardo Bufalini's map (1551) attaches the name "Turris Maecenatis" to a square building on the Esquiline with
a round central shape, while Nodot's map shows the tower as round.[110] Étienne
Du Pérac (1577) puts the Frontespizio on the Quirinal but simultaneously records a "Turris Maecenatis" on the Esquiline (shown as a formal garden surrounded by a hedge, no tower visible).[111] Some interpretations verged on the
preposterous. Fabio Calvo's engraving in his *Antiquae urbis Romae cum regionibus
simulachrum* (first edition 1527) shows the tower as centrepiece of Maecenas's
Esquiline *horti*, a beetling combination of tower and palace, evoking the Lighthouse at Alexandria (figure 9.4). Still more ambitiously monumental is the five-
tier ziggurat-like tower in Giacomo Lauro's engraving (1612; figure 9.5), which
suggests another Wonder, the Mausoleum at Halicarnassus.[112]

109. Fulvio 1588: 2.59.

110. Frutaz 1962: vol. 1, plates 192, 66.

111. Frutaz, 1962: vol. 2, plate 254.

112. Thanks to Tom True for introducing me to this image, described by Meibom (1653: ch.
28.27, pp. 176–77) with some scepticism.

HORTI MOECENATIS CV TVRRI

FIGURE 9.4 "Horti Moecenatis cum turri" by Fabio Calvo, in *Antiquae urbis Romae cum regionibus simulachrum* (Basel, 1558).
Reproduced by kind permission of the Syndics of Cambridge University Library

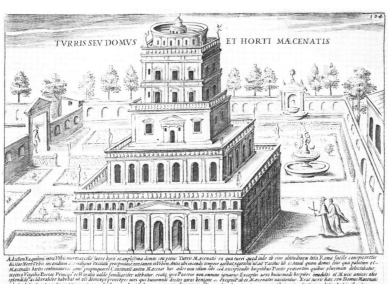

FIGURE 9.5 "Tower of Maecenas" by Giacomo Lauro, in *Antiquae urbis splendor* (Rome, 1612).
Source: The Warburg Institute Library; Artstor image

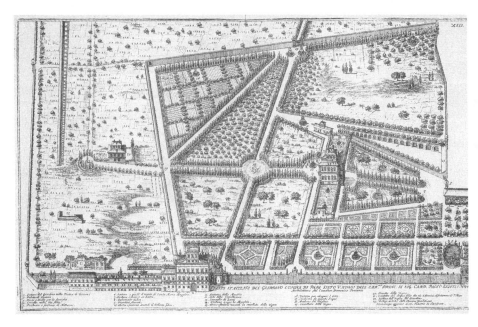

FIGURE 9.6 Villa Montalto, plan and elevation of the garden and vineyard of Pope Sixtus V, etching by Giovanni Battista Falda, *Li giardini di Roma* (Rome, 1677). *Source:* Artstor

Later in the sixteenth century, a further claim to the tower was staked at the Villa Montalto-Negroni-Massimo (the name reveals the sequence of owners). The prime mover was Felice Peretti, Cardinal Montalto (1521–90), who bought an elevated vineyard in 1576 and commissioned Domenico Fontana to build a villa and gardens straddling the Esquiline, Quirinal and Viminal hills, above Servius Tullius's Agger and overlooking the Baths of Diocletian (figure 9.6). Here he spent five years of happy Maecenas-like "exile in the city", imposed by Pope Gregory XIII, before he himself became Pope Sixtus V and developed the surrounding area by widening the streets and restoring the water source of the ancient *horti* via a new aqueduct, the Acqua Felice. He could not have known that his gardens occupied the former site of the Horti Lolliani, associated with Augustus's friend Lollius.[113] It is far more likely that he saw himself as a successor to Maecenas. The connection is suggested above all by the turret-like

113. Wiseman (1992: 71–110, esp. 77–95) gives a riveting account of the site's vicissitudes, from Horti Lolliani to California-style work-out studio. The site was confirmed by a boundary stone found in 1883 at the intersection of Via Principe Umberto and Via del Viminale, assigning ownership to Emperor Claudius (= *CIL* VI 31285).

belvedere atop the little *casino* or *palazetto* in the centre of the garden. Added to the estate in 1588, it nods to imagined versions of Maecenas's tower, evoking an earlier golden age of gardening. The site's altitude was also to its advantage: incorporated into the gardens was the peak known as Monte della Giustizia. Sixtus placed a classical statue of Rome there, popularly believed to represent Justice, marked on Bufalini's 1551 map as the highest spot in Rome (*altissimus Romae locus*) and as *Turris Maecenatis*, simultaneously.[114]

Sixtus's occupancy was, it turned out, the high point of the villa's fortunes. By 1696, his family was forced to sell up, and a century later Villa Negroni, as it became known, was a ruin as neglected and romantic as anything ancient, in William Beckford's eyes: "The air was filled with the murmurs of water, trickling down basins of porphyry, and losing itself amongst overgrown weeds and grasses."[115] In this state of delicious decay, the villa suggested "a paradise closed and idle" to Henry James, who visited in 1869.[116] One of its American artist tenants, William Story, charts its regression from Neronian belvedere to humble cabbage patch:[117]

> As one looks from the Villa Negroni windows, he cannot fail to be impressed by the strange changes through which this wonderful city has passed. The very spot on which Nero, the insane emperor-artist, fiddled while Rome was burning has now become a vast kitchen garden, belonging to Prince Massimo (himself a descendant, as he claims, of Fabius Cunctator), where men no longer, but only lettuces, asparagus, and artichokes, are ruthlessly cut down. (Story 1863: 1.155–56)

A final claim to continuity with Maecenas's tower was made in a history of the family estate (1836) by Prince Massimo's son Vittorio.[118] Logic dictated, he wrote, that if Nero wanted the best possible panorama of Rome, the Tower of Maecenas with its "deliziosi orti" (delightful vegetable gardens) must have stood on or near Monte della Giustizia and therefore, pleasingly, within the confines of the current Villa Massimo.[119] But a project more grandiose even than Nero's Domus Aurea—*Roma Capitale*—would soon lay waste to

---

114. In the Turin manuscript of his *Antichità Romane*, Pirro Ligorio associates the *horti* of Maecenas with enhanced all-round views of the city: "superba torre", "superba veduta"; Brothers 2002: 72.

115. Letter of 30 June 1782, cited by Wiseman 1992: 83; Chapman 1928: 1.273.

116. James 1903: 1.123.

117. Wiseman 1992: 91–2.

118. Sabatini 1914: 16.

119. Massimo 1836: 7–8, citing Severano 1630: 673: Nero looked out from "il più eminente luogo di Roma".

Vittorio's inheritance, as with many of the papal estates that occupied former *horti*.[120] His father barely outlived the abrupt seizure and destruction of his villa to make way for Termini Station in 1863.

Francesco Sabatini concludes: "The much-sought Tower of Maecenas is rather like the Arabian phoenix: everyone says it exists, but no one knows where it is to be found."[121] Easy though it is to mock the strenuous, not to say creative, efforts of later Romans to relocate the tower and incorporate it into family estates and personal mythologies, modern scholars can also be naïve about whether Maecenas had a personal tower. The tower stands firm in their imaginations because they want it to. It satisfies and supports their belief in the owner's contradictions: his worldliness and his unworldliness, his remoteness and his omniscience, his Epicureanism and his Machiavellianism, his aesthetics and his politics.

## The Auditorium of Maecenas

In 1874, a far more substantial relic of Maecenas's gardens came to light. In "a moment of great glory" in the course of excavations in Rome's Monti district for the new Quartiere Umbertino, architect Virginio Vespignani and archaeologist Carlo Ludovico Visconti unearthed near Via Merulana a building that soon became known as the "Auditorium of Maecenas".[122] It had survived because it was partly subterranean, embedded in part of the now sunken Servian Agger as it descended from the Porta Esquilina. Conveniently, it can be dated on the basis of its materials to the turn of the first millennium, making a desired date of around 30 BCE quite plausible.[123] As the only obviously relevant building in the area of the Horti Maecenatiani, it has, not surprisingly, taken on an exaggerated importance as a focus for the lived experience of the gardens As one scholar insists: it is "hard to imagine the rich store of history, life, poetry, art and memory hidden in this squalid shack in the middle of Piazza Leopardi".[124]

120. Pisani Sartorio 1996: 34.

121. Sabatini 1914: 16. His prize for most hare-brained suggestion goes to the amateur archaeologist who placed its foundations under the Church of San Eusebio in Piazza Vittorio Emanuele (18).

122. Vespignani and Visconti 1874. De Vos 1983; Rizzo 1983: 225: "un momento di grande gloria per l'archeologia di Roma capitale".

123. Steinby 1993–99: 3.74–75. Purcell (1996: 148) argues for an uninterrupted view of the Campagna from the (blocked up) rear window; Häuber (2014: 324) points to the newly excavated Augustan building that spoils this vision.

124. Pisani Sartorio 1996: 44.

FIGURE 9.7 The Auditorium of Maecenas.
*Source:* Author's own photo

Descending a tunnelled ramp, the modern visitor emerges into a murky, earth-floored space (once paved in white mosaic tiles) some ten by twenty metres, resembling a small, domed church (figure 9.7). An apse at the end holds seven semicircular rows of what look like seats, while along the straight walls niches are painted with trompe l'oeil windows, which seem to overlook fenced gardens and have painted Dionysiac friezes around their borders. The theatrical appearance is deceptive. The "seats" turn out to be dotted with water holes. A favourite explanation is that the building was some kind of grotto, housing an ornamental cascade, which perhaps doubled as an étagère to display plants, like a Victorian auricula theatre.[125] But the space is also the perfect size for an intimate party, and interpreters have often wanted to build in that possibility, to repopulate the building with Maecenas and friends—dining, talking and reciting poetry.[126] Labels at

125. So Christopher Smith suggests to me. Filippo Coarelli has argued persuasively (oral presentation, Florence, November 2016) that these are the drainage holes needed for any structure built into an escarpment.

126. Vespignani and Visconti 1874. See, e.g., Pisani Sartorio 1996: 44; Villetard 2018; Keith 2008: 9: "It is tempting to imagine Propertius, Horace, and even Vergil, among others, performing there at Maecenas' invitation after dinner."

the site mark it as a hybrid: a "summer nymphaeum–triclinium".[127] The name "Auditorium" has stuck, however, in the popular imagination. This feels all too temptingly like a place that might have echoed with the parties of Maecenas and the songs of Virgil, Horace and Propertius.

Moreover, texts serendipitously found in the vicinity—a poetic graffito, inscriptions on lead piping—have helped to keep alive theories about the building's use as performance space or dining room. An epigram of Callimachus is scratched on an outer wall: "Unmixed wine and love held me back. One of them dragged my steps, and the other would not keep me sane . . . I did not shout your name or your father's but kissed the doorpost."[128] The physical context neatly turns a reveller's boast about a small but extravagant erotic gesture into an apt memorial to drunken love locked out. But it is another step altogether to argue that ruin and text together make a coherent whole:

> We come closest to the reality of sympotic performance with the so-called Auditorium of Maecenas, found in the area of the Gardens of Maecenas in 1874. . . . It has been variously interpreted as an auditorium for poetic recitations or as a nymphaeum or "greenhouse"; but Lugli rightly saw difficulties in both types of interpretation. One clue as to its purpose was first noted by Thylander: a connection with sympotic poetry is demonstrated by a Greek graffito found painted on the outside wall, which is in fact a paraklausithyron of Callimachus (no. 80 GP = 42 Pfeiffer), asking pardon for bad behaviour brought on by wine and love. There could hardly be a better example of that fusion of poetry and life which we are seeking: the scribe recreates the original function of the literary genre by actually writing the poem on a wall (leaving it as a "kiss on the doorstep"); but the apology is surely for bad behaviour at the symposium, not outside the house of the loved one. Combined with the decoration, this graffito would suggest that the building was designed as an elaborate setting for literary symposia. (Murray 1985: 43)

"There could hardly be a better example of that fusion of poetry and life which we are seeking." Indeed: Callimachean memories of drunken revels are harnessed to claim a sympotic function for the building from which the graffito's speaker is apparently excluded, such that the epigram ends up being parasitic on the very scene to which it gives longed-for life and meaning. The fact that

---

127. See De Vos 1983; Rizzo 1983. Claridge et al. (1998: 330) call it "essentially a setting for dinner parties". They go on to say that water holes simply need reorienting: "The couches would be arranged in front of the apse, facing the transept at the other end, where entertainments would be staged." The photograph in William A. Johnson (2010: 141) contains a row of chairs added for scale, reinforcing the desired function of the space.

128. Callim. *Epigr.* 42.3–4, 5–6 Pfeiffer.

the same verses are translated almost verbatim inside a longer poem by
Propertius has only helped bolster the connection between the graffito on
the outside and the sympotico-literary activities of the poets on the inside:
"Imagining that Propertius drew inspiration for his elegy in the auditorium of
Maecenas is as exciting as it is impossible to verify."[129]

*In the dining room with the lead pipe . . .*

Links with another literary text are far more plausible. In a letter to his
friend and pupil the emperor Marcus Aurelius, the rhetorician Fronto (*c.* 100–
*c.* 160 CE) refers in passing to "Gardens of Maecenas", of which he claims
ownership ("Maecenatianos hortos meos"). The train of thought is abstruse,
but Fronto appears to be fishing for compliments on a recent speech. He is
pleased with his spin on a famous conversion narrative, the Greek playboy
Polemo's lightning transformation into an Academic philosopher after burst-
ing drunk into a lecture on restraint. Horace had briefly alluded to it in one of
his satires, and this is how Maecenas enters the letter:

> plane multum mihi facetiarum contulit istic Horatius Flaccus, memorabilis
> poeta mihique propter Maecenatem ac Maecenatianos hortos meos non
> alienus. is namque Horatius Sermonum libr[o] s[ecundo] fabulam istam
> Polemonis inseruit, si recte memini, hisce uersibus:
>
> mutatus Polemon ponas insignia morbi,
> fasciolas, cubital, focalia, potus ut ille
> dicitur ex collo furtim carpsisse coronas,
> postquam et impransi correptus uoce magistri. [Hor. *Sat.* 2.3.254–57]
>     (Fronto *Ad M. Caesarem* 2.1.5 [Haines 1.122] = 1.9.5 van den Hout)

Horatius Flaccus clearly gave me a lot of help with the jokes—a memorable
poet, and no stranger to me because of Maecenas and my gardens of Maecenas. Horace put the story of Polemo into the second book of his Satires,
if I remember rightly, in the following verses: "Will you take off the tokens
of your sickness, like the convert Polemo: your garters, neck-cushion and
scarf [i.e., effeminate garb]? Just so he, when drunk, is said to have sneaked
the garlands from his head, arrested by the voice of the sober master."

---

129. Wyler 2013: 543; Prop. 1.3.13–14: ". . . duplici correptum ardore iuberent / hac Amor hac
Liber, durus uterque deus". Cf. Barchiesi 2011: 515n8: "It is suggestive that Call. *Epigr.* 42 Pf. (8
GP) is epigraphically attested inside the so-called Auditorium of Maecenas, a place where a
culture of wine and poetic performance must have been important." Milnor (2014: 14) urges
caution in linking the content of graffiti to the buildings where they are found.

Miraculously, Fronto's claim to ownership of (at least part of) the Horti Maecenatiani has been confirmed by lead water -pipes found at the scene, bearing the names "Corneli<orum> Front<onis> et Quadrati" (Fronto's brother Quadratus), together with an honorific inscription possibly dedicated to his son-in-law, C. Aufidius Victorinus.[130] How these gardens became Fronto's is harder to say: by inheritance or through "princely gratitude for his unpaid services"?[131] Purcell sees evidence here of the common practice of parcelling out large imperial estates, either by sale or by gift:

> For Fronto in the second century, the *horti* that he owed to his imperial patrons were also *maecenatiani*, meaning either that he had a share in the disposable space of the same estate, or, more probably, that he understood the applicability of the prototype of Maecenas and his generosity to later examples of the display of patronage through the disposal of lots in the urban periphery.[132]

In other words, Maecenas may have inspired a tradition of benefaction (or profiteering) that continued with later owners.

The context here, a letter to another imperial patron-cum-friend, is already suggestive. But the links with Maecenas are more than just contractual. Fronto calls Horace "a memorable poet", one who is "no stranger" (non alienus) to him. Perhaps he is remembering Horace as a "mindful" follower of Maecenas (*Sat.* 2.6.31: "ad Maecenatem memori si mente recurras") or knows Maecenas's plea to Augustus to "remember" Horace after his death (Suet. *Vita Hor.*: "Horati Flacci ut mei esto memor"), along with its fulfilment, their joint burial on the Esquiline. At any rate, the memory of a paradigmatic friendship feeds this communication between two literati whose like-mindedness and shared humour similarly override differences in status. Fronto, the self-styled "nomad from Libya", has acquired his share, not just of a famous Roman property but also the textual and cultural memories that go with it (*si recte memini*). Horace is not only *non alienus* to him; he is part of his new property.[133]

Links with the world of the *horti* do not end here. The larger poem from which Fronto takes the vignette about Polemo, Horace's *Satires* 2.3, is the conversion narrative of a bankrupt estate agent, Damasippus: "Now I mind other people's business, having lost my own . . . I used to be the only man who knew how to buy and sell gardens and fine houses at a profit."[134] Historians have

---

130. *CIL* XV 7438, VI 31821; Champlin 1980: 21–22.

131. Champlin 1980: 24.

132. Purcell 2007: 373; see also Champlin 1980: 24–25.

133. Richlin 2006: 88n22. One meaning of *alienare* is "to transfer property to someone else".

134. Hor. *Sat.* 2.3.19–20, 24–25.

argued that he is very likely the real-life speculator Damasippus whom Cicero associates with parcelling up *horti* plots down by the Tiber.[135] Maecenas even plays a cameo role in the satire, as a potential customer, when Damasippus turns on Horace and accuses him of feebly imitating Maecenas's *grands projets*: "You're a developer; I mean, you're imitating the high-rise boys" (aedificas, hoc est longos imitaris; 308).[136] "Polemo and Maecenas" anticipates the chiastic opposition in Plutarch's parallel lives of Cimon and Lucullus: the first turning halfway through his life to a better way of living, the second to a worse one—symbolized by his notorious gardens.[137]

In short, Fronto is claiming to be a new Horace, as if the title deeds to the gardens came with a bonus of transferable wit (*facetiarum*). Amy Richlin writes: "Fronto's real estate purchase . . . enables him in effect to own both Horace and Maecenas."[138] Even so, there is a patronizing, arm's-length tone to *memorabilis* and *non alienus*, as if little Horace were almost beneath Fronto's notice.[139] As sentimental terms, "memory" and "memorability" screen starker notions of obligation and mutual repayment, with an eye to posterity and the permanent fixing of identities. Fronto's acquisition has freed up another role, in which he can compete with his imperial patron.[140] Put differently, "Horace and Maecenas" is complicated by the other double act available to Fronto and Marcus: "Maecenas and Augustus".[141] In his reply, Marcus begs Fronto to stop recalling (*memineris*) Horace, who as far as he is concerned is "dead and gone" (emortuus), along with Pollio.[142] Emperor and tutor are trying less to imitate the effete Augustans than to supersede them, "remembering" them in order to supplant them. They are also defusing Seneca's crisis of conscience between philosophy and gardens.

Sure enough, centuries later, a passage from Walter Pater's *Marius the Epicurean* (1885), set in the late empire, imagines Fronto the philosopher-proprietor sitting outdoors (like the Maecenas of the *Elegiae*), listening to birds and

---

135. Cic. *Att.* 12.33 = 269 Shackleton Bailey. See Purcell 2007: 371. Verboven (1997) argues that Damasippus was an aristocrat engaged in trade.

136. Earlier in Fronto's letter, rhetorical analogies with soft clothing recall Maecenas the dandified statesman of Sen. *Ep.* 114.

137. Plut. *Vit. Cim. et Luc.* 1.4.

138. Richlin 2006: 101. See Hinds 2001: 253–57, 261–62 on the "poetics of real estate".

139. Van den Hout 1999: 53.

140. Not the Fronto of boring alfresco recitations at Juv. 1.12–13 (despite the scholion "in Horatiana domo, in qua poetae recitabant"); Champlin 1980: 150n14; Rushforth 1919: 34.

141. The bantering tone recalls Augustus's letters to Maecenas.

142. *Ad M. Caesarem* 2.8 [2.4.3 van den Hout; 1.138–39 Haines]: "Polemonis tui quom memineristi, rogo ne Horatii memineris, qui mihi com Pol[l]ione est emortuus". Maecenas's name is obliterated by Pollio's (unless *Pollione* is an error for *Polemone*).

reflecting on his fame.[143] Indifferent to the compromising luxuries that surround him, he has succeeded in becoming Maecenas—or rather, a far more satisfactory version of Maecenas:

> But his sumptuous appendages, including the villa and gardens of Maecenas, had been borne with an air perfectly becoming, by the professor of a philosophy which, even in its most accomplished and elegant phase, presupposed a gentle contempt for such things. . . . Through a long life of now eighty years, he had been, as it were, surrounded by the gracious and soothing air of his own eloquence—the fame, the echoes, of it—like warbling birds, or murmuring bees. Setting forth in that fine medium the best ideas of matured pagan philosophy, he had become the favourite "director" of noble youth. (Pater [1885] 1910: 1.222)

## The Sculptures

It is no accident that two of the texts associated with the Auditorium—the Callimachean epigram and the Horatian fable of Polemo—deal with irruptions, measured or boisterous, into a sealed sanctum. Together, they recall the opposition (familiar from Plato's *Symposium*) between decorous moderation (inside) and unlicensed excess (outside).[144] The contrast nicely frames our own curious speculations: about what went on inside the Auditorium, how to reconstitute an ensemble out of its fragments and how to interpret and rearrange the sculptures that adorned the surrounding gardens. Visconti, the original excavator, imagined a relatively restrained composite of sympotico-literary activity: he grouped the Callimachus epigram with a statue of the Muse Urania (now thought to be Hygea) and one of Melpomene to stage Maecenas as a plausible patron of the muses and doyen of the Auditorium.[145] How should we imagine the activities on the inside? Serene classicizing or Dionysiac frenzy? Or some combination of the two?[146] The interior décor and the rich haul of sculptures found in the environs of the gardens cannot be interpreted, it seems, without pronouncing on Maecenas's aesthetic allegiances.

What to make of the unmistakably Dionysiac motifs that border the niches along the straight walls of the Auditorium: Silenuses riding on donkeys, raving

143. *Eleg. in Maec.* 1.33–36.

144. See also Mart. 10.20(19), discussed above, p. 336.

145. Häuber 1983: 207. Häuber (2011) would like the so-called Calliope statue found in the Horti (MC 1824) to be teamed up with the four "Muses" now in the Prado to reconstitute a lost tableau: the contest of the Muses and the Pierides, commissioned by Maecenas.

146. La Penna 1995.

Maenads, a marine thiasos and a thyrsus-waving Bacchus? Sculptural finds also include dancing Maenads, a stunning giant rhyton (drinking horn) engraved with a miniature maenad in relief, reliefs of satyrs in a rural shrine, and a lifesize statue of flayed Marsyas, his raw flesh gruesomely suggested by purple pavonazzetto marble. From these, Stéphanie Wyler has argued for a strongly Dionysiac element in high Augustan art, both as counterbalance to Augustan classicism and as a specific indicator of Maecenas's taste: "Admittedly these images were much in fashion at the time, but this does not rule out that they were highly significant in designing the aesthetic program of the gardens of Maecenas."[147] Claiming some leeway, given that the painted frieze dates from the time of Tiberius or later, she concludes: "The Dionysiac scenes are perfectly appropriate for the context of a *triclinium-nympheum* frequented by Augustan intellectuals from Maecenas' time as well as Tiberius', in the middle of a garden filled with sculptures of the Dionysiac world, Muses and poets."[148] That said, Apolline sculptures would be no less "appropriate", while a Marsyas, reunited with a Laocoön, would suggest an overwhelming taste for the Hellenistic baroque or grotesque. In any case, Maecenas cannot take full responsibility for what survives.

Similar decisions about framing need to be made when it comes to displaying the artefacts from the site. In 1903, sculptural finds from the Horti Romani were chosen by Rodolfo Lanciani to be housed in the Palazzo dei Conservatori. Originally, they were crowded into the now-demolished "Octagon Room", but since 2006 the Horti have occupied their own tranquil suite, where the cultural importance of these grand estates is newly emphasized in the accompanying labels. The Horti Maecenatiani finds, the cream of Lanciani's selection, occupy three of these rooms in an intimate enfilade that suggests an "upward" progress, from rustic and Dionysiac to classically Attic to stately and divine:

Room 1: steles of rustic scenes with satyrs, shrines and trees; a mosaic of Achilles and Orestes; three portrait busts (often identified as poets); the head of an Amazon; a dancing Maenad (figure 9.8); Marsyas; the splendid rhyton (suggesting sympotic activity) in the centre (figure 9.9).

Room 2: three statues of Muses; four archaic herms of caryatids; a charioteer reassembled from scattered fragments; a porphyry hunting dog (suggesting aristocratic recreation) in the centre.

Room 3: a female figure carrying a peplos; Attic funerary steles; Hercules fighting; Hygea; Demeter; Eros/Thanatos.

147. Wyler 2013: 544.

148. Wyler 2013: 549. Ling (1995) concludes that there is no strong tendency for Roman dining rooms to contain Dionysiac decoration.

FIGURE 9.8 Sculpture of a Maenad, Horti Maecenatiani display, Palazzo dei Conservatori, Rome.
*Source:* Author's own photo

After the crush of the Octagon Room, the arrangement is suggestively sympotic: seven to nine items per room, with an appropriate centrepiece in two
of them. For Elizabeth Fentress, who reviewed the new galleries in 2007, the
sculptures speak of a conventionally "classicizing" taste for fifth-century Athens: "The galleries showing the Horti of Maecenas . . . reveal the collector's
strong preference for the Attic, either real or re-elaborated by Augustan crafts-
men . . . a taste Maecenas clearly shared with Augustus."[149] An exception is the
green porphyry dog in Room 2, which "strikes a rare Egyptianizing note". From
this, Fentress concludes that Maecenas was not exactly swept up in the vogue
for Egyptomania after Actium: he "preferred Neo-Attic originals with Dionysiac themes", like the marble rhyton. Looked at objectively, however, the display represents nothing more than a broad cross-section of different sculptural

149. Fentress 2007.

FIGURE 9.9 Rhyton, Halls of the Horti Maecenatiani, Palazzo dei Conservatori, Rome.
*Source:* Author's own photo

styles and themes—typical, perhaps, of any grand Roman garden.[150] In the end, it is impossible to know where the sculptures belonged, how old or representative they are, how conventional or how idiosyncratic, or indeed whether they were ever personally chosen by Maecenas.[151] One thing is certain: the new ensemble in the Conservatori is bound to shape future assessments of Maecenas's tastes as collector and connoisseur.

150. Andrew Stewart (2006: 151) speculates that Laocoön, found near a Homer and a purple Marsyas ("a copyist's favorite", 142), "could suggest a wider sculptural program". For the category of "Neo-Attic", see Huet and Lissarrague (2005). Elsner (2006) and A. Stewart (2006) seek to extend the definition of "classical" to embrace other canonical styles such as Pharaonic Egyptian and Hellenistic (tragic) baroque.

151. Stuart Jones 1926: 155.

## Maecenas in the Garden

The sun, nearing its evening disappearance behind the grey garden wall, the great row of sheltering beech, the distant Burren hills, shines with a special warmth as it seems on the colossal marble bust of Macaenas [*sic*] at the end of the flower bordered gravel walk. Kiltartan tradition says this image was carried across Europe on wagons drawn by oxen; but it is likely the width of the land between its birthplace and an Italian seaport is a truer measure of its journey; and I know not from what harbour in Ireland it was carried to its resting place here.

In another garden, a thousand miles and two millennia distant, Maecenas still stands as figurehead for a legendary literary circle. The words above come from *Coole*, a short reflection by Augusta, Lady Gregory, on her house, Coole Park in County Galway, published in 1931, some decades after her heyday as literary hostess to the most celebrated figures in Irish poetry, drama and art.[152] Ten years later, Coole was demolished. But its green woods and flocks of water-birds have been immortalized by W. B. Yeats, who visited in 1896 and ended up staying two months:

> The trees are in their autumn beauty,
> The woodland paths are dry,
> Under the October twilight the water
> Mirrors a still sky;
> Upon the brimming water among the stones
> Are nine-and-fifty swans.
>
> (W. B. YEATS, *THE WHITE SWANS AT COOLE*, 1919)

By 1920, according to Danish-American visitor Signe Toksvig, the chatelaine was elderly and living alone. She still proudly showed off her "Autograph Tree", a vast copper beech on whose trunk were scratched "monograms that cover the whole Irish literary revival":[153]

> I cannot remember them all. There was "G.B.S." for George Bernard Shaw,—the boldest letters of them all,—and modest "J.M.S." for Synge, a "W.B.Y.", for Yeats, a "J.B." and a small donkey for his brother Jack, a "D.H." for Douglas Hyde, and "A.E." for George Russell, a new white "L.R." for Lennox Robinson, an "A.J." for Augustus John, and others and others and others. (Toksvig, quoted in Pihl 1994: 367)

---

152. Gregory 1931: 39.
153. Pihl 1994: 364–72: "A visit to Lady Gregory".

Beyond that, a door opened to reveal a legendary sanctum, also familiar from Yeats's poetry:

> Then we went to the big gate at the end of the garden, and in it there was a little door that I hadn't seen before, and near the door hung a large key, and the key opened the door. We were in the Seven Woods of Coole.

Today, Coole is a public park, free for all. Visitors can tramp its damp woodland paths in search of the colossal bust that Lady Gregory mentions, shipped from Italy by a nineteenth-century ancestor and placed in a natural arbour at the far end of the garden (figure 9.10a).[154] It is a copy of a Luna marble bust excavated at Carsulae on the Via Flaminia around 1830 and identified as Maecenas on the basis of its likeness to the gem attributed to Dioscorides.[155] Lauded at the time in a frothy tribute by Pietro Ercole Visconti, the find was later dismissed as a seventeenth-century forgery.[156] It is currently in storage in the Palazzo dei Conservatori (figure 9.10b). As we have seen, Thorvaldsen's two marble copies ended up in Arezzo and Naples.[157] In 1837, Pietro Manni, the excavator, presented a third copy to the British Association for the Advancement of Science, based in Liverpool.[158] This was kept in the first-floor gallery of the Liverpool Institute until the school closed in 1985 and its contents were sold, at which point the bust mysteriously disappeared.[159]

Toksvig records stumbling on the Gregory bust unexpectedly:

> Up the garden, on the other side I discovered a sort of shrine of dark bending boughs and clustering ivy screening a Roman bust—Virgil, I thought, or Quintus Horatius Flaccus, set there by eighteenth century admiration. A little further on I met Lady Gregory, red-cheeked, brown-eyed, black-robed, with a nice housewifely basket on her arm. She gave me a bunch of grapes. Encouraged by this into asking questions, I said, "Would you mind telling me the history of that bust over there?" "Not at all," she answered,

---

154. The bust was transported from Italy sometime in the 1830s by Richard, second son of Robert "Nabob" Gregory, a director of the East India Company, who had built the house in 1770. Anne Gregory (Smythe 1995: 12) recalls that it also spent many years in a large foaling box in the stables. See ibid. p. 17 for a photograph of the bust in transit.

155. Bernouilli 1882: 242; the identification was dismissed by Ashby and Fell (1921: 173) and Stuart Jones (1926: 169; no. 23, pl. 57).

156. P. Visconti et al. 1837.

157. See p. 12 above.

158. See p. 12 n. 65 above.

159. As Jim Lycett narrates: "The Liverpool Institute High School's Artefacts", Liverpool Institute High School for Boys, September 26, 2011, http://www.liobians.org/building/artifacts1 .html. See also Tiffen 1935: 166–67.

FIGURE 9.10 Busts of Maecenas: (*a*) Coole Park, County Galway, Ireland;
(*b*) Capitoline Museums, Rome, Inv. MC 1097/S.
*Sources:* AKG-Images

> "that's a bust of Maecenas. We used to have him in the little bathroom
> downstairs, and got very tired of him there, and so we put him outside."
> (Toksvig, quoted in Pihl 1994: 367)

Thanks to his owner's change of mood, Maecenas was transferred to a chilly
grove in the grounds. In *Coole*, Lady Gregory records in loftier strains how the
bust (inscribed MŒCENAS on its base, but to her always an honorary Irish-
man: *Mac-aenas*) was borne in triumph by four men to its present site:

> As if exhausted by such travel it found a resting place within our dwelling
> house for many years, until some awakening of energy, or it may be a mem-
> ory of Ben Jonson's—"Rome's past age when both her Kings and Consuls
> held the plough or garden'd well",—was the cause of its removal to the
> garden one summer day. (Gregory 1931: 39)

Among the bystanders was "Martin Ross" (of Somerville and Ross fame), but to Lady Gregory's regret the episode did not inspire her next novel. A specialist in Irish folklore herself, Augusta Gregory appreciated the simpler power of rural gossip to magnify and mythologize its surroundings. Gratifyingly, an old man turned up at Coole asking to see the image of one he had heard was "the second strongest man in the world".[160] The locals, as she put it, "had long ago created or enriched tradition round the memory of that old owner of Coole who had brought this and other Italian treasures to his western home. 'He had a room of gold,' it is said, 'that used to be turned over with a shovel'".[161]

It was Lady Gregory herself who did the heavy spadework of enriching the soil of Coole. Even these affectionate, informal accounts show something familiar happening. Maecenas, bowered in his ivy-clad grove, is conflated with his poets, Virgil and Horace. At the same time, his image is overlaid on that of its Grand Tour purchaser ("He had a room of gold . . ."). And, silently but emphatically, he functions as a figurehead for the activities of the current owner. The Roman model of "Kings and Consuls [who] . . . garden'd well", activated in Virgil's *Georgics*, fits both the ancient patron and the modern one. Kings and trees are united in Lady Gregory's vision of her role as hands-on nurturer of talent and feeder of riches back into the soil: "[She] cares for the seven woods in a very practical way, and she showed me groves of young trees and saplings she had planted. 'Nearly all my book royalties grow into trees,' she said. I liked the commonsense streak in her."[162] The stewardship of trees, like that of poets, is likewise imagined as conducive to cross-fertilization and idealized sociability: "These woods have been well loved, well tended by some who came before me, and my affection has been no less than theirs. The generations of trees have been my care, my comforters. Their companionship has often brought me peace."[163]

W. B. Yeats, Augusta Gregory's favourite poet, played an equal or even greater part in melding elderly chatelaine with ancient patron.[164] "Coole Park, 1929", written two years after the estate was sold to the Forestry Department, is composed in *ottava rima*, a metre associated with Renaissance court poetry. It remembers the group of poets as tuneful flitting birds, now flown from a hidden garden where the air was once filled with "intellectual sweetness". The "laurelled head" of a presiding genius that seals the poem stands ambiguously either for (the nicely named) Augusta or for Maecenas—or even for Yeats himself:

160. Gregory 1931: 39.
161. Gregory 1931: 40.
162. Toksvig, quoted in Pihl 1994: 368.
163. Gregory 1931: 38.
164. Bradley 2011: 69: "Yeats played Horace to Gregory's Maecenas."

I meditate upon a swallow's flight,
Upon an aged woman and her house,
A sycamore and lime tree lost in night
Although that western cloud is luminous,
Great works constructed there in nature's spite
For scholars and for poets after us,
Thoughts long knitted into a single thought,
A dance-like glory that those walls begot.

There Hyde before he had beaten into prose
That noble blade the Muses buckled on,
There one that ruffled in a manly pose
For all his timid heart, there that slow man,
That meditative man, John Synge, and those
Impetuous men, Shawe-Taylor and Hugh Lane,
Found pride established in humility,
A scene well set and excellent company.

They came like swallows and like swallows went,
And yet a woman's powerful character
Could keep a swallow to its first intent;
And half a dozen in formation there,
That seemed to whirl upon a compass-point,
Found certainty upon the dreaming air,
The intellectual sweetness of those lines
That cut through time or cross it withershins.

Here, traveller, scholar, poet, take your stand
When all those rooms and passages are gone,
When nettles wave upon a shapeless mound
And saplings root among the broken stone,
And dedicate—eyes bent upon the ground,
Back turned upon the brightness of the sun
And all the sensuality of the shade—
A moment's memory to that laurelled head.

(W. B YEATS, "COOLE PARK, 1929")

Unmoving "compass-point" to the poets who whirl around her, Lady Gregory appears in somewhat faint relation here to her more active protégés. For Yeats, her evolving status as co-author (of several of his plays) and independent literary creator complicated the recognized system of mutual exchanges and debts—money/fame, leisure/art—that traditionally circulates between artist and patron. As James Pethica has pointed out: "If a patron is independently accomplished, the artist can no longer feel that his monetary debts are repaid by shared or reflected creative acclaim; and if the patron is also a collaborator, a new category of debt arises within the creative realm to add to that of the economic."[165] After reading Castiglione's *The Courtier* and visiting Urbino with Lady Gregory, Yeats consciously modelled his patron on the Duchess of Montefeltro, a dominant woman remembered as a muse rather than an active participant in her own circle.[166] While Pethica ascribes the anomaly of patrons whose influence is both celebrated and circumscribed by their gender, there is much here that recalls the Augustan poets and their suppression of Maecenas's creative energies in favour of a more passive function: as their prop (*columen*), ornament (*decus*) or constant presence (*tuque ades*).

Like the Augustan poets, Yeats aestheticizes privilege, minimizing the wealth that safeguarded poetic autonomy at Coole and sublimating it into ethereal and generalized "riches". He elides the "aged woman" with her estate, so that credit for begetting the poets' "dance-like glory" goes more comfortably to the walls and rooms of a great house than to the individual whose material gifts the poem gestures so inadequately towards repaying.[167] "A Prayer for My Daughter" enshrines a similarly patrician model of patronage as spreading tree or cornucopia, modelled equally on Virgilian pastoral and on Yeats's own experience at Coole, a calm space protected from everything noisy, popular and ordinary:[168]

And may her bridegroom bring her to a house
Where all's accustomed, ceremonious;
For arrogance and hatred are the wares
Peddled in the thoroughfares.
How but in custom and in ceremony
Are innocence and beauty born?
Ceremony's a name for the rich horn,
And custom for the spreading laurel tree.

(W. B. YEATS, "A PRAYER FOR MY DAUGHTER", FINAL STANZA, 1921)

Serene and dignified as this environment sounds, it was maintained, as many have pointed out, on the back of brutal local suffering and against a troubled political background. Anglo-Irish landowning and the traditional

165. Pethica 1992: 61; influenced by Marcel Mauss's concept of gift exchange as both binding and competitive.

166. Pethica 1992: 78–79.

167. See Pethica (1992: 81–87) on the poem's vexed process of composition; in a letter, Lady Gregory releases Yeats from his monetary debts as she reminds him of them.

168. That Maecenas was in the poet's thoughts is suggested by a deleted stanza referring to "an echo in the wall / Above Maecenas' image".

tenant system were in decline thanks to the slaughter of the First World War, new British land legislation and the growing threat of violence. In 1921, returning with friends after a tennis doubles match, Robert Gregory's widow Margaret was the only one of the quartet to survive assassination by the IRA. The old ways were ending, so Yeats's dirges for patrician Ireland suggest.[169] As for the idyll that was Coole, it was founded on an outdated, or rather timelessly idealized, version of social relations: "Pastoral depends on the fiction of a social unity in which the interests of the wealthy and the poor are mutual and interdependent and the landed gentry who occupy the big house are guarantors of civilized ease and apolitical culture."[170]

In the corporate age, Coole Park and its portrait bust have continued to fuel nostalgia for an ideal enclosure that embraces productive artists together with their aristocratic protectors. In "From Maecenas to MacAlpine", a lecture published in a collection of essays on Irish architecture, Seamus Heaney treats Coole and its genius loci as emblems of a lost compact—classical in origin and form—between architects and patrons, one that harmoniously integrated beauty and wealth, before estate owners sold out to greedy developers:

> Maecenas in Coole Park. The classical head in the *hortus conclusus*. The image of the patron in the demesne of the landlord. This whole set of correspondences and associations is one which may well have become eroded in the Ireland of the 1980s, but it remains as an enduring emblem of the covenant which architects must surely still observe, a covenant with classical achievements, with powerful patrons, with images of order, with projects of salutary beauty and force. (Heaney 1989: 69)

Heaney is ready to admit that his model of benign aristocracy is a tendentious one: "A Marxist would maintain that the walled enclosure as an image of the good place where high civilisation is in flower is nothing but a mystification of the facts."[171] Maecenas, he recognizes, stands not just for "the possibility of a benevolent link between power and art, between imperium and imagination", he also represents "a hierarchical system of privilege between haves and have-nots".[172] Yet Heaney goes on to propose that the grand artistic products of a secure elite, driven by a coherent vision, belong to all of us—just as more modest vernacular buildings do, once age and naturalization in the landscape have turned them into "objects with emotional, historical and cultural force".[173] By

169. Bradley 2011: 69.

170. Bradley 2011: 69. Contemporary reports speak of strained relations between the Gregorys and their tenants, a far cry from Lady Gregory's "sanitized" accounts (Pethica 1992: 88n6).

171. Heaney 1989: 70.

172. Heaney 1989: 69.

173. Heaney 1989: 71.

contrast, contemporary architecture has lost its sense of sacred space, its focus (in the Latin sense of "hearth"): the concentric relationship between dweller, dwelling and outside world.

A contemporary American poet, Gibbons Ruark (b. 1941), takes a much more detached glance at Anglo-Irish patriarchy:

> In this garden now without a house to care,
> They quarreled or conspired beneath the hedges,
> The dead whose books were all they bought of heaven.
> Where the stiff-backed patroness strolled in the twenties,
> A great patron's head ennobles the scene.
> Once, and not from a heart too delicate
> For blood's obscenities, he was so moved
> Against some purge of Caesar's as to flirt
> With his own beheading, flinging these words
> Over the crowd still breathing in the stench
> Of retribution: "Break off, butcher!"
> Fast friend of poets, soldier, counselor,
> West of your head a great tree stands, its coppery
> Leaf cloud stirring like a thought to break off butchery.

> ("WITH THE BUST OF MAECENAS AT COOLE"
> [1984] = RUARK 1991: 14)

The sonnet keeps Maecenas's bust as an emblem of aristocratic custodianship, while the rustle of a nearby copper beech (recognizable as the famous Autograph Tree) conjures up the patron's familiar protective canopy. But the like-minded poetic circle that Lady Gregory cherished and Yeats commemorated, "knitted into a single thought", has dissolved into fractious intrigues "beneath the hedges"; the free-standing bust conjures up more sinister beheadings. Ruark evokes Dio's famous anecdote about Maecenas's intervention in Augustus's executions ("Break off, butcher!") to recall the carnage on which imperial paradises are built, a tide that courtiers like Maecenas could only temporarily stem. Heaney's "charmed enclosure", this idyllic Irish garden, is permeated and even maintained by the blood and stench of political violence. Across millennia, patron and patroness are superimposed, the 1920s are mapped onto the 20s BCE, and a consciously entwined legacy is surveyed from a cool distance. Once again, a face in a garden activates thoughts about inclusion and exclusion, quietism and turbulence; a picture comes to life and old gaps are filled in new ways.[174]

174. Toksvig, quoted in Pihl 1994: 366: "The quietude of Coole I shall always remember."

# 10

# The Afterlives of Maecenas

Maecenas: "A gentleman of Rome [,] minion to Augustus the Emperour: and bycause hee was the supporter of great learned men, all fauourers and succourers of learned men be so called."

—THOMAS COOPER, *THESAURUS LINGUAE ROMANAE ET BRITANNICAE* (1578)

I shall not avail myself of the right by which all poets compare their patron to Maecenas.

—VOLTAIRE, LETTER TO THE DUC DE BRANCAS (1716)

Under the rule of Augustus, men of outstanding worth and wisdom always served the state, for who can name greater men of that period than Maecenas and Agrippa? . . . At no time did arts and letters flourish more, for in that age there lived a very large number of writers from whom as from a fountain-head all peoples drew learning.

—KARL MARX, "DOES THE REIGN OF AUGUSTUS DESERVE TO BE COUNTED AMONG THE HAPPIER PERIODS OF THE ROMAN EMPIRE?" (STUDENT ESSAY, AUGUST 1835)

AS RECENTLY AS 1990, it was claimed that the afterlife of Maecenas in Western culture largely remained to be written.[1] At first sight, this seems astonishing: so central a figure, so many imitators? As soon becomes clear, however, the sheer flexibility of the prototype and the abundance of Maecenas lookalikes make the

---

1. Evenepoel 1990: 117: "The later history of Maecenas' *Nachleben* largely remains to be written. Only a few intermittent moments are presently available." I do not have space here to discuss artistic and musical patronage, but have explored Maecenas's architectural legacy in chapter 9 and visual representations of Maecenas in chapter 1.

task extraordinarily unwieldy. It would take several sprawling volumes to include every "Maecenas of Liverpool" and "Maecenas of Cincinnati"[2]—not to mention every "female Maecenas" (Hannah More's term for Elizabeth Montagu), "baby Maecenas" (Hilda Doolittle's name for her lover, novelist Bryher) or "Russian Maecenas" (Vronsky in *Anna Karenina*).[3] It would also be a dull task to record every obsequious address to every Maecenas-like figure in history.[4]

Instead, this chapter takes a more limited range of scenes from the Middle Ages to the present day to illustrate Maecenas's posthumous versatility and the multiple identities he has come to represent: among them, friend to a great ruler, successful practitioner of leisure, and patron of the arts.[5] In restricting my scope to actual citations of his name and identifiable reworkings of classic Maecenas-focused texts, I skim over a far denser historical background of changing patronage relations, political conditions and literary conventions. Some might argue that the name is what matters, along with its talismanic power to historicize personal relationships and personalize links between culture, money and power. Yet in English, at least, "Maecenas" has never been a household word.[6] What is more, the type of patronage he represents—exclusive and private or harnessed to state propaganda—is now out of fashion, tarnished by its historical associations. The aura of mystification, capital and class that surrounds him has made him a Marxist bugbear (despite the warm tribute from a young Karl Marx that heads this chapter).[7] As we will see, "Maecenas" has needed careful repurposing to survive. These days, his name is attached to more democratic, less individualized solutions to supporting the arts and redistributing wealth.

Maecenas's later appearances tend to fall into three categories: biographical, historical and other moralizing assessments; fictional creations (surprisingly rare); and above all, a type-name given to generous patrons—actual or potential, hopefully, gratefully or reproachfully. For all his iconic status as "Über-patron", Maecenas has been identified with some very contradictory notions of what

2. See Tucker 1967; Duval 1986.

3. More 1996: 8–9 ("the female Maecenas of Hill Street"); Hilda Doolittle, in a letter to Marianne Moore; Tolstoy [1877] 2014: 428 (part 5, ch. 9): "'And is it true that this Mihailov is in such penury?' asked Vronsky, thinking that he, as a Russian Mæcenas, should help the artist, regardless of whether the picture was good or bad."

4. McCabe (2016b: 1) notes the high visibility of such dedications (30,000-odd instances in early modern printed books, recorded in Franklin B. Williams's *Index of Dedications and Commendatory Verses in English Books before 1641*, London, 1962), while cautioning that they do not count as evidence of actual patronal relationships.

5. The three main roles listed by Beugnot (1985).

6. Wilson-Okamura (2014: 60–64) contrasts *mesenaatti* in Finnish, меценат in Russian.

7. Marx 1975.

that might mean: a patron who endorses freedom of choice; one who gives ineluctable orders; a "threshold patron"—that is, a conduit to a higher source of support; an exclusive benefactor; an operator across private, semi-private and public spheres.[8] Aristocrats and former slaves, satirists and sycophants, men and women: petitioners have approached him and his surrogates with remarkably divergent agendas. In some periods, his role as ideal friend and adviser to an emperor has been at least as important a cultural template as his role as an artistic supporter. After the ambivalence of the ancient lives, he emerges as something of a paragon, one who fitted comfortably into the coteries and salons of later eras as an exemplary representative of humanistic or anti-establishment values, as well as being the focus of many flattering comparisons. As Richard McCabe writes: "In seeking to model themselves on Horace, both ancient and early modern poets were taking the exception as the rule, but no-one had any interest in debunking so useful a myth."[9]

Maecenas would find a particularly congenial home in Renaissance and early modern court culture. Here he functioned as a role model, a shield for protégés against direct contact with an autocrat, and a mascot for new cultural alternatives to pomp and state business, such as informality, leisure, retreat and sentimental friendship. The seventeenth century saw the first wave of Maecenas biographies, a time when poetic coteries flourished in France and Spain and absolute power served by prominent counsellors developed alongside private patronage—trends that would become institutionalized in eighteenth-century England with the birth of political parties and the expansion of the press as an instrument of mass propaganda.[10] Later, Maecenas's fortunes adjusted to rapid social, commercial and technological change. In the New World, he represented both a decadent hangover from old Europe and a benchmark for the latest standards in consumer style. Even today, when traditional patron–client relationships have been displaced by broader forces—global production, international markets and more transparent employment procedures—and when patronage has shifted from a private or personal activity to charitable foundations, national committees and the state itself, "Maecenas" has proved astonishingly resilient. These days, his name lends its cachet to funding bodies and luxury goods alike.

Picking up the story in late antiquity, we find the imperial debate around Maecenas's character and morals continuing to simmer in the critical scholia to

8. "Threshold patron" is McCabe's coinage (2016a).

9. McCabe 2016b: 33.

10. See Mousnier and Mesnard (1985), Beugnot (1985) and Shoemaker (2007) on the figure of Maecenas in seventeenth-century France; Voisin (2000) on the enduring influence of the "circle of Maecenas".

Virgil, Horace and Juvenal. Porphyrio and Pseudo-Acro (fourth and fifth centuries CE) tend to see through the Horatian rhetoric of friendship to a more transactional patron–client relationship.[11] They also make much of Maecenas's rejection of senatorial dignity.[12] An anonymous fifth-century scholiast, on the other hand, when confronted with the litter-borne forger in Juvenal's first satire, "reminiscent of a recumbent Maecenas" (multum referens de Maecenate supino; 1.66), interprets supinus, startlingly, as "proud [superbus] or dead: dead or more probably proud and bold because of his nobility".[13] Maecenas's haughtiness and arrogance as Augustus's "secretary and chamberlain" (signator ... et cancellarius) would become a tradition in later medieval commentary.

Otherwise, Maecenas's name appears only fleetingly in the Middle Ages.[14] He makes a brief appearance in Osbert de Clare's fulsome Latin panegyric for the Angevin king Henry II, who presided over the so-called twelfth-century Renaissance. Presenting Maecenas in familiar guise as the patron of Horace and Virgil who introduced them to Augustus and rewarded their poems with cash, Osbert hints at similar promotions and compensation for Henry's most exceptional subjects.[15] It is not until the early Renaissance, when miniature courts and literary circles began to proliferate on classical models, and public magnificence became inextricable from self-promotion, that Maecenas once again makes an obvious blueprint for a statesman who was also patron of the arts. In many respects, his post-medieval appearances continue the story of his posthumous fortunes in Rome: swords drawn between "ins" and "outs" and nostalgic lip service paid to an elusive ideal of friendly mediation between artists and those in authority. Maecenas remained associated with sympathetic support for all the arts, not just literature, and the promise of financial generosity, often sublimated in claims of like-mindedness and good taste.

---

11. Porph. *ad* Hor. *Epod.* 1.1: "Non uidetur uerecundiae Horati conuenire, ut amicum se Maecenatis dicat, cum clientem debeat dicere"; cf. Porph. *ad* Hor. *Epod.* 1.31: "donatum sibi in Sabinis fundum a Maecenate Horatius saepe testatus est". See further Costa 2015: 454–56.

12. Costa 2015: 454; e.g., Ps.-Acro *ad* Hor. *Sat.* 1.2.1–2.

13. Costa 2015: 455–56.

14. Holzknecht (1923) 2018: 75–76.

15. Williamson (1929) 1998: 132 (letter 38): "Vir Horatio Maecenas / Amoris laxans habenas, / Suo tempore dilexit / Et in multis hunc provexit / Et Virgilio, venusto / Carmine gratus Augusto, / Auctus est mercede bona, / Ampla satis sumens dona" (A man called Maecenas, relaxing his reins of love for Horace, chose him in his time and promoted him among many. And Virgil, pleasing to Augustus for his charming verse, was enriched with generous funds, having received ample enough gifts from him [the Latin is loose]).

## Maecenas's Renaissance

The Renaissance period, particularly in Italy, offers more frequent sightings of "Maecenas" as a main or subsidiary patron. Not only did smaller courts, supplying papal and imperial ones, function as springboards for ambitious poetic careers—more significantly, patronage relationships were consciously framed by classic scenes from antiquity, especially those staged by Horace, thanks to whom systemic unease between patrons and emerging celebrities features as often as idealized friendship in contemporary discourse.[16] Petrarch goes through all the permutations in turn. Crowned poet laureate in 1341 with the support of King Robert of Naples, he leaned in his epic *Africa* on Cicero's exaltation of the public-serving poet in *Pro Archia* and the recollections there of glory sharing between Scipio and Ennius. In his *Oration*, he recalls that laurel wreaths once belonged fittingly to Caesars and poets alike, partners in fame—yet it is his Daphne (Laura) who truly crowns a poet who already transcends earthly bonds.

When after Robert's death Petrarch transferred his loyalties to the Colonna brothers, Giacomo and Giovanni, in Avignon, he began to register the strain involved in being "almost an equal" (ex aequo prope) to his patrons.[17] In his eighth eclogue (*Divortium*, "Rupture"), he turns to Horace's renegotiation with Maecenas in *Epistles* 1.7 and its metaphors of voluntary enslavement (calling Giovanni "Ganymede", after Jupiter's favourite cupbearer, presumably because he in turn danced attendance on the papal court).[18] More compromisingly "tyrannical" relationships followed, first with the powerful Visconti in Milan, then with Holy Roman Emperor Charles IV in Prague. Looking back over his various experiences in his "Letter to Posterity", Petrarch smooths over his grievances and acknowledges his good fortune. To explain the episodic nature of his ties with his patrons, he invents a narrative of personal integrity under threat: "I derived many advantages and no annoyances from their eminence. I fled, however, from many of those whom I loved a great deal; such love for freedom was implanted in me that I studiously avoided anyone whose very name seemed incompatible with it" (*Seniles* II, 673).[19]

As ever, the imaginative character of the patron was customized to suit genre as well as circumstance. Since satire and pastoral were the ancient *loci classici* for discussions of patrons, appeals to a "Maecenas" functioned as something of a generic badge when those contexts were revived; they did not

---

16. McCabe 2016b: 29–42.

17. Petrarch, *Epistolae familiares* 1.230.

18. Probably recalling Martial 8.55 (56); see pp. 304–306 above.

19. See for more detail McCabe (2016b: 107–20).

necessarily guarantee the lack of patrons they bemoan. By far the most celebrated Renaissance adaptation of Horace's classic attempt to detach himself
from Maecenas (*Epist.* 1.7) is Ludovico Ariosto's first satire. Originally sent in
draft (1517) to his brother Alessandro and friend Ludovico da Bagno, it complains, behind his back, about Cardinal Ippolito d'Este, who has just demanded his client's attendance on an extended trip to Hungary.[20] Ariosto had
concealed his odium well enough in his dedication of *Orlando Furioso* (first
edition 1516) where, echoing Horace's first ode, he calls the cardinal "the ornament and splendour of our age", and also in the fulsome eulogy in the forty-
sixth canto (somewhat undercut by a general lament about the meanness of
most contemporary patrons).[21] In the satire, he grumbles far more frankly
about the discomforts of travel in a great man's retinue, reviving Horace's jaded
comments on the chains that enslave protégés humiliatingly to their patrons.
The end of the poem clearly builds on the Horatian fox and weasel fable (*Epist.*
1.7.29–33) with a startling new image, a guzzling donkey driven to vomit out
its stuffing—the climax of an outpouring apparently more acerbic and bitter
(*acerbo e acro*) than any of Horace's subtler attempts at evasion.

The fact that the satire was not actually published until 1534, long after Ippolito d'Este's death, has only bolstered the assumption that it must have been
shockingly inflammatory: "Horace with the dampers off".[22] For all the
venom, however, the cardinal emerges as something of a tailor-made foil for a
satirist—a no-nonsense, egalitarian patron who has no truck with flattery
("He does not consider his praises, composed by me, as work worthy of any
thanks. . . . If I have praised him in my verses, he says I have done so to please
myself and at my leisure"; 106–8). For his part, Ariosto makes it clear that he
is no ordinary dish-washing servant but a self-standing poet who has received
regular rewards. He even claims that it is not the gifts but his patron's "affection
and good graces" (l'amor e grazia; 132) that he risks losing; he is forced in any
case to admit that the gifts have been generous enough ("Oh, but your lord
has given you . . ." "Yes, I grant you that, enough to make more than one cape";
91–92).[23] The poem is as much about Ariosto's self-construction, then, as an
independent, ungrateful curmudgeon as it is about an indifferent patron. Amid

20. McCabe 2016b: 129: in common with Petrarch's eighth eclogue, the poem "bear[s] witness
to systemic problems in patronal relationships" between the fourteenth and sixteenth
centuries.

21. By contrast with the "villas, farmlands and palaces" (35.25) doled out to Augustan poets.

22. Burrow 1993: 33.

23. The triple print run of *Orlando Furioso*, a poem the cardinal allegedly dismissed as "little
stories", had in any case relieved Ariosto of some of his need for personal patronage, and the
satire marks this shift in his fortunes; McCabe 2016b: 123.

a flood of unctuous eulogies in all periods, such moments of candour and disobedience stand out. In England, John Marston also paraded his credentials as an independent-minded satirist when he dedicated his comedy *Antonio and Mellida* (1602) "To the only rewarder, and most just poiser of virtuous merits, the most honourably renowned No-body, bounteous Mecaeanas of Poetry, and Lord Protector of oppressed innocence, *Do, Dedicoque.*"

Some of the most curious Maecenas-inspired works of this time, continuing in the subversive spirit of Tasso and Ariosto, come from the pen of Cesare Caporali (1531–1601), poet in residence at courts in Rome, Florence and Perugia. Three *terza rima* skits offer light-hearted, often lewd entertainment for the Roman emperors' Renaissance heirs by portraying Etruria's maverick son as prototype for any pretentious courtier-statesman. *Esequie di Mecenate* (*Maecenas' Funeral*, 1578) is dedicated to Francesco I de' Medici, while *Orti di Mecenate* (*Gardens of Maecenas*, 1599), a humorous catalogue of the medicinal herbs, fruit and vegetables imagined growing on Maecenas's Esquiline estate, is offered to Ascanio Della Corna, Marchese di Castiglione, at whose Umbrian lakeside palace Caporali lodged. The *Vita di Mecenate* (*Life of Maecenas*, 1604), also written for Ascanio, is the climax of the sequence, a saga in ten books that conjures a Rabelaisian vision of the civil wars, centred on the Perusine campaign.

Introduced as an ordinary man with a nose and two eyes, ears, arms and legs, just like anyone else, Maecenas soon reveals his true colours as a flamboyant sensualist.[24] While the second triumvirs are busy dividing up the great tart (*torta*) of the world, he is distracted by the delights of the table, vegetable and otherwise, where his refined and adventurous gastronomic tastes are apparently code for ambidextrous sexual proclivities ("sometimes boiled, sometimes roast"; 4.164), such that the deft skinning of a capon (4.169) suggests the peeling back of a foreskin and "eating fatty meat in winter" (4.181) denotes sex with menstruating women.[25] Cannibalizing anecdotes from Pliny, Seneca and others into a parodic life history tinged with all "the corrosive vinegar of the court" (il corrosivo aceto della Corte; 6.3), the *Vita* set the tone for the contentious Maecenas biographies that followed.

More broadly, Renaissance poets loved to echo Martial's and Juvenal's complaints about the dearth of imperial patrons compared with the Augustan Age. Joachim du Bellay's opinion is typical: "Surely if we had Maecenases and Augustuses, Heaven and Nature are not so hostile to our century, that we should not also have our Virgils."[26] In 1589, playwright and satirist Thomas

---

24. See p. 17 above.

25. Caporali even etymologizes Maecenas's name from "dine with me" (ceniate meco; 4.36).

26. Du Bellay (1549) 1966: 132–33; cited by Wilson-Okamura 2014: 61.

Nashe wrote "To the Gentlemen Students of Both Universities" that if contemporary poetry "wanders abroad unrewarded in the mouths of ungratefull monsters" it is because possible patrons are ignoring "the remembrance of *Mæcenas* liberalitie extended to *Maro*, and men of like qualitie".[27] Elizabethan pastoral, with its laments for lost worlds and mirages of miraculous benefactors, was often the setting for such evocations, and, following Martial, tended to import Maecenas, inaccurately, as a patron of the bucolic Virgil. In his third eclogue (1595), Thomas Lodge voices similar discontent:

> Oh were the world so forward to affect
> The high conceits of artists as of yore,
> When least deserts were held in high respect;
> Did wise Maecenas flourish still to adore
> The heavenly lines his Virgil did erect,
> Or he whom Rome admired for wisdom's store;
> Want should not wring good wits, and this our age
> For science, should with theirs, the battle wage.
>
> But now, these frugal patrons, who begin
> To skantle [i.e., stint] learning with a servile pay,
> Make poets count their negligence, no sin:
> The cold conceit of recompense doth lay
> Their fiery fury when they should begin,
> The priest unpaid, can neither sing, nor say:
> Nor poets sweetly write, except they meet
> With sound rewards, for sermoning so sweet.

Lodge's lament draws on an earlier pastoral poem, devoted to "October", in Edmund Spenser's *The Shepheardes Calender* (1579), where Cuddie, a disgruntled rustic, grumbles that he, too, cannot find a patron. "Romish Tityrus" (i.e., Virgil, another poet disguised as a herdsman) had Maecenas to guide his progress from pastoral to epic, but that was long ago:

> But ah, Maecenas is yclad in clay,
> And great Augustus long ago is dead:
> And all the Worthies liggen wrapp'd in lead,
> That matter made for Poets on to play.
> For ever, who in derring doe were dread,
> The loftie verse of hym was loved aye.

(*THE SHEPHEARDES CALENDER*, 61–66)

27. Preface to Robert Greene's *Menaphon* (1589), in Nashe (1958: 3.322).

It is no secret that Cuddie's complaint veils Spenser's own anxieties. The obvious equivalents to Augustus and Maecenas in his time were Queen Elizabeth and her favourite, the Earl of Leicester. But the lack of a direct approach here suggests some obstacle. As so often, Maecenas's name stands in for a perceived deficiency, recalling a ready enabler who took a poet to a higher plane where the ruler stood waiting, on the model of the Virgilian or Horatian career. Elizabeth and Leicester had perhaps been less than receptive to this poet's overtures; the wistful parallel indicates all too clearly that "the Classical template had not been realized".[28]

As his career as poet and public servant developed, Spenser was nothing if not pragmatic in his choice of patrons. His magnum opus, *The Faerie Queene* (1590–96), written during "exile" to Ireland in the train of Arthur Grey, Lord Wilton, was launched, for all its polish, as the product of cultural isolation, "the wild fruit which savage soil hath bred". Dutifully, Spenser made Queen Elizabeth the principal dedicatee. But his return to civilization came with a flourish the like of which had never been seen: no fewer than seventeen additional sonnets, each one addressing a past or potential benefactor. Among these, Sir Francis Walsingham alone, the queen's secretary and spymaster and father-in-law of Sir Philip Sidney (an earlier object of Spenser's attentions, until his death), is honoured with the name of Maecenas:

> To the right honourable Sir Fr. Walsingham knight, Secretary to her Maiesty, and of her honourable priuy Counsell.

> That Mantuan Poet's incompared spirit,
> Whose garland now is set in highest place,
> Had not *Maecenas* for his worthy merit,
> It first advanced to great *Augustus'* grace,
> Might long perhaps have lain in silence base,
> Nor been so much admired of later age.
> This lowly Muse, that learns like steps to trace,
> Flies for like aid unto your Patronage;
> That are the great *Maecenas* of this age,
> As well to all that civil arts profess
> As those that are inspired with martial rage,
> And craves protection of her feebleness:
> Which if you yield, perhaps you may her raise
> In bigger tunes to sound your living praise. E. S.

But Maecenas's legacy can be traced in many of the other dedications, too. Grey himself is called "Most noble Lord, the pillar of my life, And patron of

---

28. McCabe 2016a: 25.

my Muses' pupillage" (1–2). Lord Burleigh is portrayed as overwhelmed by cares of state: "To you, right noble Lord, whose careful breast / To manage of most grave affairs is bent, / And on whose mighty shoulders most doth rest / The burden of this kingdom's government" (1–4). Spenser also engages with some familiar ancient debates: how best to distribute time and effort between statecraft and leisure; the role of the patron in polishing raw material; and the competing claims of ancestry and true nobility, worldly deeds and poetic immortality. As a result, the legacy of Maecenas's divided life as statesman and patron of the arts ends up being diffused across the entire sequence. The queen may be pre-eminent, but her courtiers are appointed "threshold patrons" to her presence. Lacking one reliable patron, Spenser generates a solid insurance policy, a multiplicity of possible "Maecenases" to underwrite her unique but volatile "Augustus". In the event, however, his stratagems were in vain: Walsingham gave Spenser nothing.[29]

Maecenas features occasionally as a dramatic character in this period—though, somewhat unexpectedly, his infinite variety did little to inspire Shakespeare. Another sequined queen takes centre stage in Antony and Cleopatra, leaving him only a cameo role, first as the Rosencrantz to Agrippa's Guildenstern ("Half the heart of Caesar, worthy Maecenas!—my honourable friend, Agrippa!") and then as sounding board for Enobarbus's eye-opening reports from Alexandria.[30] Despite this, aspects of his ancient character shine through: his appetite for pleasure ("Eight wild boars roasted whole at a breakfast, and but twelve persons there. Is this true?"), his shrewd statesmanship ("Give him no breath, but now / Make boot of his distraction: never anger / Made good guard for itself") and his firm hand at matchmaking ("If beauty, wisdom, modesty, can settle / The heart of Antony, Octavia is / A blessed lottery to him").[31] He is also on the receiving end of one of Caesar's most laconically funny lines: "I do not know, Maecenas, ask Agrippa."[32] Only on Antony's death does the man who was himself a mirror to others utter something more philosophical:

When such a spacious mirror's set before him [Caesar],
He needs must see himself.

(ANTONY AND CLEOPATRA, ACT V, SCENE 1, 42–43)

---

29. An early eighteenth-century engraving of Walsingham by Adriaen van de Werff bears the inscription: "Tel que fut Mecenas, apliqué pour Auguste, tel pour Elisabeth devoiié tout entire, on me vit comme lui vigilant, sage, juste, et content comme lui du rang de chevalier."

30. Antony and Cleopatra, act II scene 2, 208–9.

31. Antony and Cleopatra, act II scene 2, 215–16; act IV scene 1, 10–12; act II scene 2, 282–84.

32. Antony and Cleopatra, act II scene 2, 20. Thanks to Julia Griffin for reminding me of this line.

In Ben Jonson's *Poetaster* (1601), by contrast, Maecenas has a far more dynamic role. Here, the literary in-fighting of Elizabethan London is displaced to the Rome of Horace's *Satires*, with its aesthetic skirmishes between genuine poets, on the one hand, and fake "poetasters", on the other.[33] Maecenas and Horace, two joined-at-the-hip men about town, mingle in the streets with Virgil, Gallus, Tibullus and Augustus, while Jonson reworks Horatian scenes crucial for differentiating the poet of taste from the poet with none—in particular, the duel with Crispinus (Hor. *Sat.* 1.4) and the meeting with the Pest (*Sat.* 1.9), now elided with Crispinus. Even more than in the original, these little dramas are conceived as originating inside Horace's head:

> *Hor.* Umph. Yes, I will begin an ode so; and it shall be to Maecenas.
> *Crisp.* 'Slid, yonder's Horace! They say he's an excellent poet:
>     Maecenas loves him. I'll fall into his acquaintance, if I can; I think
>     he be composing as he goes in the street. Ha! 'Tis a good humour, if
>     he be: I'll compose too.

(<small>POETASTER, ACT III, SCENE 1,1–7</small>)

When "Horace" defends Maecenas's house, he offers nothing less than a smooth translation of his own original Latin:

>         Sir, your silkness
> Clearly mistakes Maecenas and his house,
> To think there breathes a spirit beneath his roof,
> Subject unto those poor affections
> Of undermining envy and detraction,
> Moods only proper to base grovelling minds.
> That place in Rome is not, I dare affirm,
> More pure, or free from such low common evils.
> There's no man grieved, that this is thought more rich,
> Or this more learned; each man hath his place,
> And to his merit, his reward of grace,
> Which with a mutual love they all embrace.

(<small>POETASTER, ACT III, 1.250–55 = HOR. SAT. 1.9.48–52</small>)

The remote, idealized space envisaged here—a "detraction-free zone"—contrasts starkly with the rivalrous pit where Caesar's potential protégés (poets and informers alike) squabble, and, by implication, with the minefields

---

33. See Moul (2010: 135–58) on *Poetaster* as a "translated play".

confronted by any Elizabethan author.[34] Jonson's "Maecenas" even starts to blur with his "Horace". First, as if imitating his protégé, he heralds *his* superior, Caesar, as an enlightened friend to high culture:

> Your majesty's high grace to poesy,
> Shall stand 'gainst all the dull detractions
> Of leaden souls; who, for the vain assumings
> Of some, quite worthless of her sovereign wreaths,
> Contain her worthiest prophets in contempt.
>
> (ACT V, 1.33–37)

Then he continues to ape Horace by acting as a suspicious bouncer at Caesar's gate, fending off a vindictive magistrate, Asinius Lupus ("asinine wolf"):[35]

> Caesar doth know it, wolf, and to his knowledge,
> He will, I hope, reward your base endeavours.
> Princes that will but hear, or give access
> To such officious spies, can ne'er be safe:
> They take in poison with an open ear,
> And, free from danger, become slaves to fear.
>
> (ACT V, 8.26–31)

Only the parenthetical "I hope" lets slip a glimmer of doubt about the ruler's reliability.[36]

Meanwhile, Horace himself helps by deflecting Lupus from challenging Maecenas's privileged role as "props and columns of his [Caesar's] safety" (act IV, 8.21–22). He knows that his own protected relationship with his patron shields him, as a critical and outspoken satirist, from full complicity with the state.[37] In minimizing Maecenas's friction with his various associates while hinting at external dangers, Jonson masks a history of systematic ruptures with his own patrons.[38] His Maecenas is an emperor's yes-man, a lubricant between ruler and protégé, a nostalgic reminder of the lost ideals of social harmony,

---

34. Sinfield 1996: 12.

35. Moul (2010: 147–58) points to meaningful allusions here to Horace's dialogue with Trebatius about Caesar's unpredictable ear in *Sat.* 2.1.

36. Moul 2010: 157.

37. As Moul (2010: 157n39) notes, "Horace" reuses Horatian metaphors for Maecenas: *Carm.* 2.17.34 ("columen"); *Carm.* 1.1.12 ("praesidium"); *Epod.* 1.3–4 ("paratus omne Caesaris periculum / subire, Maecenas, tuo?").

38. Sinfield 1996: 3–18.

shared taste and like-mindedness that Horace himself promoted. By contrast, Jonson's *Sejanus His Fall* is a study in the sinister pathology of a court favourite who knows no boundaries; the milder portrait of Maecenas in *Poetaster* is pitted against the monster he might have become as imperialism took hold.

## Maecenas in Seventeenth-Century France

If ever there was a golden age and place for Maecenas's afterlife, it was seventeenth-century France.[39] The conditions were ripe: absolute monarchy, combined with court culture and a wealth of independent salons, together with strong intellectual curiosity about the compatibility of a strong state with support for the arts and the potential for combining life in the public arena with the delights of privacy. Maecenas represented a historical figurehead for contemporary royal counsellors and a focus for more abstract political reflection. For many thinkers, he exemplified "a certain idealized type of relationship between culture and power, predicated on intimate exchanges between sovereign, patron, and client ... part of a larger vision of a society of peace, prosperity, and leisure".[40] Thanks to the effective balance he was thought to have achieved between politics and leisure, he put most of his later imitators in the shade. In political discourse, he was often pitted against either his military counterpart Agrippa or the darker Sejanus, especially following the assassination in 1618 of Louis XIII's favourite, Concino Concini, and the rise of Cardinals Richelieu and Mazarin as royal deputies.[41] Pierre Perrin dedicated his translation of the *Aeneid* to Mazarin, including some pertinent reflections on his own time:

> In effect, Sir, the famous century of this grand author, does it not seem to have come around again in the present? Is Paris not now a Rome triumphant, like her enormous in population and territory, like her queen of cities, mistress of nations, capital of the world? Is our monarch not a nascent Augustus, in his first years already the most victorious, already the most august of kings? And your eminence, sir, are you not a faithful Maecenas, like him a Roman, like him the most grand and the most cherished minister, and the sacred depository of his secrets and his power? To complete these illustrious connections, does not Heaven require for France a French Virgil?[42]

39. Mousnier and Mesnard (1985) call it "L'âge d'or du mécénat"; Beugnot 1985.

40. Shoemaker 2007: 48.

41. Amstutz 2011.

42. M. P. Perrin, *Leneide de Virgile fidellement traduitte en vers heroiques avec le latin a costé* (Paris 1664), fos. 31r–v; cited in Kallendorf 2007: 12.

One might assume that Maecenas's reputation would only benefit from the Tacitists' demonization of Sejanus, archetype of the powerful favourite ("Grand-Mignon") in many a political agitator's treatise and pamphlet war.[43] However, Sejanus's rapid rise and fall also lent itself to tragic dramatization, with the result that he was sometimes surprisingly cast as a sympathetic figure, the hapless victim of tyranny.[44] Meanwhile, Maecenas, less dramatic all round, made fewer fictional appearances, but was swept up into the general hostility to favourites; for example, in the distinctly ambivalent assessment of Nicolas Coeffeteau in his *Histoire romaine* (1680) or in this guarded verdict on his symbiosis with Augustus, from Jean Puget de La Serre:[45]

> Augustus loved Maecenas because Maecenas made Augustus loved; and as the virtue of this illustrious sage was heroic, it became necessary that this great Hero venerated him; and the special esteem that he had for this virtue obliged the entire world to venerate him especially.[46]

Parisian salons, little courts in their own right, were sites of independence, withdrawal and experimentation where even the pursuit of luxury could be justified as a laboratory for modelling human improvement. At the same time, they did not exist in a complete vacuum from politically motivated court patronage.[47] In this special configuration of circles, Maecenas found a place as a figure of "linkage and connection", socially and ideologically, who guaranteed "the articulation between public and private, politics and culture, republican past and imperial future".[48] As it happens, two authors who showed a strong interest in Maecenas—Jean-Louis Guez de Balzac and Madeleine de

43. Pierre Matthieu, historian to Louis XIII, wrote a novel, *Aelius Sejanus* (1617), and Cyriacus Hardesheim (Herdesianus) a political biography, *Sejanus Grand-Mignon seu De ortu et occasu aulicorum. Problema aulico-politicum posthumum ex analectis praelectionum ad Tacit lib. 14 annal. in. pr.* (1640).

44. In Cyrano de Bergerac's *La mort d'Agrippine* (1654), Agrippina survives, and Sejanus dies tragically; cf. Jean Magnon's *Sejanus* (1647). Amstutz (2011: 342n11) claims that Jonson had little influence on French Tacitism since he was not translated until the eighteenth century.

45. Coeffeteau 1680: 1.481–92. Maecenas has a walk-on role in Jean Mairet's *Marc-Antoine ou la Cléopâtre* (performed 1635, pub. 1637) and informs the figure of Cinna in Corneille's tragedy of that name; Amstutz 2011.

46. Puget de la Serre 1664: 107: "Auguste aimait Mécène, parce que Mécène faisait aimer Auguste: et comme la vertu de cet illustre sage était heroïque, il fallait de nécessité que ce grand heros l'eût en véneration; et l'estime particulière qu'il avait pour elle, obligeait tout le monde à l'estimer particulièrement."

47. Fumaroli 1985: 8.

48. Shoemaker 2007: 45.

Scudéry—belonged to the same salon, that of the Marquise de Rambouillet. In Guez de Balzac's biography, *Mecenas* (1644), dedicated to Madame de Rambouillet, the spotlight is as much on Maecenas as friend and spin doctor to Augustus as it is on his role as patron to Horace and other poets.

*Mecenas* opens with a typical antithesis, influenced by Tacitus (*Ann.* 14.53) and the Plutarchan tradition of parallel lives, by pitting the "bon capitaine" (good captain) Agrippa against the "habile courtisan" (clever courtier) Maecenas.[49] Far from being Tacitus's Machiavellian figure, Maecenas comes across as a guileless amateur endowed with "pleasant social skills" (des vertus douces et sociables): "the most perfect gentleman of his age, who had nothing about him that was not carefully shaped by nature and polished by literature and experience of the world".[50] Guez de Balzac seems to be reproducing the soft-focus view of the *Elegiae*, in particular the alignment of Maecenas's serene temperament with the Roman people's inclination to embrace the pax Augusta:

> In place of freedom, which now seemed like an illusory pleasure to them, they embraced peace, which they took to be the highest of goods. Everyone was glad to have a little leisure after so much misfortune, and sweet idleness insinuated itself so easily into their souls that frankly they would not have returned to their past lives if Augustus had offered them the choice.[51]

Against this backdrop, Maecenas could be seen to have pulled off the twin feats of calming Augustus and making his subjects receptive to tyranny: "Equal parts confidant, confessor, image consultant, and psychotherapist . . . a veritable partner in power, a kind of imperial "alter-ego'".[52] This oxymoronic figure who balanced frank-talking intimacy ("familiarité piquante") with mildness in his dealings with his sovereign usefully linked ancient ideals with their humanistic revival in contemporary France.[53] He could be credited, for example, with having launched a model of intimate friendship of the kind

---

49. Beugnot 1985: 286.

50. Guez de Balzac 1664: 176 = 1995: 140: "le plus honnête homme de son temps, et n'avait rien en sa personne que la nature n'eût formé avec soin, et que les belles lettres et le grand monde n'eussent poli".

51. Guez de Balzac 1664: 73 = 1995: 138: "Le repos, qu'ils crurent être un bien essential, leur tint lieu de liberté, qui ne leur sembla plus qu'un plaisir de fantaisie. Chacun fut bien-aise d'être de loisir, après tant de fâcheuses affaires; et la douceur de l'oisiveté se coula si agréablement dans leur âme qu'ils n'eussent pas voulu de leur première condition, quand Auguste la leur eût voulu rendre de bonne foi."

52. Shoemaker 2007: 44.

53. Guez de Balzac 1664: 81 = 1995: 144; Shoemaker 2007: 44.

recently recreated on classical lines by Montaigne with La Boétie (*Essais* 1.28).[54] Guez de Balzac spoke from a superior position about "Maecenas, of whom so many people speak, without knowing him".[55] Equally, Maecenas could be said to have lived out the happy medium of social interaction prescribed by Aristotle in the *Nicomachean Ethics*, while appearing to pioneer fashionable modern virtues such as "familiarité", "politesse", "negligence" and "conversation". He knew how to manage leisure productively, despite appearances, in a manner attractive to the doyens of salon culture: "The solitude that he established in the city, and the shade of his gardens, kept half of his virtue hidden. His activities were concealed by the outer appearance of indolence."[56] Indeed, it is assumed that were Maecenas transported from Rome to modern Paris, he would instantly choose to take up residence at the Hôtel de Rambouillet.[57]

Guez de Balzac's sympathetic, sophisticated portrait is a far cry from a life published shortly afterwards in Latin (*Maecenas*, 1653) by a German contemporary, Johann Heinrich Meibom (1590–1655). Meibom came from a well-known family of physicians; his other works include a treatise *De usu flagrorum*, on the venereal uses of flogging. In composing the life that broke ground for many later biographies, that of Abbé Henri Richer (1746) and its close imitation in English, by Ralph Schomberg (1766), Meibom laments that he has inherited not a complete corpus but a collection of fragments, "torn apart like Pentheus".[58] He has no qualms about supplementing this battered testimony with ancient parallels, including, for example, chapters on Maecenas's early life and education (using a description by Claudian of Stilico to plug the gap), and treating the *Elegiae* (attributed to C. Pedo Albinovanus and printed at the end of the volume) as a reliable source for the dubious war record. He is refreshingly blank on the matter of physique: "I have nothing to say about the bearing and stature of Maecenas."[59] But turning from virtue to vice (following Plutarch in his lives of Cimon and Lucullus), he is "reluctantly" forced to list Maecenas's voluptuous habits and tastes: casual dress, jewels and pearls,

54. Beugnot 1985: 287.

55. Guez de Balzac 1664: 75 = 1995: 139.

56. Guez de Balzac 1664: 80 = 1995: 143: "La solitude qu'il bâtit dans la ville, et les ombrages de ses jardins, cachaient la moitié de sa vertu. Ses occupations étaient couvertes d'une apparence extérieure d'oisivité."

57. Guez de Balzac 1664: 88 = 1995: 150.

58. Meibom 1653: ch. 1.24, p. 7: "quod integrum optarem daemonium illud hominis, non Penthei instar distractum"; ch. 4.20, p. 27, wishing that Varro on placenames had been clearer: "et contextus esset integer, nec mutilus, aut, quod videtur, etiam corruptus".

59. Meibom 1653: ch. 5.41, p. 39: "De corporis habitu aut statura Maecenatis, nihil habeo dicere."

parasites, actors, women, boys, and lax literary style.[60] This is capped by a concerted effort to rescue his subject from wholesale character assassination by Seneca, whom he tries to hoist with his own petard as a walking specimen of luxury and dissimulation.[61] Even Maecenas's notorious taste for donkey meat might, he surmises, have been doctor's orders from the imperial physician, Antonius Musa.[62]

In his preface, Meibom swipes at another contemporary, Juan Pablo Mártir Rizo, for anachronistically moulding his life of Maecenas (*Historia vitae Maecenatis lingua castillana descripta*, 1626, dedicated to the Count-Duke of Olivares) to fit the model of the Spanish court.[63] Mártir Rizo had praised Olivares as a "father of good letters, protector of the muses, defender of philosophy" and minister "of a more august emperor [Philip IV], to whom peace owes greater successes, and war more glorious triumphs" (despite the fact that Guez de Balzac had joked that patrons like Olivares were far too grand to appreciate casual affability).[64] But dedicating his biography to the Bishop of Lübeck (so offering "Maecenas" to another Maecenas, as he quaintly expresses it), Meibom proceeds to plug another of his own works, the *Historia medica, seu Catalogus medicorum*. Indeed, his systematic dissection of Maecenas has a similarly clinical or diagnostic flavour. Guez de Balzac, meanwhile, had a vested interest in using the Ciceronian *otium cum dignitate* he detected in Maecenas's life to dignify his own forced retreat from politics, harnessing an ancient exemplar to argue for the compensations of literature and private *liberté*.[65] As usual, Maecenas offered his observers a malleable template, allowing the powerful to soften their authority and the dispossessed to mask political failure with cultural achievements.

There is often a self-reflexive quality to these lives of Maecenas, many of them fulsomely dedicated to the author's own patron, who is openly compared

60. Meibom 1653: ch. 19.9, p. 119: "habitus laxus et discinctus, caput palliolatum, mollicies in incessu, gemmarum unionumque studium, in histriones, parasitos et pueros amor; tum adulteriorum insimulatio; stilus denique a mollitie nusquam abiens, sed congruens vitae, congenerque".

61. Meibom 1653: ch. 19.20, p. 121 ("Et haec de Maecenatis habitu, incessu, deliciis, voluptatibus, unus Seneca"); ch. 22.2–3, p. 132 ("nam quis, quaeso fuit tandem Seneca, ut vel solius eius arbitrio, stilo et calculo Maecenas stet cadatque?"). Cf. ch. 7.17–18, pp. 54–55, where he defends Maecenas against Seneca's charges of *dissimulatio* (a case of the pot calling the kettle black: "scapha ibi scapha appellatur").

62. Meibom 1653: ch. 26.14–17, p. 165.

63. Meibom, 1653: *praeloquium*: "aulicum is describere sub Maecenatis nomine voluit" (he chose to describe his own court life under the name of Maecenas).

64. Mártir Rizo 1626: fol. 80 and dedication; Elliott 1986: 174.

65. Beugnot 1985: 288.

to the subject under discussion. Maecenas held out an appealing vision of power without power, and harmonious mediation between state and individual. For example, Henri Richer presents his *Vie de Mecenas* (1746) to the recently dispossessed Prince of Monaco, Honoré, Duc de Valentinois, to whom he offers the doubtless hollow consolation that "great captains and wise ministers, who through their valour and their counsel have contributed to the glory of monarchs and the happiness of peoples" deserve no less prestige than rulers themselves. Ralph Schomberg's English translation of Richer (1766) is dedicated to William Pitt the Elder, known as "the Great Commoner" for his refusal of honours. In a blistering review of Schomberg's bland compilation, comic novelist Tobias Smollett likened the book to a watch made of entirely imported parts, "about a hundred and forty-eight pages of as unimportant fluff as any to be met with in the remains of antiquity".[66]

When Madeleine de Scudéry (1607–1701), a learned bluestocking who invented the delicious fantasy map of erotic feeling, "Carte du tendre", departed the Hôtel Rambouillet to preside over a high-minded salon of her own, she became a patron in her own right. Her Société du Samedi would be mercilessly satirized in Molière's *Les précieuses ridicules* and *Les femmes savantes*. I claimed earlier that Maecenas and Livia never appear side by side, but one of de Scudéry's dialogues in *Les femmes illustres* (or *The heroic harangues of illustrious women*, 1642) offers a rare exception. This series of fictional speeches by Sappho, Cleopatra, Lucretia, Zenobia and others reimagines Ovid's *Heroides* in prose, showcasing the rhetorical versatility of a female intellectual (who, ironically, published under her brother's name). Livia claims that conversations with Augustus and Maecenas have equipped her to discuss poetry on an equal footing, but she does not engage her husband directly. Instead, she uses Maecenas as mediator, knowing that he will champion her preference for poetry over buildings, statues and the rewards of empire as the surest route to immortality:

> Conquerors make efforts to erect trophies, build triumphal arches, have their statues put up in public places and engrave magnificent inscriptions on their tombs to immortalize their glory. All those things fall eventually into ruin, they destroy themselves, they bury themselves underground and in oblivion, and their memory perishes with the marbles they have raised.[67]

Maecenas appears against the symbolic backdrop of a secluded ornamental park, a cultivating influence who implanted in his poet-friends both courtly sophistication and a stable environment for their labours:

66. Smollett 1766: 192.
67. De Scudéry 1642: 337–38.

They [poets] have spoken of forests and rivers, because these universal beauties are in the power of all the world. But that does not prevent these same muses who search the woods from walking in a cultivated garden. Art does not spoil nature: it perfects it. And trees regularly planted do not hinder, if I am not deceived, the poets from working under their shade with pleasure and with glory.[68]

In return for her go-between's services, Livia guarantees his immortality (of course, historically a fait accompli):

Yes, Maecenas, you shall reign over the most illustrious of all ages: and if conjecture deceives me not, your name shall be so venerable to posterity, principally among the learned that all those who render themselves their protectors, shall esteem it an honour to bear it. They shall be called the Maecenases of these times, and from age to age, that glory renewing itself every day, your name shall be in the memory and in the mouths of all men, so long as the sun shall give light to the world.[69]

It is easy to see how de Scudéry might latch onto the doyen of an artistic coterie, "cet illustre protecteur des muses" (this illustrious protector of the muses), as a kindred spirit. Dedicating her address "à la gloire des belles lettres" (to the glory of literature), she draws on the authority of ancient Rome to imagine her own future glory. In fact, her precious phrases would suffer the same fate as Maecenas's own arcane literary style. Molière's caricature nails "a society of snobs obsessed with distinguishing themselves from the crowd via an artificially constructed language rich in metaphors, where speech becomes ever more exaggerated into the incomprehensible, hermetic gibberish of heroines Cathos and Madelon".[70] Draw on past glories as she might, the philosophical virtues of de Scudéry's writing and her attempts to rescue women from low intellectual aspirations would wait centuries to be better appreciated.

The race for patronage is pictured quite differently, from the point of view of one of its more frantic participants, in Nicolas Boileau's *First Satire* (Boileau 1666: 1–11):

Il est vrai que du roi la bonté secourable
Jette enfin sur la muse un regard favorable;
Et, réparant du sort l'aveuglement fatal,
Va tirer désormais Phébus de l'hôpital.

68. De Scudéry 1642: 344–45.
69. De Scudéry 1642: 353.
70. Claude Maignien, preface to de Scudéry 2012 (which omits "Livia and Maecenas").

On doit tout espérer d'un monarque si juste,
Mais sans un Mécénas à quoi sert un Auguste?
Et fait comme je suis, au siècle d'aujourd'hui,
Qui voudra s'abaisser à me servir d'appui?
Et puis, comment percer cette foule effroyable
De rimeurs affamés dont le nombre l'accable;
Qui, dès que sa main s'ouvre, y courent les premiers,
Et ravissent un bien qu'on devoit aux derniers
Comme on voit les frelons, troupe lâche et stérile,
Aller piller le miel que l'abeille distille?   (First Satire, 81–94)

It is true that the king's welcome bounty casts a benign glance on the muses,
and preventing his fatal blindness, rescues Phoebus from the hospital. One
ought to hope for everything from so just a monarch, but without a Maecenas what can an Augustus do? And given who I am, living in today's age, who
would want to humiliate himself to support me? And then, how to penetrate
this frightful crowd of starving rhymesters in their overwhelming numbers;
to whom, as soon as his hand opens, the frontrunners flock, to raid all the
goods that the latecomers ought to have, looking just like hornets, a lazy,
sterile swarm, who go to plunder the honey that the bee distils?

This poem conflates and updates some of the most memorable complaints
of ancient Rome: Juvenal's disillusioned émigré Umbricius (*Satires* 3, with
Rome replaced by Paris); Juvenal's own appeal to an emperor (*Satires* 7); and
the anxiety of a Horatian Pest in search of preferment (Hor. *Sat.* 1.9). Boileau
represents the opportunities of his own day as equally limited. While Louis XIV
had embraced the muses and spared many poets from a cramped old age, a poet
still needed a Maecenas to fast-track his progress, which risked being obstructed
by a horde of pest-like rivals, the "hornets" (frelons) who swarmed around the
royal honeypot. Boileau's celebrated outcry—"Mais sans un Mécénas à quoi
sert un Auguste?" (But what use is an Augustus without a Maecenas?)—
acknowledges the role of an intermediary in negotiating potential pitfalls, such
as competition for a monarch's attention, the monarch's other distracting concerns and the limited resources available to needy poets. Underlying the slogan,
however, is a deep-seated belief in the collaborative potential of culture and
power to stimulate great literary moments.[71] Unlike many satirists, Boileau
never considers the downsides of losing one's independence. Having always
had the leisure to write, thanks to a legacy from his father, he was approached
by Louis XIV to abandon his satiric voice for panegyric and then richly

71. Beugnot 1985: 290.

rewarded. Like Horace, on whom he closely based his literary persona, he moved swiftly from disregarded outsider to smug insider.

## To Maecenas

By the eighteenth century, dedications to one's own "Maecenas" had become a cliché. Voltaire mocks the tradition in a letter to the Duc de Brancas (1716): "I shall not avail myself of the right by which all poets compare their patron to Maecenas."[72] In his case, however, the joke is part of the double compliment his letter is delicately negotiating. Trying to persuade his addressee to wave a poem he has written for the Prince Regent (who had exiled Voltaire) before the prince's eyes at a propitious time, he admits him behind the scenes of power, flattering him not just as a protector of the arts and man of taste but also as a peacemaker and intimate friend. Later, Tobias Smollett would scoff at Ralph Schomberg's strained comparison between Pitt the Elder and Maecenas:

> between the minister of an amiable king, ruling over a free people, and favourite of an usurper, whom he persuades to rivet the chains he had already imposed upon his country; between a minister whose eloquence in the senate unites the force of Demosthenes with the embellishments of Cicero, and one whose style was so affected and enervated, that it became the ridicule of his best friends . . . between a minister whose pleasures were never known to break in upon his business, and one whose life was spent in an uninterrupted course of sensuality and effeminacy.[73]

Among a host of bland conventional approaches, there are a few outliers. This late eighteenth-century encomiastic ode by Phillis Wheatley, for example, offers a very different perspective on the unreachability of Maecenas:

> MAECENAS, you, beneath the myrtle shade,
> Read o'er what poets sung, and shepherds play'd.
> What felt those poets but you feel the same?
> Does not your soul possess the sacred flame?
> Their noble strains your equal genius shares
> In softer language, and diviner airs.
>
> While *Homer* paints lo! circumfus'd in air,
> Celestial Gods in mortal forms appear;

72. Voltaire (1877–85) 33.33: "Je ne me servirai point ici du droit qu'ont tous les poètes de comparer leur patron à Mécène."
73. Smollett 1766: 192–93.

Swift as they move hear each recess rebound,
Heav'n quakes, earth trembles, and the shores resound.
Great Sire of verse, before my mortal eyes,
The lightnings blaze across the vaulted skies,
And, as the thunder shakes the heav'nly plains,
A deep-felt horror thrills through all my veins.
When gentler strains demand thy graceful song,
The length'ning line moves languishing along.
When great *Patroclus* courts *Achilles'* aid,
The grateful tribute of my tears is paid;
Prone on the shore he feels the pangs of love,
And stern *Pelides* tend'rest passions move.

Great *Maro's* strain in heav'nly numbers flows,
The *Nine* inspire, and all the bosom glows.
O could I rival thine and *Virgil's* page,
Or claim the *Muses* with the *Mantuan* Sage;
Soon the same beauties should my mind adorn,
And the same ardors in my soul should burn:
Then should my song in bolder notes arise,
And all my numbers pleasingly surprize;
But here I sit, and mourn a grov'ling mind,
That fain would mount, and ride upon the wind.

Not you, my friend, these plaintive strains become,
Not you, whose bosom is the *Muses* home;
When they from tow'ring *Helicon* retire,
They fan in you the bright immortal fire,
But I less happy, cannot raise the song,
The fault'ring music dies upon my tongue.

The happier *Terence*[1] all the choir inspir'd,
His soul replenish'd, and his bosom fir'd;
But say, ye *Muses*, why this partial grace,
To one alone of *Afric's* sable race;
From age to age transmitting thus his name
With the first glory in the rolls of fame?

Thy virtues, great *Mæcenas!* shall be sung
In praise of him, from whom those virtues sprung:
While blooming wreaths around thy temples spread,
I'll snatch a laurel from thine honour'd head,
While you indulgent smile upon the deed.

As long as *Thames* in streams majestic flows,
Or *Naiads* in their oozy beds repose,
While *Phœbus* reigns above the starry train,
While bright *Aurora* purples o'er the main,
So long, great Sir, the muse thy praise shall sing,
So long thy praise shall make *Parnassus* ring:
Then grant, *Mæcenas*, thy paternal rays,
Hear me propitious, and defend my lays.

Note 1. He was an *African* by birth.[74]

("TO MAECENAS", IN WHEATLEY 1773: 9–12)

This poem might read like any other piece of post-Popean heroic verse were it not for the unusual background of its author, to which the single footnote gives a clue. Phillis Wheatley (1753–84) was born in West Africa and bought as a sickly child at the Boston slave market for his wife by tailor John Wheatley, from whom she took her surname (just as his own freedmen, and Petronius's Trimalchio, had taken their names from Maecenas). Educated at her master's expense, Wheatley read Homer via Pope's translation of the *Iliad* and Horace and Virgil in the original. But her precocity was always under suspicion, to the point where she had to be forcibly quizzed on her knowledge of classical mythology in front of a panel of judges. Despite catching the attention of British evangelical abolitionist Selina Hastings, Countess of Huntingdon, who oversaw the publication of her collected poems and then her manumission, and being praised by George Washington, Wheatley ended up a scullery maid and died in poverty.

The frontispiece to Wheatley's collected poems, captioned "Negro servant to Mr John Wheatley, of Boston, in New England", makes it possible to hear something other than conventional politeness in the dedication to Selina Hastings: "By her much obliged, Very humble, And devoted servant, Phillis Wheatley."[75] For Wheatley, the word "patron", left unvoiced in her petition to "Maecenas", would always have two meanings: an artist's protector or a slave's former master. Until recently, her work was dismissed as derivative, often via avian metaphors that make her sound both subhuman and a mere imitator: "songbird of Africa" or "canary in a cage".[76] New interest in Wheatley has focused not just on her anxieties about her African origins but also on her social and literary ambitions: "Knowledge of Wheatley's enslaved status *colours*

74. Wheatley's own note.
75. Wheatley 1773: 4.
76. Greenwood 2011: 160.

(quite literally) judgements about her originality and her relation to the white literary tradition."[77] Classicizing verse functioned as a cultural currency, no less, which moved her up in the world and allowed her voice to be heard, enabling her to challenge on their own terms the humanist, Christian and Republican ideals of the circles to which she had been so tentatively admitted.[78] It also offered scattered parallels for her disadvantaged origins, which she could use to support her appeals.

Even so, it is unclear which of any of Wheatley's real-life patrons is the "Maecenas" she so boldly approaches. Strikingly, she starts by flattering her addressee as an "equal genius", not just a shadowy sounding board for her compositions but somehow "softer" and "diviner", a sympathizer whose experience was entirely caught up with those he supported:

> What felt those poets but you feel the same?
> Does not your soul possess the sacred flame?
>
> . . .
>
> Thy virtues, great *Mæcenas!* shall be sung
> In praise of him, from whom those virtues sprung

This tactic enables her to plead not so much for patronal support as for equal opportunities in relation to her contemporaries.[79] Their hostility and indifference contrasts with the interested attention of an idealized authority figure relied on to offer artists a friendly ear.

Wheatley proceeds to engage with various ancient poets. First of these is Homer, specifically Pope's Homer, conceived as an independent-minded genius whose inspired tones modulated from sublime horror to intimate tenderness. Virgil, by contrast, is seen as a collaborator, a model for Wheatley's more modest symbiosis with her patrons. Yet as soon as she aspires to join this timeless pantheon, a focus on her "grov'ling mind", "plaintive strains" and "fault'ring music" exaggerates both her need for a prop and her distance from the ancient source. It also plays to a prevailing conception of African Americans as abject and incapable.[80] "Here I sit" suggests not just "here in the eighteenth century" but also

---

77. Greenwood 2011: 159.

78. Flanzbaum 1993; Felker 1997.

79. See Greenwood (2011: 169) on equality as a theme of the poem.

80. Greenwood 2011: 153: Wheatley "was fully aware of the cultural presumption constituted by an enslaved African reading and writing about classical themes". Cynthia Smith (1989: 586) claims that only the former interpretation applies. In *Niobe in Distress*, Wheatley characterizes herself as "the last and meanest of the rhyming train"; Cynthia Smith 1989: 583.

"here as a slave oppressed by racial prejudice".[81] Wheatley's final appropriation, that of the comic playwright Terence, as her ancestor and ally is also, as her footnote indicates, racially determined. According to tradition (on the basis of his cognomen Afer), he, too, was an African slave, taken up and launched on the Roman scene by powerful patrons, then wrongly accused of plagiarism.[82]

Another poet is strikingly absent from the list, not just given the title and the lyric form, but also because of his well-known association with a bid for insertion into a canon. Horace, even more consciously than Terence, had paraded his freedman origins. Like him, Wheatley aspires to sublimity and immortality, making it clear that she "considered herself a full-fledged participant in the poetic tradition of Western writing".[83] Her claim to be recreating the spirit of ancient writers is also curiously close to the arguments of *Epistles* 1.19, where Horace appeals to Maecenas to bless his attempt to reanimate Greek texts.[84] And by chance, her name echoes that of Phyllis, Horace's handmaiden, pupil and appointed heir (*Carm.* 4.11.30–31: "meorum / finis amorum" [last of my loves]). Yet the very next poem in her collection, "On Being Brought from Africa to America" (Wheatley 1773: 18), is far more defeatist about the racial prejudices that stood in her way and the sense of exclusion from a patron's "paternal rays" that they engendered: "Some view our sable race with scornful eye, / 'Their colour is a diabolic die.'"

A far more caustic note sounds from another piece from the same century, addressed to the same talismanic name. In a formerly unpublished verse draft from the 1750s, Gotthold Ephraim Lessing, philosopher and author of *Laocoön: An Essay on the Limits of Painting and Poetry*, took time out to compose a skit casting himself and his fellow Germans as "barbarians" who inhabit a new Iron Age relative to classical antiquity. Lessing's imagined "Maecenas" is a barely disguised portrait of Frederick II (the Great), painted here as a chilly ruler surrounded by sycophants (Frederick was in fact a sincere devotee of music and the other arts). Chafing at having to write in praise of an emperor, Lessing assumes the familiar persona of the indigent, humiliated poet. Meanwhile, he introduces an unknown contemporary called Corner, a decadent reincarnation of the Greek lyric poet Anacreon, afflicted by gout and syphilis, whose hospitality comes with strings attached.[85] Corner's voluptuous lifestyle and the allusion to Anacreon (who like Maecenas had a lover called Bathyllus) suggest that he

81. Cynthia Smith (1989: 586) claims that only the former applies.

82. *Vita Terenti.*

83. Smith 1989: 590.

84. Smith 1989: 589.

85. H. Nisbet 2013: 236.

is being conceived as a lesser Maecenas, just one who is further down the pyramid:

### An Mäcen [To Maecenas]

You, through whom Horace once lived, to live without rest, without comfort, without wine, without the enjoyment of a beloved, would have been no life; you, who now live through Horace; for to live without glory in the memory of posterity is worse than to be unknown to them; you, O Maecenas, have left us your name, which the rich and powerful seize, and give away to the hungry scribblers [Du, o Mäcen, hast uns deinen Namen hinterlassen, den die Reichen und Mächtigen an sich reißen, und die hungrigen Skribenten verschenken]; but did you leave us with more than your name? Who in our iron days, here in a country whose inhabitants are still the ancient barbarians from within, who will host a spark of your philanthropy, of your virtuous ambition to protect the favourites of the Muses? How could I not look for a faint imprint of yourself? Looked around with the eyes of a needy man! What sharp eyes! At last I have become tired of searching, and want to pour out a bitter laugh over your replicas [Endlich bin ich des Suchens müde geworden, und will über deine Afterkopien ein bitteres Lachen ausschütten]. There, the regent nourishes a lot of beautiful spirits, and needs them in the evening, when he wants to recover from the troubles of the state through farce, in his comic councils. How much he misses being a Maecenas! Never shall I feel able to play such a low role; even if medal ribbons were to be won. After all, a king may rule over me; he was more powerful, but he did not think he was better. He cannot give me such graces that I should consider worthy of infuriating. Corner, the voluptuary, fell in love with my songs. He considers me his equal. He is looking for my company. I could feast with him daily, get drunk with him for nothing, and in vain embrace the most expensive prostitute; if only I did not respect my life; and wanted to praise him as a second Anacreon. An Anacreon, that heaven has mercy! has the podagra and the gout, and yet another disease which is doubted whether Columbus brought it from America. (Lessing 1922: 1.149–50)

Lessing's aesthetic interests are not hard to detect in the contrast he draws between the original Maecenas and his Iron Age imitators: like his post-Augustan acolytes, they are cast as copies that fall short of an idealized prototype. For this, Lessing coins a term that smacks of connoisseurship: *Afterkopien*, "after-copies" (or, more accurately, "bum-copies"[86]). He fetishizes the first Maecenas by deploring those successors who are not "even a faint imprint" (einem

---

86. As my anonymous referee points out.

nur schwachen Abdrucke) of the original and lack "any whiff of his philan-thropic spirit" (einen Funken von deiner Menschenliebe) but who simply steal his name as an imprimatur for their corrupt activities. In his treatment, the elegant Francophile coteries of Sanssouci are transformed into tense soirées where hungry scribblers snatch sustenance in exchange for poems (in the best satirical tradition: cf. Persius, *Satires* 1). In another poem, "An seinen Bruder" (To his brother), playwright Karl Gotthelf Lessing is addressed as the "darling of Maecenases" (Liebling des Mäcenen). A decade later, in a review of Meinhard's *Essays* "On the Character and Works of the Best Italian Poets" (1763–64), Lessing draws attention to the author's view that the Medici had fostered no great poets because they were too indulgent to their protégés. This strikes an immediate chord: "A remark as acute as it is true, very applicable to the external condition of contemporary German literature, one that should silence forever those scribblers who are loud in their complaints of want of patronage and overrate the influence of the great in tones of fawning flattery."[87]

## Maecenas goes to America

"Without wealth, there can be no Maecenas."[88] With these hard-hitting words, from his essay "Wealth" (1889), the steel magnate Andrew Carnegie urged a new duty, philanthropy, on his more affluent countrymen. The model he adopted was a paternalistic one: rational and strategic giving for the public good, rather than conventional "charity", whose needy beneficiaries could not be trusted to spend their hand-outs responsibly.[89] Yet Carnegie had no wish to go back to the past. That would mean sacrificing "our wonderful material development"—modern institutions like the Cooper Institute and the New York Public Library, which at once enshrined the public-spirited generosity of their donors, ensured their immortality and enabled social progress.[90]

Around the same time, sociologist Thorstein Veblen, better known for inventing the notion of "conspicuous consumption", coined the terms "Maecenas function" and "Maecenas relation". The original context was a comparison between the mechanisms of patronage then underpinning US institutions of higher education (Veblen's own University of Chicago, for example, founded by John D. Rockefeller) and the longer tradition of personal relationships between scholars and their protectors:

87. *Literaturbrief* 332 (review of Johann Nicolaus Meinhard's *Versuche über den Charackter und die Werke der besten Italienischen Dichter*); Lessing 1922: 8.283.

88. Carnegie 1889: 653.

89. Malamud 2008: 110–11.

90. Carnegie 1889: 655.

The scholar under patronage performs the duties of a learned life vicariously for his patron, to whom a certain repute inures after the manner of the good repute imputed to a master for whom any form of vicarious leisure is performed. It is also to be noted that, in point of historical fact, the furtherance of learning or the maintenance of scholarly activity through the Maecenas relation has commonly been a furtherance of proficiency in classical lore or in the humanities. This knowledge tends to lower rather than to heighten the industrial efficiency of the community. (Veblen [1899] 1992: 246–47)

Veblen's analogy between universities and private patronage is a contrived, if idealistic one. He enlists "Maecenas" somewhat awkwardly to support the economic argument for abandoning the humanities in favour of scientific subjects (an early example of its kind).

In both cases, the choice of Maecenas to label a public-facing patron is an arresting one. A symbol of an outdated model of private, artistic Greco-Roman patronage was being deployed in the service of new paradigms, particularly those involving the interface between private wealth and public benefaction. A few decades later, historian Guglielmo Ferrero would find a more appropriate Roman model in the builder of the Pantheon and restorer of the city's waterworks: "Agrippa and Carnegie were moved by the same notions of civic zeal."[91] By contrast, Veblen's assimilation of the patronal activities of a newly moneyed American middle class to traditional aristocratic or feudal connections was no longer very convincing. What's more, the power dynamics in these new-style relationships sometimes reversed the expected hierarchies— for example, in the case of connoisseur Bernard Berenson, a forceful tastemaker, and Isabella Stewart Gardner, his acquisitive but meek Bostonian patron.[92] To this day, philanthropy remains an essential component of US arts funding, whether it stems from individuals, corporations or foundations. But from the beginning it excited suspicion as a potential sweetener that might perpetuate both capitalism and individualism: "Philanthropic gestures were seen by many American workers as [an] attempt to compensate for their economic exploitation by plutocrats."[93]

What place was there for Maecenas among the swamps, prairies and skyscrapers of the New World? His name is invoked surprisingly often in American literature of the late nineteenth and early twentieth centuries, a period of social

91. Ferrero 1914: 26 (cited in Malamud 2008: 110). Cf. Ferrero (1914: 28) on ancient Rome: "Every little city, then, had her own millionaire benefactors, her little Carnegies, her Huntingtons, Morgans, and in miniature."
92. See Fisher 2013: viii–ix ("The Maecenas Relation in High Culture").
93. Malamud 2008: 111.

realignment negatively framed for posterity by modernist authors disillusioned with bourgeois values. For the artistically inclined, a visit to Europe
continued to hold out the promise of the cultural capital Veblen saw as the
finishing "ornament" to American wealth. It often helps to see Maecenas in
the context of stereotypes familiar from the novels of Henry James: the ex-
perienced, cultivated, decadent European in confrontation with the naïve,
materialistic, forward-thrusting American; old versus new money. James's late
novel *The Outcry* (1910) encapsulates in the outrageous figure of "Breckenridge
Bender" the entire band of "robber barons"—self-made butchers, bankers,
steel and railroad men, like P.A.B. Widener, William Walters and Henry Clay
Frick (along with those who built on inherited wealth, like J. Pierpont Morgan,
Isabella Stewart Gardner and Andrew Mellon)—who were busy stripping
Europe of its treasures and shipping them back to form their own world-class
art collections. As Gorman Beauchamp writes:

> Any garden variety plutocrat . . . could build himself a huge mansion, buy
> himself a yacht or private Pullman car, or load his wife up with diamonds
> and pearls; but the supply of Raphaels and Vermeers was finite and small
> and maddeningly hard to come by, so that possession of a trove of such
> pleasures raised one above the ruck of run-of-the-mill millionaires and con-
> ferred a princely status.[94]

In their defence, these pirates could be said to have enabled the westward
spread of cultural capital and eventually widened access to art, since most of
their collections are now on public display.[95]

But where did Maecenas really belong: with the old or the new? Fascinat-
ingly often, his name appears alongside those of Petronius and Petronius's fictional freedman "Trimalchio", a far more obvious role model for American
nouveaux riches, especially when viewed by alienated aesthetes. The qualities
he more usually represents—private, exclusive, European, cultivated, old,
enervated—are never quite the diametrical opposite of stereotypically "American" values. Sometimes he is a focus for successful attempts to combine the
cultural hegemony of Europe with the wealth of the New World; sometimes,
less positively, a symbol of the vulgar fusion of European decadence and American enterprise. More often than one might expect, his figure even merges with
Trimalchio. His glamour was, after all, inseparable from his wealth. As F. Scott
Fitzgerald might have said of him: "His voice is full of money."[96]

94. Beauchamp 2006.
95. Beauchamp 2006.
96. F. S. Fitzgerald 2000: ch. 7, p. 115.

Fitzgerald's *The Great Gatsby* (1925) must vie with *Citizen Kane* for first place as the twentieth century's supreme fictional portrait of the triumph and failure of a self-made man. It is no accident that the novel alludes in passing to both Trimalchio and Maecenas, though it is left to the reader to find the links between the two figures. But first it is worth looking at two short stories from a few decades earlier, both of which also feature versions of Maecenas in relation to the American dream. In Bret Harte's "A Maecenas of the Pacific Slope" (1891), Robert Rushbrook, a self-made man, builds a Californian coastal villa in many instalments, marking his business successes and the upward trajectory of his life: "an exciting though irritating state of transition to something better".[97] Jokingly referred to as "Maecenas", he is more obviously a socially mobile Trimalchio, judging from the author's satire on the villa, with its "pillared pretensions", "a wonderful temple of white and silver plaster, formal, yet friable like the sugared erection of a wedding cake". Even the furniture reeks of new money, having "so much of the attitude of the show-room still lingering about it that one almost expected to see the various articles of furniture ticketed with their prices". Rushbrook's friends have assisted him in procuring old-style knickknacks from Europe and furnishing his library with musty volumes "from the spoils of foreign collections", bound with spanking new leather. Indoors, on the dessert table, nature vies, *Satyrica*-style, with art: pyramids of giant Californian fruits are served on silver dishes, "as outrageous in dimensions and glaring color as any pasteboard banquet". Outside lies primeval America, the "still virgin solitude" of the canyon, absorbing all domestic noise:[98]

> For it was remarkable that even the various artists, musicians, orators, and poets whom Maecenas had gathered in his cool business fashion under that roof, all seemed to become, by contrast with surrounding Nature, as new and artificial as the house, and as powerless to assert themselves against its influence.[99]

While business is good, Mr Rushbrook's protégés have little to complain of, thanks to his reliable spread of investments ("His name was associated with the oldest and safest schemes—as well as the newest and boldest—with an equal guarantee of security"). So long as his largesse flows, they turn a blind eye to his poor taste. Then Rushbrook, who treats every human interaction as a business arrangement, is deceived into underwriting a young chancer's marriage to an outspoken Californian heiress, Grace Nevil (who has tactfully

97. Harte 1891: 242.
98. Harte 1891: 241, 243–44, 245–46, 264, 262, 247.
99. Harte 1891: 247.

rearranged some of Rushbrook's shiny new furniture). As he admits: "Jack Somers has brains, knowledge of society, tact, accomplishments, and good looks: that's HIS capital as much as mine is money."[100]

When Somers's deception is discovered, Rushbrook is isolated by the friends who have no further reason to flatter him ("I grieve to say that the *protégés* and parasites of Maecenas deserted him in a body")[101] and so force him to sell his awful "daubs" at auction.[102] However, there is a happy ending: Miss Nevil returns, offers Rushbrook money, is refused on the grounds of his love for her, and they are swiftly engaged. Unlike *Gatsby*, this parable decisively celebrates the triumph of pioneering grit, native business sense and instinctive good taste over the inherited capital and shady manoeuvres of wily Europhiles.

Nearer to Fitzgerald's heyday, another Maecenas, or rather a "Mrs Maecenas", is transplanted to a campus setting in Kenneth Burke's story of that name, published in 1920 in the *Dial*, a progressive New York magazine.[103] Following the death of her husband, the president of a fictitious American university, a young widow stays on in a determined attempt to sustain the arts. A cultural desert in a rich agricultural area, the university in question cheerfully churns out soccer stars and future leaders of America who will later donate "a sun-dial, or a gate, or iron railing" to their alma mater. Mrs Maecenas craves more satisfaction than is offered by endless cycles of regeneration: "Everywhere, everywhere, typical young Americans were springing up, sturdy tough daisy-minds that were cheerful, healthy, and banal." Among these energetic plants cowers a lone, etiolated aesthete, Siegfried, to whom she unveils the inmost sanctum of her husband's library: a collection of rare early modern editions, along with the later products of decadence, which reflect fin de siècle interest in obscene or late Latin. Bound volumes of Gourmont and Huysmans rub shoulders with the authors they revered, Prudentius and (again) Petronius. Siegfried reacts with mock alarm: "You are worse than a pagan: you are a lover of art. I am scandalized."[104]

100. Harte 1891: 270, 277.

101. Harte 1891: 302.

102. Uncannily close to Petronius's legend of Proculus the ruined auctioneer (*Sat.* 38.11–16), who made a fortune but who, when his pot went off the boil, lost all his friends and was reduced to selling his unwanted possessions.

103. Later included in *The White Oxen & Other Stories* (Charles A. Boni, 1924) and *The Complete White Oxen* (University of California Press, 1868). The story is reprinted in *Harvard Review* 27 (2004) 71–81. I suspect that the name "Mrs Maecenas" derives from Eugene Field's translation of *Epod.* 3, "A Counterblast against Garlic", in *Echoes from the Sabine Farm* (Eugene and Roswell M. Field, New Rochelle, 1891).

104. Burke 1920: 348, 347, 350.

Soon, the couple are meeting regularly for clandestine worship at the shrine of Art, Mrs Maecenas describing their evenings in the catacombs as "something rare and wonderful": "Love, art, death, renunciation, the beautiful—the two of them drank long draughts of these deep red vintages, for they each loved art eloquently." This intimacy seems all too likely to culminate in the neophyte's physical seduction by the high priestess, when the spell suddenly breaks: Siegfried erupts in a pimply rash, exemplifying all too realistically the "glorious unhealthiness of Baudelaire".[105] Kenneth Burke is better known now as a literary critic, philosopher and theorist of rhetoric. His satirical reduction of artistic cult to sex drive in "Mrs Maecenas" reads as a detached and somewhat schizophrenic prelude to his later intellectual involvement with Marxism and his growing belief that interpersonal ploys such as courtship, identification and mystification function as sociological and ideological as well as rhetorical tools. For now, the story's comic ending leaves the old conflict between bohemian and bourgeois values unresolved. "Maecenas" is identified with a lofty notion of art for art's sake and a decadent, Catholic or pagan image of old Europe, out of place in the United States and potentially undercut by corrupt motives.

"It was when curiosity about Gatsby was at its highest that the lights in his house failed to go on one Saturday and, as obscurely as it had begun, his career as Trimalchio was over."[106] F. Scott Fitzgerald's classical education was equally short-lived, but it is hard not to see a meaningful link in a novel whose provisional title was *Trimalchio in West Egg* and which was published following a revival of interest in all things Petronian (three years after the New York obscenity trial of an unexpurgated translation of the *Satyrica* and two years after T. S. Eliot made Petronius's Sibyl's words the epigraph to "The Waste Land").[107]

What is less obvious is how deep the engagement with Petronius goes in this tale of the transformation and fall of James Gatz of North Dakota, told by social climber Nick Carraway, as unreliable a narrator as Petronius's rootless Encolpius.[108] The superficial similarities between Gatsby and Trimalchio are clear enough: their journey from distant origins (Asia and the Midwest) to riches in Naples and New York (via naval speculation in one case and bootleg liquor and fake bonds in the other); their partial success in acquiring a veneer of culture (the books in Gatsby's library may be more "absolutely real" than Trimalchio's, but their pages are still uncut); their joint obsession with the

---

105. Burke 1920: 351, 351, 354.

106. F. S. Fitzgerald 2000: ch. 7, p. 108.

107. Briggs 1999: 226. For the engagement of Eliot, Pound, Lawrence, Huxley and others with Petronius, see Schmeling and Rebmann (1975).

108. MacKendrick 1950.

passing of time; and above all their lavish entertainments.[109] Gatsby's "gleaming, dazzling" Long Island parties closely replicate the menus of Proculus, a legendary Petronian millionaire:[110]

> On buffet tables, garnished with glistening hors d'oeuvre, spiced baked hams crowded against salads of harlequin designs and pastry pigs and turkeys bewitched to a dark gold. (F. S. Fitzgerald 2000: ch. 3, p. 33)

> He used to dine like a king: pigs in blankets, pastry confections, roast fowl, cooks, bakers. Not a human but a fairy prince. (Petron. *Sat.* 38.15)

At the same time, these descriptions capture the differences between the authors: one exquisitely aesthetic, the other matter of fact. Petronius simply lists, while Fitzgerald adds the gleaming surface (garnished, glistening, spiced, harlequin, bewitched) that makes so seductive an appetizer to his narrative of disappointment.[111] True, he leans heavily on Petronius's explorations of a guest's blurred experience of reality and illusion when confronted by an unknowable host.[112] Like Encolpius, Nick feels his way through a world of the senses where not all that glitters is genuine gold but might at any moment turn to dust, like Long Island's symbolic "valley of ashes".[113] But Fitzgerald's novel is a far subtler characterization of a variegated world, one aesthetically overloaded with "many-coloured, many-keyed commotion".[114] Gatsby is fragile (his simulacrum "broken up like glass against Tom's hard malice"), while Trimalchio, like the shatter-free glass he celebrates, remains unbreakable.[115] Emotionally, the gulf between the two men is vast: Gatsby is "no vulgarian, but a romantic dreamer", while the freedman is a cartoon.[116] If Daisy represents for Gatsby the glamour of a "rich, full life", that is what Gatsby represents for Nick.[117] If Fitzgerald's charming "Mr Nobody from Nowhere" is presented more

109. MacKendrick 1950: 309: "These Nabobs, ancient and modern, have in common not only their music and their *objets d'art*, but their parasites, the types that prey upon them."

110. F. S. Fitzgerald 2000: ch. 9, p. 170. By contrast, Nick bolts down "little pig sausages and mashed potatoes and coffee" in New York restaurants (ch. 3, p. 57). T. Tanner (1990: ix–x) links East and West Egg with Trimalchio's peahen egg and its surprise beccafico filling.

111. Sklenář (2007–8: 122) calls it "beautiful". T. Tanner (1990: xiii) speaks of Fitzgerald's "personal lexicon of ineffable glitteringness".

112. See Endres (2009) for this and other parallels.

113. Another projected title was "Among Ash Heaps and Millionaires". See Endres (2009) on similarities between the two narrators.

114. F. S. Fitzgerald 2000: ch. 6, p. 100.

115. F. S. Fitzgerald 2000: ch. 7, p. 115. Trimalchio tells the story of the invention of unbreakable glass at *Sat.* 51.1–6.

116. Sklenář 2007–8: 121. Cf. Briggs 1999: 229.

117. F. S. Fitzgerald 2000: ch. 8, p. 142.

sympathetically than tough, straight-talking Trimalchio, that is because he is diffused for us through the double lens of an aspirational narrator and an as-pirational author, each caught up in similar dreams and disillusionments.

Maecenas, too, is mentioned only in passing. Nick inserts his name when recalling his first preparations for the financial career that might bring him closer to the rich and powerful:

> I bought a dozen volumes on banking and credit and investment securities, and they stood on my shelf in red and gold like new money from the mint, promising to unfold the shining secrets that only Midas and Morgan and Maecenas knew. (F. S. Fitzgerald 2000: ch. 1, p. 10)

In this alliterative triad, J. Pierpont Morgan, the philanthropist and banker who controversially bailed out the US government from a gold shortage in 1895, receives legendary status next to the Augustan patron and the Lydian king with the golden touch (Maecenas is displaced till last, weighted down by his extra syllable). As a naïve gold digger seduced by "new", "promising" and "shining", Nick apparently includes him for his exceptional wealth, rather than as a patron of the arts. But Morgan was a collector, too, who bequeathed his sumptuous library of medieval manuscripts to New York City in 1924, while Midas also judged the artistic contest between Pan's music and Apollo's. In the next sentence, Nick, too, will confess to having latent literary ambitions.

No direct connection is made between Maecenas and the novel's other an-cient figure, Trimalchio. Yet just as he cast his long shadow over both elegant Petronius and his vulgar creation (not to mention emperor Nero), Maecenas becomes the missing link that helps calibrate the essential similarities and dif-ferences between Trimalchio and Gatsby.[118] Like both of them, he could be said to "drift coolly out of nowhere", a mysterious profiteer with a war record and murky sources of wealth, who lived like a "young rajah" but was a "turbaned 'character' leaking sawdust at every pore".[119] Yet while Fitzgerald's allusion to Trimalchio can be read as a bleak warning about the ruthlessness and emptiness of American materialism stripped of aesthetics, Maecenas's combination of wealth with aesthetics anticipates the more complex allure of a Jay Gatsby, whose stacks of shirts, selected for him in England, are prized for their exquisite melange of colours and patterns, not just their cost and their abundance:

> the soft rich heap mounted higher—shirts with stripes and scrolls and plaids in coral and apple-green and lavender and faint orange, and mono-graphs of Indian blue. (F. S. Fitzgerald 2000: ch. 5, p. 89)

118. See Byrne (2007) on Maecenas and Trimalchio; Byrne (2018) on Terentia and Fortunata (Mrs Trimalchio).

119. F. S. Fitzgerald 2000: ch. 3, p. 50; ch. 4, p. 64.

His parties, likewise, promise blue-hued mystery and romance as much as opulence:

> There was music from my neighbor's house through the summer nights. In his blue gardens men and girls came and went like moths among the whisperings and the champagne and the stars. (F. S. Fitzgerald 2000: ch. 3, p. 41)

Gatsby is even made into a sun god, an "ecstatic patron of recurrent light", flashing a radiant smile at each of his protégés in turn:

> one of those rare smiles with a quality of eternal reassurance in it, that you may come across four or five times in life. It faced—or seemed to face—the whole eternal world for an instant, and then concentrated on you with an irresistible prejudice in your favor. It understood you just so far as you wanted to be understood, believed in you as you would like to believe in yourself, and assured you that it had precisely that impression of you that, at your best, you hoped to convey. (F. S. Fitzgerald 2000: ch. 3, p. 49)

If Fitzgerald's passing allusion to Maecenas tells us anything significant, it is that money does not just underpin glamour and romance: it is an intrinsic component, even when softened or purified by aesthetics. Trimalchio had money but no aesthetics; Maecenas had both. For all its cachet, decadent Europe is being dwarfed by something more intoxicating and illusory. Newness and promise brought the founding fathers to America, to what Fitzgerald calls the "fresh, green breast of the new world", inspiring the "transitory enchanted moment" of its original viewers (in one of the novel's most sublime passages).[120] Their heirs continue to grasp at a dream of mythical, bucolic plenitude, a future imagined out of idealized versions of their pasts. It is Gatsby who represents this for Nick, while he in turn is drawn by his ever-fresh Daisy to spring-like meadows of vitality:

> There was a ripe mystery about it, a hint of bedrooms upstairs more beautiful and cool than other bedrooms, of gay and radiant activities taking place through its corridors and of romances that were not musty and laid away already in lavender but fresh and breathing and redolent of this year's shining motor cars and of dances whose flowers were scarcely withered. (F. S. Fitzgerald 2000: ch. 8, p. 141)

The old myth of Maecenas's unreachable world has been updated with new forms of enchantment—lucre, youth, sport, energy, cars, sex. These are powerful fantasies with which to transcend for a while the mass production and grinding poverty that undergirds them:

---

120. F. S. Fitzgerald 2000: ch. 9, p. 171.

Gatsby was overwhelmingly aware of the youth and mystery that wealth imprisons and preserves, of the freshness of many clothes, and of Daisy, gleaming like silver, safe and proud above the hot struggles of the poor. (F. S. Fitzgerald 2000: ch. 8, p. 142)

Back in Europe, around the same time, "Maecenas" continues to play a more familiar role, as a code name for cultural distinction tainted by decadence. The setting is the salon of the upstart Verdurins, aspiring husband-and-wife patrons of a bohemian demi-monde, a "little clan" (petit clan), in the "Sodome et Gomorrhe" episode of Marcel Proust's *À la recherche du temps perdu* (1923). The Baron de Charlus, a mysterious closet homosexual, a "man-woman" with camp mannerisms, has been boasting about his aristocratic ancestors to impress a younger man. This prompts the pedantic Professeur Brichot to inject a Horatian tag into the conversation: "Maecenas atauis edite regibus" (Maecenas, issue of ancestral kings; Hor. *Carm.* 1.1.1). Proust has already mocked those socialites who hoard a stock of meaningless classical mottoes for all occasions.[121] But this one cleaves the party in two. M. de Charlus understands the reference, while the ignorant hostess needs enlightening. Brichot enjoys explaining to her that "Maecenas" was a decadent *avant la lettre*—a "dandy who was the crème de la crème" (un dandy qui était la fleur du gratin) and a "bookworm" (rat de bibliothèque), elevated by sycophantic poets to pseudo-royal status, as well as being the first apostle of the oriental god "Jemenfou" (Dontgiveatoss).[122] In short, he was a forerunner of today's opium-eating symbolists:[123]

these intellectuals worshipping art with a capital A, who, when they can no longer intoxicate themselves upon Zola, inject themselves with Verlaine. Having become etheromaniacs out of Baudelairean devotion, they would no longer be capable of the virile effort which the country may one day or another demand of them, anaesthetised as they are by the great literary neurosis in the heated, enervating atmosphere, heavy with unwholesome vapours, of a symbolism of the opium-den. (Proust 1981: 2.988)

121. E.g., the pretentious Dr Cottard, who cites Ovid's "Os homini sublime dedit cœlumque tueri" out of context; Proust (1922–31) 1954: 2.1072.

122. Proust (1922–31) 1954: 2.955.

123. Proust (1922–31) 1954: 2.956: "ces intellectuels adorant l'Art, avec un grand A, et qui, quand il ne leur suffit plus de s'alcooliser avec du Zola, se font des piqûres de Verlaine. Devenus éthéromanes par dévotion baudelairienne, ils ne seraient plus capables de l'effort viril que la patrie peut un jour ou l'autre leur demander, anesthésiés qu'ils sont par la grande névrose littéraire, dans l'atmosphère chaude, énervante, lourde de relents malsains, d'un symbolisme de fumerie d'opium."

Dropped into the conversation, the tag is a litmus test of the cultural credentials of the various guests, dividing "ins" from "outs" against a background of swooning aestheticism, snobbery and repression, where Latin performs a function akin to the secret codes of homosexuality.[124] To further his erotic goals and flatter his host at the same time, M. de Charlus offers another explanation: Maecenas was nothing less than "the Verdurin of his day". Even as Madame Verdurin misguidedly believes her "little clan" to be "something so matchless throughout the world, one of those perfect wholes which it takes centuries of time to produce",[125] the Horatian tag hangs above the little salon, reflecting a grimier version of its ancient prototype and exposing all later circles as self-important and degenerate.

Not long after, Maecenas the decadent would be engulfed by more sinister impulses in world politics. In his biography *Augustus* (1937), John Buchan was the first to call the emperor's henchman an *éminence grise* (after Cardinal Richelieu's confidant Père Joseph), complete with "all the foibles of the aesthete and the foppishness of the *petit maître*".[126] Writing in the shadow of fascism, he also launched the Nazi-influenced "minister of propaganda" label, calling Maecenas "the physician who watched over the soul and spirit of Rome". In *The Roman Revolution* (1939), Ronald Syme chose the variant "chief of propaganda".[127] At the same time, developments in psychology made this unusually complex personality a canvas for amateur analysts. Buchan, again: "Maecenas is an eternal enigma. The rugged face was no index to a character which was a compound of the effeminate hedonist and the provident and subtle statesman. . . . it is clear that there was something in him of the antic and the grotesque."[128] Fast-forward to Jean-Marie André in his psycho-biography, *Mécène* (1967), concluding that Maecenas was a romantic, "a wounded soul which bears within it, like a torment, a sense of human limitation".[129] In his historical novel *Augustus* (1972), John Williams presents Maecenas as a closet homosexual stuck in a marriage of convenience, whose repressed psyche erupts in violent mood swings: "a harsh-featured but oddly effeminate youth who flounces rather than walks, and who flutters his eyelashes in a most repulsive

---

124. Madeline Gowers reminds me that M. de Charlus mistakes an ambiguous remark of M. Verdurin's for a discovery of his homosexuality: "Or dès les premiers mots que nous avons échangés, j'ai compris que vous en étiez!" (Even from the first words we exchanged, I knew you for what you were!; Proust [1922–31] 1954: 2.941).

125. Proust 1981: 2.914.

126. Buchan 1937: 144, 187.

127. Buchan 1937: 164; Syme 1939: 460; see Dalzell 1956; Reckford 1959: 199n12.

128. Buchan 1937: 187.

129. André 1967: 61: "un 'romantique' de l'antiquité . . . cette âme blessée porte en elle, comme un tourment, le sentiment de la finitude humaine".

way", but also "deadly, cold (when he is serious, drops all mannerisms and even his body seems to harden), sees no possibility of conciliation, wants none".[130]

## Modern Maecenas

Today, "Maecenas" is used to sell luxury brands, from pens and paintings to books and swimming pools. For all its associations with antiquity and exclusivity, the name has been astonishingly adaptable to more commercial, more democratic models of patronage. It has been bestowed on a venture capital site in Australia, publishing imprints in New York and Budapest, a philanthropic foundation in the Netherlands, funding councils in Germany and France, the annual fundraiser for the Pittsburgh opera house, and, most recently, a digital platform offering the public shares in fine art.[131] Less meaningfully, but appropriately for a silent presence or cipher, "Maecenas" often appears in the "lorem ipsum" Latinate dummy text used by printers to fill empty spaces.

In the late twentieth century, the use of Maecenas's name tracks the evolution of patronage from exclusive personal relationships into global processes of consumption and benefaction. A short Pathé film from 1958, "Maecenas of the Past and Our Time", pairs scenes of old-style bounty—the opulent rococo rooms of the Amalienburg Palace, built by Prince Karl Albrecht of Bavaria for his wife—with the present-day activities of the "Kulturpreis" (Circle of Culture), a sober group of men in suits deliberating around a table in Duisburg before inspecting the works of beret-wearing painters and sculptors. In present-day France, "Maecenas" has moved a stage further towards institutionalization and centralization. Since 2003, Le Mécénat, a scheme administered by the French government, has offered tax breaks to stimulate corporate giving for institutions or events "of general interest". There must otherwise be no obvious benefit to the donor, while individual artists are not eligible for support. Taking inspiration from the United States, philanthropy is expected to be a long-term relationship, not a one-off donation. As a result, publicly siphoned funding for the arts, around €2.5 billion a year, now outstrips that from the private sector; Le Mécénat is said to provide 40 per cent of the Louvre's budget, 25 per cent of that of Versailles. The aim has

130. J. Williams (1972) 2014: 36.

131. Australia: "Funding Alternatives: A Seat at the Table", Maecenas Capital, http://www.maecenascapital.com.au. UK: "The Art Investment Platform: Build Your Own Portfolio of Tokenised Masterpieces", Maecenas, www.maecenas.co; all accessed May 10, 2023; James Totcomb, "Fancy Buying Shares in a Masterpiece? This Site Will Let You", *Telegraph*, May 20, 2017, https://www.telegraph.co.uk/technology/2017/05/20/fancy-buying-shares-masterpiece-site-will-let/. Maecenas Press was an illustrated books division of Random House, based in New York City, in the 1960s and 1970s; it is also the name of a contemporary press in Budapest.

been to remove patronage from negative associations with favouritism, exploitation and tax avoidance, while keeping centre-stage the legendary by-product—
universal good—claimed by and for its practitioners in ancient Rome. Meanwhile, in the United Kingdom, Maecenas has given his name to a new
blockchain-based platform with global reach, which in theory allows any member of the public to use crypto-wallets full of tokens to buy and trade shares in
fine art: a modern marriage of capitalism and democracy.

In some quarters, the "circle of Maecenas" continues to exercise its magnetic
powers. In Malostranské Square in Prague, for example, the restaurant U Me-
cenáse (Chez Maecenas) doles out generous portions of goulash, beef with
dumplings and apple strudel, while trading off its history as a hostelry with
sixteenth-century roots. Its website boasts that rival astronomers Tycho Brahe
and Johannes Kepler, sculptor Adriaen de Vries and imperial executioner Jan
Mydlar used to drink there—without much historical backing.[132] So it is that all
the cachet of the eccentric court of Rudolph II (the patron whom Giuseppe Arcimboldo portrayed as a collage of fruits, a changeable Vertumnus for his times)
has been harnessed in the service of contemporary "heritage": yet another imaginary little clique has been invented under the convenient sign of Maecenas.

"Are you the next Maecenas?" is the challenge posed by the title of a set of
charcoal drawings by Eveline van der Griend (Saatchi Art, 2013). She refers
tangentially to a hallowed Dutch philanthropic institution that supports deserving artists and cultural activities. In the title picture, a ruffed, cloaked
couple are shown gingerly proffering a dead chicken on a string to a gorilla,
one in a series of images that appeal for continued sustenance in wintry times
by cheekily and knowingly looking back to the Golden Age of Dutch art. The
image is easily identified as a parody of Aelbert Cuyp's *The Commander of the
Homeward-Bound Fleet* (Amsterdam, Rijksmuseum, *c.* 1640–60), a picture ripe
for postcolonial deconstruction, with its parasol-carrying slave and harbour
view of the Dutch-Indonesian settlement of Batavia. Together with its whee-
dling caption, the drawing frames the ongoing tradition of fishing for patrons
as a laughable anachronism. As ever, Maecenas attracts a question. Perhaps
this one reminds us above all in these bleak times that what he has always
represented to artists—the hand on the shoulder, the intimate meeting of eyes
and minds, the open but exclusive space for creative possibility—is above all
a tool of the imagination, predicated on its being an ungraspable dream.

132. "U Mecenáše Restaurant in Prague, Malá Strana: Your Favourite Restaurant throughout
the Centuries", U Mecenáše, accessed May 10, 2023, https://www.restauraceumecenase.com.

# REFERENCES

Adler, Eric (2012) "Cassius Dio's Agrippa–Maecenas Debate: An Operational Code Analysis", *AJPhil.* 133: 477–520.

Ahmed, Sara (2006) *Queer Phenomenology: Orientations, Objects, Others.* Durham, NC.

Aigner-Foresti, Luciana (1996) "L'uomo Mecenate", in *Atti del convegno per il bimillenario della nascita di Mecenate, Rivista storica di antichità* 26: 7–26.

Algazi, Gadi, and Rina Drory (2000) "L'amour à la cour des Abbassides: Un code de compétence sociale", *Annales* 35: 1255–82.

Amat, Jacqueline (1991) *Calpurnius Siculus, Bucoliques; Pseudo-Calpurnius, Éloge de Pison.* Paris.

Ampolo, Carmine (1996) "Livio I, 44, 3: La casa di Servio Tullio, l'Esquilino e Mecenate", *Parola del passato* 51: 27–32.

Amstutz, Delphine (2011) "Mécène et Séjane: sur la figure du favori au xviie siècle", *Dix-septième siècle* 251: 333–50.

Ancona, Ronnie (1994) *Time and the Erotic in Horace's Odes.* Durham, NC.

Anderson, William S. (1963) *Pompey, His Friends, and the Literature of the First Century B.C.* Berkeley, CA.

——— (2010) "Horace's Friendship: Adaptation of a Circular Argument", in G. Davis, ed., *A Companion to Horace.* Chichester, 34–52.

André, Jean-Marie (1967). *Mécène: Essai de biographie spirituelle.* Paris.

——— (1983) "Mécène écrivain (avec en appendice, les fragments de Mécène)", *ANRW* II 30.3: 1765–87.

Andreae, Bernard (2005–6) "Die Bildnisse des Gaius Cilnius Maecenas in Arezzo und an der Ära Pacis", *Mitteilungen des deutschen archäologischen Instituts, Römische Abteilung* 112: 121–61.

Ariosto, Ludovico (1954) *Ludovico Ariosto: Opere minori*, ed. Cesare Segre. Milan.

Armisen-Marchetti, Mireille (1989) *Sapientiae facies: Étude sur les images de Sénèque.* Paris.

Ashby, Thomas, and Roland Fell (1921) "The Via Flaminia", *JRS* 11: 125–90.

Austin, Roland G. (1964) *Aeneidos liber secundus P. Vergilii Maronis.* Oxford.

Auvray, Clara (1987) "La citation virgilienne dans les lettres à Lucilius de Sénèque: Dès praecepta aux decreta du Stoïcisme", in Gérard Freyburger, ed., *De Virgile à J. Balde: Hommage à Mme A. Thill.* Mulhouse, France, 29–34.

Avallone, Ricardo ([1962/63]) *Mecenate.* Naples.

Baldwin, Barry (1984) "Trimalchio and Maecenas", *Latomus* 43: 402–3.

Ball, Sydney H. (1950) *A Roman Book on Precious Stones.* Los Angeles.

Barber, Eric A. (1960) *Sexti Properti Carmina.* Oxford, 2nd ed.

Barchiesi, Alessandro (1996) "Poetry, Praise, and Patronage: Simonides in Book 4 of Horace's *Odes*", *Cl. Ant.* 15: 5–47.

—— (2000) "Rituals in Ink: Horace on the Greek Lyric Tradition", in Mary Depew and Dirk Obbink, eds, *Matrices of Genre*. Cambridge, MA, 167–82. Reprinted in Lowrie (2009): 418–40.

—— (2009a) "Final Difficulties in an Iambic Poet's Career," in Lowrie (2009), 232–46.

—— (2009b) "Lyric in Rome", in Felix Budelmann, ed., *Cambridge Companion to Greek Lyric*. Cambridge, 319–35.

—— (2011) "Roman Callimachus", in Benjamin Acosta-Hughes, Luigi Lehnus and Susan Stephens, eds, *Brill's Companion to Callimachus*. Leiden, 509–33.

Bardon, Henri (1949) "Trois écrivains du temps d'Auguste", *Revue des études latines* 27: 163–68.

—— (1952) *La littérature latine inconnue*. Paris, 2 vols.

Barham, Nicola (2018) "Esteemed Ornament: An Overlooked Value for Approaching Roman Visual Culture", in Nikolaus Dietrich and Michael Squire, eds, *Ornament and Figure in Graeco-Roman Art*. Berlin, 279–98.

Barkan, Leonard (1999) *Unearthing the Past: Archaeology and Aesthetics in the Making of Renaissance Culture*. New Haven, CT.

Bartalucci, Aldo (1979) "Presenza di Mecenate nelle Satire di Persio", in Giovanni D'Anna et al., eds, *Studi di poesia latina in onore di Antonio Traglia*. Rome, 2 vols; 2.669–92.

Barthes, Roland (1982) "Tacitus and the Funerary Baroque", in Susan Sontag, ed., *A Barthes Reader*. London, 162–66.

Barton, Carlin (1994). "All Things Beseem the Victor: Paradoxes of Masculinity in Early Imperial Rome", in Richard Trexler, ed., *Gender Rhetorics*. Binghamton, NY, 83–92.

—— (2007) "Hercules in a Skirt, Or the Feminization of Victory During the Roman Civil Wars and Early Empire", in Alexandra Cuffel and Brian Britt, eds, *Religion, Gender, and Culture in the Pre-modern World*. Basingstoke, UK, 63–73.

Barton, Tamsyn (1994a) *Ancient Astrology*. London.

—— (1994b) *Power and Knowledge: Astrology, Physiognomics, and Medicine under the Roman Empire*. Ann Arbor, MI.

Bartsch, Shadi (1994) *Actors in the Audience: Theatricality and Doublespeak from Nero to Hadrian*. Cambridge, MA.

—— (2005) "Eros and the Roman Philosopher", in Bartsch and Thomas Bartscherer, eds, *Erotikon: Essays on Eros, Ancient and Modern*. Chicago, 59–83.

—— (2006) *The Mirror of the Self: Sexuality, Self-Knowledge, and the Gaze in the Early Roman Empire*. Chicago.

Bastomsky, Saul J. (1972) "Tacitus: *Annals*, 14,53,2: The Pathos of the Tacitean Seneca's Request to Nero", *Latomus* 31: 174–78.

Batinski, Emily E. (1990–91) "Horace's Rehabilitation of Bacchus", *CW* 84: 361–78.

Batstone, William (1988) "On the Surface of the *Georgics*", *Arethusa* 21: 227–45. Revised in Stephanie Quinn, ed. (2000) *Why Vergil?* Rome, 275–84.

—— (1997) "Virgilian Didaxis: Value and Meaning in the *Georgics*", in Charles Martindale, ed., *The Cambridge Companion to Virgil*. Cambridge, 125–44.

Bauman, Richard A. (1982) "Hangman, Call a Halt", *Hermes* 110: 102–10.

Baxter, Robert T. S. (1968) "Virgil's Influence on Tacitus". Dissertation, Stanford University.

Bayet, Jean (1956) "Catulle, la Grèce et Rome", *Entretiens Fondation Hardt* 2. Vandoeuvres, Switzerland, 3–40.

Beard, Mary (1993) "Looking (Harder) for Roman Myth: Dumézil, Declamation and the Problems of Definition", in Fritz Graf, ed., *Mythos in mythenloser Gesellschaft: Das Paradigma Roms.* Stuttgart, 44–64.

———— (1997) "Vita Inscripta", in W. W. Ehlers, ed., *La biographie antique*, Entretiens sur l'antiquité classique 44. Geneva, 83–114.

———— (1998) "Imaginary *Horti*: Or Up the Garden Path", in Cima and La Rocca (1998): 23–32.

Beard, Mary, and John Henderson (2001) *Classical Art from Greece to Rome.* Oxford.

Beauchamp, Gorman (2006) "Henry James vs. the Robber Barons: The Novelist Thought Italian Art Should Stay in England, Where It Belongs, and Not Fall into the Hands of His Countrymen", *American Scholar* 75.2: 100–108.

Bellandi, Franco (1995) "L'immagine di Mecenate protettore delle lettere nella poesia tra I e II sec. d. C.", *Atene e Roma* 40: 78–101.

Bennett, Alva W. (1967) "*Sententia* and Catalogue in Propertius (3, 9, 1–20)", *Hermes* 95: 222–43.

———— (1968) "The Patron and Poetical Inspiration", *Hermes* 96: 318–41.

Bernardi Perini, G. (1966–67) "*Suspendere naso*: Storia di una metafora", *Memorie dell'Accademia patavina: Classe di scienze morali, lettere ed arti* 79: 233–64.

Bernhardy, Gottfried (1865) *Grundriss der römischen Litteratur.* Braunschweig, Germany, 4th ed.

Berno, Francesca Romana (2013) "Eccellente ma non troppo: L'exemplum di Augusto in Seneca", in Mario Labate and Gianpiero Rosati, eds, *La costruzione del mito augusteo.* Heidelberg, 181–96.

Bernoulli, Johann Jacob (1882) *Römische Ikonographie.* Stuttgart, 2 vols.

Bernstein, Neil (2009) "Adoptees and Exposed Children in Roman Declamation: Commodification, Luxury, and the Threat of Violence", *CPhil.* 104: 331–53.

———— (2012) "Torture Her until She Lies: Torture, Testimony, and Social Status in Roman Rhetorical Education", *G & R* 59: 165–77.

———— (2013) *Ethics, Identity, and Community in Later Roman Declamation.* Oxford.

Berti, Emanuele (2007) *Scholasticorum studia: Seneca il Vecchio e la cultura retorica e letteraria della prima età imperiale.* Pisa.

———— (2014) "Su alcuni frammenti di Mecenate trasmessi da Seneca (*Ep.* 114.5)", *Prometheus* 40: 224–40.

Bertrand-Dagenbach, Cécile (1992) "La mort de Pétrone et l'art de Tacite", *Latomus* 51: 601–5.

Beugnot, Bernard (1985) "La figure de Mécénas", in Mousnier and Mesnard (1985): 285–93.

Beulé, Charles-Ernest (1868) *Auguste, sa famille et ses amis.* Paris. 2nd ed.

Bickel, Ernestus (1950) "*De Elegiis in Maecenatem monumentis biographicis et historicis*", *Rh. Mus.* 83: 97–133.

Bielfeldt, Ruth (2018) "Candelabrus and Trimalchio: Embodied Histories of Roman Lampstands and Their Slaves", *Art History* 41: 420–43.

Bing, Peter (2005) "The Politics and Poetics of Geography in the Milan Posidippus, Section One: On Stones (AB 1–20)", in Gutzwiller (2005): 119–40.

Biondo, Fabio ([1444–46] 1940–53) *Roma instaurata*, in Roberto Valentini and Giuseppe Zucchetti, eds, *Codice topografico della città di Roma.* Rome, 4 vols; 4.247–323.

Bischoff, Heinrich (1932) "Der Warner bei Herodot". Dissertation, University of Marburg.

Bitarello, Beatrice (2009) "The Construction of Etruscan 'Otherness' in Latin Literature", *G & R* 56: 211–33.

Bloomer, Martin (1997a) "A Preface to the History of Declamation: Whose Speech? Whose History?", in Thomas Habinek and Alessandro Schiesaro, eds, *The Roman Cultural Revolution*. Cambridge, 199–215.

——— (1997b) "Schooling in Persona: Imagination and Subordination in Roman Education", *Cl. Ant.* 16: 57–78.

——— (2007) "Roman Declamation: The Elder Seneca and Quintilian", in William Dominik and Jon Hall, eds, *A Companion to Roman Rhetoric*. Malden, MA, 297–306.

Boardman, John (1970) *Greek Gems and Finger Rings: Early Bronze Age to Late Classical*. London.

Boardman, John, and Donna Kurtz (1986) "Booners", in Jiri Frel and Marion True, eds, *Greek Vases in the J. Paul Getty Museum* 3: 35–70.

Boatwright, Mary T. (1998) "Luxuriant Gardens and Extravagant Women: The *horti* of Rome between Republic and Empire", in Cima and La Rocca (1998): 71–82.

Bodel, John (1989) "Trimalchio's Coming of Age", *Phoenix* 43: 72–74.

——— (1994) *Graveyards and Groves. A Study of the Lex Lucerina*. Cambridge, MA.

——— (1997) "Monumental Villas and Villa Monuments", *JRA* 10: 5–35.

——— (2014) "The Life and Death of Ancient Roman Cemeteries: Living with the Dead in Imperial Rome", in Chrystina Häuber, Franz X. Schütz and Gordon M. Winder, eds, *Reconstruction and the Historic City: Rome and Abroad—an Interdisciplinary Approach*. Munich, 177–95.

Boileau, Nicolas (1666) *Satires du sieur D\*\*\* (Despréaux)*. Paris.

Bonner, Stanley (1949) *Roman Declamation in the Late Republic and Early Empire*. Berkeley, CA.

Boucher, Jean-Paul (1958) "L'oeuvre de L. Varius Rufus d'après Properce II, 34", *Rév.Ét. Anc.* 60: 307–22.

Bourdieu, Pierre (1977) *Outline of a Theory of Practice*, trans. Richard Nice. Cambridge.

——— (1984) *Distinction: A Social Critique of the Judgment of Taste*. London.

Bowditch, Phebe Lowell (2001) *Horace and the Gift Economy of Patronage*. Berkeley, CA.

——— (2010) "Horace and Imperial Patronage", in Gregson Davis, ed., *A Companion to Horace*. Chichester, 53–74.

——— (2011) "Tibullus and Egypt: A Postcolonial Reading of Elegy 1.7", *Arethusa* 44: 89–122.

Bowie, Ewen (2009) "Wandering Poets, Archaic Style", in Hunter and Rutherford (2009): 105–36.

Bradley, Anthony (2011) *Imagining Ireland in the Poems and Plays of W. B. Yeats: Nation, Class, and State*. New York.

Bradshaw, Arnold (1970) "Some Stylistic Oddities in Horace, *Odes*, III 8", *Philologus* 114: 145–50.

——— (1989) "Horace *in Sabinis*", in Carl Deroux, ed., *Studies in Latin Literature and Roman History* 5, Collection Latomus 206. Brussels, 160–86.

——— (2002) "Horace's Birthday and Deathday", in Tony Woodman and Denis Feeney, eds, *Traditions and Contexts in the Poetry of Horace*. Cambridge, 1–16.

Bramble, John (1974) *Persius and the Programmatic Satire*. Cambridge.

Breed, Brian W. (2009) "Perugia and the Plots of the Monobiblos", *Cambridge Classical Journal* 55: 24–48.

———— (2010) "Propertius on Not Writing about Civil Wars", in Breed, C. Damon, and A. Rossi, eds, *Citizens of Discord: Rome and Its Civil Wars*. New York, 233–48.

Briant, Pierre (2002) *From Cyrus to Alexander: A History of the Persian Empire*. Winona Lake, IN.

Briggs, Ward (1999) "Petronius and Virgil in 'The Great Gatsby'", *International Journal of the Classical Tradition*, 6: 226–35.

Brink, Charles (1982) *Horace on Poetry: Epistles Book II*. Cambridge.

Broise, Henri, and Vincent Jolivet (1998) "Il giardino e l'acqua: L'esempio degli Horti Luculliani", in Cima and La Rocca (1998): 189–202.

Brothers, Cammy (2002) "Reconstruction as Design: Giuliano da Sangallo and the 'Palazo di Mecenate' on the Quirinal Hill", *Annali di architettura* 14: 55–72.

———— (2022) *Giuliano Sangallo and the Ruins of Rome*. Princeton, NJ.

Brown, Edwin L. (1963) *Numeri Vergiliani: Studies in Eclogues and Georgics*. Brussels.

Brunt, Peter (1965) "*Amicitia* in the Late Roman Republic", *PCPS* 11: 1–20.

———— (1988) *The Fall of the Roman Republic and Related Essays*. Oxford.

Buchan, John (1937) *Augustus*. London.

Buchheit, Vincenz (1972) *Der Anspruch des Dichters in Vergils Georgika: Dichtertum und Heilsweg*. Darmstadt.

———— (1977) "Würdigung des Dichterfreundes und Dichterpatrons bei Catull und Vergil", *Philologus* 121: 66–82.

Burke, Kenneth (1920) "Mrs Maecenas", *Dial* 68: 346–58.

Burrow, Colin (1993) "Horace at Home and Abroad: Wyatt and Sixteenth Century Horatianism", in Charles Martindale and David Hopkins, eds, *Horace Made New: Horatian Influences on British Writing from the Renaissance to the Twentieth Century*. Cambridge, 27–49.

Butrica, James L. (1996) "The Amores of Propertius: Unity and Structure in Books II–IV", *ICS* 21: 87–158.

Byrne, Shannon N. (1999a) "Maecenas in Seneca and Other Post-Augustan Authors", in Byrne and Edmund P. Cueva, eds, *Veritatis Amicitiaeque Causa: Essays in Honor of Anna Lydia Motto and John R. Clark*. Wauconda, IL, 21–40.

———— (1999b) "Pointed Allusions: Maecenas and Sallustius in the *Annals* of Tacitus", *Rh. Mus.* 142: 339–45.

———— (2004) "Martial's Fiction: Domitius Marsus and Maecenas", *CQ* 54: 255–65.

———— (2006) "Petronius and Maecenas: Seneca's Calculated Criticism", in Byrne, Edmund P. Cueva and Jean Alvares, eds, *Authors, Authority, and Interpreters in the Ancient Novel: Essays in Honor of Gareth L. Schmeling*, Ancient Narrative Suppl. 5: 83–111.

———— (2007) "Maecenas and Petronius' Trimalchio Maecenatianus", *Ancient Narrative* 6: 31–49.

———— (2018) "Fortunata and Terentia: A Model for Trimalchio's Wife", in Marília P. Futre Pinheiro, David Konstan and Bruce D. MacQueen, eds, *Cultural Crossroads in the Ancient Novel*. Berlin, 65–78.

Cairns, Francis (2006) *Sextus Propertius: The Augustan Elegist.* Cambridge.

——— (2007) "The Power of Implication: Horace's Invitation to Maecenas (*Odes* 1.20)", in Tony Woodman and Jonathan Powell, eds, *Author and Audience in Latin Literature.* Cambridge, 85–109. Reprinted in Cairns (2012): 213–43.

——— (2010) "The Mistress's Midnight Summons: Propertius 3.16", *Hermes* 138: 70–91.

——— (2012) *Roman Lyric: Collected Papers on Catullus and Horace.* Berlin.

Cameron, Alan (1995) *Callimachus and His Critics.* Princeton.

Caporali, Cesare (1762) *Rime di Cesare Caporali, part 1, Vita di Mecenate.* Naples.

——— (2018) *Vita di Mecenate,* ed. Danilo Romei. N.p. https://www.nuovorinascimento.org /n-rinasc/testi/pdf/caporali/TestoNR.pdf.

Capponi, Livia (2002) "Maecenas and Pollio", *ZPE* 140: 181–84.

Carandini, Andrea (2010) *Le case del potere nell'antica Roma.* Rome.

Carnegie, Andrew (1889) "Wealth", *North American Review,* 148.391: 653–4.

Carson, Anne (1991) "Putting Her in Her Place: Woman, Dirt, and Desire", in David M. Halperin, John, J. Winkler and Froma I. Zeitlin, eds, *Before Sexuality: The Construction of Erotic Experience in the Ancient Greek World.* Princeton, NJ, 135–70.

Casali, Sergio (2004) "Nisus and Euryalus: Exploiting the Contradictions in Virgil's 'Doloneia'", *Harv. Stud.* 102: 319–54.

Cassio, Alberto (1757) *Corso delle acque.* Rome, 2 vols.

Champlin, Edward (1980) *Fronto and Antonine Rome.* Cambridge, MA.

——— (1982) "The Suburbium of Rome", *AJAH* 7: 97–117.

——— (1989) "The Life and Times of Calpurnius Piso", *Museum Helveticum* 46: 101-124.

——— (2003) *Nero.* Cambridge, MA.

Chapman, Guy, ed. (1928) *The Travel-Diaries of William Beckford of Fonthill.* Cambridge, 2 vols.

Chillet, Clément (2011) "Limites de la ville et symbols du pouvoir à Rome: Les ambiguïtés des jardins de Mécène", *Histoire urbaine* 31: 151–70.

——— (2016) *De l'Étrurie à Rome: Mécène et la fondation de l'empire.* Rome.

Christian, Kathleen Wren (2010) *Empire without End: Antiquities Collections in Renaissance Rome c. 1350–1527.* New Haven, CT.

Cianfriglia, Laura (1976–77) "Horti di Mecenate", unpublished BA thesis, Istituto di Topografia Antica, Università di Roma 1, Facoltà di Lettere e Filosofia.

Cima, Maddalena, and Eugenio La Rocca, eds (1986) *Le tranquille dimore degli dei: La residenza imperiale degli horti Lamiani.* Rome.

———, eds (1998) *Horti Romani.* Rome.

Cioffi, Robert L. (2014) "Seeing Gods: Epiphany and Narrative in the Greek Novels", *Ancient Narrative,* 11: 1–42.

Citroni, Mario (1975) *M. Valerii Martialis Epigrammaton liber primus.* Florence.

——— "Produzione letteraria e forme del potere: Gli scrittori Latini nel I secolo dell'impero", in Andrea Schiavone, ed., *Storia di Roma, vol. 2/3, L'impero mediterraneo: La cultura e l'impero.* Turin, 383–491.

——— (1995) *Poesia e lettori in Roman antica.* Rome, Italy.

——— (2005) "Orazio, Cicerone, e il tempo della letteratura", in J. P. Schwindt, ed., *La représentation du temps dans la poésie augustéenne; Zur Poetik der Zeit in augusteischer Dichtung.* Heidelberg, 123–39.

——— (2009) "Occasions and Levels of Address", in Lowrie (2009): 72–105.

Claridge, Amanda, Judith Toms and Tony Cubberley, eds (1998) *Rome: An Oxford Archaeological Guide*. Oxford.

Clay, Jenny Strauss (1981) "The Old Man in the Garden: 'Georgic' 4.116–48", *Arethusa* 14: 57–65.

Clément-Tarantino, Séverine (2006) "La poétique romaine comme hybridation féconde: Les leçons de la greffe (Virgile, *Géorgiques*, 2, 9–82)", Interférences, *Ars scribendi* 4, June 1, 2006, http://ars-scribendi.ens-lsh.fr/article.php3?id_article=37var_affichage=vf.

Coarelli, Filippo (2004) *Lexicon topographicum urbis Romae. Suppl 2: Scavi di Rome*. Rome.

——— (2014) *Roma 1878–1921 and Environs: An Archaeological Guide*. Berkeley, CA.

Coeffeteau, Nicholas (1680) *Histoire romaine, contenant tout ce qui s'est passé de plus memorable, depuis le commencement de l'Empire d'Auguste, jusqu'à celuy de Néron*. Rouen, 3 vols.

Colaizzi, Randall M. (1993) "A New Voice in Roman Elegy: The *Poeta* of Propertius 2.1", *Rh. Mus.* 136: 126–43.

Coleman, Kathleen (1986) "The Emperor Domitian and Literature", *ANRW* II 32.5: 3087–115.

——— (1988) *Statius Silvae IV*. Oxford.

Colini, Antonio Maria (1979) "La torre di Mecenate", *Rendiconti dell'Accademia dei Lincei* 34: 239–50.

Collinge, Nevil E. (1961) *The Structure of Horace's Odes*. Oxford.

Colton, Robert E. (1991) *Juvenal's Use of Martial's Epigrams: A Study of Literary Influence*. Amsterdam.

Comber, Michael (1998) "A Book Made New: Reading Propertius, Reading Pound. A Study in Reception", *JRS* 88: 37–55.

Commager, Steele (1962) *The Odes of Horace: A Critical Study*. New Haven, CT.

Connolly, Joy (2016) "Imaginative Fiction beyond Morals and Moralism", in Martin Dinter, Charles Guérin and Marcos Martinho, eds, *Roman Declamation*. Berlin, 191–208.

Connors, Catherine (1998) *Petronius the Poet*. Cambridge.

——— (1994) "Famous Last Words: Authorship and Death in the Satyricon and in Neronian Rome", in Jaś Elsner and Jamie Masters, eds, *Reflections of Nero*. London, 225–35.

Conte, Gian Biagio (1992) "Proems in the Middle", *YClS* 29: 147–59.

Coo, Lyndsay (2007) "Polydorus and the *Georgics*: Virgil *Aeneid* 3.13–68", *MD* 59: 193–99.

Corbeill, Anthony (1996) *Controlling Laughter: Political Humor in the Late Roman Republic*. Princeton, NJ.

——— (1997) "Dining Deviants in Roman Political Invective", in Judith Hallett and Marilyn Skinner, eds, *Roman Sexualities*. Princeton, NJ, 99–128.

——— (2004) *Nature Embodied: Gesture in Ancient Rome*. Princeton, NJ.

——— (2015) *Sexing the World: Grammatical Gender and Biological Sex in Ancient Rome*. Princeton, NJ.

Corbett, Philip B. (1986) *The Scurra*. Edinburgh.

Corbier, Mireille (1991a) "Constructing Kinship in Rome: Marriage and Divorce, Filiation and Adoption", in David I. Kertzer and Richard P. Saller, eds, *The Family in Italy from Antiquity to the Present*. New Haven, CT, 127–44.

——— (1991b) "Divorce and Adoption as Roman Familial Strategies", in Beryl Rawson, ed., *Marriage, Divorce, and Children in Ancient Rome*. Oxford, 47–78.

Cornell, Tim (1995) *The Beginnings of Rome: Italy and Rome from the Bronze Age to the Punic Wars (c. 1000–264 BC)*. London.

Costa, Stefano (2014) *Mecenate: Frammenti e testimonianze latine*. Milan.

——— (2015) "Maecenas between Apologies and Anthologies: Past Scholarship and New Researches", *Acta antiqua Academiae Scientiarum Hungaricae* 55: 443–56.

Courtil, Jean-Christophe (2014) "Torture in Seneca's Philosophical Works: Between Justification and Condemnation", in Julia Wildberger and Marcia L. Colish, eds, *Seneca philosophus*. Berlin, 189–207.

Courtney, Edward (1980) *A Commentary on the Satires of Juvenal*. London.

——— (2003) *The Fragmentary Latin Poets*. Oxford, rev. 2nd ed.

Cowan, Robert (2018) "You Too: The Narratology of Apostrophe and Second-Person Narrative in Virgil's *Georgics*", *Arethusa* 51: 269–98.

Cramer, David (2000) "The Power of Gender and the Gender of Power in Ancient Rome". Dissertation, University of Texas at Austin.

Cresci, Giovannella (1995) "*Maecenas, Equitum Decus*", *RSA* 25: 169–76.

Crook, John (1955) *Consilium principis*. Cambridge.

Crum, Richard H. (1952) "Petronius and the Emperors, I: Allusions in the *Satyricon*", *CW* 45: 161–68, 197–201.

Cucchiarelli, Andrea (2001) *La satira e il poeta: Orazio tra Epodi e Sermones*. Pisa.

——— (2019) *Orazio, Epistole I: Introduzione, traduzione e commento*. Pisa.

Curtius, Ernst Robert (1953) *European Literature and the Latin Middle Ages*, trans. W. R. Trask. Princeton, NJ.

Dahlmann, Hellfried (1954) "Der Bienenstaat in Vergils Georgika", *AAWM* 10: 545–62. Reprinted in Philip Hardie, ed. (1999) *Virgil: Critical Assessments*, New York, 2.253–67.

Dakouras, Panayotes (2006) "Maecenas Eques: A Study in the Creation and Development of an Image". PhD thesis, New York University.

Dalzell, Alexander (1956) "Maecenas and the Poets", *Phoenix* 10: 151–62.

——— (1997) *The Criticism of Didactic Poetry*. Toronto.

Damon, Cynthia (1997) *The Mask of the Parasite: A Pathology of Roman Patronage*. Ann Arbor, MI.

Dang, Karen (2010) "Rome and the Sabine Farm: Aestheticism, Topography, and the Landscape of Production", *Phoenix* 64: 102–27.

D'Angour, Armand (1999) "*Ad unguem*", *AJPhil.* 120: 411–27.

D'Anna, Giovanni (1997) s.v. "recusatio", in *Orazio: Enciclopedia oraziana* II, Rome, 737–39.

D'Arms, John H. (1981) *Commerce and Social Standing in Ancient Rome*. Cambridge, MA.

——— (1998) "'Between Public and Private': The *Epulum Publicum* and Caesar's *Horti Trans Tiberim*", in Cima and La Rocca (1998): 33–43.

Davies, Penelope J. (2010) "Living to Living, Living to Dead: Communication and Political Rivalry in Roman Tomb Design", in Avril Maddrell and James D. Sidaway, eds, *Deathscapes: Spaces for Death, Dying, Mourning and Remembrance*. Farnham, 225–42.

Davis, Gregson (1991) *Polyhymnia: The Rhetoric of Horatian Lyric Discourse*. Berkeley, CA.

Davis, Peter J. (1987) "Structure and Meaning in the *Eclogues* of Calpurnius Siculus", *Ramus* 16: 32–54.

Davis, Tracy C. (2008) "Introduction", in T. Davis, ed., *The Cambridge Companion to Performance Studies*. Cambridge, 1–8.

DeBrohun, Jeri (1994) "Redressing Elegy's Puella: Propertius IV and the Rhetoric of Fashion", *JRS* 84: 41–63.

Degl'Innocenti Pierini, Rita (2013) "Seneca, Mecenate e il 'ritratto in movimento' (a proposito dell'epistola 114)", in Fabio Gasti, ed., *Atti della IX giornata di filologia classica, Pavia 22 ottobre 2010 "Seneca e la letteratura greca e latina", per i settanti'anni di Giancarlo Mazzoli.* Pavia, 45–66.

De Grummond, Nancy T. (2005) "Roman Favor and Etruscan Thuf(ltha): A Note on Propertius 4.2.34", *Ancient West and East* 4: 296–317.

De Lacy, Philip (1964) "Distant Views: The Imagery of Lucretius 2", *CJ* 60: 49–55.

Della Corte, Francesco (1974–75) *Appendix Vergiliana.* Genoa, 2 vols.

———(1992) "Agrippa e Mecenate: Due politiche culturali a confronto", in Della Corte, *Opuscula.* Genoa, 13: 119–35.

De Man, Paul (1979) "Autobiography as De-facement", *Modern Language Notes* 94: 919–30.

Deremetz, Alain (1986) "L'élégie de Vertumne: L'oeuvre trompeuse", *Rev. Ét. Lat.* 64: 116–49.

——— (2009) "The Question of the Marvellous in the *Georgics* of Virgil", in P. Hardie (2009a): 113–25.

Derrida, Jacques (2005) *Rogues: Two Essays on Reason.* Stanford, CA.

De Scudéry, Madeleine (1642) *Les femmes illustres, ou Les harangues héroïques de Mr de Scudéry: Avec les véritables portraits de ces héroïnes, tirez des médailles antiques.* Paris.

——— (2012) *Les femmes illustres ou Les harangues héroïques, 1642,* with a preface by Claude Maignien. Paris.

De Vos, Mariette (1983) "Funzione e decorazione dell'auditorium di Mecenate", in Giuseppina Pisani Sartorio and Lorenzo Quilici, eds, *Roma capitale 1870–1911,* vol. 7, *L'archeologia in Roma capitale tra sterro e scavo.* Venice, 231–47.

Dewald, Carolyn (2003) "Form and Content: The Question of Tyranny in Herodotus", in K. Morgan (2003): 25–58.

Di Benedetto, Andrea (1960) "La satira oraziana del seccatore, Lucilio, ed alcune reminiscenze dell' *Eunuchus* di Terenzio", *Rendiconti della reale Accademia di Archeologia, Lettere e Belle Arti* 35: 57–64.

Di Brazzano, Stefano (2004) *Laus Pisonis: Introduzione, edizione critica, traduzione e commento.* Pisa.

Dinerstein, Joel (2017) *The Origins of Cool in Post-War America.* Chicago.

Dolven, Jeff (2018) *Senses of Style: Poetry before Interpretation.* Chicago.

Douglas, Mary (1966). *Purity and Danger.* London.

Drew, Douglas L. M. (1927) *The Allegory of the Aeneid.* Oxford.

Du Bellay, Joachim ([1549] 1966) *La deffence et illustration de la langue francoyse,* ed. Henri Chamard. Paris, 3rd ed.

Dufallo, Basil (2015) "Publicizing Political Authority in Horace's *Satires*, Book 1: The Sacral and the Demystified", *CPhil.* 110: 313–32.

Dugan, John (2001) "How to Make (and Break) a Cicero: Epideixis, Textuality, and Self-Fashioning in the *Pro Archia* and *In Pisonem*", *Cl. Ant.* 20: 35–77.

Dunkle, J. Roger (1967) "The Greek Tyrant and Roman Political Invective of the Late Republic", *TAPA* 98: 151–71.

Dunn, Francis M. (1989) "Horace's Sacred Spring (*Ode* I.1)", *Latomus* 48: 97–109.

DuQuesnay, Ian M. LeM. (1984) "Horace and Maecenas: The Propaganda Value of *Sermones* I", in T. Woodman and D. West, eds, *Poetry and Politics in the Age of Augustus*. Cambridge, 19–58.

―――― (1992) "*In Memoriam Galli*: Propertius I.21", in Anthony J. Woodman and Jonathan Powell, eds, *Author and Audience in Latin Literature*. Cambridge, 52–83.

―――― (2002) "*Amicus certus in re incerta cernitur*: Epode I", in Woodman and Feeney (2002): 17–37.

Duval, M. Susan (1986)"F.R. Leyland: A Maecenas from Liverpool", *Apollo* 124: 110–15.

Edmunds, Lowell (2009) "Horace's Priapus: A Life on the Esquiline (*Sat.* 1.8)", *CQ* 59: 125–31.

Edwards, Catharine (1993) *The Politics of Immorality in Ancient Rome*. Cambridge.

―――― (2005) "Response to Shadi Bartsch", in Shadi Bartsch and Thomas Bartscherer, eds, *Erotikon: Essays on Eros, Ancient and Modern*. Chicago, 84–90.

―――― (2019) *Seneca: Selected Letters*. Cambridge.

Eidinow, John (2009) "Horace: Critics, Canons and Canonicity", in Houghton and Wyke (2009): 80–95.

Eilers, Claude F. (2002) *Roman Patrons of Greek Cities*. Oxford.

Elliott, John H. (1986) *The Count-Duke of Olivares: The Statesman in an Age of Decline*. New Haven, CT.

Elsner, Jaś (2006) "Classicism in Roman Art", in Porter (2006): 270–97.

―――― (2014) "Lithic Poetics: Posidippus and His Stones", *Ramus* 43: 152–72.

Endres, Nikolai (2009) "Petronius in West Egg: *The Satyricon* and *The Great Gatsby*", *F. Scott Fitzgerald Review* 7: 65–79.

Erskine, Andrew (2001) *Troy between Greece and Rome: Local Tradition and Imperial Power*. Oxford.

Evenepoel, Willy (1990) "Maecenas: A Survey of Recent Literature", *Anc. Soc.* 21: 99–117.

Fabbrini, Delphina (2007) *Il migliore dei mondi possibili: Gli epigrammi ecfrastici di Marziale per amici e protettori*. Florence.

Fairweather, Janet (1981) *Seneca the Elder*. Cambridge.

Fantham, Elaine (2013) *Roman Literary Culture from Plautus to Macrobius*. Baltimore, MD, 2nd ed.

Faralli, Sara (2019) "Il busto di 'Mecenate' all'anfiteatro romano: La rappresentazione di Gaio Cilnio Mecenate ad Arezzo nell'Ottocento e Novecento tra erronee iconografiche e celebrazione municipalistica", *Atti e memorie dell'Accademia Petrarca di Lettere Arti e Scienze di Arezzo* 80: 79–91.

Farney, Gary F. (2007). *Ethnic Identity and Aristocratic Competition in Republican Rome*. Cambridge.

Farrell, Joseph (1991) *Vergil's Georgics and the Traditions of Ancient Epic*. Oxford.

Fedeli, Paolo (2005) *Properzio: Elegie Libro II, introduzione, testo e commento*. Cambridge.

Feeney, Denis (1991) *The Gods in Epic*. Oxford.

―――― (1993) "Horace and the Greek Lyric Poets", in Niall Rudd, ed., *Horace 2000: a Celebration. Essays for the Millennium*. London, 41–63. Reprinted in Lowrie (2009): 202–31.

―――― (1994) Review of *Promised Verse: Poets in the Society of Augustan Rome* by Peter White [1993], *Bryn Mawr Classical Review*, June 16, 1994.

―――― (1999) "Epic Violence, Epic Order: Killings, Catalogues, and the Role of the Reader in *Aeneid* 10", in Christine Perkell, ed., *Reading Vergil's Aeneid*. Norman, OK, 178–94.

——— (2002a) "The Odiousness of Comparisons: Horace on Literary History and the Limitations of Synkrisis", in Michael Paschalis, ed., *Horace and Greek Lyric Poetry*. Rethymnon,
Crete, 7–18.

——— (2002b) *"Vna Cum Scriptore Meo*: Poetry, Principate and the Traditions of Literary
History in the Epistle to Augustus", in Woodman and Feeney (2002): 172–87.

——— (2007) *Caesar's Calendar: Ancient Time and the Beginnings of History*. Berkeley, CA.

——— (2009) "Becoming an Authority: Horace on His Own Reception", in Houghton and
Wyke (2009): 16–38.

Felker, Christopher (1997) "'The Tongues of the Learned are Insufficient': Phillis Wheatley,
Publishing Objectives, and Personal Liberty", in Philip Cohen, ed., *Texts and Textuality:
Textual Instability, Theory, and Interpretation*. New York, 81–119.

Fentress, Elizabeth (2007) "Around the Temple: The New Galleries of the Capitoline Museum",
*AJArch*. 111: 365–69.

Ferrero, Guglielmo (1914) *Ancient Rome and Modern America: A Comparative Study of Morals
and Manners*. New York.

Fisher, Paul (2013) *Artful Itineraries: European Art and American Careers in High Culture, 1865–
1920*. Abingdon, UK.

Fitzgerald, F. Scott (2000) *The Great Gatsby*. London.

Fitzgerald, William (1988) "Power and Impotence in Horace's *Epodes*", *Ramus* 17: 176–91.

——— (1995) *Catullan Provocations*. Berkeley, CA.

——— (2000) *Slavery and the Roman Literary Imagination*. Cambridge.

——— (2007) *Martial: The World of the Epigram*. Chicago.

——— (2016) *Variety: The Life of a Roman Concept*. Oxford.

——— (2018) "Pliny and Martial: Dupes and Non-dupes in the Early Empire", in Alice Konig
and Christopher Whitton, eds, *Roman Literature under Nerva, Trajan and Hadrian: Literary
Interactions, AD 96–138*. Cambridge, 108–25.

Fitzgerald, William, and Emily Gowers, eds (2007) *Ennius Perennis: The Annals and Beyond*.
Cambridge.

Flanzbaum, Hilene (1993) "Unprecedented Liberties: Re-reading Phillis Wheatley", *MELUS*
18: 71–81.

Flobert, Pierre (2003) "Considérations intempestives sur l'auteur et la date du *Satyricon* sous
Hadrien", in József Herman and Hannah Rosén, eds, *Petroniana: Gendenkschrift für Hubert
Petersmann*. Heidelberg, 109–22.

Flower, Harriet (2001) "A Tale of Two Monuments: Domitian, Trajan, and Some Praetorians
at Puteoli (*AE* 1973, 137)", *AJArch*. 105: 625–48.

Ford, Andrew (1992) *Homer: The Poetry of the Past*. Ithaca, NY.

Foster, Philip. E. (1978) *A Study of Lorenzo de' Medici's Villa at Poggio a Caiano*. New York.

Fougnies, Armand (1947) *Mécène: Ministre d'Auguste, protecteur des lettres*. Brussels.

Fowler, Don (1995) "Horace and the Aesthetics of Politics", in Stephen Harrison, ed., *Homage
to Horace*. Oxford, 248–66. Reprinted in Lowrie (2009): 247–70.

——— (2002) "Masculinity under Threat: The Poetics and Politics of Inspiration in Latin Poetry", in Efrossini Spentzou and Fowler, eds, *Cultivating the Muse: Struggles for Power and
Inspiration in Classical Literature*. Oxford, 140–59.

——— (2004) "The Didactic Plot", in Mary Depew and Dirk Obbink, eds, *Matrices of Genre:
Authors, Canons, and Society*. Cambridge, MA, 205–19.

—— (2008) "Lectures on Horace's *Epistles*", *Cambridge Classical Journal* 54: 80–114.

Fox, Matthew (1996) *Roman Historical Myths: The Regal Period in Augustan Literature.* Oxford.

Fraenkel, Eduard (1957) *Horace.* Oxford.

—— (2007) *Plautine Elements in Plautus*, trans. Frances Muecke and Tomas Drevikovsky. Oxford.

Fraschetti, Augusto, and Francesco Ursini (2016) *Poesia anonima latina.* Rome.

Freudenburg, Kirk (1993) *The Walking Muse: Horace on the Theory of Satire.* Princeton, NJ.

—— (2001) *Satires of Rome: Threatening Poses from Lucilius to Juvenal.* Cambridge.

—— (2014) "*Recusatio* as Political Theatre: Horace's Letter to Augustus", *JRS* 104: 105–32.

Friedman, Susan (1987) "Creativity and the Childbirth Metaphor: Gender Difference in Literary Discourse", *Feminist Studies* 13: 49–82.

Frischer, Bernard, Jane Crawford and Monica De Simone, eds (2006) *The Horace's Villa Project, 1997–2003.* Oxford, 2 vols.

Frontisi-Ducroux, Françoise, and François Lissarrague (1990) "From Ambiguity to Ambivalence: A Dionysiac Excursion through the 'Anakreontic' Vases", in David M. Halperin, John, J. Winkler and Froma I. Zeitlin, eds, *Before Sexuality: The Construction of Erotic Experience in the Ancient Greek World.* Princeton, NJ, 211–56.

Frutaz, Amato (1962) *Le piante di Roma.* Rome, 3 vols.

Fulvio, Andrea (1588) *Le antichità di Roma.* Venice.

Fumaroli, Marc (1985) Introduction to Mousnier and Mesnard (1985): 1–12.

Fumerton, Patricia (1991) *Cultural Aesthetics.* Chicago.

Gagné, Renaud (2006) "What Is the Pride of Halicarnassus?", *Cl. Ant.* 25: 1–33.

Gaisser, Julia H. (1971) "Tibullus 1.7: A Tribute to Messalla", *CPhil.* 66: 221–29.

Gale, Monica (1991) "Man and Beast in Lucretius and the *Georgics*", *CQ* 41: 414–26.

—— (2000) *Virgil on the Nature of Things: The Georgics, Lucretius and the Didactic Tradition.* Cambridge.

Gambato, Maria (2000) "The Female King: Some Aspects of Representation of Eastern Kings in the *Deipnosophistae*", in David Braund and John Wilkins, eds, *Athenaeus and His World.* Exeter, 227–30.

Garber, Marjorie (1992) *Vested Interests: Cross-Dressing and Cultural Anxiety.* New York.

Gardthausen, Viktor (1964) "Maecenas", in *Augustus und seine Zeit.* Aalen, Germany, 6 vols; 1.762–84.

Gelder, Ken (2007) *Subcultures: Cultural Histories and Social Practice.* London.

Gelsomino, Remo (1958) "Augusti epistula ad Maecenatem. Macrobius, *Saturn.* II 4.12", *Rh. Mus.* 101: 147–52.

Gelzer, Matthias (1969) *The Roman Nobility.* Oxford.

Geue, Tom (2018) "Soft Hands, Hard Power: Sponging off the Empire of Leisure (Virgil, *Georgics* 4)", *JRS* 108: 115–140.

—— (2019) *Author Unknown: The Power of Anonymity in Ancient Rome.* Cambridge, MA.

Giangrande, Giuseppe (1967) "Sympotic Literature and Epigram", in *L'épigramme grecque.* Vandoeuvres, 91–174.

Gibbon, Peter, and Michael D. Higgins (1974) "Patronage, Tradition and Modernisation: The Fate of the Irish 'Gombeenman'", *Economic and Social Review* 6: 27–44.

Gibson, Roy (2011) "Aristocrats, Equestrians and the Ethos of Roman Love Elegy", in P. Millett, S. P. Oakley and R.J.E. Thompson, eds, *Ratio et Res Ipsa: Classical Essays Presented by Former Pupils to James Diggle on His Retirement*. Cambridge, 97–113.

Gigante, Marcello, and Mario Capasso (1989) "Il ritorno di Virgilio a Ercolano", *SIFC* 82: 3–6.

Gildenhard, Ingo (2003) "The 'Annalist' before the Annalists: Ennius and His *Annales*", in Ulrich Eigler, Ulrich Gotter, Nino Luraghi and Uwe Walter, eds, *Formen römischer Geschichtsschreibung von den Anfängen bis Livius: Gattungen, Autoren, Kontexte*. Darmstadt, Germany, 93–114.

Gilman, Richard (1979) *Decadence: The Strange Life of an Epithet*. New York.

Giraldi, Lilio Gregorio (1545) *De historia poetarum tam Graecorum quam Latinorum dialogi decem*. Basel.

Giugliano, Dario (2001) "The Obese Etruscan", *Journal of Endocrinological Investigation* 24: 206.

Giusti, Elena (2014) "Virgil's Carthaginians at *Aen.* 1.430–6: Cyclopes in Bees' Clothing", *Cambridge Classical Journal* 60: 37–58.

Gleason, Maud (1995) *Making Men: Sophists and Self-Presentation in Ancient Rome*. Princeton, NJ.

Goffman, Erving (1956) *The Presentation of Self in Everyday Life*. Edinburgh.

Gold, Barbara K., ed. (1982a) *Literary and Artistic Patronage in Ancient Rome*. Austin, TX.

———— (1982b) "Propertius 3.9: Maecenas as *Eques, Dux, Fautor*", in Gold (1982a): 103–17.

———— (1987) *Literary Patronage in Greece and Rome*. Chapel Hill, NC.

———— (1992) "Openings in Horace's *Satires* and *Odes*: Poet, Patron, and Audience", in Francis Dunn and Thomas Cole, eds, *Beginnings in Classical Literature*. Cambridge, 161–85.

———— (2012) "Patronage and the Elegists: Social Reality or Literary Construction?", in Gold, ed., *A Companion to Roman Love Elegy*. Malden, MA, 303–17.

Goldberg, Sander (1989) "Poetry, Politics, and Ennius", *TAPA* 119: 247–61.

Gowers, Emily (1993) *The Loaded Table: Representations of Food in Roman Literature*. Oxford.

———— (1994) "Persius and the Decoction of Nero", in Jaś Elsner and Jamie Masters, eds, *Reflections of Nero*. London, 131–50. Reprinted in M. Plaza, ed. (2009) *Oxford Readings: Persius and Juvenal*. Oxford, 173–98.

———— (2000) "Vegetable Love: Virgil, Columella, and Garden Poetry", *Ramus* 29: 127–48.

———— (2003) "Fragments of Autobiography in Horace, *Satires* I", *Cl. Ant.* 22: 55–91.

———— (2009) "A Cat May Look at a King: Difference and Indifference in Horace, Satire 1.6", in G. Urso, ed., *Ordine e sovversione nel mondo greco e romano, Atti del convegno internazionale, Fondazione Niccolò Canussio, Cividale del Friuli, 25–27 settembre 2008*. Pisa, 301–16.

———— (2010) "Augustus and 'Syracuse'", *JRS* 100: 69–87.

———— (2011a) "Trees and Family Trees in the *Aeneid*", *Cl. Ant.* 30: 87–118.

———— (2011b) "The Road to Sicily: Lucilius to Seneca", *Ramus* 40: 168–97.

———— (2012) *Horace: Satires Book I*. Cambridge.

———— (2016a) "Girls Will Be Boys and Boys Will Be Girls, Or, What Is the Gender of Horace's *Epodes*?", in P. Bather and C. Stocks, eds, *Horace, Epodes: Contexts, Intertexts, and Reception*. Oxford, 103–30.

———— (2016b) "Under the Influence: Maecenas and Bacchus in *Georgics* 2", in P. Hardie (2016): 134–52.

———— (2017a) "Maecenas, Gaius", in Simon Hornblower, Anthony Spawforth and Esther Eidinow, eds, *Oxford Classical Dictionary*. Oxford, digital ed.

———— (2017b) "*Rus in urbe*: L'intimité urbaine chez Horace", in Bénédicte Délignon and Nathalie Dauvois, eds, *L'invention de la vie privée et le modèle d'Horace*. Paris, 43–57.

Granados de Arena, Dolores, and Laura López de Vega (1993) "La personalidad de Mecenas a través del poeta Horacio", *Revista de estudios clásicos* 23: 51–76.

Graver, Margaret (1998) "The Manhandling of Maecenas: Senecan Abstractions of Masculinity", *AJPhil.* 119: 608–32.

Graverini, Luca (1997) "Un secolo di studi su Mecenate", *RSA* 27: 231–89.

—— (1999) "Mecenate e la pace di Augusto", *Notizie di storia* 2: 5–6, 18.

—— (2006) "Mecenate, mecenatismo e poesia augustea", *Annali Aretini* 12: 49–71.

Gray, Vivienne (1986) "Xenophon's Hiero and the Meeting of the Wise Man and the Tyrant in Greek Literature", *CQ* 36: 115–23.

Green, Carol M. C. (1996) "Did the Romans Hunt?", *Cl. Ant.* 15: 222–60.

Greene, Ellen (2000) "Gender Identity and the Elegiac Hero in Propertius 2.1", *Arethusa* 33: 241–61.

Greenwood, Emily (2011) "The Politics of Classicism in the Poetry of Phillis Wheatley", in Edith Hall, Richard Alston and Justine McConnell, eds, *Ancient Slavery and Abolition: From Hobbes to Hollywood*. Oxford, 153–79.

Gregory, Augusta (1931) *Coole*. Dublin.

Griffin, Jasper (1977) "Propertius and Antony", *JRS* 67: 17–26. Reprinted in Griffin (1994): 32–47.

—— (1979) "The Fourth 'Georgic', Virgil, and Rome", *G & R* 26: 61–80.

—— (1984) "*Caesar qui cogere posset*", in Fergus Millar and Erich Segal, eds, *Caesar Augustus: Seven Aspects*. Oxford, 189–218.

—— (1994) *Latin Poets and Roman Life*. Bristol, 2nd ed.

Griffin, Miriam (1976) *Seneca: A Philosopher in Politics*. Oxford.

—— (1990) Review of *Patronage in Ancient Society* by Andrew Wallace-Hadrill [1989a], *CR* 40: 399–403.

—— (2000) "The Flavians", in Alan K. Bowman, Peter Garnsey and Dominic Rathbone, eds, *Cambridge Ancient History*, vol. 9, *The High Empire, AD 70–192*. Oxford, 1–83.

Griffiths, Alan (2002) "The *Odes*: Just Where Do You Draw the Line?", in Woodman and Feeney (2002): 65–79.

Grimal, Pierre (1943) *Les jardins romains*. Paris.

—— (1953) "Notes sur Properce: La composition de l'élégie à Vertumne", *Revue des Études Latines* 23: 110–19.

Gruen, Erich (1974) *The Last Generation of the Roman Republic*. Berkeley, CA.

—— (1992) *Culture and National Identity in Republican Rome*. Ithaca, NY.

Gruendler, Beatrice (2005) "Meeting the Patron: An Akhbār Type and Its Implications for Muḥdath Poetry", in Sebastian Günther, ed., *Ideas, Images, and Methods of Portrayal: Insights into Classical Arabic Literature and Islam*. Wiesbaden, Germany, 59–88.

Guarino, Antonio (1992) "Mecenate e Terenzia", *Labeo* 38: 137–46.

Guez de Balzac, Jean-Louis (1664) *Oeuvres diverses*. Rouen, 2 vols.

—— (1995) *Oeuvres diverses*, ed. and comm. Roger Zuber. Geneva.

Gundersheimer, W. L. (1981) "Patronage in the Renaissance: An Exploratory Approach", in Guy Fitch Lytle and Stephen Orgel, eds, *Patronage in the Renaissance*. Princeton, NJ, 3–23.

Gunderson, Erik (2003) *Declamation, Paternity, and Roman Identity: Authority and the Rhetorical Self*. Cambridge.

———— (2015) *The Sublime Seneca: Ethics, Literature, Metaphysics*. Cambridge.

Gutzwiller, Kathryn J. (2002) "Posidippus on Statuary", in G. Bastianini and A. Casanova, eds, *Il papiro de Posidippo un anno dopo*. Florence, 41–60.

————, ed. (2005) *The New Posidippus: A Hellenistic Poetry Book*. Oxford.

Habinek, Thomas N. (2005) "Satire as Aristocratic Play", in Kirk Freudenburg, ed., *Cambridge Companion to Roman Satire*. Cambridge, 177–91.

Hallett, Judith P. (1977) "Perusinae Glandes and the Changing Image of Augustus", *AJAH* 2: 151–71.

Hammond, Mason (1980) "An Unpublished Latin Funerary Inscription of Persons Connected with Maecenas", *Harv. Stud.* 84: 263–77.

Hardie, Alex (2002) "The Georgics, the Muses and the Mysteries at Rome", *PCPS* 48:175–208.

Hardie, Colin (1971) *The Georgics: A Transitional Poem*. Abingdon, UK.

Hardie, Philip (1986) *Virgil's Aeneid: Cosmos and Imperium*. Oxford.

———— (1995) *Virgil Aeneid Book IX*. Cambridge.

———— (1998) *Virgil*, Greece & Rome: New Surveys in the Classics no. 28. Oxford.

———— (2004) "Political Education in Virgil's *Georgics*", *SIFC* 97: 83–111.

———— (2007a) "Images of the Persian Wars in Rome", in Emma Bridges, Edith Hall and Peter J. Rhodes, eds, *Cultural Responses to the Persian Wars: Antiquity to the Third Millennium*. Oxford, 127–44.

———— (2007b) "Poets, Patrons, Rulers: The Ennian Traditions", in Fitzgerald and Gowers (2007): 129–44.

————, ed. (2009a) *Paradox and the Marvellous in Augustan Literature and Culture*. Oxford.

———— (2009b) "Virgil: A Paradoxical Poet?", in Hardie (2009a): 95–112.

————, ed., (2016) *Augustan Poetry and the Irrational*. Oxford.

Harrison, Stephen J. (1988) "Horace *Odes* 3.7: An Erotic Odyssey", *CQ* 38: 186–92.

———— (2007) *Generic Enrichment in Vergil and Horace*. Oxford.

Harte, Bret (1891) "A Maecenas of the Pacific Slope", in *A Sappho of Green Springs, and Other Stories*. Boston, 241–310.

Hartswick, Kim J. (2004) *The Gardens of Sallust: A Changing Landscape*. Austin, TX.

Häuber, Chrystina (1983) "Ricerca sui confini e apparato decorativo degli Horti Mecenaziani", in Giuseppina Pisani Sartorio and Lorenzo Quilici, eds, *Roma capitale 1870–1911*, vol. 7, *L'archeologia in Roma capitale tra sterro e scavo*. Venice, 204–22.

———— (1990) "Zur Topographie der Horti Maecenatis und der Horti Lamiani auf dem Esquilini in Rome", *Kölner Jahrbuch für Vor- und Frühgeschichte* 23: 11–107, maps 1–4.

———— (2011) "The *Horti* of Maecenas on the Esquiline Hill in Rome", November 30, 2011, https://fortvna-research.org/texte/hm_text1.html.

———— (2014) *The Eastern Part of the Mons Oppius in Rome*. Rome.

Hawley, Richard (2007) "Lords of the Rings: Ring-Wearing, Status, and Identity in the Age of Pliny the Elder", *BICS* 100: 103–11.

Haynes, Holly (2010) "The Tyrant Lists: Tacitus' Obituary of Petronius", *AJPhil.* 131: 69–99.

Heaney, Seamus (1989) "From Maecenas to MacAlpine", in John Graby, ed., *150 Years of Architecture in Ireland*. Dublin, 68–72.

Heckster, Olivier, and Robert Fowler, eds (2005) *Imaginary Kings: Royal Images in the Ancient Near East, Greece and Rome*. Stuttgart.

Heindorf, Ludwig F. (1815) *Des Q. Horatius Flaccus satiren.* Breslau, Poland.

Hellegouarc'h, Joseph (1963) *Le vocabulaire latin des relations et des partis politiques sous la ré-publique.* Paris.

Henderson, John (1987) "Suck It and See (Horace, Epode 8)", in Michael Whitby, Philip Hardie and Mary Whitby, eds, *Homo Viator: Classical Essays for John Bramble.* Bristol, 105–18.

—— (1993) "Be Alert (Your Country Needs Lerts): Horace, *Satires* 1.9". *PCPS* 39: 67–93. Reprinted in Henderson (1999): 202–27.

—— (1996) "Polishing off the Politics: Horace's Ode to Pollio, 2, 1", *MD* 37: 59–136. Reprinted in Henderson (1998a): 108–64.

—— (1998a) *Fighting for Rome: Poets and Caesars, History and Civil War.* Cambridge.

—— (1998b) "Virgil, *Eclogue* 9: Valleydiction", *PVS* 23: 149–76.

—— (1999) *Writing Down Rome: Satire, Comedy and Other Offences in Latin Poetry.* Oxford.

—— (2001a) "Going to the Dogs / Grattius <&> the Augustan Subject", *Cambridge Classical Journal* 47: 1–22.

—— (2001b) *Telling Tales on Caesar: Roman Stories from Phaedrus.* Oxford.

Henig, Martin (1994) *Classical Gems: Ancient and Modern Intaglios and Cameos in the Fitzwilliam Museum, Cambridge.* Cambridge.

Henkel, John H. (2009) "Writing on Trees: Genre and Metapoetics in Vergil's *Eclogues* and *Georgics*". Dissertation, University of North Carolina, Chapel Hill.

Henrichs, Albert (1993) "He Has a God in Him: Human and Divine in the Modern Perception of Dionysus", in Thomas H. Carpenter and Christopher A. Faraone, eds, *Masks of Dionysus.* Ithaca, NY: 13–43.

Henry, Denis, and Bessie Walker (1963) "Tacitus and Seneca", *G & R* 10: 98–110.

Herman, Gabriel (1980–81) "The 'Friends' of the Early Hellenistic Rulers: Servants or Officials?", *Talanta* 12/13: 103–49.

Heslin, Peter (2011) "Metapoetic Pseudonyms in Horace, Propertius and Ovid", *JRS* 101: 51–72.

Heurgon, Jacques (1961) *La vie quotidienne chez les Étrusques.* Paris.

Heyworth, Stephen J. (2007a) *Cynthia: A Companion to the Text of Propertius.* Oxford.

—— (2007b) "Propertius, Patronage and Politics", *BICS* 50: 93–128.

—— (2007c) *Sexti Properti Elegos.* Oxford.

—— (2010) "An Elegist's Career: From Cynthia to Cornelia", in Philip Hardie and Helen Moore, eds, *Classical Literary Careers and Their Reception.* Oxford, 89–104.

Heyworth, Stephen J., and James H. W. Morwood, (2011) *A Commentary on Propertius, Book 3.* Oxford.

Hill, Timothy (2004) *Ambitiosa Mors: Suicide and Self in Roman Thought and Literature.* New York.

Hinds, Stephen (1998) *Allusion and Intertext: Dynamics of Appropriation in Roman Poetry.* Cambridge.

—— (2000) "Essential Epic: Genre and Gender from Macer to Statius", in Mary Depew and Dirk Obbink, eds, *Matrices of Genre: Authors, Canons, and Society.* Cambridge, MA, 221–44.

—— (2001) "Cinna, Statius, and 'immanent literary history' in the cultural economy", in Ernst A. Schmidt, ed., *L'histoire littéraire immanente dans la poésie latine.* Vandoeuvres, 221–57.

Hollis, Adrian S. (2007) *Fragments of Roman Poetry, c. 60 BC–AD 20.* Oxford.

Holmes, Daniel (2008) "Practicing Death in Petronius' 'Cena Trimalchionis' and Plato's 'Phaedo'", *CJ* 104: 43–57.

Holzknecht, Karl Julius ([1923] 2018) *Literary Patronage in the Middle Ages*. Abingdon, UK.

Hornblower, Simon (2009) "Greek Lyric and the Politics and Sociologies of Archaic and Classical Greek Communities", in Felix Budelmann, ed., *Cambridge Companion to Greek Lyric*. Cambridge, 39–57.

Horsfall, Nicholas (1988) Review of *Literary and Artistic Patronage in Ancient Rome* by Barbara K. Gold [1982a], *CR* 38: 268–70.

——— (1995) *Companion to the Study of Virgil*. Leiden.

——— (2003) *Virgil Aeneid 11: A Commentary*. Leiden.

Houghton, Luke B. T. (2011) "Death Ritual and Burial Practice in the Latin Love Elegists", in Valerie M. Hope and Janet Huskinson, eds, *Memory and Mourning: Studies on Roman Death*. Oxford, 61–77.

Houghton, Luke B. T., and Maria Wyke, eds (2009) *Perceptions of Horace: A Roman Poet and His Readers*. Cambridge.

Housman, A. E. (1972) *The Classical Papers of A. E. Housman*, ed. James Diggle and Frank R. D. Goodyear. Cambridge, 3 vols.

Howell, Peter (1980) *A Commentary on Book One of the Epigrams of Martial*. London.

Huet, Valérie, and François Lissarrague (2005) "Un 'relief néo-attique': Icarios, le retour", in Huet and Emmanuelle Valette-Cagnac, eds, *Dossier: Et si les Romains avaient inventé la Grèce?*, *Mètis* 3: 85–100.

Hulme, B. J. (2011) "*Naturalis historiae* 37.3–4: Pliny, Livia, and the Sardonyx of Polycrates", *Phoenix* 65: 395–97.

Hunter, Richard (1985) "Horace on Friendship and Free Speech", *Hermes* 113: 480–90.

——— (1996) *Theocritus and the Archaeology of Greek Poetry*. Cambridge.

——— (2003) *Theocritus: Encomium of Ptolemy Philadelphus*. Berkeley, CA.

——— (2006) "The Prologue of the *Periodos to Nicomedes* ('Pseudo-Scymnus')", in M. A. Harder, R. F. Regtuit and G. C. Wakker, eds, *Beyond the Canon*. Leuven, Belgium, 123–40.

Hunter, Richard, and Ian Rutherford, eds (2009) *Wandering Poets in Ancient Greek Culture: Travel, Locality and Pan-Hellenism*. Cambridge.

Hutchinson, Gregory (2003) "The Catullan Corpus, Greek Epigram, and the Poetry of Objects", *CQ* 53: 206–21.

——— (2006) *Propertius: Elegies Book IV*. Cambridge.

Huysmans, Joris-Karl ([1891] 1998) *Against Nature*, trans. Margaret Mauldon. Oxford.

Jaeger, Mary (1995) "Reconstructing Rome: The Campus Martius and Horace, *Ode* 1.8", *Arethusa* 28: 177–91.

James, Henry (1903) *William Wetmore Story and His Friends*. Boston, MA.

Jenkyns, Richard (1998) *Virgil's Experience: Nature and History; Times, Names, and Places*. Oxford.

Jocelyn, Harry D. (1979) "Vergilius Cacozelus (Donatus Vita Vergilii 44)", *PLLS* 2: 67–142.

Johnson, Terry, and Christopher Dandeker (1989) "Patronage: Relation and System", in Wallace-Hadrill (1989a): 219–42.

Johnson, W. Ralph (1982) *The Idea of Lyric*. Berkeley, CA.

——— (1993) *Horace and the Dialectic of Freedom: Readings in Epistles I*. Ithaca.

Johnson, William A. (2010) *Readers and Reading Culture in the High Roman Empire*. Oxford.

Johnston, Patricia A. (2009) "The Mystery Cults and Virgil's *Georgics*", in Giovanni Casadio and Johnston, eds, *Mystic Cults in Magna Graecia*. Austin, TX, 251–73.

Johnstone, Steven (1994) "Virtuous Toil, Vicious Work: Xenophon on Aristocratic Style", *CPhil.* 89: 219–40.

Jolivet, Vincent (1987) "*Xerxes togatus*: Lucullus en Campanie", *Mélanges de l'école française de Rome* 99: 875–904.

Jones, Christopher P. (1986) "Suetonius in the Probus of Giorgio Valla", *Harv. Stud.* 90: 245–51.

Kallendorf, Craig (2007) *The Other Virgil: 'Pessimistic' Readings of the Aeneid in Early Modern Culture*. Oxford.

Kappelmacher, Alfred (1928) "C. Maecenas (6)", *RE* 14: 207–29.

Kaster, Robert A. (1988) *Guardians of Language: The Grammarian and Society in Late Antiquity*. Berkeley, CA.

—— (1995) *C. Suetonius Tranquillus: De Grammaticis et Rhetoribus*. Oxford.

—— (1997) "The Shame of the Romans", *TAPA* 127: 1–19.

—— (2001) "Controlling Reason: Declamation in Rhetorical Education at Rome", in Yun Lee Too, ed., *Education in Greek and Roman Antiquity*. Leiden, 317–37.

—— (2002) "The Taxonomy of Patience, Or When is *Patientia* Not a Virtue?", *CPhil.* 97: 133–44.

—— (2005) *Emotion, Restraint, and Community in Ancient Rome*. New York.

—— (2010) *Studies on the Text of Macrobius' Saturnalia*. New York.

——, ed. and trans. (2011) *Macrobius, Saturnalia*. Cambridge, MA, 2 vols.

Kay, Nigel M. (1985) *Martial Book IX*. London.

Kehoe, Denis (1985) "Tacitus and Sallustius Crispus", *CJ* 80: 247–54.

Keith, Alison (1999) "Slender Verse: Roman Elegy and Ancient Rhetorical Theory", *Mnemosyne* 52: 41–62.

—— (2008) *Propertius: Poet of Love and Leisure*. London.

Kelly, Joan (1984) "Did Women Have a Renaissance?", in *Women, History, and Theory: The Essays of Joan Kelly*. Chicago, 19–50.

Kennedy, Duncan (1992) "'Augustan' and 'Anti-Augustan': Reflections on Terms of Reference", in Anton Powell, ed., *Roman Poetry and Propaganda in the Age of Augustus*. Bristol, UK, 26–58.

—— (1993). *The Arts of Love*. Cambridge.

Klingner, F. (1963) *Vergils Georgica*. Zürich.

Knox, Peter E. (2006) "An Unnoticed Imitation of Callimachus, *Aetia* fr. 1.1 Pf.", *CQ* 2: 639–40.

Konstan, David (1995) "Patrons and Friends", *CPhil.* 90: 328–42.

Kovacs, David (2010) "The Second Person Indefinite and the Logic of Horace, *Odes* 1.12.29–36", *Philologus* 154: 306–15.

Kraggerud, Emil (1987) "La 'ballata di Paride' di Orazio (carm. I 15)", in Sandro Boldrini, ed., *Filologia e forme letterarie: Studi offerti a F. Della Corte*. Urbino, Italy, 3.47–56.

Kraus, Christina S. (1994) "No Second Troy: Topoi and Refoundation in Livy, Book V", *TAPA* 124: 267–89.

Kuhlmann, Peter (2010) "Die Maecenas-Rede bei Cassius Dio: Anachronismen und intertextuelle Bezüge", in Dennis Pausch, ed., *Stimmen der Geschichte: Funktionen von Reden in der antiken Historiographie*. Berlin, 109–21.

Kurke, Leslie (1991) *The Traffic in Praise: Pindar and the Poetics of Social Economy*. Ithaca, NY.

——— (1992). "The Politics of ἁβροσύνη in Archaic Greece", *Cl. Ant.* 11: 91–120.

Kuttner, Ann (2005) "Cabinet Fit for a Queen: The 'Lithika' as Posidippus' Gem Museum", in Gutzwiller (2005): 141–63.

Labate, Mario (1984) *L'arte di farsi amare: Modelli culturali e progetto didascalico nell'elegia ovidiana*. Pisa.

——— (2005) "Poetica minore e minima: Mecenate e gli amici nelle Satire di Orazio", *MD* 54: 47–63.

——— (2012) "Mecenate senza poeti, poeti senza Mecenate: La distruzione di un mito augusteo", in Guido Bastianini, Walter Lapini and Mauro Tulli, eds, *Harmonia: Scritti di filologia classica in onore di Angelo Casanova*. Florence, 405–24.

——— (2016) "The Night of Reason: The Esquiline and Witches in Horace", in P. Hardie (2016): 74–94.

La Bua, Giuseppe (2013) "Between Poetry and Politics: Horace and the East", *Harv. Stud.* 107: 265–96.

Lakoff, George, and Mark Johnson (1980) *Metaphors We Live By*. Chicago.

La Penna, Antonio (1963) *Orazio e l'ideologia del principato*. Turin.

——— (1976) "Il ritratto paradossale da Silla a Petronio", *Rivista di Filologia e di Istruzione Classica* 104: 270–93. Reprinted in La Penna (1978): *Aspetti del pensiero storico latino*. Turin, 193–221.

——— (1977) "Senex Corycius", in *Atti del convegno virgiliano sul bimillenario delle Georgiche*. Naples, 37–66.

——— (1981) "Mobilità dei modelli etici e relativismo dei valori: Da Cornelio Nepote a Valerio Massimo e al Laus Pisonis", in Andrea Giardina and Aldo Schiavone, eds, *Società romana e produzione schiavistica III, Modelli etici, diritto e formazioni sociali*. Rome, 183–206.

——— (1987) s.v. "Mecenate" in *Enc. Virg.* 3.410–14.

——— (1995) "Il vino di Orazio: Nel *modus* e contro il *modus*", in Oswyn Murray, ed., *In vino veritas*. Oxford, 266–82.

——— (1996) s.v. "Mecenate" in *Orazio: Enciclopedia oraziana* I. Rome, 792–803.

Lattimore, Richmond (1939) "The Wise Adviser in Herodotus", *CPhil.* 34: 24–35.

Leach, Elinor W. (1993) "Horace's Sabine Property in Lyric and Hexameter Verse", *AJPhil.* 114: 271–302.

Le Doze, Philippe (2012) "*Quomodo Maecenas uixerit*: A propos du Mécène de Sénèque", *Latomus* 71: 734–52.

——— (2014) *Mécène: Ombres et flamboyances*. Paris.

——— (2019) "Maecenas and the Augustan Poets: The Background of a Cultural Ambition", in Josiah Osgood, Kit Morrell and Kathryn Welch, eds, *The Alternative Augustan Age*. Oxford, 231–46.

Lee-Stecum, Parshia (2006) "*Tot in uno corpore formae*: Hybridity, Ethnicity and Vertumnus in Propertius Book 4", *Ramus* 34: 22–46.

Leigh, Matthew (2010) "The Garland of Maecenas (Horace, *Odes* 1.1.35)", *CQ* 60: 268–71.

Leitao, David (2012) *The Pregnant Male as Myth and Metaphor in Classical Greek Literature*. Cambridge.

Lenski, Noel (2013) "Working Models: Functional Art and Roman Conceptions of Slavery", in Michele George, ed., *Roman Slavery and Roman Material Culture*. Toronto, 129–57.

Lentano, Mario (2005) "'Un nome più grande di qualsiasi legge': declamazione latina e *patria potestas*", *Bollettino di studi Latini* 35: 558–89.

Leppin, Hartmut (1992) "Die *Laus Pisonis* als Zeugnis senatorischer Mentalität", *Klio* 74: 221–36.

Lerouge, Charlotte (2007) *L'image des Parthes dans le monde greco-romain*. Stuttgart.

Lessing, Gotthold Ephraim (1922) *Sämmtliche Schriften*, ed. Karl Lachmann and Franz Muncker. Berlin, 17 vols.

Liebert, Rana Saadi (2010) "Apian Imagery and the Critique of Poetic Sweetness in Plato's *Republic*", *TAPA* 140: 97–115.

Liebert, Yves (2006) *Regards sur la truphè étrusque*. Limoges.

Lindheim, Sara (1998) "I Am Dressed, Therefore I Am?: Vertumnus in Propertius 4.2 and in *Metamorphoses* 14.622–771", *Ramus* 27: 27–38.

Ling, Roger (1995) "The Decoration of Roman *Triclinia*", in Oswyn Murray, ed., *In vino veritas*. Oxford, 239–51.

Lloyd-Jones, Hugh (1999) "The Pride of Halicarnassus", *ZPE* 124: 1–14.

Lowe, Dunstan (2010) "The Symbolic Value of Grafting in Ancient Rome", *TAPA* 140: 461–88.

Lowrie, Michèle (1995) "A Parade of Lyric Predecessors: Horace C. 1.12–18", *Phoenix* 49: 33–48. Reprinted in Lowrie (2009): 337–55.

——— (1997) *Horace's Narrative Odes*. Oxford.

——— (2002) Review of *Horace and the Gift Economy of Patronage* by Phebe Lowell Bowditch [2001], *AJPhil.* 123: 305–8.

———, ed. (2009) *Oxford Readings: Horace's Odes and Epodes*. Oxford.

——— (2011) "Divided Voices and Imperial Identity in Propertius 4.1 and Derrida, *Monolingualism of the Other* and *Politics of Friendship*", *Dictynna* 8, https://journals.openedition.org/dictynna/711.

Lucot, Robert (1953) "Vertumne et Mécène", *Pallas* 1: 66–80.

Lugli, Giuseppe (1930–38) *I monumenti antichi di Roma e suburbio*. Rome, 3 vols.

Lunderstedt, Paul (1911) *De C. Mecenatis fragmentis*, Commentationes philologae Ienenses 9. Leipzig.

Lyne, R. Oliver A. M. (1995) *Horace: Behind the Public Poetry*. New Haven, CT.

Ma, John (2003) "Kings", in A. Erskine, ed., *A Companion to the Hellenistic World*. Oxford. 177–95.

Macaulay-Lewis, Elizabeth (2008) "The Fruits of Victory: Generals, Plants, and Power in the Roman World", in Edward Bragg, Lisa Irene Hau and Macaulay-Lewis, eds, *Beyond the Battlefields: New Perspectives on Warfare and Society in the Graeco-Roman World*. Cambridge, 205–25.

Macfarlane, Roger T. (1996) "*Tyrrhena Regum Progenies*: Etruscan Literary Figures from Horace to Ovid", in John F. Hall, ed., *Etruscan Italy: Etruscan Influences on the Civilization of Italy from Antiquity to the Modern Era*. Provo, UT: 241–65.

Mac Góráin, Fiachra (2009a) "Microcosm and the Virgilian Persona", in Frédéric Nau, ed., *Autoportraits de poètes: Les paratopies romaines et leur postérité, Camenae* 7.

——— (2009b) "Tragedy and the Dionysiac in Virgil's *Aeneid*". DPhil thesis, Oxford University.

—— (2013) "Virgil's Bacchus and the Roman Republic", in Joseph Farrell and Damien P. Nelis, eds, *Augustan Poetry and the Roman Republic*. Oxford, 124–45.

—— (2014) "The Mixed Blessings of Bacchus in Virgil's *Georgics*", *Dictynna* 11, https://journals.openedition.org/dictynna/1069.

Mack, John (2007) *The Art of Small Things*. London.

MacKay, Louis (1942). "Notes on Horace", *CPhil.* 37: 79–81.

MacKendrick, Paul (1950) "*The Great Gatsby* and Trimalchio", *CJ* 45: 307–14.

Macleod, Colin W. (1983) *Collected Essays*. Oxford.

Magnelli, Enrico (2006), "Bucolic Tradition and Poetic Programme in Calpurnius Siculus", in Marco Fantuzzi and Theodore Papanghelis, eds, *Brill's Companion to Greek and Latin Pastoral*. Leiden, 467–77.

Makowski, John F. (1985) "*Georgic* 3.41: A Vergilian Wordplay at the Expense of Maecenas", *Vergilius* 31: 57–58.

—— (1991) "*Iocosus Maecenas*: Patron as Writer", *Syllecta Classica* 3: 25–35.

Malamud, Margaret (2008) *Ancient Rome and Modern America*. Malden, MA.

Mannering, Jonathan E. (2008) "Momentous Masks: Verse Quotation in Roman Authorship from the Late Republic to the Early Empire". PhD thesis, University of Cambridge.

Marangoni, Claudio (2002–3) "*Tua, Maecenas, haud mollia iussa*: Materiali e appunti per la storia di un *topos* proemiale", *Incontri triestini di filologia classica* 2: 77–90.

Marquis, E. (1974) "Vertumnus in Propertius IV, 2", *Hermes* 102: 491–500.

Martin, Richard (2009) "Read on Arrival", in Hunter and Rutherford (2009): 80–104.

Martini, Remo (1995) "Di una causa giudiziaria, *inter Terentiam et Maecenatem*", *RSA* 25: 177–85.

Mártir Rizo, Juan Pablo (1626) *Historia de la vida de Mecenas*. Madrid.

Marx, Karl ([1835] 1975) "Does the Reign of Augustus Deserve to be Counted among the Happier Periods of the Roman Empire?", *Archiv für die Geschichte des Sozialismus und der Arbeiterbewegung*. Reprinted in *Marx/Engels Collected Works*, London, 1.639.

Massa-Pairault, Françoise-Hélène (1999) "Mythe et identité politique: L'Étrurie du IVe siècle à l'époque héllenistique", in Massa-Pairault, ed., *Le mythe grec dans l'Italie antique: Fonction et image*. Rome, 521–54.

Massimo, Vittorio (1836) *Notizie istoriche della villa Massimo alle Terme Diocleziane*. Rome.

Mattiacci, Silvia (1995) "L'attività poetica di Mecenate tra neoterismo e novellismo", *Prometheus* 21: 67–86.

Mayer, Roland (2012) *Horace: Odes Book I*. Cambridge.

Mazzoli, Giancarlo (1968) "L'epicureismo di Mecenate e il *Prometheus*", *Athenaeum* 46: 300–326.

McCabe, Richard (2016a) "Patrons", in Andrew Escobedo, ed., *Edmund Spenser in Context*. Cambridge, 23–32.

—— (2016b) *"Ungainefull Arte": Poetry, Patronage, and Print in the Early Modern Era*. Oxford.

McCarter, Stephanie (2015) *Horace between Freedom and Slavery: The First Book of Epistles*. Madison, WI.

McCarthy, Kathleen (1998) "*Servitium amoris: Amor servitii*", in Sandra Joshel and Sheila Murnaghan, eds, *Women and Slaves in Greco-Roman Culture*. London, 174–92.

McDermott, Emily (1982) "Horace, Maecenas, and *Odes* 2.17", *Hermes* 110: 211–28.

McGann, Michael (1969) *Studies in Horace's First Book of Epistles*. Brussels.

McGill, Scott (2012) *Plagiarism in Latin Literature*. Cambridge.

McGinn, Thomas A. (1998) *Prostitution, Sexuality, and the Law in Ancient Rome*. Oxford.

Meibom [Meibomius], Johann Heinrich (1653) *Maecenas, sive de C. Cilnii Maecenatis vita, moribus et rebus gestis liber singularis*. Leiden.

Meyer, Paul (1891) "De Maecenatis oratione a Dione ficta", PhD thesis, University of Berlin.

Meyer, Reinhold (1986) "In Praise of Cassius Dio", *Antiquité classique* 55: 213–22.

Miles, Gary (1980) *Virgil's Georgics: A New Interpretation*. Berkeley, CA.

Millar, Fergus (1977) *The Emperor in the Roman World*. London.

Miller, John F. (1991) "Propertius' Hymn to Bacchus and Contemporary Poetry", *AJPhil.* 112: 77–86.

Miller, Paul Allen (2001) "Why Propertius Is a Woman: French Feminism and Augustan Elegy", *CPhil.* 96: 127–46.

Millett, Paul (1989) "Patronage and Its Avoidance in Classical Athens", in Wallace-Hadrill (1989a): 15–47.

Milnor, Kristina (2014) *Graffiti and the Literary Landscape in Roman Pompeii*. Oxford.

Missirini, Melchior (1835) *Della scoperta di un busto marmoreo colossale di Mecenate*. Naples.

Mitchell, Elizabeth (2010) "Time for an Emperor: Old Age and the Future of the Empire in Horace *Odes* 4", *MD* 64: 43–76.

—— (2012) "Horace *Odes* 3.27: A New World for Galatea", *Cambridge Classical Journal* 58: 165–180.

Möller, Melanie (2004) *Talis oratio—qualis vita*. Heidelberg, Germany.

Mommsen, Theodor (1856) *Römische Geschichte*, vol. 1, book 1, *Bis zur Abschaffung des römischen Königtums*. Berlin.

Morales, Helen (1996) "The Torturer's Apprentice: Parrhasius and the Limits of Art", in Jaś Elsner, ed., *Art and Text in the Roman World*. Cambridge, 182–209.

More, Hannah (1996) *Selected Writings of Hannah More*, ed. Robert Hole. London.

Moretti, Giuseppe (1948) *Ara Pacis Augustae*. Rome.

Morgan, Kathryn, ed. (2003) *Popular Tyranny. Sovereignty and Its Discontents in Ancient Greece*. Austin, TX.

—— (2013) "Imaginary Kings: Visions of Monarchy in Sicilian Literature from Pindar to Theokritos", in Claire L. Lyons, Michael Bennett and Clemente Marconi, eds, *Sicily: Art and Invention between Greece and Rome*. Los Angeles, 98–109.

Mörland, Henning (1965) "Zu Horaz, *carm*. II 17", *Symb. Osl.* 40: 75–80.

Morris, Ian (1996) "The Strong Principle of Equality and the Archaic Origins of Greek Democracy", in Josiah Ober and Charles Hedrick, eds, *Demokratia*. Princeton, 19–48.

Morris, Sarah (2003) "Imaginary Kings: Alternatives to Monarchy in Early Greece", in K. Morgan (2003): 1–24.

Most, Glenn W. (1993) "Hesiod and the Textualization of Personal Temporality", in G. Arrighetti and F. Montanari, eds, *La componente autobiografica nella poesia greca e latina: Fra realtà e artificio letterario, Atti del Convegno Pisa 16–17 maggio 1991*. Pisa, 73–92.

Motto, Anna L., and John R. Clark (1993) "Seneca and the Paradox of Adversity", in Motto and Clark, eds, *Essays on Seneca*. New York, 65–86.

Moul, Victoria (2010) *Jonson, Horace and the Classical Tradition*. Cambridge.

Mountford, Peter (2019) *Maecenas*. London.

Mouritsen, Henrik (2011) *The Freedman in the Roman World*. Cambridge.

Mousnier, Roland, and Jean Mesnard, eds (1985) *L'âge d'or du Mécénat (1598–1661)*. Paris.

Muecke, Frances (1979) "Poetic Self-Consciousness in *Georgics* II", *Ramus* 8: 87–107.

——— (1982) "A Portrait of the Artist as a Young Woman", *CQ* 32: 41–55.

Murray, Oswyn (1985) "Symposium and Genre in the Poetry of Horace", *JRS* 75: 39–50.

Mutschler, Fritz-Heiner (1978) "Kaufmannsliebe: Eine Interpretation der Horazode 'Quid fles Asterie?' (c. 3, 7)", *Symb. Osl.* 53: 111–31.

Mynors, Roger (1990) *Virgil Georgics*. Oxford.

Naldi, Naldo (1934) *Elegiarum libri III ad Laurentium Medicen*, ed. Ladislaus Juhász. Leipzig.

Nappa, Christopher (2005) *Reading after Actium: Vergil's Georgics, Octavian, and Rome*. Ann Arbor, MI.

Nashe, Thomas (1958) *The Works of Thomas Nashe*, ed. Ronald B. McKerrow. Oxford, 5 vols.

Naumann, Heinrich (1981) "Was wissen wir von Vergils Leben?" *Altsprachliche Unterricht* 24: 5–16.

Nauta, Ruurd R. (2002) *Poetry for Patrons: Literary Communication in the Age of Domitian*. Leiden.

Nelis, Damien P. (2013) "Past, Present, and Future in Virgil's *Georgics*", in Joseph Farrell and Nelis, eds, *Augustan Poetry and the Roman Republic*. Oxford, 244–62.

Nenci, Giuseppe (1983) "Tryphé e colonizzazione", in *Modes de contacts et processus de transformation dans les societes anciennes, Actes du colloque de Cortona (24–30 mai 1981)*. Rome, 1019–31.

Netz, Reviel (2020) *Scale, Space and Canon in Ancient Literary Culture*. Cambridge.

Newlands, Carole (1987) "Urban Pastoral: The Seventh Eclogue of Calpurnius Siculus", *Cl. Ant.* 6: 218–31.

Newman, John K. (1997) *Augustan Propertius*. Hildesheim, Germany.

Nicastri, Luciano (1980) "Sul Maecenas pseudovirgiliano", *Vichiana* 9: 258–98.

Nichols, Marden (2010) "Contemporary Perspectives on Luxury Building in Second-Century Rome", *Papers of the British School at Rome* 78: 39–61.

Nicolet, Claude (1966) *L'ordre équestre a l'époque républicaine (312–43 av. J.-C.)*. Paris.

Nielson, Kristina P. (1984) "Tarchon Etruscus: Alter Aeneas", *Pacific Coast Philology* 19: 28–34.

Nigro, Maria-Antonietta (1998) "La prima *Elegia a Mecenate*: Apologia di un ministro e propaganda di regime", *Ant. Class.* 67: 137–48.

Nisbet, Hugh Barr H. (2013) *Gotthold Ephraim Lessing: His Life, Works, and Thought*. Oxford.

Nisbet, Robin G. M., and Margaret Hubbard (1970) *A Commentary on Horace Odes Book I*. Oxford.

——— (1978) *A Commentary on Horace Odes Book II*. Oxford.

Nisbet, Robin G. M., and Niall Rudd (2004) *A Commentary on Horace Odes Book III*. Oxford.

Nisetich, Frank (2005) "The Poems of Posidippus", in Gutzwiller (2005): 17–66.

Nugent, Georgia (1990) "This Sex Which Is Not One: De-constructing Ovid's Hermaphrodite", *Differences* 2: 160–85.

Nünlist, René (2012) "Homer as a Blueprint for Speechwriters: Eustathius' Commentaries and Rhetoric", *GRBS* 52: 493–509.

Oberhelman, Steven, and David Armstrong (1995) "Satire as Poetry and the Impossibility of Metathesis in Horace's *Satires*", in Dirk Obbink, ed., *Philodemus and Poetry: Poetic Theory and Practice in Lucretius, Philodemus, and Horace*. Oxford, 233–54.

O'Gorman, Ellen (2000) *Irony and Misreading in the Annals of Tacitus*. Cambridge.

Oliensis, Ellen (1997) "The Erotics of *Amicitia*: Readings in Tibullus, Propertius, and Horace", in Judith Hallett and Marilyn Skinner, eds, *Roman Sexualities*. Princeton, NJ, 151–71.

———— (1998) *Horace and the Rhetoric of Authority*. Cambridge.

———— (2002) "Feminine Endings, Lyric Seductions," in Woodman and Feeney (2002): 93–106.

Olson, Kelly (2006) "*Matrona* and Whore: Clothing and Definition in Roman Antiquity", in Christopher A. Faraone and Laura K. McClure, eds, *Prostitutes and Courtesans in the Ancient World*. Madison, WI, 186–204.

Omrani, Bijan (2014) "Horace and the Persians", in Horatian Society (London), [Addresses delivered before the Society]. British Library, General Reference Collection Ac. 1188.h, system no. 002231506.

O'Neill, Kerill (2000) "Propertius 4.2: Slumming with Vertumnus?", *AJPhil.* 121: 259–77.

Osgood, Josiah (2006) *Caesar's Legacy*. Cambridge.

Pagán, Victoria E. (2007–8) "Teaching Torture in Seneca *Controversiae* 2.5", *CJ* 103: 165–82.

Pallottino, Massimo (1975) *The Etruscans*. London, Rev. 2nd ed.

Pandey, Nandini (2018) *The Poetics of Power in Augustan Rome*. Cambridge.

Papaioannou, Sophia (2000) "Vergilian Diomedes Revisited: The Re-evaluation of the *Iliad*", *Mnemosyne* 53: 193–217.

Papi, Emanuele (1996) "Horti Caesaris (trans Tiberim)", in Steinby (1993–99), 3.55–56.

Parassoglou, George M. (1978) *Imperial Estates in Roman Egypt*. Amsterdam.

Paratore, Ettore (1966) "La Persia nella letteratura latina", in *La Persia e il mondo greco-romano, Atti dei convegni della Accademia Nazionale dei Lincei*. Rome, 505–58.

Parker, Grant (2008) *The Making of Roman India*. Cambridge.

———— (2011) "India, Egypt and Parthia in Augustan Verse: The Post-Orientalist Turn", *Dictynna* 8, https://journals.openedition.org/dictynna/684.

Pater, Walter ([1885] 1910) *Marius the Epicurean*. London, 2 vols.

Paturzo, Franco (1999) *Mecenate, il ministro d'Augusto: Politica, filosofia, letteratura nel periodo augusteo*. Cortona, Italy.

Pease, Arthur Stanley (1926) "Things without Honor", *CPhil.* 21: 27–42.

Peirano, Irene (2012) *The Rhetoric of the Roman Fake: Latin Pseudepigrapha in Context*. Cambridge.

Pelletier, André (1948) "L'image du 'frelon' dans la *République* de Platon", *Rev. Phil.* 22: 131–46.

Pelling, Christopher (2009) "Was There a Genre of the Memoir? Or, Did Augustus Know What He Was Doing?", in Christopher Smith and Anton Powell, eds, *The Lost Memoirs of Augustus and the Development of Roman Autobiography*. Swansea, UK, 41–64.

Penella, Robert J. (2007) *Man and the Word: The Orations of Himerius*. Berkeley, CA.

Perkell, Christine G. (1989) *The Poet's Truth: A Study of the Poet in Virgil's Georgics*. Berkeley, CA.

———— (1981) "On the Corycian Gardener in Vergil's Fourth *Georgic*", *TAPA* 111: 167–77.

Perrin, Yves (1996) "Turris Maecenatiana: Une note d'histoire et de topographie", *Latomus* 55: 399–410.

Pethica, James (1992) "Patronage and Creative Exchange: Yeats, Lady Gregory, and the Economy of Indebtedness", *Yeats Annual* 9: 60–94.

Petrain, David (2005) "Gems, Metapoetics, and Value: Greek and Roman Responses to a Third-Century Discourse on Precious Stones", *TAPA* 135: 329–57.

Pihl, Lis, ed. (1994) *Signe Toksvig's Irish Diaries, 1926–1937*. Dublin.

Pinotti, Paola (1983) "Properzio e Vertumno: Anticonformismo e restaurazione augustea", in Salvatore Vivona, ed., *Colloquium Propertianum (tertium): Atti: Assisi, 29–31 maggio 1981.* Assisi, 75–96.

Pisani Sartorio, Giuseppina (1996) "Mecenate sull' Esquilino", *RSA* 26: 33–45.

Plass, Paul (1988) *Wit and the Writing of History: Rhetoric of Historiography in Imperial Rome.* Madison, WI.

Platner, Samuel Ball, and Thomas Ashby (1929) *A Topographical Dictionary of Ancient Rome.* London.

Platt, Verity (2006) "Making an Impression: Replication and the Ontology of the Greco-Roman Seal Stone", *Art History* 29: 233–57.

Pollitt, Jerome J. (1974) *The Ancient View of Greek Art: Criticism, History, and Terminology.* New Haven, CT.

Pomeroy, Arthur J. (1992) "Trimalchio as 'Deliciae'", *Phoenix* 46: 45–53.

Porter, James I., ed. (2006) *Classical Pasts: The Classical Traditions of Greece and Rome.* Princeton, NJ.

——— (2011) "Against Λεπτοτης: Rethinking Hellenistic Aesthetics", in Andrew Erskine and Lloyd Llewellyn Jones, eds, *Creating a Hellenistic World.* Swansea, UK, 271–312.

Potolsky, Matthew (2004) "Introduction", *New Literary History* 35: v–xi.

Powell, Anton (2017) "Sinning against Philology? Method and the Suetonian-Donatan Life of Virgil", in Powell and Philip Hardie, eds, *The Ancient Lives of Virgil: Literary and Historical Studies.* Swansea, UK, 173–98.

Powell, Lindsay (2015) *Marcus Agrippa: Right-Hand Man of Caesar Augustus.* Barnsley, UK.

Préaux, Jean-G. (1959) *"Tua, Maecenas, haud mollia iussa"*, *Revue belge de philologie et d'histoire* 37: 92–103.

Priuli, Stefano (1975) *Ascyltus: Note di onomastica petroniana.* Brussels.

Proust, Marcel ([1922–31] 1954) *À la recherche du temps perdu.* Paris, 3 vols.

——— (1981) *Remembrance of Things Past*, trans. C. K. Scott Moncrieff and Terence Kilmartin. London.

Pucci, Joseph (1998) *The Full-Knowing Reader: Allusion and the Power of the Reader in the Western Literary Tradition.* New Haven, CT.

Puget de la Serre, Jean (1664) *Les maximes politiques de Tacite, ou La conduit des gens de cour.* Paris.

Purcell, Nicholas (1987) "Tomb and Suburb", in Henner Von Hesberg and Paul Zanker, eds, *Römische Gräberstrassen: Selbstdarstellung-Status-Standard.* Munich, 25–41.

——— (1996) "The Roman Garden as a Domestic Building", in Ian M. Barton, ed., *Roman Domestic Buildings.* Exeter, UK, 121–51.

——— (2007) "The *Horti* of Rome and the Landscape of Property", in Anna Leone, Domenico Palombi and Susan Walker, eds, *Res bene gestae: Ricerche di storia urbana su Roma antica in onore di Eva Margareta Steinby.* Rome, 361–77.

Putnam, Michael C. J. (1979) *Virgil's Poem of the Earth: Studies in the "Georgics".* Princeton, NJ.

——— (1982) "Horace *Odes* 3.9: The Dialectics of Desire", in Putnam, ed., *Essays on Latin Lyric, Elegy, and Epic*. Princeton, NJ, 107–25.

——— (1995–96) Review of *The Walking Muse: Horace on the Theory of Satire* by Kirk Freudenburg [1993], *Arion* 3: 303–16.

——— (1996) "Horace's Arboreal Anniversary (*C.* 3.8)", *Ramus* 25: 27–38.

——— (2000) *Horace's Carmen Saeculare: Ritual Magic and the Poet's Art*. New Haven, CT.

——— (2006) "Horace to Torquatus: 'Epistle 1.5' and 'Ode 4.7'", *AJPhil.* 127: 387–413.

——— (2008) "Italian Virgil and the Idea of Rome", in Katharina Volk, ed., *Oxford Readings in Classical Studies: Vergil's Georgics*. Oxford, 138–60.

Race, William (1978) "*Odes* 1.20: A Horatian *Recusatio*", *California Studies in Classical Antiquity* 11: 179–96.

Rankin, H. D. (1971) *Petronius the Artist: Essays on the Satyricon and Its Author*. The Hague.

Rawson, Elizabeth (1976) "The Ciceronian Aristocracy and Its Properties", in Moses I. Finley, ed., *Studies in Roman Property*. Cambridge, 85–102.

Reckford, Kenneth (1959) "Horace and Maecenas", *TAPA* 90: 195–208.

Redford, Bruce (1992–94) *The Letters of Samuel Johnson*. Oxford, 5 vols.

Reynolds, Leighton (1965) *L. Annaei Senecae ad Lucilium Epistulae Morales*. Oxford.

Richardson, Lawrence, Jr (1992) *A New Topographical Dictionary of Ancient Rome*. Baltimore, MD.

Richer, Henri (1746) *Vie de Mecenas: Avec des notes historiques et critiques*. Paris.

Richlin, Amy (2006) *Marcus Aurelius in Love*. Chicago.

——— (2015) "Reading Boy-Love and Child-Love in the Greco-Roman World", in Mark Masterson, Nancy Sorkin-Rabinowitz and James Robson, eds, *Sex in Antiquity: Exploring Gender and Sexuality in the Ancient World*. London, 352–73.

——— (2016) "The Kings of Comedy", in Stavros Frangoulidis, Stephen J. Harrison and Gesine Manuwald, eds, *Roman Drama and Its Contexts*. Berlin, 67–95.

Richter, Gisela M. A. (1956) *Catalogue of Engraved Gems: Greek, Etruscan, and Roman*. Rome, 2nd ed.

Ridley, Ronald T. (2020) "The Man in the Background: The Search for Maecenas", *Antichthon* 54: 54–79.

Rimell, Victoria (2002) *Petronius and the Anatomy of Fiction*. Cambridge.

——— (2009) *Martial's Rome: Empire and the Ideology of Epigram*. Cambridge.

——— (2015) *The Closure of Space in Roman Poetics: Empire's Inward Turn*. Cambridge.

Rizzo, Silviana (1983) "L'Auditorium di Mecenate", in Giuseppina Pisani Sartorio and Lorenzo Quilici, eds, *Roma capitale 1870–1911*, vol. 7, *L'archeologia in Roma capitale tra sterro e scavo*. Venice, 225–30.

Robinson, Jenefer M. (1985) "Style and Personality in the Literary Work", *Philosophical Review* 94: 227–47.

Rodríguez-Almeida, Emilio (1987) "Qualche osservazione sulle Esquiliae patrizie e il Lacus Orphei", *Publications de l'École Française de Rome* 98: 415–28.

Rojas, Felipe (2010) "Empire of Memories: Anatolian Material Culture and the Imagined Past in Hellenistic and Roman Lydia". Dissertation, University of California, Berkeley.

——— (2013) "Antiquarianism in Roman Sardis", in Alain Schnapp, Lothar von Falkenhausen, Peter N. Miller and Tim Murray, eds, *World Antiquarianism: Comparative Perspectives*. Los Angeles, 176–200.

Roller, Matthew (1997) "*Color*-Blindness: Cicero's Death, Declamation, and the Production of History", *CPhil*. 92: 109–30.

Roman, Luke (2014) *Poetic Autonomy in Ancient Rome*. Oxford.

Rosati, Gianpiero (2002) "Muse and Power in the Poetry of Statius", in Efrossini Spentzou and Don Fowler, eds, *Cultivating the Muse: Struggles for Power and Inspiration in Classical Literature*. Oxford, 229–51.

———— (2005) "Elegy after the Elegists: From Opposition to Assent", *PLLS* 12: 133–50.

Rosen, Ralph (1990) "Poetry and Sailing in Hesiod's *Works and Days*", *Cl. Ant.* 9: 99–113.

Ross, David O. (1980) "*Non sua poma*: Varro, Virgil, and Grafting", *ICS* 5: 63–71.

———— (1987) *Virgil's Elements: Physics and Poetry in the Georgics*. Princeton, NJ.

Rossbach, Otto (1920) "Zwei Schriften des Maecenas", *B. phil. Woch.* 15: 356–60.

Rossi, Andreola (2000) "The Tears of Marcellus: History of a Literary Motif in Livy", *G & R* 47: 56–66.

———— (2004) *Contexts of War: Manipulation of Genre in Virgilian Battle Narrative*. Ann Arbor, MI.

Rossini, Orietta (2006) *Ara pacis*. Milan.

Rostovtzeff, Mikhail (1957) *The Social and Economic History of the Roman Empire*. Oxford, 2 vols.

Rothstein, Max (1920) *Die Elegien des Sex. Propertius*. Berlin, 2nd ed., 2 vols.

Rouzer, Paul (2001) *Articulated Ladies: Gender and the Male Community in Early Chinese Texts*. Cambridge, MA.

Ruark, Gibbons (1991) *Rescue the Perishing*. Baton Rouge, LA.

Rudich, Vasily (1997) *Dissidence and Literature under Nero: The Price of Rhetoricization*. London.

Rushforth, Gordon McNeil (1919) "Magister Gregorius de Mirabilibus Urbis Romae: A New Description of Rome in the Twelfth Century", *JRS* 9: 14–58.

Sabatini, Francesco (1914) *La torre delle Milizie erroneamente denominata Torre di Nerone*. Rome.

Sailor, Dylan (2008) *Writing and Empire in Tacitus*. Cambridge.

Saller, Richard (1982a) "Martial on Patronage and Literature", *CQ* 33: 246–57.

———— (1982b) *Personal Patronage under the Early Empire*. Cambridge.

Santirocco, Matthew (1984) "The Maecenas Odes", *TAPA*. 114: 241–53.

Santoro L'Hoir, Francesca (2006) *Tragedy, Rhetoric, and the Historiography of Tacitus' Annales*. Ann Arbor, MI.

Scaglia, Gustina (1992) "Il frontespizio di Nerone, la Casa Colonna e la scala di età romana in un disegno nel Metropolitan Museum of Art di New York", *Bollettino d'arte* 72: 35–62.

Schiesaro, Alessandro (1993) "Il destinatario discreto: Funzioni didascaliche e progetto culturale nelle Georgiche", in Schiesaro, Philip Mitsis and Jenny Strauss Clay, eds, *Mega nepios: Il destinatario nell'epos didascalico, MD* 31: 129–47.

———— (1994) "The Palingenesis of *De rerum natura*", *PCPS* 40: 81–107.

———— (1997) "The Boundaries of Knowledge in Virgil's *Georgics*", in Thomas Habinek and Schiesaro, eds, *The Roman Cultural Revolution*. Cambridge, 63–89.

———— (2009) "Horace's Bacchic Poetics", in Houghton and Wyke (2009): 61–79.

———— (2015) "Seneca and Epicurus: The Allure of the Other", in Shadi Bartsch and Schiesaro, eds, *The Cambridge Companion to Seneca*. Cambridge, 239–52.

Schlegel, Catherine (2000) "Horace and His Fathers: Satires 1.4 and 1.6", *AJPhil*. 121: 93–119.

Schmeling, Gareth L. (2011) *A Commentary on the Satyrica of Petronius*. Oxford.

Schmeling, Gareth L., and David R. Rebmann (1975) "T. S. Eliot and Petronius", *Comparative Literature Studies* 12: 393–410.

Schmid, Alfred (2005) *Augustus und die Macht der Sterne: Antike Astrologie und die Etablierung der Monarchie in Rom*. Cologne.

Schmidt, Ernst A. (1972) *Poetische Reflexion: Vergils Bukolik*. Munich.

Schneider, Rolf M. (1998) "Die Faszination des Feindes: Bilder der Parther und des Orients in Rom", in J. Wiesehöfer, ed., *Das Partherreich und seine Zeugnisse*. Stuttgart, 95–146.

Schomberg, Ralph (1766) *The Life of Maecenas*. London.

Schoonhoven, Hendrik (1980) *Elegiae in Maecenatem: Prolegomena, Text, Commentary*. Gröningen.

Schork, R. Joseph (1971) "*Aemulos Reges*: Allusion and Theme in Horace 3.16", *TAPA* 102: 515–39.

Scullard, Howard H. (1967) *The Etruscan Cities and Rome*. Oxford.

Sedley, David (2004) *The Midwife of Platonism*. Cambridge.

Severano, Giovanni (1630) *Memorie sacre delle sette chiese di Roma e di altri luoghi*. Rome.

Shackleton Bailey, David R. (1982) *Profile of Horace*. Cambridge, MA.

——— (1993) *Martial Epigrams*. Cambridge, MA, 3 vols.

Sharlet, Jocelyn (2011) *Patronage and Poetry in the Islamic World*. London.

Sharrock, Alison R. (1997) "Haud Mollia Iussa: A Response to Roy Gibson", in Catherine Atherton, ed., *Form and Content in Didactic Poetry*. Bari, Italy, 99–115.

Shea, Chris (1985) "The Vertumnus Elegy and Propertius Book IV", *ICS* 13: 63–71.

Shey, H. James (1971) "The Poet's Progress: Ode I.1", *Arethusa* 4: 185–96.

Shoemaker, Peter W. (2007) *Powerful Connections: The Poetics of Patronage in the Age of Louis XIII*. Newark, DE.

Sijpesteijn, Pieter J. (1985) "Further Evidence of Imperial Estates in Roman Egypt", *ZPE* 60: 279–82.

Simpson, Chris J. (1996) "Two Small Thoughts on 'Cilnius Maecenas'", *Latomus* 55: 394–98.

——— (2005) "Rome's 'Official Imperial Seal'? The Rings of Augustus and His First Century Successors", *Historia* 54: 180–88.

Sinclair, Patrick (1995) "Political Declensions in Latin Grammar and Oratory, 55 BCE–CE 39", in Anthony J. Boyle, ed., *Roman Literature and Ideology: Ramus Essays for J. P. Sullivan*. Bendigo, Australia, 92–109.

Sinfield, Alan (1996) "Poetaster, the Author, and the Perils of Cultural Production", *Renaissance Drama* 27: 3–18.

Skinner, Marilyn (2001) "Among Those Present: Catullus 44 and 10", *Helios* 28: 57–73.

Sklenář, Robert (2007–8) "Anti-Petronian Elements in *The Great Gatsby*", *F. Scott Fitzgerald Review* 6: 121–28.

——— (2017) *Plant of a Strange Vine: "Oratio corrupta" and the Poetics of Senecan Tragedy*. Berlin.

Skutsch, Otto (1968) *Studia Enniana*. London.

Smith, Cynthia J. (1989) "'To Maecenas': Phillis Wheatley's Invocation of an Idealized Reader", *Black American Literature Forum* 23: 579–92.

Smith, R. Alden (2007) "'In vino civitas': The Rehabilitation of Bacchus in Virgil's *Georgics*", *Vergilius* 53: 53–87.

Smollett, Tobias (1766) Review of *The Life of Maecenas, with Critical, Historical, and Geographical Notes* by Ralph Schomberg, *Critical Review/Annals of Literature* 22: 192–97.

Smyshlyayev, Alexander L. (1991) "'The Maecenas Speech' (Dio Cass., LII): The Dating and Ideological and Political Orientation", *GLP* 13:137–55.

Smythe, Colin (1995) *A Guide to Coole Park, Co. Galway: The Home of Lady Gregory.* Gerrards Cross, UK.

Snyder, Jane M. (1974) "Aristophanes' Agathon as Anacreon", *Hermes* 102: 244–46.

Soldo, Janja (2021) *Seneca, Epistulae Morales Book 2.* Oxford.

Sordi, Marta (1995) "La centralità di Etruria nella politica di Mecenate", *RSA* 25: 149–56. Reprinted in Sordi (2002) *Scritti di storia romana*, Milan, 489–96.

Sourvinou-Inwood, Christine (2004) "Hermaphroditos and Salmakis: The Voice of Halikarnassos", in Signe Isager and Poul Pedersen, eds, *The Salmakis Inscription and Hellenistic Halikarnassos.* Odense, Denmark, 59–84.

Spawforth, Anthony J. (2001) "Shades of Greekness: A Lydian Case Study", in Irad Malkin, ed., *Ancient Perceptions of Greek Ethnicity.* Cambridge, MA, 375–400.

Spencer, Diana (2003) "Horace and the Company of Kings: Art and Artfulness in *Epistle* 2, 1", *MD* 51: 135–60.

——— (2006) "Horace's Garden Thoughts: Rural Retreats and the Urban Imagination", in Ralph Rosen and Ineke Sluiter, eds, *City, Countryside, and the Spatial Organization of Value in Classical Antiquity.* Leiden, 239–74.

Spineto, Natale (1998) "Tradizione e miti dionisiaci, epifanie e ritorni del 'Dio che viene'", *Storiografia* 2: 115–28.

Squire, Michael (2011) *The Iliad in a Nutshell: Visualizing Epic on the Tabulae Iliacae.* Oxford.

Stahl, Hans-Peter (1985) *Propertius: "Love" and "War"; Individual and State under Augustus.* Berkeley, CA.

Star, Christopher (2012) *The Empire of the Self: Self-Command and Political Speech in Seneca and Petronius.* Baltimore, MD.

Steinby, Eva Margarethe (1993–99) *Lexicon topographicum vrbis Romae.* Rome, 5 vols.

Stevenson, Thomas R. (1992) "The Ideal Benefactor and the Father Analogy in Greek and Roman Thought." *CQ* 42: 421–36.

Stewart, Andrew (1990) *Greek Sculpture: An Exploration.* New Haven, CT, 2 vols.

——— (2005) "Posidippus and the Truth in Sculpture", in Gutzwiller (2005): 183–205.

——— (2006) "Baroque Classics: The Tragic Muse and the Exemplum", in Porter (2006): 127–70.

Stewart, Susan (1984) *On Longing: Narratives of the Miniature, the Gigantic, the Souvenir, the Collection.* Durham, NC.

Stoddard, Kathryn B. (2003) "The Programmatic Message of the 'Kings and Singers' Passage, Hesiod, *Theogony* 80–103", *TAPA* 133: 1–16.

Story, William W. (1863) *Roba di Roma*, London, 2 vols.

Stroup, Sarah (2010) *Catullus, Cicero, and a Society of Patrons.* Cambridge.

Stuart Jones, Henry (1926) *A Catalogue of the Ancient Sculptures Preserved in the Municipal Collections of Rome: The Sculptures of the Palazzo dei Conservatori.* Oxford, 2. vols (text and plates).

Suerbaum, Werner, ed. (2002) *Die archaische Literatur von den Anfängen bis Sullas Tod: Die vorliterarische Periode und die Zeit von 240 bis 78 v Chr.* Munich.

Summers, Walter C. (1908) "On Some Fragments of Maecenas", *CQ* 2: 170–74.

———— (1910) *Select Letters of Seneca*. London.

Sussman, Lewis A. (1995) "Sons and Fathers in the Major Declamations Ascribed to Quintilian", *Rhetorica* 13: 179–92.

Swain, Simon C. R. (1992) "Plutarch's Characterization of Lucullus", *Rh. Mus.* 135: 307–16.

Swan, Peter M. (2004) *The Augustan Succession: An Historical Commentary on Cassius Dio's Roman History Books 55–56, 9 BC–AD 14*. Oxford.

Syme, Ronald (1939) *The Roman Revolution*. Oxford.

———— (1958) *Tacitus*. Oxford, 2 vols.

———— (1978) *History in Ovid*. Oxford.

Syndikus, Hans Peter (1972) *Die Lyrik des Horaz: Eine Interpretation der Oden*. Darmstadt, Germany, vol. 1.

Tait, Hugh, ed. (1984) *The Art of the Jeweller; A Catalogue of the Hull Grundy Gift to the British Museum: Jewellery, Engraved Gems and Goldsmiths' Work*. London.

Tandoi, Vincenzo (1968) "Giovenale e il mecenatismo a Roma fra il I e II secolo", *Atene e Roma* 13: 125–45.

Tanner, R. G. [Godfrey] (1970–71) "Some Problems in *Aeneid* 7–12", *PVS* 10: 37–44.

Tanner, Tony, ed. (1990) Introduction and notes to F. Scott Fitzgerald's *The Great Gatsby*. London.

Taplin, Oliver (2010) "Echoes from Mount Cithaeron", in Philip Mitsis and Christos Tsagalis, eds, *Allusion, Authority, and Truth: Critical Perspectives on Greek Poetic and Rhetorical Praxis*, Berlin, 235–48.

Tarpin, Michel (1995) "*TRIMALCHIO MAECENATIANVS*", *Lettre de Pallas* 3: 15.

Tarrant, Dorothy (1946) "Imagery in Plato's *Republic*", *CQ* 40: 27–34.

Tarrant, Richard (1976) *Seneca: Agamemnon*. Cambridge.

———— (2012) *Virgil Aeneid Book XII*. Cambridge.

Thibodeau, Philip (2001) "The Old Man and His Garden (Verg. *Georg.* 4,116–148)". *MD* 47: 175–95.

———— (2011) *Playing the Farmer: Representations of Rural Life in Vergil's Georgics*. Berkeley, CA.

Thomas, Richard F. (1982) *Lands and Peoples in Roman Poetry: The Ethnographic Tradition*, Cambridge Philological Society Suppl. 7. Cambridge.

———— (1983) "Callimachus, the Victoria Berenices, and Roman Poetry", *CQ* 33: 92–113. Reprinted in Thomas (1999): 68–100.

———— (1987) "Prose into Poetry: Tradition and Meaning in Virgil's *Georgics*", *Harv. Stud.* 91: 229–60.

———— (1988a) "Tree Violation and Ambivalence in Virgil", *TAPA* 118: 261–73.

———— (1988b) *Virgil Georgics*. Cambridge, 2 vols.

———— (1999) *Reading Virgil and His Texts: Studies in Intertextuality*. Ann Arbor, MI.

———— (2011) *Horace: Odes IV and Carmen Saeculare*. Cambridge.

Tiffen, Herbert J. (1935) *History of the Liverpool Institute Schools, 1825–1935*. Liverpool.

Tischer, Ute (2006) *Die zeitgeschichtliche Anspielung in der antiken Literaturerklärung*. Tübingen, Germany.

Tolstoy, Leo ([1877] 2014) *Anna Karenina*, ed. Gary S. Morton, trans. Marian Schwartz. New Haven, CT.

Torelli, Mario (1969) "Senatori etruschi della tarda reppublica e dell'impero", *Dial. di Arch.* 3: 285–363.

Townend, Gavin B. (1973) "The Literary Substrata to Juvenal's *Satires*", *JRS* 63: 148–60.

Traina, Alfonso (1995) *Lo stile "drammatico" del filosofico Seneca.* Bologna, 5th ed.

Trinacty, Christopher (2014) *Senecan Tragedy and the Reception of Augustan Poetry.* Oxford.

Tröster, Manuel (2008) *Themes, Character, and Politics in Plutarch's Life of Lucullus: The Construction of a Roman Aristocrat.* Stuttgart.

Tucker, Louis Leonard (1967) "'Old Nick' Longworth, the Paradoxical Maecenas of Cincinnati", *Cincinnati Historical Society Bulletin* 25: 246–59.

Turnbull, George (1740) *A Treatise on Ancient Painting Containing Observations on the Rise, Progress, and Decline of that Art amongst the Greeks and Romans.* London.

Turpin, William (1998) "The Epicurean Parasite: Horace, *Satires* 1.1–3", *Ramus* 27: 127–40.

Tylawsky, Elizabeth I. (2002) *Saturio's Inheritance: The Greek Ancestry of the Roman Comic Parasite.* New York.

Urbanik, Jakub (2016) "Husband and Wife", in Paul J. du Plessis, Clifford Ando and Kaius Tuori, eds, *The Oxford Handbook of Roman Law and Society.* Oxford, 473–86.

Vance, Norman (2004) "Decadence from Belfast to Byzantium", *New Literary History* 35: 563–72.

Van Den Berg, Christopher (2008) "*Malignitas* and Aesthetic Rivalry", in Ralph Rosen and Ineke Sluiter, eds, *Kakos: Badness and Anti-Value in Classical Antiquity.* Leiden, 399–431.

Van den Hout, Michel J. P. (1999) *A Commentary on the Letters of M. Cornelius Fronto.* Leiden.

Vanderpool, Eugene (1968) "Three Inscriptions from Eleusis", *Archaiologikon deltion* 23: 1–9.

Vardi, Amiel D. (1996) "*Diiudicatio Locorum*: Gellius and the History of a Mode in Ancient Comparative Criticism", *CQ* 46: 492–514.

Veblen, Torstein ([1899] 1992) *The Theory of the Leisure Class: An Economic Study of Institutions.* New Brunswick, NJ.

Verboven, Koenraad (1997) "Damasippus, the Story of a Businessman?", in Carl Deroux, ed., *Studies in Latin Literature and Roman History* 8, Collection Latomus 239. Brussels, 195–214.

Verzár-Bass, Monika (1998) "A proposito dei mausolei negli horti e nelle ville", in Cima and La Rocca (1998): 401–24.

Vespignani, Virginio, and Carlo Ludovico Visconti (1874) "Antica sala di recitazione, ovvero *auditorio*, scoperto fra le ruine degli orti di Mecenate, sull'Esquilino", *Bulletino della Commissione Archeologica di Roma* 2: 137–73.

Vilatte, Sylvie (1986) "La femme, l'esclave, le cheval, et le chien: Les emblèmes du *kalós kagathós* Ischomaque", *DHA* 12: 271–94.

Villetard, Michèle (2018) "L'auditorium de Mécène: Une réévaluation à la lumière des auditoriums d'Alexandrie", *Mètis* 16: 261–91.

Visconti, Ennio Quirino (1818) *Iconografia Romana.* Milan, 2 vols.

Visconti, Pietro Ercole, et al. (1837) *Di un busto colossale in marmo di Caio Cilnio Mecenate scoperto e posseduto dal cavaliere Pietro Manni.* Paris.

Voisin, Dominique (2000) "Les cercles littéraires à Rome à l'époque d'Auguste". PhD thesis, Université Bordeaux 3.

Volk, Katharina (2002) *The Poetics of Latin Didactic.* Oxford.

——— (2009) *Manilius and His Intellectual Background.* Oxford.

Voltaire (1877–85) *Oeuvres complètes de Voltaire*, ed. Louis Moland. Paris, 52 vols.

Von Stackelberg, Katharine T. (2009) *The Roman Garden: Sense, Space, and Society*. Abingdon, UK.

Vout, Caroline (2007) *Power and Eroticism in Imperial Rome*. Cambridge.

—— (2009) "The Satyrica and Neronian Culture", in Jonathan Prag and Ian Repath, eds, *Petronius: A Handbook*. Oxford, 101–13.

—— (2012) *The Hills of Rome: Signature of an Eternal City*. Cambridge.

Walker, Bessie (1960) *The Annals of Tacitus*. Manchester, 2nd ed.

Walker, Jeffrey (2000) *Rhetoric and Poetics in Antiquity*, Oxford.

Wallace-Hadrill, Andrew (1982) "Civilis Princeps: Between Citizen and King", *JRS* 72: 32–48.

—— (1989a) *Patronage in Ancient Society*. London.

—— (1989b) "Rome's Cultural Revolution", Review of *The Power of Images in the Age of Augustus* by Paul Zanker, *JRS* 79: 157–64.

—— (1998) "Horti and Hellenization", in Cima and La Rocca (1998): 1–12.

—— (2008) *Rome's Cultural Revolution*. Cambridge.

Wallis, Jonathan (2008) "Reading Backwards and Looking Forwards in Propertius Book 3". PhD thesis, University of Cambridge.

—— (2018) *Introspection and Engagement in Propertius: A Study of Book 3*. Cambridge.

Watson, A.J.M. (1991) "An Attempt at a Psychological Analysis of Maecenas", *Akroterion* 36: 25–35.

Watson, Lindsay (2003) *A Commentary on Horace's Epodes*. Oxford.

Watson, Lindsay, and Patricia Watson (2003) *Martial: Select Epigrams*. Cambridge.

Wehrli, Fritz (1944) "Horaz und Kallimachos", *Museum Helveticum* 1: 69–76.

West, David (1991) "'Cur me querelis' (Horace, *Odes* 2.17)", *AJPhil.* 112: 45–52.

—— (1995) *Horace Odes I: Carpe diem*. Oxford.

West, Martin L. (1978) *Hesiod: Works & Days*, Oxford.

Wheatley, Phillis (1773) *Poems on Various Subjects*. London.

White, Peter (1991) "Maecenas' Retirement", *CPhil.* 86: 130–38.

—— (1993) *Promised Verse: Poets in the Society of Augustan Rome*. Cambridge, MA, 2 vols.

—— (2007) "Friendship, Patronage and Socio-Poetics", in Stephen Harrison, ed., *Cambridge Companion to Horace*. Cambridge, 195–206.

Whitehead, Jane (1993) "The Cena Trimalchionis and Biographical Narration in Roman Middle-Class Art", in Peter J. Holliday, ed., *Narrative and Event in Ancient Art*. Cambridge, 299–325.

Whitlatch, Lisa (2013) "The Hunt for Knowledge: Hunting in Latin Didactic Poets", Dissertation, Rutgers University.

—— (2014) "Empiricist Dogs and the Superiority of Philosophy in Lucretius' *De Rerum Natura*", *CW* 108: 45–66.

Whitmarsh, Tim (2000) "The Politics and Poetics of Parasitism: Athenaeus on Parasites and Flatterers", in David Braund and John Wilkins, eds, *Athenaeus and His World: Reading Greek Culture in the Roman Empire*. Exeter, UK, 304–16.

—— (2013) *Beyond the Second Sophistic: Adventures in Greek Postclassicism*. Berkeley, CA.

Wiggers, Nancy (1977) "Reconsideration of Propertius II.1", *CJ* 72: 334–41.

Wilde, Oscar (2019) *The Complete Works of Oscar Wilde*, vol. 10, *Plays 3: The Importance of Being Earnest; "A Wife's Tragedy" (fragment)*, ed. Joseph Donohue. Oxford.

Wilkinson, Lancelot Patrick (1969) *The Georgics of Virgil: A Critical Survey*. Cambridge.

Williams, Craig A. (2010) *Roman Homosexuality*. Oxford, 2nd ed.

——— (2012) *Reading Roman Friendship*. Cambridge.

Williams, Gareth (2012) *The Cosmic Viewpoint: A Study of Seneca's Natural Questions*. Oxford.

——— (2016) "Style and Form in Seneca's Writings", in S. Bartsch and A. Schiesaro, eds, *Cambridge Companion to Seneca*. Cambridge, 135–49.

Williams, Gordon (1982) "Phases in Political Patronage of Literature in Rome", in Gold (1982a): 3–27.

——— (1990) "Did Maecenas Fall from Favor? Augustan Literary Patronage", in Kurt Raaflaub and Mark Toher, eds, *Between Republic and Empire: Interpretations of Augustus and His Principate*. Berkeley, CA, 258–75.

Williams, John ([1972] 2014) *Augustus*. New York.

Williamson, E. W. ([1929] 1998) *The Letters of Osbert of Clare*. Oxford, repr. ed.

Wilson, Michael (1987) "Seneca's Epistles to Lucilius: A Revaluation", *Ramus* 16: 102–21.

Wilson-Okamura, David Scott (2014) *Virgil in the Renaissance*. Cambridge.

Wimmel, Walter (1960) *Kallimachos in Rom: Die Nachfolge seines apologetischen Dichtens in der Augusteerzeit*. Wiesbaden, Germany.

Winterbottom, Michael (1974) *The Elder Seneca: Declamations*. Cambridge, MA.

Winterling, Alois (1999) *Aula Caesaris: Studien zur Institutionalisierung des römischen Kaiserhofes in der Zeit von Augustus bis Commodus (31 v. Chr. -192 n. Chr.)*. Munich.

Wiseman, T. Peter (1971) *New Men in the Roman Senate, 139 B.C.–A.D. 14*. Oxford.

——— (1987) "Legendary Genealogies in Late-Republican Rome", in *Roman Studies: Literary and Historical*. Liverpool, 207–18.

——— (1992) "A Roman Villa", in Wiseman, ed., *Talking to Virgil*. Exeter, UK, 71–110.

——— (1998) "A Stroll on the Rampart", in Cima and La Rocca (1998): 13–22.

——— (2016) "Maecenas and the Stage", *PBSR* 84: 131–55 (plates 357–58).

Wisseman, Michael (1982) *Die Parther in der augusteischen Dichtung*. Frankfurt.

Wohl, Victoria (1999) "The Eros of Alcibiades", *Cl. Ant.* 18: 349–85.

——— (2002) *Love among the Ruins: The Erotics of Democracy in Classical Athens*. Princeton, NJ.

Wolfe, Jessica (2015) *Homer and the Question of Strife from Erasmus to Hobbes*. Toronto.

Woodman, Anthony J. (1983) *Velleius Paterculus: The Caesarian and Augustan Narrative (2.41–93)*. Cambridge.

——— (2002) "*Biformis Vates*: The *Odes*, Catullus and Greek Lyric", in Woodman and Feeney (2002): 53–64.

Woodman, Anthony J., and Denis Feeney (2002) *Traditions and Contexts in the Poetry of Horace*. Cambridge.

Woodman, Anthony J., and Ronald H. Martin (1996) *The Annals of Tacitus Book 3*. Cambridge.

Wyke, Maria (1987) "The Elegiac Woman at Rome", *PCPS* 33: 153–78.

Wyler, Stéphanie (2013) "An Augustan Trend towards Dionysos: Around the 'Auditorium of Maecenas'", in Alberto Bernabé, Miguel Herrero de Jáuregui, Ana Jiménez San Cristóbal and Raquel Martín Hernández, eds, *Redefining Dionysos*. Berlin: 541–53.

Zanker, Paul (1988) *The Power of Images in the Age of Augustus*. Ann Arbor, MI.

Zetzel, James E. G. (1972) "Cicero and the Scipionic Circle", *Harv. Stud.* 76: 173–79.

—— (1980) "Horace's *Liber Sermonum*: The Structure of Ambiguity", *Arethusa* 13: 59–77.

—— (1982) "The Poetics of Patronage in the Late First Century BC", in Gold (1982a): 87–102.

Ziolkowski, Theodore (1998) *The View from the Tower: Origins of an Anti-Modernist Image*. Princeton, NJ.

Zwierlein, Otto (1999) *Die Ovid- und Vergil-Revision in tiberischer Zeit*, vol. 1, *Prolegomena*. Berlin.

# INDEX

Page numbers in *italics* indicate figures.

A NOTE ON THE TYPE

This book has been composed in Arno, an Old-style serif typeface in the
classic Venetian tradition, designed by Robert Slimbach at Adobe.